SAXON®

# GEOMETRY

# Solution Manual

SAXON®

HOUGHTON MIFFLIN HARCOURT
Supplemental Publishers

www.SaxonPublishers.com
800-531-5015

ISBN 13: 978-1-6027-7561-9
ISBN 10: 1-6027-7561-3



Printed in the United States of America



27 2266 22
4500862171

## LESSON 1

### Warm Up 1

1. coordinate
2. The length of pipe she needs is 140% of the length of pipe she already has. So, $140\% \times 7 = 1.4 \times 7 = 9.8$ inches.
3. $\sqrt[4]{81}$
$= \sqrt[4]{3 \times 3 \times 3 \times 3}$
$= 3$
4. $\frac{4(2+6)}{2(2)}$
$= \frac{4(8)}{4}$
$= \frac{32}{4}$
$= 8$

### Lesson Practice 1

a. *w*, *x*, and *y* are the lines.
b. Any two points are collinear. Sample: points *A* and *B*, points *C* and *D*
c. *R* and *S* are the two planes.
d. Sample: Points *A*, *B*, and *D* are coplanar.
e. Sample: *w* and *x* are coplanar lines.
f. Sample: *w* and *y* are noncoplanar lines.
g. point *P*
h. point *K*, point *M*

### Practice 1

1. *A*, *B*, and *C* are collinear. Point *D* is not collinear to any two of the other three points.
2. No, a ruler can be used to line up any two points making them collinear.
3. No, even if two lines appear noncoplanar, once they intersect, they are coplanar.
4. point, line, and plane
5. intersecting
6. No, a plane can always be oriented so that the three points lie in one plane.
7. *A*, *C*, and *E*
8. See student work; lines; Sample: The edges of the classroom are formed where the walls and floor of the room meet. These edges represent lines.
9. $\overleftrightarrow{AD}$
10. $\overleftrightarrow{CD}$ is coplanar with each of the other lines, but not both at once, since $\overleftrightarrow{AD}$ and $\overleftrightarrow{CH}$ are not coplanar.
11. There is no intersection between $\overleftrightarrow{BC}$ and line *x* because they are noncoplanar and do not intersect at the intersection of the planes.
12. Choice A is false because there can be two lines on different planes. Choice B is false because there can be three lines on three different planes. Choice **C** is true because once two lines intersect, they are by nature coplanar. Choice D is false because two intersecting lines are by nature coplanar.
13. A line can contain an infinite number of points.
14. A plane can contain an infinite number of lines.
15. Choice A is false because the intersection of two lines is a point that is zero-dimensional. Choice B is false because the intersection of two planes forms a line that is one-dimensional. Choice **C** is true because the intersection of two planes forms a line that is one-dimensional. Choice D is false because the intersection of two lines is a point that is zero-dimensional.
16. Two points can be used to name a line, but at least three noncollinear points are needed to define a plane.
17. $5 - (7 + 8) \div 5 + (-2)^3$
$= 5 - 15 \div 5 + (-8)$
$= 5 - 3 - 8$
$= -6$
18. The Commutative Property of Addition, which says that the order of the numbers does not matter for addition.

**19.** Jacob is correct. −3 can be represented as a fraction using integers, which makes it a rational number.

**20.** It is rational because, even though it does not terminate, it does repeat and is equal to the fraction of integers $\frac{1}{3}$.

**21.** $\frac{\text{Non-Hits}}{\text{At Bats}} = \frac{\text{At Bats} - \text{Hits}}{\text{At Bats}}$

$= \frac{55 - 33}{55} = \frac{22}{55}$ or $22 \div 55 = 0.4$

**22.** $(-3)^3 - \left(\frac{1}{3}\right)^{-3}$

$= -27 - (3)^3$
$= -27 - 27$
$= -54$

**23.** $2\sqrt{12} + 6\sqrt{27}$
$= 2\sqrt{4} \cdot \sqrt{3} + 6\sqrt{9} \cdot \sqrt{3}$
$= 2 \cdot 2\sqrt{3} + 6 \cdot 3\sqrt{3}$
$= 4\sqrt{3} + 18\sqrt{3}$
$= 22\sqrt{3}$

**24.** 4 inches $= \frac{4}{12} = \frac{1}{3}$ ft

Cubic yards is a measure of volume.

$V = lwh = 9 \times 9 \times \frac{1}{3} = 27 \text{ ft}^3$

Change cubic feet to cubic yards.

$27 \text{ ft}^3 \times \left(\frac{1 \text{ yd}}{3 \text{ ft}}\right) \times \left(\frac{1 \text{ yd}}{3 \text{ ft}}\right) \times \left(\frac{1 \text{ yd}}{3 \text{ ft}}\right)$

$= \frac{27}{27} \text{ yd}^3 = 1 \text{ yd}^3$

**25.** mean: $(0.5 + 2 + 0 + 4 + 2.5 + 5 + 7) \div 7$
$= 21 \div 7 = 3$ mm

median: 0, 0.5, 2, **2.5**, 4, 5, 7 → median = 2.5

**26.** $\frac{9.760}{9.807} = 0.9952 = 99.52\%$ correct

To find the percent error, we can subtract this percent from 100:
$100 - 99.52 = 0.48\%$.

**27.**

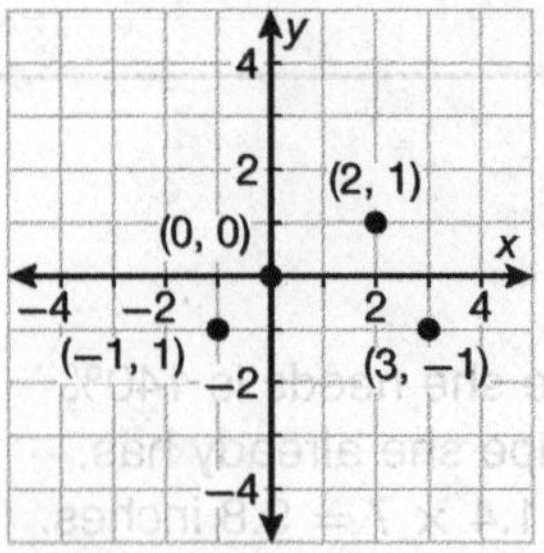


**28.** $xy^{-2} + \frac{x}{y}$
$= (-2)\left(\frac{1}{2}\right)^{-2} + \frac{-2}{\frac{1}{2}}$
$= (-2)(2)^2 + (-2)(2)$
$= (-2)(4) + (-4)$
$= -8 - 4$
$= -12$

**29.** $Prt = I$
$r = I \div Pt$
$r = \frac{I}{Pt}$

**30.** $3x + 4y - 15 = 0$
$4y = -3x + 15$
$y = -\frac{3}{4}x + \frac{15}{4}$

The slope is $-\frac{3}{4}$.

## LESSON 2

### Warm Up 2

**1.** collinear

**2.** $5x + 6 = 2x - 5$
$5x - 2x = -5 - 6$
$3x = -11$
$x = -\frac{11}{3}$

**3.** $5(2x - 6) + 3x - 7$
$= 10x - 30 + 3x - 7$
$= 13x - 37$

### Lesson Practice 2

**a.** Symmetric Property of Congruence

**b.** $|(-4) - 3| = |-7| = 7$

c. $AC = AB + BC$

$AC = x^2 - x + 3 + 2x + 7$

$AC = x^2 + x + 10$

d. If $M$ is the midpoint between Seattle, $W$, to San Francisco, $C$:

$WC = WM + MC$

$WM = MC$

$WC = WM + WM$

$811 = 2(WM)$

$405.5 = WM$

The midpoint is 405.5 miles from either city.

**Practice 2**

1. $\overline{AB} \cong \overline{EF}$ because their measures are equal.

2. $\sqrt{32}$ is between 5 and 6, but closer to 6 because $5^2 = 25$ and $6^2 = 36$.

$5.6^2 = 31.36$

$5.7^2 = 32.49$

$5.7^2$ is the number to the nearest tenth that is closest to 32. So, $\sqrt{32} \approx 5.7$.

3. Commutative Property of Addition

4. The correct choice is **C** because it takes at least three noncollinear points to define a plane.

5. $AD = |(-7) - 3| = |-10| = 10$

6. $BC = |9 - (-5)| = |14| = 14$

7. $DA = |3 - (-7)| = |10| = 10$

8. $AC = |(-7) - (-5)| = |-2| = 2$

9. The mode is the number that occurs the most in the data set. The mode is 83.

10. $3m^2 - 5m + 17$

$= 3(-3)^2 - 5(-3) + 17$

$= 3(9) - (-15) + 17$

$= 27 + 15 + 17$

$= 59$

11. Quadrant IV

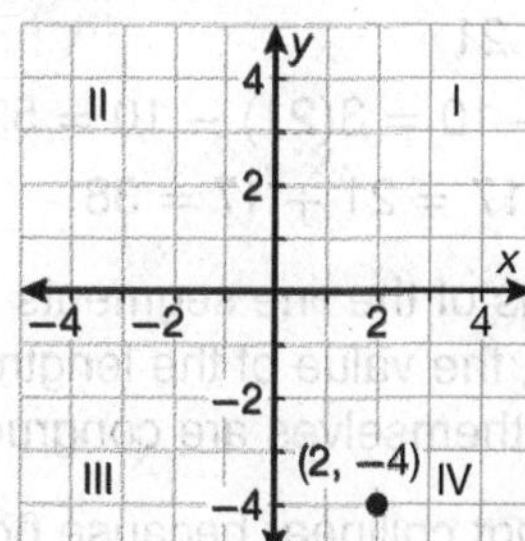


12. Since the data are written in order, the median is the middle number, 6.

13. $AC = AB + BC$

$AC = 5x - 19 + 3x + 4$

$AC = 8x - 15$

14. There are lights at the beginning and the end of the walkway. The three remaining lights must be spaced evenly along the 60-yard walkway. The first light divides the walkway in half and the remaining two lights divide each half in half. So, they divide the walkway into four equal sections. $60 \div 4 = 15$. The lights should be spaced every 15 yards.

15. To define a unique plane, the points must be noncollinear. Sample: Sunil could say, "Three noncollinear points determine a unique plane."

16. $AB = BC$

$3x = 2y + 16$

$AC = AB + BC$

$60 = 3x + 2y + 16$

$60 = 3x + (3x)$

$60 = 6x$

$10 = x$

$3(10) = 2y + 16$

$30 = 2y + 16$

$14 = 2y$

$7 = y$

17. D 15 E x + 17 F

3x − 10

$DF = DE + EF$

$3x - 10 = 15 + x + 17$

$3x - x = 15 + 17 + 10$

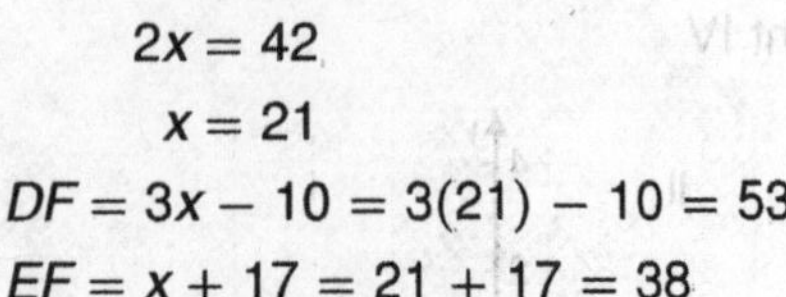

$2x = 42$

$x = 21$

$DF = 3x - 10 = 3(21) - 10 = 53$

$EF = x + 17 = 21 + 17 = 38$

**18.** The lengths of the line segments are equal (i.e., the value of the length) and the segments themselves are congruent.

**19.** They are not collinear because points *B* and *C* are not on the same line. They are coplanar because they all lie on the same plane.

**20.** Two points are required to determine a line.

**21.** Choice **C** is false because space is determined by four noncoplanar points.

**22.**

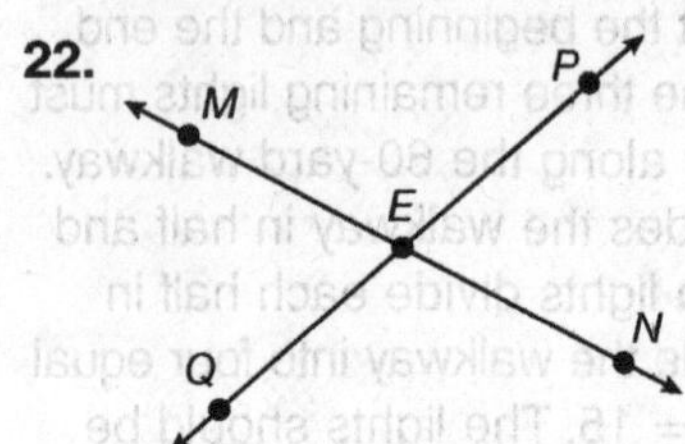


Points *M, N,* and *E* are collinear. Points *P, Q,* and *E* are collinear.

**23.** $2x^2 - 16x - 66$

$= 2(x^2 - 8x - 33)$

$= 2(x - 11)(x + 3)$

**24.** $(x - 4)(x + 7)$

$= x^2 + 7x - 4x - 28$

$= x^2 + 3x - 28$

**25.** 7 feet 4 inches $= 7\frac{1}{3}$ feet

$8 - 7\frac{1}{3} = \frac{24}{3} - \frac{22}{3} = \frac{2}{3}$ foot

**26.** $\frac{-36x^{-4}y^5}{12x^2y^{-3}} = \frac{-3y^5y^3}{x^2y^4} = \frac{-3y^8}{x^6}$

**27.** \$48.99 is close to \$50. 10% of \$50 is \$5. It is a little more than \$2.50, which is half of \$5. A good estimate would be approximately \$3.00.

**28.** $1.8 + 2.345 + 0.65 + 13.56$

$\approx 2 + 2 + 1 + 14$

$\approx 19$

**29.** $V = (8)(4)(1.5) = 48\text{ m}^3$

liters $= 48 \times 1000 = 48{,}000$ liters

$48{,}000\text{ liters} \times \left(\frac{1\text{ gal}}{3.85\text{ liters}}\right) \approx 12{,}468\text{ gallons}$

**30.** $9.8\text{ m/s}^2 \times \left(\frac{100\text{ cm}}{1\text{ m}}\right) \times \left(\frac{1\text{ in.}}{2.54\text{ cm}}\right) \times \left(\frac{1\text{ ft}}{12\text{ in.}}\right) \approx 32.15\text{ ft/s}^2$

## LESSON 3

### Warm Up 3

**1.** congruent

**2.** $\frac{1}{2}\left(\frac{2^2}{2} - 2\right) = \frac{1}{2}\left(\frac{4}{2} - 2\right)$

$= \frac{1}{2}(2 - 2) = \frac{1}{2}(0) = 0$

**3.** $22 \div 7 \approx 3.\overline{142857}$; It is a repeating decimal.

### Lesson Practice 3

**a.** Rays: $\overrightarrow{SR}, \overrightarrow{ST}, \overrightarrow{SP}$

Angles: $\angle RST, \angle TSP, \angle RSP$

**b.** The angle is greater than 90° making it an obtuse angle. The angle measures 125°.

**c.** $m\angle AED = m\angle AEB + m\angle BEC + m\angle CED$

$120° = m\angle AEB + 22° + 33°$

$m\angle AEB = 65°$

**d.** Since *XY* bisects $\angle WXZ$, it divides $\angle WXZ$ into two congruent angles. So, $m\angle WXY = m\angle YXZ = 32°$.

Using the congruence marks in the diagram, $m\angle ZXU = m\angle UXV = 35°$.

$m\angle YXU = m\angle YXZ + m\angle ZXU$

$m\angle YXU = 32° + 35° = 67°$

The measure of $\angle YXU = 67°$.

**e.** $10\% \times 360° = 36°$

### Practice 3

**1.** $\angle AFC$ is a right angle and thus measures 90°.

**2.** $\angle CFD$ is an acute angle because it is smaller than 90°.

$m\angle CFD = 90° - 36° = 54°$

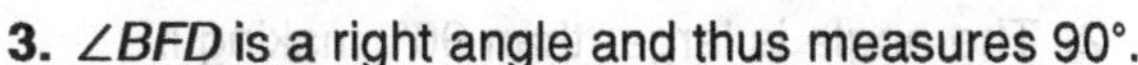

3. $\angle BFD$ is a right angle and thus measures 90°.

4. $\angle AFD$ is an obtuse angle because it is greater than 90°.
$m\angle AFD = 90° + 54° = 144°$

5. $m\angle GLH = 36°$
$m\angle HLI = 90°$
$m\angle ILK = 180° - m\angle GLI$
$m\angle ILK = 180° - (36° + 90°) = 54°$
$m\angle ILJ = \frac{1}{2}(m\angle ILK) = \frac{1}{2}(54°) = 27°$
$m\angle GLJ = m\angle GLH + m\angle HLI + m\angle ILJ$
$m\angle GLJ = 36° + 90° + 27° = 153°$
The correct choice is **D**.

6. 180°

7. $AB = |(-7) - 4| = |-11| = 11$

8. A: $\frac{1}{2} = 50\% = 5{:}10 \rightarrow$ true
B: $\frac{20}{20} = 100\% = 7{:}7 \rightarrow$ true
C: $\frac{30}{36} = \frac{5}{6} = 0.8333 = 83.\overline{3} = 5{:}6 \rightarrow$ true
So, choice **D**, all of the above, is correct.

9. 2

10. There are 5 significant digits since the first digit is 1 and all of the other digits are to the left of the decimal.

11. Sample: He needs to remember that congruence refers to a figure whereas equality refers to numbers. Two segments having the same length are congruent segments, but their lengths are equal.

12. Since $\overrightarrow{BD}$ bisects $\angle ABC$, we know that $m\angle ABD = m\angle DBC$.
$x^2 + x + 12 = x^2 + 3x + 4$
$x^2 - x^2 + x - 3x = 4 - 12$
$-2x = -8$
$x = 4$
$m\angle ABC = (x^2 + x + 12) + (x^2 + 3x + 4)$
$= 2x^2 + 4x + 16$
$= 2(4)^2 + 4(4) + 16$
$= 2(16) + 16 + 16$
$= 64°$

13. 16 m/8 posts = 2 m/post
The posts should be spaced apart every 2 meters.

14. Transitive Property of Congruence

15. A 12 B $4x - 1$ C; $7x + 5$
$7x + 5 = 12 + 4x - 1$
$7x - 4x = 12 - 1 - 5$
$3x = 6$
$x = 2$

16. $\frac{-142 + 53}{2} = -44.5$

17. Yes, since any line can be contained in a plane.

18. $\frac{\text{Boys}}{\text{Total}} = \frac{14}{31} = \frac{B}{186}$
$14(186) = 31B$
$2604 = 31B$
$84 = B$
Of the 186 children, there are 84 boys.

19. $10x^2 + x - 21$
$= 10x^2 + 15x - 14x - 21$
$= 5x(2x + 3) - 7(2x + 3)$
$= (5x - 7)(2x + 3)$

20. The mean of these numbers is the sum of all the numbers divided by 6. So,
$\frac{25.14 + 17.22 + x + 23.04 + 20.21 + 21.27}{6}$
$= 20.38$
$106.88 + x = 6(20.38)$
$x = 122.28 - 106.88$
$x = 15.4$

21.

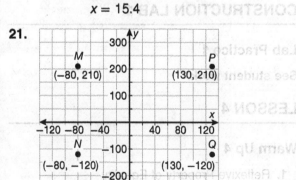

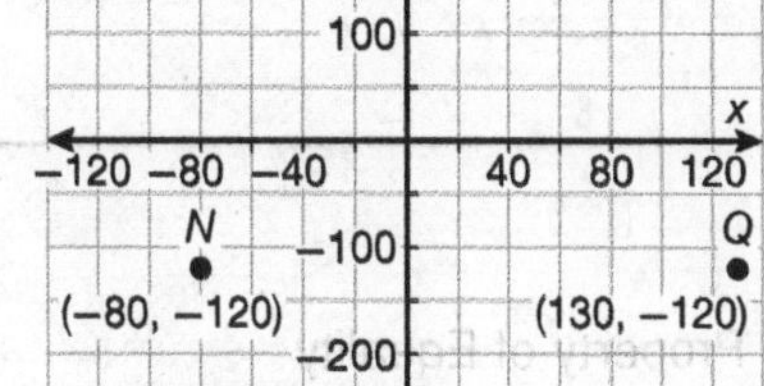

$A = lw$
$A = (210)(330) = 69{,}300$
The area of the lot is 69,300 $ft^2$.

22. $0.015x = \$12{,}000$
$x = 800{,}000\ yd^2$

23. The graph of $y = f(x) + 3$ is the graph of $y = f(x)$ translated up 3 units.

24. $\sqrt{6g} = (j + y)$
$6g = (j + y)^2$
$6g = (j + y)(j + y)$
$6g = j^2 + 2jy + y^2$
$g = \frac{j^2 + 2jy + y^2}{6}$

25. $h(1.7) = 82 - 4.9(1.7)^2$
$= 82 - 4.9(2.89)$
$\approx 67.8$
The height of the stone is approximately 67.8 meters at 1.7 seconds.

26. $8.6(9.46 \times 10^{15})$
$= 81.4 \times 10^{15}$
$= 8.14 \times 10^{16}$ kilometers

27. $\frac{1 \text{ concentrate}}{6 \text{ total}} = \frac{500 \text{ mL concentrate}}{x \text{ total}}$
$x = 6 \times 500 = 3000$ mL
This can make 3000 milliliters of juice.

28. integer, rational number, and real number

29. Yes, it will be a rational or irrational number. The exception is negative numbers, for which the square roots are undefined.

30. $|(-346) - (-320)| = |-26| = 26°$ F

## CONSTRUCTION LAB 1

### Lab Practice 1

**See student work.**

## LESSON 4

### Warm Up 4

1. Reflexive Property of Equality
2. The angle is larger than 90°, making it obtuse.
3. $\overleftrightarrow{CD}$ goes through and is not on plane $ABC$. Choice **B** is correct.

### Lesson Practice 4

a. No; Postulate 6: Through any three noncollinear points there is only one plane.

b. $\overleftrightarrow{AB}$ is a line on plane $M$. The intersection of $\overleftrightarrow{CD}$ and $\overleftrightarrow{AB}$ is point $O$. The intersection of planes $M$ and $N$ is $\overleftrightarrow{AB}$. Points $E$ and $F$ are coplanar.

c. Three legs are steadier on uneven surfaces by Postulate 6. Four legs are less steady on uneven surfaces because the legs must be in the same plane in order to be steady.

### Practice 4

1. Points $H$, $I$, and $K$ are noncollinear points. Choice **C** is correct.
2. Collinear points are points that lie on the same line. Coplanar lines are lines that lie in the same plane.
3. Theorem 4-1: If two lines intersect, then they intersect in exactly one point.
4. 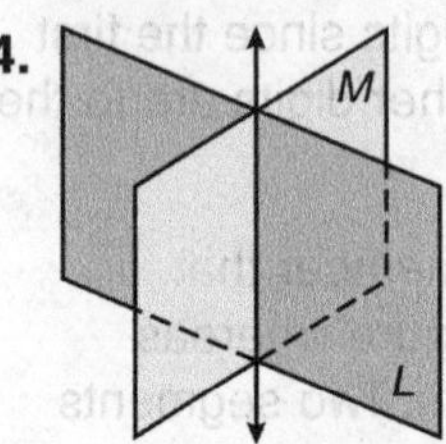

5. 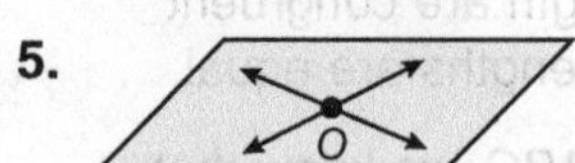

6. This is always true because Theorem 4-3 says if two lines intersect, then there exists exactly one plane that contains them.
7. Answers may vary. Sample: $\overrightarrow{BA}$ and $\overrightarrow{BC}$.
8. This is a straight line, which measures 180°.
9. This is called a straight angle.
10. $30° + 13° = 43°$

11. $m\angle ABD = \frac{1}{2} m\angle ABC$

$m\angle ABD = \frac{1}{2}(62°)$

$m\angle ABD = 31°$

12. Locate the midpoint of $AB$ and label it $C$. Then locate the midpoint of $AC$, label it $D$, and locate the midpoint of $CB$ and label it $E$. These are the quarter points.

13. A  2x + 5  B  5x − 16  C

$AC = (2x + 5) + (5x - 16)$

$= 7x - 11$

14. The probability is still $\frac{1}{2}$ because each flip is an independent event.

15. 1  75 yd  2  x  3

120 yd

$120 - 75 = 45$

The second light is 45 yards from the third one.

16. Theorem 4-3 tells us that choice **B** is true. Answers may vary for the drawings. Samples:

Choice A:

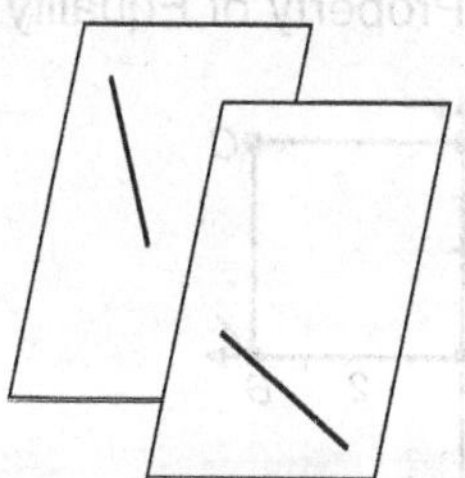

Choice C:

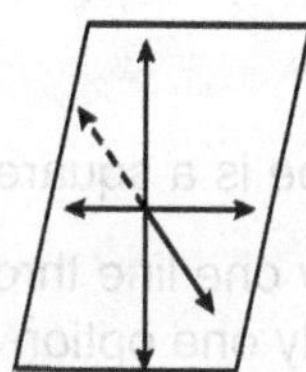

Choice D:

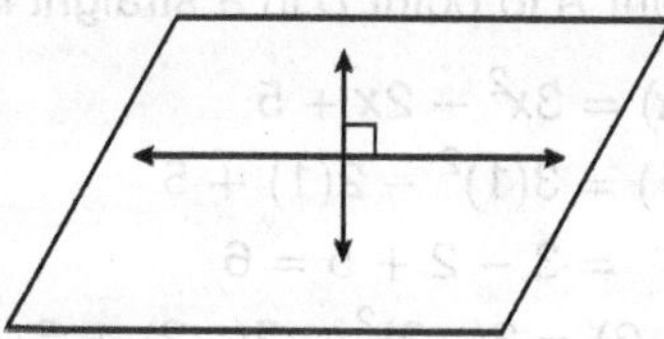

17. An infinite number of points can lie between any two points on a line.

18. parallel

19. $\frac{15 - 6x^2}{2}$ is the parent function $y = x^2$ after some transformations.

20.

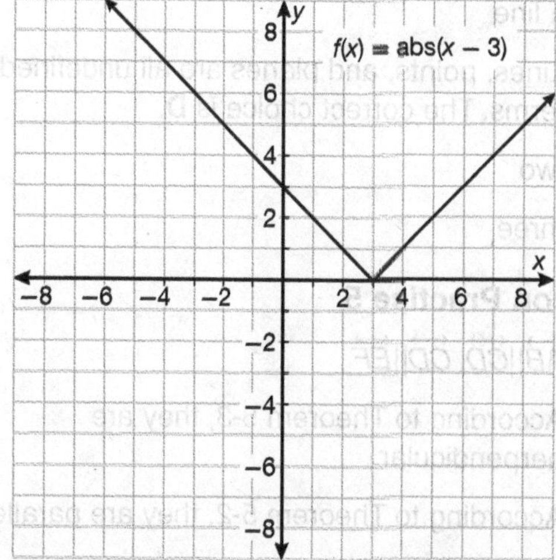


Yes, it is a function because it passes the vertical line test.

21. $\frac{4j - 12x^2}{3} = j$

$4j - 12x^2 = 3j$

$4j - 3j = 12x^2$

$j = 12x^2$

22. $-4m + 2 < 26$

$-4m < 24$

$m > -6$

23. $AC = |(-4) - 5| = |-9| = 9$

24. $1.15 \div 1.25 = 0.92$ or 92%. To find the percent error, we can subtract: $100\% - 92\% = 8\%$. Jaime's percent error is 8%.

25. $18 \text{ cm} \times \left(\frac{1 \text{ in.}}{2.54 \text{ cm}}\right) \approx 7.1 \text{ in.}$

26. $0.5 \text{ mi} \times \left(\frac{5280 \text{ ft}}{1 \text{ mi}}\right) \times \left(\frac{12 \text{ in.}}{1 \text{ ft}}\right) = 31{,}680 \text{ in.}$

27. $23{,}000{,}000 = 2.3 \times 10^7$

28. $3^5 = 3 \times 3 \times 3 \times 3 \times 3 = 243$

29. 34,020

30. Multiplication Property of Zero

## LESSON 5

### Warm Up 5

1. coplanar

2. a line
3. Lines, points, and planes are all undefined terms. The correct choice is **D**.
4. two
5. three

**Lesson Practice 5**

a. $\overleftrightarrow{AB} || \overleftrightarrow{CD}$, $\overleftrightarrow{CD} || \overleftrightarrow{EF}$
b. According to Theorem 5-3, they are perpendicular.
c. According to Theorem 5-2, they are parallel.
d. They are congruent right angles.
e. The Parallel Postulate states that there is only one line through a point not on a line that is parallel to that line. Since $\overleftrightarrow{XY} || \overleftrightarrow{CD}$ and passes through $M$, and $\overleftrightarrow{JK}$ also passes through point $M$, it cannot also be parallel to $\overleftrightarrow{CD}$.
f. If all adjacent boards are parallel to each other, then all the boards will be parallel to one another by the Transitive Property of Parallel Lines.

**Practice 5**

1.
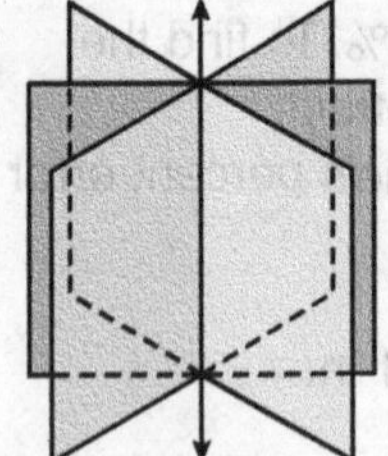

2. Damon is incorrect as it takes only three noncollinear points to determine a plane.
3. The three points are collinear, and an infinite number of planes contain them all. Three noncollinear points are needed to define a plane.
4. 6, 8, 10, or any multiple of 3, 4, 5, as well as values such as 5, 12, 13 and 7, 24, 25 and 8, 15, 17 and 9, 40, 41 and so on, as well as multiples of these triples. Yes, there are an infinite number.
5. Two opposite rays form a straight line. So, the measure of the angle is 180°.
6.
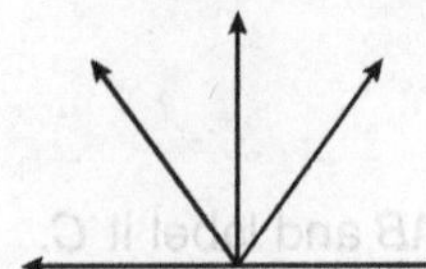

Only one line can be drawn that is perpendicular to the given line from the point, but two lines can be drawn that meet the given line at 45°, one on each side of the perpendicular.

7. 10,000; Square the number of centimeters in $1 \text{ m} = (100)^2$.
8. $\frac{2(2+4)}{6} - |-2|$

$= \frac{2(6)}{6} - 2$

$= 2 - 2$

$= 0$

9. Answers will vary. Sample: parallel $\overline{DC}$, perpendicular $\overline{AD}$, skew $\overline{EH}$
10. Symmetric Property of Equality
11.
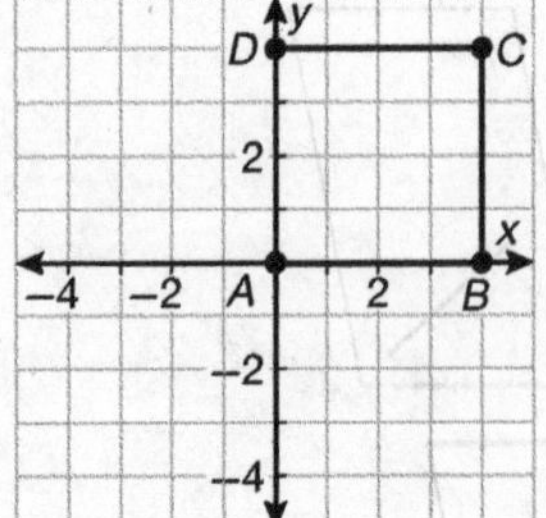


The resulting shape is a square.

12. Since there is only one line through any two points, there is only one option to get from point $A$ to point $B$ in a straight line.
13. $f(x) = 3x^2 - 2x + 5$

$f(1) = 3(1)^2 - 2(1) + 5$

$= 3 - 2 + 5 = 6$

$f(-2) = 3(-2)^2 - 2(-2) + 5$

$= 12 - (-4) + 5 = 21$

$f(a) = 3a^2 - 2a + 5$

14. The coordinates are located at $W(-3, 2)$, $Y(3, -3)$, $X(3, 0)$, $Z(0, -3)$; The correct choice is **B**.

15. Any three points define a plane (Postulate 9), so a tripod will always be steady. A stand with four or more legs could easily wobble on many surfaces.

16. According to Theorem 5-3, $\overrightarrow{UT}$ must be perpendicular to $\overleftrightarrow{XY}$.

17. $\frac{1 \text{ concentrate}}{8 \text{ total}} = \frac{250 \text{ mL concentrate}}{x \text{ total}}$

$x = 8 \times 250 = 2000$ mL

This can make 2000 mL, or 2 L, of juice.

18.

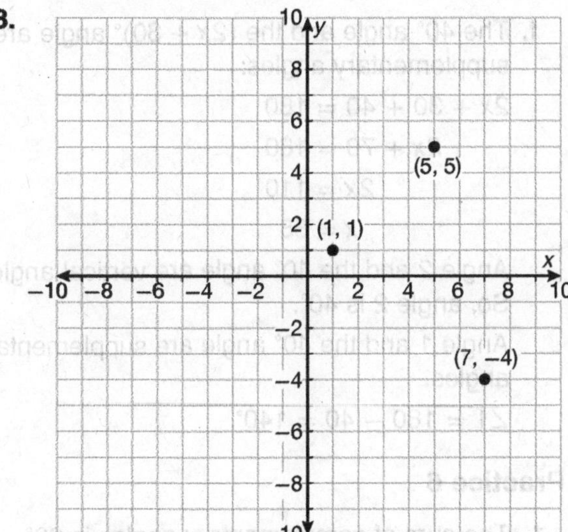


They are coplanar, since they are not on the same line.

19. $a^3 + b^3 + c^3 = d^3$

$b^3 = d^3 - a^3 - c^3$

$b = \sqrt[3]{d^3 - a^3 - c^3}$ or $(d^3 - a^3 - c^3)^{\frac{1}{3}}$

20. Even numbers: 2, 4, or 6

Probability: $\frac{3}{6} = \frac{1}{2}$

21. Measure each segment to verify that *AM* is the same length as *MB*.

22. Yes, it makes a difference. If paid after the tax, the amount left as a tip would be higher than before the tax is added.

23. Only one line exists through any two points. The curved path does not represent a line.

24. They all have a negative value for *x* and a positive value for *y*.

25. They are congruent because they both have a measure of 70°.

26. $A = \frac{1}{2}bh$

$2A = bh$

$\frac{2A}{b} = h$

27. The floor and the ceiling are parallel because if two lines in a plane are perpendicular to the same line, then they are parallel to each other.

28. $m\angle A = 35°$, $m\angle B = 25°$

So, $m\angle A + m\angle B = 35° + 25° = 60°$, which is acute.

$m\angle C = 45°$, $m\angle D = 85°$

So, $m\angle C + m\angle D = 45° + 85° = 130°$, which is obtuse.

29. Going from $C_4$ to $C_5$ is one octave, which means the frequency doubles.

261.63 hertz × 2 = 523.26 hertz

30. No, because $\overleftrightarrow{DE}$ is not shown to be parallel to $\overleftrightarrow{KL}$.

## CONSTRUCTION LAB 2

### Lab Practice 2

a. Step 1: Use a ruler to draw a line segment that is 3 inches long and label the endpoints *A* and *B*. Measure 1.75 inches from point *A* and mark point *P*.

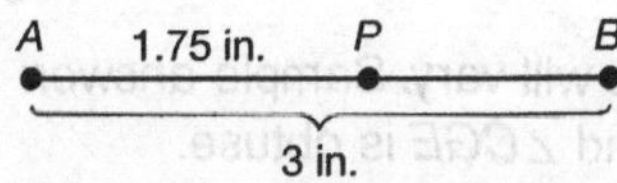


Step 2: Follow steps 1–4 of the lab to construct a bisector through point *P*.

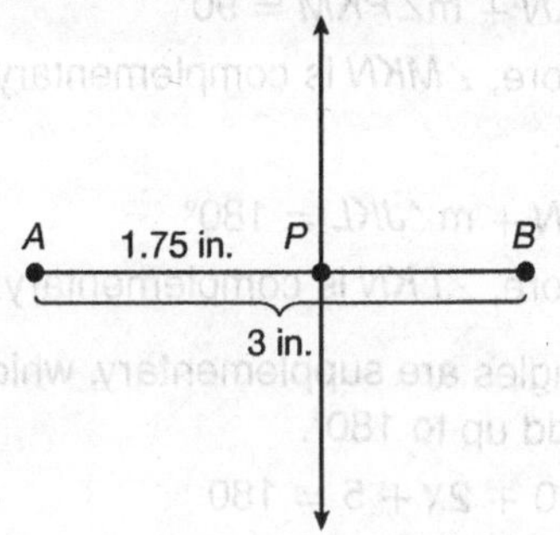

**b.** Step 1: Use a ruler to draw a line segment that is 6 inches long and label the endpoints *M* and *N*. Measure 2 inches from point *N* and mark point *P*.

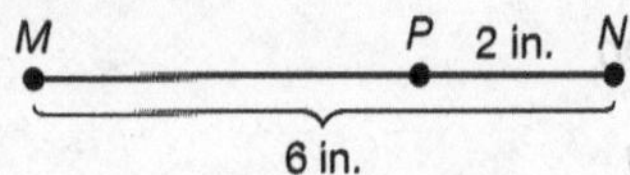


Step 2: Follow steps 1–4 of the lab to construct a bisector through point *P*.

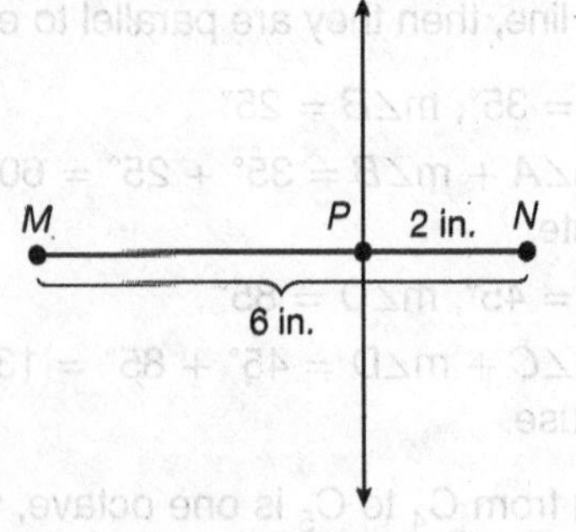


## LESSON 6

### Warm Up 6

1. congruent angles
2. $x + 135 = 180$
   $x = 180 - 135$
   $x = 45$
3. Collinear means on the same line (B). Space is the set of all points (C). Coplanar means in the same plane (D). Intersection is the point or set of points common to different figures (A).
4. Answers will vary. Sample answer: $\angle HGB$ is acute and $\angle CGE$ is obtuse.

### Lesson Practice 6

**a.** $m\angle MKN + m\angle PKM = 90°$
Therefore, $\angle MKN$ is complementary to $\angle PKM$.

**b.** $m\angle LKN + m\angle JKL = 180°$
Therefore, $\angle LKN$ is complementary to $\angle JKL$.

**c.** The angles are supplementary, which means they add up to 180°.
$3x + 10 + 2x + 5 = 180$
$5x + 15 = 180$
$5x = 165$
$x = 33$

**d.** Sample: adjacent angles: $\angle JKN$ and $\angle NKH$, $\angle JKN$ and $\angle NKL$, $\angle NKH$ and $\angle HKL$; Linear pairs: $\angle JKN$ and $\angle NKL$, $\angle NKH$ and $\angle HKM$

**e.** The marked angles are vertical angles, which are congruent.
$6x - 13 = 3x + 11$
$3x = 24$
$x = 8$

**f.** The 40° angle and the $(2x + 30)°$ angle are supplementary angles:
$2x + 30 + 40 = 180$
$2x + 70 = 180$
$2x = 110$
$x = 55$
Angle 2 and the 40° angle are vertical angles. So, angle 2 is 40°.
Angle 1 and the 40° angle are supplementary angles.
$\angle 1 = 180 - 40 = 140°$

### Practice 6

1. The sum of complementary angles is 90°.
   $2x - 16 + 32 = 90$
   $2x + 16 = 90$
   $2x = 74$
   $x = 37$
2. The sum of complementary angles is 180°.
   $180° - 51° = 129°$
3. $|3 \times 2 - 8| \times 2$
   $= |6 - 8| \times 2$
   $= |-2| \times 2$
   $= 2 \times 2$
   $= 4$
4. Yes they can, as two of the points create a line, and this line plus one of the other noncollinear points define one plane while this line and the other noncoplanar point form another unique plane.
5. The marked angles are vertical angles.
   $5x - 30 = 3x + 22$

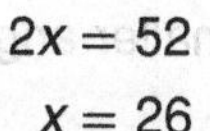

$2x = 52$

$x = 26$

**6.** Since an infinite number of planes can be drawn through a line, and the point is also on the line, the statement should be, "If a point is on a line, there are an infinite number of planes that contain this line and the point."

**7.** midpoint of the $x$-coordinates:

$\frac{1}{2}(-11 + 7)$

$\frac{1}{2}(-4)$

$-2$

midpoint of the $y$-coordinates:

$\frac{1}{2}(3 + 3) = \frac{1}{2}(6)$

$= 3$

The halfway point is at $(-2, 3)$.

**8.** $3xy + 5x + 2y$ for $x = 2$ and $y = -1$

$3(2)(-1) + 5(2) + 2(-1)$

$-6 + 10 - 2$

$2$

**9.** Two equal angles that are complementary must each be 45°.

**10.** $P(\text{red}) = \frac{20 \text{ red}}{100 \text{ total}} = \frac{1}{5}$ or 20%

**11.** No. A plane is defined by noncollinear points, and a space is defined by noncoplanar points.

**12.** $x$-axis: $\frac{1}{2}(4 + 8) = \frac{1}{2}(12) = 6$

$y$-axis: $\frac{1}{2}(1 + 7) = \frac{1}{2}(8) = 4$

**13.** $m\angle ABC = m\angle ABD + m\angle DBC$

$74° = 32° + m\angle DBC$

$m\angle DBC = 42°$

**14.** There are a total of three possibilities on each turn. So, the probability is one out of three or $\frac{1}{3}$ that two competitors will have the same combination.

**15.** She will not succeed, since the two lines can only be perpendicular to the same line if they are parallel to each other.

**16.** Both parallel planes will be intersected by the third plane at a line and the two lines of intersection will be parallel.

**17.** $-x^y + 3xy - \frac{x}{y}$ for $x = 4$ and $y = 2$

$= -(4)^2 + 3(4)(2) - \frac{4}{2}$

$= -16 + 24 - 2$

$= 6$

**18.** The correct choice is **D** because in order for an angle to be described by only one point, that point must be at the vertex.

**19.** Answers will vary. Sample: Find the sum by rounding: 23.52 + 19.37.

**20.** Students should use a protractor and find the measure of the angle to be 10°.

**21.** $|(-7) - 11| = |-18| = 18$

**22.** Since these lines are parallel to a common line, they are parallel to each other (Theorem 5-7).

**23.** $654 \times 20\% = 654 \times 0.20 = 130.8$

**24.** Yes, subtraction exhibits the closure property as the difference of any two real numbers is always a real number.

Subtraction is not commutative. The order in which you subtract the numbers does matter (i.e., $5 - 4 \neq 4 - 5$).

**25.** The sum of complementary angles is 90°.

$90° - 40° = 50°$

**26.** One; If two lines intersect, then there exists exactly one plane that contains them (Theorem 4-3).

**27.** $\overleftrightarrow{EF}, \overleftrightarrow{GH}$

**28.** Apples are cheaper by weight. Since 1 lb = 0.454 kg, \$1.59 per kg is the equivalent of \$0.72/lb, which is cheaper than the oranges.

**29.** If they are both complementary to $\angle PQR$, then they are congruent angles.

$m\angle PQR + m\angle DEF = 90°$

$= m\angle PQR + m\angle KLM$

$m\angle PQR + m\angle DEF = m\angle PQR + m\angle KLM$

$3x + 5 = x + 31$

$2x = 26$

$x = 13$

$m\angle KLM = x + 31 = 13 + 31 = 44$

Both angles have a measure of 44°.

**30.** $f(x) = \frac{5}{x+2}$ for $x = \frac{2}{3}$

$f\left(\frac{2}{3}\right) = \frac{5}{\frac{2}{3}+2} = \frac{5}{\frac{2+6}{3}} = \frac{5}{\frac{8}{3}} = 5 \times \frac{3}{8}$

$= \frac{15}{8}$

## CONSTRUCTION LAB 3

### Lab Practice 3

**a.** Students should use a ruler to draw a segment measuring 4 inches long. Students should follow steps 1–6 for constructing a perpendicular bisector which divides the segment into two 2 inch segments.

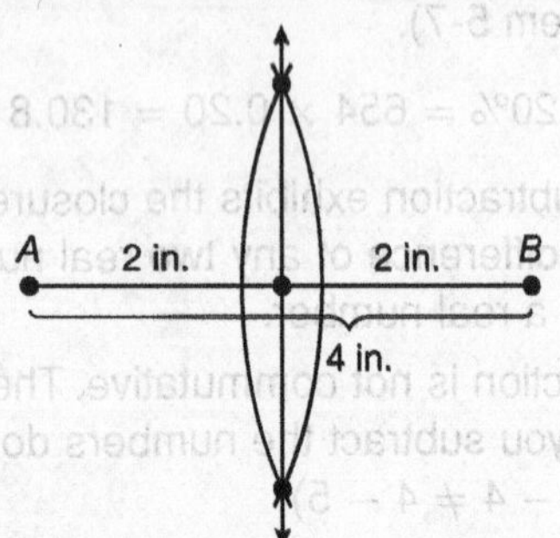


**b.** See student work. The two halves of the segment should have the same measure.

**c.** Students should use a protractor to draw an angle that measures 108°. Students should follow steps 1–5 for constructing an angle bisector, which divides the angle into two congruent angles measuring 54° each.

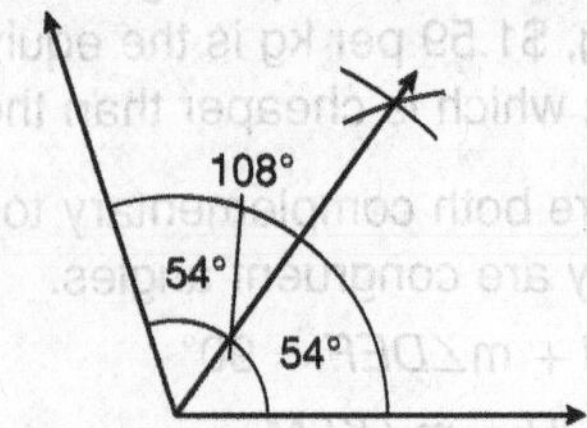


**d.** See student work. Both smaller angles should have congruent measures.

## LESSON 7

### Warm Up 7

1. theorem
2. Choice **A** is false because a postulate is not a proven statement, but rather a statement that is assumed to be true.
3. Choice A is true by the definition of perpendicular. Choice B is false because parallel lines never intersect. Therefore, choice **A** is the correct answer.

### Lesson Practice 7

**a.** The value that comes next in the sequence is found by adding the previous two values in the sequence.

**b.** Every even integer between 4 and 14 can be written as the sum of two prime numbers is a true statement. Proof:

$4 = 2 + 2; 6 = 3 + 3; 8 = 3 + 5;$
$10 = 3 + 7$ or $5 + 5; 12 = 5 + 7;$
$14 = 7 + 7$ or $3 + 11.$

**c.** Find an example of a fruit that does not grow on trees (e.g., grapes or strawberries).

### Practice 7

1. Yes, since all terminating or repeating decimal numbers can be expressed as a ratio of two integer numbers, which is the definition of a rational number.
2. Yes. The median of the coordinates of two points is the midpoint of the segment connecting them.
3. The angles are supplementary.

$m\angle ABD + m\angle DBC = 180°$

$4x + 2x = 180$

$6x = 180$

$x = 30$

**4.** Answers will vary. Sample: In this diagram, $\overleftrightarrow{AC}$ and $\overleftrightarrow{DE}$ are an example of skew lines.

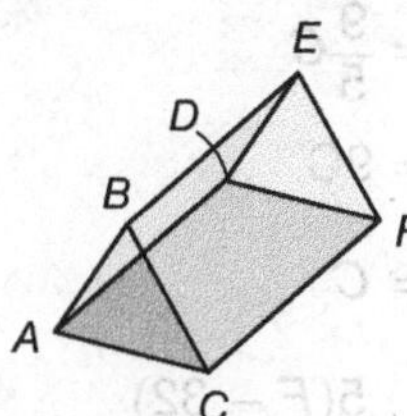


**5.** Sample: It is a sequence of the squares of even whole numbers.

$4, 16, 36, 64, 100, 144, \ldots$
$= 2^2, 4^2, 6^2, 8^2, 10^2, 12^2, \ldots$

**6.** The two airplanes must be at different altitudes.

**7.** No, as there is no way to determine if the zero values in the hundreds, tens, and ones places were measured to be zero or if they are simply place holders.

**8.** The angle marked as 30° and the angle marked as $3x$ are complementary angles.

$3x + 30 = 90$
$3x = 60$
$x = 20$

Also, the angles marked $x$, 40°, and 30° have a sum of 90°.

$x + 40 + 30 = 90$
$x + 70 = 90$
$x = 20$

**9.** Three noncollinear points is the fewest number of points that can define a plane (Postulate 9).

**10.** Sample: If the object were a helium-filled balloon, it would not fall to the ground once released from a position of rest.

**11.** Yes. Proof:

<u>1 through 5:</u>

$1 + 2 + 3 + 4 + 5 = \frac{1}{2}(5)(5 + 1)$
$15 = \frac{1}{2}(30)$
$15 = 15$

<u>1 through 10:</u> (use 15 for the sum of 1 to 5)

$(15) + 6 + 7 + 8 + 9 + 10$
$= \frac{1}{2}(10)(10 + 1)$
$55 = \frac{1}{2}(110)$
$55 = 55$

<u>1 through 15:</u> (use 55 for the sum of 1 to 10)

$55 + 11 + 12 + 13 + 14 + 15$
$= \frac{1}{2}(15)(15 + 1)$
$120 = \frac{1}{2}(240)$
$120 = 120$

**12.** $\$3450 \div \$4000 \approx 0.86$ or 86%

She made 86% of what she thought she would make. This means that her percent error was 100% − 86% = 14%.

**13.** Any mathematical term that is undefined is a term that cannot be defined without using the term itself.

**14.** $\frac{2x - 5}{3} = \frac{x + 10}{4}$ (cross-multiply)

$4(2x - 5) = 3(x + 10)$
$8x - 20 = 3x + 30$
$8x - 3x = 30 + 20$
$5x = 50$
$x = 10$

**15.** $l = 2w + 3$

$A = lw$
$119 = (2w + 3)(w)$
$119 = 2w^2 + 3w$
$0 = 2w^2 + 3w - 119$
$2w^2 + 3w - 119 = 0$
$2w^2 - 14w + 17w - 119 = 0$
$2w(w - 7) + 17(w - 7) = 0$
$(2w + 17)(w - 7) = 0$
$2w + 17 = 0$ and $w - 7 = 0$
$w = -\frac{17}{2}$ and $w = 7$

Since the width cannot be negative, the width must be 7 yards. To find the length,

$119 = 7(l)$
$l = 17$ yd

The dimensions of the field are 17 yd by 7 yd.

**16.** The distance she drives along the $x$-axis is the distance between 4 and $-3$.

$|4 - (-3)| = |7| = 7$ miles

The distance she drives along the $y$-axis is the distance between 22 and $-4$.

$|22 - (-4)| = |26| = 26$ miles

The total distance is 26 miles + 7 miles = 33 miles.

**17.** A conjecture can only be proved by the study of examples relating to the conjecture if all possible cases are tested, but if one result that is not predicted by the conjecture is found, the conjecture can be disproved.

**18.** Since $\overrightarrow{BD}$ bisects $\angle ABC$, $m\angle ABD = m\angle DBC$.

$$3x + 2 = 4x - 20$$
$$3x - 4x = -20 - 2$$
$$-1x = -22$$
$$x = 22$$

**19.** Answers will vary. Sample:

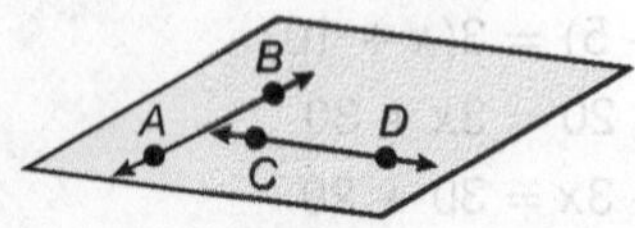


**20.** There are 3 significant digits: In 0.0100, the one and two trailing zeros are significant.

**21.** From this diagram, it can be seen that the two perpendicular lines through $K$ and $L$ are parallel to each other and the two parallel lines through $K$ and $L$ are parallel to each other.

**22.** It is a valid use of inductive reasoning because it is based on several true observations. However, it may be proven false by further observations, such as a car that runs on diesel or electricity.

**23.** $m = 1.609k$

$$\frac{m}{1.609} = k$$

For 539 miles, $k = \frac{539}{1.609} \approx 335$ km

For 7380 miles, $k = \frac{7380}{1.609} \approx 4587$ km

**24.** No, because acute angles have to measure less than 90°, so two of them cannot add to 180°, which is the definition of a linear pair.

**25.** $F = \frac{9}{5}C + 32$

$$F - 32 = \frac{9}{5}C$$
$$5(F - 32) = 9C$$
$$\frac{5(F - 32)}{9} = C$$
$$C = \frac{5(F - 32)}{9}$$

**26.** Choice A is false because the two coplanar lines intersect at only one point. Choice B is true. Choice C is false because two distinct lines will not coincide, and, therefore, will intersect at only one point or never intersect if they are parallel. Choice D is false because parallel lines will never intersect. Choice **B** is the correct option.

**27.** The measures of the three congruent angles whose sum is 180° is $\frac{180°}{3} = 60°$. Therefore, the complementary angle to one of these angles would be 30° because 60° + 30° = 90°.

**28.** It is possible. Sample:

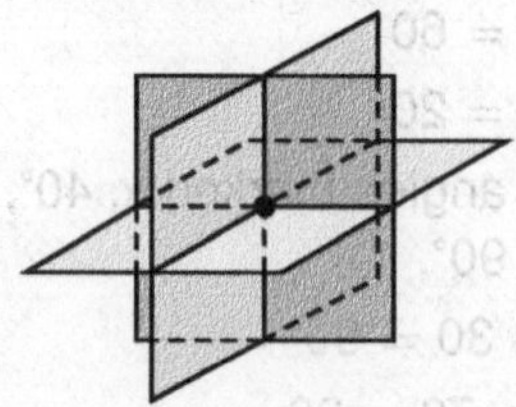

**29.** Since $B$ is the midpoint of the segment, $\overline{AB} \cong \overline{BC}$.

$$2x - 2 = x + 11$$
$$2x - x = 11 + 2$$
$$x = 13$$

**30.** An angle bisector divides an angle into two equal parts.

$$\frac{110°}{2} = 55°$$

## LESSON 8

### Warm Up 8

**1.** Parallel; Perpendicular lines intersect at 90°, and skew lines are noncoplanar lines that do not intersect.

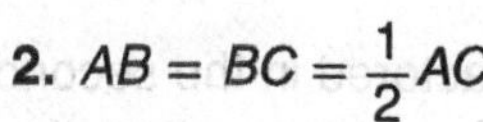



2. $AB = BC = \frac{1}{2}AC$

$\frac{1}{2}(12) = 6$

$AB = BC = 6$

3. Choice **D** is a property, not a theorem.

### Lesson Practice 8

a. $6.5 \text{ m} + 6.5 \text{ m} + 6.5 \text{ m} = 19.5 \text{ m}$

b. $P = 2l + 2w$

$P = 2(145) + 2(123)$

$= 290 + 246$

$= 536$

The perimeter of the rectangle is 536 cm.

c. $P = 6 \times 16 = 96$

The perimeter of the rectangle is 96 in.

d. $A = lw$

$A = 21.2 \times 14.5 = 307.4$

The area of the rectangle is 307.4 ft$^2$.

e. $A = lw$

$12 = 6w$

$2 = w$

The base of the rectangle is 2 cm.

f. $a^2 + b^2 = c^2$

$8^2 + b^2 = 10^2$

$64 + b^2 = 100$

$b^2 = 36$

$\sqrt{b^2} = \sqrt{36}$

$b = 6 \text{ m}$

g.

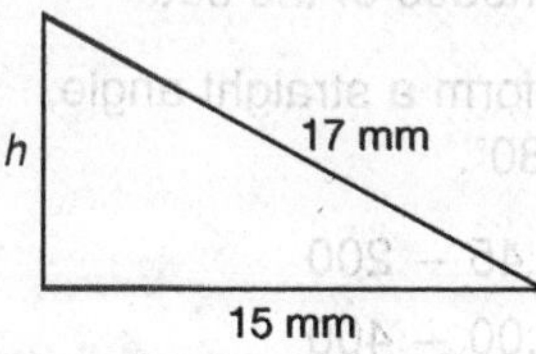


First, find the length of $h$.

$h^2 + 15^2 = 17^2$

$h^2 + 225 = 289$

$h^2 = 64$

$\sqrt{h^2} = \sqrt{64}$

$h = 8$

Now use $A = \frac{1}{2}bh$ to find the area of the triangle.

$A = \frac{1}{2}(15)(8) = \frac{1}{2}(120) = 60$

The area of the triangle is 60 mm$^2$.

h. $C = \frac{5}{9}(F - 32)$ for $F = 0°$

$C = \frac{5}{9}(0 - 32) = \frac{5(-32)}{9}$

$= \frac{-160}{9}$

$\approx -17.8$

The temperature is $-17.8$°C.

i. $C = \frac{5}{9}(F - 32)$ for $C = 100°$

$100 = \frac{5}{9}(F - 32)$

$900 = 5(F - 32)$

$180 = F - 32$

$212 = F$

The temperature is 212°F.

### Practice 8

1. Even; When a number is multiplied by an even number, the product is always even.

2. Each week's growth is found by multiplying the previous week's growth by $\frac{2}{3}$. 1.333 is the same as $\frac{4}{3}$. So, $\frac{4}{3} \times \frac{2}{3} = \frac{8}{9}$ in. or 0.888 in.

3. point, line, and plane

4.

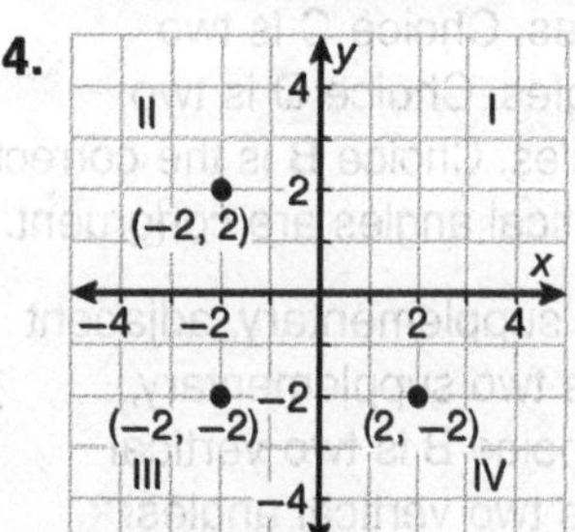


a. Quadrant III

b. Quadrant II

c. Quadrant IV

5. Since the median weight is the middle weight of all of the turtles, half the turtles' weights will be more than the median weight.

$P(> \text{median weight}) = \frac{6}{12} = \frac{1}{2}$ or 0.5

6. $$(2x + 1)(x + 2) = 54$$
$$2x^2 + 5x + 2 = 54$$
$$2x^2 + 5x - 52 = 0$$
$$2x^2 - 8x + 13x - 52 = 0$$
$$2x(x - 4) + 13(x - 4) = 0$$
$$(2x + 13)(x - 4) = 0$$
$$2x + 13 = 0 \text{ and } x - 4 = 0$$
$$x = -\frac{13}{2} \text{ and } x = 4$$
Since the sides of the rectangle cannot be negative, $x = 4$. Now substitute this value for $x$ to find the length of the sides.
$x + 2 = 4 + 2 = 6$
$2x + 1 = 2(4) + 1 = 9$
The sides measure 6 cm and 9 cm.

7. A line cannot be intersected at the same point with two different perpendicular lines. Using any point on a line as the vertex, a line has a 180° angle and to intersect it at 90° means there is only one trajectory from which the line can come.

8. $\frac{0 + 0.25}{2} = 0.125$ mi

9. Each term in the sequence is two times the previous term. So, the next term is $32 \times 2 = 64$.

10. Choice A is two unrelated angles. Choice B is two vertical angles. Choice C is two supplementary angles. Choice D is two supplementary angles. Choice **B** is the correct option because vertical angles are congruent.

11. A linear pair is two supplementary, adjacent angles. Choice A is two supplementary, adjacent angles. Choice B is two vertical angles. Choice C is two vertical angles. Choice D is two unrelated angles. Choice **A** is the correct option.

12. $\angle 5$ and $\angle 6$, $\angle 6$ and $\angle 8$, $\angle 5$ and $\angle 7$, and $\angle 7$ and $\angle 8$

13. No; Three noncollinear points define a plane.

14. Doubled side lengths: 60 m and 72 m; New perimeter: 264 m, which is double the original perimeter measuring 132 m.

15. The student incorrectly factored in the second step.
$$5^2 + 12^2 = c^2$$
$$25 + 144 = c^2$$
$$169 = c^2$$
$$\sqrt{169} = \sqrt{c^2}$$
$$13 = c$$

16. $\overleftrightarrow{LN}$ or $m$

17. $\overrightarrow{NL}$ and $\overrightarrow{NA}$

18. a point

19. Choice **B** is the correct choice because line segments can be congruent but lines cannot.

20. $\frac{x + (3x)^2 + x}{2}$ for $x = \sqrt{2}$
$$= \frac{\sqrt{2} + (3\sqrt{2})^2 + \sqrt{2}}{2} = \frac{2\sqrt{2} + (9 \cdot 2)}{2}$$
$$= \frac{2\sqrt{2} + 18}{2} = \sqrt{2} + 9$$

21. Since an increase in one octave results in the doubling of the frequency, moving down one octave would cut the frequency in half.
$261.63 \div 2 \approx 130.82$

22. $136 \times 3 = 408$
The perimeter of the triangle is 408 mm.

23. $f(x) = 3x + x^2$
$f(2) = 3(2) + (2)^2 = 6 + 4 = 10$

24. The mode is the members that appear most frequently in the set. M and H both show up twice and are the modes of the set.

25. Two opposite rays form a straight angle, which measures 180°.

26.

| | |
|---|---|
| 2:00 – 25 | 2:45 – 200 |
| 2:15 – 50 | 3:00 – 400 |
| 2:30 – 100 | 3:15 – 800 |

The number of bacteria doubles every 15 minutes.

27. Reflexive Property

28. $\frac{1.5 \text{ cups}}{6 \text{ people}} = \frac{x \text{ cups}}{8 \text{ people}}$

$1.5 \times 8 = 6 \times x$

$12 = 6x$

$2 = x$

2 cups of flour should be used to serve 8 people.

29. Since one side will be the house and the sides of the fence are equal in length, you multiply the length of a side by 3, $3s$.

30. <u>Showing Associative Property:</u>

$[f(x) + g(x)] + h(x) = f(x) + [g(x) + h(x)]$

$[3x + 2 + (-2x) + 3] + 0$
$= 3x + 2 + [-2x + 3 + 0]$

$[x + 5] + 0 = 3x + 2 + [-2x + 3]$

$x + 5 = x + 5$

<u>Showing Commutative Property:</u>

$f(x) + g(x) = g(x) + f(x)$

$(3x + 2) + (-2x + 3) = (-2x + 3) + (3x + 2)$

$[x + 5] + 0 = 3x + 2 + [-2x + 3]$

$x + 5 = x + 5$

## LESSON 9

### Warm Up 9

1. absolute value
2. Quadrant IV
3. $\frac{|5x - 8|}{2}$ when $x = 3$

$= \frac{|5(3) - 8|}{2} = \frac{|15 - 8|}{2}$

$= \frac{|7|}{2} = \frac{7}{2} = 3.5$

### Lesson Practice 9

a. $d = |a_1 - a_2| = |-7 - 5| = |-12| = 12$

b. Use the distance formula to find the distance between $S(-5, -3)$ and $T(-2, -6)$.

$d = \sqrt{(x_2 - x_1)^2 + (y_2 - y_1)^2}$

$= \sqrt{(-2 - -5)^2 + (-6 - -3)^2}$

$= \sqrt{(3)^2 + (-3)^2}$

$= \sqrt{9 + 9}$

$= \sqrt{18}$

$\approx 4.24$

c. $d = \sqrt{(2 - 2)^2 + (-4 - 3)^2}$

$= \sqrt{0^2 + (-7)^2}$

$= \sqrt{49}$

$= 7$

d. $d = \sqrt{(0 - 120)^2 + (125 - 0)^2}$

$= \sqrt{(-120)^2 + 125^2}$

$= \sqrt{14{,}400 + 15{,}625}$

$= \sqrt{30{,}025}$

$\approx 173.277$ units

Since each unit is 10 meters, we need to multiply our result by 10.

$173.277 \times 10 \approx 1732.8$ m

### Practice 9

1. $A(-3, 3)$, $B(1, 1)$

$d = \sqrt{(1 - -3)^2 + (1 - 3)^2}$

$= \sqrt{4^2 + (-2)^2}$

$= \sqrt{16 + 4}$

$= \sqrt{20}$

$\approx 4.47$

2. Distance from $E(-4, -4)$ to $F(1, -1)$.

$d = \sqrt{(1 - -4)^2 + (-1 - -4)^2}$

$= \sqrt{5^2 + 3^2}$

$= \sqrt{25 + 9}$

$= \sqrt{34}$

$\approx 5.83$

Distance from $F(1, -1)$ to $E(-4, -4)$.

$d = \sqrt{(-4 - 1)^2 + (-4 - -1)^2}$

$= \sqrt{(-5)^2 + (-3)^2}$

$= \sqrt{25 + 9}$

$= \sqrt{34}$

$\approx 5.83$

Yes, they are the same distance.

**3.** $9x^2 - 18x - 7$

$= 9x^2 - 21x + 3x - 7$

$= 3x(3x - 7) + 1(3x - 7)$

$= (3x + 1)(3x - 7)$

**4.** (9, 14), (−5, 13)

$d = \sqrt{(-5 - 9)^2 + (13 - 14)^2}$

$= \sqrt{(-14)^2 + (-1)^2}$

$= \sqrt{196 + 1}$

$= \sqrt{197}$

$\approx 14.04$

**5.** For 4:00, the hour hand is rotated around 20 out of 60 minutes. Since there are 360° in a circle, the angle can be found as follows:

$\frac{20}{60} \times 360° = \frac{1}{3} \times 360° = 120°$

**6.** The angle must be acute because a right angle or an obtuse angle will make the sum greater than 180°.

**7.** The student has confused a decagon with a dodecagon, which has 12 sides instead of 10. The correct formula is $P = 12n$.

**8.** $\frac{2(2 + 4)}{6} - |-2|$

$= \frac{2(6)}{6} - 2$

$= 2 - 2$

$= 0$

**9.** Never; Two planes intersect at a line.

**10.** Each number is found by adding the two numbers directly above it. The next line will be:

1, 4, 6, 4, 1

**11.** No; By the parallel postulate, two lines that are each parallel to a third line are parallel to each other.

**12.** A postulate is a statement that is accepted as true without proof. A theorem is a statement that is accepted as true only when proven.

**13.** The angles are vertical angles, which are congruent. So,

$4x^2 + 3x + 3 = 6x^2 - 4x + 6$

$2x^2 - 7x + 3 = 0$

$2x^2 - 6x - 1x + 3 = 0$

$2x(x - 3) + -1(x - 3) = 0$

$(2x - 1)(x - 3) = 0$

$2x - 1 = 0$ and $x - 3 = 0$

$x = \frac{1}{2}, 3$

**14.** Two distinct nonparallel planes intersect in a line.

**15.** $a^2 + b^2 = c^2$

$\sqrt{a^2 + b^2} = \sqrt{c^2}$

$\sqrt{a^2 + b^2} = c$

It is similar to the distance formula because when you calculate the difference in the $x$-variable, you are calculating one of the legs of a right triangle. When you calculate the difference in the $y$-variable, you are calculating the other leg.

**16.** $5^2 + 7^2 = c^2$

$74 = c^2$

$8.60 \text{ m} \approx c$

**17.** $\frac{7 \text{ apples}}{15 \text{ total}} \times \frac{2 \text{ oranges}}{14 \text{ total}} = \frac{14}{210}$ or $\frac{1}{15}$

**18.** $m\angle BXC = 180° - m\angle AXB - m\angle CXD$

$= 180° - 13° - 129°$

$= 38°$

**19.** There is not a protractor formula. Choice **D** is correct. There is a Protractor Postulate.

**20.** $(2x - 2)(x + 1)$

$= 2x^2 + 2x - 2x - 2$

$= 2x^2 - 2$

**21.** Transitive Property of Congruence

**22.** No, Sample: if two lines intersect, then there is a plane containing both lines.

23. Sample: $\frac{10}{2} = 5$. You can buy 5 cartons if they cost \$2. But they cost slightly more than \$2, so you can only buy 4 cartons.

24. Choice **C** is correct because a right angle is a single angle.

25. Since $B$ is the midpoint. $BC = AB = \frac{1}{2}AC$.

$$BC = \frac{5}{2}x + 12 = \frac{1}{2}(12x - 4)$$
$$2\left[\frac{5}{2}x + 12\right] = (12x - 4)$$
$$5x + 24 = 12x - 4$$
$$-7x = -28$$
$$x = 4$$
$$BC = \frac{5}{2}(4) + 12$$
$$= 10 + 12$$
$$= 22$$

26. The domain is all nonnegative real numbers. The square root of negative numbers is undefined.

27. The formula $d = |y_2 - y_1|$ can be used rather than the distance formula.

28. $-3w + 2 < 4w + 16$
$$-7w < 14$$
$$w > -2$$

29. They are right angles. Yes, all right angles are congruent.

30. A conjecture becomes a theorem only after being proved true.

## LESSON 10

### Warm Up 10

1. inductive

2. conjecture

3. $2x + 7 = 4$
$$2x = -3$$
$$x = -\frac{3}{2}$$

### Lesson Practice 10

a. Hypothesis: $x = 4$ and $y = 2$
Conclusion: $2x + 3y = 14$

b. Hypothesis: An apple is a golden delicious apple.
Conclusion: The apple is yellow in color.

c. True; Two collinear points are coplanar.

d. If $x = 3$ or $-3$, then $x^2 = 9$; True.

e. If it is Thursday, then it is Thanksgiving Day; False.

f. If a cardinal is bright red, then it is a male; True.

### Practice 10

1. Orangebourgh — $x$ — Dawson City — 19 mi — Danteville; 32 mi

$$32 = x + 19$$
$$13 = x$$

Using the Segment Addition Postulate, we find the distance to be 13 miles.

2. A regular triangle has three sides with equal lengths.
$$15 + 15 + 15 = 45$$
The perimeter is 45 inches.

3. Yes, by definition, parallel lines are coplanar.

4. If a number is an integer, then it is a rational number.

5. $x^2 - 4x - 21 = (x - 7)(x + 3)$

6. The statement is always nonnegative for all real numbers $x$, because the numerator is always nonnegative, and the denominator is positive.

7. Use the distance formula to check each point.
Choice A:
$A(4, 7)$, $B(1, 4)$
$$d = \sqrt{(1 - 4)^2 + (4 - 7)^2}$$
$$= \sqrt{(-3)^2 + (-3)^2}$$
$$= \sqrt{9 + 9}$$

$= \sqrt{18}$

$\approx 4.24$

Choice B:

$A(4, 7), B(1, 11)$

$d = \sqrt{(1 - 4)^2 + (11 - 7)^2}$

$= \sqrt{(-3)^2 + (4)^2}$

$= \sqrt{9 + 16}$

$= \sqrt{25}$

$= 5$

The distance between (4, 7) and (1, 11) is 5.

**8.** The Ruler Postulate refers to measures of distance whereas the Protractor Postulate refers to angle measures.

**9.** No; A statement's converse can be false even if the statement itself is true. For example:

Statement: If it is Easter, then it is Sunday. (true)

Converse: If it is Sunday, then it is Easter. (false)

**10.** Yes; If an animal's expected life span is approximately 70 years, then it is a loggerhead sea turtle.

**11.** $\frac{768}{770} = 0.9974$ or 99.74%

768 is 99.74% of 770. So, the percent error is 100% − 99.74% = 0.26%.

**12.** $E = mc^2$

$\frac{E}{c^2} = m$

**13.**

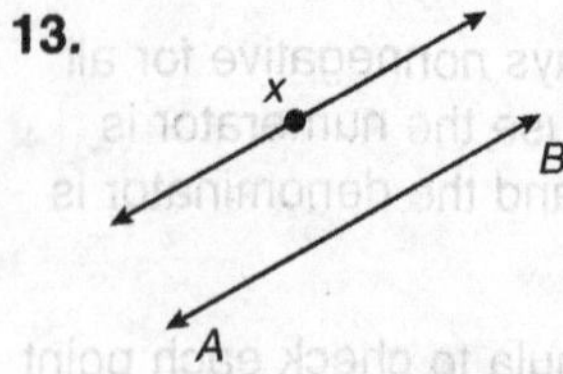


It is impossible to draw a second line because of the Parallel Postulate.

**14.** (2, 3), (−4, 1)

$d = \sqrt{(-4 - 2)^2 + (1 - 3)^2}$

$= \sqrt{(-6)^2 + (-2)^2}$

$= \sqrt{36 + 4}$

$= \sqrt{40}$

$\approx 6.32$

**15.** $d = 7$

$7 = \sqrt{(k - 1)^2 + (3 - 3)^2}$

$7 = \sqrt{(k - 1)^2 + (0)^2}$

$7^2 = \left(\sqrt{(k - 1)^2}\right)^2$

$49 = (k - 1)^2$

$\sqrt{49} = \sqrt{(k - 1)^2}$

$\pm 7 = k - 1$

$\pm 7 + 1 = k$

$+7 + 1 = 8$ and $-7 + 1 = -6$

$k = 8$ or $k = -6$; There are two solutions because the segment can extend in either of two directions.

**16.** It is not possible because the lines are straight. They intersect at the same angle on both sides of the line. Therefore, the vertical angles will be equal.

**17.** These would be the corners that are opposite each other, called vertical angles.

**18.** Yes, as long as they are measuring the same types of units (i.e. both are units of length), but you must convert one into the unit of the other.

**19.** Answers will vary. Sample: expressing the distances between planets.

**20.** Reflexive Property of Equality

**21.**

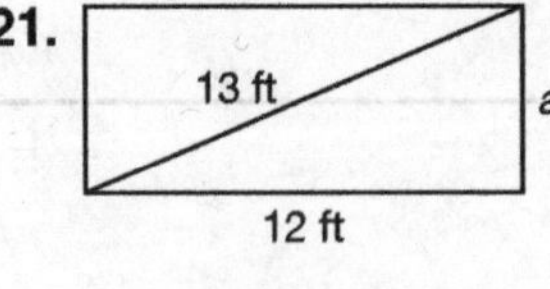


$a^2 + 12^2 = 13^2$

$a^2 = 169 - 144$

$\sqrt{a^2} = \sqrt{25}$

$a = 5$

$A = \frac{1}{2}bh$

$= \frac{1}{2}(5)(12)$

$= 30$

The area of one of the triangles is 30 ft$^2$.

22. The pattern is to multiply the previous term by three to get the next term. The next term is $81 \times 3 = 243$.

23. $(1)(3 \times 10^8)^2$
$= 3^2 \times (10^8)^2$
$= 9 \times 10^{16}$

24. $2x + 7 = 13$
$2x = 6$
$x = 3$
If $2x + 7 = 13$, then $x = 3$.

25. There could be one obtuse angle and two acute angles whose measures would add to 180°. The student could say, "If the measures of three angles add to 90°, then the angles are all acute."

26. $(x + 2)(x - 3)$
$= x^2 - 3x + 2x - 6$
$= x^2 - x - 6$
The student incorrectly added the center term. The answer should be $x^2 - x - 6$.

27. rational numbers and real numbers.

28. $|3 + (-4) + 6|$
$= |5|$
$= 5$
$|3| + |-4| + |6|$
$= 3 + 4 + 6$
$= 13$
The answers are different because in the first, the magnitude of the numbers' sum is found, but in the second, the magnitude of each number is found before adding.

29. Choice A: Supplementary angles add up to 180° and vertical angles are equal.
Choice B: Complementary angles add up to 90° and vertical angles are equal.
Choice C: A linear pair is two adjacent, supplementary angles.
Choice D: Adjacent angles are not necessarily supplementary.
Choice **C** is the correct choice.

30.


## INVESTIGATION 1

1. Line $n$ is the transversal because it intersects two coplanar lines.
2. There are 8 angles formed by the transversal crossing two lines.
3. Answers could be any one of the following: ∠1 and ∠5, ∠2 and ∠6, ∠3 and ∠7, ∠4 and ∠8.
4. Answers could be any one of the following: ∠3 and ∠6, ∠4 and ∠5.
5. Answers could be any one of the following: ∠2 and ∠7, ∠1 and ∠8.
6. Answers could be any one of the following: ∠4 and ∠6, ∠3 and ∠5.
7. One will increase and the other will decrease.
8. Main St. is a transversal intersecting Third and Second Avenues.
9. Mille's Restaurant and Jake's Restaurant represent corners that are alternate exterior angles.
10. These represent same-side interior angles.
11. corresponding angles
12. Students should find that both angles measure 70°.
13. Their measures are the same.
14. 50°; They are corresponding angles.
15. Yes, it is equal to the measure of ∠4; They are a pair of alternate interior angles.
16. Same-side interior angles formed by a transversal intersecting parallel lines are supplementary. 180° − 75° = 105°
17. a. The angle pair are alternate interior angles.

b. Alternate interior angles are congruent.

$5b - 45° = 36°$

$5b = 81°$

$b = 16.2°$

c. $\angle 1$ is supplementary to 36°.

$180° - 36° = 144°$

## Investigation Practice 1

a. alternate exterior

b. same-side interior

c. corresponding

d. alternate exterior

e. alternate interior

f. $\angle 2$ and $\angle 5$ or $\angle 3$ and $\angle 4$

g. Answers could be any one of the following: $\angle 3$ and $\angle 9$, $\angle 2$ and $\angle 8$, or $\angle 1$ and $\angle 10$.

h. $\angle 6$ and $\angle 9$ or $\angle 5$ and $\angle 8$

i. transversal $c$

j. The hill represents the transversal. The posts represent the two lines it intersects.

k. $\angle 1$ and $\angle 2$ are supplementary angles.

$m\angle 1 = 180° - 135° = 45°$

This is true because of the Same-Side Interior Angles Theorem.

l. By the Alternate Exterior Theorem,

$\angle LMP \cong \angle ONQ$

$m\angle LMP = m\angle ONR$

$4x + 25 = 3x + 50$

$x + 25 = 50$

$x = 25$

$m\angle LMP = m\angle ONR = 125°$

m. Yes; See student work. Sample:

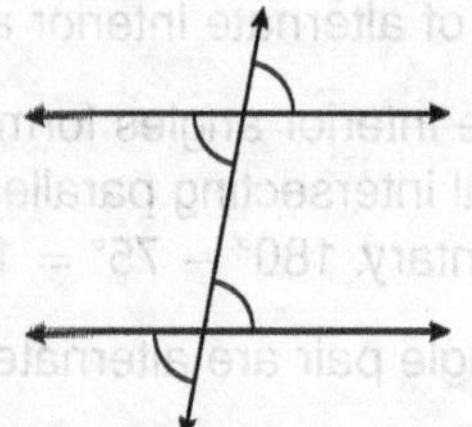

Marked acute angles are congruent.

## LESSON 11

### Warm Up 11

1. coordinates
2. distance $= |C - D| = |-4 - 6| = |-10| = 10$
3. $\frac{-3 + 5}{2} = \frac{2}{2} = 1$

The correct choice is **C**.

### Lesson Practice 11

a. midpoint $= \frac{1 + 4}{2} = \frac{5}{2} = 2.5$

b. $M\left(\frac{x_1 + x_2}{2}, \frac{y_1 + y_2}{2}\right)$

$= M\left(\frac{5 + 3}{2}, \frac{1 + 7}{2}\right)$

$= M\left(\frac{8}{2}, \frac{8}{2}\right)$

$= M(4, 4)$

c. $M\left(\frac{-3 + 4}{2}, \frac{2 + 2}{2}\right)$

$= M\left(\frac{1}{2}, \frac{4}{2}\right)$

$= M(0.5, 2)$

d. $M$ of $\overline{JK}\left(\frac{x_1 + x_2}{2}, \frac{y_1 + y_2}{2}\right)$

$= M$ of $\overline{JK}\left(\frac{-3 + 1}{2}, \frac{0 + 3}{2}\right)$

$= M$ of $\overline{JK}\left(\frac{-2}{2}, \frac{3}{2}\right)$

$= M$ of $\overline{JK}(-1, 1.5)$

$M$ of $\overline{KL}\left(\frac{x_1 + x_2}{2}, \frac{y_1 + y_2}{2}\right)$

$= M$ of $\overline{KL}\left(\frac{1 + 3}{2}, \frac{3 + -1}{2}\right)$

$= M$ of $\overline{KL}\left(\frac{4}{2}, \frac{2}{2}\right)$

$= M$ of $\overline{KL}(2, 1)$

$M$ of $\overline{JL}\left(\frac{x_1 + x_2}{2}, \frac{y_1 + y_2}{2}\right)$

$= M$ of $\overline{JL}\left(\frac{-3 + 3}{2}, \frac{0 + -1}{2}\right)$

$= M \text{ of } \overline{JL}\left(\frac{0}{2}, \frac{-1}{2}\right)$

$= M \text{ of } \overline{JL}(0, -0.5)$

**e.** $A(-3, 5)$, $B(4, 3)$, $C(0, -2)$

$M \text{ of } \overline{AB}\left(\frac{x_1 + x_2}{2}, \frac{y_1 + y_2}{2}\right)$

$= M \text{ of } \overline{AB}\left(\frac{-3 + 4}{2}, \frac{5 + 3}{2}\right)$

$= M \text{ of } \overline{AB}\left(\frac{1}{2}, \frac{8}{2}\right)$

$= M \text{ of } \overline{AB}(0.5, 4)$

$M \text{ of } \overline{BC}\left(\frac{x_1 + x_2}{2}, \frac{y_1 + y_2}{2}\right)$

$= M \text{ of } \overline{BC}\left(\frac{4 + 0}{2}, \frac{3 + -2}{2}\right)$

$= M \text{ of } \overline{BC}\left(\frac{4}{2}, \frac{1}{2}\right)$

$= M \text{ of } \overline{BC}(2, 0.5)$

$M \text{ of } \overline{AC}\left(\frac{x_1 + x_2}{2}, \frac{y_1 + y_2}{2}\right)$

$= M \text{ of } \overline{AC}\left(\frac{-3 + 0}{2}, \frac{5 + -2}{2}\right)$

$= M \text{ of } \overline{AC}\left(\frac{-3}{2}, \frac{3}{2}\right)$

$= M \text{ of } \overline{AC}(-1.5, 1.5)$

## Practice 11

1. $\frac{2 + 9}{2} = \frac{11}{2} = 5.5$

2. $M\left(\frac{x_1 + x_2}{2}, \frac{y_1 + y_2}{2}\right)$

   $= M\left(\frac{3 + 7}{2}, \frac{2 + 4}{2}\right)$

   $= M\left(\frac{10}{2}, \frac{6}{2}\right)$

   $= M(5, 3)$

3. $M\left(\frac{x_1 + x_2}{2}, \frac{y_1 + y_2}{2}\right)$

   $= M\left(\frac{-3 + 2}{2}, \frac{2 + -2}{2}\right)$

   $= M\left(\frac{-1}{2}, \frac{0}{2}\right)$

   $= M(-0.5, 0)$

4. $\frac{a + 5}{2} = 2$

   $a + 5 = 4$

   $a = -1$

5. He only added the coordinates instead of finding their average.

6. $\angle EFD = 90° + 17° = 107°$

   $\angle EFD = \angle AEF = 107°$

7. $\angle BEG = \angle AEF = 107°$

   $11x + 19 = 107$

   $11x = 88$

   $x = 8$

8. Alternate Exterior Angles Theorem

9. False; February is another possible winter month.

10. False; $x = 1$ and $y = 2$ is another possible solution.

11. $d = \sqrt{(x_2 - x_1)^2 + (y_2 - y_1)^2}$

    $= \sqrt{(-9 - 3)^2 + (7 - 4)^2}$

    $= \sqrt{(-12)^2 + 3^2}$

    $= \sqrt{144 + 9}$

    $= \sqrt{153}$

    $\approx 12.37$

12. $d = \sqrt{(x_2 - x_1)^2 + (y_2 - y_1)^2}$

    $= \sqrt{(5 - -1)^2 + (-6 - 4)^2}$

    $= \sqrt{(6)^2 + (-10)^2}$

    $= \sqrt{36 + 100}$

    $= \sqrt{136}$

    $\approx 11.66$

13. $a^2 + b^2 = c^2$

    $120^2 + b^2 = 180^2$

    $b^2 = 32{,}400 - 14{,}400$

    $b^2 = 18{,}000$

    $\sqrt{b^2} = \sqrt{18{,}000}$

    $b \approx 134$ yd

14. To find the hypotenuse,
$a^2 + b^2 = c^2$
$6^2 + 6^2 = c^2$
$36 + 36 = c^2$
$72 = c^2$
$\sqrt{72} = \sqrt{c^2}$
$8.49 \approx c$
The perimeter is $6 + 6 + 8.49 = 20.49$ units.

15. Perimeter of a square $= 4s$
$4s = 458$
$s = \frac{458}{4}$
$s = 114.5$ cm

16. Each number is the sum of the two numbers directly above it.
1, 5, 10, 10, 5, 1
1, 6, 15, 20, 15, 6, 1
1, 7, 21, 35, 35, 21, 7, 1

17. The value that comes next in the sequence is found by multiplying the previous value by 3.

18. Her conjecture has no foundation in fact. There would be no evidence to support a team playing better based on an event unrelated to the game.

19. $90° - 14° = 76°$

20. $180° - 85° = 95°$

21. No, the three planes could all be perpendicular to each other. For example,

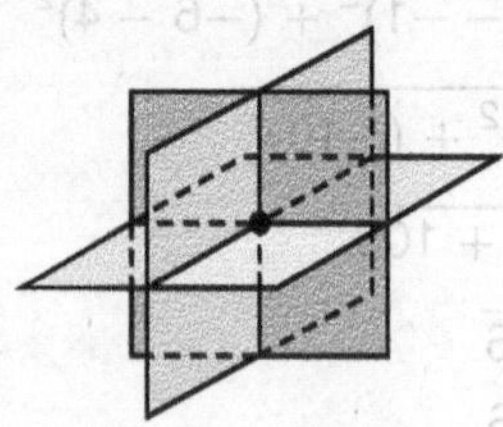

22. $18k = 90°$
$k = \frac{90}{18}$
$k = 5$

23. Greatest: There could be an infinite number of planes by moving the three points around.
Least: There is only one plane that goes through three noncoplanar points that are set in place.

24. Sometimes; The lines could be parallel or skew.

25. 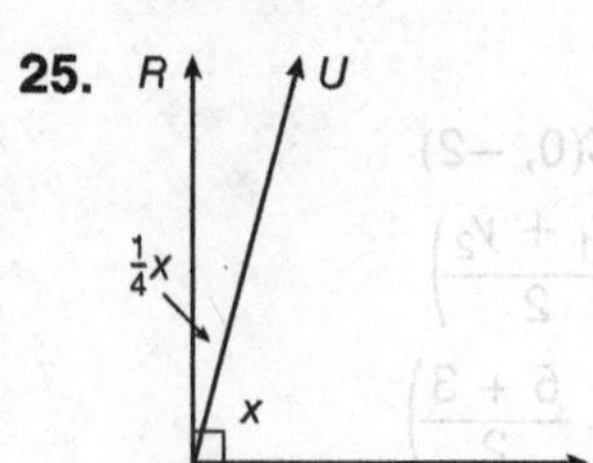


$x + \frac{1}{4}x = 90$
$\frac{5}{4}x = 90$
$x = 90 \times \frac{4}{5}$
$x = 72$
$m\angle UST = 72°$

26. 

Each number on the clock represents $\frac{360°}{12} = 30°$. There are 3.5 numbers on the clock between the 2:30 and the 6:00. So, the angle measurement is $3.5 \times 30° = 105°$.

27. Figures are congruent and numbers are equal. If $\overline{AB}$ is congruent to $\overline{CD}$, and $\overline{AB}$ has a length of 6, then $AB = 6 = CD$.

28. Segment Addition Postulate

29. Three points can be noncollinear, but if they are on the same line, then they are collinear. The student could say, "Any two distinct points are collinear."

30. Choice A: False. If two planes are coplanar, they are the same plane.
Choice B: False. Two points are collinear.
Choice **C**: True
Choice D: False. Two lines can be noncoplanar.

## LESSON 12

### Warm Up 12

1. transversal
2. alternate exterior angles
3. Choice **A**: alternate interior angles

### Lesson Practice 12

**a.** m∠1 = m∠2, so ∠1 ≅ ∠2; angles 1 and 2 are corresponding angles; by Postulate 12, *a* and *b* are parallel

**b.** Since ∠2 and ∠3 form a linear pair and thus are supplementary angles, m∠2 + 111° = 180°. So m∠2 = 69°. Since m∠1 = 69°, ∠1 ≅ ∠2. Since ∠1 and ∠2 are alternate interior angles, by Theorem 12-1, lines *u* and *v* are parallel.

**c.** ∠1 and ∠7, ∠4 and ∠6

**d.** ∠1 and ∠7 are ≅ alternate exterior angles; lines *m* and *n* are parallel by Theorem 12-2.

**e.** ∠2 and ∠5, ∠3 and ∠8

**f.** Angles 5 and 6 are supplementary. Since ∠2 ≅ ∠6, ∠2 and ∠5 are supplementary. Lines *m* and *n* are parallel by Theorem 12-3.

**g.** transversal

**h.** Angles marked at Fox St. and Elati St. are congruent and corresponding angles. By Postulate 12, Fox St. and Elati St. are parallel. By the same argument, Elati St. and Delaware St. are parallel. Since two lines that are parallel to the same line are also parallel to each other, all three streets are parallel to each other.

### Practice 12

1. The pair of marked angles in the figure are both congruent and are alternate interior angles. So, by the Converse of the Alternate Interior Angles Postulate, lines *m* and *n* are parallel.
2. Inductive reasoning is being used.
3. **a.** Angles 1 and 5 are corresponding angles and ∠1 ≅ ∠5. Lines *x* and *y* are parallel by the Converse of the Corresponding Angles Postulate.

   **b.** ∠1 and ∠8, ∠2 and ∠7
4. If the two lines are parallel, then the same-side interior angles are supplementary. So, we add the two expressions together and set them equal to 180° and solve for *x*. If *x* = 34, then the lines are parallel.
5. $\frac{4+8}{2} = \frac{12}{2} = 6$
6. Midpoint between 1 in. and 6 in.:
   $\frac{1+6}{2} = \frac{7}{2} = 3.5$ in.

   Midpoint between 6 in. and 11 in.:
   $\frac{6+11}{2} = \frac{17}{2} = 8.5$ in.
7. Draw a picture and use the Pythagorean Theorem. The line segment will make a right triangle with the segment's rise and run. The run is known to be 4 units. The rise is unknown, call it *y*. The segment's length is *a*. Using the Pythagorean Theorem, *y* can be found for any given length. The coordinates of the endpoint will be (4, *y*).
8. Midpoint of $\overline{SR}$:
   $$M\left(\frac{x_1+x_2}{2}, \frac{y_1+y_2}{2}\right)$$
   $$= M\left(\frac{0+4}{2}, \frac{3+3}{2}\right)$$
   $$= M\left(\frac{4}{2}, \frac{6}{2}\right)$$
   $$= (2, 3)$$
   Midpoint of $\overline{RT}$:
   $$M\left(\frac{x_1+x_2}{2}, \frac{y_1+y_2}{2}\right)$$
   $$= M\left(\frac{4+4}{2}, \frac{3+0}{2}\right)$$
   $$= M\left(\frac{8}{2}, \frac{3}{2}\right)$$
   $$= (4, 1.5)$$

**9.** Midpoint of $\overline{ST}$:

$M\left(\frac{x_1 + x_2}{2}, \frac{y_1 + y_2}{2}\right)$

$= M\left(\frac{0 + 4}{2}, \frac{3 + 0}{2}\right)$

$= M\left(\frac{4}{2}, \frac{3}{2}\right)$

$= (2, 1.5)$

**10.** true

**11.** true

**12.** $(4x + 2) + (6x + 8) = 180$

$10x + 10 = 180$

$10x = 170$

$x = 17$

**13.** $3^2 + 5^2 = c^2$

$9 + 25 = c^2$

$34 = c^2$

$\sqrt{34} = \sqrt{c^2}$

$5.83 \approx c$

The diagonal is approximately 5.83 ft.

**14.** $M\left(\frac{x_1 + x_2}{2}, \frac{y_1 + y_2}{2}\right)$

$= M\left(\frac{-3 + 4}{2}, \frac{-4 + 3}{2}\right)$

$= M\left(\frac{1}{2}, \frac{-1}{2}\right)$

$= (0.5, -0.5)$

**15.** always

**16.** $A = s^2$

$182.25 = s^2$

$\sqrt{182.25} = \sqrt{s^2}$

$13.5 = s$

**17.** $A_{room} = 12 \times 18$

$= 216 \text{ ft}^2$

18 in. = 1.5 ft

$A_{tile} = 1.5 \times 1.5$

$= 2.25$

Number of tiles $= 216 \div 2.25 = 96$

**18.** $\overleftrightarrow{PQ} \parallel \overleftrightarrow{RS}$

**19.** Angles 1 and 2 have equal measures, so they are congruent alternate exterior angles. The Converse of the Alternate Exterior Angles Theorem implies lines *a* and *b* are parallel.

**20.** $x + 32° = 90°$

$x = 58°$

**21.** Choice A: $y = 2(1)^2 - 5$

$= 2 - 5$

$= -3$

Choice B: $y = 2(2)^2 - 5$

$= 8 - 5$

$= 3$

Choice C: $y = 2(3)^2 - 5$

$= 18 - 5$

$= 13$

Choice D: $y = 2(100)^2 - 5$

$= 20{,}000 - 5$

$= 19{,}995$

Choice **A** is correct.

**22.** Yes, since $\overleftrightarrow{XY}$ and $\overleftrightarrow{TU}$ are parallel, and $\overleftrightarrow{AB}$ is perpendicular to $\overleftrightarrow{TU}$, and $\overleftrightarrow{DF}$ is perpendicular to $\overleftrightarrow{XY}$, $\overleftrightarrow{AB}$ and $\overleftrightarrow{DF}$ must be parallel.

**23.** **D**

**24.** Two lines can intersect at one point (with different slopes); they can be non-intersecting (parallel lines that have a different *y*-intercept); or they can have an infinite number of points of intersection (if they are coincidental lines).

**25.** $P = 2l + 2w$

$84 = 2(5x - 5) + 2(3x - 7)$

$84 = 10x - 10 + 6x - 14$

$84 = 16x - 24$

$108 = 16x$

$6.75 = x$

$l = 5(6.75) - 5 = 28.75$

$w = 3(6.75) - 7 = 13.25$

$A = lw = (28.75)(13.25) \approx 381 \text{ in.}^2$

**26.** The lines could be skew.

27. 

Each number on the clock represents $\frac{360^\circ}{12} = 30^\circ$. There are 4 numbers on the clock between the 8 and the 12. So, the angle measurement is $4 \times 30^\circ = 120^\circ$.

28. Choice **A**: This is not a property.

29. 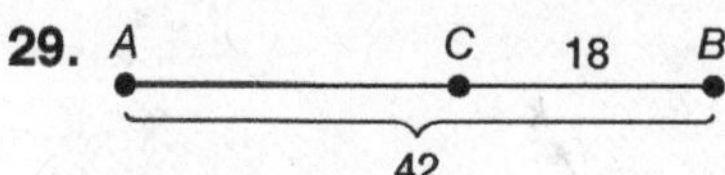


$AC = AB - CB = 42 - 18 = 24$

30. They can have zero (all three parallel), one (two coincidental), two (two parallel), or three (none parallel or coincidental) points of intersection.

## CONSTRUCTION LAB 4

### Lab Practice 4

Answers will vary. Check student work with a protractor.

## LESSON 13

### Warm Up 13

1. obtuse
2. $P = 3.5 + 3 + 6 = 12.5$ units
3. Angles $X$ and $Z$ are both acute angles. Choice **B** is correct.

### Lesson Practice 13

a. $\triangle UVW$

b. $\triangle XYZ$

c. $\triangle RST$

d. Yes, $\triangle XYZ$ has no congruent sides, making it scalene.

e. $P = 13.2 + 13.2 + 18.7 = 45.1$ cm

f. $A = \frac{1}{2}bh$

$= \frac{1}{2}(13.2)(13.2)$

$= 87.12 \text{ cm}^2$

g. The boundary fencing is the perimeter of the triangle.

$P = 766 + 987 + 1254 = 3007$ yd

h. $0.95A = 0.95\left(\frac{1}{2}\right)(1254)(603)$

$\approx 359{,}177 \text{ yd}^2$

### Practice 13

1. $\angle 2$ and $\angle 5$ or $\angle 3$ and $\angle 8$ are both sets of same-side interior angles.
2. Answers may vary. Sample: If a triangle is equilateral, then the triangle is isosceles.
3. Since $\angle A$ is obtuse, $\triangle ABC$ is obtuse.
4. It is not possible with three points. Four noncoplanar points can be drawn.
5. $n = 3$: $n^2 = 3^2 = 9$; $1 + 3 + 5 = 9$

   $n = 5$: $n^2 = 5^2 = 25$; $1 + 3 + 5 + 7 + 9 = 25$

   $n = 7$: $n^2 = 7^2 = 49$; $1 + 3 + 5 + 7 + 9 + 11 + 13 = 49$
6. $Y(-3, 4)$, $Z(3, 6)$

   $d = \sqrt{(x_2 - x_1)^2 + (y_2 - y_1)^2}$

   $= \sqrt{(3 - -3)^2 + (6 - 4)^2}$

   $= \sqrt{6^2 + 2^2}$

   $= \sqrt{36 + 4}$

   $= \sqrt{40}$

   $\approx 6.32$
7. $W(-1, -2)$, $X(1, 2)$

   $d = \sqrt{(x_2 - x_1)^2 + (y_2 - y_1)^2}$

   $= \sqrt{(1 - -1)^2 + (2 - -2)^2}$

   $= \sqrt{2^2 + 4^2}$

   $= \sqrt{4 + 16}$

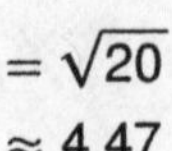



$= \sqrt{20}$

$\approx 4.47$

**8.** Northern hedge runs from (−3, 3) to (6, 5).

$M\left(\frac{x_1 + x_2}{2}, \frac{y_1 + y_2}{2}\right)$

$= M\left(\frac{-3 + 6}{2}, \frac{3 + 5}{2}\right)$

$= M\left(\frac{3}{2}, \frac{8}{2}\right)$

$= (1.5, 4)$

Southern hedge runs from (−3, −2) to (5, −3).

$M\left(\frac{x_1 + x_2}{2}, \frac{y_1 + y_2}{2}\right)$

$= M\left(\frac{-3 + 5}{2}, \frac{-2 + -3}{2}\right)$

$= M\left(\frac{2}{2}, \frac{-5}{2}\right)$

$= (1, -2.5)$

**9.** There is a chance of the conclusion being true, but not for the reasons given. So, the conjecture is invalid.

**10.** No, because $\overleftrightarrow{DE}$ is not parallel to $\overleftrightarrow{KL}$.

**11.** Since ∠3 and ∠8 are same-side interior angles, the Converse of the Same-Side Interior Angles Theorem should be used.

**12.** Choice **D**: 6; Sample:

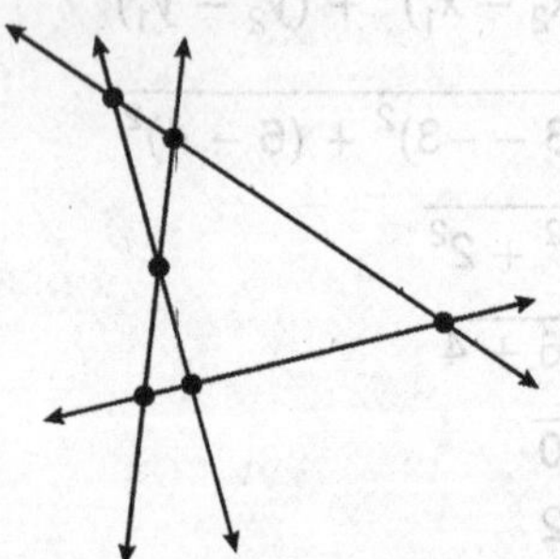

**13.** Isosceles; No, because $\overline{EF}$ is not congruent to the other two sides.

**14.** There is not enough data to determine who is correct. There is no indication as to whether the numbers increase by adding 2, by multiplying by 2, or by squaring the previous term.

**15.** $\frac{-4 + 11}{2} = \frac{7}{2} = 3.5$

This is choice **C**.

**16.** Because an angle greater than 90° cannot be equal to an angle less than 90°

**17.** If a person is born in the United States, then that person can have an American passport.

**18.** $A = lw$

$40 = (8)(w)$

$5 = w$

The length of the other side is 5 feet.

**19.** Sample:

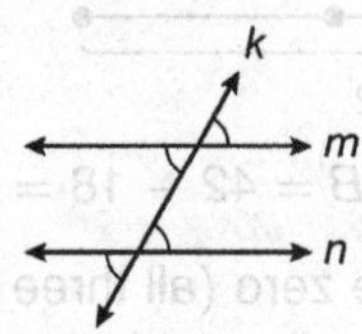


**20.** $A = \frac{1}{2}bh$

$= \frac{1}{2}(200)(1280)$

$= 128{,}000 \text{ ft}^2$

$128{,}000 \div 45 \approx 2844.44$

Approximately 2845 panes of glass are needed to cover one of the faces of the tower.

**21.** If a bird is pink, then it is a flamingo.

**22.** The two angles are congruent because they are vertical angles.

**23.** always true

**24.** **a.** △*PQR*

**b.** △*MNO*

**c.** △*JKL*

**25.** **a.** $\frac{-5 + 0}{2} = \frac{-5}{2} = -2.5$

**b.** [number line with points at −5, −2.5, 0; labels −6, −4, −2, 0]

**26.** $P = 2 + 2 + 5 + 5 + 3 = 17$

**27.** $CD = 2DE$

$2x + 7 = 2(4x - 13)$

$2x + 7 = 8x - 26$

$-6x = -33$

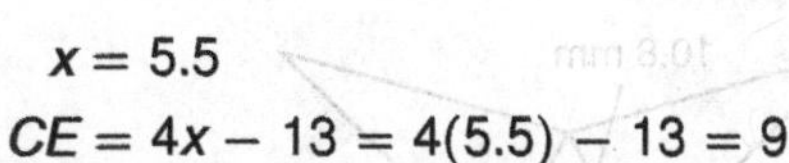



$x = 5.5$

$CE = 4x - 13 = 4(5.5) - 13 = 9$

**28.** No, because none of the planes are parallel, it is impossible to know if their lines of intersection are parallel.

**29. a.** Angles 1 and 2 are congruent alternate interior angles. So, by the Converse of the Alternate Interior Angles Theorem, the upper and lower girders are parallel.

**b.** Angles 1 and 3 are supplementary. Show that angles 2 and 3 are also supplementary. Then use the Converse of the Same-Side Interior Angles Theorem.

**30.** If $x$ were 5, the angle would be a right angle. Since acute angles need to have smaller measures than right angles, but larger measures than zero degrees,

$0 < 12x + 30 < 90$

$-30 < 12x < 60$

$-2.5 < x < 5$

## LESSON 14

### Warm Up 14

1. conjecture
2. Choice **A** is the hypothesis.
3. Choice **B** is the conclusion.

### Lesson Practice 14

**a.** Hypothesis: Line $a$ is perpendicular to line $b$ and to line $c$.
Conclusion: Lines $b$ and $c$ are perpendicular.

**b.** Counterexample: Lines $b$ and $c$ are parallel, so they are not perpendicular.

**c.** Hypothesis: $x^2 = 9$
Conclusion: $x = 3$

**d.** Counterexample: $x = -3$

**e.** The mass-volume ratios are not equal. The data provide a counterexample.

$$\frac{327}{275} \stackrel{?}{=} \frac{568}{501}$$

$$(327)(501) \stackrel{?}{=} (275)(568)$$

$$163{,}827 \neq 156{,}200$$

### Practice 14

**1. a.** No; There are no data in the table for a triangle with an area less than 10 cm$^2$ and base length of 3 cm or greater.

**b.** Sample:

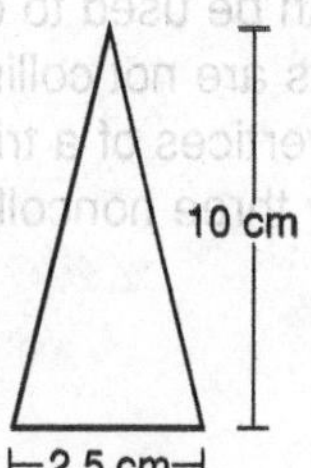


**2.** This is never true because three points define a plane. Any three points are always coplanar, or never noncoplanar.

**3.** It is possible. First, double the area and then find the square root. You will then have one of the leg lengths. Then find the hypotenuse using the Pythagorean Theorem. Once you have determined the leg lengths, you can find the perimeter by adding them together.

**4.** Sample: $\angle AFB$ and $\angle BFC$, $\angle BFC$ and $\angle CFD$ are adjacent angle pairs and $\angle BFC$ and $\angle CFE$ are a linear pair.

**5.** All three sides of a regular triangle are congruent. So, to find the length of one side, divide the perimeter by 3.

$$\frac{12x + 3}{3} = 4x + 1$$

**6.** Alternate exterior angles are congruent.

$2x - 10 = -3x + 20$

$5x = 30$

$x = 6$

$2(6) - 10 = 2$

The angles both measure 2°.

**7. a.** Hypothesis: A shape is a pentagon.
Conclusion: All of its interior angles are obtuse.

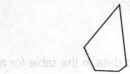

b. Sample:

8. $\frac{-13+5}{2} = \frac{-8}{2} = -4$; Choice **B**

9. These lines can be used to define a plane, as the three points are not collinear, since they are the three vertices of a triangle. A plane is defined as any three noncollinear points.

10. a. $\triangle JKL$

b. $\triangle MNO$

c. $\triangle JKL$

11. No, they do not need to be adjacent. Their measures just need to add up to 90°.

12. 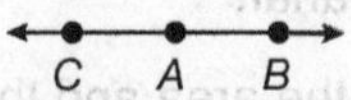


13. Hypothesis: One dozen eggs cost $2.49.
Conclusion: Two dozen eggs cost $4.98.

14. The student found the difference between the *x*- and *y*-coordinates instead of between the *x*-coordinates and the *y*-coordinates. This is their wrong calculation:

$$d = \sqrt{(x_1 - y_1)^2 + (x_2 - y_2)^2}$$
$$= \sqrt{(12-4)^2 + (12-2)^2}$$
$$= \sqrt{8^2 + 10^2}$$
$$= \sqrt{64 + 100}$$
$$= \sqrt{164}$$
$$\approx 12.81$$

They should have done the following:

$$d = \sqrt{(x_2 - x_1)^2 + (y_2 - y_1)^2}$$
$$= \sqrt{(12-12)^2 + (2-4)^2}$$
$$= \sqrt{0^2 + (-2)^2}$$
$$= \sqrt{0 + 4}$$
$$= \sqrt{4}$$
$$= 2$$

The answer should be 2.

15. 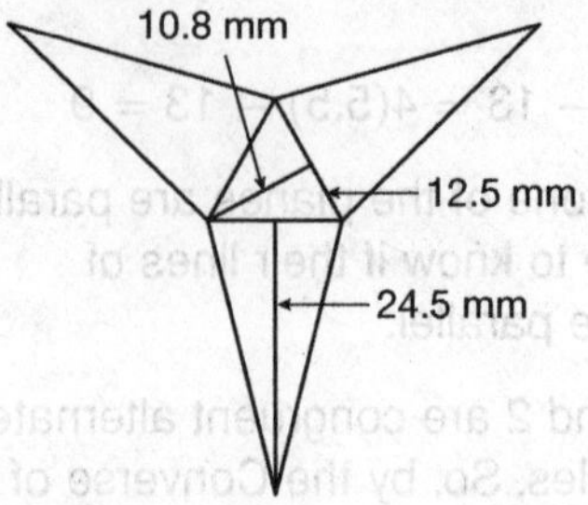


The total area will be the sum of the areas of the four triangles.

$$A = 3\left[\frac{1}{2}(12.5)(24.5)\right] + \frac{1}{2}(12.5)(10.8)$$
$$\approx 527 \text{ mm}^2$$

16. If two lines are parallel, then alternate interior angles are congruent when the parallel lines are cut by a transversal.

17. If the kicker makes a field goal, then the team scores three points.

18. If a number is squared, then the result is positive.

19. Sample: $a = 1$, $b = 50$:
$(1 - 1)(1 - 50) = (0)(-49) = 0$

20. There are two congruent sides making it an isosceles triangle. One of the angles is obtuse making it an obtuse triangle.

21. Answers may vary. Sample: Same-side interior angles, any linear pairs that are formed, same-side exterior angles

22. There are an infinite number of endpoints. If you think about the length as the radius of a circle, then there are an infinite number of points along the outside of a circle.

23. Two of the marked angles are alternate exterior angles and are congruent. By the Converse of the Alternate Exterior Angles Theorem, the lines are parallel.

24. To become a theorem, a conjecture must be proved true.

25. $K(-2, -5)$, $L(-7, 4)$, $M(0, -1)$

$$\text{midpoint} = \left(\frac{x_1 + x_2}{2}, \frac{y_1 + y_2}{2}\right)$$

$$M \text{ of } \overline{KL}\left(\frac{-2 + -7}{2}, \frac{-5 + 4}{2}\right) = (-4.5, -0.5)$$

$M$ of $\overline{KM}\left(\frac{-2+0}{2}, \frac{-5+-1}{2}\right) =$
$(-1, -3)$
$M$ of $\overline{LM}\left(\frac{-7+0}{2}, \frac{4+-1}{2}\right) =$
$(-3.5, 1.5)$

**26.** Three non-parallel planes can intersect at one point, one line, or in three lines, any two of which are parallel. If two of the planes are parallel, then the intersection of the three planes will result in two parallel lines. If the three planes are parallel, there will not be an intersection.

**27.** The pattern is adding 3 to the previous term. The next term is 5.

**28.** Sample:

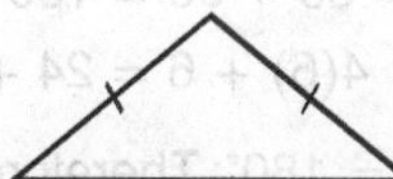

This is an isosceles triangle that is not equilateral.

**29.** Area $= (10)(12) + (10)(12) + (10)(10) + (10)(10)$
$= 440 \text{ ft}^2$

**30. a.** Midpoint of Baltimore $(-4, -2)$ and Philadelphia $(4, 2)$:

$$\left(\frac{x_1 + x_2}{2}, \frac{y_1 + y_2}{2}\right)$$
$$= \left(\frac{-4+4}{2}, \frac{-2+2}{2}\right)$$
$$= (0, 0)$$

**b.** Elkton is the closest town to the midpoint of the towns where they live. Its coordinates are $(1, 1)$.

## LESSON 15

### Warm Up 15

**1.** endpoints

**2.** A ray has one endpoint and extends in the other direction indefinitely.

**3.** The first triangle has three acute angles and two congruent sides, making it an acute and isosceles triangle. The second triangle contains a right angle and has no congruent sides, making it a right and scalene triangle. The third triangle has three equal angles and three congruent sides, making it an equilateral and equiangular triangle.

### Lesson Practice 15

**a.** Polygon A has 6 sides, so it is a hexagon. It is equilateral but not equiangular, so it is irregular. Polygon B has 8 sides, so it is an octagon. It is equiangular and irregular. Polygon C is a nonagon. It is irregular. Polygon D is a regular pentagon.

**b.** $\overline{HK}$ or $\overline{HL}$

**c.** Concave; $\overline{WY}$ and $\overline{WZ}$ both contain points in the exterior of the polygon.

**d.** Yes, corresponding pairs of angles and sides are congruent, making the polygons congruent.

**e.** $\angle 1$ is interior; $\angle 2$ is exterior; $\angle 3$ is interior; $\angle 4$ is exterior.

**f.** The polygons have 6 sides making them hexagons. All sides and angles of the polygons are congruent making them regular.

**g.** The polygons are all congruent because their corresponding angles and sides are congruent. They are convex because there are no diagonals that contain points in the exterior of the polygon.

### Practice 15

**1.** For the statement to be true, 3 and 3 would both have to be even since $3 + 3 = 6$. This is false.

**2.** Since the canal and the road are parallel, perpendicular lines drawn from the road will also meet the canal at a right angle. The farmer can simply measure perpendicular lines to the road that are equally spaced and these lines will give an equal exposure to the canal for each divided area.

**3.** The wallpaper will go 6 feet up each wall.
$A = 4(6)(14) = 336 \text{ ft}^2$

**4.** Interior angles:
$\angle KLM, \angle MNJ, \angle JKL, \angle NJK, \angle NML$
Exterior angles: $\angle QMN, \angle NJP$

**5.** If you find the absolute value of a number, then it is nonnegative.

**6.** If a person is bilingual, then he or she speaks two languages.

**7.** $X(0, 2)$ and $Y(6, 1)$

$$\text{midpoint} = \left(\frac{x_1 + x_2}{2}, \frac{y_1 + y_2}{2}\right)$$
$$= \left(\frac{0 + 6}{2}, \frac{2 + 1}{2}\right) = \left(\frac{6}{2}, \frac{3}{2}\right)$$
$$= (3, 1.5)$$

**8.** Sample: a drawing where the third coplanar line is parallel to one of the other two.

**9.** Double the previous number, then subtract 1.

**10.** Transitive Property of Equality

**11.** alternate exterior angles, alternate interior angles, corresponding angles

**12.** (1.3, 4.1) and (2.8, 6.1)

$$d = \sqrt{(x_2 - x_1)^2 + (y^2 - y_1)^2}$$
$$= \sqrt{(2.8 - 1.3)^2 + (6.1 - 4.1)^2}$$
$$= \sqrt{1.5^2 + 2^2}$$
$$= \sqrt{2.25 + 4}$$
$$= \sqrt{6.25}$$
$$= 2.5$$

**13. a.** $A = lw = (8)(3) = 24 \text{ cm}^2$

**b.** The area of $\Delta PQS$ is half the area of the rectangle. $\frac{1}{2}(24) = 12 \text{ cm}^2$

**c.** $A = \frac{1}{2}bh = \frac{1}{2}(8)(3) = \frac{1}{2}(24) = 12 \text{ cm}^2$

**14.** The polygon is a quadrilateral. It is equilateral, but not equiangular based on the markings. Since it is not equiangular, it is not regular.

**15. a.** They are corresponding angles.

**b.** The angles are congruent because their measures are equal, and since they are corresponding angles, the Converse of the Corresponding Angles Postulate implies that the rails are parallel.

**16.** A kite is a counterexample as it is a quadrilateral with exactly two pairs of congruent consecutive sides and the opposite sides are not parallel.

**17.** Same-side interior angles are supplementary.

$$(10x + 90) + (4x + 6) = 180$$
$$14x + 96 = 180$$
$$14x = 84$$
$$x = 6$$
$$10(6) + 90 = 60 + 90 = 150°$$
$$4(6) + 6 = 24 + 6 = 30°$$

**18.** $m\angle 1 + m\angle 2 = 180°$; Therefore, $\angle 1$ and $\angle 2$ are supplementary. $\angle 1$ and $\angle 2$ are same-side interior angles. By the Converse of the Same-Side Interior Angles Theorem, lines $m$ and $n$ are parallel.

**19. a.** Sample:

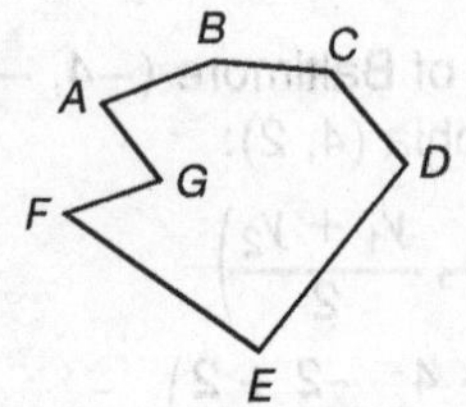


**b.** Sample:

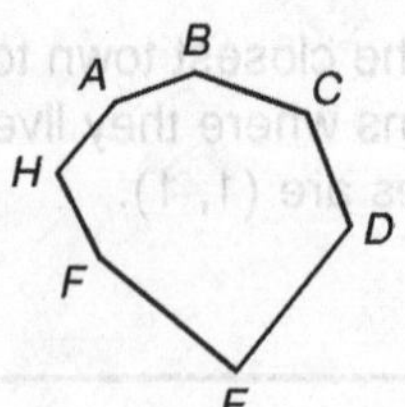


**20.** $\angle 1$ and $\angle 5$, $\angle 2$ and $\angle 6$, $\angle 3$ and $\angle 7$, $\angle 4$ and $\angle 8$

21.

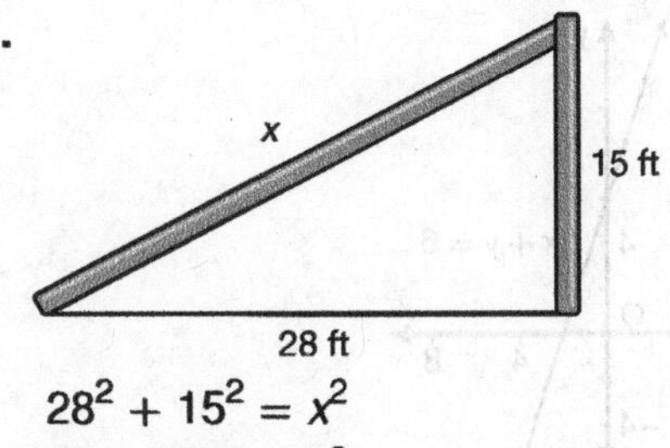


$28^2 + 15^2 = x^2$

$784 + 225 = x^2$

$1009 = x^2$

$31.76 \approx x$

The beam should be approximately 31.76 feet long.

22. midpoint $= \left(\frac{x_1 + x_2}{2}, \frac{y_1 + y_2}{2}\right)$

$M$ of $\overline{AB}$ $\left(\frac{2+3}{2}, \frac{4+-1}{2}\right) = \left(\frac{5}{2}, \frac{3}{2}\right)$

$= (2.5, 1.5)$

$M$ of $\overline{AC}$ $\left(\frac{2+-2}{2}, \frac{4+0}{2}\right) = \left(\frac{0}{2}, \frac{4}{2}\right)$

$= (0, 2)$

$M$ of $\overline{BC}$ $\left(\frac{3+-2}{2}, \frac{-1+0}{2}\right) = \left(\frac{1}{2}, \frac{-1}{2}\right)$

$= (0.5, -0.5)$

23. $A = \frac{1}{2}bh$

$31.75 = \frac{1}{2}(b)v(12.7)$

$63.5 = (b)(12.7)$

$5 = b$

The base length is 5 cm.

24. The intersection of two planes is always a line. Choice **A** is correct.

Choice B: Two lines can be noncoplanar.
Choice C: Two lines can intersect at zero, 1, or an infinite number of points.

Choice D: Four points can be contained in more than one plane.

25. ∠1 and ∠2 are corresponding angles. Choice **C** is correct.

26. The next term would be 33. The pattern is "multiply by 2, subtract 1."

27. $A = s^2$

$289 = s^2$

$17 = s$

$P = 4s = 4(17) = 68$ cm

28. The four interior angles include two sets of supplementary angles.

$180° + 180° = 360°$

29. A hexagon has six sides.

$P = 6s = 6(6.8) = 40.8$ in.

30. concave

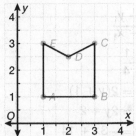

## LESSON 16

### Warm Up 16

1. ordered pair

2. $3 + 2y = 8$

$2y = 5$

$y = \frac{5}{2}$

$y = 2.5$

3. Choice A: $x - 2 = 0$

$x = 2$

Choice B: $-2 + x = 0$

$x = 2$

Choice C: $2 + x = 0$

$x = -2$

Choice D: $2 - x = 0$

$-x = -2$

$x = 2$

Choice **C** is correct.

## Lesson Practice 16

**a.** slope $= \frac{\text{rise}}{\text{run}} = \frac{6}{2} = 3$

**b.** $m = \frac{y_2 - y_1}{x_2 - x_1} = \frac{4-2}{3-1} = \frac{2}{2} = 1$

**c.** The $y$-intercept is 4.

slope $= \frac{\text{rise}}{\text{run}} = \frac{-1}{2}$

$y = -\frac{1}{2}x + 4$ or $y = 4 - \frac{1}{2}x$

**d.** $m = \frac{y_2 - y_1}{x_2 - x_1}$

$\frac{3}{2} = \frac{y+1}{x-4}$

$3(x-4) = 2(y+1)$

$3x - 12 = 2y + 2$

$-2y = -3x + 14$

$y = \frac{3}{2}x - 7$

**e.** $m = \frac{y_2 - y_1}{x_2 - x_1} = \frac{2 - -2}{5 - 0} = \frac{4}{5}$

$y = \frac{4}{5}x + b$

Substitute one point in for $x$ and $y$.

$2 = \frac{4}{5}(5) + b$

$2 = 4 + b$

$-2 = b$

$y = \frac{4}{5}x - 2$

**f.**

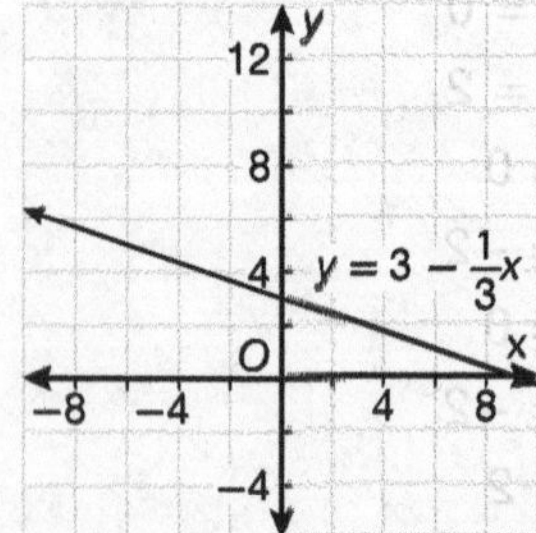


Plot a point at the $y$-intercept, 3. Rise is $-1$ and run is 3. Use this to plot another point and draw the line.

**g.**

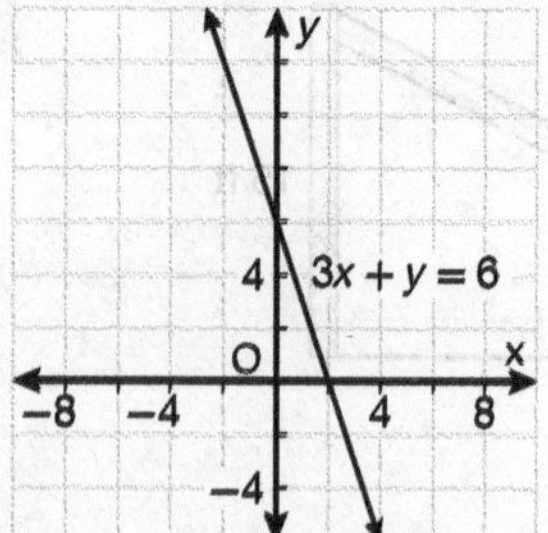


Change the equation to $y = -3x + 6$. The $y$-intercept is at 6. Draw a point and use the slope $\frac{-3}{1}$ to find the next point and draw the line.

## Practice 16

**1. a.** It is neither.

**b.** The shape is irregular.

**c.** It is concave because several diagonals cross the exterior of the shape.

**2.** $m = \frac{y_2 - y_1}{x_2 - x_1} = \frac{5-1}{5-3} = \frac{4}{2} = 2$

**3.** Angles 2 and 3 are corresponding angles. So, we can use the Converse of the Corresponding Angles Postulate to show the lines are parallel. $\angle 1$ and $\angle 2$ are vertical angles, so they are congruent; since $\angle 1 \cong \angle 2$ and $\angle 2 \cong \angle 3$, $\angle 1 \cong \angle 3$; $\angle 1$ and $\angle 3$ are also alternate exterior angles, so by the Converse of the Alternate Exterior Angles Theorem, lines $x$ and $y$ are parallel.

**4. a.** slope $= \frac{\text{rise}}{\text{run}} = \frac{-4}{2} = -2$

**b.** The $y$-intercept is at 3.

$y = -2x + 3$

**5.** Sample: If two polygons are congruent, then they have the same area.

**6.** $A = (17)(14) = 238 \text{ ft}^2$

238 tiles are needed at $1.29 per tile.

$238 \times 1.29 = \$307.02$

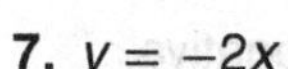



**7.** $y = -2x$

The $y$-intercept is at 0 and the slope is $\frac{-2}{1}$.

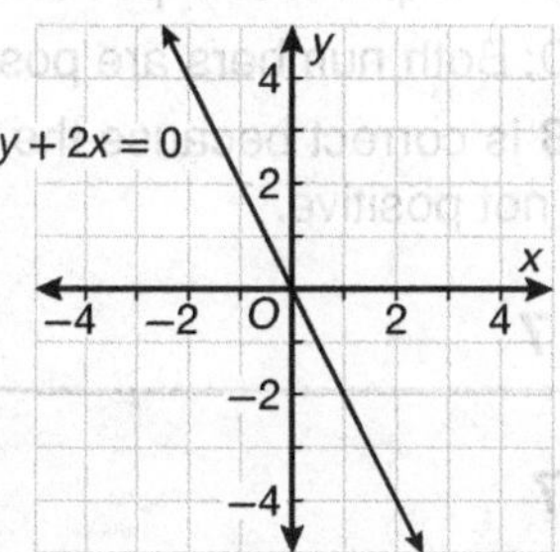


**8.** Corresponding angles are congruent.

$$2x = 4x - 60$$
$$-2x = -60$$
$$x = 30$$
$$2(30) = 60°$$
$$4(30) - 60 = 120 - 60 = 60°$$

They are both 60°.

**9.** $\frac{-8 + x}{2} = y$ and $\frac{x + 4x}{2} = y$

$$-8 + x = 2y \text{ and } 5x = 2y$$
$$y = 2.5x$$
$$-8 + x = 2(2.5x)$$
$$-8 + x = 5x$$
$$-8 = 4x$$
$$x = -2$$
$$y = \frac{-8 + x}{2} = \frac{-8 + -2}{2}$$
$$= \frac{-10}{2} = -5$$

**10.** midpoint $= \left(\frac{x_1 + x_2}{2}, \frac{y_1 + y_2}{2}\right)$

$$\left(\frac{-100 + 40}{2}, \frac{40 + -60}{2}\right) = \left(\frac{-60}{2}, \frac{-20}{2}\right)$$
$$= (-30, -10)$$

**11.** $a^2 + b^2 = c^2$

$$4^2 + b^2 = 6^2$$
$$4^2 + b^2 = 6^2$$
$$b^2 = 36 - 16$$
$$\sqrt{b^2} = \sqrt{20}$$
$$b \approx 4.47$$
$$4.47 + 0.5 = 4.97 \text{ ft}$$

**12.**

$$\angle ABD = \frac{1}{8}\angle DBC$$

If $\angle DBC = x$,

$$x + \frac{1}{8}x = 180$$
$$\frac{9}{8}x = 180$$
$$x = 180\left(\frac{8}{9}\right)$$
$$x = 160°$$
$$\angle DBC = 160°$$

**13.** $A = \frac{1}{2}bh$

$$24.75 = \frac{1}{2}(4.5)(h)$$
$$49.5 = 4.5h$$
$$11 = h$$

The height of the triangle is 11 inches.

**14.** In two dimensions, he is correct, but in three dimensions, he is not. The line that is perpendicular in two dimensions is part of the plane that is perpendicular to the line. This plane contains an infinite number of lines that are perpendicular to the given line through a point on the line.

**15.**

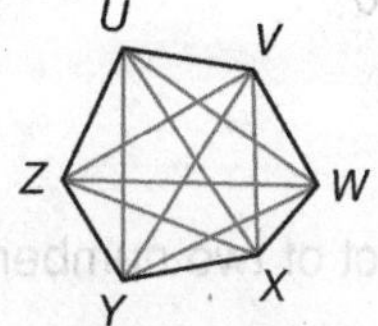


The polygon is convex because none of the diagonals contain points on the exterior of the polygon.

**16.** First, find the height.

$$15^2 + h^2 = 36^2$$
$$h^2 = 1296 - 225$$
$$h \approx \sqrt{1071}$$
$$A = \frac{1}{2}bh = \frac{1}{2}(15)(\sqrt{1071}) \approx 245.45 \text{ in.}^2$$

**17.** Sample: $\overleftrightarrow{AB} \perp \overleftrightarrow{BE}$, $\overleftrightarrow{AC}$ is skew to $\overleftrightarrow{DE}$, $\overleftrightarrow{AC} \parallel \overleftrightarrow{DF}$.

**18.** Yes, if two points lie in the same plane, then the line containing those points lies in the plane.

**19.** $n = 3: 2(3) - 1 = 6 - 1 = 5$: true
$n = 4: 2(4) - 1 = 8 - 1 = 7$: true

**20.** $180° - 80° = 100°$
Choice **A** is correct.

**21.** Yes, as both angles are complementary to $\angle CBD$, they are congruent to each other.

**22.** The slope is negative. So, the line slopes down as you move left to right.

**23.** No, two planes will always intersect at a line, never a point.

**24.** The angles that are marked congruent are alternate interior angles. By the Converse of the Alternate Interior Angles Theorem, the lines are parallel.

**25.** The pattern is "plus 5 to get the next term, then minus 1, plus 5, minus 1, etc." The next term will be 28.

**26.** $2x + 40$ is equal to 120° and $3y - 30$ is supplementary to 120°.
$2x + 40 = 120$
$2x = 80$
$x = 40$
$(3y - 30) + 120 = 180$
$3y + 90 = 180$
$3y = 90$
$y = 30$

**27.** Hypothesis: The product of two numbers is at least 4.
Conclusion: Both numbers are at least 2. This conclusion is not true because 1 and 100 is a counterexample.

**28.** slope $= \frac{\text{rise}}{\text{run}} = \frac{3}{3} = 1$

**29.** Sample:

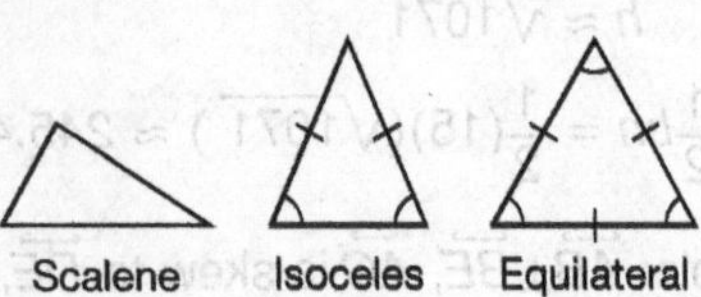


**30.** Choice A: One number is not negative.
Choice B: Zero is not positive or negative.
Choice C: The product is positive.
Choice D: Both numbers are positive.
Choice **B** is correct because the result is 0, which is not positive.

## LESSON 17

### Warm Up 17

1. hypothesis
2. If I am not dehydrated, then I drink enough water.
3. Choice **C** is correct because a regular polygon must be equilateral.

### Lesson Practice 17

**a.** Hypothesis: A polygon is regular.
Conclusion: A polygon is convex.
Converse: If a polygon is convex, then it is regular.

**b.** No, there are irregular convex polygons.

**c.** Hypothesis: Durrell buys juice.
Conclusion: Durrell buys pretzels.
Negation of each: Durrell does not buy juice. Durrell does not buy pretzels.

**d.** For two lines that are cut by a transversal, if the lines are not parallel, then same-side interior angles are not congruent. Neither the statement nor the inverse is true because same-side interior angles are supplementary.

**e.** If the sum of their measures is not 90°, then two angles are not complementary.

**f.** If two angles are not complementary, then the sum of their measures is not 90°. This is the inverse of the original statement.

### Practice 17

**1. a.** The height of the triangle is 9.75 in. and the base is 15 in.
$A = \frac{1}{2}bh = \frac{1}{2}(15)(9.75) \approx 73 \text{ in.}^2$

**b.** Multiply the perimeter by $\frac{3}{4}$.

$\frac{3}{4}(15 + 11.5 + 13.25) \approx 30 \text{ in.}^2$

**2.** Sample: $x = 1$

Acme: $300(1) + 500 = 800$

Amalgamated: $420(1) + 250 = 670$

When $x = 1$, Acme's cost are higher than Amalgamated's.

**3.** $c^2 = 6^2 + 12^2 = 36 + 144$

$\sqrt{c^2} = c = \sqrt{180} \approx 13$

**4. a.** Midpoint of $x$-coordinates:

$\frac{7 + -1}{2} = \frac{6}{2} = 3$

Midpoint of $y$-coordinates:

$\frac{1 + 4}{2} = \frac{5}{2} = 2.5$

The midpoint of $\overline{GH}$ is (3, 2.5).

**b.** $\left(\frac{7 + -1}{2}\right), \left(\frac{1 + 4}{2}\right) = (3, 2.5)$

**5.** If Noah does not have pasta for lunch, then it is not Tuesday.

**6.** By the definition of skew lines (lines that are noncoplanar), this is always true.

**7.** If a student is a PE student, then they wear blue shorts to class.

Hypothesis: A student is a PE student.

Conclusion: They wear blue shorts to class.

**8.** $\angle 5$ and $\angle 4$ are alternate exterior angles. Choice **D** is correct.

**9.** $\angle 2 \cong \angle 3$ because they are vertical angles, $m\angle 2 = m\angle 3 = 48°$; so $m\angle 1 + m\angle 2 = 180°$, therefore $\angle 1$ and $\angle 2$ are supplementary; $\angle 1$ and $\angle 2$ are same-side interior angles; by the Converse of the Same-Side Interior Angles Theorem, lines $x$ and $y$ are parallel.

**10.** slope $= \frac{\text{rise}}{\text{run}} = \frac{-3}{6} = -0.5$ Choice **C**

**11.** This statement is false because it could also be $x < -2$.

Converse: If $x > 2$, then $x^2 > 4$.

This is a true statement.

**12.** $\frac{a + (-a)}{2} = \frac{0}{2} = 0$, or 0 is $|a|$ units away from both $a$ and $-a$.

**13.** slope $= \frac{\text{rise}}{\text{run}} = \frac{60}{40} = \frac{3}{2} = 1.5$

This represents the speed of the train in miles per minute.

**14.** Symmetric Property of Equality

**15.** Answers will vary as to the size and the shape of each triangle, but, in all cases, the conjecture should be found true. Sample: the angle and the side that are marked are the largest

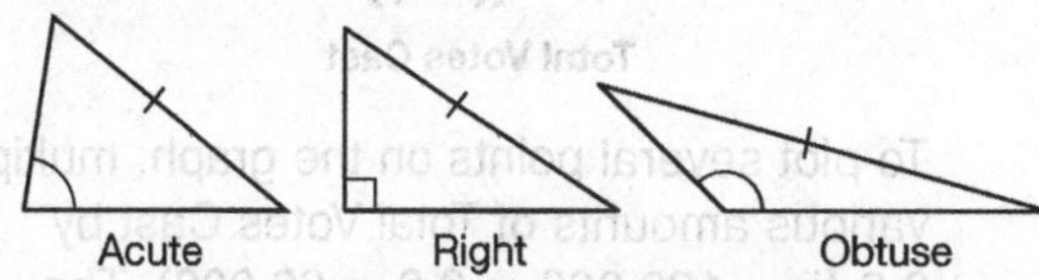


**16.** The angles marked congruent are corresponding angles. By the Converse of Corresponding Angles Postulate, lines $r$ and $q$ are parallel.

**17.**

| Side Lengths | Isosceles or Scalene? | Equilateral? |
|---|---|---|
| 3, 4, 5 | scalene | no |
| 7, 13, 7 | isosceles | no |
| 39, 39, 39 | isosceles | yes |

Scalene has no congruent sides, isosceles has two congruent sides, and equilateral has three congruent sides. An equilateral triangle is also isosceles.

**18.** Contrapositive: "If a bird is a swan, then it is not black."

No, there might be other swans that are black.

No, because there might be swans you have not seen that are black.

Yes, if you have seen many white swans and no black swans, it is probable, although not certain, that most or all swans are not black.

**19.** $5^2 = 4^2 + 3^2$

$25 = 16 + 9$

$25 = 25$

This is a right triangle with no congruent sides.

20. The baseboards are two planes whose intersection forms a line. Choice **D** is correct.

21. Hypothesis: A drink has bubbles.
Conclusion: The drink is a soda.

22.

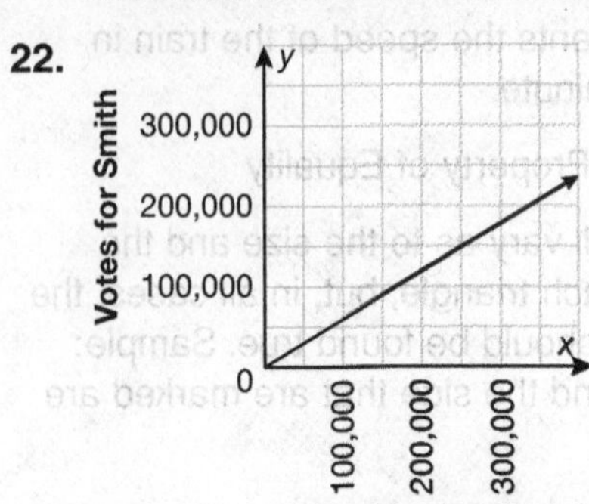


To plot several points on the graph, multiply various amounts of Total Votes Cast by 0.6 (i.e., $100{,}000 \times 0.6 = 60{,}000$). The coordinate for this point is at (60,000, 100,000).

23. any three non-parallel lines that meet at a single point

24. If the sum of the angle measures of a polygon is 180°, then it is a triangle.

25. Sample: $x = 0$, $y = 2$
$(0)(2) < 1$, but $y$ is not less than 1.

26. $EF$:

$$d = \sqrt{(x_2 - x_1)^2 + (y_2 - y_1)^2}$$
$$= \sqrt{(4-1)^2 + (1-2)^2}$$
$$= \sqrt{3^2 + (-1)^2}$$
$$= \sqrt{9+1} = \sqrt{10} \approx 3.16$$

$GH$:

$$d = \sqrt{(x_2 - x_1)^2 + (y_2 - y_1)^2}$$
$$= \sqrt{(-4 - -1)^2 + (-1 - 1)^2}$$
$$= \sqrt{(-3)^2 + (-2)^2}$$
$$= \sqrt{9+4} = \sqrt{13} \approx 3.61$$

$EF \neq GH$

27. The perimeter is divisible by 7. Since the heptagon is regular, there are 7 sides and they all have the same measure.

28. $c^2 = a^2 + b^2$
$17^2 = 10^2 + b^2$
$b^2 = 289 - 100$
$\sqrt{b^2} = \sqrt{189}$
$A = \frac{1}{2}bh = \frac{1}{2}(10)(\sqrt{189}) \approx 68.74 \text{ cm}^2$

29. If both legs (base and height) are $x$:
$A = \frac{1}{2}bh$
$32 = \frac{1}{2}x^2$
$64 = x^2$
$8 = x$

Find the length of the hypotenuse:
$c^2 = 8^2 + 8^2$
$c^2 = 64 + 64$
$\sqrt{c^2} = \sqrt{128}$
$c \approx 11.31$

Find the perimeter by adding the sides together:
$P \approx 8 + 8 + 11.31 = 27.31$ m

30. Sample:

The angles are supplementary.

## LESSON 18

### Warm Up 18

1. acute
2. There are two acute angles and one right angle in a right triangle.
3. It would be an isosceles right triangle.
Sample:

## Lesson Practice 18

**a.** $m\angle R + m\angle S + m\angle T = 180°$

$50° + 60° + m\angle T = 180°$

$m\angle T = 70°$

**b.** $60° + 60° + m\angle T = 180°$

$m\angle T = 60°$

**c.** $90° + 20° + x = 180°$

$x = 70°$

**d.** $m\angle DAB = m\angle B + m\angle C$

$m\angle DAB = 28° + 37° = 65°$

**e.**

J
100° 60°
L K

**f.** $100° = 60° + m\angle J$

$40° = m\angle J$

**g.**

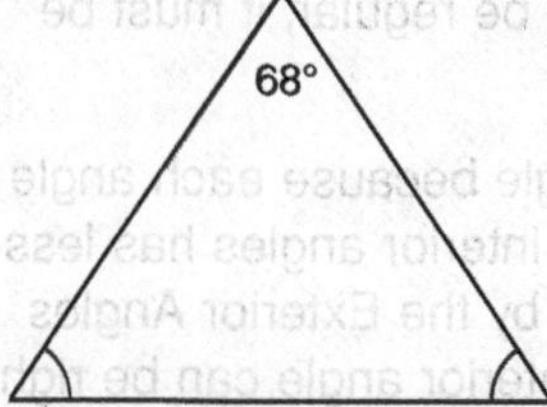


Base angles are congruent, so we can call them both $x$.

$x + x + 68° = 180°$

$2x = 112°$

$x = 56°$

Both base angles measure 56°.

## Practice 18

**1. a.** $(YZ)^2 = \left(3\frac{1}{8}\right)^2 + \left(5\frac{1}{2}\right)^2$

$(YZ)^2 = (3.125)^2 + (5.5)^2$

$(YZ)^2 = 9.765625 + 30.25$

$(YZ)^2 \approx 40$

$YZ \approx 6.32$

This is closest to $6\frac{3}{8}$ in.

**b.** $P \approx 6\frac{3}{8} + 3\frac{1}{8} + 5\frac{1}{2} = 15$ in.

**2.** Since both angles are complementary to 22°,

$(3x + 5) + 22 = 90$

$3x + 27 = 90$

$3x = 63$

$x = 21$

$(7y - 2) + 22 = 90$

$7y + 20 = 90$

$7y = 70$

$y = 10$

**3. a.** If a rock is not metamorphic, then it is not crystalline.

**b.** No, simply because the original statement is true does not make the inverse true.

**4.** By observing the graph, we should test segment $ADE$ first.

$A(4, -3)$, $E(-2, 2)$

$$\text{midpoint} = \left(\frac{x_1 + x_2}{2}, \frac{y_1 + y_2}{2}\right)$$

$$= \left(\frac{4 + -2}{2}, \frac{-3 + 2}{2}\right)$$

$$= \left(\frac{2}{2}, \frac{-1}{2}\right) = (1, -0.5)$$

This is also the location of point $D$. Point $D$ is the midpoint of segment $AE$.

**5.** Converse: If $x^2 = 16$, then $x = -4$.

Counterexample: $x = 4$

**6.** Choice A:

$$d = \sqrt{(x_2 - x_1)^2 + (y_2 - y_1)^2}$$

$$= \sqrt{(3 - 0)^2 + (-2 - 1)^2}$$

$$= \sqrt{3^2 + (-3)^2}$$

$$= \sqrt{9 + 9}$$

$$= \sqrt{18}$$

$\approx 4.24$ No

Choice B:

$$d = \sqrt{(x_2 - x_1)^2 + (y_2 - y_1)^2}$$

$$= \sqrt{(3 - -1)^2 + (-2 - 2)^2}$$

$$= \sqrt{4^2 + (-4)^2}$$

$$= \sqrt{16 + 16}$$

$= \sqrt{32} \approx 5.66$ No

Choice C:

$$d = \sqrt{(x_2 - x_1)^2 + (y_2 - y_1)^2}$$

$$= \sqrt{(3 - -1)^2 + (-2 - 1)^2}$$

$$= \sqrt{4^2 + (-3)^2} = \sqrt{16 + 9} = \sqrt{25} = 5$$

Yes

Choice **C** is correct.

**7.** Yes, due to the fact that $\overleftrightarrow{CD} \parallel \overleftrightarrow{AB}$ by the Corresponding Angles Postulate. For the same reason $\overleftrightarrow{CD} \parallel \overleftrightarrow{EF}$. Since lines parallel to the same line are parallel, $\overleftrightarrow{EF} \parallel \overleftrightarrow{AB}$.

**8.** $P = 2l + 2w$

$40 = 2(4x + 8) + 2(3x - 2)$

$40 = 8x + 16 + 6x - 4$

$40 = 14x + 12$

$28 = 14x$

$2 = x$

Longer side: $4(2) + 8 = 8 + 8 = 16$ in.

Shorter side: $3(2) - 2 = 6 - 2 = 4$ in.

The rectangle is 16 in. by 4 in.

**9.** The third angle in the triangle is $180° - 60° - 40° = 80°$.

This angle and $\angle 1$ are alternate interior angles. Since alternate interior angles are congruent, $\angle 1 = 80°$.

**10.** It has six unequal sides, making it an irregular hexagon. It is neither equilateral nor equiangular. It is concave because the diagonal from $B$ to $A$ contains points on the exterior of the polygon.

**11.** Since the transversal is perpendicular, all angles formed equal 90°. Therefore, all pairs of angles will be supplementary.

**12.** Alternate interior pairs are $\angle 3$ and $\angle 5$, $\angle 2$ and $\angle 8$. Since $m$ and $n$ are parallel, by the Alternate Interior Angles Theorem, $\angle 3 \cong \angle 5$. Since $\angle 1$ and $\angle 3$ are vertical angles, $\angle 1 \cong \angle 3$. Since congruence is transitive, $\angle 1 \cong \angle 5$. A similar argument can be made for $\angle 2 \cong \angle 8$; then $\angle 4 \cong \angle 8$.

**13.**

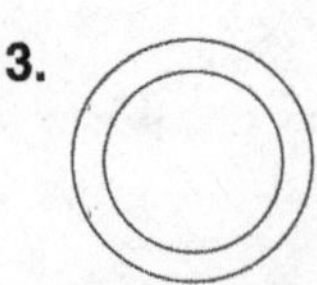

**14.** Since the sum of the measures of the angles of a triangle is 180°:

$180° - 30° - 45° = 105°$

**15.** $x - 3y = 6$

$-3y = -x + 6$

$y = \frac{1}{3}x - 2$

**16.** $m\angle ACD = m\angle A + m\angle B$

$m\angle ACD = 46° + 57° = 103°$

**17.** **a.** Converse: If a polygon is concave, then it is irregular.

**b.** Inverse: If a polygon is regular (not irregular), then it is convex (not concave).

**c.** Both statements are true because in order for a polygon to be regular, it must be convex.

**18.** It is an acute triangle because each angle in any pair of remote interior angles has less than 90° measure, by the Exterior Angles Theorem. So, no interior angle can be right or obtuse.

**19.** **a.** When inputs are 1 and 0, the output is 1.

**b.** The counterexample would be inputs 0 and 0 result in an output of 1. There is no counterexample in the table.

**20.** Inverse: If a triangle does not have all three sides congruent, then it is not obtuse. Neither the statement nor the inverse is true because there are counterexamples for each.

**21.** Answers will vary. Sample:

Statement: If it is Christmas, then it is December 25th.

Converse: If it is December 25th, then it is Christmas.

**22.** A regular hexagon has six congruent sides.

$P = 6(2x - 6) = 12x - 36$

23. $\angle 3$ and $\angle 5$; Converse of the Alternate Interior Angles Theorem. Since $\angle 3$ and $\angle 5$ are alternate interior angles, if they are congruent, the lines are parallel.

24. The polygon is convex, equilateral, and equiangular. It is a regular five-sided polygon. Choice **D** is correct.

25. Four true statements:
If *p*, then *q*.
If *p*, then *r*.
If *q*, then *r*.
If *q*, then *p*.

26. The slope should be $\frac{1}{2}$; the *y*-intercept has been read from given equation, not from the slope-intercept form (should be 2).

27. The slope formula can be used to see if the slope is the same between all three points.

28. $m\angle D = m\angle E + m\angle F$
$58° = 36° + \angle F$
$22° = \angle F$

29. Since $\angle F = 22°$ and $\angle E = 36°$, the interior angle at *D* must be
$180° - 36° - 22° = 122°$
$\triangle DEF$ is an obtuse triangle.

30. If they pass through the plane at the same point, they have one point of intersection. If they pass through different points on the plane, they have two points of intersection.

## LESSON 19

### Warm Up 19

1. regular
2. quadrilateral
3. It is a rectangle because it has 4 right angles, but only two sets of congruent sides.
4. Choice **D** is correct because choices A, B, and C are all true about the interior angles of a square.

### Lesson Practice 19

a. rhombus, parallelogram

b. Sample:

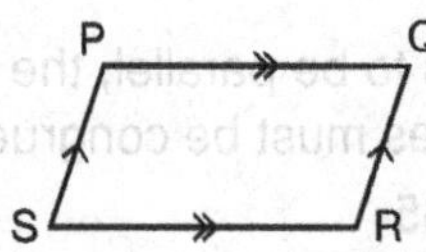


c. $P = 2l + 2w$
$= 2(25) + 2(50)$
$= 150$ m
$A = lw$
$= (25)(50)$
$= 1250 \text{ m}^2$

d. $P = 4s$
$= 4(4.3)$
$= 17.2$ cm
$A = lw$
$= (4.3)(4.3)$
$= 18.49 \text{ cm}^2$

### Practice 19

1.

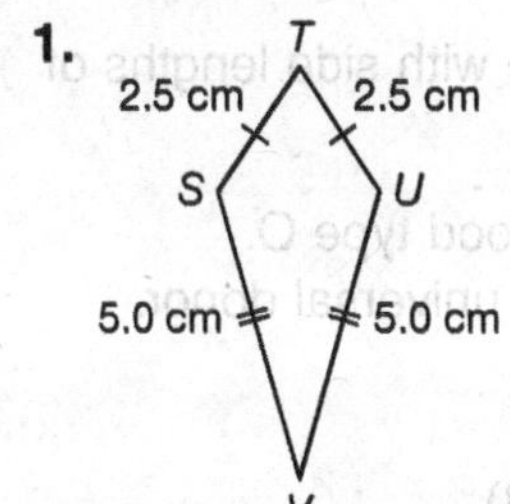


2. Right triangle; Choice **A**

3. For a pair of lines cut by a transversal, if alternate exterior angles are not congruent, then the lines are not parallel.

4. The length of the third side of the triangle is found by subtracting:
$133.1 - 23.8 - 49.3 = 60$

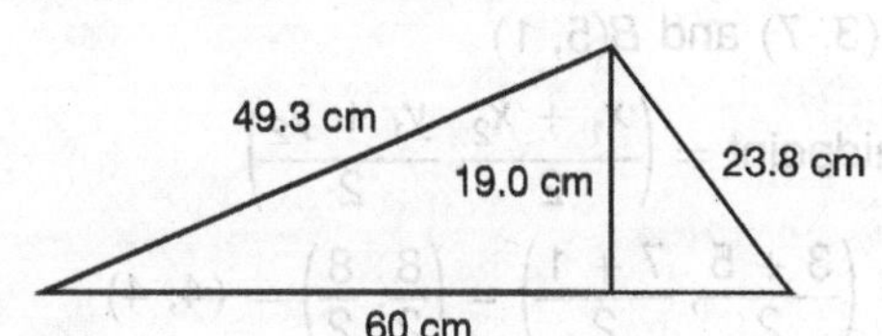


$A = \frac{1}{2}bh = \frac{1}{2}(60)(19) = 570 \text{ cm}^2$

5. slope $= \frac{\text{rise}}{\text{run}} = \frac{-6}{6} = -1$

6. This is a list of prime numbers in order. The missing value is 29.

7. For the lines to be parallel, the alternate interior angles must be congruent.
$3x - 17 = 85$
$3x = 102$
$x = 34$
If $x = 34$, then the lines are parallel.

8. the point

9. $\overline{SU}$, $\overline{SV}$, or $\overline{TV}$; The polygon is concave because there are diagonals that contain points that are exterior to the polygon.

10. $180° - 68° - 43° = 69°$

11. It is a rectangle because it has four right angles, but only two sets of congruent sides.

12. 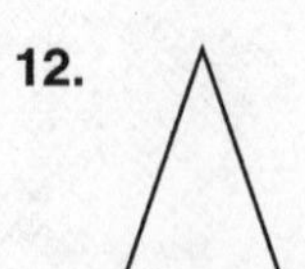 5-5-3 triangle
This is an acute triangle with side lengths of 5, 5, and 3.

13. Hypothesis: You have blood type O.
Conclusion: You are the universal donor.

14. Parallel Postulate

15. $P(-3, 0)$ and $Q(-7, -3)$
midpoint $= \left(\frac{x_1 + x_2}{2}, \frac{y_1 + y_2}{2}\right)$
$= \left(\frac{-3 + -7}{2}, \frac{0 + -3}{2}\right) = \left(\frac{-10}{2}, \frac{-3}{2}\right)$
$= (-5, -1.5)$

16. If an animal is not warm-blooded, then it is not a mammal.

17. $A(3, 7)$ and $B(5, 1)$
midpoint $= \left(\frac{x_1 + x_2}{2}, \frac{y_1 + y_2}{2}\right)$
$= \left(\frac{3 + 5}{2}, \frac{7 + 1}{2}\right) = \left(\frac{8}{2}, \frac{8}{2}\right) = (4, 4)$
$M$ lies on $\overleftrightarrow{AB}$ because the slope from $A$ to $M$ is the same as the slope from $M$ to $B$.
$AM = \sqrt{(4 - 3)^2 + (4 - 7)^2}$
$= \sqrt{1^2 + (-3)^2}$
$= \sqrt{1 + 9}$
$= \sqrt{10}$
$BM = \sqrt{(4 - 5)^2 + (4 - 1)^2}$
$= \sqrt{(-1)^2 + 3^2}$
$= \sqrt{1 + 9}$
$= \sqrt{10}$
$AM = BM$

18. Represent the length as $x$ and the width as $2x$.
$A = lw = (x)(2x) = 2x^2$

19. a. $A_{\text{ceiling}} = (16)(10) = 160 \text{ ft}^2$
b. The height is 7.5 ft.
$A = 2(7.5)(10) + 2(7.5)(16)$
$= 390 \text{ ft}^2$
c. door $= (2)(6) = 12 \text{ ft}^2$
window $= (3)(4) = 12 \text{ ft}^2$
$390 - 12 - 12 = 366 \text{ ft}^2$

20. Yes, each product is different (1295, 1680, and 1650, respectively). Any two data pairs give a counterexample.

21. They are congruent.

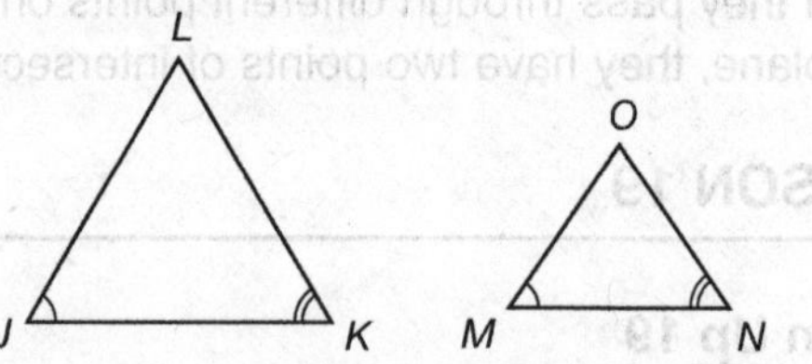


22. Since both pairs of opposite sides are parallel, it is a parallelogram.

23. midpoint $= \left(\frac{x_1 + x_2}{2}, \frac{y_1 + y_2}{2}\right)$
$= \left(\frac{-4 + 4}{2}, \frac{1 + -1}{2}\right) = \left(\frac{0}{2}, \frac{0}{2}\right) = (0, 0)$

24. While it is true that all the geese in the study flew south for the winter, it cannot be concluded that all geese fly south because there are geese that were not observed.

25. $A(4, 2)$ and $B(6, 3)$:

$AB = \sqrt{(4-6)^2 + (2-3)^2}$

$= \sqrt{(-2)^2 + (-1)^2}$

$= \sqrt{4+1} = \sqrt{5}$

$C(-1, 3)$ and $D(-2, 5)$:

$CD = \sqrt{(-1 - -2)^2 + (3-5)^2}$

$= \sqrt{1^2 + (-2)^2}$

$= \sqrt{1+4} = \sqrt{5}$

$\overline{AB} \cong \overline{CD}$

26. Symmetric Property of Congruence

27. Same-side interior pairs are ∠2 and ∠5, and ∠3 and ∠8. Since *m* and *n* are parallel, ∠2 and ∠5 are supplementary angles. Since ∠1 and ∠2 are also supplementary angles, ∠1 ≅ ∠5. A similar argument can be made, if ∠3 and ∠8 are supplementary; ∠4 ≅ ∠8. Similar arguments can be used to show ∠2 ≅ ∠6 and ∠3 ≅ ∠7.

28. $m = \frac{-1-0}{5-3} = \frac{-1}{2}$

$y = -\frac{1}{2}x + b$

$0 = -\frac{1}{2}(3) + b$

$\frac{3}{2} = b$

$y = -\frac{1}{2}x + \frac{3}{2}$

29. The measure of an exterior angle is equal to the sum of the remote interior angles.

$90° + 28° = 118°$

30. Shen is correct. Two angles whose measures add to 180° are supplementary.

## LESSON 20

### Warm Up 20

1. converse
2. If the product of two numbers is positive, then the numbers are both positive.
3. The statement is true. The converse is false because the product of two negative numbers is also positive.

### Lesson Practice 20

a. If a quadrilateral is a rhombus, then it is equiangular.

b. The statement is false because a rhombus is equilateral, not necessarily equiangular. The converse is also false for the same reason.

c. A quadrilateral is equiangular if and only if it is a rhombus. False, neither the statement nor its converse is true.

d., e.

| Hypothesis: filet mignon | Conclusion: leek soup | Statement: If filet mignon then leek soup | Converse: If leek soup, then filet mignon | Biconditional: Filet mignon if and only if leek soup |
|---|---|---|---|---|
| T | T | T | T | T |
| T | F | F | F | F |
| F | T | F | F | F |
| F | F | T | T | T |

| Hypothesis: grilled salmon | Conclusion: spinach salad | Statement: If grilled salmon then spinach salad | Converse: If spinach salad, then grilled salmon | Biconditional: grilled salmon if and only if spinach salad |
|---|---|---|---|---|
| T | T | T | T | T |
| T | F | F | F | F |
| F | T | F | F | F |
| F | F | T | T | T |

**f.** A customer orders a filet mignon entrée and receives a baby spinach salad appetizer. This is false.

**g.** A customer orders a filet mignon entrée or receives a baby spinach salad appetizer. This is true.

## Practice 20

**1.**

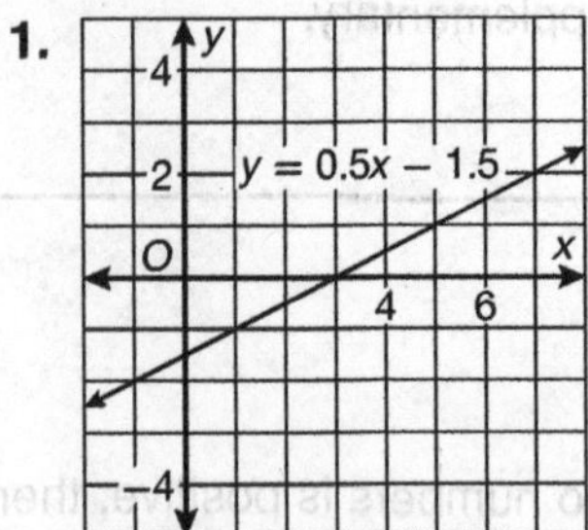


The *y*-intercept is at −1.5 and it rises 1 and runs 2.

**2.** There are 2 congruent sides, making it an isosceles triangle.

**3.** Converse: If the measures of two angles are equal, then the angles are congruent.
Biconditional: Two angles are congruent if and only if their measures are equal.

**4. a.** Area × windows × floors

$= (57)(38)(30)(23)$

$= 1{,}494{,}540 \text{ in.}^2$

**b.** $1{,}494{,}540 \text{ in.}^2 \times \left(\frac{1 \text{ ft}}{12 \text{ in.}}\right) \times \left(\frac{1 \text{ ft}}{12 \text{ in.}}\right)$

$= 10{,}378.75 \text{ ft}^2$

**5.**

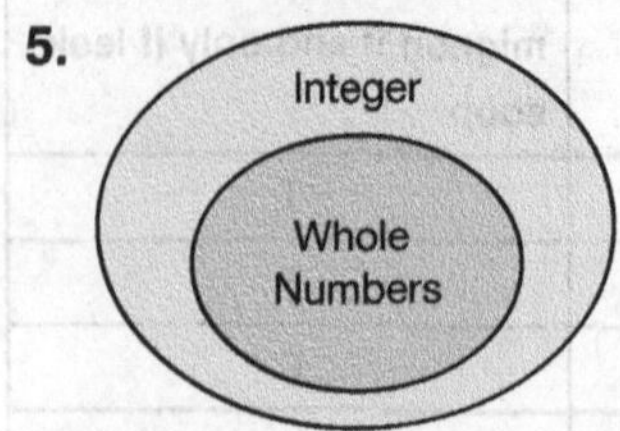


**6.** Only one direction because there is only one line between any two points on a plane.

**7.** If you do not have a brother, then you are an only child.

**8.** Choice **A** is correct. A rectangle that is not a rhombus has four equal angles and two pairs of congruent sides.

**9.** If a state is one of the lower 48 states, then it lies to the east of longitude 125°W.

**10.** They can make a straight angle. They cannot make a right angle because an obtuse angle is greater than a right angle.

**11.** Testing by example only shows the conjecture to be true for the given values. This is not proof as there are other values that can be tested.

**12. a.** Let ∠1 and ∠2 be a pair of alternate exterior angles formed by *l*, *m*, and *n*. Let ∠3 be the vertical angle to ∠1, and let ∠4 be the vertical angle to ∠2. Statement *p* implies ∠3 ≅ ∠4. Since vertical angles are congruent, ∠1 ≅ ∠3 and ∠2 ≅ ∠4. Since congruence is transitive, ∠1 ≅ ∠2; this proves statement *q*.

**b.** Part a is, "If statement *p* is true, then statement *q* is true." The Converse of the Alternate Exterior Angles Theorem is, "If statement *q* is true, then lines *m* and *n* are parallel." Using the Law of Syllogism, conclude: "If statement *p* is true, then statement *r* is true: lines *m* and *n* are parallel." This is the Converse of the Alternate Interior Angles Theorem.

**13.** $M \text{ of } \overline{AD}\left(\frac{1+1}{2}, \frac{2+7}{2}\right) = \left(\frac{2}{2}, \frac{9}{2}\right)$

$= (1, 4.5)$

$M \text{ of } \overline{AB}\left(\frac{1+6}{2}, \frac{2+2}{2}\right) = \left(\frac{7}{2}, \frac{4}{2}\right)$

$= (3.5, 2)$

$M \text{ of } \overline{BC}\left(\frac{6+6}{2}, \frac{2+7}{2}\right) = \left(\frac{12}{2}, \frac{9}{2}\right)$

$= (6, 4.5)$

$M \text{ of } \overline{CD}\left(\frac{1+6}{2}, \frac{7+7}{2}\right) = \left(\frac{7}{2}, \frac{14}{2}\right)$

$= (3.5, 7)$

**14.** If one example can be found that is not supported by the conjecture, the conjecture has been disproved by counterexample.

**15.** The perimeter should be $2(3) + 2(7.5) = 21$ cm.

16. **a.** If a quadrilateral has four congruent sides, then it is square; A quadrilateral is square if and only if it has four congruent sides.

**b.** No; the second row corresponds to a non-square rhombus and is a counterexample.

| Hypothesis $p$: four congruent sides | Conclusion $q$: square | $p \to q$: if four congruent sides, then square | $q \to p$: if square, then four congruent sides | Biconditional: four congruent sides if and only if square |
|---|---|---|---|---|
| T | T | T | T | T |
| T | F | F | T | F |
| F | T | T | F | F |
| F | F | T | T | T |

17. There is a square and a parallelogram.

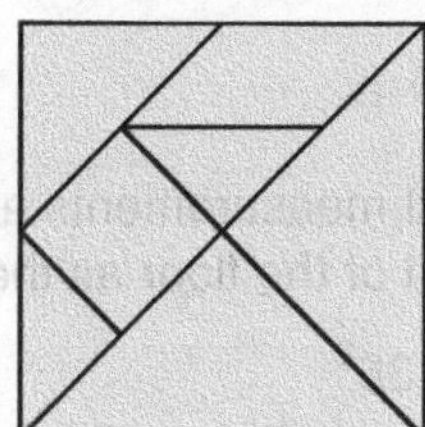

18. They are complementary. By the Exterior Angles Theorem, the sum of their measures is 90°.

19. The Converse of the Corresponding Angles Theorem says if the corresponding angles are congruent, then the lines are parallel. So, if $x = 40$, then the corresponding angles are congruent. This means that the lines are parallel.

20. $m = \frac{0-6}{6-3} = \frac{-6}{3} = -2$

21. No; By definition, only two angles can be supplementary angles, even if the measures of three angles add to 180°.

22. $A(1, 7)$ and $B(4, 2)$

$d = \sqrt{(x_2 - x_1)^2 + (y_2 - y_1)^2}$
$= \sqrt{(4-1)^2 + (2-7)^2}$
$= \sqrt{3^2 + (-5)^2}$
$= \sqrt{9 + 25} = \sqrt{34} \approx 5.83$

23. $C(-1, 3)$ and $D(2, -4)$

$d = \sqrt{(x_2 - x_1)^2 + (y_2 - y_1)^2}$
$= \sqrt{(2 - -1)^2 + (-4 - 3)^2}$
$= \sqrt{3^2 + (-7)^2}$
$= \sqrt{9 + 49}$
$= \sqrt{58}$
$\approx 7.62$

24. Sample: "Soo-Lin takes cheese sandwiches or she takes a salad", "Soo-Lin takes milk or she takes a salad."

25. Yes; By definition, a regular polygon has all angles congruent.

26. They are complementary and acute.

27. **a.** If the month has 31 days, then it is December.

**b.** The statement is true because December does have 31 days. The converse is false because there are counterexamples of other months that have 31 days.

28. $P = 2l + 2w$
$= 2(14) + 2(7)$
$= 28 + 14$
$= 42$ in.

29. $M$ of $\overline{KL}\left(\frac{-3+1}{2}, \frac{8+4}{2}\right) = \left(\frac{-2}{2}, \frac{12}{2}\right)$
$= (-1, 6)$

$M \text{ of } \overline{KM}\left(\frac{-3+5}{2}, \frac{8+2}{2}\right) = \left(\frac{2}{2}, \frac{10}{2}\right)$

$= (1, 5)$

$M \text{ of } \overline{LM}\left(\frac{1+5}{2}, \frac{4+2}{2}\right) = \left(\frac{6}{2}, \frac{6}{2}\right)$

$= (3, 3)$

30. Alternate exterior angles have equal measures.

$160 - 2x = 5x + 55$

$-7x = -105$

$x = 15$

$5x + 55 = 5(15) + 55 = 75 + 55 = 130°$

## INVESTIGATION 2

1. right triangle
2. The square with 10-cm sides should match the hypotenuse of the triangle.
3. The 10-cm square has the largest area of 100 cm$^2$.
4. Yes, when cut up, they should fit inside the larger square. The sum of the areas of the two smaller squares equals the area of the largest square.
5. 36 cm$^2$, 64 cm$^2$, and 100 cm$^2$; Yes, it shows numerically that the sum of the areas of the two smaller squares equals the area of the largest square.
6. Sample: They show that when you square each side of a right triangle (to obtain the area of each square), the squares of the two legs will add to the square of the hypotenuse.
7. $c^2 = 5^2 + 12^2$

   $c^2 = 25 + 144$

   $c^2 = 169$

   $c = 13$
8. $b^2 = 20^2 - 16^2$

   $b^2 = 400 - 256$

   $b^2 = 144$

   $b = 12$
9. $c^2 = 6^2 + 8^2$

   $c^2 = 36 + 64$

   $c^2 = 100$

   $c = 10$

### Investigation Practice 2

a. The length of the hypotenuse will get longer. The right angle stays the same. The angle on the constant leg increases while the angle on the lengthened leg decreases.

b. $x^2 = 25^2 - 24^2$

$x^2 = 625 - 576$

$x^2 = 49$

$x = 7$ m

c. $x^2 = 15^2 - 12^2$

$x^2 = 225 - 144$

$x^2 = 81$

$x = 9$ in.

d. Use the wall measurements as the legs and the diagonal of the floor as the hypotenuse.

e. $x^2 = 48^2 + 36^2$

$x^2 = 2304 + 1296$

$x^2 = 3600$

$x = 60$ feet

## LESSON 21

### Warm Up 21

1. conditional
2. False; Not all of the school's athletes are on the bus.
3. $x - 6 = 9$

   $x - 6 + 6 = 9 + 6$

   $x = 15$ True
4. False, 9 is an odd number that is not prime.
5. true

### Lesson Practice 21

a. Therefore, Lorissa is left-handed.

b. Therefore, the pond is frozen.

c. Therefore, Michael got a perfect score on the test.

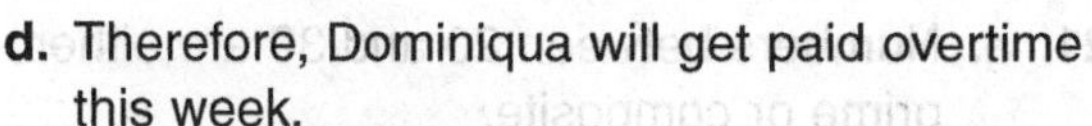



**d.** Therefore, Dominiqua will get paid overtime this week.

**e.** Therefore, the gift has four wheels.

**f.** If Nafeesa enrolls in an elective, then she will play the violin this semester.

**g.** If I oversleep tomorrow morning, then I will be late for my appointment.

**h.** Law of Syllogism

**i.** If a gumble is hungry, then he must hunt for gloop; Law of Syllogism

**j.** Therefore, this vehicle has only one wheel; Law of Detachment

## Practice 21

**1.** Therefore, our company will purchase the granite.

**2.**

$$P = 2l + 2w$$
$$300 = 2(l) + 2(32)$$
$$300 = 2(l) + 64$$
$$300 - 64 = 2(l) + 64 - 64$$
$$236 = 2(l)$$
$$\frac{236}{2} = \frac{2(l)}{2}$$
$$118 = l$$

The length is 118 ft.

**3.** $m = \frac{y_2 - y_1}{x_2 - x_1}$

$$= \frac{5 - 1}{5 - 1}$$
$$= \frac{4}{4}$$
$$= 1$$

Yasmini is correct. Slope is a ratio of rise to run and is not a point. Yasmini's calculation of the slope is correct.

**4.** Converse: If all the socks in the drawer are red, then it is certain that a sock I pull out of the drawer will be red.

True; It is certain that a sock I pull out of a drawer will be red if and only if all the socks in the drawer are red.

**5.** Yes, if two parallel lines are cut by a transversal, then alternate exterior angles are congruent (Alternate Exterior Angles Theorem).

**6.** Since the sides of the squares on the edge are all 10 ft,

$$P = 22 + 10 + 10 + 10 + 22 + 10 + 10 + 8 + 34 + 8 + 10 + 10 = 164 \text{ ft}$$

**7.** Distance from $A(4, 5)$ to $B(7, 1)$.

$$d = \sqrt{(x_2 - x_1)^2 + (y_2 - y_1)^2}$$
$$= \sqrt{(7 - 4)^2 + (1 - 5)^2}$$
$$= \sqrt{3^2 + (-4)^2}$$
$$= \sqrt{9 + 16}$$
$$= \sqrt{25}$$
$$= 5 \text{ units}$$

**8.** The statement is a compound statement and a disjunction (uses "or"). Choice **C** is correct.

**9.**

$$a = 4b$$
$$16^2 = (4b)^2 + b^2$$
$$256 = 16b^2 + b^2$$
$$256 = 17b^2$$
$$15.06 \approx b^2$$
$$3.88 \approx b$$

To change 0.88 feet to inches, $0.88 \times 12 \approx 11$ in.

The ladder should be placed approximately 3.88 feet or 3 ft 11 in. from the base of the wall.

**10.** Sample: Twenty-five is one more than 24, which is a multiple of 6, but it is not prime.

**11.**

$$x = x$$
$$80^\circ + x + x = 180^\circ$$
$$80^\circ + 2x = 180^\circ$$
$$2x = 100^\circ$$
$$x = 50^\circ$$

**12.** Converse: If $x = 2$, then $3x + 4 = 10$. The statement is true.

$$3(2) + 4 = 10$$
$$6 + 4 = 10$$
$$10 = 10$$

The converse is true.

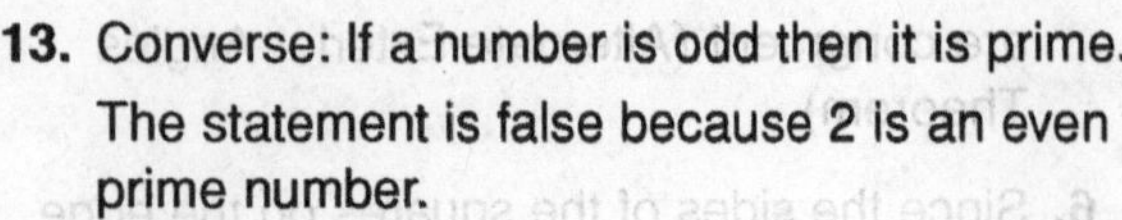



**13.** Converse: If a number is odd then it is prime.
The statement is false because 2 is an even prime number.
The converse is false because 9 is an odd number that is not prime.

**14. a.** It is a parallelogram because it has two pairs of parallel sides.

**b.** It is a trapezoid because it has exactly one pair of parallel sides.

**15.** $\text{midpoint} = \left(\frac{x_1 + x_2}{2}, \frac{y_1 + y_2}{2}\right)$

$= \left(\frac{6 + -2}{2}, \frac{9 + 5}{2}\right)$

$= \left(\frac{4}{2}, \frac{14}{2}\right)$

$= (2, 7)$

**16.** Therefore, the bread is fresh.

**17.** Sample:

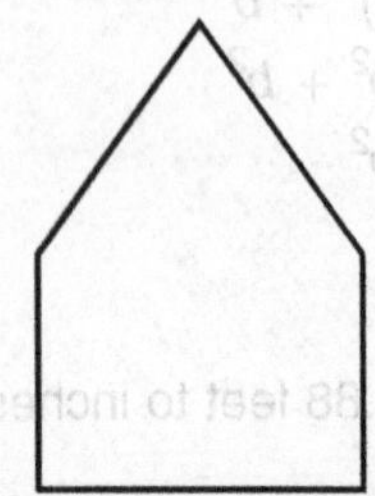

This is a convex, irregular polygon.

**18.** Yes, the alternate exterior angles are congruent.

**19.** Since $\angle b$ is part of a triangle with the angles measuring 71° and 52°,

$m\angle b = 180° - 71° - 52° = 57°$.

$m\angle b = m\angle a$ because they are alternate interior angles.

$m\angle b = m\angle a = 57°$

$m\angle c = 52°$ because they are alternate interior angles.

**20.** $E(4, 2)$, $F(1, 8)$

$m = \frac{8 - 2}{1 - 4}$

$= \frac{6}{-3}$

$= -2$

**21. a.** Numbers between 20 and 30 are either prime or composite.

**b.** The lunch special can come with soup or a salad.

**22.** The polygon is concave because a diagonal can be drawn so that part of the diagonal contains points in the exterior of the polygon.

**23.** If the season is rainy, then there will be plenty of corn for the livestock.

**24.** Lucy is the tallest in her class at school.

**25.** $m = \frac{19 - 7}{5 - 1} = \frac{12}{4} = 3$

$y = 3x + b$

$7 = 3(1) + b$

$4 = b$

$y = 3x + 4$

**26.** $A = \frac{1}{2}bh$

$= \frac{1}{2}(4)(4.5) = 9 \text{ ft}^2$

**27.** No, the alternate interior angles are not equal.

**28. a.** Today it is cold and snowing.

**b.** Later this week is the big game at our school and Anita is playing.

**29.** $m\angle 2 = 2(m\angle 1)$

$\angle 1$ and $\angle 2$ are supplementary.

$m\angle 1 + m\angle 2 = 180°$

$m\angle 1 + 2(m\angle 1) = 180°$

$3\,m\angle 1 = 180°$

$m\angle 1 = 60°$

$m\angle 2 = 120°$

**30.** $(5x + 10) + (2x - 5) = 180°$

$7x + 5 = 180$

$7x = 175$

$x = 25$

$m\angle AMF = m\angle NMB = m\angle CNM = m\angle END = 5(25) + 10 = 125 + 10 = 135°$

$m\angle FMB = m\angle AMN = m\angle CNE = m\angle MND = 2(25) - 5 = 50 - 5 = 45°$

## LESSON 22

### Warm Up 22

1. height
2. a. It is a right triangle because it has one right angle
   b. It is an equilateral triangle because it has three equal sides.
   c. It is an obtuse isosceles triangle because it has two equal sides and one angle greater than 90°.
3. a. It is a trapezoid because it has exactly one pair of parallel sides.
   b. It is a parallelogram because it has two pairs of parallel sides.
   c. It is a rhombus because it has four congruent sides.
4. $2(-2)^2 + 3(-2)(1) - (1)^2$
   $= 2(4) + 3(-2) - 1$
   $= 8 - 6 - 1$
   $= 1$

### Lesson Practice 22

a. $A = bh = (14)(8) = 112 \text{ yd}^2$

b. $A = bh = (16)(4) = 64 \text{ ft}^2$

c. $A = \frac{1}{2}(b_1 + b_2)h$
$= \frac{1}{2}(14 + 21)(13)$
$= \frac{1}{2}(35)(13)$
$= 227.5 \text{ cm}^2$

d. $A = \frac{1}{2}(b_1 + b_2)h$
$= \frac{1}{2}(4 + 6)(2)$
$= \frac{1}{2}(10)(2)$
$= 10 \text{ yd}^2$

e. $A = \frac{1}{2}d_1d_2 = \frac{1}{2}(8)(11) = 44 \text{ in}^2$

f. $A = \frac{1}{2}d_1d_2$
$12 = \frac{1}{2}(6)(d_2)$
$12 = 3d_2$
$4 \text{ m} = d_2$

g. Since the cafeteria is a rhombus, he should measure the base and height, or the diagonals of the cafeteria.

### Practice 22

1.

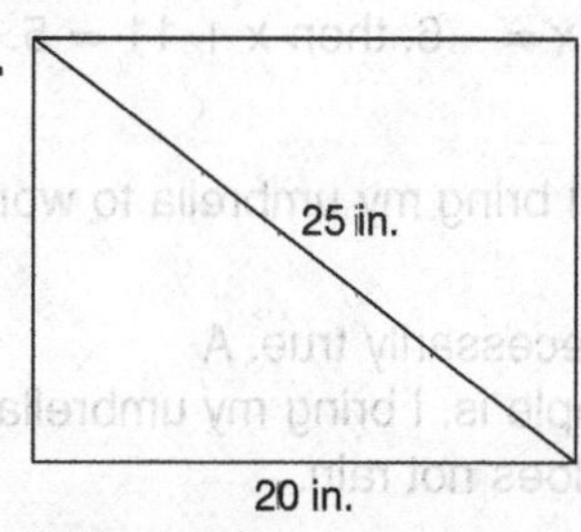


$25^2 = 20^2 + x^2$
$625 = 400 + x^2$
$225 = x^2$
$15 = x$
$A = lw = (15)(20) = 300 \text{ in}^2$

2. a. Yes, the corresponding sides and angles are the same.
   b. No, one is larger than the other.

3. Choice A: $-30 = \frac{9}{5}(-30) + 32$
$-30 = -54 + 32$
$-30 \neq -22$

Choice B: $30 = \frac{9}{5}(30) + 32$
$30 = 54 + 32$
$30 \neq 86$

Choice C: $-40 = \frac{9}{5}(-40) + 32$
$-40 = -72 + 32$
$-40 = -40$

Choice D: $40 = \frac{9}{5}(40) + 32$
$40 = 72 + 32$
$40 \neq 104$

Choice **C** is correct.

**4.** The game involving Allentown and Holdenville was decided by one run.

**5. a.** $A = bh = (14)(14) = 196 \text{ cm}^2$

**b.** $A = \frac{1}{2}(b_1 + b_2)h$

$= \frac{1}{2}(12 + 8)(16)$

$= \frac{1}{2}(20)(16)$

$= 160 \text{ in}^2$

**6. a.** Converse: If $x = -6$, then $x + 11 = 5$.

This is true.

**b.** Converse: If I bring my umbrella to work, then it rains.

This is not necessarily true. A counterexample is, I bring my umbrella to work and it does not rain.

**7.** $180° - 90° - 31° = 59°$

The measures of the interior angles of a triangle add up to 180°.

**8. a.** true

**b.** False; The sum of complementary angles is 90°.

**c.** False; Vertical angles are opposite each other, not adjacent.

**d.** true

**9.** $(x + 10)° + (4x + 50)° + (2x + 50)° = 180°$

$7x + 110 = 180$

$7x = 70$

$x = 10$

$10° + 10° = 20°$

$4(10°) + 50° = 40° + 50° = 90°$

$2(10°) + 50° = 20° + 50° = 70°$

**10.** It is Mrs. Wu's turn to drive the children to their piano lesson.

**11.** Distance from $A(3, 11)$ to $B(14, 26)$.

$d = \sqrt{(x_2 - x_1)^2 + (y_2 - y_1)^2}$

$= \sqrt{(14 - 3)^2 + (26 - 11)^2}$

$= \sqrt{11^2 + 15^2}$

$= \sqrt{121 + 225}$

$= \sqrt{346}$

$\approx 18.6$ units

Since each unit on the grid is 5 $\text{mi}^2$,

$5 \times 18.6 = 93$ miles

The stations are approximately 93 miles apart.

**12. a.** Two angles are congruent if and only if they have the same measure.

**b.** A triangle is equilateral if and only if it has three lines of symmetry.

**13.** This is a disjunction because it is an "or" statement.

**14. a.** $A = bh = (24)(9) = 216 \text{ ft}^2$

**b.** $A = \frac{1}{2}d_1d_2$

$= \frac{1}{2}(16)(20) = 160 \text{ yd}^2$

**15. a.** $y = -2x + b$

$5 = -2(0) + b$

$5 = b$

$y = -2x + 5$

**b.** $y = \frac{1}{2}x + b$

$11 = \frac{1}{2}(4) + b$

$11 = 2 + b$

$9 = b$

$y = \frac{1}{2}x + 9$

**16. a.** It is isosceles because it has two equal sides.

**b.** It is scalene because it has no sides that are equal.

**17.** $d^2 = 6^2 + 8^2$

$d^2 = 36 + 64$

$d^2 = 100$

$d = 10$

The race covers the perimeter of the right triangle.

$P = 10 + 6 + 8 = 24$ miles

**18.** To find the equation of the line through (1, 5) and (5, 17):

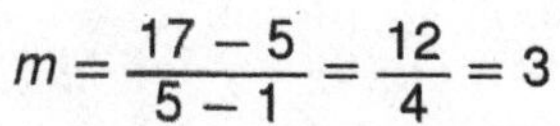

$m = \frac{17-5}{5-1} = \frac{12}{4} = 3$

$y = 3x + b$

$5 = 3(1) + b$

$2 = b$

$y = 3x + 2$

She has switched the slope and the *y*-intercept. The correct equation is $y = 3x + 2$.

**19. a.** No, the same-side interior angles do not add to 180°.

**b.** Yes, the same-side interior angles add to 180°.

**20.**

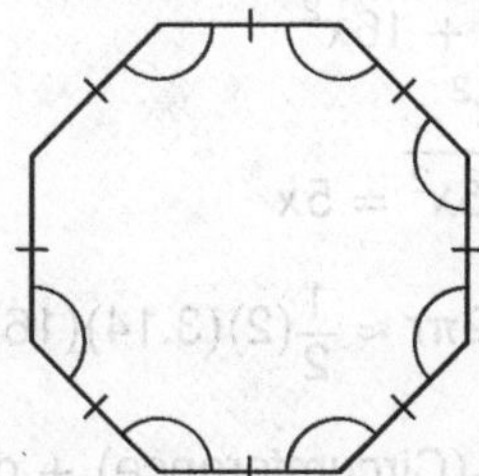

See student work. Yes, a polygon that is both equilateral and equiangular is regular by definition.

**21.** $13^2 = 5^2 + x^2$

$169 = 25 + x^2$

$144 = x^2$

$12 = x$

$A = lw = (12)(5) = 60 \text{ ft}^2$

**22.** $\overline{AB}_{\text{midpoint}} = \left(\frac{5+4}{2}, \frac{-4+9}{2}\right) = \left(\frac{9}{2}, \frac{5}{2}\right)$

$\overline{AC}_{\text{midpoint}} = \left(\frac{8+5}{2}, \frac{17+9}{2}\right) = \left(\frac{13}{2}, \frac{26}{2}\right)$

$= \left(\frac{13}{2}, 13\right)$

$\overline{BC}_{\text{midpoint}} = \left(\frac{8+4}{2}, \frac{17+-4}{2}\right)$

$= \left(\frac{12}{2}, \frac{13}{2}\right)$

$= \left(6, \frac{13}{2}\right)$

**23.**

| $x$ | $y = 3x + 1$ | $y$ |
|---|---|---|
| −1 | $y = 3(-1) + 1$ | −2 |
| 0 | $y = 3(0) + 1$ | 1 |
| 1 | $y = 3(1) + 1$ | 4 |

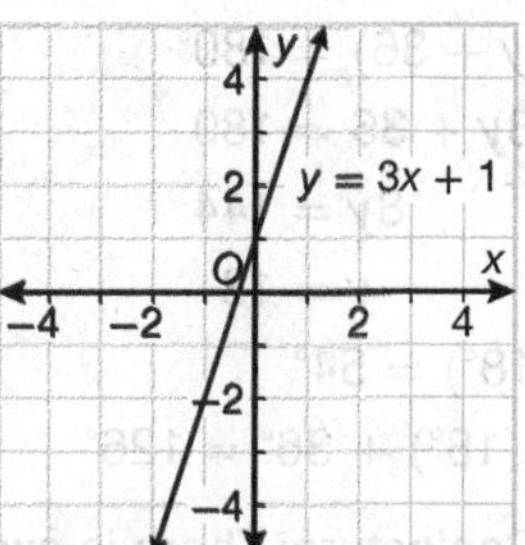


**24. a.** Hypothesis: Today is Wednesday.

Conclusion: Jasmine needs to take out the trash.

**b.** Hypothesis: $x - 3 = 5$

Conclusion: $x = 8$

**25.** Distance from $A(4, 8)$ to $F(9, 21)$.

$d = \sqrt{(x_2 - x_1)^2 + (y_2 - y_1)^2}$

$= \sqrt{(9-4)^2 + (21-8)^2}$

$= \sqrt{5^2 + 13^2}$

$= \sqrt{25 + 169} = \sqrt{194}$

$\approx 13.93$ miles

Distance from $B(17, 29)$ to $F(9, 21)$.

$d = \sqrt{(x_2 - x_1)^2 + (y_2 - y_1)^2}$

$= \sqrt{(9-17)^2 + (21-29)^2}$

$= \sqrt{(-8)^2 + (-8)^2}$

$= \sqrt{64 + 64}$

$= \sqrt{128}$

$\approx 11.31$ miles

The fire station at point *B* should respond.

**26.** If Mark's pen runs out of ink, then he must go to the store.

**27.** $F = 2C + 30$

To convert 25°C,

$F = 2(25) + 30 = 50 + 30 = 80°$

To convert −30°C,

$F = 2(-30) + 30 = -60 + 30 = -30°$

**28.** $A = lw + lw + lw + lw$

$= (34)(18) + (10)(10) + (10)(10) + (10)(10)$

$= 612 + 100 + 100 + 100$

$= 912 \text{ ft}^2$

29. $(3y) + (5y + 36) = 180°$

$$8y + 36 = 180$$
$$8y = 144$$
$$y = 18$$

Acute: $3(18°) = 54°$

Obtuse: $5(18°) + 36° = 126°$

30. Sample: Conjecture: There is exactly one unique line through point $P$ not on line $l$ that is parallel to $l$.

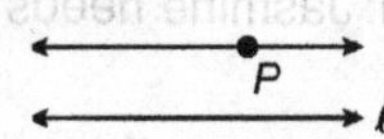


## LESSON 23

### Warm Up 23

1. perimeter
2. $2(3) + 5(-2) = 6 - 10 = -4$
3. Therefore, the dog got out.
4. $2(15)^2 = 2(225) = 450$
5. $3.27(6.5)^2 = 3.27(42.25) \approx 138.16$

### Lesson Practice 23

a. Sample:

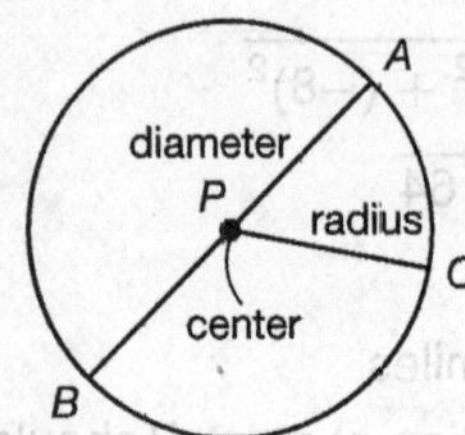


b. $C = 2\pi r \approx 2(3.14)(0.5) = 3.14$ meters

c. $A = \pi r^2$

$$\approx (3.14)(31^2)$$
$$= (3.14)(961)$$
$$= 3017.54 \text{ cm}^2$$

d. $r = 0.5$ yd

$$A = \pi r^2$$
$$\approx (3.14)(0.5^2)$$
$$= (3.14)(0.25)$$
$$= 0.79 \text{ yd}^2$$

e. $r = 17.5$ in.

$$3C = 3(2)(\pi)(r)$$
$$\approx 3(2)\left(\frac{22}{7}\right)(17.5)$$
$$= 330 \text{ in.}$$

### Practice 23

1. $C = 2\pi r \approx 2(3.14)(6378) \approx 40{,}054$ km

2. The statement has not been proved or disproved. Sample: If $n$ is even, then $n + 1$ is odd.

3. $c^2 = (3x)^2 + (4x)^2$

$$c^2 = 9x^2 + 16x^2$$
$$c^2 = 25x^2$$
$$c = \sqrt{25x^2} = 5x$$

4. $\frac{1}{2}C = \frac{1}{2}2\pi r \approx \frac{1}{2}(2)(3.14)(16) \approx 50.2$ ft

tape $= \frac{1}{2}(\text{Circumference}) + \text{diameter}$

$$= 50.2 + 32$$
$$= 82.2 \text{ ft}$$

5. midpoint $= \left(\frac{11 + 1}{2}, \frac{6 + 4}{2}\right) = \left(\frac{12}{2}, \frac{10}{2}\right)$

$$= (6, 5)$$

Distance between (6, 5) and (5, 7):

$$d = \sqrt{(x_2 - x_1)^2 + (y_2 - y_1)^2}$$
$$= \sqrt{(5 - 6)^2 + (7 - 5)^2}$$
$$= \sqrt{(-1)^2 + 2^2}$$
$$= \sqrt{1 + 4}$$
$$= \sqrt{5} \text{ units}$$

6. $A = \frac{1}{2}(b_1 + b_2)h$

$$= \frac{1}{2}(12 + 10)(12)$$
$$= \frac{1}{2}(22)(12)$$
$$= 132 \text{ cm}^2$$

7. $\frac{1}{2}bh = 36$

$$bh = 72$$

The base and the height must be factors of 72. Sample: 6 in. by 12 in.; 8 in. by 9 in.; 4 in. by 18 in.

**8.** no

**9.** $D(3, 4)$, $E(11, 9)$, $F(5, -3)$

$$\overline{DE}_{\text{midpoint}} = \left(\frac{11+3}{2}, \frac{9+4}{2}\right)$$
$$= \left(\frac{14}{2}, \frac{13}{2}\right)$$
$$= (7, 6.5)$$
$$\overline{DF}_{\text{midpoint}} = \left(\frac{3+5}{2}, \frac{4+-3}{2}\right)$$
$$= \left(\frac{8}{2}, \frac{1}{2}\right)$$
$$= (4, 0.5)$$
$$\overline{EF}_{\text{midpoint}} = \left(\frac{11+5}{2}, \frac{9+-3}{2}\right)$$
$$= \left(\frac{16}{2}, \frac{6}{2}\right)$$
$$= (8, 3)$$

**10.**

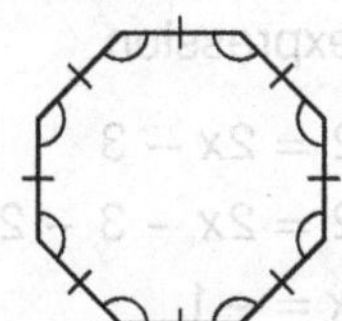

**11.** Therefore, I can open the safe.

**12.** $c^2 = b^2 + b^2$
$c^2 = 2b^2$
$c = \sqrt{2b^2} = b\sqrt{2}$

**13.** Statement 1: If the rooms in the arena get a new coat of paint, then the new funding from the local council was approved.

Statement 2 (converse): If the new funding from the local council is approved, then the rooms at the arena will get a new coat of paint.

**14.** A curved side cannot describe a polygon because a polygon consists of straight line segments. Choice **B** is correct.

**15. a.** $180° - 75° = 105°$

**b.** $180° - 126° = 54°$

**16.**

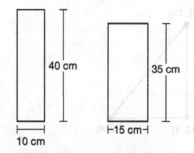

40 cm
10 cm
Area = 400 cm²

35 cm
15 cm
Area = 525 cm²

Area 1st rectangle = $(10)(40) = 400 \text{ cm}^2$
Area 2nd rectangle = $(15)(35) = 525 \text{ cm}^2$

**17.** $\angle A$ and $\angle B$ are alternate interior angles. If they are congruent, then the sides are parallel by the Converse of the Alternate Interior Angles Theorem.

**18.** Choice **B** is correct.

**19.** $180° - 90° - 47° = 43°$

Dustin is incorrect. The missing angle is 43°.

**20.** $r = 9$ in.

$C = 2\pi r \approx 2(3.14)(9) \approx 56.5 \text{ in}^2$

**21.** Sample: If it is the first day of the school week, then it is Monday.

Inverse: If it is not the first day of the school week, then it is not Monday.

**22.** $A_{\text{triangle}} = \frac{1}{2}bh = \frac{1}{2}(18)(12) = 108 \text{ ft}^2$

$108 \div 32 = 3.375$

It will take 4 cans of spray paint.

**23.** $m = \frac{\text{rise}}{\text{run}}$

$0.08 = \frac{24}{x}$

$0.08x = 24$

$x = \frac{24}{0.08}$

$x = 300$ meters

**24.** Sample: Any open figure with five points.

**25.** $r = 3$ ft

$A = \pi r^2 \approx (3.14)(3)^2 = (3.14)(9)$
$= 28.26 \text{ ft}^2$

Since there are 2 circles,

$2 \times 28.26 \approx 56.5 \text{ ft}^2$

**26.**

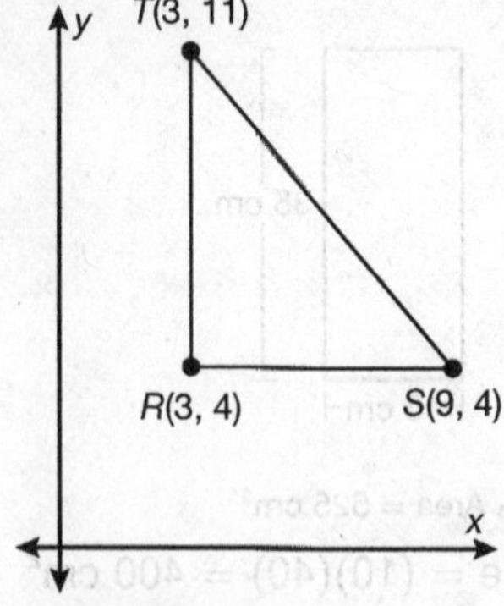


Perimeter: $RS = 6$, $RT = 7$

$ST^2 = RS^2 + RT^2$
$ST^2 = 6^2 + 7^2$
$ST^2 = 36 + 49$
$ST^2 = 85$
$ST = \sqrt{85}$
$ST \approx 9.22$ ft
$P = 6 + 7 + 9.22 \approx 22$ ft

Area: $A = \frac{1}{2}bh = \frac{1}{2}(6)(7) = 21$ ft$^2$

**27.** Alternate Exterior Angles Theorem

**28.** Since the hypotenuse is 39 cm, the base and height are 15 cm and 36 cm.
$A = \frac{1}{2}bh = \frac{1}{2}(15)(36) = 270$ cm$^2$

**29.** $A = \frac{1}{2}(b_1 + b_2)h$
$= \frac{1}{2}(3x + 5x)\left(\frac{1}{4}x\right)$
$= \frac{1}{2}(8x)\left(\frac{1}{4}x\right) = x^2$
$= (4x)\left(\frac{1}{4}x\right)$
$= x^2$

**30.** Since the bases have the same average and the heights are the same, the areas will be the same.
$\frac{1}{2}(b_1 + b_2)h = \frac{1}{2}(b_1 + b_2)h$
$\frac{1}{2}(15 + 28)(10) = \frac{1}{2}(11 + 32)(10)$
$\frac{1}{2}(43)(10) = \frac{1}{2}(43)(10)$
$215 = 215$

## LESSON 24

### Warm Up 24

**1.** Syllogism

**2. a.** subtraction
**b.** multiplication
**c.** squaring an expression

**3.** $3x - 2 = 2x - 3$
$3x - 2 - 2x + 2 = 2x - 3 - 2x + 2$
$x = -1$

Choice **A** is correct.

**4.** Converse: If a parallelogram is a rhombus, then all of its sides are congruent. Inverse: If all of the sides of a parallelogram are not congruent, then it is not a rhombus.

### Lesson Practice 24

**a.**

| | |
|---|---|
| $x + 5 = 4x + 2$ | Given |
| $x + 5 - 5 = 4x + 2 - 5$ | Subtraction Property of Equality |
| $x = 4x - 3$ | Simplify. |
| $x - 4x = 4x - 3 - 4x$ | Subtraction Property of Equality |
| $-3x = -3$ | Simplify. |
| $\frac{-3x}{-3} = \frac{-3}{-3}$ | Division Property of Equality |
| $x = 1$ | Simplify. |

b. $\dfrac{4x+5}{3} = \dfrac{5x+7}{4}$ Given

$12\left(\dfrac{4x+5}{3} = \dfrac{5x+7}{4}\right)$ Multiplication Property of Equality

$16x + 20 = 15x + 21$ Distributive Property

$16x + 20 - 20 = 15x + 21 - 20$ Subtraction Property of Equality

$16x = 15x + 1$ Simplify.

$16x - 15x = 15x + 1 - 15x$ Subtraction Property of Equality

$x = 1$ Simplify.

c. The correct order is:

$\frac{2}{3}x + 6 = 4 - 2x$ Given

$2x + 18 = 12 - 6x$ Multiplication Property of Equality

$2x = -6 - 6x$ Subtraction Property of Equality

$8x = -6$ Addition Property of Equality

$x = -\frac{2}{3}$ Division Property of Equality

d. $A = 40$, $l = (x + 2)$, and $w = (x - 1)$ Given

$A = lw$ Area formula for a rectangle

$40 = (x + 2)(x - 1)$ Substitution Property of Equality

$40 = x^2 + x - 2$ Simplify.

$40 - 40 = x^2 + x - 2 - 40$ Subtraction Property of Equality

$0 = x^2 + x - 42$ Simplify.

$x^2 + x - 42 = 0$ Symmetric Property of Equality

$(x - 6)(x + 7) = 0$ Factor.

The solution cannot come from $x + 7 = 0$, as the sides of the rectangle must be positive.

$x - 6 = 0$

$x - 6 + 6 = 0 + 6$

$x = 6$

Substitute to find the dimensions.

length $= (x + 2)$ yd

$= (6 + 2)$ yd

$= 8$ yd

width $= (x - 1)$ yd

$= (6 - 1)$ yd

$= 5$ yd

The length is 8 yd and the width is 5 yd.

**Practice 24**

1. $20^2 = (4x)^2 + (3x)^2$

$400 = 16x^2 + 9x^2$

$400 = 25x^2$

$16 = x^2$

$4 = x$

horizontal: $4x = 4(4) = 16$ in.

vertical: $3x = 3(4) = 12$ in.

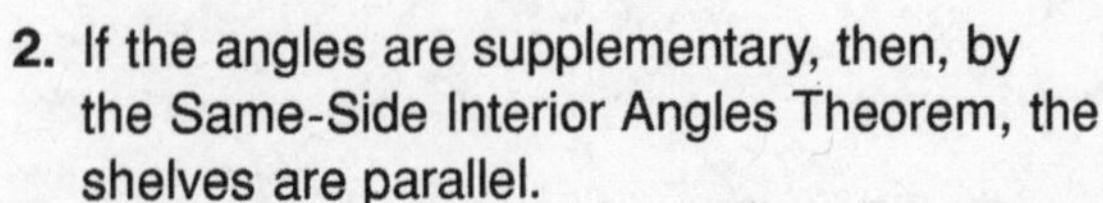



2. If the angles are supplementary, then, by the Same-Side Interior Angles Theorem, the shelves are parallel.

3. Converse: If two lines are cut by a transversal and the same side-interior angles are supplementary, then the lines are parallel. Yes this is true.

4. They are both correct. The Distributive Property can be avoided if the Division Property of Equality is used first.

5. Converse: If the window is not closed, then it is open.

   The converse is true.

6. Choice A: Symmetric Property of Equality: If $a = b$, then $b = a$.

   Choice B: Reflexive Property of Equality: $a = a$.

   Choice C: Transitive Property of Equality: If $a = b$ and $b = c$, then $a = c$.

   Choice D: Comparative Property of Equality is not a property of equality.

   Choice **C** is correct.

7. $27 \text{ yd} \times \left(\frac{3 \text{ ft}}{1 \text{ yd}}\right) = 81 \text{ ft}$

   $A = lw$

   $2592 = (81)(w)$

   $32 \text{ ft} = w$

8. The sum of the interior and its adjacent exterior angle at any vertex of a polygon is always 180°.

9. Triangle $A = \frac{1}{2}bh = \frac{1}{2}(10)(2) = 10 \text{ ft}^2$

   Triangle $B = \frac{1}{2}bh = \frac{1}{2}(4)(5) = 10 \text{ ft}^2$

10. Sample answer:

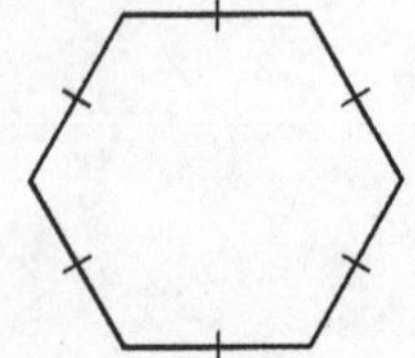

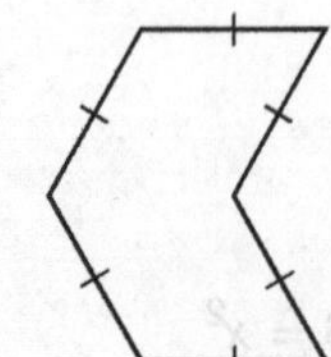

11. If the school receives a new computer lab from the district, then all of the students in the school achieved over 70% on the state exams. The converse is not necessarily true.

12. Obtuse; the diagonals form a linear pair of angles. So, the other triangles each have a 120° angle.

13.

| | |
|---|---|
| $2x - 1 = 5$ | Given |
| $2x - 1 + 1 = 5 + 1$ | Addition Property of Equality |
| $2x = 6$ | Simplify. |
| $\frac{2x}{2} = \frac{6}{2}$ | Division Property of Equality |
| $x = 3$ | Simplify. |

14. Choice **D**, a counterexample, is what she used to disprove the conjecture.

15. $A = 6^2 + 12^2 = 36 + 144 = 180$

    The total area of one of each type of square is 180 square centimeters.

    $4500 \text{ cm}^2 \div 180 \text{ cm}^2 = 25$

16. $2x + 3y - 15 = 0$

    $3y = -2x + 15$

    $y = -\frac{2}{3}x + 5$

    The slope of the line is $-\frac{2}{3}$ and the $y$-intercept is 5.

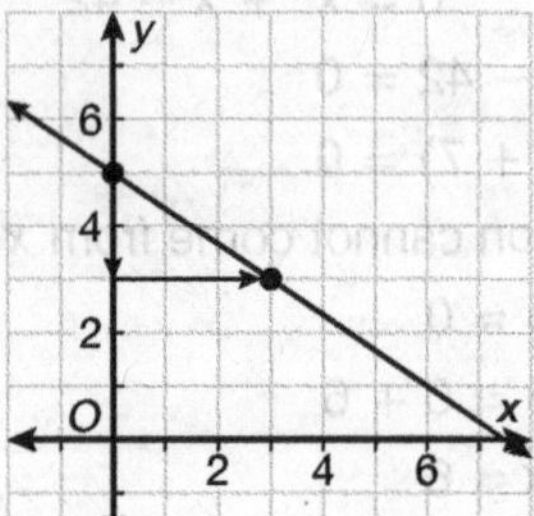


17. $A = \frac{1}{2}(b_1 + b_2)h$

    $= \frac{1}{2}(20 + 32)(14)$

    $= \frac{1}{2}(52)(14)$

    $= 364 \text{ ft}^2$

18. Total distance = 5 trips × 2 circle's circumference

    $d = (5)(2)(2\pi r)$

    $d \approx 20(3.14)(15)$

    $d \approx 942 \text{ ft}$

19. $a^2 = 10^2 - 6^2$
$a^2 = 100 - 36$
$a^2 = 64$
$a = 8$ in.

20. Inverse: If it is not raining, then I will not use my umbrella.
This inverse may be true, but you might have reasons to use an umbrella when it is not raining.

21. Since the hypotenuse is 52 m, the base and height are 48 m and 20 m.
$A = \frac{1}{2}bh = \frac{1}{2}(48)(20) = 480 \text{ m}^2$

22. Sample: interior $\angle ABC$; exterior $\angle XEA$

23. $x$-coordinate: $\frac{4 + x}{2} = 7$
$4 + x = 14$
$x = 10$
$y$-coordinate: $\frac{5 + y}{2} = 1$
$5 + y = 2$
$y = -3$
The other point is (10, –3).

24. Both the angle the box inclines and the angle of the ramp are complementary to angle ABC, so they are congruent. The greatest value $\angle EBC$ can have is 30°.

25. $A = \pi r^2 \approx (3.14)(3)^2 \approx 28 \text{ ft}^2$

26. The slope of 30 represents the amount per month that must be paid for membership.
$C = 30(5) + 200 = 150 + 200 = \$350$

27. There may be birds without brown feathers that have not been seen.

28. Conclusion: The angle cannot be acute. This conclusion uses the Law of Detachment.

29. $y = \frac{1}{2}x + b$
$4 = \frac{1}{2}(3) + b$
$4 = \frac{3}{2} + b$
$2\frac{1}{2} = b$
$y = \frac{1}{2}x + 2\frac{1}{2}$

30. She is incorrect because she is not following the Order of Operations.

## LESSON 25

### Warm Up 25

1. scalene

2. $\frac{3.5}{x} = \frac{17.5}{40}$
$17.5x = (3.5)(40)$
$17.5x = 140$
$x = 8$

3. $\angle 4$ is congruent to $\angle 2$ because they are vertical angles.

4. $x^2 = 13^2 - 12^2$
$x^2 = 169 - 144$
$x^2 = 25$
$x = 5$ in.

5. 180° – 80° – 45° = 55°

### Lesson Practice 25

a. $\angle Q$ corresponds to $\angle U$, $\angle P$ corresponds to $\angle S$, and $\angle R$ corresponds to $\angle T$. $\overline{PR}$ corresponds to $\overline{ST}$, $\overline{RQ}$ corresponds to $\overline{TU}$, and $\overline{PQ}$ corresponds to $\overline{SU}$.

b. Since $A$ corresponds to $D$, $B$ corresponds to $E$, and $C$ corresponds to $F$, $\triangle ABC \cong \triangle DEF$.

c. $\angle J \cong \angle S$, $\angle K \cong \angle T$, $\angle L \cong \angle U$, $\overline{JL} \cong \overline{SU}$, $\overline{LK} \cong \overline{UT}$, and $\overline{KJ} \cong \overline{TS}$

d. The measure of the other obtuse angle is 110° because the obtuse angles are congruent. The other two angles in each triangle must add up to 70°, since a triangle's angles add up to 180°. Therefore, the sum of the other angles in both triangles is 140°.

## Practice 25

1. $P = 7.7 + 12 + 7.7 + \left(\frac{2\pi(6)}{2}\right)$
   $\approx 27.4 + 18.8$
   $\approx 46.2$ m

2. $A = \pi r^2$
   $400 = \pi r^2$
   $127.4 \approx r^2$
   $11.3 \approx r$
   $d = 2r = 2(11.3) = 22.6$ m

3. $\triangle ABC \cong \triangle DCB$

4. It is a kite because it has exactly two pairs of congruent consecutive sides.

5. $P = 90 + 90 + 90 + 90 = 360$ ft

6. Yes, the rails are not parallel. If two lines are cut by a transversal and alternate interior angles are not congruent, then the lines are not parallel.

7. F, E, G, L, N, M

8. Sample: $n > 4$
   $4(5) > 5^2$
   $20 > 25$
   This is false, making it a counterexample.

9. $d^2 = 2^2 + 3^2$
   $d^2 = 4 + 9$
   $d^2 = 13$
   $d \approx 3.6$ units
   $3.6 \times 0.1 = 0.36$ mi

10. $d^2 = 7^2 + 3^2$
    $d^2 = 49 + 9$
    $d^2 = 58$
    $d \approx 7.6$ units
    $7.6 \times 0.1 = 0.76$ mi

11.

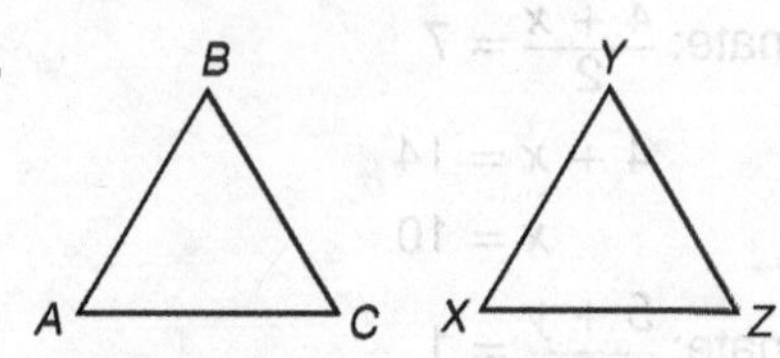


The angle statements are correct, but $\overline{BC} \cong \overline{XZ}$ and $\overline{AC} \cong \overline{YZ}$ are not. She has the last two corresponding sides reversed.

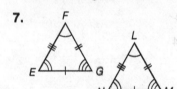

12.

| | |
|---|---|
| $2x + 10 = 4x - 20$ | Given |
| $2x + 10 - 10 = 4x - 20 - 10$ | Subtraction Property of Equality |
| $2x = 4x - 30$ | Simplify. |
| $2x - 4x = 4x - 30 - 4x$ | Subtraction Property of Equality |
| $-2x = -30$ | Simplify. |
| $\frac{-2x}{-2} = \frac{-30}{-2}$ | Division Property of Equality |
| $x = 15$ | Simplify. |

13. Choice **C** is a valid concluding statement.

14. The quadrilateral is a trapezoid because it has exactly one pair of parallel sides.

15. Kelly is wearing a blue shirt.

16. yes; yes

17.

| | |
|---|---|
| $\frac{x+5}{3} = 3$ | Given |
| $3\left(\frac{x+5}{3} = 3\right)$ | Multiplication Property of Equality |
| $x + 5 = 9$ | Simplify. |
| $x + 5 - 5 = 9 - 5$ | Subtraction Property of Equality |
| $x = 4$ | Simplify. |

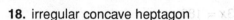

18. irregular concave heptagon

19. This is not a polygon because it does not consist of line segments.

20. False; A rhombus is a quadrilateral whose sides have equal length.

21. $\angle A \cong \angle L, \angle B \cong \angle M,$
$\overline{AB} \cong \overline{LM}, \overline{BC} \cong \overline{MN}$

22.

| | |
|---|---|
| $x + (3x + 20) = 180$ | Given |
| $4x + 20 = 180$ | Simplify. |
| $4x + 20 - 20 = 180 - 20$ | Subtraction Property of Equality |
| $4x = 160$ | Simplify. |
| $\frac{4x}{4} = \frac{160}{4}$ | Division Property of Equality |
| $x = 40$ | Simplify. |

23. $m = \frac{-4 - 4}{6 - -3} = \frac{-8}{9}$

Since *A*'s *y*-coordinate is larger than *B*'s, the road is going downhill from *A* to *B*.

24. It is biconditional because it contains "if and only if."

25. Counterexample: $n = 0$
$\frac{1}{0}$ is undefined.

26. $r = 20$
$C \approx 2(3.14)(20) \approx 126$ ft

27. Conclusion: The team will make the playoffs. This is valid by the Law of Detachment.

28. If a bee leaves the hive, then it is not the queen bee.

29.

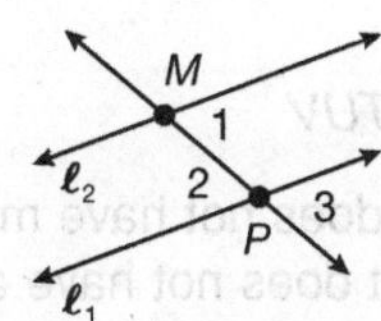


Sample answer: ∠1 and ∠2 are alternate interior angles, and ∠1 and ∠3 are corresponding angles.

30.
$$m\angle 1 = m\angle 2$$
$$2x^2 + 2x + 3 = 3x^2 - 5x + 3$$
$$0 = x^2 - 7x$$
$$x^2 - 7x = 0$$
$$x(x - 7) = 0$$
$$x = 7$$

$$m\angle 1 = m\angle 2 = 2(7)^2 + 2(7) + 3$$
$$= 98 + 14 + 3$$
$$= 115°$$

## LESSON 26

### Warm Up 26

1. radius

2. The area of a semicircle is one-half the area of the full circle. Choice **D** is correct.

3. $x = 90 - 40 = 50$

4. $\frac{45}{360} = \frac{x}{100\%}$
$360x = (45)(100)$
$360x = 4500$
$x = 12.5\%$

### Lesson Practice 26

a.

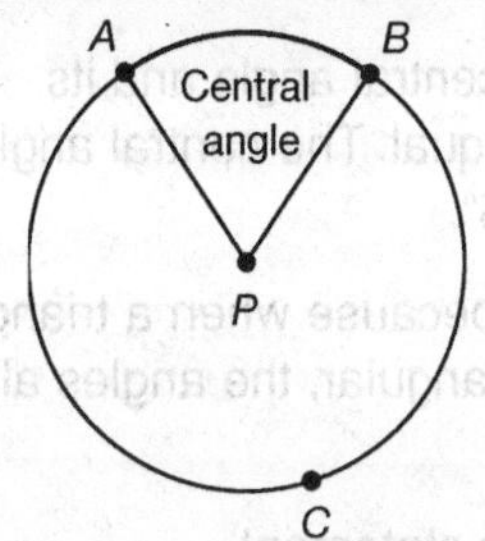


b. $m\widehat{RS} = 115°$

c. $2x - 15 = x + 30$

$x = 45$

$m\widehat{JK} = m\widehat{LM} = 45 + 30 = 75°$

d. $m\widehat{AB} = m\widehat{AD} + m\widehat{DC} + m\widehat{CB}$

e. $m\widehat{DEG} = 360° - m\widehat{DG} = 360° - 140° = 220°$

f. $\frac{360°}{100°} = 3.6$

4 lamps would be needed to ensure full coverage.

4 lamps provide 400° of total coverage which means the overlap is 400° − 360° = 40°.

## Practice 26

1. $m = \frac{-2 - 3}{12 - 7} = \frac{-5}{5} = -1$

2. A cactus requires water to develop.

3. $x^2 - x + 5 = 5x - 4$

$x^2 - 6x + 9 = 0$

$(x - 3)(x - 3) = 0$

$x = 3$

$AB = BC = 5(3) - 4 = 11$

$AC = 3(3)^2 - 2(3) - 1$

$= 27 - 6 - 1$

$= 20$

4. $r = 6.5$ km

$C = 2\pi r \approx 2(3.14)(6.5) \approx 41$ km

5.

| P | Q | ~P | ~Q | ~P∧~Q |
|---|---|---|---|---|
| T | T | F | F | F |
| T | F | F | T | F |
| F | T | T | F | F |
| F | F | T | T | T |

6. The measures of a central angle and its associated arc are equal. The central angle has a measure of 65°.

7. Choice **D** is correct because when a triangle is equilateral or equiangular, the angles all measure 60°.

8. *A* and not *B* is a true statement.

9. $180 - x = 4(90 - x)$

$180 - x = 360 - 4x$

$3x = 180$

$x = 60$

The angle is 60°.

10. Sample: $n = 2$

$2^3 = 8$

$3(2) = 6$

$8 > 6$

11. $m = \frac{3 - k}{2 - -1} = 0$

$\frac{3 - k}{3} = 0$

$3 - k = 0$

$k = 3$

12. $\angle A \cong \angle B = 30°$ because they are alternate interior angles.

Same-side interior angles are supplementary. So,

$\angle A + \angle C = 180°$

$30° + \angle C = 180°$

$\angle C = 150°$

13. 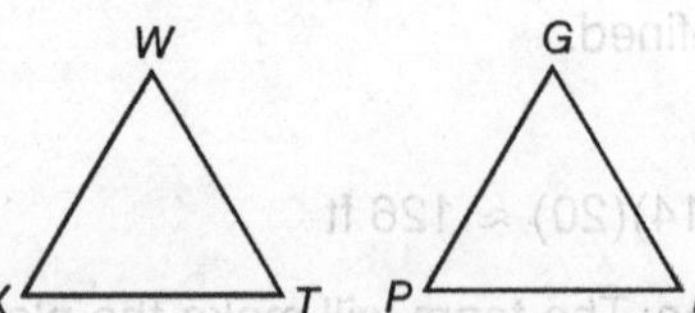


$\overline{XT}$ corresponds to $\overline{PR}$.

14. Counterexample: $y < 0$

If *y* is a negative number, then the answer will be negative.

15. $\triangle FGH \cong \triangle TUV$

16. If a building does not have more than four floors, then it does not have an elevator.

17. $(5x - 18)° + 33° = 180°$

$5x + 15 = 180$

$5x = 165$

$x = 33$

18. Choice **D** is correct because the Arc Addition Postulate says that the larger arc is equal to the sum of the smaller adjacent arcs.

19. The figure is not a polygon because each segment is not connected to exactly two other segments at the endpoints.

20. $A = \frac{1}{2}bh = \frac{1}{2}(12)(26) = 156 \text{ ft}^2$

21. Symmetric Property of Equality

22. The vertical intercept is 60 and represents the monthly fixed cost of using the phone.

23. $3x + 10 = 50 - 2x$
$5x = 40$
$x = 8$
$3(8) + 10 = 24 + 10 = 34°$

24. $\angle A \cong \angle W, \angle B \cong \angle X, \angle C \cong \angle Y,$
$\overline{AB} \cong \overline{WX}, \overline{BC} \cong \overline{XY}$, and $\overline{AC} \cong \overline{WY}$

25. Contrapositive: If a polygon does not have three sides, then it is not a triangle.

26. Subtraction Property of Equality

27. $x^2 = 253^2 + 188^2$
$x^2 = 64{,}009 + 35{,}344$
$x^2 = 99{,}353$
$x \approx 315$ mi

28. $360° - 227° = 133°$

29. Each term is the sum of the previous two terms. The next four terms are 34, 55, 89, 144.

30. square, rhombus, rectangle, parallelogram

## LESSON 27

### Warm Up 27

1. proof
2. Division Property of Equality
3. Symmetric Property of Equality
4. $180° - 90° - 43° = 47°$
Choice **D** is correct.

### Lesson Practice 27

a. The sum of two other angles must be less than 90°. By definition, an obtuse triangle contains one obtuse angle (i.e., between 90° and 180°). Since the Triangle Angle Sum Theorem states that the sum of the angle measures of a triangle is 180°, each of the other angles must be less than 90°.

b.

| Statements | Reasons |
|---|---|
| 1. $\angle LNM \cong \angle LNP$ | 1. Given |
| 2. $m\angle LNM = m\angle LNP$ | 2. Definition of congruent angles |
| 3. $m\angle MNP = 180°$ | 3. Definition of straight angle |
| 4. $m\angle LNM + m\angle LNP = m\angle MNP$ | 4. Angle Addition Postulate |
| 5. $2m\angle LNM = 180°$ | 5. Substitute. |
| 6. $m\angle LNM = 90°$ | 6. Division Property of Equality |
| 7. $LN \perp MP$ | 7. Definition of perpendicular lines |

c.

| Statements | Reasons |
|---|---|
| 1. $\angle ACD$ is an exterior angle of $\triangle ABC$. | 1. Given |
| 2. $m\angle ACD + m\angle ACB = 180°$ | 2. Linear Pair Theorem |
| 3. $m\angle CAB + m\angle ACB + m\angle ABC = 180°$ | 3. Triangle Angle Sum Theorem |
| 4. $m\angle ACD + m\angle ACB = m\angle CAB + m\angle ACB + m\angle ABC$ | 4. Transitive Property of Equality |
| 5. $m\angle ACD = m\angle CAB + m\angle ABC$ | 5. Subtraction Property of Equality |

### Practice 27

1. A minor arc has the same measure as the central angle and has measures between 0° and 180°. A major arc measures between 180° and 360°.

2. always true

3. No, he used a side length instead of the height of the triangle for his calculation.

4.

| Statements | Reasons |
|---|---|
| 1. $m \parallel n$ | 1. Given |
| 2. $\angle 2 \cong \angle 3$ | 2. If parallel lines are cut by a transversal, the corresponding angles are congruent. |
| 3. $\angle 1 \cong \angle 3$ | 3. Vertical angles are congruent |
| 4. $\angle 1 \cong \angle 2$ | 4. Transitive Property of Congruence |

5. $A = \pi r^2 \approx \left(\frac{22}{7}\right)(20^2) \approx 1257 \text{ ft}^2$

6.

| Statements | Reasons |
|---|---|
| 1. $M$ is the midpoint of $\overline{AB}$ | 1. Given |
| 2. $\overline{AM} \cong \overline{MB}$ | 2. Definition of midpoint |
| 3. $AM = MB$ | 3. Definition of congruence |
| 4. $AM + MB = AB$ | 4. Segment Addition Postulate |
| 5. $AM + AM = AB$ | 5. Substitution Property of Equality |
| 6. $2AM = AB$ | 6. Simplify. |
| 7. $\frac{2AM}{2} = \frac{AB}{2}$ | 7. Division Property of Equality |
| 8. $AM = \frac{1}{2}AB$ | 8. Simplify. |

7. $\overline{AB}_{\text{midpoint}} = \left(\frac{8 + 14}{2}, \frac{1 + 7}{2}\right) = \left(\frac{22}{2}, \frac{8}{2}\right)$

$= (11, 4)$

$\overline{CD}_{\text{midpoint}} = \left(\frac{7 + 5}{2}, \frac{11 + 5}{2}\right)$

$= \left(\frac{12}{2}, \frac{16}{2}\right)$

$= (6, 8)$

8. If all the math classes are full, then Raymond will enroll in theater.

9. $r = 7$ in.

$A = \pi r^2 \approx 3.14(7)^2 \approx 153.9 \text{ in}^2$

10. $w = l - 2$

$A = lw$

$35 = (l)(l - 2)$

$35 = l^2 - 2l$

$0 = l^2 - 2l - 35 \; (l - 7)(l + 5) = 0$

$l = 7$ (since the length must be positive)

$w = 7 - 2 = 5$

The dimensions are 5 ft by 7 ft.

11. Priyanka takes the bus or goes to work early.

12.

| Statements | Reasons |
|---|---|
| 1. $\angle 1$ and $\angle 2$ are right angles. | 1. Given |
| 2. $\angle 1 = 90°$, $\angle 2 = 90°$ | 2. Definition of right angles |
| 3. $m\angle 1 = m\angle 2$ | 3. Transitive Property of Equality |
| 4. $\angle 1 \cong \angle 2$ | 4. Definition of congruent angles |

13. No, Her statement is only true when the lines it intersects are parallel.

14. $A = bh = (11)(5) = 55 \text{ m}^2$

15.

| Statements | Reasons |
|---|---|
| 1. $\overleftrightarrow{AB} \parallel \overleftrightarrow{DE}$ and $\overleftrightarrow{EF} \parallel \overleftrightarrow{CD}$ | 1. Given |
| 2. $\angle 2 \cong \angle 2$ | 2. Corresponding angles are congruent |
| 3. $\angle 2 \cong \angle 3$ | 3. Corresponding angles are congruent |
| 4. $\angle 1 \cong \angle 3$ | 4. Transitive Property of Congruence |
| 5. $\overleftrightarrow{AB} \parallel \overleftrightarrow{EF}$ | 5. If two lines are cut by a transversal and the corresponding angles are congruent, the lines are parallel. |

16. Sample: any trapezium

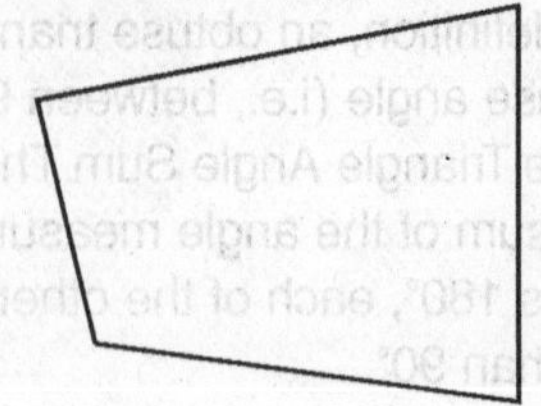

17.

| Statements | Reasons |
|---|---|
| 1. $\angle 1 \cong \angle 2$ | 1. Given |
| 2. $\angle 1 \cong \angle 3$ | 2. Vertical angles are congruent |
| 3. $\angle 2 \cong \angle 3$ | 3. Transitive Property of Congruence |
| 4. $m \parallel n$ | 4. If lines that are cut by a transversal form congruent corresponding angles, then they are parallel. |

18. $r = 5$ m

$\frac{1}{4}C = \frac{1}{4}(2\pi r) \approx \frac{1}{2}3.14(5) \approx 7.85 \text{ m}^2$

19. She should measure the lengths of each side of both triangles. If three pairs of sides are congruent, then the triangles are congruent by the SSS Postulate.

20.

| Statements | Reasons |
|---|---|
| 1. $4x = 8 - 2x$ | 1. Given |
| 2. $4x + 2x = 8 - 2x + 2x$ | 2. Addition Property of Equality |
| 3. $6x = 8$ | 3. Simplify |
| 4. $\frac{6x}{6} = \frac{8}{6}$ | 4. Division Property of Equality |
| 5. $x = \frac{4}{3}$ | 5. Simplify. |

21. $\frac{y - -3}{-5 - -2} = -\frac{2}{3}$

$\frac{y+3}{-3} = \frac{2}{-3}$

$y + 3 = 2$

$y = -1$

22. $\angle T$

23. Right, acute, and equiangular are terms that pertain to the angles of a triangle. Choice **A** is correct.

24. A rhombus has four congruent sides.

$4x + 7 = 8x - 5$

$-4x = -12$

$x = 3$

$QR = 8(3) - 5 = 24 - 5 = 19$

25. $3(x + 4) = 4(x - 5)$

$3x + 12 = 4x - 20$

$-x = -32$

$x = 32$

26.

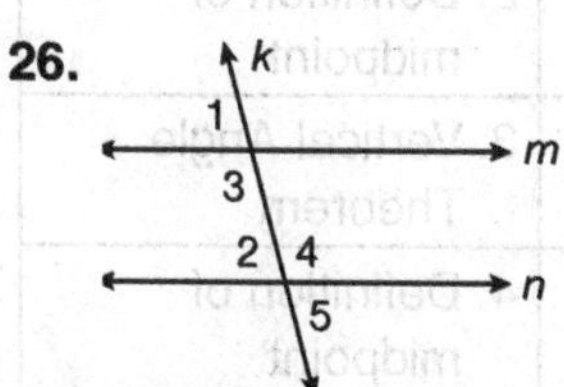


27. Sample: $4 - 6 = -2$

28. Transitive Property of Equality

29. Central angle = associated arc measure = 45°

30. It is acute because it has three acute angles. It is isosceles because it has two congruent sides.

## LESSON 28

### Warm Up 28

1. congruent
2. $\angle 4$
3. $90° - 25° = 65°$

   Choice **C** is correct.
4. The letters are in the wrong order. The correct statement is $\triangle ABC \cong \triangle EFD$.

### Lesson Practice 28

a. Yes, they are congruent by SAS because two sides and the included angle are congruent.

b. $3x - 12 = 2x + 8$

$x = 20$

c.

| Statements | Reasons |
|---|---|
| 1. $\overline{WZ} \cong \overline{WX}$ | 1. Given |
| 2. $\angle ZWY \cong \angle XWY$ | 2. Given |
| 3. $\overline{WY} \cong \overline{WY}$ | 3. Reflexive Property |
| 4. $\triangle WXY \cong \triangle WZY$ | 4. SAS Postulate |

**d.**

| Statements | Reasons |
|---|---|
| 1. Point $C$ is the midpoint | 1. Given of $\overline{AD}$, $\overline{BE}$ |
| 2. $\overline{AC} \cong \overline{DC}$ | 2. Definition of midpoint |
| 3. $\angle ACB \cong \angle DCE$ | 3. Vertical Angle Theorem |
| 4. $\overline{BC} \cong \overline{EC}$ | 4. Definition of midpoint |
| 5. $\Delta ABC \cong \Delta DEC$ | 5. SAS Postulate |

## Practice 28

1. Henry can hang the frame on the wall such that the edges of the frame and the stripes on the wallpaper create 45° angles.

2. It is not valid because not all skates that fit well are expensive.

3. $x^2 - 4x - 1 = x^2 - 3x + 10$
$-x = 11$
$x = -11$

4.

| Statements | Reasons |
|---|---|
| 1. $\angle 1$ and $\angle 2$ are a linear pair | 1. Given |
| 2. $m\angle ABC = 180°$ | 2. Definition of straight angle |
| 3. $m\angle 1 + m\angle 2 = m\angle ABC$ | 3. Angle Addition Postulate |
| 4. $m\angle 1 + m\angle 2 = 180°$ | 4. Substitute |

5. $x^2 = 105^2 + 88^2$
$x^2 = 11{,}025 + 7744$
$x^2 = 18{,}759$
$x = 137$ meters

6. $360° - 122° = 238°$

7. The exterior angle equals the sum of the remote interior angles.
$9x - 12 + 4x = 157$
$13x - 12 = 157$
$13x = 169$
$x = 13$
$\angle P = 9(13) - 12 = 117 - 12 = 105°$

8. $1, \frac{1}{4}, \frac{1}{9}, \frac{1}{16}, \ldots$
$= \frac{1}{1^2}, \frac{1}{2^2}, \frac{1}{3^2}, \frac{1}{4^2}, \ldots$
The general formula is $\frac{1}{n^2}$. The sequence will never equal 0 because $\frac{1}{n}$ can never equal zero.

9. The proof is incorrect because $\angle ABC$ is not the included angle of the two congruent sides.

10. midpoint
$= \left(\frac{-3+1}{2}, \frac{5+1}{2}\right)$
$= \left(\frac{-2}{2}, \frac{6}{2}\right) = (-1, 3)$
The correct choice is **C**.

11.

| Statements | Reasons |
|---|---|
| 1. $\overleftrightarrow{ST} \perp \overleftrightarrow{PQ}$, $\overleftrightarrow{RU} \perp \overleftrightarrow{PQ}$ | 1. Given |
| 2. $m\angle PST = 90°$, $m\angle SRU = 90°$ | 2. Definition of perpendicular |
| 3. $\overleftrightarrow{ST} \parallel \overleftrightarrow{RU}$ | 3. If two lines are cut by a transversal and the corresponding angles are congruent, then the lines are parallel. |

12. Inverse: If John is not at least 5'10", then he is not taller than Herschel.

13. The SAS Postulate can be used when two corresponding sides of triangles are congruent and the included angles are also congruent.

14. $r_1 = 17$ ft, $r_2 = 15$ ft, $r_3 = 13$ ft
$C_1 + C_2 + C_3 = (2\pi r_1) + (2\pi r_2) + (2\pi r_3)$
$= 2\pi(17) + 2\pi(15) + 2\pi(13)$
$\approx 107 + 94 + 82$
$\approx 283$ feet

15. Both line segments are radii of the circle.

16.

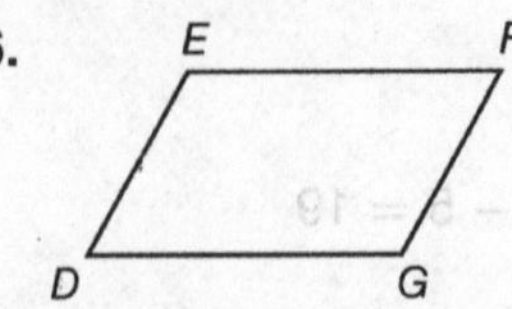

Since angles $D$ and $E$ are not opposite angles, they are supplementary.

$8x + 17 + 5x^2 - 2 = 180$

$5x^2 + 8x + 15 = 180$

$5x^2 + 8x - 165 = 0$

$5x^2 + 33x - 25x - 165 = 0$

$x(5x + 33) - 5(5x + 33) = 0$

$(x - 5)(5x + 33) = 0$

$x = 5$ (since the factor $5x + 33$ will result in a negative angle)

$m\angle F = m\angle D = 8(5) + 17 = 57°$

$m\angle G = m\angle E = 5(5)^2 - 2 = 123°$

**17.** $\triangle TUV \cong \triangle XZY$; SSS Postulate

**18.** $m = \frac{-3-(-1)}{-2-2} = \frac{-2}{-4} = \frac{1}{2}$

$y = \frac{1}{2}x + b$

$-1 = \frac{1}{2}(2) + b$

$-1 = 1 + b$

$-2 = b$

$y = \frac{1}{2}x - 2$

**19.** The conclusion is valid.

**20.** No, $\angle K$ corresponds to $\angle T$, not $\angle U$.

**21.** $A = \frac{1}{2}d_1d_2 = \frac{1}{2}(22)(14) = 154 \text{ in}^2$

**22.** Therefore, Clark lives in the 25th state to enter the union.

**23.** The radius after three days will be 6 meters.

$A = \pi r^2 = \pi(6)^2 \approx 113 \text{ m}^2$

**24.** They must also be congruent.

**25.** The slope is 2 or $\frac{2}{1}$ and the $y$-intercept is 4.

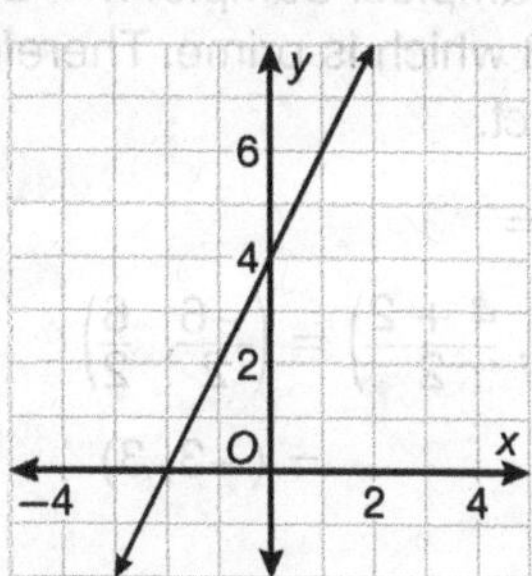


**26.**

| Statements | Reasons |
|---|---|
| 1. $\overline{BA} \cong \overline{BD}$ | 1. Given |
| 2. $\angle ABE \cong \angle DBC$ | 2. Vertical Angles Theorem |
| 3. $\overline{BE} \cong \overline{BC}$ | 3. Given |
| 4. $\triangle ABE \cong \triangle DBC$ | 4. SAS Theorem |

**27.** 18 in. = 1.5 ft; 24 in. = 2 ft

$2A = 2\left(\frac{1}{2}bh\right) = bh = (1.5)(2) = 3 \text{ ft}^2$

**28.** $x^2 = (a)^2 + (\sqrt{3}a)^2$

$x^2 = a^2 + 3a^2$

$x^2 = 4a^2$

$x = \sqrt{4a^2}$

$x = 2a$

**29.** $m\angle W = m\angle J$

$9x - 4 = 7x + 26$

$2x = 30$

$x = 15$

$m\angle W = m\angle J = 9(15) - 4 = 131°$

**30.** $A = \frac{1}{2}(b_1 + b_2)h$

$= \frac{1}{2}(7 + 3)(2)$

$= \frac{1}{2}(10)(2)$

$= 10 \text{ ft}^2$

## LESSON 29

### Warm Up 29

1. hypotenuse
2. It is isosceles because it has two congruent sides. It is right because it contains a right angle.
3. $\sqrt{3^2 + 4^2} = \sqrt{9 + 16} = \sqrt{25} = 5$

   Choice **B** is correct.
4. $\sqrt{640} = \sqrt{64 \cdot 10} = \sqrt{64} \cdot \sqrt{10} = 8\sqrt{10}$

### Lesson Practice 29

**a.** $x^2 = 20^2 + 21^2$

$x^2 = 400 + 441$

$x^2 = 841$
$x = \sqrt{841}$
$x = 29$ yd
Yes, the sides lengths form a Pythagorean triple.

**b.** $41^2 = 40^2 + p^2$
$1681 - 1600 = 1600 + p^2 - 1600$
$81 = p^2$
$9 = p$
$p$ is 9 inches long, and they form a Pythagorean triple.

**c.** $s^2 = 6^2 + 14^2$
$s^2 = 36 + 196$
$s^2 = 232$
$s = \sqrt{232}$
$s = \sqrt{232} = \sqrt{4 \cdot 58} = 2\sqrt{58}$

**d.** $20^2 = 2^2 + y^2$
$400 - 4 = 4 + y^2 - 4$
$396 = y^2$
$\sqrt{396} = y$
$y = \sqrt{396} = \sqrt{36 \cdot 11} = 6\sqrt{11}$

**e.** $\frac{w}{h} = \frac{16}{9}$
$\frac{32}{h} = \frac{16}{9}$
$16h = (32)(9)$
$16h = 288$
$h = 18$
$d^2 = 18^2 + 32^2$
$d^2 = 324 + 1024$
$d^2 = 1348$
$d = \sqrt{1348} = \sqrt{4 \cdot 337} = 2\sqrt{337}$

## Practice 29

**1. a.** $m\angle 1 = 5^2 + 3(5) - 5$
$= 25 + 15 - 5$
$= 35°$
$m\angle 2 = 5^3 - 2(5)^2 - 2(5) - 10$
$= 125 - 50 - 10 - 10$
$= 55°$

**b.** No, they are not parallel. If the lines were parallel, then angles 1 and 2 would be supplementary. They are complementary angles.

**2.** $A = \pi r^2$
$250{,}000 = \pi r^2$
$79{,}577 \approx r^2$
$282 \approx r$
The radius is approximately 282 km.

**3.**

| *s* | *t* | ~*t* | *s*∧~*t* |
|---|---|---|---|
| True | True | False | False |
| True | False | True | True |
| False | True | False | False |
| False | False | True | False |

**4.** They are not congruent. One pair of corresponding sides is not congruent.

**5.** SAS can be used when two pairs of corresponding sides of a triangle are congruent and the included angles are also congruent.

**6.** The measure of an exterior angle is equal to the sum of the two remote interior angles.
$m\angle F = m\angle D + m\angle E$
$107° = 71° + m\angle E$
$36° = m\angle E$

**7.** Choice **C** is correct because it is not equilateral.

**8.** My family room is quiet.

**9.** $\Delta RSC \cong \Delta EDC$

**10.** $\overline{DE} \cong \overline{PQ}$
$5 = y$
$\overline{EF} \cong \overline{QR}$
$x = 14$

**11.** Choice B is the only option that has counterexamples. Sample: $x = 2$; $2 + 1 = 3$ which is prime. Therefore, choice **B** is correct.

**12.** midpoint =
$\left(\frac{-10+4}{2}, \frac{4+2}{2}\right) = \left(\frac{-6}{2}, \frac{6}{2}\right)$
$= (-3, 3)$

13.

| Statements | Reasons |
|---|---|
| 1. $A$ lies on the perpendicular bisector of $\overline{BC}$ | 1. Definition of perpendicular bisector |
| 2. $\overline{AD} \cong \overline{AD}$ | 2. Reflexive Property of Congruence |
| 3. $\angle ADC \cong \angle ADB$ | 3. Perpendicular lines form congruent adjacent angles. |
| 4. $\Delta ADB \cong \Delta ADC$ | 4. SAS Triangle Congruence |
| 5. $\overline{AB} \cong \overline{AD}$ | 5. CPCTC |
| 6. $AB = AC$ | 6. Definition of congruent segments |

14. $A = \pi r^2 = \pi(22)^2 \approx 1521 \text{ ft}^2$

15. $9x - 12 + 4x = 157$

$13x - 12 = 157$

$13x = 169; x = 13$

$m\angle Q = 4(13) = 52°$

16. $x^2 + 15^2 = 17^2$

$x^2 = 289 - 225$

$x^2 = 64; x = 8 \text{ mi}$

17. $120° \div 3 = 40°$

18.

| Statements | Reasons |
|---|---|
| 1. $m \parallel n$ | 1. Given |
| 2. $\angle 1$ is supplementary to $\angle 3$ | 2. Linear pairs are supplementary. |
| 3. $\angle 1 + m\angle 3 = 180°$ | 3. Def. supp. angles |
| 4. $\angle 3 \cong \angle 4$ | 4. If parallel lines are cut by a transversal, the corresponding angles are congruent. |
| 5. $\angle 2 \cong \angle 4$ | 5. Vertical angle are congruent. |
| 6. $\angle 2 \cong \angle 3$ | 6. Trans. Prop. of $\cong$ |
| 7. $m\angle 2 = m\angle 3$ | 7. Def. $\cong \angle$s |
| 8. $m\angle 1 + m\angle 2 = 180°$ | 8. Substitute. |
| 9. $\angle 1$ is supplementary to $\angle 2$ | 9. Definition of supplementary angles |

19. $C = 2\pi r = 2\pi\,(380{,}000) \approx 2{,}387{,}610$ km

20. The slope is $-3$ or $\frac{-3}{1}$ and the $y$-intercept is $-6$.

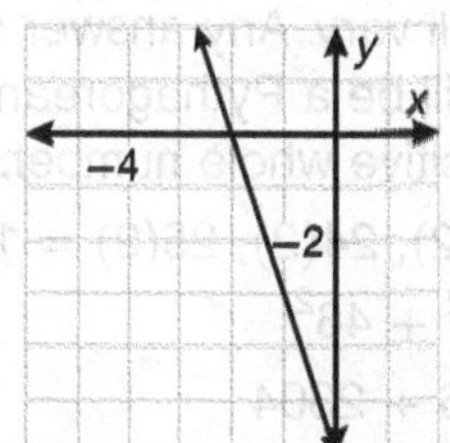


21. Since it contains a right angle, it is a right triangle. It has no sides that are congruent, making it scalene.

22.

| Statements | Reasons |
|---|---|
| 1. Planes $CDE$ and $ABF$ are parallel | 1. Given |
| 2. $\overline{AB}$ and $\overline{CD}$ do not intersect | 2. Definition of parallel planes |
| 3. Plane $ABC$ intersects both planes. | 3. Given |
| 4. $\overline{AB}$ and $\overline{CD}$ lie on $ABC$ | 4. Planes intersect in a line |
| 5. $\overline{AB} \parallel \overline{CD}$ | 5. Definition of parallel lines |

23. fence: $P = 2(110) + 2(60)$

$= 220 + 120 = 340$ yd

tarp: $A = (110)(60) = 6600 \text{ yd}^2$

24. true

25. $x^2 = 13^2 - 5^2$

$x^2 = 169 - 25$

$x^2 = 144; x = 12$

His answer is incorrect. The hypotenuse is always the longest side in a right triangle. His error was that he substituted 13 and 5 for $a$ and $b$, and solved xfor $c$.

26. $\angle K \cong \angle T, \angle L \cong \angle V$

$m\angle T = 40°$

$m\angle V = 30°$

$m\angle U = 180° - 40° - 30° = 110°$

So, $y = 110$.

$\overline{LM} \cong \overline{UV}$; $x = 22$ cm

**27.** No; Counterexample:

$\frac{1}{2}, \frac{2}{3}, \frac{3}{4}, \frac{4}{5}, \ldots$

**28.** Answers will vary. Any answer of the form $7n$, $24n$, $25n$ will be a Pythagorean triple, with $n$ being a positive whole number.

Sample: 7(2), 24(2), 25(2) = 14, 48, 50

$50^2 = 14^2 + 48^2$

$2500 = 196 + 2304$

$2500 = 2500$

**29.** sometimes true

**30.** $s^2 = 3^2 + 4^2$

$s^2 = 9 + 16$

$s^2 = 25$

$s = 5$ ft

## LESSON 30

### Warm Up 30

1. included
2. $x^2 + 14^2 = (x + 2)^2$

   $x^2 + 196 = x^2 + 4x + 4$

   $196 = 4x + 4$

   $192 = 4x$

   $48 = x$
3. SAS and SSS Postulates can both be used to prove two triangles congruent, AAA cannot. Choice **A** is correct.

### Lesson Practice 30

**a.** ASA

$AB = DE = 10$ cm

$CB = FE = 15$ cm

$CA = FD = 11$ cm

**b.**

| Statements | Reasons |
|---|---|
| 1. $\overline{AB} \parallel \overline{DE}$ | 1. Given |
| 2. $\overline{AB} \cong \overline{DE}$ | 2. Given |
| 3. $\angle BAC \cong \angle EDC$ | 3. Alternate Interior Angles Theorem |
| 4. $\angle ABC \cong \angle DEC$ | 4. Alternate Interior Angles Theorem |
| 5. $\Delta ABC \cong \Delta DEC$ | 5. ASA Postulate |

**c.** $4x + 6 = 2x + 10$

$2x = 4$

$x = 2$

$h = 4(2) + 6 = 14$

$A = \frac{1}{2}bh = \frac{1}{2}(8)(14) = 56$ square units

**d.**

| Statements | Reasons |
|---|---|
| 1. $\angle A \cong \angle B$ | 1. Given |
| 2. $\angle ADC \cong \angle BDC$ | 2. Given |
| 3. $\overline{DC} \cong \overline{DC}$ | 3. Reflexive Property of Congruence |
| 4. $\Delta ADC \cong \Delta BDC$ | 4. AAS Postulate |

**e.**

| Statements | Reasons |
|---|---|
| 1. $\angle IJK \cong \angle LMN$ | 1. Given |
| 2. $\overline{JK} \cong \overline{MN}$ | 2. Property of a rectangle |
| 3. $\angle IKJ \cong \angle LNM$ | 3. Given |
| 4. $\Delta IJK \cong \Delta LMN$ | 4. ASA Postulate |
| 5. $\overline{JI} \cong \overline{ML}$ | 5. CPCTC |

### Practice 30

**1.**

| $x$ | $y$ | $x \to y$ | $y \to x$ | $(x \to y) \wedge (y \to x)$ |
|---|---|---|---|---|
| T | T | T | T | T |
| T | F | F | T | F |
| F | T | T | F | F |
| F | F | T | T | T |

**2.** Since the distance traveled is one-third the total distance, She needs to go 3(0.5) or 1.5 km north and 3(0.4) or 1.2 km east. When she travels this distance, she will be at coordinate (1 + 1.2, 2 + 1.5) or (2.2, 3.5).

**3.** The wire is the hypotenuse of a right triangle.

$4^2 = 1.5^2 + h^2$

$16 - 2.25 = h^2$

$13.75 = h^2$

$3.7 \approx h$

The wire should be attached approximately 3.7 meters up the tree.

**4.** No, the angle that is congruent is not located between the corresponding congruent sides in both triangles.

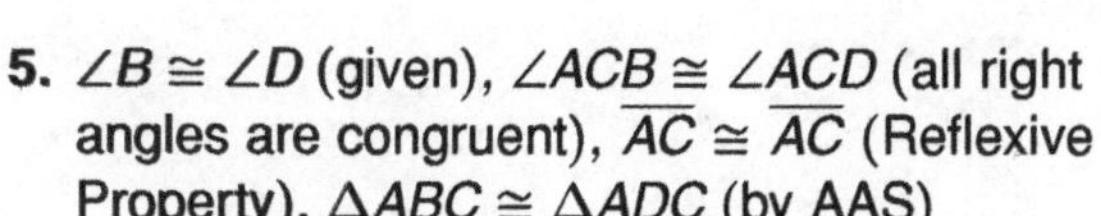



**5.** $\angle B \cong \angle D$ (given), $\angle ACB \cong \angle ACD$ (all right angles are congruent), $\overline{AC} \cong \overline{AC}$ (Reflexive Property), $\Delta ABC \cong \Delta ADC$ (by AAS)

**6.**

| Statement | Reason |
|---|---|
| $\frac{2x-5}{5} = 3$ | Given |
| $5\left(\frac{2x-5}{5}\right) = 5(3)$ | Multiplication Property of Equality |
| $2x - 5 = 15$ | Simplify. |
| $2x - 5 + 5 = 15 + 5$ | Addition Property of Equality |
| $2x = 20$ | Simplify. |
| $\frac{2x}{2} = \frac{20}{2}$ | Division Property of Equality |
| $x = 10$ | Simplify. |

**7.**

| Statements | Reasons |
|---|---|
| 1. *PQRS* is a parallelogram | 1. Given |
| 2. $\overline{PQ} \parallel \overline{RS}$ and $\overline{PR} \parallel \overline{QS}$ | 2. Definition of parallelogram |
| 3. $\angle 2 \cong \angle 4$ | 3. Alternate interior angles are congruent. |
| 4. $\angle 6 \cong \angle 3$ | 4. Alternate interior angles are congruent. |
| 5. $m\angle 2 = m\angle 4$ $m\angle 6 = m\angle 3$ | 5. Def. $\cong$ angles |
| 6. $m\angle 1 + m\angle 2 + m\angle 3 = 180°$ and $m\angle 4 + m\angle 5 + m\angle 6 = 180°$ | 6. Triangle Angle Sum Theorem |
| 7. $m\angle 1 + m\angle 2 + m\angle 3 = m\angle 4 + m\angle 5 + m\angle 6$ | 7. Substitute. |
| 8. $m\angle 1 + m\angle 2 + m\angle 3 = m\angle 2 + m\angle 5 + m\angle 3$ | 8. Substitute |
| 9. $m\angle 1 = m\angle 5$ | 9. Simplify. |
| 10. $\angle 1 \cong \angle 5$ | 10. Def. $\cong$ angles |

**8.** $C = 2\pi r = 14;\ r \approx 2.23$

$A = \pi r^2 = \pi(2.23)^2 \approx 15.6 \text{ ft}^2$

**9.** $\overline{EF} \cong \overline{PQ}$

$3x - 55 = x + 5$

$2x = 60;\ x = 30$

$x + 5 = 30 + 5 = 35$

$P = 22 + 28 + 35 = 85$ units

**10.** $12x - 62 = 8x + 86$

$4x = 148;\ x = 37$

**11.** $\angle T \cong \angle H$

$9x = 54;\ x = 6$

**12.** $\angle A \cong \angle D$, $\angle B \cong \angle E$, $\angle C \cong \angle F$, $\overline{AB} \cong \overline{DE}$, $\overline{BC} \cong \overline{EF}$, $\overline{AC} \cong \overline{DF}$

**13.** Choice **B**: They are contrapositives.

**14.** Since the given congruent side is included within the two given congruent angles, the ASA Postulate applies. Alternatively, by the Triangle Sum Theorem, $\angle F$ and $\angle P$ can be shown to be congruent, and then the AAS Triangle Congruence Theorem applies.

**15.** Since statement *a* is true, the disjunction is also true.

**16.** Counterexample: $x = 2$ and $y = 4$; $2 - 4 = -2$, which is negative.

**17.** $24^2 = x^2 + x^2$

$576 = 2x^2$

$288 = x^2;\ 17 \approx x$

The length of each leg is about 17 inches.

**18.** Therefore, the clerk made a mess.

**19.** major arc $= 360° - 135° = 225°$

$225° \div 5 = 45°$

**20.** $x^2 = 660^2 + 60^2$

$x^2 = 435{,}600 + 3600$

$x^2 = 439{,}200$

$x \approx 663$ yd

**21.** The exterior angle is equal to the sum of the remote interior angles.

$m\angle I = m\angle G + m\angle H$

$141° = 33° + m\angle H$

$108° = m\angle H$

**22.** $A_{\text{Rhombus}} = \frac{1}{2}d_1 d_2$

$= \frac{1}{2}(14)(22) = 154 \text{ cm}^2$

$A_{\text{Rectangle}} = lw$

$154 = (l)(5)$

$30.8 = l$

The length of the rectangle is 30.8 cm.

**23.** If $\overline{AB} \cong \overline{DE}$, then that would show $\Delta ABC$ congruent to $\Delta EDC$, not $\Delta DEC$.

**24.**

| Statements | Reasons |
|---|---|
| 1. $K$ lies on the angle bisector of $\angle HIJ$ | 1. Given |
| 2. Draw $\overline{HK}$ and $\overline{KJ}$ | 2. The shortest distance between a point and a line is a perpendicular segment. |
| 3. $m\angle KHI = m\angle KJI = 90°$ | 3. Definition of perpendicular segments |
| 4. $\angle KHI \cong \angle KJI$ | 4. Definition of congruent angles |
| 5. $\overline{KI} \cong \overline{KI}$ | 5. Reflexive Property of Congruence |
| 6. $\angle HIK \cong \angle JIK$ | 6. Definition of angle bisector |
| 7. $\Delta HIK \cong \Delta JIK$ | 7. AAS Triangle Congruence |
| 8. $\overline{HK} \cong \overline{JK}$ | 8. CPCTC |

**25.** $m = \frac{3-1}{-2-1} = \frac{2}{-3} = -\frac{2}{3}$

$y = -\frac{2}{3} + b$

$1 = -\frac{2}{3}(1) + b$

$\frac{5}{3} = b$

**26.** $42 = \pi r^2$

$13.37 \approx r^2$

$3.66 \approx r$

$8C = 8(2\pi r) = 8(2\pi)(3.66) \approx 184$ in.

**27.** Only one, because of the SSS Postulate

**28.** Since the two acute angles are complementary, $(90 - y)°$.

**29.** $A = \frac{1}{2}(b_1 + b_2)h = \frac{1}{2}(4 + 3)(2) = 7 \text{ ft}^2$

**30.** They are inverses.

## INVESTIGATION 3

1.

| Regular Polygon | Triangle | Quadrilateral | Pentagon | Hexagon |
|---|---|---|---|---|
| Interior Angle Measure | 60° | 90° | 108° | 120° |
| Sum of Interior Angle Measures | 180° | 360° | 540° | 720° |

2. If the number of sides in one regular polygon is greater than the number of sides in another regular polygon, then the interior angle measure of the first regular polygon is greater than that of the second regular polygon.

3. Since the number of sides is equal to the number of interior angles, the sum can be calculated by multiplying the measure of one interior angle by the number of sides of the polygon.

4. Answers may vary: There is an increase in the sum that is proportional to the increase in number of sides.

5. a. $\frac{(n-2)180°}{n} = \frac{(3-2)180°}{3} = \frac{180°}{3} = 60°$

triangle: 60°

$\frac{(n-2)180°}{n} = \frac{(4-2)180°}{4} = \frac{360°}{4} = 90°$

square: 90°

$\frac{(n-2)180°}{n} = \frac{(5-2)180°}{5} = \frac{540°}{5} = 108°$

pentagon: 108°

$\frac{(n-2)180°}{n} = \frac{(6-2)180°}{6} = \frac{720°}{6} = 120°$

hexagon: 120°

b. Students should have the same or very similar values for each method.

6.

| Regular Polygon | Triangle | Quadrilateral | Pentagon | Hexagon |
|---|---|---|---|---|
| Exterior Angle Measure | 120° | 90° | 72° | 60° |
| Sum of Exterior Angle Measures | 360° | 360° | 360° | 360° |

7. The exterior angle measures will be the same for each vertex polygon.

8. If the number of sides in one regular polygon is greater than in a different regular polygon, then the exterior angle measure of the first regular polygon is less than the second different regular polygon.

9. The sum of the exterior angle measures for each polygon is 360°.

10. a. $\frac{360°}{n} = \frac{360°}{3} = 120°$

triangle: 120°

$\frac{360°}{n} = \frac{360°}{4} = 90°$

square: 90°

$\frac{360°}{n} = \frac{360°}{5} = 72°$

pentagon: 72°

$\frac{360°}{n} = \frac{360°}{6} = 60°$

hexagon: 60°

**b.** Students should have the same or very similar values for each method.

**11.**

| Regular Polygon | Triangle | Quadrilateral | Pentagon | Hexagon |
|---|---|---|---|---|
| Central Angle Measure | 120° | 90° | 72° | 60° |
| Sum of Central Angle Measure | 360° | 360° | 360° | 360° |

**12.** The central angle measures will be the same for each polygon.

**13.** For each polygon, the central angles are equivalent. See student work.

**14.** They are all 360°, the same.

**15.** triangle: 3; square: 4; pentagon: 5; hexagon: 6

**16.** The number of sides equals the number of central angles.

**17. a.** $\frac{360°}{n} = \frac{360°}{3} = 120°$

triangle: 120°

$\frac{360°}{n} = \frac{360°}{4} = 90°$

square: 90°

$\frac{360°}{n} = \frac{360°}{5} = 72°$

pentagon: 72°

$\frac{360°}{n} = \frac{360°}{6} = 60°$

hexagon: 60°

**b.** Students should have the same or very similar values for each method.

**Investigation Practice 3**

**a.** As the number of sides of a regular polygon increases, the measure of each interior angle increases, the measure of each exterior angle decreases, and the measure of each central angle decreases.

**b.** $\frac{(n-2)180°}{n} = \frac{(8-2)180°}{8}$

$= \frac{1080°}{8} = 135°$

**c.** $\frac{(n-2)180°}{n} = \frac{(20-2)180°}{20}$

$= \frac{3240°}{20} = 162°$

**d.** $\frac{360°}{n} = \frac{360°}{10} = 36°$

**e.** $\frac{360°}{n} = \frac{360°}{30} = 12°$

**f.** No, irregular polygons are not equiangular.

**g.** No, it would not be possible for an angle's vertex to be at a center point in irregular polygons.

## LESSON 31

**Warm Up 31**

**1.** deductive

**2.** Choice A: $1^2 + 2^2 = 3^2$

$1 + 4 = 9$

$5 \neq 9$

Choice B: $1^2 + 1^2 = (\sqrt{2})^2$

$1 + 1 = 2$

$2 = 2$

But, since $\sqrt{2}$ is not an integer, this is not a Pythagorean triple.

Choice C: $1^2 + 1^2 = 1^2$

$1 + 1 = 1$

$2 \neq 1$

Choice D: $3^2 + 4^2 = 5^2$

$9 + 16 = 25$

$25 = 25$

Choice **D** is correct.

3. I will go to the store. Law of Detachment

## Lesson Practice 31

a.

| Statements | Reasons |
|---|---|
| 1. $\angle 1$ and $\angle 2$ are complementary. | 1. Given |
| 2. $\angle 1$ and $\angle 3$ are congruent. | 2. Given |
| 3. $m\angle 1 + m\angle 2 = 90°$ | 3. Definition of complementary angles |
| 4. $m\angle 1 = m\angle 3$ | 4. Definition of congruent angles |
| 5. $m\angle 3 + m\angle 2 = 90°$ | 5. Substitution Property of Equality |
| 6. $\angle 3$ and $\angle 2$ are complementary. | 6. Definition of complementary angles |

b.

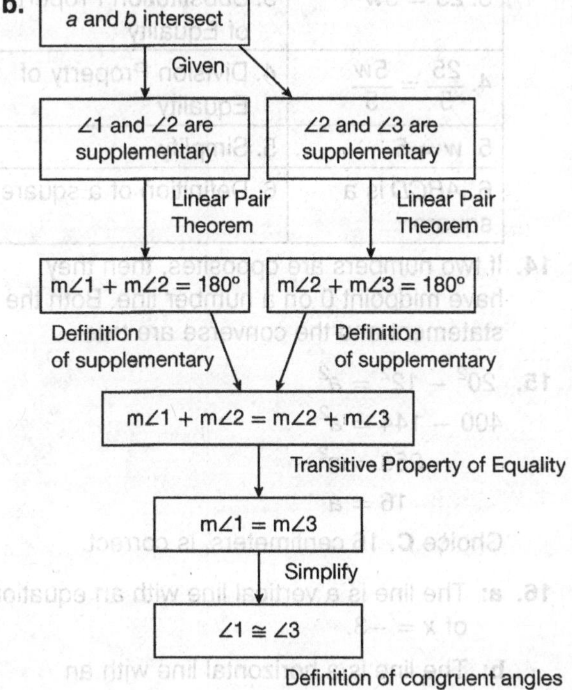


c.

| Statements | Reasons |
|---|---|
| 1. $\angle 1$ and $\angle 4$ are complementary. | 1. Given |
| 2. $m\angle 1 + m\angle 4 = 90°$ | 2. Definition of complementary angles |
| 3. $\angle 1$ and $\angle 3$ are congruent. $\angle 2$ and $\angle 4$ are congruent. | 3. Vertical Angles Theorem |
| 4. $m\angle 1 = m\angle 3$, $m\angle 2 = m\angle 4$ | 4. Definition of congruent angles |
| 5. $m\angle 2 + m\angle 3 = 90°$ | 5. Substitution Property of Equality |
| 6. $\angle 2$ and $\angle 3$ are complementary. | 6. Definition of complementary angles |

d. It is given that $s$ and $t$ are perpendicular lines. By the definition of perpendicular lines, angles 1 and 2 are right angles. Angles 1 and 2 are congruent by Theorem 5-3: All right angles are congruent. Angles 1 and 2 are adjacent by the definition of adjacent angles. Therefore, angles 1 and 2 are congruent adjacent angles.

## Practice 31

1. $(n - 2)180° = (4 - 2)180° = 360°$

$$\frac{360°}{4} = 90°$$

2.

| Statements | Reasons |
|---|---|
| 1. $\overline{AE} \cong \overline{CE}$, $\overline{DE} \cong \overline{BE}$ | 1. Given |
| 2. $AE = CE$, $DE = BE$ | 2. Definition of congruent segments |
| 3. $\angle AED \cong \angle CEB$ | 3. Vertical Angles Theorem |
| 4. $m\angle AED = m\angle CEB$ | 4. Def. $\cong$ angles |
| 5. $\triangle AED \cong \triangle CEB$ | 5. SAS Postulate |
| 6. $\overline{AD} \cong \overline{CB}$ | 6. CPCTC |

3. $180° - 58° - 62° = 60°$

4. $A = bh$

$18 = (6)(h)$

$3 = h$

The height was 3 cm.

5. $360° - 70° = 290°$

6. By the Vertical Angles Theorem, $\angle 1 \cong \angle 2$. Then by the Same-Side Interior Angles Theorem, $\angle 2$ and $\angle 3$ are supplementary. By the Alternate Interior Angles Theorem, $\angle 3 \cong \angle 4$. By substitution, $\angle 2$ and $\angle 4$ are supplementary. By the definition of a linear pair, $\angle 4$ and $\angle 5$ are supplementary. Using the Congruent Supplements Theorem, $\angle 2 \cong \angle 5$. Finally, $\angle 1 \cong \angle 5$ by the Transitive Property of Congruence.

7.

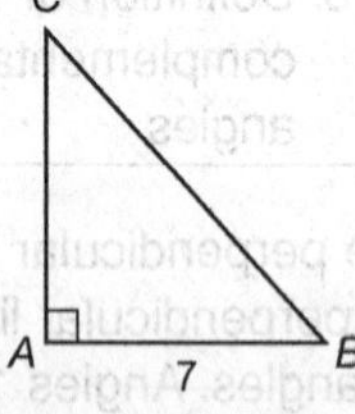


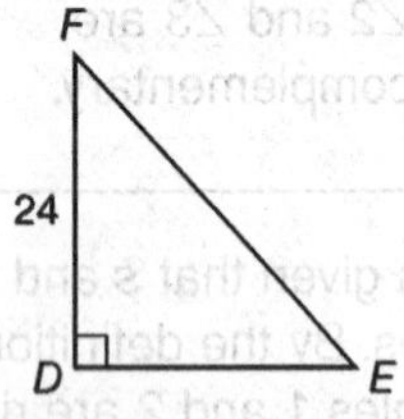


$x^2 = 24^2 + 7^2$

$x^2 = 576 + 49$

$x^2 = 625$

$x = 25$

8. $4^2 = 3.8^2 + 1.5^2$

$16 = 14.44 + 2.25$

$16 < 16.69$

The ladder is not long enough.

9. $(n - 2)180° = (8 - 2)180° = 1080°$

$\frac{1080°}{8} = 135°$

10. $A = \frac{1}{2}d_1d_2$

$224 = \frac{1}{2}(14)(x)$

$448 = 14x$

$32 = x$

The other diagonal crosspiece is 32 inches.

11.

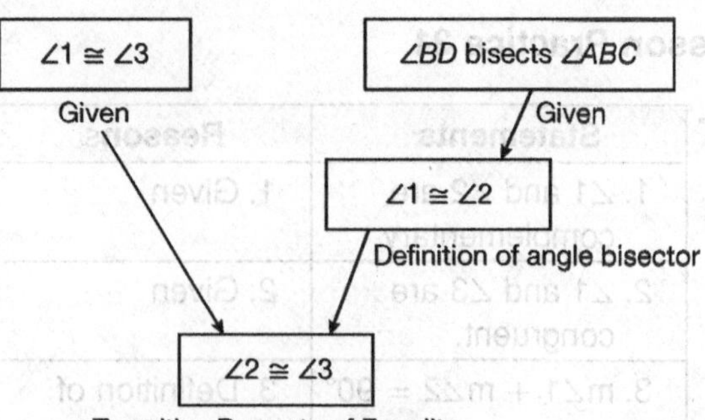


12. The Transitive Property of Congruence tells that $\triangle ABC$ and $\triangle XYZ$ are congruent. Since the corresponding parts of the congruent triangles are congruent,

$\angle A \cong \angle X, \angle B \cong \angle Y, \angle C \cong \angle Z,$

$\overline{AB} \cong \overline{XY}, \overline{BC} \cong \overline{YZ}, \overline{CA} \cong \overline{ZX}.$

13.

| Statements | Reasons |
|---|---|
| 1. $A = 25$, $l = 5$ | 1. Given |
| 2. $A = lw$ | 2. Area of a rectangle |
| 3. $25 = 5w$ | 3. Substitution Property of Equality |
| 4. $\frac{25}{5} = \frac{5w}{5}$ | 4. Division Property of Equality |
| 5. $w = 5$ | 5. Simplify. |
| 6. *ABCD* is a square | 6. Definition of a square |

14. If two numbers are opposites, then they have midpoint 0 on a number line. Both the statement and the converse are true.

15. $20^2 - 12^2 = a^2$

$400 - 144 = a^2$

$256 = a^2$

$16 = a$

Choice **C**, 16 centimeters, is correct.

16. **a:** The line is a vertical line with an equation of $x = -3$.

**b:** The line is a horizontal line with an equation of $y = 2$.

**17.** There is a good chance of wind and rain later in the day.

**18.** Gayle is correct because, according to the ASA Theorem or the AAS Postulate, corresponding sides must be congruent in order for the triangles to be congruent.

**19.** Sample: The equation $x + 1 = x + 2$ has no solutions.

**20.**

| Statements | Reasons |
|---|---|
| 1. $\overline{AD} \parallel \overline{BC}$, $\overline{AD} \cong \overline{BC}$ | 1. Given |
| 2. $AD = BC$ | 2. Definition of congruent segments |
| 3. $m\angle ADE = m\angle CBE$ | 3. Alternate Interior Angles Theorem |
| 4. $m\angle AED = m\angle CEB$ | 4. Vertical Angles Theorem |
| 5. $\triangle ADE \cong \triangle CBE$ | 5. AAS Theorem |
| 6. $\overline{AE} = \overline{CE}$ | 6. CPCTC |

**21.** Since $\overline{AD}$ bisects $\overline{CB}$, $\overline{CD} \cong \overline{BD}$ by the definition of a bisector. Because $\overline{AD} \perp \overline{CB}$, $\angle ADC$ and $\angle ADB$ are right angles by the definition of perpendicular. Then $\angle ADC \cong \angle ADB$, because all right angles are congruent. From the drawing, $\overline{AD} \cong \overline{AD}$ by the Reflexive Property. Finally, $\triangle ACD \cong \triangle ABD$ by the SAS Postulate.

**22.**

| Statements | Reasons |
|---|---|
| 1. $\sqrt{((x-3)-1)^2 + ((4x+1)-1)^2} = 5$ | 1. Distance Formula |
| 2. $\sqrt{(x-4)^2 + (4x)^2} = 5$ | 2. Simplify. |
| 3. $\sqrt{x^2 - 8x + 16 + 16x^2} = 5$ | 3. Expand exponents. |
| 4. $\sqrt{17x^2 - 8x + 16} = 5$ | 4. Simplify. |
| 5. $\left(\sqrt{17x^2 - 8x + 16}\,)^2\right) = 5^2$ | 5. Square both sides. |
| 6. $17x^2 - 8x + 16 = 25$ | 6. Simplify. |
| 7. $17x^2 - 8x + 16 - 25 = 25 - 25$ | 7. Subtraction Property of Equality |
| 8. $17x^2 - 8x - 9 = 0$ | 8. Simplify. |
| 9. $(17x + 9)(x - 1) = 0$ | 9. Factor. |
| 10. $x - 1 = 0$ | 10. $17x + 9 = 0$ gives a negative solution. |
| 11. $x - 1 + 1 = 0 + 1$ | 11. Addition Property of Equality |
| 12. $x = 1$ | 12. Simplify. |
| 13. $(1 - 3, 4(1) + 1)$ | 13. Substitute $x = 1$ into the original coordinates. |
| 14. $(-2, 5)$ | 14. Simplify. |

So the coordinates are $(-2, 5)$.

**23.** $y - 2 = 4(x + 3)$
$y - 2 = 4x + 12$
$y = 4x + 14$

**24.**

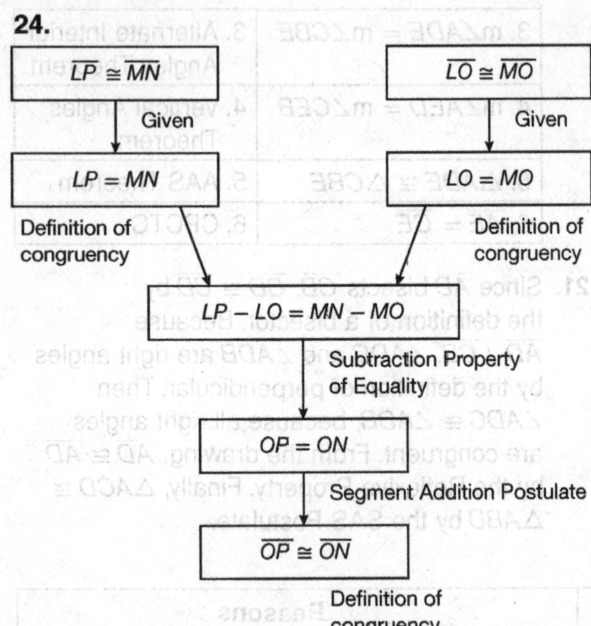


**25.** Yes.

| Statements | Reasons |
|---|---|
| 1. $\angle B$ and $\angle E$ are right angles, $AB = DE$, $AC = DF$ | 1. Given |
| 2. $AB^2 + BC^2 = AC^2$ | 2. Pythagorean Theorem |
| 3. $DE^2 + EF^2 = DF^2$ | 3. Pythagorean Theorem |
| 4. $AB^2 + BC^2 = DE^2 + EF^2$ | 4. Transitive Property of Equality |
| 5. $BC^2 = EF^2$ | 5. Subtraction Property of Equality |
| 6. $BC = EF$ | 6. Square root |
| 7. $\overline{BC} \cong \overline{EF}$ $\overline{AB} \cong \overline{DE}$ | 7. Def. of congruence |
| 8. $\angle ABC \cong \angle DEF$ | 8. All right angles are congruent. |
| 9. $\triangle ABC \cong \triangle DEF$ | 9. SAS Postulate |

**26. a.** $A = \frac{1}{2}bh = \frac{1}{2}(1.5)(1.2) = 0.9 \text{ m}^2$

**b.** $P = 1.5 + 1.2 + 1.9 \approx 4.6 \text{ m}$

**27. a.** Sample: $\sim p$ or $q$ **b.** $\sim p$ and $\sim q$

**c.** $p$ and $\sim q$

**28.** interior: $\angle TSZ$, $\angle WVU$

exterior: $\angle AZY$, $\angle SZB$, and $\angle WVC$

**29.** $C = 2\pi r$

$= 2\pi\left(\frac{13}{2}\right) = 13\pi \approx 13(3.14) = 40.82$ cm

Sal forgot to divide the diameter by 2 to find the radius.

**30.**

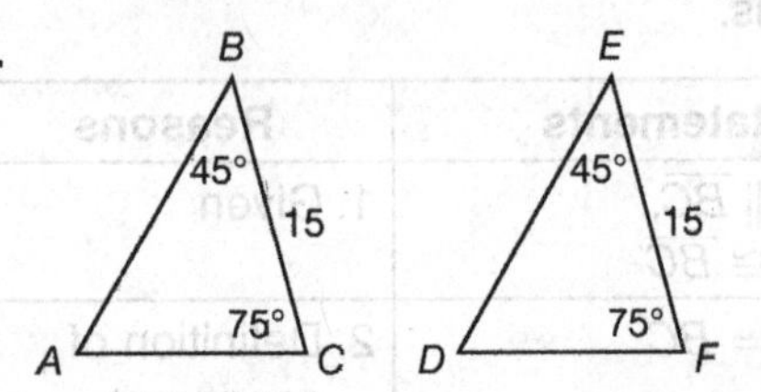


By the ASA Theorem, $\triangle ABC \cong \triangle DEF$. So, by CPCTC, $\overline{AB} \cong \overline{DE}$ and $AB = DE$.

$3x + 11 = 7x - 9$

$-4x = -20$

$x = 5$

## LESSON 32

### Warm Up 32

1. equiangular
2. False, the height of an obtuse triangle is on the exterior of the triangle.
3. $m = \left(\frac{x_1 + x_2}{2}, \frac{y_1 + y_2}{2}\right) = \left(\frac{-3 + 2}{2}, \frac{4 + 8}{2}\right)$

   $= \left(\frac{-1}{2}, \frac{12}{2}\right) = (-0.5, 6)$
4. $m = \left(\frac{x_1 + x_2}{2}, \frac{y_1 + y_2}{2}\right)$

   $= \left(\frac{4 + -1}{2}, \frac{2 + 3}{2}\right)$

   $= \left(\frac{3}{2}, \frac{5}{2}\right) = (1.5, 2.5)$

### Lesson Practice 32

**a.** To find $OD$: $\frac{1}{3}(AD)$

$= \left(\frac{1}{3}\right)(5)$

$= 1.67$

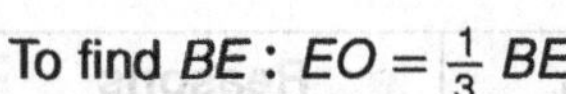



To find $BE : EO = \frac{1}{3} BE$

$4.2 = \frac{1}{3}(BE)$

$\overline{BE} = 3(4.2)$

$= 12.6$

**b.** Find the midpoints of $\overline{JK}$ and $\overline{KL}$.

$\overline{JK}$: $\left(\frac{-9 + -1}{2}, \frac{1 + 5}{2}\right) = (-5, 3)$

$\overline{KL}$: $\left(\frac{-1 + -5}{2}, \frac{5 + 9}{2}\right) = (-3, 7)$

The slope of the median that extends from $J$ to $(-3, 7)$ is:

$m = \frac{1 - 7}{-9 - -3} = \frac{-6}{-6} = 1$

$y - y_1 = m(x - x_1)$

$y - 7 = 1(x - -3)$

$y = x + 10$

The slope of the median that extends from $L$ to $(-5, 3)$ is

$m = \frac{9 - 3}{-5 - -5} = \frac{6}{0} = 0$

When slope is undefined, the line is vertical.

$x = -5$

Solve these two equations as a system.

$y = x + 10$

$y = -5 + 10$

$y = 5$

The coordinates of the centroid are $(-5, 5)$.

**c.** The orthocenter is located on the vertex of the right angle.

**d.** $\frac{2}{3}(3.6) = 2.4$ in.

$\frac{2}{3}(6.9) = 4.6$ in.

$\frac{2}{3}(4.5) = 3$ in.

## Practice 32

**1.** $\left(\frac{180°}{360°}\right)\pi r^2 = \frac{1}{2}\pi r^2$

**2.** trapezoid only

**3.** $A = \frac{1}{2}(b_1 + b_2)h$

$22 = \frac{1}{2}(x + 2 + 3x - 3)(4)$

$22 = 2(4x - 1)$

$22 = 8x - 2$

$24 = 8x$

$3 = x$

**4.** As the list progresses, the number of sides of the polygon described in each term increases by one. Therefore, the next item in the list would be an octagon.

**5.** midpoint

**6. a.** hexagon (6 sides)

**b.** irregular

**c.** It is concave because the diagonal between the left-most points lies outside the polygon.

**7. a.** Hypothesis: $\triangle MNO$ is an acute triangle, $D$ lies on $\overline{MN}$, and $E$ lies on $\overline{MO}$.

Conclusion: $\triangle MDE$ is an acute triangle.

**b.** For example,

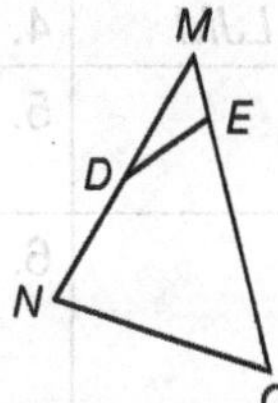


**8.**

| Statements | Reasons |
|---|---|
| 1. $\overline{SR} \cong \overline{UT}$ | 1. Given |
| 2. $\overline{SO} \cong \overline{UO}$ | 2. Radii of the same circle are congruent. |
| 3. $\overline{RO} \cong \overline{TO}$ | 3. Radii of the same circle are congruent. |
| 4. $\triangle SRO \cong \triangle UTO$ | 4. SSS Postulate |
| 5. $\angle SRO \cong \angle UTO$ | 5. CPCTC. |
| 6. $m\angle SRO = m\angle UTO$ | 6. Definition of congruent angles |

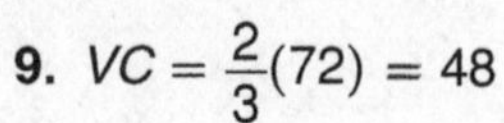



**9.** $VC = \frac{2}{3}(72) = 48$

**10.** $18 = \frac{1}{3}(UX)$

$54 = UX$

$UC = 54 - 18 = 36$

**11.**

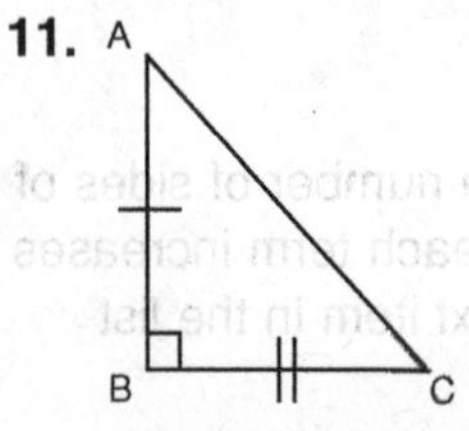


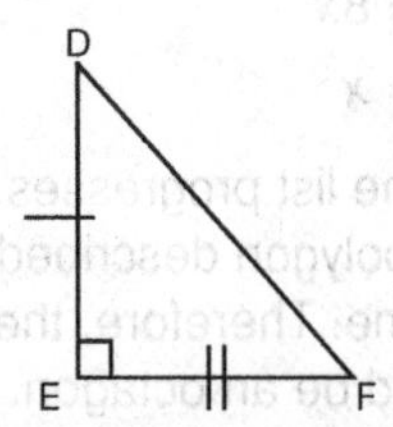


They are congruent by the SAS postulate.

**12.**

| Statements | Reasons |
|---|---|
| 1. $\angle KJM \cong \angle LJM$ $\angle JMK$ is a right angle. $JML$ is a right angle. | 1. Given |
| 2. $\angle JMK \cong \angle JML$ | 2. Right angles are congruent. |
| 3. $JM \cong JM$ | 3. Reflexive Property of Congruence |
| 4. $\triangle KJM \cong \triangle LJM$ | 4. ASA Postulate |
| 5. $\overline{KM} \cong \overline{LM}$ | 5. CPCTC. |
| 6. $KM = LM$ | 6. Definition of congruent segments |

**13.** $A = \frac{1}{2}(b_1 + b_2)h$

$= \frac{1}{2}(3 + 4)(3)$

$= 2(7)(3)$

$= 10.5 \text{ in}^2$

**14.** It is given that $\overline{AB} \cong \overline{BC}$ and $\overline{BC} \cong \overline{DE}$, so by the Transitive Property of Congruence, $\overline{AB} \cong \overline{DE}$.

**15.**

| Statements | Reasons |
|---|---|
| 1. $m\angle P = m\angle Q = m\angle R$ | 1. Given |
| 2. $m\angle P + m\angle Q + m\angle R = 180°$ | 2. Triangle Sum Theorem |
| 3. $m\angle P + m\angle P + m\angle P = 180°$ | 3. Substitution Property of Equality |
| 4. $3m\angle P = 180°$ | 4. Simplify. |
| 5. $\frac{3m\angle P}{3} = \frac{180°}{3}$ | 5. Division Property of Equality |
| 6. $m\angle P = 60°$ | 6. Simplify. |
| 7. $m\angle P = m\angle Q = m\angle R = 60°$ | 7. Transitive Property of Equality |

**16.** $\sqrt{360} = \sqrt{6^2 \cdot 10} = 6\sqrt{10}$;
Beatrice's answer is incorrect, because she did not take the square root of 36.

**17.** Given that $\angle 1$ and $\angle 2$ are complementary and $\angle 3$ and $\angle 4$ are complementary, by the definition of complementary angles, $m\angle 1 + m\angle 2 = 90°$ and $m\angle 3 + m\angle 4 = 90°$ and $m\angle 1 + m\angle 2 = m\angle 3 + m\angle 4$. It is given that angle 2 is congruent to $\angle 3$ and, by the definition of congruency, $m\angle 2 = m\angle 3$. By substitution, $m\angle 1 + m\angle 2 = m\angle 2 + m\angle 4$. Simplification makes $m\angle 1 = m\angle 4$. By the definition of congruency, $\angle 1$ is congruent to $\angle 4$.

**18.**

| Statements | Reasons |
|---|---|
| $4x - 4 = 3x + 7$ | Vertical Angles Theorem |
| $4x - 4 + 4 = 3x + 7 + 4$ | Addition Property of Equality |
| $4x = 3x + 11$ | Simplify. |
| $4x - 3x = 3x + 11 - 3x$ | Subtraction Property of Equality |
| $x = 11$ | Simplify. |
| $4x - 4 = 4(11) - 4$ | Substitution. |
| $= 44 - 4$ $= 40°$ | Simplify. |

**19. a.** Hypothesis: The product of three numbers is positive.
Conclusion: All three numbers are positive.

**b.** Sample: The product of −3, −1, and 1 is positive.

**20.** If $M$ is the midpoint of $\overline{WX}$, then $WM = MX$.

**21.** The second interior angle measures 49°. 49° + 49° = 98°

**22. a.** The circumference of the first gear is 0.77 the circumference of the second.

**b.** $C_1 = 0.77C_2$

$2\pi(10) = 0.77(2\pi r_2)$

$20\pi = 1.54\pi r_2$

$\frac{20\pi}{1.54\pi} = r_2$

$13 \approx r_2$

The second gear's radius is about 13 centimeters.

**23.**

| Statements | Reasons |
|---|---|
| 1. Two parallelograms with base $b$ and heights $h_1$ and $h_2$ lie on parallel lines | 1. Given |
| 2. $h_1 = h_2$ | 2. Equal distance between parallel lines |
| 3. $A_1 = bh_1$ | 3. Area of parallelogram 1 |
| 4. $A_2 = bh_2$ | 4. Area of parallelogram 2 |
| 5. $A_2 = bh_1$ | 5. Substitution Property of Equality |
| 6. $A_1 = A_2$ | 6. Transitive Property of Equality |

**24.** $\frac{1}{3}(4.5) = 1.5$; Choice **D** is correct.

**25.**

| Statements | Reasons |
|---|---|
| 1. m∠ACB = 90°, m∠ABD = 90° $\overline{AB} \cong \overline{BD}$, $\overline{AC} \cong \overline{BC}$ | 1. Given |
| 2. m∠BAC + m∠ABC = 90° | 2. Acute angles in a right triangle are complementary |
| 3. m∠ABC + m∠DBC = 90° | 3. Definition of complementary angles |
| 4. m∠BAC + m∠ABC = m∠ABC + ∠DBC | 4. Substitution Property of Equality |
| 5. m∠BAC + m∠ABC − m∠ABC = m∠ABC + m∠DBC − m∠ABC | 5. Subtraction Property of Equality |
| 6. m∠BAC = m∠DBC | 6. Simplify |
| 7. ∠BAC ≅ ∠DBC | 7. Def. ≅ angles |
| 8. △ABC ≅ △BDC | 8. SAS Postulate |

**26.**

| Statements | Reasons |
|---|---|
| If $p$, then $q$ | If ~$q$, then ~$p$ |
| If ~$p$, then $q$ | If ~$q$, then $p$ |
| If $p$, then ~$q$ | If $q$, then ~$p$ |
| If ~$p$, then ~$q$ | If $q$, then $p$ |

**27.** m∠WVY = m∠WXY, or m∠WYV = m∠WYX

**28.**

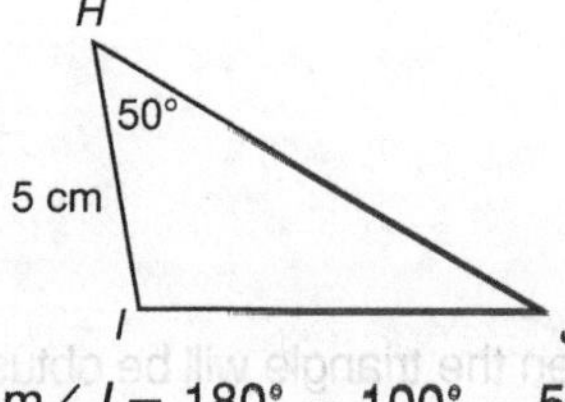


m∠J = 180° − 100° − 50° = 30°

**29.**

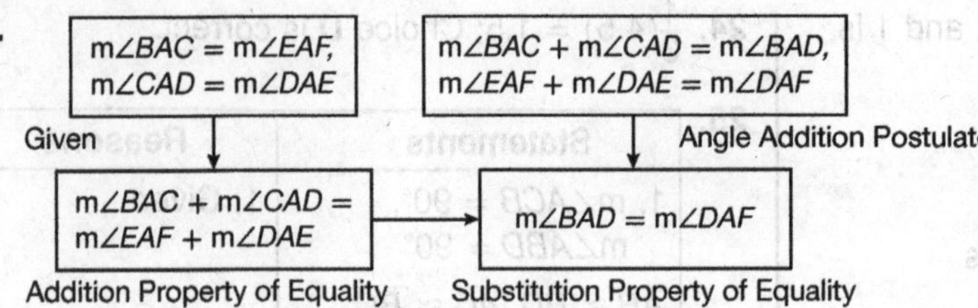


**30.** $p$ and $\sim q$; See student work.
Sample:

| Statement: $p$ | Statement: $q$ | Conjunction: $p$ and $q$ | Negation: $p$ and $\sim q$ |
|---|---|---|---|
| T | T | T | F |
| T | F | F | T |
| F | T | F | F |
| F | F | F | F |

## LESSON 33

### Warm Up 33

1. converse
2. $(PQ)^2 = 4^2 + 3^2$
   $(PQ)^2 = 16 + 9$
   $\sqrt{(PQ)^2} = \sqrt{25}$
   $PQ = 5$
3. Converse: If two angles are congruent, then they are vertical angles.
   This is false. A counterexample would be a right angle divided into two 45° angles.

### Lesson Practice 33

**a.** $27^2 = a^2 + 20^2$
$729 = a^2 + 400$
$329 = a^2$
$\sqrt{329} = a$

**b.** $15^2 = 8^2 + 14^2$
$225 = 64 + 196$
$225 \neq 260$
This triangle is not a right triangle by the Converse of the Pythagorean Theorem.

**c.** $13^2 = 7^2 + 8^2$
$169 = 49 + 64$
$169 > 113$
Since $c^2 > a^2 + b^2$, the triangle is obtuse.

**d.** $25^2 = 24^2 + 7^2$
$625 = 576 + 49$
$625 = 625$
Since $c^2 = a^2 + b^2$, the triangle is a right triangle.

**e.** $10^2 = 6^2 + 7.5^2$
$100 = 36 + 56.25$
$100 > 92.25$
No. $6^2 + 7.5^2 < 10^2$, so the triangle is obtuse.

### Practice 33

1. $\angle F \cong \angle T$, $\angle G \cong \angle U$, $\angle H \cong \angle V$
   $\overline{FG} \cong \overline{TU}$, $\overline{GH} \cong \overline{UV}$, $\overline{HF} \cong \overline{VT}$
2. 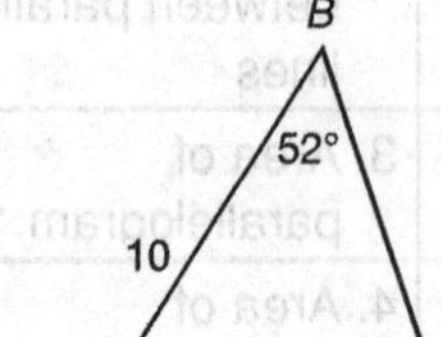

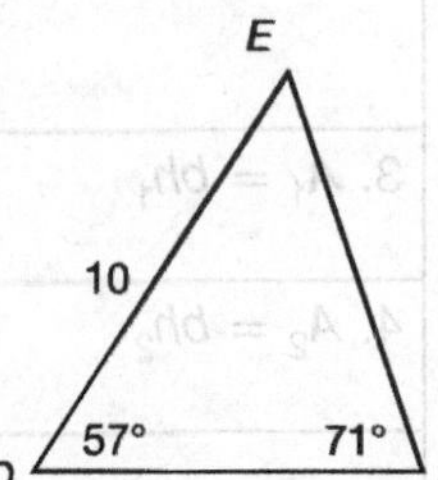

   Yes, by the Triangle Angle Sum Theorem, m∠DEF = 52°. So, the triangles are congruent by the ASA Theorem.
3. $(3x)^2 = x^2 + 8^2$
   $9x^2 = x^2 + 64$
   $8x^2 = 64$
   $x^2 = 8$
   $x = 8$
   $x = \sqrt{4 \cdot 2}$
   $x = 2\sqrt{2}$
   So, if $x > 2\sqrt{2}$, then the triangle will be obtuse.
4. If a triangle is obtuse, then it is isosceles.

**5.** Since $\angle STU$ and $\angle UVS$ are congruent, $m\angle STU = m\angle UVS$, by definition of congruent angles. $\angle STV$ and $\angle TVU$ must also have the same measure, for the same reason. By the Angle Addition Postulate, $m\angle STU = m\angle STV + m\angle UTV$, and $m\angle UVS = m\angle UVT + m\angle SVT$. By the Subtraction Property of Equality, $m\angle STU - m\angle STV = m\angle UTV$, and $m\angle UVS - m\angle UVT = m\angle SVT$. By substitution, $m\angle UVS - m\angle UVT = m\angle UTV$. By the Transitive Property of Equality, $m\angle SVT = m\angle UTV$, and by the definition of congruent angles, $\angle SVT \cong \angle UTV$.

**6.**

A D
9x − 77°
5x + 17°
B C E F
6x − 33°

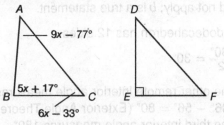

$(9x - 77°) + (6x - 33°) + (5x + 17°) = 180°$

$20x - 93° = 180°$

$20x = 273°$

$x = 13.65°$

$\angle ABC = 5(13.65°) + 17° = 85.25°$

since $\angle ABC \ncong \angle DEF$, the triangles are not congruent.

**10.**

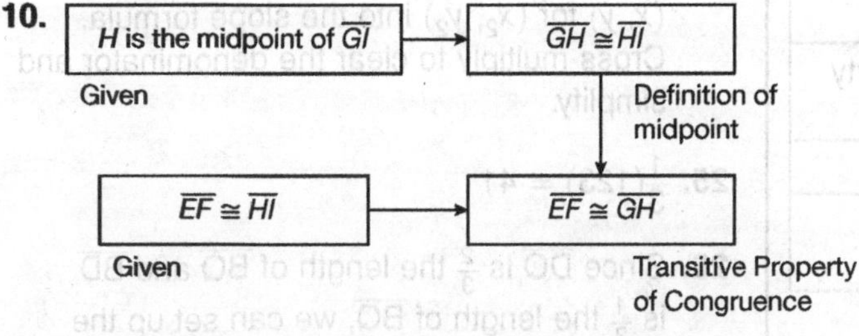


**11. a.** A circle has an infinite number of radii.

**b.** They all have the same measure.

**12.** For the triangle to be obtuse $c^2 > a^2 + b^2$

$11^2 > x^2 + 7^2$

$121 > x^2 + 49$

$72 > x^2$

$\sqrt{72} > x$

$\sqrt{36 \cdot 2} > x$

$6\sqrt{2} > x$

**7.** $A = bh$

$= (2y)(3x) = 6xy$

**8. a.** $y^2 = 80^2 + 185^2$

$y^2 = 6400 + 34,225$

$y^2 = 40,625$

$y \approx 201.6$ feet

$(201.6)^2 \approx 40,643$

$40,643 > 40,625$

Since $y^2 > 80^2 + 185^2$, the triangle is obtuse and $y$ must be at least 201.6 ft.

**b.** $y^2 = 125^2 + 185^2$

$x^2 = 15,625 + 34,225$

$x^2 = 49,850$

$x \approx 223.3$ feet

Select a value for $x$ that is less than 223.3,

$(223)^2 = 49,729$

$49,729 < 49,850$

For values of $x$ less than the maximum length of 223.3 feet, the triangle is acute.

**9.** Inverse: If a triangle has an obtuse angle, then it is not acute.

The inverse is true. Any right triangle is a counterexample for the statement, but a triangle cannot have an obtuse angle if it is acute.

**13.** For each increase of 1 in $x$, $y$ increases by $m$. Use this fact to plot two or three points, starting at the $y$-intercept, $(0, b)$.

**14. a.** Conjunction: A volcano is active and not expected to erupt again.
No, by definition, an active volcano is expected to erupt again.

**b.** Disjunction: A volcano is active or it is not expected to erupt again.
No, a volcano might be dormant. Thus, it is not active, but it is expected to erupt again.

**15.**

| Statements | Reasons |
|---|---|
| $\frac{1}{2}((x+1)+(x+5))(x) = 40$ | Area of a trapezoid |
| $\frac{1}{2}(2x+6)(x) = 40$ | Simplify. |
| $x^2 + 3x = 40$ | Distributive Property |
| $x^2 + 3x - 40 = 40 - 40$ | Subtraction Property of Equality |
| $x^2 + 3x - 40 = 0$ | Simplify. |
| $(x+8)(x-5) = 0$ | Factor. |
| $x - 5 = 0$ | $x + 8 = 0$ would give a negative solution. |
| $x - 5 + 5 = 0 + 5$ | Addition Property of Equality |
| $x = 5$ | Simplify. |
| Base 1 = 5 + 1 = 6 ft<br>Base 2 = 5 + 5 = 10 ft | Substitution |

**16.** Choice **A**: orthocenter

**17.** interior: $\angle EDC$, $\angle ABC$, and $\angle BAF$
exterior: $\angle CDJ$ and $\angle LFE$

**18.** The polygon has 5 sides. So, the sum of the interior angles is $(n-2)180° = (5-2)180° = 540°$.

$$(x+4) + (2x+5) + (3x+6) + (4x+7) + (5x+8) = 540$$
$$15x + 30 = 540$$
$$15x = 510$$
$$x = 34$$

**19.** $a^2 = 8^2 + 2.5^2$
$a^2 = 64 + 6.25$
$a^2 = 70.25$
$a \approx 8.4$ feet or 8 ft 5 in.

Each section is approximately 2 ft 1 in. along the hypotenuse.

$a_1 = 2'\ 1''$
$a_2 = 4'\ 2''$
$a_3 = 6'\ 3''$
$a_4 = 8'\ 5''$

**20.** The student used the Law of Syllogism when it did not apply; $b$ is a true statement.

**21.** A dodecahedron has 12 sides.

$$\frac{360°}{12} = 30°$$

**22.** The other remote interior angle measures $136° - 56° = 80°$ (Exterior Angle Theorem). The third interior angle measures $180° - (56° + 80°) = 44°$ (Triangle Angle Sum Theorem).

**23.** $6x + 50 = 5x + 10 + 3x + 12$
$6x + 50 = 8x + 22$
$-2x = -28$
$x = 14$

**24.** Substitute $-1$ for $m$, $(4, 5)$ for $(x_1, y_1)$, and $(x, y)$ for $(x_2, y_2)$ into the slope formula. Cross-multiply to clear the denominator and simplify.

**25.** $\frac{1}{3}(123) = 41$

**26.** Since $\overline{DQ}$ is $\frac{2}{3}$ the length of $\overline{BQ}$ and $\overline{BD}$ is $\frac{1}{3}$ the length of $\overline{BQ}$, we can set up the following proportion and solve.

$$\frac{BD}{\frac{1}{3}} = \frac{DQ}{\frac{2}{3}}$$

$$\frac{63}{\frac{1}{3}} = \frac{DQ}{\frac{2}{3}}$$

$$\frac{1}{3}DQ = \frac{2}{3}(63)$$

$$\frac{1}{3}DQ = 42$$

$$DQ = 126$$

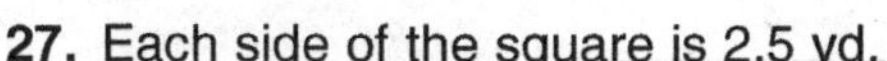

27. Each side of the square is 2.5 yd.
$h^2 = 2.5^2 + 2.5^2$
$h^2 = 6.25 + 6.25$
$h^2 = 12.5$
$h \approx 3.5$ yd

28. $m\,\widehat{AC} = m\,\widehat{AB} + m\,\widehat{BC}$
$m\,\widehat{AC} = 23° + 33° = 56°$

29. $m = \left(\frac{x_1 + x_2}{2}, \frac{y_1 + y_2}{2}\right)$
$= \left(\frac{0+5}{2}, \frac{6+2}{2}\right) = \left(\frac{5}{2}, \frac{8}{2}\right) = (2.5, 4)$

30. $C = 2\pi r = 2\pi(7x) = 14\pi x$

## LESSON 34

### Warm Up 34

1. midpoint
2. The $y$-intercept is 4. The line goes through points (0, 4) and (2, 3).
$m = \frac{3-4}{2-0} = \frac{-1}{2}$
So, the equation is $y = -\frac{1}{2}x + 4$
3. Choice A: A parallelogram has two sets of parallel sides.
Choice B: A rhombus is equilateral, but not necessarily equiangular.
Choice C: A square is equilateral and equiangular.
Choice D: A trapezium is not equilateral nor equiangular.
Choice **C** is correct.

### Lesson Practice 34

a. $4y - 10 = 2y + 5$
$2y = 15$
$y = 7.5$

b. Value of $x$:
$5x - 3 = 4x + 2$
$x = 5$
Value of $z$:
$2z + 4 = 3z - 2$
$-z = -6$
$z = 6$

c. Value of $x$:
$(13x + 8) + (7x - 8) = 180°$
$20x = 180$
$x = 9$
Value of $y$:
$(7y - 22) + (12y - 7) = 180°$
$19y - 29 = 180$
$19y = 209$
$y = 11$

d. $\overline{AB} \parallel \overline{DC}$ and $\overline{AD} \parallel \overline{BC}$ by the definition of parallelograms. $\angle EAB \cong \angle ECD$ and $\angle EBA \cong \angle EDC$ by the Alternate Interior Angles Theorem. $\overline{AB} \cong \overline{DC}$ by Property 3 of parallelograms. $\triangle AEB \cong \triangle CED$ by ASA triangle congruence. Therefore, by CPCTC, $\overline{AE} \cong \overline{EC}$ and $\overline{BE} \cong \overline{ED}$. So, the diagonals bisect each other by the definition of a segment bisector.

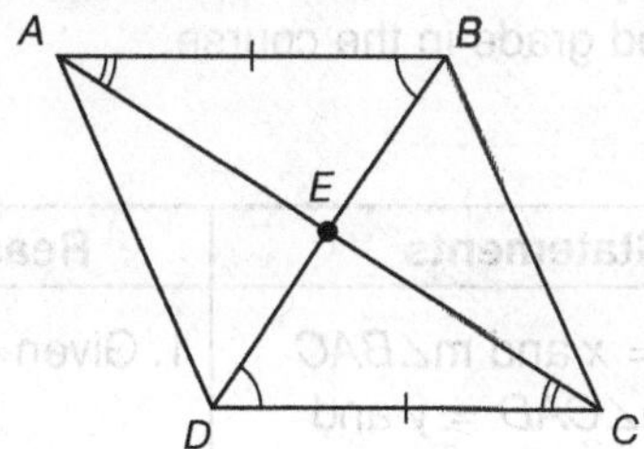


e. 1. $KO = OM$
$3x = -x + 6$
$4x = 6$
$x = \frac{3}{2}$
$KM = 3\left(\frac{3}{2}\right) + \left(-\frac{3}{2} + 6\right) = 4.5 + 4.5 = 9$
2. $KO = 3\left(\frac{3}{2}\right) = 4.5$

### Practice 34

1. $KM$: $x^2 - 3 = 5x - 7$
$x^2 - 5x + 4 = 0$
$(x - 4)(x - 1) = 0$
$x = 4, 1$
Since $x = 1$ will give us a negative length, $x = 4$ is correct.

$KM$: $(4)^2 - 3 + 5(4) - 7 = 13 + 13 = 26$

$LN$: $y^2 - 9 = -2y + 6$

$y^2 + 2y - 15 = 0$

$(y + 5)(y - 3) = 0$

$y = -5, 3$

Check of both these solutions:

$(3)^2 - 9 + -2(3) + 6$

$= 9 - 9 + -6 + 6 = 0$

Zero is not an acceptable length.

$(-5)^2 - 9 + -2(-5) + 6$

$16 + 16$

$LN$ is 16 + 16 = 32.

**2.** $m\angle ACB = m\angle DFE$

$9x - 77 = 4x + 33$

$5x = 110$

$x = 22°$

**3.** It is a trapezoid because there is exactly one pair of parallel sides.

**4.** If Molly does her homework, then she will get a good grade in the course.

**5.**

| Statements | Reasons |
|---|---|
| 1. $m\angle B = x$ and $m\angle BAC = x$, $m\angle CAD = y$ and $m\angle D = y$ | 1. Given |
| 2. $m\angle BCE = m\angle ABC + m\angle BAC$ | 2. Exterior Angle Property |
| 3. $m\angle BCE = x + x$ | 3. Substitution Property of Equality |
| 4. $m\angle BCE = 2x$ | 4. Simplify. |
| 5. $m\angle DCE = m\angle ADC + m\angle DAC$ | 5. Exterior Angle Property |
| 6. $m\angle DCE = y + y$ | 6. Substitution Property of Equality |
| 7. $m\angle DCE = 2y$ | 7. Simplify. |
| 8. $m\angle BCD = m\angle BCE + m\angle DCE$ | 8. Adjacent Angle Sum |
| 9. $m\angle BCD = 2x + 2y$ | 9. Substitute. |

**6.**

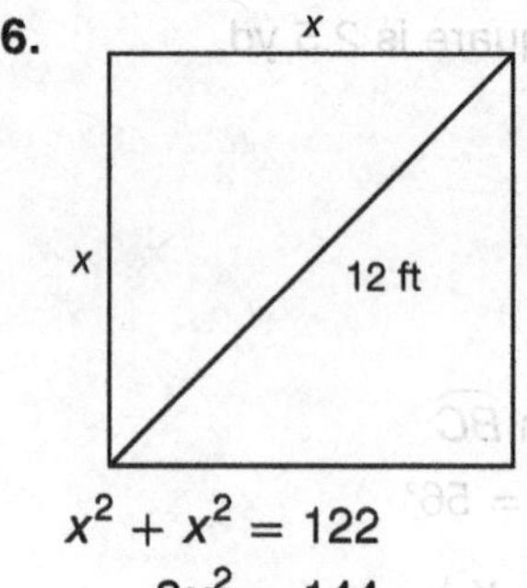


$x^2 + x^2 = 122$

$2x^2 = 144$

$x^2 = 72$

Since the area of the square is $x^2$, the area is 72 ft$^2$.

**7.** Choice **D**: the converse

**8.**

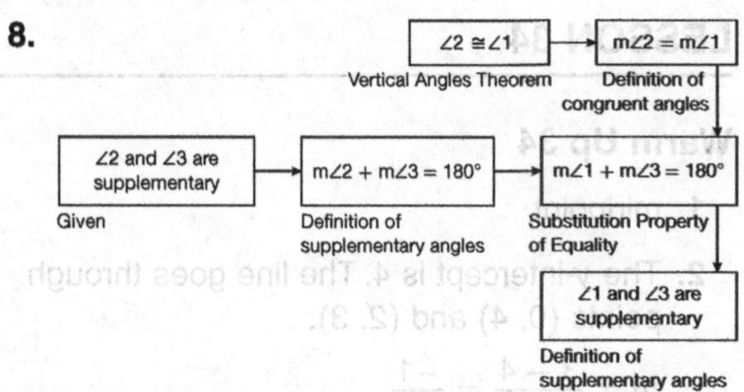


**9.** The sum of the interior angles of a hexagon (6 sides):

$(n - 2)180° = (4)(180°) = 720°$

Exterior angles: 360°

Central angles: 360°

$720° + 360° + 360° = 1440°$

**10.** Because the exterior angle and its associated interior angle form a linear pair, they are supplementary and add to 180°. Because the sum of the measures of the interior angles and the two remote angles is also 180°, by subtracting the common term, the sum of the remote angle measures equals the exterior angle measure.

**11.**
1. Opposite sides are congruent.
2. Opposite angles are congruent.
3. Consecutive angles are supplementary.
4. Diagonals bisect each other.

12. 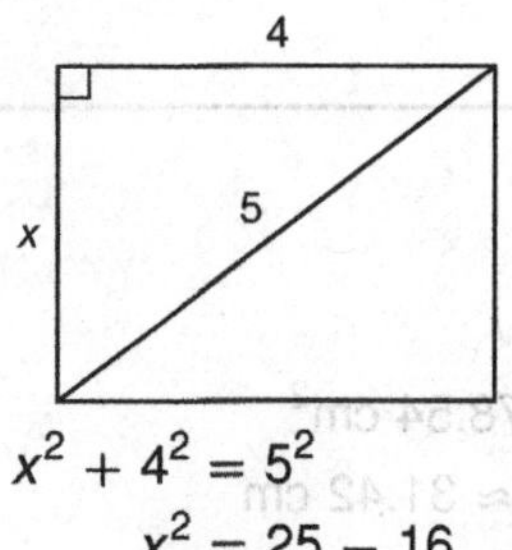


$x^2 + 4^2 = 5^2$
$x^2 = 25 - 16$
$x = 3$
$A = (3)(4) = 12$

13. She has not switched the hypothesis and the conclusion.

14. Choice **C** is correct because the vertices are in the correct order based on congruency.

15. $A = \pi r^2 = \pi(150)^2 \approx 3.14(150)^2 = 70{,}650 \text{ ft}^2$

16. For a triangle to be acute, $c^2 < a^2 + b^2$ must be true.
Choice **A**: $8^2 < 7^2 + 4^2$
$64 < 49 + 16$
$64 < 65$
This is the correct choice.

17. $m = \frac{6 - 4}{2} - 1 = \frac{2}{1} = 2$
$y = 2x + b$
$4 = 2(1) + b$
$2 = b$
$y = 2x + 2$

18. Draw one pair of parallel lines. Draw second pair of parallel lines as transversals of first pair. Mark and label the four intersections as the vertices. Mark the parallel sides.

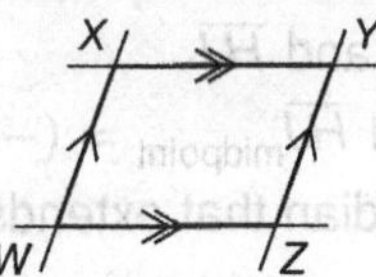


19. Angles $H$ and $I$ are supplementary.
$(3x^2 + 10x + 7) + (4x^2 - 31x + 103) = 180$
$7x^2 + 21x + 110 = 180$
$7x^2 + 21x - 70 = 0$
$7(x^2 + 3x - 10) = 0$
$7(x - 5)(x + 2) = 0$
$x = 5 \text{ or } -2$
Since $x = -2$ results in a negative angle measure, $x = 5$:
$\angle H = \angle J = 3(5)^2 + 10(5) + 7 = 132°$
$\angle K = \angle I = 4(5)^2 - 31(5) + 103 = 48°$

20. $\angle SRT$ **or** $\angle TRS$

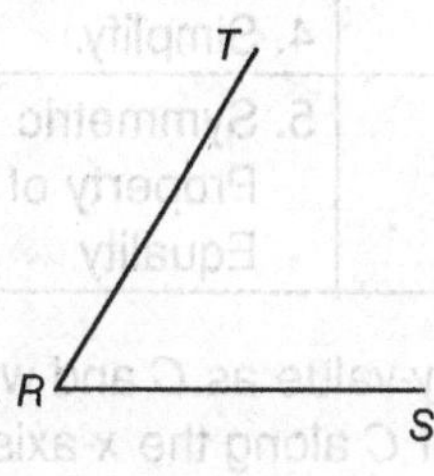


21. $184^2 + 160^2 = x^2$
$33{,}856 + 25{,}600 = x^2$
$59{,}456 = 2^2$
$244 \approx x$
The person is about 244 meters from the top.

22. No, because either method of proof can contain the same information. They are only different formats.

23. 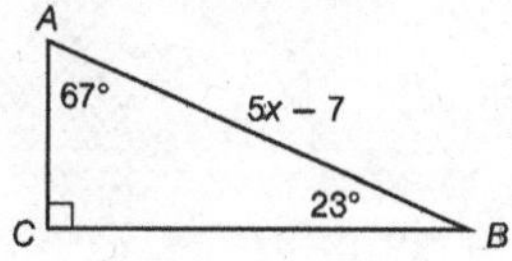

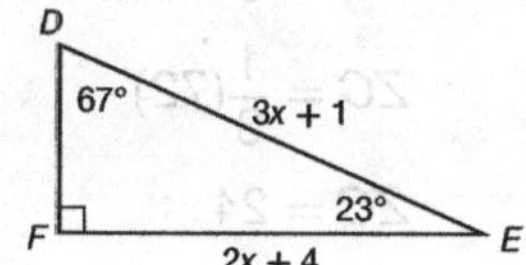


Since the triangles are congruent, $\overline{DE} \cong \overline{AB}$.
So, $3x + 1 = 5x - 7$.
$-2x = -8$
$x = 4$
$EF = 2(4) + 4 = 8 + 4 = 12$ units

24. 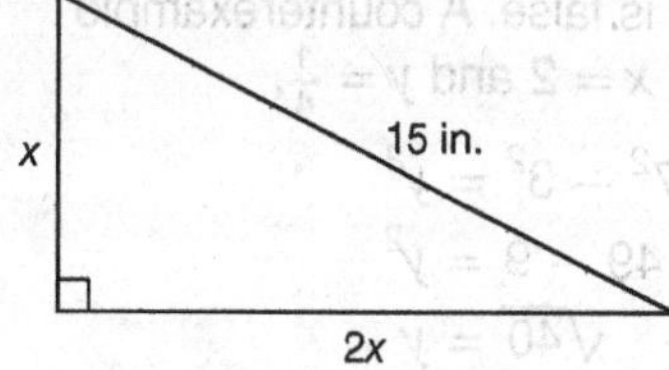


$x^2 + (2x)^2 = 15^2$
$5x^2 = 225$
$x^2 = 45$
$x \approx 6.7 \text{ in.}$
$2x \approx 13.4 \text{ in.}$

25.

| Statements | Reasons |
|---|---|
| 1. $3(x-2) = 4(x+1)$ | 1. Given |
| 2. $3x - 6 = 4x + 4$ | 2. Distributive Property |
| 3. $3x - 6 - 3x - 4 = 4x + 4 - 3x - 4$ | 3. Subtraction Property of Equality |
| 4. $-10 = x$ | 4. Simplify. |
| 5. $x = -10$ | 5. Symmetric Property of Equality |

26. $D$ will have the same $y$-value as $C$ and will be 5 units to the left of $C$ along the $x$-axis because the length of $CD$ is the same as the length of $AB$. The coordinates are $(-2, 2)$.

27. $CX = \frac{1}{3}(UX)$

$18 = \frac{1}{3}(UX)$

$54 = UX$

28. $ZC = \frac{1}{3}(ZV)$

$ZC = \frac{1}{3}(72)$

$ZC = 24$

29. a. Sample: If $0 < x < 1$ and $0 < y < 1$, then $0 < xy < 1$.

b. Sample converse: If $0 < xy < 1$, then $0 < y < 1$ and $0 < x < 1$.
Sample biconditional: $0 < x < 1$ and $0 < y < 1$ if and only if $0 < xy < 1$.
No, the biconditional is false because the converse is false. A counterexample would be $x = 2$ and $y = \frac{1}{4}$.

30.
$$7^2 - 3^2 = y^2$$
$$49 - 9 = y^2$$
$$\sqrt{40} = y$$
$$2\sqrt{10} = y$$
$$(\sqrt{50})^2 - (2\sqrt{10})^2 = x^2$$
$$50 - 40 = x^2$$
$$\sqrt{10} = x$$

## LESSON 35

### Warm Up 35

1. diameter

2. $A = \pi r^2 = \pi 5^2 \approx 78.54 \text{ cm}^2$
$C = 2\pi r = 2\pi(5) \approx 31.42 \text{ cm}$

3. $40 = \pi r^2$
$\frac{40}{\pi} = r^2$
$3.57 \approx r$

4. $A = \frac{\pi r^2}{2} = \frac{\pi(5)^2}{2} = \frac{25\pi}{2} \approx 39.27 \text{ in}^2$

### Lesson Practice 35

a. $L = 2\pi(12)\left(\frac{125°}{360°}\right) \approx 26.18$ miles

b. $A = \pi r^2\left(\frac{35°}{360°}\right) = \pi(7.5)^2\left(\frac{35°}{360°}\right) \approx 17.18 \text{ in}^2$

c. $78 = \pi r^2\left(\frac{101°}{360°}\right)$
$9.41 \approx r$; $r$ is 9.41 centimeters.

d. $2 = \pi r^2\left(\frac{50°}{360°}\right)$
$2.14 \approx r$
$D = 2r = 4.28$ miles

### Practice 35

1. The formula finds the portion of the circle that is contained in the arc by multiplying by a factor of $\frac{m°}{360°}$.

2. Label the points $H(-6, 10)$, $I(-4, 2)$, and $J(-14, 6)$.
Find the midpoint of $\overline{HI}$ and $\overline{HJ}$.
$\overline{HI}_{midpoint} = (-5, 6)$ and $\overline{HJ}_{midpoint} = (-10, 8)$
The equation of the median that extends from $J$ to $(-5, 6)$ is $y = 6$.
The slope of the median that extends from $I$ to $(-10, 8)$ is $-1$.
$y - y_1 = m(x - x_1)$
$y - 8 = -1(x - -10)$
$y - 8 = -1x - 10$
$y = -1x - 2$

Now, solve these two equations as a system.

$y = 6 = -1x - 2$

$6 = -1x - 2$

$x = -8$

$y = -1(-8) - 2 = 6$

The centroid is located at $(-8, 6)$.

**3.** $\angle B \cong \angle E, \angle C \cong \angle F, \angle D \cong \angle G,$ $\overline{BC} \cong \overline{EF}, \overline{CD} \cong \overline{FG}, \cong \overline{BD} \cong \overline{EG}$

**4.** Therefore, I will restart it.

**5.**

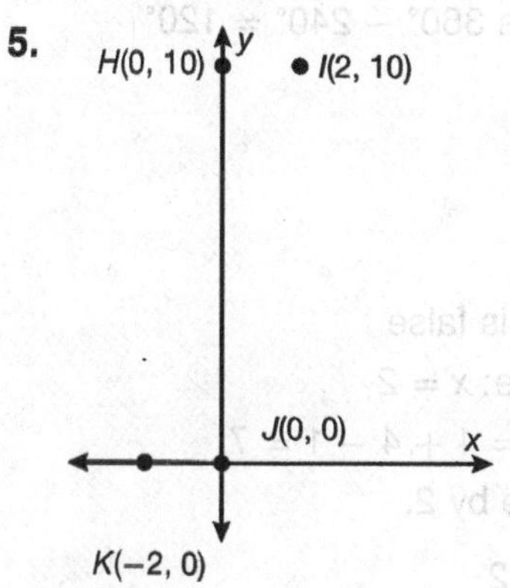


$J(0, 0)$

**6.** By examining the triangles $y = 52$ and $z = 35$. $x$, $y$, and $z$ compose a straight line, so the sum of their measures is 180°.

$180° - 52° - 35° = 93°; x = 93$

**7.** $(5x + 20)° + (8x - 50)° = 360°$

$13x - 30 = 360$

$13x = 390$

$x = 30$

Choice **B** is correct.

**8. a.** Converse: If a triangle has exactly two acute angles, then it is obtuse.

**b.** The statement is true. The converse is false because a right triangle has exactly two acute angles.

**9.** $\overline{TR}: x + 5 = 2x - 3$

$8 = x$

$TR = 8 + 5 + 2(8) - 3 = 26$

$\overline{QS}: y + 6 = 3y - 4$

$10 = 2y$

$5 = y$

$QS = 5 + 6 + 3(5) - 4 = 22$

**10.** A hexagon has 6 sides.

$(n - 2)180° = (6 - 2)180° = 720°$

$720° \div 6 = 120°$

**11.**

| Statements | Reasons |
|---|---|
| $x + 3 = \frac{4x + 5}{2}$ | Given |
| $2(x + 3) = 2\left(\frac{4x+5}{2}\right)$ | Multiplication Property of Equality |
| $2x + 6 = 4x + 5$ | Distributive Property |
| $2x + 6 - 5 = 4x + 5 - 5$ | Subtraction Property of Equality |
| $2x + 1 = 4x$ | Simplify. |
| $2x + 1 - 2x = 4x - 2x$ | Subtraction Property of Equality |
| $1 = 2x$ | Simplify. |
| $\frac{1}{2} = \frac{2x}{2}$ | Division Property of Equality |
| $\frac{1}{2} = x$ | Simplify |

**12.** $x^2 = 15^2 - 13^2$

$x^2 = 225 - 169$

$x^2 = 56$

$x \approx 7.5$ ft

No, because a Pythagorean triple is made up of three integers.

**13.**

| Statements | Reasons |
|---|---|
| 1. $\widehat{JK} \approx \widehat{HI}$ | 1. Given |
| 2. $m\widehat{HI} = 2\pi r\left(\frac{m\angle 1}{360°}\right)$ and $m\widehat{JK} = 2\pi r\left(\frac{m\angle 2}{360°}\right)$ | 2. Formula for length of an arc |
| 3. $m\angle 1 = 360°\frac{m\widehat{HI}}{2\pi r}$ and $m\angle 2 = 360°\frac{m\widehat{JK}}{2\pi r}$ | 3. Solve for $m\angle 1$ and $m\angle 2$. |
| 4. $m\angle 1 = m\angle 2$ | 4. Transitive Property of Equality |
| 5. $\angle 1 \cong \angle 2$ | 5. Definition of angle congruence |

**14.** $9^2 = (4\sqrt{2})^2 + (4\sqrt{3})^2$
$81 = (16 \cdot 2) + (16 \cdot 3)$
$81 = 32 + 48$
$81 \neq 80$
No, it is not a right triangle.

**15.** $A_{page} = (10)(12.25) = 122.5 \text{ in}^2$
The page is divided into $5 \times 7 =$ 35 boxes: $122.5 \div 35 = 3.5 \text{ in}^2$

**16.**

| Statements | Reasons |
|---|---|
| 1. ∠*KLM* and ∠*NML* are right angles | 1. Given |
| 2. ∠*KLM* ≅ ∠*NML* | 2. Right Angle Theorem |
| 3. m∠*KLM* = m∠*NML* | 3. Definition of congruent angles |
| 4. m∠*KLM* = m∠1 + m∠2 m∠*NLM* = m∠3 + m∠4 | 4. Angle Addition Postulate |
| 5. m∠1 + m∠2 = m∠3 + m∠4 | 5. Substitution Property of Equality |
| 6. ∠2 ≅ ∠3 | 6. Given |
| 7. m∠2 = m∠3 | 7. Definition of congruent angles |
| 8. m∠1 + m∠2 = m∠2 + m∠4 | 8. Substitution Property of Equality |
| 9. m∠1 = m∠4 | 9. Simplify. |
| 10. ∠1 ≅ ∠4 | 10. Definition of congruent angles |

**17.** Marc is incorrect. He used the formula for arc length instead of the formula for sector area.

**18.** If I lose my driver's license, then I will have to go to the DMV.

**19.** $\frac{3}{8} = \frac{x}{360}$
$8x = 3(360)$
$8x = 1080 \quad x = 135°$

**20.** $\overline{AB} \cong \overline{MN}$
$x + 25 = 2x + 18$
$7 = x$
$AB = 7 + 25 = 32$
$P = 32 + 27 + 24$
$= 83$ units

**21.** Disjunction: A triangle is acute or has exactly two acute angles.
The disjunction is true.

**22.** The minor arc is $360° - 240° = 120°$
$\frac{120°}{240°} = \frac{x}{18}$
$240x = 2160$
$x = 9$ cm

**23.** The conjecture is false.
Counterexample: $x = 2$
$2^2 + 2(2) - 1 = 4 + 4 - 1 = 7$
7 is not divisible by 2.

**24.** $6x - 4 = 4x + 2$
$2x = 6$
$x = 3$
$SR = 6(3) - 4 = 14$
$A = \frac{1}{2}(14)(8)$
$= 56$ square units

**25.** Converse: If a triangle has two acute angles, then it is a right triangle.

**26.** $2\pi r\left(\frac{60°}{360°}\right) = 40$
$2\pi r = 240$
$r \approx 38.2$ cm

**27.** $10^2 = 8^2 + 7^2$
$100 = 64 + 49$
$100 < 113$
Therefore, the triangle is acute.

**28.** $A = \pi r^2 = \pi(7)^2 \approx 153.94 \text{ in}^2$
No, the actual area is about $153.94 \text{ in}^2$.

**29.** Sample: 2(5, 12, 13) = (10, 24, 26)
4(5, 12, 13) = (20, 48, 52)

30. $m\angle D = m\angle B$

$10x - 5 = 8x + 5$

$2x = 10$

$x = 5$

$m\angle D = m\angle B = 10(5) - 5 = 45°$

$m\angle A = m\angle C = 180° - 45° = 135°$

## LESSON 36

### Warm Up 36

1. Side-Angle-Side
2. By ASA, the triangles are congruent.

   $6x - 10 = 3x + 20$

   $3x = 30$

   $x = 10$

   $\angle W = 3(10) + 20 = 50°$
3. Choice **C**: sides and angles

### Lesson Practice 36

a. $\triangle ABC$ and $\triangle DEF$ are right triangles, legs $\overline{AB}$ and $\overline{DE}$ are congruent, and acute angles $A$ and $D$ are congruent. Therefore, by the Leg-Angle Triangle Congruence Theorem, $\triangle ABC \cong \triangle DEF$.

b. $\triangle ABC$ and $\triangle DEF$ are right triangles, hypotenuses $\overline{AC}$ and $\overline{DF}$ are congruent, and acute angles $A$ and $D$ are congruent. Therefore, by the Hypotenuse-Angle Triangle Congruence Theorem, $\triangle ABC \cong \triangle DEF$.

c. $\triangle ABC$ and $\triangle DEF$ are right triangles, legs $\overline{AB}$ and $\overline{DE}$ are congruent, and legs $\overline{BC}$ and $\overline{EF}$ are congruent. Therefore, by the Leg-Leg Triangle Congruence Theorem, $\triangle ABC \cong \triangle DEF$.

d. $\triangle ABC$ and $\triangle DEF$ are right triangles, hypotenuses $\overline{AC}$ and $\overline{DF}$ are congruent, and legs $\overline{BC}$ and $\overline{EF}$ are congruent. Therefore, by the Hypotenuse-Leg Triangle Congruence Theorem, $\triangle ABC \cong \triangle DEF$.

e. $PR$ and $QR$ are the hypotenuse and a leg respectively. The Hypotenuse-Leg Triangle Congruence Theorem will prove that the cover will fit.

### Practice 36

1. $\triangle OPQ$ and $\triangle TRS$ are right triangles, hypotenuses $\overline{PQ} \cong \overline{RS}$, and acute $\angle P \cong \angle R$; by Hypotenuse-Angle Congruence Theorem, $\triangle OPQ \cong \triangle TRS$.
2. $m\widehat{AB} + m\widehat{BC} + m\widehat{CD} = m\widehat{AD}$
3. The square's right angles are still present in these triangles, so they are right triangles. Their hypotenuses are congruent because they are the kite's sides. Their legs are congruent because they are the square's sides. Therefore, by the Hypotenuse-Leg Congruence Theorem, the triangles are congruent.
4. Greta used the diameter, not the radius, in her calculation.
5. $1.3^2 - 1.2^2 = x^2$

   $1.69 - 1.44 = x^2$

   $0.25 = x^2$

   $0.5 = x$

   The third side is 0.5 yards.
6. $\triangle JKL$ and $\triangle MNO$ are right triangles, $\overline{JK} \cong \overline{MN}$, and $\overline{KL} \cong \overline{NO}$; by the Leg-Leg Congruence Theorem, $\triangle JKL \cong \triangle MNO$.
7. $C = 2\pi r = 2\pi(4) \approx 25$ cm
8. a. $A = \frac{1}{2}(b_1 + b_2)h$

   b. $2A = (b_1 + b_2)h$

   $\frac{2A}{b_1 + b_2} = h$
9. Draw a line that is perpendicular to $\overline{AB}$ at $Y$. So $m\angle AYX$ and $m\angle BYX$ are both 90° by the definition of perpendicular lines. It is given that $AX = BX$, so $\overline{AX} \cong \overline{BX}$ by definition of congruent segments. By the Reflexive Property of Congruence, $\overline{XY} \cong \overline{XY}$, so by the Hypotenuse-Leg Congruence Theorem, $\triangle AXY \cong \triangle BXY$. So by CPCTC, $\overline{AY} \cong \overline{BY}$. By the definition of midpoint, $Y$ is the midpoint of $\overline{AB}$, and since $\overline{XY}$ is perpendicular to $\overline{AB}$ at its midpoint, it is the perpendicular bisector of $\overline{AB}$. Since $X$ is on $\overline{XY}$, it is on the perpendicular bisector of $\overline{AB}$.
10. $A = \pi r^2 = \pi(6)^2 \approx 113.10 \text{ cm}^2$

11. $A = \pi r^2 = \pi(4)^2 \approx 50.3 \text{ in.}^2$

$A_{sector} = \frac{50.3}{4} \approx 12.6 \text{ in.}^2$

12. $5x + 11 = 7x - 9$

$-2x = -20$

$x = 10$

13. By AAS, the triangles are congruent.

$A_1 = A_2 = \frac{1}{2}(10)(5) = 25 \text{ units}^2$

14. Choice **A** is not true because each interior angle is 60°. So, the sum of any pair of interior angles is 120°.

15. $4h = 12$

$h = 3$

16. The midpoint of the side opposite of the origin is:

$m = \left(\frac{x_1 + x_2}{2}, \frac{y_1 + y_2}{2}\right) = \left(\frac{2 + 4}{2}, \frac{2 + 0}{2}\right)$

$= (3, 1)$

The line goes through (0, 0) and (3, 1).

slope $= \frac{1 - 0}{3 - 0} = \frac{1}{3}$

$y = \frac{1}{3}x$

17.

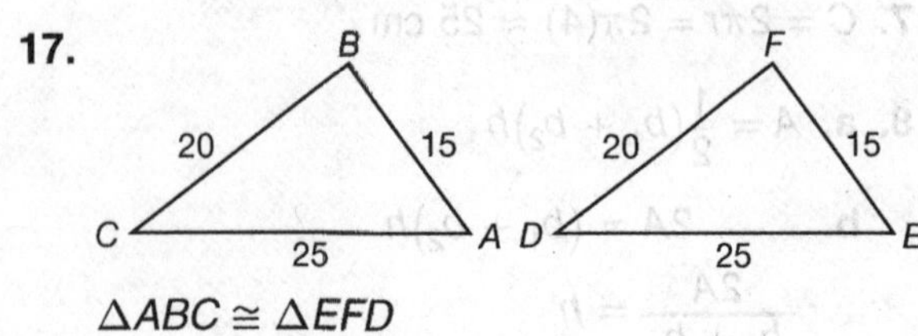


$\triangle ABC \cong \triangle EFD$

18. $\frac{1}{6}(360°) = 60°$

$A = \frac{1}{6}\pi r^2 = \frac{1}{6}\pi(12)^2 = \frac{1}{6}\pi(144) = 24\pi$

19.

| Statements | Reasons |
|---|---|
| 1. $\overline{AE} \cong \overline{CE}$, $\angle BAE \cong \angle DCE$ | 1. Given |
| 2. $\angle AEB \cong \angle CED$ | 2. Vertical Angles Theorem |
| 3. $\angle ABE \cong \angle CDE$ | 3. ASA Postulate |

20. The triangles are not congruent since the first has a side length of 12 units and the second does not have a corresponding side length of 12 units.

21.

| Statements | Reasons |
|---|---|
| 1. $VX \perp YX$, $VZ \perp YZ$, $VX = VZ$ | 1. Given |
| 2. $\overline{VX} \cong \overline{VZ}$ | 2. Def. $\cong$ segments |
| 3. $\angle VXY$ and $\angle VZY$ are right angles. | 3. Definition of perpendicular |
| 4. $\overline{YV} \cong \overline{YV}$ | 4. Reflexive Property |
| 5. $\triangle YXV \cong \triangle YZV$ | 5. HL Theorem |
| 6. $\angle XYV \cong \angle ZYV$ | 6. CPCTC |
| 7. $\overrightarrow{YV}$ bisects $\angle XYZ$. | 7. Definition of angle bisector |

22. $13x + 37 = 180$

$13x = 143; x = 11$

23. $14^2 = 5^2 + 13^2$

$196 = 25 + 169$

$196 > 194$; No, the triangle is obtuse.

24. Sample: Since all sides of a square are congruent, each triangle has two sides which are congruent. Also, since the included angle of the sides of each triangle is a right angle, the triangles are congruent by the SAS Congruence Postulate.

25. $x^2 - x = 11x - 35$

$x^2 - 12x + 35 = 0$

$(x - 5)(x - 7) = 0; x = \{5, 7\}$

26. a.

| Organism is an animal | Organism has leaves | Organism is an animal or has leaves |
|---|---|---|
| T | T | T |
| T | F | T |
| F | T | T |
| F | F | F |

**b.** The truth table shows that the disjunction is false when both statements are false: An organism can be a nonanimal without leaves, such as algae.

27. $\triangle JKL$ and $\triangle MNO$ are right triangles, $\overline{JK} \cong \overline{MN}$, and $\angle J \cong \angle M$; so, by the Leg-Angle Congruence Theorem, $\triangle JKL \cong \triangle MNO$.

28. $5^2 + 8^2 = 9^2$

$25 + 64 = 81$

$89 > 81$

She is correct because by the converse of the Pythagorean Theorem, $5^2 + 8^2 > 9^2$, so the triangle is acute.

29.

| Statements | Reasons |
|---|---|
| 1. $\triangle ABC$ and $\triangle DEF$ are right triangles | 1. Given |
| 2. $\overline{AB} \cong \overline{DE}$ | 2. Given |
| 3. $\angle A \cong \angle D$ | 3. Given |
| 4. $\angle B$ and $\angle E$ are right angles | 4. Given |
| 5. $\angle B \cong \angle E$ | 5. Right Angle Congruence Theorem |
| 6. $\triangle ABC \cong \triangle DEF$ | 6. ASA Postulate |

30. Because multiple different lines can only intersect in a single point, the intersection of two altitudes will be the same point as the intersection of all three.

## LESSON 37

### Warm Up 37

1. slope

2. $y - 4 = \frac{1}{2}(x + 4)$

$y - 4 = \frac{1}{2}x + 2$

$y = \frac{1}{2}x + 6$

3. Choice **A** is correct because it is degree 1 and the other choices are all degree 2.

### Lesson Practice 37

a. Parallel: By the Parallel Lines Theorem, parallel lines have the same slope.

$$m = \frac{y_1 - y_2}{x_1 - x_2} = \frac{3 - 1}{5 - 0} = \frac{2}{5}$$

Perpendicular: By the Perpendicular Lines Theorem, the slopes of perpendicular lines are opposite reciprocals.

The opposite reciprocal of $\frac{2}{5}$ is $-\frac{5}{2}$.

b. $3y + x = 6$

$3y = -x + 6$

$y = -\frac{1}{3}x + 2$

Since $-\frac{1}{3}$ and 3 are opposite reciprocals, the lines are perpendicular.

c. $4y = 2x + 3$

$y = \frac{1}{2}x + \frac{3}{4}$

$y + 2x = 9$

$y = -2x + 9$

Since $\frac{1}{2}$ and $-2$ are opposite reciprocals, the lines are perpendicular.

d. $y = -2x$

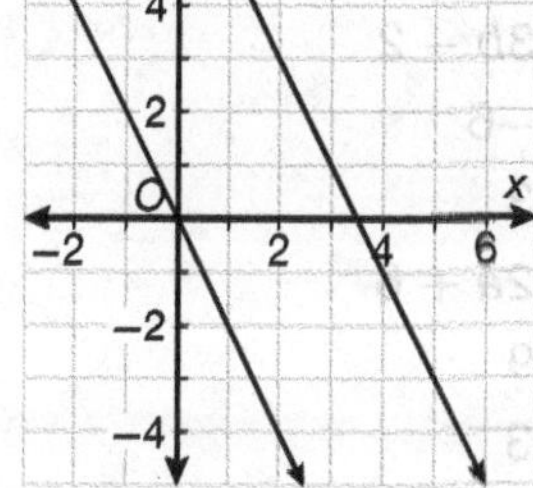


e. The slope of the line perpendicular to $y = -\frac{4}{3}x + 3$ is $\frac{3}{4}$.

$y = \frac{3}{4}x + b$

$3 = \frac{3}{4}(2) + b$

$3 = \frac{3}{2} + b$

$\frac{3}{2} = b$

$y = \frac{3}{4}x + \frac{3}{2}$

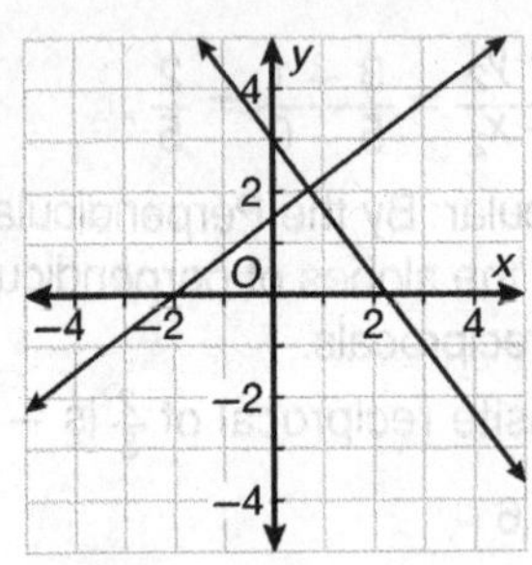


f. $y = 2x + 4$ and $y = 2.1x$; Yes, the lines are not parallel, so they will eventually intersect.

## Practice 37

1. $50^2 - 14^2 = x^2$
$2500 - 196 = x^2$
$2304 = x^2$
$48 = x$
Yes, (14, 48, 50) form a Pythagorean triple.

2. $\frac{30}{360}(\pi)(9^2) = \frac{1}{12}(81\pi)$
$= 6.75\pi$ square miles

3. yes

4. $b + 4 = 3b - 2$
$-2b = -6$
$b = 3$
$5a - 3 = 2a + 6$
$3a = 9$
$a = 3$

5. The slope of the line perpendicular to the line with a slope of 3 is $-\frac{1}{3}$.
$y = -\frac{1}{3}x + b$
$7 = -\frac{1}{3}(3) + b$
$7 = -1 + b$
$8 = b$
$y = -\frac{1}{3}x + 8$

6. Yes, the sum will always be 360° since there are 360° in a full rotation.

7. $0.16 \approx \pi r^2$
$0.226 \approx r$
The diameter is 2(0.226) or about 0.45 meters.

8. $A = bh = (13)(5) = 65\ \text{cm}^2$

9.
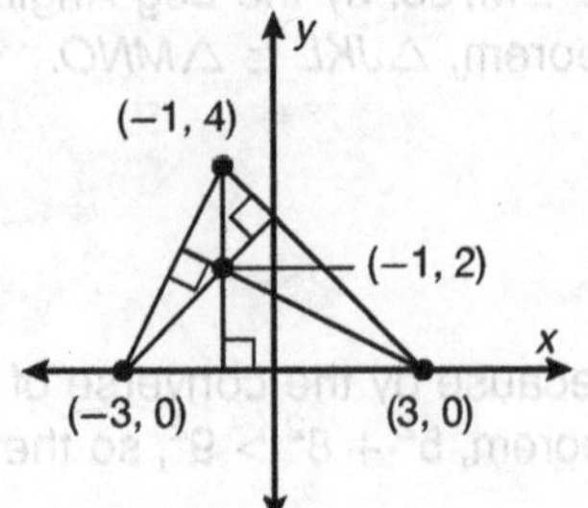


The orthocenter is located at (−1, 2).

10. One possibility: Since the slopes of parallel lines are equal, $k = 2$ and $h = 3$.

11. a. Hypothesis: *a*, *b*, and *c* are lines in a plane. Conclusion: *a*, *b*, and *c* divide the plane into seven regions.
b. Counterexample: Any example of three lines in a plane, at least two of which are parallel, or where all three lines pass through the same point.

12. Leg-Leg Right Triangle Congruence Theorem

13.

| Statements | Reasons |
|---|---|
| 1. $\overline{AB} \cong \overline{DE}$, $\overline{BC} \cong \overline{EF}$ | 1. Given |
| 2. $\angle B$ and $\angle E$ are right angles. | 2. Definition of right triangle |
| 3. $\angle B \cong \angle E$ | 3. All right angles are congruent. |
| 4. $\triangle ABC \cong \triangle DEF$ | 4. SAS Postulate |

14. Vertical Angles Theorem

15. Transitive Property of Congruence

16. The student forgot to find the opposite reciprocal of the slope. The slope should be $-\frac{13}{12}$.

17. From the diagram, $\triangle ABC$ and $\triangle DBC$ are right triangles and $\angle ACB \cong \angle DCB$. Also, $\overline{BC} \cong \overline{BC}$ by the Reflexive Property. So, by the Leg-Angle Congruence Theorem, $\triangle ABC \cong \triangle DBC$.

18. $GI = \frac{2}{3}FI$
$4.6 = \frac{2}{3}FI$
$6.9 = FI$

$GF = FI - GI = 6.9 - 4.6 = 2.3$

$GE = \frac{1}{3}HE = \frac{1}{3}(12) = 4$

**19.** Choice A: $6^2 + 9^2 = 10^2$

$36 + 81 = 100$

$117 \neq 100$

Choice B: $7^2 + 24^2 = 25^2$

$49 + 576 = 625$

$625 = 625$

Choice **B** is a Pythagorean triple.

**20.** $\widehat{KL} = 2\pi r\left(\frac{m°}{360°}\right)$

$1.2 = 2\pi(8)\left(\frac{m°}{360°}\right)$

$8.6 \approx m$; 8.6°

**21.**

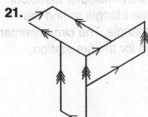

**22.** In order for the parallelogram to be a rectangle, the sides of the triangle must be a Pythagorean triple.

$13^2 + 17^2 = 20^2$

$169 + 289 = 400$

$458 \neq 400$

It is not a rectangle.

**23.**

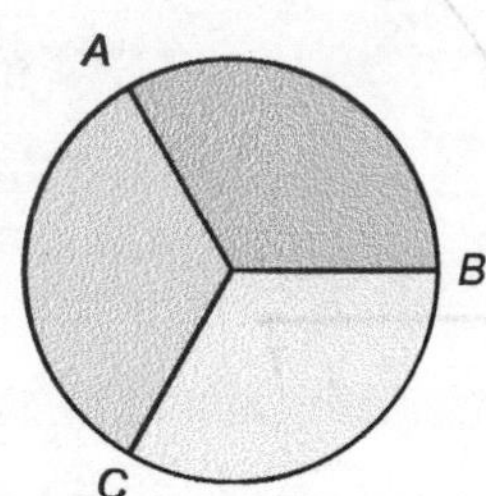


$360° - m\widehat{AB} - m\widehat{BC}$

**24.** $3x + (x - 6) = 180$

$4x = 186$

$x = 46.5$

$2y - 8 = 6y - 32$

$-4y = -24$

$y = 6$

**25.** $\frac{(n-2)(180°)}{11}$, where $n$ = number of sides $\frac{(11-2)(180°)}{11} \approx 147°$

Each angle should be approximately 147°.

**26.** The westbound lane is parallel and will have the same slope.

$y = \frac{4}{3}x$

The bridge is perpendicular to the highway and will have a slope that is the opposite reciprocal.

$y = -\frac{3}{4}x$

**27.** Vertex $M$ will have the same $y$-coordinate as $L$, but be shifted to the left 6 units along the $x$-axis. The coordinate of $M$ is $(-4, 6)$.

**28.** Hypotenuse-Angle Theorem

**29.** $1^2 + 1^2 = x^2$

$\sqrt{2} = x$

The ratio is $\sqrt{2}:1$.

A higher ratio would indicate $c^2 > a^2 + b^2$, making the triangle obtuse.

**30.** $A = \frac{1}{2}d_1d_2 = \frac{1}{2}(8)(6) = \frac{1}{2}(48) = 24\text{ cm}^2$

## LESSON 38

### Warm Up 38

**1.** median

**2.** **a.** C **b.** C **c.** B **d.** A

**3.** $m\angle SRT = 78° \div 2 = 39°$

### Lesson Practice 38

**a.**

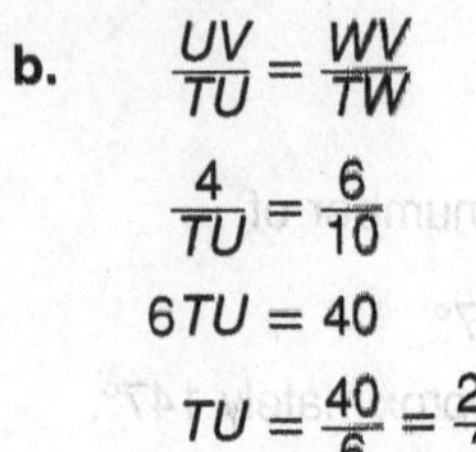



**b.** $\frac{UV}{TU} = \frac{WV}{TW}$

$\frac{4}{TU} = \frac{6}{10}$

$6TU = 40$

$TU = \frac{40}{6} = \frac{20}{3}$

**c.** Label the points $A(-3, -1)$, $B(3, -1)$, and $C(-1, -4)$.

The midpoint of $\overline{AB}$ is $(0, -1)$.

The midpoint of $\overline{AC}$ is $(-2, -2.5)$.

The line perpendicular to $\overline{AB}$ through $(0, -1)$ is $x = 0$.

To find the line perpendicular to $\overline{AC}$:

$m_{AC} = -\frac{3}{2}$ $m_{\perp AC} = \frac{2}{3}$

$y = \frac{2}{3}x + b$

$-2.5 = \frac{2}{3}(-2) + b$

$-\frac{7}{6} = b$

$y = \frac{2}{3}x - \frac{7}{6}$

The line perpendicular to $AC$ through $(-2, -2.5)$ is $y = \frac{2}{3}x - \frac{7}{6}$.

To find the circumcenter, solve the system of equations.

$x = 0$

$y = \frac{2}{3}x - \frac{7}{6}$

$y = \frac{2}{3}(0) - \frac{7}{6}$

$y = -\frac{7}{6}$

The circumcenter is located at $\left(0, -\frac{7}{6}\right)$.

**d.** Find the circumcenter.

The midpoint of $\overline{AB}$ is $(2, 0)$.

The midpoint of $\overline{AC}$ is $(0, 3)$.

The line perpendicular to $\overline{AB}$ through $(2, 0)$ is $x = 2$.

The line perpendicular to $\overline{AC}$ through $(0, 3)$ is $y = 3$.

The circumcenter is located at $(2, 3)$. This is where the restaurant should be located.

## Practice 38

**1. a.** $12^2 \stackrel{?}{=} 9^2 + 5^2$

$144 \stackrel{?}{=} 81 + 25$

$144 > 106$

Since $c^2 > a^2 + b^2$, the triangle is obtuse.

**b.** $17.5^2 \stackrel{?}{=} 17^2 + 5^2$

$306.25 \stackrel{?}{=} 289 + 36$

$306.25 < 325$

Since $c^2 < a^2 + b^2$, the triangle is acute.

**c.** $15^2 \stackrel{?}{=} 12^2 + 9^2$

$225 \stackrel{?}{=} 144 + 81$

$225 < 225$

Since $c^2 = a^2 + b^2$, the triangle is right.

**2.** On the map, draw a triangle with each town at a vertex. Find the perpendicular bisectors of all three sides of the triangle to find the circumcenter of the triangle. The circumcenter is the optimal location for the fire station.

**3.** $x^2 = 8^2 + 6^2$

$x^2 = 64 + 36$

$x = 10$ m

Yes, they form a Pythagorean triple.

**4.** See student work. Sample: $n = 3$ represents the sum of the first 3 squares or $1^2 + 2^2 + 3^2 = 14$.

$\frac{1}{6}(3)(3 + 1)(2(3) + 1) = \frac{1}{6}(3)(4)(7) = 14$

**5.** Addition Property of Equality

**6.** $\overrightarrow{RQ}$ s

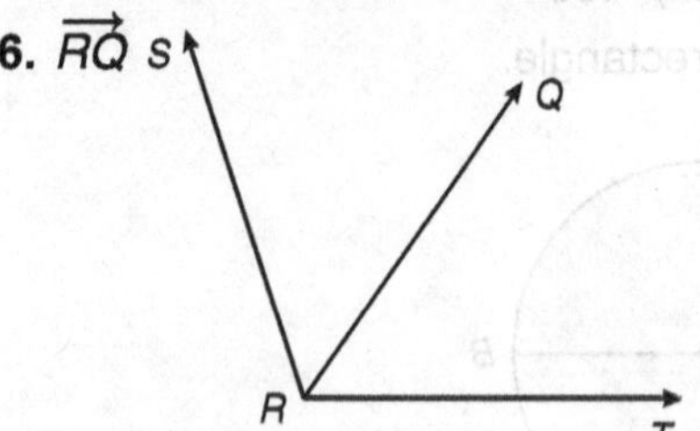


**7.**

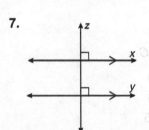

They are perpendicular.

8. $148{,}000 = \pi r^2 = 3.14r^2$
$47{,}133.76 = r^2$
$217.10 \text{ ft} = r$

9. $250° + 50° + 120° + 120° + 120° + 60° = 720°$

10. The heights are equal.

11. The logic is flawed because two things are not necessarily the same just because they have a common function. It is not true that sunglasses are safety glasses.

12. The slopes of parallel lines are equal.
$y = -\frac{1}{2}x + b$
$0 = -\frac{1}{2}(0) + b$
$0 = b$
$y = -\frac{1}{2}x$

13. $20^2 - 12^2 = (PT)^2$
$400 - 144 = (PT)^2$
$256 = (PT)^2$
$16 = PT$

14. $\frac{1}{3}(\pi 5^2) \approx 26.18 \text{ in.}^2$

15. Yes, the triangles are congruent. No, the Leg-Angle Congruence Theorem does not apply because the parts of the triangles marked congruent are the hypotenuse and the angle, not the leg and the angle. Therefore, by the Hypotenuse-Leg Congruence Theorem, the triangles are congruent.

16. She should mark the center of the circle at the incenter of the triangle because it is equidistant from each side of the triangle. This would ensure the largest circle possible from the scrap piece.

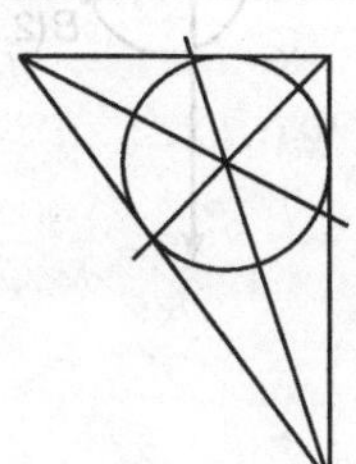

17. Label the points $A(1, 4)$, $B(5, 6)$, and $C(5, 0)$. Find the midpoint of $\overline{AB}$ and $\overline{BC}$.
$\overline{AB}_{\text{midpoint}} = (3, 5)$ and $\overline{BC}_{\text{midpoint}} = (5, 3)$
The slope of the median that extends from $C$ to $(3, 5)$ is $-\frac{5}{2}$.
$y - y_1 = m(x - x_1)$
$y - 5 = -\frac{5}{2}(x - 3)$
$y - 5 = -\frac{5}{2}x + 7\frac{1}{2}$
$y = -\frac{5}{2}x + 12\frac{1}{2}$
The slope of the median that extends from $A$ to $(5, 3)$ is $-\frac{1}{4}$.
$y - y_1 = m(x - x_1)$
$y - 3 = -\frac{1}{4}(x - 5)$
$y - 3 = -\frac{1}{4}x + \frac{5}{4}$
$y = -\frac{1}{4}x + \frac{17}{4}$
Now, solve these two equations as a system.
$y = -\frac{5}{2}x + \frac{25}{2}$
$y = -\frac{1}{4}x + \frac{17}{4}$
$-\frac{1}{4}x + \frac{17}{4} = -\frac{5}{2}x + \frac{25}{2}$
$\frac{9}{4}x = \frac{33}{4}$
$x = \frac{11}{3} \approx 3.67$
$y = -\frac{1}{4}\left(\frac{11}{3}\right) + \frac{17}{4}$
$y = \frac{10}{3} \approx 3.33$
The centroid is located at (3.67, 3.33).

18. $A = \frac{1}{2}(b_1 + b_2)h = \frac{1}{2}(1.5 + 2)(3)$
$= 5.25 \text{ in.}^2$

19. Yes, the step using the Division Property of Equality is incorrect. Since $x = y$ is given, $x - y = 0$, and the Division Property of Equality is not defined for dividing by 0.

20. Opposite angles are congruent in a rhombus, not complementary. Choice **C** is correct.

**21.** Sample: It is given that $\overline{AB} \parallel \overline{BC}$ and $\overline{DC} \parallel \overline{AB}$. Since these sets of parallel lines are cut by transversals, we know that the alternate interior angles they form must be congruent, so $\angle DAC \cong \angle BCA$ and $\angle DCA \cong \angle BAC$. $\triangle ACB$ and $\triangle CAD$ share a common side, $\overline{AC}$. By the Reflexive Property, $\overline{AC}$ is congruent to itself. This shows that two angles and an included side of $\triangle ACB$ are congruent to two angles and an included side of $\triangle CAD$, so $\triangle ACB \cong \triangle CAD$ by ASA.

**22.** $25^2 + 10^2 = x^2$
$625 + 100 = x^2$
$725 = x^2$
$27 \approx x$
He will need a 27 foot ladder.

**23.** $28^2 - 22^2 = x^2$
$300 = x^2$
$17.32 \approx x$

**24.** Conjunction: A bus is a downtown bus and is green.
This is false.

**25.** $x^2 = 10^2 + 24^2$
$x^2 = 100 + 576$
$x^2 = 676$
$x = 26$ in.

**26.** $\frac{44°}{360°}(\pi 5^2) = \frac{44°}{360°}(78.54) \approx 9.60 \text{ cm}^2$

**27.** $y = \frac{3}{2}x + b$
$4 = \frac{3}{2}(3) + b$
$4 = \frac{9}{2} + b$
$-\frac{1}{2} = b$
$y = \frac{3}{2}x - \frac{1}{2}$ or $y = \frac{3}{2}x - 0.5$

**28.** Since $\angle J$ and $\angle P$ are right angles, $\triangle JKL$ and $\triangle PQR$ are right triangles; $\overline{KL} \cong \overline{QR}$ and $\angle Q \cong \angle K$; by the Hypotenuse-Angle Congruence Theorem, $\triangle JKL \cong \triangle PQR$.

**29.**

| Statements | Reasons |
|---|---|
| 1. $m\angle ABC = m\angle ACB$ | 1. Given |
| 2. $\angle ABC \cong \angle ACB$ | 2. Def. ≅ angles |
| 3. $\angle ACB \cong \angle ABC$ | 3. Sym. Prop. ≅ |
| 4. $\overline{BC} \cong \overline{CB}$ | 4. Sym. Prop. ≅ |
| 5. $\triangle ABC \cong \triangle ACB$ | 5. ASA Postulate |
| 6. $\overline{AB} \cong \overline{AC}$ | 6. CPCTC |
| 7. $AB = AC$ | 7. Def. ≅ |

**30.** $(2y + 30) + y = 180$
$3y = 150$
$y = 50$
$(3x + 23) + (x^2 + 49) = 180$
$x^2 + 3x - 108 = 0$
$(x + 12)(x - 9) = 0$
$x = 9$ ($-12$ will give you a negative angle.)

## LAB 6

### Lab Practice

**a.** See student work. Sample:

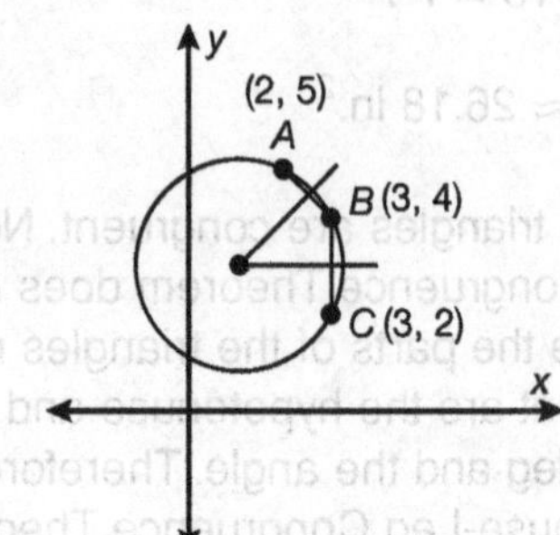


**b.** See student work. Sample:

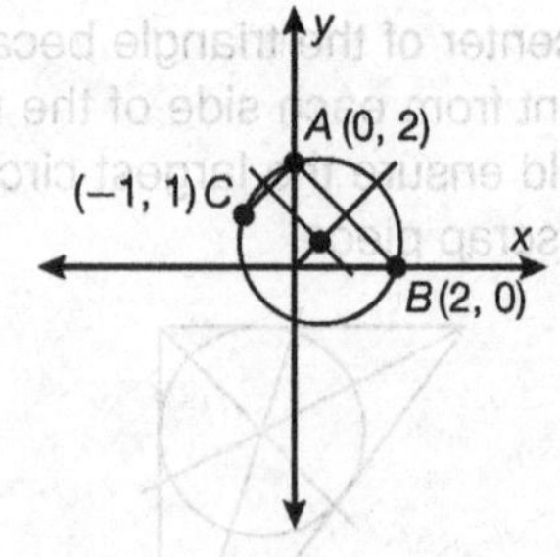


 

## LESSON 39

### Warm Up 39

1. exterior
2. $180° - 58° - 44° = 78°$
3. Choice **C**: The triangle has three acute angles, making it an acute triangle.

### Lesson Practice 39

a. $\overline{EF}, \overline{DE}, \overline{DF}$

b. $\angle Q, \angle P, \angle R$

c. $a = 120°$. Using the Exterior Angle Theorem and the given values of 50° for vertex $Y$ and 70° for vertex $X$, it can clearly be seen that $a$ is larger than the angle at either of the remote interior angles.

d. Using the Triangle Inequality Theorem, the following statements can be made:

1) $215 + 165 > x$

$380 > x$

2) $x + 215 > 165$

$x > -50$

3) $x + 165 > 215$

$x > 50$

Since all three inequalities must be true, $x > -50$ and $x > 50$ is just $x > 50$. Combining the three inequalities, we get $50 < x < 215$.

### Practice 39

1. Since $\angle G$ and $\angle K$ are right angles, $\triangle GHJ$ and $\triangle KLM$ are right triangles. Legs $\overline{GH}$ and $\overline{KL}$ are congruent, and acute angles, $\angle H$ and $\angle L$, are congruent. So, by the Leg–Angle Congruence Theorem, $\triangle GHJ \cong \triangle KLM$.
2. $\overline{BC}, \overline{AB}, \overline{AC}$
3. $10^2 = x^2 + x^2$

   $100 = 2x^2$

   $50 = x^2$

   $7.1 \text{ in.} \approx x$
4. $\frac{360°}{75°} = 4.8$

   Five cameras are necessary to view the entire area.
5. 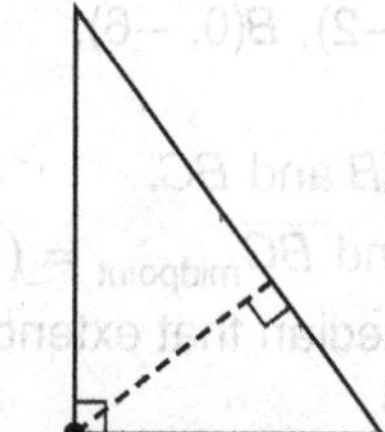


   The orthocenter is located on the vertex of the right angle. It will be located at the same place on every right triangle.
6. We can use the Triangle Inequality Theorem.

   Choice A: The sum of the two shorter sides is less than the longer side.

   Choice B: The sum of the two shorter sides is less than the longer side.

   Choice C: The sum of the two shorter sides is less than the longer side.

   Choice D: There is no combination of two sides whose sum is less than the third side.

   Choice **D** is correct.
7. Since $34 + 14 < 51$, these three side lengths cannot form a triangle.
8. $A = (ST)(TU)$

   $27 = (3TU)(TU)$

   $27 = 3TU^2$

   $9 = TU^2$

   $3 = TU = SV$

   $9 = ST = UV$
9. To show that $AB = CD$, the Transitive Property must be used, not the Reflexive Property.
10. 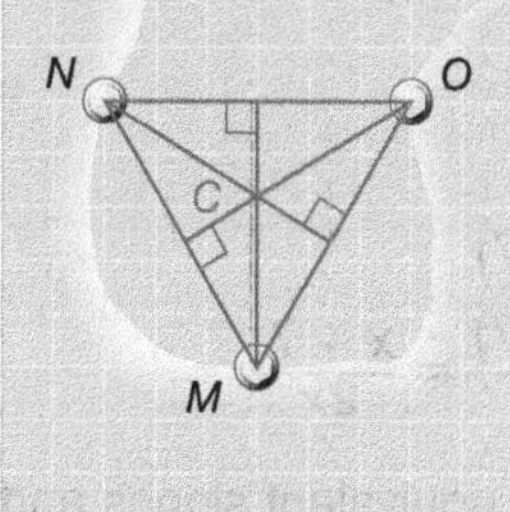

11. For any two sections, by definition of congruent segments, both pairs of legs are congruent. By the Leg-Leg Congruence Theorem, the sections are congruent.
12. $A = lw = (11)(13) = 143 \text{ ft}^2$

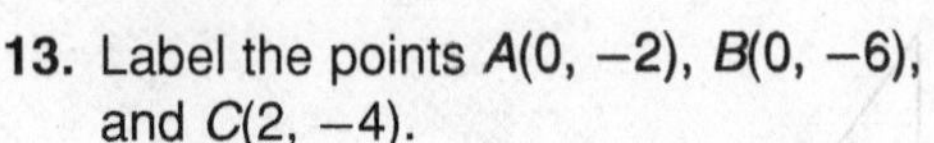



**13.** Label the points $A(0, -2)$, $B(0, -6)$, and $C(2, -4)$.

Find the midpoint of $AB$ and $BC$.

$\overline{AB}_{\text{midpoint}} = (0, -4)$ and $\overline{BC}_{\text{midpoint}} = (1, -5)$

The equation of the median that extends from $C$ to $(0, -4)$ is $y = -4$.

The slope of the median that extends from $A$ to $(1, -5)$ is $-3$.

$$y - y_1 = m(x - x_1)$$
$$y - -5 = -3(x - 1)$$
$$y + 5 = -3x + 3$$
$$y = -3x - 2$$

Now, solve these two equations as a system.

$$y = -4$$
$$y = -3x - 2$$
$$-4 = -3x - 2$$
$$3x = 2$$
$$x = \frac{2}{3}$$
$$y = -3\left(\frac{2}{3}\right) - 2$$
$$y = -4$$

The centroid is located at (0.67, −4).

**14.** 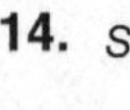

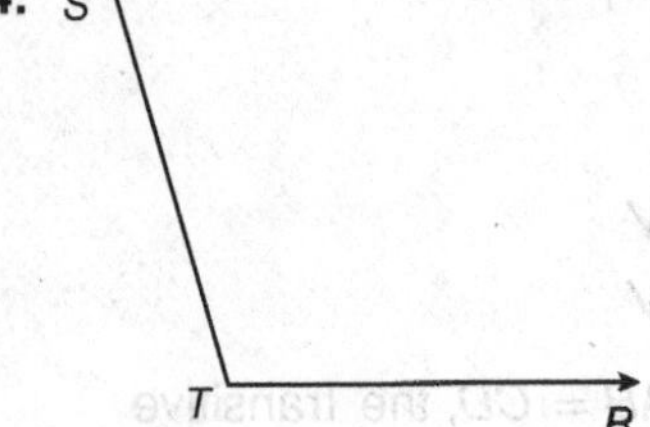


$\angle RTS$ or $\angle STR$

**15.**
$$\frac{NO}{MN} = \frac{OP}{MP}$$
$$\frac{2}{MN} = \frac{4x}{x + 7}$$
$$4x(MN) = 2(x + 7)$$
$$MN = \frac{2(x + 7)}{4x} = \frac{x + 7}{2x}$$

**16.** Choice **B** has two equivalent slopes and different $y$-intercepts.

**17.** $c = 1296 + 2500$

$c = 3796 \text{ ft}^2$

See student work. Sample: The buildings will be arranged to form a park that is in the shape of a right triangle. Based on the proof model of the Pythagorean Theorem, the sum of the squares sharing the sides with the legs of a right triangle are equal to the sum of the square sharing the hypotenuse side, which is the third building.

**18.**
$$50^2 - 35^2 = PU^2$$
$$2500 - 1225 = PU^2$$
$$1275 = PU^2$$
$$35.71 \approx PU$$

**19.** The central angles will always sum to 360°, so as the number of sides increases, the number of central angles will increase so that there are fewer degrees for each angle.

**20.**

| Statements | Reasons |
|---|---|
| 1. $16 = 4(3x - 8)$ | 1. Given |
| 2. $\frac{16}{4} = \frac{4(3x - 8)}{4}$ | 2. Division Property of Equality |
| 3. $4 = 3x - 8$ | 3. Simplify. |
| 4. $4 + 8 = 3x - 8 + 8$ | 4. Addition Property of Equality |
| 5. $12 = 3x$ | 5. Simplify. |
| 6. $\frac{12}{3} = \frac{3x}{3}$ | 6. Division Property of Equality |
| 7. $4 = x$ | 7. Simplify. |
| 8. $x = 4$ | 8. Symmetric Property of Equality |

**21.**
$$y = 2x + b$$
$$-1 = 2(-1) + b$$
$$1 = b$$
$$y = 2x + 1$$

**22.** $x$ is the hypotenuse, $c$.

$$c^2 > a^2 + b^2$$
$$x^2 > 8^2 + 7^2$$
$$x^2 > 64 + 49$$
$$x^2 > 113$$
$$x > \sqrt{113}$$

**23.** $\frac{50°}{360°}(\pi 7^2) = \frac{50°}{360°}(153.94) \approx 21.38 \text{ cm}^2$

24.

| Statements | Reasons |
|---|---|
| 1. $2x + 1 = 15$ | 1. Given |
| 2. $2x + 1 - 1 = 15 - 1$ | 2. Subtraction Property of Equality |
| 3. $2x = 14$ | 3. Simplify. |
| 4. $\frac{2x}{2} = \frac{14}{2}$ | 4. Division Property of Equality |
| 5. $x = 7$ | 5. Simplify. |

Therefore, Preetha is 7 years old.

25. It is given that $\overline{AB} \parallel \overline{DE}$. The Exterior Angle Theorem says that the measure of an exterior angle is equal to the sum of the two remote interior angles, so in $\triangle ABC$, we know that $m\angle CAB + m\angle ACB = m\angle ABE$.
Since $\overline{AB} \parallel \overline{DE}$, the corresponding angles formed by a transversal are congruent. $\angle ABE$ and $\angle DEF$ are corresponding angles, so $m\angle ABE = m\angle DEF$. Since they are equal to one another, $\angle DEF$ can be substituted for $\angle ABE$. Doing this with the earlier equation yields $m\angle CAB + m\angle ACB = m\angle DEF$.

26. $C = 2\pi r = 2\pi(6) \approx 37.7$ m

$C_{circle} - C_{sector} = 37.7 - \frac{35°}{360°}(37.7)$
$\approx 34.0$ m

27. a. $(\sqrt{34})^2 \stackrel{?}{=} 4^2 + 4^2$ obtuse
$34 \stackrel{?}{=} 16 + 16$
$34 > 32$

b. $8^2 \stackrel{?}{=} 6^2 + 5^2$ obtuse
$64 \stackrel{?}{=} 36 + 25$
$64 > 61$

c. $26^2 \stackrel{?}{=} 24^2 + 10^2$ right
$676 \stackrel{?}{=} 576 + 100$
$676 = 676$

28. $\overline{TU}$ is the smallest piece because it is across from the smallest angle in the smallest triangle.

29.

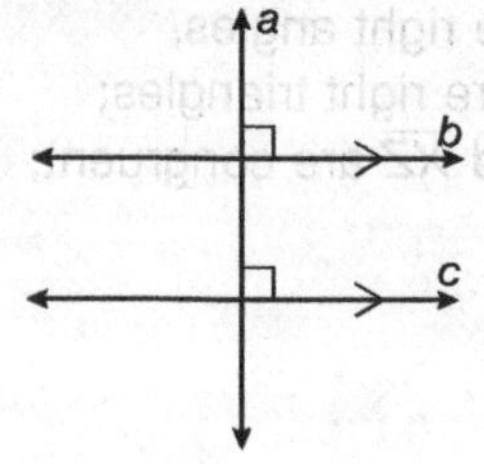


They are parallel.

30. $x^2 = 12^2 + 24^2$
$x^2 = 144 + 576$
$x^2 = 720$
$x = \sqrt{720}$
$x = \sqrt{144 \cdot 5}$
$x = 12\sqrt{5}$ in.

## LESSON 40

### Warm Up 40

1. area
2. $x^2 = 25^2 + 60^2$
$x^2 = 625 + 3600$
$x^2 = 4225$
$x = 65$
$P = 65 + 60 + 25 = 150$ mm
3. Choice **B**

### Lesson Practice 40

a. $P = 4.5 + 4.5 + 3 + 4 + 4 = 20$ in.

b. $A = lw + \frac{\pi r^2}{2} = (4)(4) + \frac{4\pi}{2}$
$= (16 + 2\pi)$ cm$^2$

c. $(16 + 2\pi) - (3)(1.5) = (16 + 2\pi) - 4.5$
$= (11.5 + 2\pi)$ cm$^2$

d.

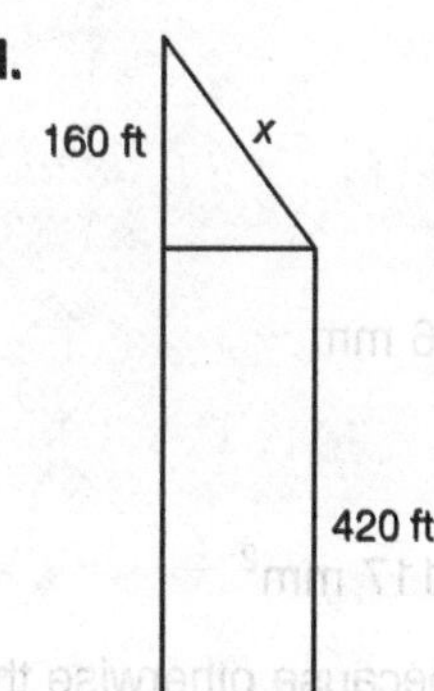


$x^2 = 160^2 + 120^2$
$x^2 = 25{,}600 + 14{,}400$
$x^2 = 40{,}000$
$x = 200$

$P = 200 + 420 + 120 + 420 + 160$
$= 1320$ ft

**e.** $A = lw + \frac{1}{2}bh$

$= (420)(120) + \frac{1}{2}(120)(160)$

$= 60{,}000 \text{ ft}^2$

## Practice 40

**1.** $m = \frac{1 - -3}{4 - 2} = \frac{4}{2} = 2$

$m_{\perp} = -\frac{1}{2}$

$y = -\frac{1}{2}x + b$

$2 = -\frac{1}{2}(-2) + b$

$2 = 1 + b$
$1 = b$

$y = -\frac{1}{2}x + 1$

**2.** The hypotenuse is always the longest side and would be the 75 cm length.

**3.** $(4x)^2 = (2x)^2 + (3x)^2$
$16x^2 = 4x^2 + 9x^2$
$16x^2 > 13x^2$ obtuse

**4.** $m_{\perp} = -4$
$y = -4x + b$
$0 = -4(0) + b$
$0 = b$
$y = -4x$

**5.** $P_1 = 9 + 9 + 9 + 9 = 36$ mm
$A_1 = (9)(9) = 81 \text{ mm}^2$
$P_2 = (20)(3) = 60$ mm
$A_2 = (9)(9) + 4(3)(3) = 117 \text{ mm}^2$

**6.** The statement *p* is false because otherwise the Law of Detachment would fail.

**7.** $\triangle HJK$ and $\triangle LMN$ are right triangles; hypotenuses $\overline{HJ}$ and $\overline{LN}$ are congruent; and legs $\overline{HK}$ and $\overline{LM}$ are congruent; so by the Hypotenuse-Leg Congruence Theorem, $\triangle HJK \cong \triangle LNM$.

**8.** $A = \pi r^2 = \pi(8.96)^2 \approx 252 \text{ mm}^2$

**9.**

y, x, 2, O, (0, 0), −2, 2, 4, N, (−1, −4), (5, −3)

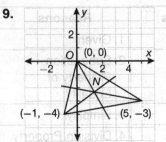

**10.** $\sqrt{490} = \sqrt{49 \cdot 10} = 7\sqrt{10}$

**11.** $QW = \frac{2}{3}QV = 14$

$21 = QV$

$TW = \frac{1}{3}TR = \frac{1}{3}(9) = 3$

**12.** $56° - 34° + 67° = 89°$

**13.** The angle across from the 31-yard side because it is the longest side.

**14.** $9 = \frac{65°}{360°}\pi r^2$

$58.91 = \pi r^2$; $r \approx 3.98$ units

**15.** Lily claims the triangles are congruent by AAA, but only ASA, AAS, SSS, and SAS can be used to determine congruence.

**16.**

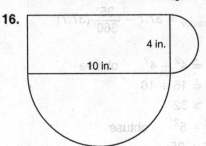

4 in.
10 in.

$P = 10 + 4 + \frac{10\pi}{2} + \frac{4\pi}{2} = (14 + 7\pi)$ in.

$A = (10)(4) + \frac{\pi 5^2}{2} + \frac{\pi 2^2}{2}$

$= 40 + 12.5\pi + 2\pi$

$= (40 + 14.5\pi) \text{ in.}^2$

**17.** $\angle P$, $\angle E$, $\angle S$

**18.** Since $\angle V$ and $\angle Y$ are right angles, $\triangle UVW$ and $\triangle XYZ$ are right triangles; hypotenuses $\overline{UW}$ and $\overline{XZ}$ are congruent;

acute angles $\angle U$ and $\angle X$ are congruent; by the Hypotenuse-Angle Congruence Theorem, $\triangle UVW \cong \triangle XYZ$.

**19.** $\frac{45°}{360°} = \frac{1}{8}$; Therefore, it would take 8 cameras to look in all directions.

**20.** $\sqrt{3^2 + 4^2} = \sqrt{25} = 5$

$2x - 3 = 5 = AC$

$2x = 8$

$x = 4$

**21.** $4.75 \text{ feet} = \pi D$

$1.5 \text{ feet} \approx D$

The tree trunk is 1 ft 6 in. wide.

**22.** Choice A: $2x - 3y = 4$

$-3y = -2x + 4$

$y = \frac{2}{3}x - \frac{4}{3}$

The slopes are not opposite reciprocals.

Choice B: The slopes are not opposite reciprocals.

Choice C: $-3y + 2x + 7 = 0$

$-3y = -2x - 7$

$y = \frac{2}{3}x + \frac{7}{3}$

$-3x + 2y - 4 = 0$

$2y = 3x + 4$

$y = \frac{3}{2}x + 2$

The slopes are not opposite reciprocals.

Choice D: $2x + y = 8$

$y = -2x + 8$

$x - 2y = 1$

$-2y = -x + 1$

$y = \frac{1}{2}x - \frac{1}{2}$

The slopes are opposite reciprocals.

Choice **D** is correct.

**23.** The exterior angles will always sum to 360°. So, as we increase the number of sides, the number of exterior angles will increase so that there are fewer degrees for each angle.

**24.** Since $8 + 8 = 16$, these three side lengths cannot form a triangle.

**25.** $P = 5 + 5 + 3 + 4 + 9 + 4 = 30$ in.

**26.** $A = lw + \frac{1}{2}bh$

$= (4)(9) + \frac{1}{2}(6)(4)$

$= 48 \text{ in.}^2$

**27.** $25^2 - 24^2 = (7x)^2$

$49 = 49x^2$

$1 = x^2$

$x = 1$

**28.** $x^2 = 20^2 + 45^2$

$x^2 = 400 + 2025$

$x^2 = 2425$

$x \approx 49.24$ miles

**29.** $A(-4, -1)$, $B(6, 2)$

$d = \sqrt{(x_2 - x_1)^2 + (y_2 - y_1)^2}$

$= \sqrt{(6 - -4)^2 + (2 - -1)^2}$

$= \sqrt{10^2 + 3^2}$

$= \sqrt{100 + 9}$

$= \sqrt{109}$

$\approx 10.44$

**30.** $B(6, 2)$, $C(3, -5)$

$d = \sqrt{(x_2 - x_1)^2 + (y_2 - y_1)^2}$

$= \sqrt{(3 - 6)^2 + (-5 - 2)^2}$

$= \sqrt{(-3)^2 + (-7)^2}$

$= \sqrt{9 + 49}$

$= \sqrt{58}$

$\approx 7.62$

## INVESTIGATION 4

**1.** The third side becomes longer as the door is opened.

**2.** Answers will vary. See student work. Sample:

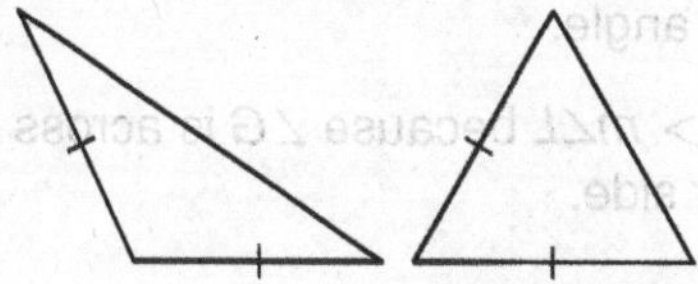

3. The third sides are not congruent.

4. Answers will vary. See student work. Sample:

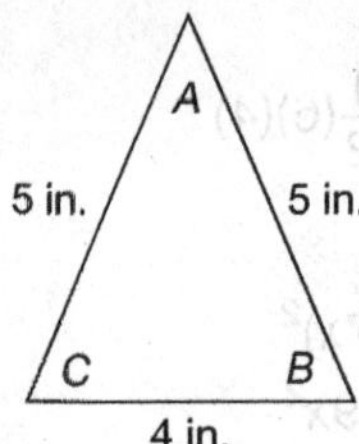


5. Answers will vary. See student work. Sample:

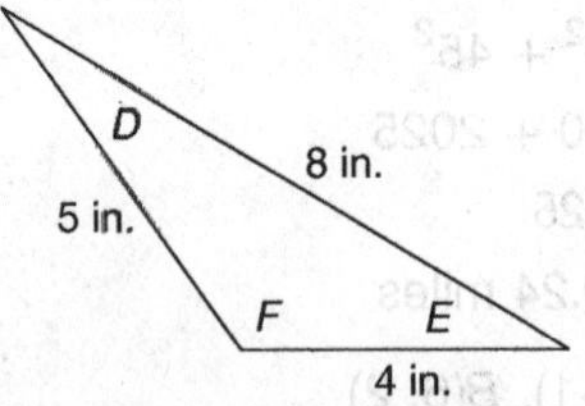


6. The angle measure corresponds to the length of the opposite side, so the larger angle is opposite the longer side.

7. Converse: If two sides of one triangle are congruent to two sides of another triangle and the third side of the first triangle is longer than the third side of the second triangle, then the measure of the angle opposite the third side of the first triangle is greater than the measure of the angle opposite the third side of the second triangle.

   Yes, it is true for the triangles drawn.

8. *BC* is opposite $\angle BAC$, which is larger than $\angle DAE$, so *BC* will be longer than *DE*.

9. Angle *a* is largest in the relaxed position and smallest in the writing position. The lengths opposite angle a in these positions are the largest and smallest, respectively.

10. $0 < 2x + 4 < 18$

    $-4 < 2x < 14$

    $-2 < x < 7$

## Investigation 4 Practice

**a.** $XY > TV$ because *XY* is across from the larger angle.

**b.** $m\angle G > m\angle L$ because $\angle G$ is across from the longer side.

**c.** Sample: As the hood of a car is raised, the hood and the engine frame form two sides of a triangle. The support brace holding the hood up extends as the angle between the hood and the frame grows larger.

**d.** *EF* must be less than FG because the angle across from FG is 90°, which is greater than the angle across from EF, which is 60°, so the correct choice is **B**.

**e.** $0 < 3x - 9 < 54$

$9 < 3x < 63$

$3 < x < 21$

**f.** The door that opens a straight-line distance of 48 inches needs the larger sweep angle.

**g.** The larger angle of 47° will correspond to the longer swing distance, so Kelvin is swinging through the greatest distance.

## LESSON 41

### Warm Up 41

1. proportion

2. True, by the SSS Congruence Theorem.

3. $\overline{AB} \cong \overline{DE}$, $\overline{BC} \cong \overline{EF}$, $\overline{AC} \cong \overline{DF}$

4. 

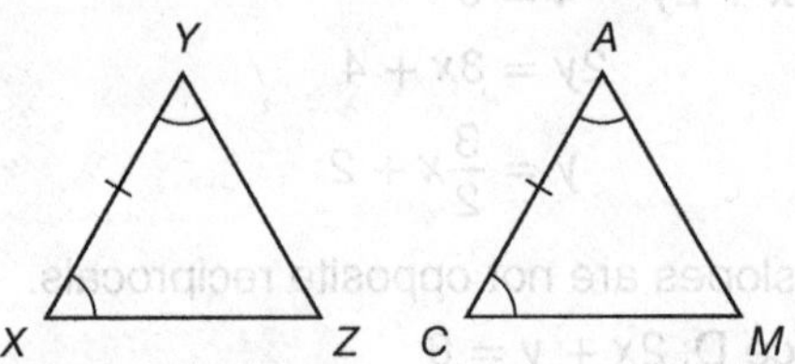


The ASA Congruence Theorem, since two angles and the included side are congruent

### Lesson Practice 41

**a.** 4:9:6

**b.** $\frac{9}{27} = \frac{1}{3}$

$\frac{1}{3}$, 1:3, or 1 to 3

**c.** $\frac{6}{18} = \frac{9}{27}$

d. $\frac{8}{7} = \frac{x}{21}$

$(8)(21) = (7)(x)$

$168 = 7x$

$24 = x$

e. $\frac{8}{20} = \frac{10}{x}$

$(8)(x) = (20)(10)$

$8x = 200$

$x = 25$

f. $m\angle O = m\angle S = 62°$

$m\angle N = 360° - m\angle O - m\angle P - m\angle M$

$= 360° - 62° - 95° - 81°$

$= 122°$

$m\angle R = m\angle N = 122°$

g. $\frac{4}{12} = \frac{3}{x}$

$(4)(x) = (12)(3)$

$4x = 36$

$x = 9$

$\frac{4}{12} = \frac{5}{y}$

$(4)(y) = (12)(5)$

$4y = 60$

$y = 15$

$\frac{4}{12} = \frac{9}{z}$

$(4)(z) = (12)(9)$

$4z = 108$

$z = 27$

h. $\frac{21}{18} = \frac{12}{x}$

$(21)(x) = (18)(12)$

$21x = 216$

$x \approx 10$

The ladder will reach approximately 10 feet.

**Practice 41**

1. No, he must have added the interior angles $(3 \times 180° + 2 \times 180°)$. All of the exterior angles combined would have equaled 720° $(360° + 360°)$.
2. $m\angle E = m\angle X = 73°$

   $\frac{2}{3} = \frac{b}{15}$

   $(3)(b) = (2)(15)$

   $3b = 30$

   $b = XY = 10$ units
3. On the map, draw a triangle with each friend's home at a vertex. Find the perpendicular bisectors of all three sides of the triangle to find the circumcenter of the triangle. The circumcenter is equidistant from all three vertices and is the optimal location for the reunion.
4. Since $\angle C$ is larger than $\angle F$, $\overline{AB}$ is longer than $\overline{DE}$.
5. They are perpendicular.
6. $\frac{9}{x+2} = \frac{27}{9}$

   $(27)(x + 2) = (9)(9)$

   $27x + 54 = 81$

   $27x = 27$

   $x = 1$
7. Transitive Property of Equality
8. It is a heptagon because it has 7 sides. It is equiangular but not equilateral, making it irregular.
9. 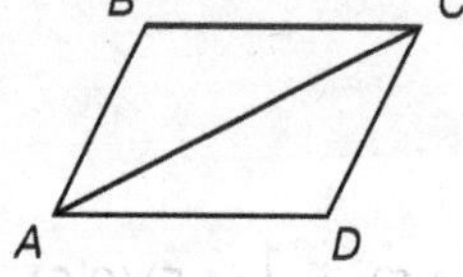

| Statements | Reasons |
|---|---|
| 1. *ABCD* is a quadrilateral, draw $\overline{AC}$ | 1. Given |
| 2. m∠*ABC* + m∠*BCA* + m∠*CAB* = 180° | 2. Triangle Angle Sum Theorem |
| 3. m∠*ACD* + m∠*CDA* + m∠*DAC* = 180° | 3. Triangle Angle Sum Theorem |
| 4. m∠*ABC* + m∠*BCA* + m∠*CAB* + m∠*ACD* + m∠*CDA* + m∠*DAC* = 180° + 180° | 4. Addition Property of Equality |
| 5. m∠*ABC* + m∠*BCA* + m∠*CAB* + m∠*ACD* + m∠*CDA* + m∠*DAC* = 360° | 5. Simplify |
| 6. m∠*ABC* + m∠*BCD* + m∠*CDA* + m∠*DAB* = 360° | 6. Angle Addition Postulate |

**10.** Since all triangles are convex, the sum of the interior angles in a triangle = 180(3 − 2) = 180°.

**11.** $A = \frac{1}{2}bh + lw + \frac{\pi r^2}{2}$

$A = \frac{1}{2}(3)(4) + (5)(8) + \frac{\pi(2.5)^2}{2}$

$A = 6 + 40 + \frac{\pi(6.25)}{2}$

$A = (46 + 3.125\pi) \text{ in.}^2$

**12.** distance $= 4(2\pi r) = 4(2\pi)(9) \approx 226.19$ in.

**13.** Answers will vary. Any answer of the form 7*n*, 24*n*, 25*n*, where *n* is a nonzero whole number other than 1. For example, 14, 48, 50 when *n* = 2.

**14.** $A = lw + lw + \frac{1}{2}bh$

$= (4.5)(6.5) + (2)(4.5) + \frac{1}{2}(4.5)(2.5)$

$= 29.25 + 9 + 5.625$

$= 43.875 \text{ in.}^2$

**15.** △*LJK*

**16.**

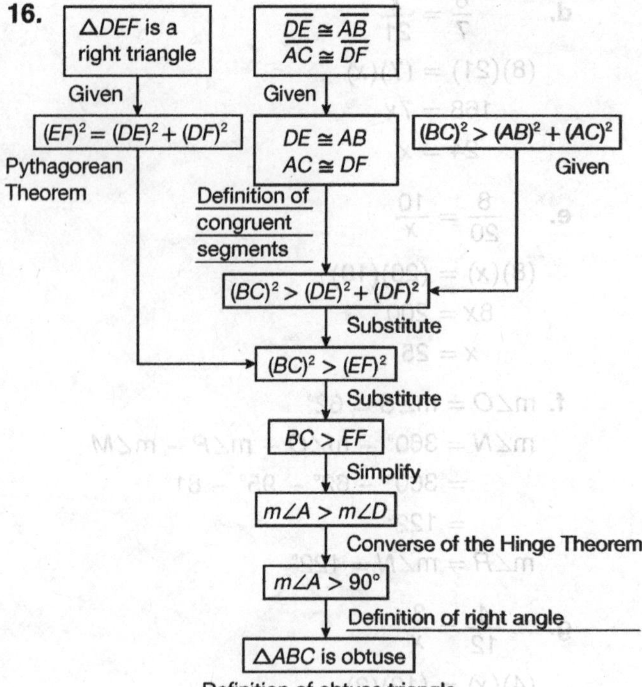


**17.** $\frac{2}{3}(70.2) = 46.8$

*DC* = 46.8 cm; Centroid Theorem

**18.** $A = \frac{1}{2}(b_1 + b_2)h$

$= \frac{1}{2}((g - h) + (g + h))(2)$

$= 2g$

**19.**

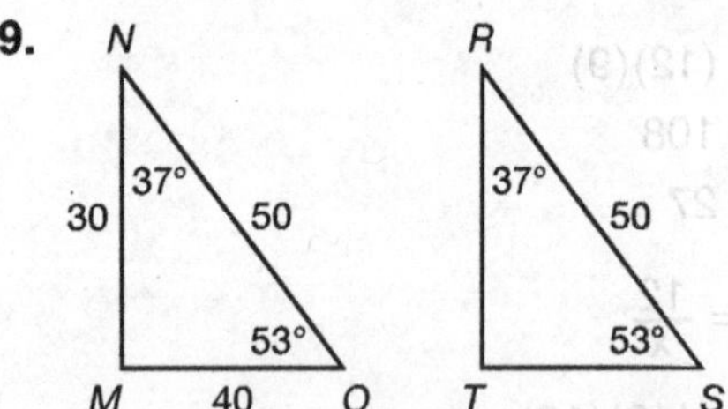


By ASA, the triangles are congruent.

*RT* = 30 ft; *ST* = 40 ft

**20.** The triangles are right triangles, and the hypotenuses are congruent; so by the Alternate Exterior Angles Theorem, the angles at Madison/Broadway and Marion/Broadway are congruent; by the HA Congruence Theorem, the triangles are congruent.

**21.** $\frac{1}{4}(8) = 2$

$\frac{1}{4}(10) = 2.5$

2-by-2.5-inches

**22.** $9x - 18 = 7x + 12$

$2x = 30$

$x = 15$

$m\angle P = m\angle R = 9(15) - 18 = 117°$

$m\angle Q = m\angle S = 180° - 117° = 63°$

**23.** $10y - 4 = 5y + 8$

$5y = 12$

$y = 2.4$

$PS = 10(2.4) - 4 = 20$

$PQ = 2PS = 2(20) = 40$

Perimeter $= 2(20) + 2(40) = 120$

**24.** triangle; angle; side

**25.** No, a side length can never be greater than or equal to the sum of the other two lengths.

**26.**

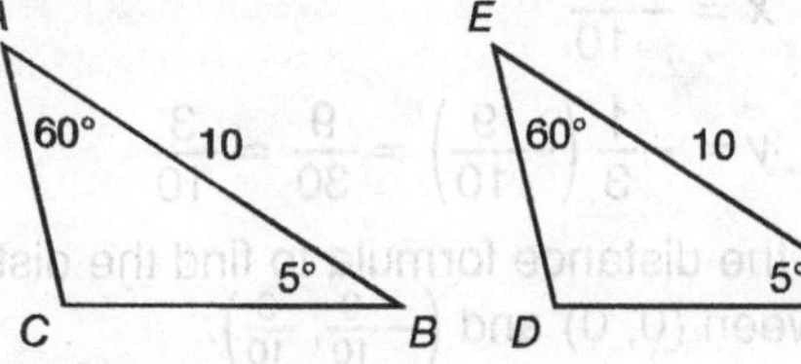


$\triangle ABC \cong \triangle EFD$ by $ASA$ congruency

**27.** $WV = 2(1) + 1 = 2 + 1 = 3$

$WU = 1 + 3 = 4$

$VU = 1 + 5 = 6$

Since $WV$ is the shortest side, $\angle U$ has the least measure.

**28.** $C_1 = 2(3.14)(0.5) = 3.14$ units

$A_2 = (3.14)(3.14)^2 \approx 30.96$ units$^2$

**29.** The first shape is a square.

$A_{square} = s^2$

The second shape is a parallelogram.

$A_{parallelogram} = bh$

Choice **C** is correct.

**30.** Sample: If a figure is a square, then it is a rhombus; and if a figure is a rhombus, its area is half the product of its diagonals; so by the Law of Syllogism, if a figure is a square, then its area is half the product of its diagonals.

## LESSON 42

### Warm Up 42

**1.** perpendicular

**2.** $a^2 + b^2 = c^2$

**3.** $d = \sqrt{(x_2 - x_1)^2 + (y_2 - y_1)^2}$

**4.** $m = 3$

**5.** Slopes of perpendicular lines are opposite reciprocals of each other.

$m = -2$

$m_{\perp} = \frac{1}{2}$

### Lesson Practice 42

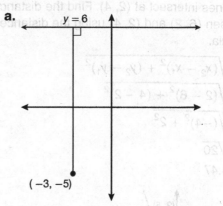

**a.** y = 6

(−3, −5)

The distance between the point (−3, −5) and the line is 11 units.

**b.**

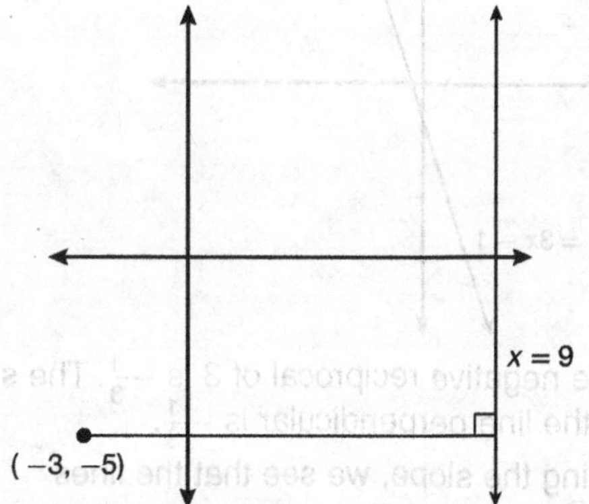


The distance between the point (−3, −5) and the line is 12 units.

**c.**

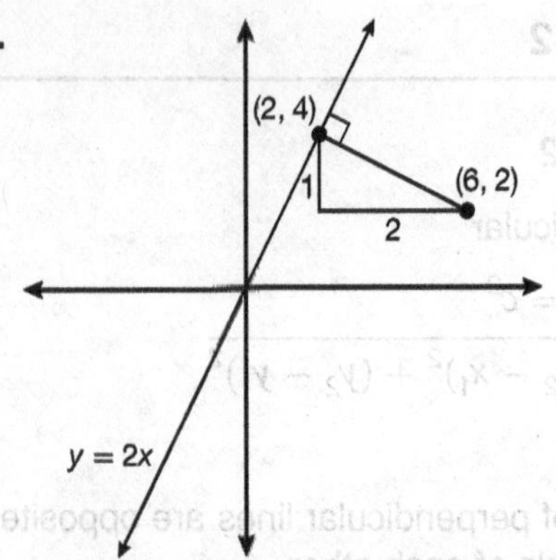


The slope of the perpendicular line is the negative reciprocal of the line $y = 2x$, which is $-\frac{1}{2}$.

Start at point (6, 2). Use the slope to find the point of intersection and draw the line.

The lines intersect at (2, 4). Find the distance between (6, 2) and (2, 4) using the distance formula.

$$d = \sqrt{(x_2 - x_1)^2 + (y_2 - y_1)^2}$$
$$= \sqrt{(2 - 6)^2 + (4 - 2)^2}$$
$$= \sqrt{(-4)^2 + 2^2}$$
$$= \sqrt{20}$$
$$\approx 4.47$$

**d.**

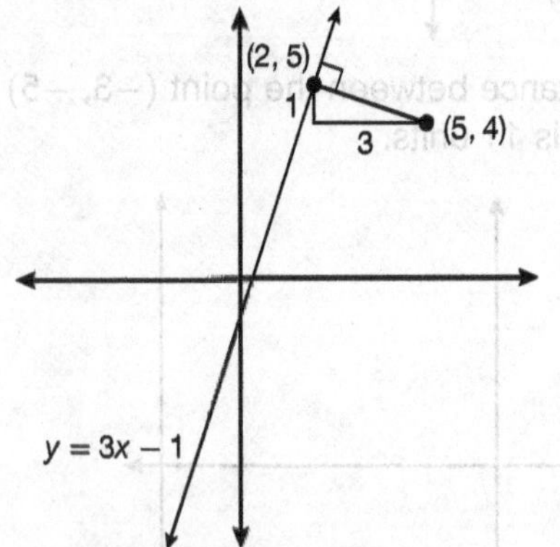


The negative reciprocal of 3 is $-\frac{1}{3}$. The slope of the line perpendicular is $-\frac{1}{3}$.

Using the slope, we see that the lines intersect at (2, 5).

**e.**

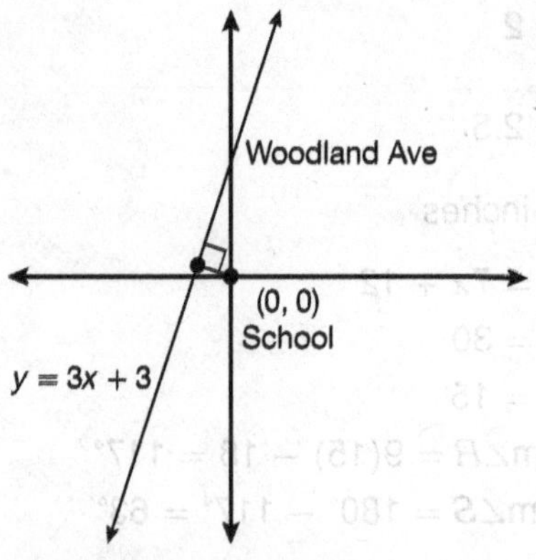


The opposite reciprocal of 3 is $-\frac{1}{3}$.

$$y - y_1 = m(x - x_1)$$
$$y - 0 = -\frac{1}{3}(x - 0)$$
$$y = -\frac{1}{3}x$$
$$-\frac{1}{3}x = 3x + 3$$
$$-\frac{10}{3}x = 3$$
$$x = -\frac{9}{10}$$
$$y = -\frac{1}{3}\left(-\frac{9}{10}\right) = \frac{9}{30} = \frac{3}{10}$$

Use the distance formula to find the distance between (0, 0) and $\left(-\frac{9}{10}, \frac{3}{10}\right)$.

$$d = \sqrt{(x_2 - x_1)^2 + (y_2 - y_1)^2}$$
$$= \sqrt{\left(-\frac{9}{10} - 0^2\right) + \left(\frac{3}{10} - 0\right)^2}$$
$$= \sqrt{\left(\frac{81}{100}\right)^2 + \left(\frac{9}{100}\right)^2}$$
$$= \sqrt{\frac{90}{100}}$$
$$\approx 0.95$$

He lives 0.95 miles away, so he cannot ride the bus.

## Practice 42

1. By making the new support 18 in. long, Denzel can make sure that hypotenuses are congruent. By fixing it 10 in. below the roof, he can make sure that a pair of legs are congruent. By the HL Congruence Theorem, this makes sure that triangles are congruent.

2. $C = 2\pi r$
$328 = 2\pi r$
$52.2 \approx r$
The radius is about 52.2 feet.

3. 100°

4. $c = 14$
$14^2 = 5^2 + 12^2$
$196 = 25 + 144$
$196 > 169$
The triangle is obtuse.
$c = 13$
$13^2 = 5^2 + 12^2$
$169 = 25 + 144$
$169 = 169$
The triangle is right.
$c = 12$
$12^2 = 5^2 + 12^2$
$144 = 25 + 144$
$144 < 169$
The triangle is acute.

5. Using the Triangle Sum Theorem, $\angle C$ is equal to 23°, which is smaller than the corresponding angle in the second triangle at vertex $F$. So, $\overline{DE}$ is longer.

6.

| Statements | Reasons |
|---|---|
| 1. $\angle 1$ and $\angle 2$ are straight angles | 1. Given |
| 2. $m\angle 1 = 180°$, $m\angle 2 = 180°$ | 2. Definition of straight angles |
| 3. $m\angle 1 = m\angle 2$ | 3. Substitute |
| 4. $\angle 1 \cong \angle 2$ | 4. Definition of congruent angles |

7. $\frac{6}{19.2} = \frac{12}{x}$
$(6)(x) = (12)(19.2)$
$6x = 230.4$
$x = 38.4$ in.
Choice **D** is correct.

8. Since $\angle B$ and $\angle E$ are right angles, $\triangle ABC$ and $\triangle DEF$ are right triangles. We are given that $\overline{BC} \cong \overline{EF}$ and $\angle C \cong \angle F$. By the LA Theorem, $\triangle ABC \cong \triangle DEF$.

9. The negative reciprocal of $-\frac{3}{2}$ is $\frac{2}{3}$.
The slope of the line perpendicular is $\frac{2}{3}$.
$(y - 5) = \frac{2}{3}(x - 4)$
$(y - 5) = \frac{2}{3}x - \frac{8}{3}$
$y = \frac{2}{3}x + \frac{7}{3}$
To find the point of intersection, set the equations equal.
$-\frac{3}{2}x - 2 = \frac{2}{3}x + \frac{7}{3}$
$-\frac{13}{6}x = \frac{13}{3}$
$x = -2$
$y = \frac{2}{3}(-2) + \frac{7}{3}$
$y = -\frac{4}{3} + \frac{7}{3}$
$y = 1$
Find the distance between $(-2, 1)$ and $(4, 5)$.
$d = \sqrt{(x_2 - x_1)^2 + (y_2 - y_1)^2}$
$= \sqrt{(4 - -2)^2 + (5 - 1)^2}$
$= \sqrt{6^2 + 4^2}$
$= \sqrt{52}$
$\approx 7.21$

10. $m_j = \frac{2 - 6}{3 - 4} = \frac{-4}{-1} = 4$
For the lines to be parallel, $m_k = 4$.
$\frac{3 - -1}{-3 - x} = \frac{4}{1}$
$\frac{4}{-3 - x} = \frac{4}{1}$
$4(-3 - x) = 4$
$-12 - 4x = 4$
$-4x = 16$
$x = -4$

11. $A = lw + lw = (6)(4) + (4)(2) = 32 \text{ cm}^2$

12. $x^2 = 27^2 + 36^2$
$x^2 = 729 + 1296$
$x^2 = 2025$
$x = 45$ inches

**13.** Answers will vary. Any answer of the form $5n$, $12n$, $13n$ will be a Pythagorean triple, where $n$ is a positive integer. For example, 10, 24, and 26 when $n = 2.15$, 36, and 39 when $n = 3$.

**14.**

| Statements | Reasons |
|---|---|
| 1. m∠$ABC$ = 60°, m∠$BCD$ = 60°, m∠$CDE$ = 75°, m∠$CED$ = 45° | 1. Given |
| 2. m∠$ACD$ = m∠$CDE$ + m∠$CED$ | 2. Exterior Angle Theorem |
| 3. m∠$ACD$ = 75° + 45° | 3. Substitute |
| 4. m∠$ACD$ = 120° | 4. Simplify |
| 5. m∠$ACB$ + m∠$BCD$ = m∠$ACD$ | 5. Adjacent Angle Sum |
| 6. m∠$ACB$ + 60° = 120° | 6. Substitute |
| 7. m∠$ACB$ + 60° − 60° = 120° − 60° | 7. Subtraction Property of Equality |
| 8. m∠$ACB$ = 60° | 8. Simplify |
| 9. m∠$ABC$ + m∠$ACB$ + m∠$BAC$ = 180° | 9. Triangle Sum Theorem |
| 10. 60° + 60° + m∠$BAC$ = 180° | 10. Substitute |
| 11. 120° + m∠$BAC$ = 180° | 11. Simplify |
| 12. 120° + m∠$BAC$ − 120° = 180° − 120° | 12. Subtraction Property of Equality |
| 13. m∠$BAC$ = 60° | 13. Simplify |
| 14. m∠$BAC$ = m∠$ABC$ | 14. Transitive Property of Equality |

**15.** $y = 4x - 1$

$15 = 4(4) - 1$

$15 = 15$

The distance is zero because the point is on the line.

**16.** The point is 13.45 units to the left of the line $x = 11.3$. The perpendicular distance is the difference in the $x$-coordinates. The distance is 13.45 units.

**17.**

| Statements | Reasons |
|---|---|
| 1. $AB = CD$, m∠$BAE$ = m∠$DCE$ | 1. Given |
| 2. $\overline{AB} \cong \overline{CD}$ | 2. Def. ≅ line seg. |
| 3. ∠$BAE$ ≅ ∠$DCE$ | 3. Def. ≅ angles |
| 4. m∠$AEB$ = m∠$CED$ | 4. Vertical Angle Theorem |
| 5. △$ABE$ ≅ △$CDE$ | 5. AAS Congruence Theorem |

**18.** $\overline{RS}$

**19.** Angles 2 and 3 are vertical angles, so they are congruent; Since ∠1 ≅ ∠3 and ∠2 ≅ ∠3, by the Transitive Property of Congruence ∠1 ≅ ∠2; ∠1 and ∠2 are also corresponding angles, so by the Converse of the Corresponding Angles Postulate, lines $p$ and $q$ are parallel.

**20.** Since $4x$ is the longest side, it is opposite the angle with the greatest measure.

**21.** $m = \dfrac{4-3}{3 - -1} = \dfrac{1}{4}$

$y = \frac{1}{4}x + b$

$2 = \frac{1}{4}(4) + b = 1 + b$

$1 = b$; $y = \frac{1}{4}x + 1$

**22.** Given; Distributive Property; Subtraction Property of Equality; Simplify; Division Property of Equality; Simplify

**23.** The point is 4.2 units to the left of the line $x = 3$. The perpendicular distance is the difference in the $x$-coordinates. The distance is 4.2 units.

**24.** Converse: If the product of two numbers is positive, then the two numbers are positive.

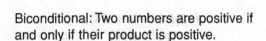

Biconditional: Two numbers are positive if and only if their product is positive.

25.

| | |
|---|---|
| $A = 4$, $b = 2x + 4$, $h = x - 1$ | Given |
| $A = \frac{bh}{2}$ | Area of a triangle |
| $\frac{(2x + 4)(x - 1)}{2} = 4$ | Substitution Property of Equality |
| $x^2 + x - 2 = 4$ | Simplify |
| $x^2 + x - 2 - 4 = 4 - 4$ | Subtraction Property of Equality |
| $x^2 + x - 6 = 0$ | Simplify |
| $(x + 3)(x - 2)$ | Factoring |
| $x - 2 = 0$ | $(x + 3) = 0$ gives a negative length |
| $x - 2 + 2 = 0 + 2$ | Addition Property of Equality |
| $x = 2$ | Simplify |

26. $\frac{x}{x + 5} = \frac{4}{9}$

$(9)(x) = (4)(x + 5)$

$9x = 4x + 20$

$5x = 20$

$x = 4$

$KL = 4$

$QR = KL + 5 = 4 + 5 = 9$

27. $x + 7 = 2(x + 1)$

$x + 7 = 2x + 2$

$5 = x$

$PC = 5 + 7 = 12$

$CM = 5 + 1 = 6$

$PM = 12 + 6 = 18$

28. **a.** True, because all angles in squares are congruent 90° angles, and since all the sides of a square have the same measure, each side of one square is proportional to the sides of another square.

**b.** False, because although all angles in rectangles and squares are congruent, the sides are not proportional (unless the rectangle is a square).

29. $11^2 = 5^2 + 8^2$

$121 = 25 + 64$

$121 > 89$

The triangle is obtuse by the Pythagorean Inequality Theorem.

30. **a.** $x^2 + x^2 = 4^2$

$2x^2 = 16$

$x = \sqrt{8} = 2\sqrt{2}$

$A = \frac{1}{2}bh = \frac{1}{2}(2\sqrt{2})(2\sqrt{2}) = \frac{1}{2}(8)$

$= 4 \text{ cm}^2$

**b.** $A = \frac{1}{2}bh = \frac{1}{2}(2)(2) = 2 \text{ cm}^2$

**c.** $A = bh = (4)(2) = 8 \text{ cm}^2$

**d.** $A = s^2 = 2^2 = 4 \text{ cm}^2$

**e.** $A = \frac{1}{2}bh = \frac{1}{2}(4)(4) = \frac{1}{2}(16) = 8 \text{ cm}^2$

## LESSON 43

### Warm Up 43

1. circumference
2. Radius; Choice **C** is correct.
3. Choice **A**, major arc and minor arc, is correct.
4. $A = \pi r^2$

$125 = \pi r^2$

$39.79 \approx r^2$

$6.31 \approx r$

The radius of the circle is 6.31 cm.

### Lesson Practice 43

**a.** $FG$ is a chord and a diameter, line $m$ is a tangent, and line $l$ is a secant.

**b.** Since the diameter is perpendicular to the chord, the chord is bisected by the diameter. So, $a = 7$.

**c.** Since the diameter bisects the chord, the chord is perpendicular to the diameter. Therefore, $x = 90°$.

d.

| Statements | Reasons |
|---|---|
| 1. $\overline{CD} \perp \overline{EF}$ | 1. Given |
| 2. $\angle CME$ and $\angle CMF$ are rt. $\angle$s | 2. Def. $\perp$ lines |
| 3. Draw radii $\overline{CE}$ and $\overline{CF}$ | 3. Two points determine a line |
| 4. $\triangle CME$ and $\triangle CMF$ are rt. $\triangle$s | 4. Def. rt. $\triangle$s |
| 5. $\overline{CE} \cong \overline{CF}$ | 5. Definition of radius |
| 6. $\overline{CM} \cong \overline{CM}$ | 6. Reflexive Property |
| 7. $\triangle CMF \cong \triangle CME$ | 7. HL Right Triangle Congruence |
| 8. $\overline{FM} \cong \overline{EM}$ | 8. CPCTC |
| 9. $\overline{CD}$ bisects $\overline{EF}$ | 9. Definition of bisector |

e.

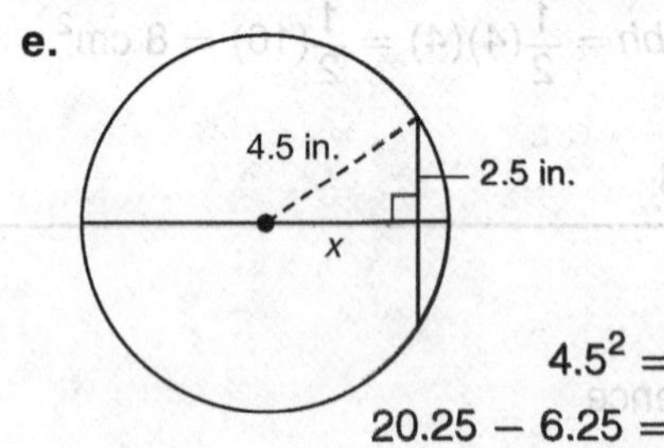


$$4.5^2 = 2.5^2 + x^2$$
$$20.25 - 6.25 = x^2$$
$$14 = x^2; 3.74 \text{ in.} \approx x$$

f.

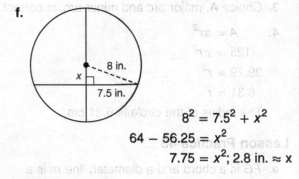

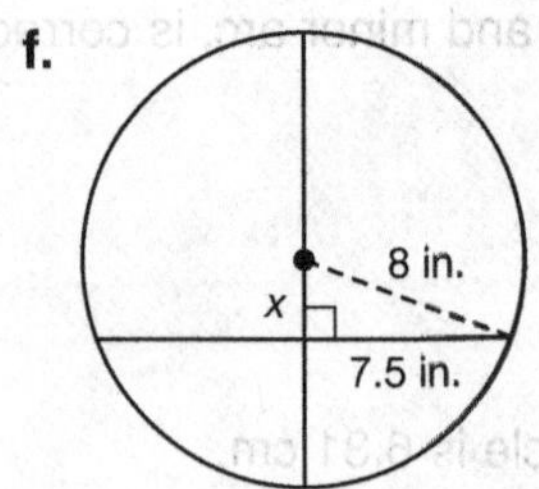


$$8^2 = 7.5^2 + x^2$$
$$64 - 56.25 = x^2$$
$$7.75 = x^2; 2.8 \text{ in.} \approx x$$

## Practice 43

1. Choice **D**, a trapezoid, is not a parallelogram.

2. Short side: $\frac{3}{12} = \frac{x}{264}$
$$(12)(x) = (3)(264)$$
$$12x = 792; x = 66 \text{ ft}$$
Middle side: $\frac{4}{12} = \frac{x}{264}$
$$(12)(x) = (4)(264)$$
$$12x = 1056$$
$$x = 88 \text{ ft}$$
Long side: $\frac{5}{12} = \frac{x}{264}$
$$(12)(x) = (5)(264)$$
$$12x = 1320$$
$$x = 110 \text{ ft}$$

3. $(4x + 10) + (5x + 2) + (x + 8) = 360°$
$$10x + 20 = 360$$
$$10x = 340$$
$$x = 34$$

4. The slope of the line perpendicular is 4.
$$y = 4x + b$$
$$-4 = 4(1) + b$$
$$-8 = b$$
$$y = 4x - 8$$
$$-0.25x + 9 = 4x - 8$$
$$-4.25x = -17$$
$$x = 4$$
$y = 4(4) - 8 = 16 - 8 = 8$
The point is (4, 8).

5. $m\widehat{NP} = m\widehat{MP} - m\widehat{MN}$
$m\widehat{NP} = 80° - 50° = 30°$

6. $\left(\frac{m\angle 1}{360°}\right)(\pi r^2) + \left(\frac{m\angle 2}{360°}\right)(\pi r^2)$
$= \left(\frac{m\angle 1 + m\angle 2}{360°}\right)(\pi r^2)$

7. $\overline{AB}$, $\overline{AC}$, and $\overline{AD}$ are chords, the lines through $\overleftrightarrow{AB}$, $\overleftrightarrow{AC}$, and $\overleftrightarrow{AD}$ are secants and $A$ is a point of tangency with the tangent line $m$.

8. $m = \frac{6 - 2}{-3 - 4} = \frac{4}{-7} = -\frac{4}{7}$
The slope of the line perpendicular will be $\frac{7}{4}$.
$$y = \frac{7}{4}x + b$$
$$2 = \frac{7}{4}(-1) + b$$
$$2 + \frac{7}{4} = b$$
$$\frac{15}{4} = b$$
$$y = \frac{7}{4}x + \frac{15}{4}$$

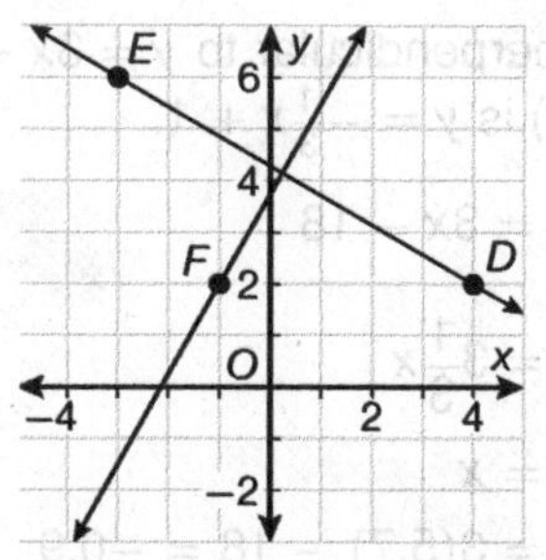


**9.** Derek did not divide the circumference, $\pi d$, by 2.

$P = 3 + 3 + 5 + \frac{1}{2}\pi(5) = (11 + 2.5\pi)$ cm

**10.** $25^2 = (4x)^2 + (3x)^2$

$625 = 16x^2 + 9x^2$

$625 = 25x^2$

$25 = x^2$

$5 = x$

$4(5) = 20$

$3(5) = 15$

The dimensions are 15 feet by 20 feet.

**11.** The medians and altitudes of a triangle are congruent only when it is an equilateral triangle.

**12.** Since the hypotenuse and an angle in each right triangle is congruent, choice **D**, the Hypotenuse-Angle Theorem, is correct.

**13.** Since the sum of the central angles is 360°, the polygon has 360 sides.

**14.**

| Statements | Reasons |
|---|---|
| $3(2x - 1) = 15$ | Given |
| $6x - 3 = 15$ | Distributive Property |
| $6x - 3 + 3 = 15 + 3$ | Addition Property of Equality |
| $6x = 18$ | Simplify |
| $\frac{6x}{6} = \frac{18}{6}$ | Division Property of Equality |
| $x = 3$ | Simplify |

**15.**

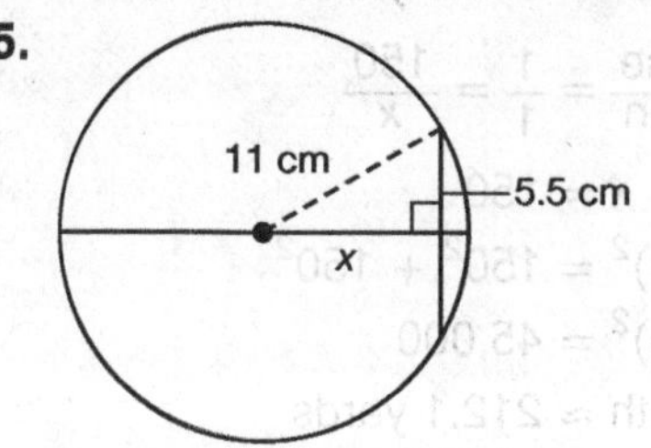


$11^2 = 5.5^2 + x^2$

$121 - 30.25 = x^2$

$90.75 = x^2$

$\sqrt{90.75} = \sqrt{30.25 \cdot 3}$

$= \sqrt{5.5^2 \cdot 3} = 5.5\sqrt{3} = x$

The exact distance from the chord to the center of the circle is $5.5\sqrt{3}$ centimeters.

**16.**

| Statements | Reasons |
|---|---|
| 1. $\overline{BE}$ is ⊥ bisector of $\overline{AC}$ at pt. $D$ | 1. Given |
| 2. $\overline{AD} \cong \overline{DC}$ | 2. Def. ⊥ bisector |
| 3. $\angle ADB$ and $\angle CDB$ are rt. ∠s | 3. Def. ⊥ bisector |
| 4. $\angle ADB \cong \angle CDB$ | 4. All rt. ∠s are ≅ |
| 5. $\overline{BD} \cong \overline{BD}$ | 5. Reflexive Property |
| 6. $\triangle ABD \cong \triangle CBD$ | 6. SAS Postulate |

**17.** The slope of the line perpendicular will be $-\frac{1}{2}$.

$y = -\frac{1}{2}x + b$

$4 = -\frac{1}{2}(4) + b; 6 = b$

$y = -\frac{1}{2}x + 6$

$-\frac{1}{2}x + 6 = 2x + 1$

$-2\frac{1}{2}x = -5; x = 2$

$y = 2(2) + 1 = 5$

The point is located at (2, 5).

**18.** Find the equation of the line that runs through the median and is perpendicular to $\overline{NP}$ and $\overline{MP}$.

$m_{NP} = \frac{8 - 4}{2 + 6} = \frac{4}{8} = \frac{1}{2}$

So, the slope of the line perpendicular to $\overline{NP}$ is −2. The midpoint of $\overline{NP}$ is (−2, 6).

$y = -2x + b$

$6 = -2(-2) + b$

$6 = 4 + b; 2 = b$

$y = -2x + 2$

$m_{MP} = \frac{4 - 2}{-6 - 2} = \frac{2}{-8} = \frac{-1}{4}$

The slope of the line perpendicular to $\overline{MP}$ is 4. The midpoint of $\overline{MP}$ is (−2, 3).

$y = 4x + b$
$3 = 4(-2) + b$
$3 = -8 + b$
$11 = b$
$y = 4x + 11$

The orthocenter is at the intersection of these two lines. To find the intersection, set the two lines equal to each other.

$4x + 11 = -2x + 2$
$6x = -9$
$x = -1.5$
$y = 4(-1.5) + 11 = -6 + 11 = 5$

The orthocenter is at (−1.5, 5).

**19.** $\frac{180°}{360°}(2\pi r) + 2r = \frac{1}{2}(2\pi r) + 2r = \pi r + 2r$

**20.** $x = 180° - 47° - 69° = 64°$
Since 47° is the smallest angle, the shortest side is opposite of the 47° angle. Targets 2 and 3 are closest together.

**21.** Hypothesis: Two planes intersect.
Conclusion: They intersect on exactly one line.

**22.** The two chords are congruent if they are the same distance from the center of the circle.

**23.** $A = \pi r^2$
$40.6 = \pi r^2$
$3.6 \approx r$
$C = 2\pi r \approx 2\pi(3.6) \approx 22.62$
$\frac{2.8}{22.62} = \frac{x}{360}$
$22.62x = (2.8)(360)$
$22.62x = 1008$
$x \approx 45°$

**24.** $(\text{Exeter})^2 = 2.2^2 + 3.4^2$
$(\text{Exeter})^2 = 4.84 + 11.56$
$(\text{Exeter})^2 = 16.4$
$\text{Exeter} \approx 4$
The distance she traveled on the detour was 2.2 + 3.4 = 5.6 miles.
5.6 − 4 = 1.6; She traveled about 1.6 miles farther on the detour.

**25.** The line perpendicular to $y = 3x + 1$ at the point (0,1) is $y = -\frac{1}{3}x + 1$.
$-\frac{1}{3}x + 1 = 3x - 18$
$19 = 3\frac{1}{3}x$
$5.7 = x$
$y = 3(5.7) - 18 = -0.9$
Find the distance between (5.7, −0.9) and (0, 1).
$d = \sqrt{(x_2 - x_1)^2 + (y_2 - y_1)^2}$
$= \sqrt{(5.7 - 0)^2 + (-0.9 - 1)^2}$
$= \sqrt{5.7^2 + (-1.9)^2}$
$= \sqrt{36.1}$
$\approx 6.01$ units

**26.** **a.** possibly
**b.** Impossible; All equilateral triangles have congruent angles and proportional sides.

**27.** Given that ∠1 and ∠2 are congruent, m∠1 = m∠2 by definition of congruent angles. m∠1 + m∠3 = 180° by the Linear Pair Theorem. By substitution, m∠2 + m∠3 = 180°. By the definition of supplementary angles, ∠2 and ∠3 are supplementary.

**28.** Green run: $\frac{\text{rise}}{\text{run}} = \frac{1}{3} = \frac{150}{x}$
$x = 450$
$(\text{length})^2 = 150^2 + 450^2$
$(\text{length})^2 = 225{,}000$
$\text{length} \approx 474.3$ yards

Blue run: $\frac{\text{rise}}{\text{run}} = \frac{1}{2} = \frac{150}{x}$
$x = 300$
$(\text{length})^2 = 150^2 + 300^2$
$(\text{length})^2 = 112{,}500$
$\text{length} \approx 335.4$ yards

Black run: $\frac{\text{rise}}{\text{run}} = \frac{1}{1} = \frac{150}{x}$
$x = 150$
$(\text{length})^2 = 150^2 + 150^2$
$(\text{length})^2 = 45{,}000$
$\text{length} \approx 212.1$ yards

29. 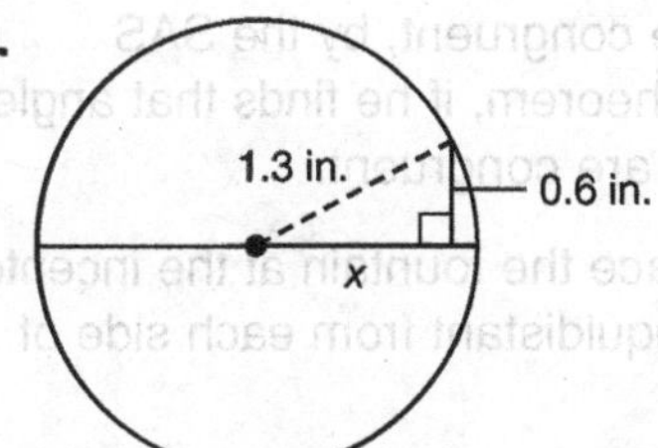


$$1.3^2 = 0.6^2 + x^2$$
$$1.69 - 0.36 = x^2$$
$$1.33 = x^2$$
$$1.15 \approx x$$

The distance from the center to the chord is 1.15 inches.

30. The longer side is $y$, since it is opposite the larger angle, with the other two corresponding pairs of sides being congruent.

## LESSON 44

### Warm Up 44

1. extremes

2. $1x + 2x + 3x = 180°$
$$6x = 180°$$
$$x = 30$$
So, $1x$, $2x$, and $3x$ are 30°, 60°, and 90°, respectively.

3. $$\frac{5}{7} = \frac{3}{2x}$$
$$(5)(2x) = (7)(3)$$
$$10x = 21$$
$$x = 2.1$$
$$\frac{5}{7} = \frac{2}{4y}$$
$$(5)(4y) = (7)(2)$$
$$20y = 14$$
$$y = 0.7$$

4. $$\frac{y}{5} = \frac{6}{4}$$
$$(4)(y) = (5)(6)$$
$$4y = 30$$
$$y = 7.5$$
$$\frac{8}{2x} = \frac{6}{4}$$
$$(6)(2x) = (8)(4)$$
$$12x = 32$$
$$x = 2.67$$

5. Choice A: $\frac{2}{4.1} = \frac{4}{8.1}$
$$(2)(8.1) = (4)(4.1)$$
$$16.2 \neq 16.4$$
Choice B: $\frac{2}{4.1} = \frac{3}{6.1}$
$$(2)(6.1) = (3)(4.1)$$
$$12.2 \neq 12.3$$
Choice C: $\frac{2}{4.1} = \frac{6}{12.3}$
$$(2)(12.3) = (6)(4.1)$$
$$24.6 = 24.6$$
Choice D: $\frac{2}{4.1} = \frac{5}{10}$
$$(2)(10) = (5)(4.1)$$
$$20 \neq 20.5$$
Choice **C** is correct.

### Lesson Practice 44

a. $$\frac{11}{33} = \frac{x}{21}$$
$$(33)(x) = (11)(21)$$
$$33x = 231$$
$$x = 7$$
$$\frac{11}{33} = \frac{y}{27}$$
$$(33)(y) = (11)(27)$$
$$33y = 297$$
$$y = 9$$

b. $$\frac{x^2 - 7}{6} = \frac{5}{15}$$
$$(15)(x^2 - 7) = (6)(5)$$
$$15x^2 - 105 = 30$$
$$15x^2 = 135$$
$$x^2 = 9$$
$$x = \pm 3$$
$$\frac{y + 4}{12} = \frac{5}{15}$$
$$(15)(y + 4) = (12)(5)$$
$$15y + 60 = 60$$
$$15y = 0$$
$$y = 0$$

 

The ratio of the perimeters of $\Delta ABC$ to $\Delta DEF$ is 11:33 or 1:3.

**c.** $\frac{3}{5} = \frac{x}{45}$

$(5)(x) = (3)(45)$

$5x = 135$

$x = 27$ inches

**d.** $\frac{2}{9} = \frac{32}{x}$

$(2)(x) = (9)(32)$

$2x = 288$

$x = 144$ cm

**e.** $\frac{4}{5} = \frac{3}{x}$

$(4)(x) = (3)(5)$

$4x = 15$

$x = 3.75$ feet tall

$\frac{4}{2} = \frac{3}{w}$

$(4)(w) = (3)(2)$

$4w = 6$

$w = 1.5$ feet wide

$P = 2(3.75) + 2(1.5) = 10.5$ feet

## Practice 44

1. $\frac{5}{15} = \frac{3}{x}$

$(5)(x) = (3)(15)$

$5x = 45$

$x = 9$

$\frac{5}{15} = \frac{4}{y}$

$(5)(y) = (4)(15)$

$5y = 60$

$y = 12$

2. 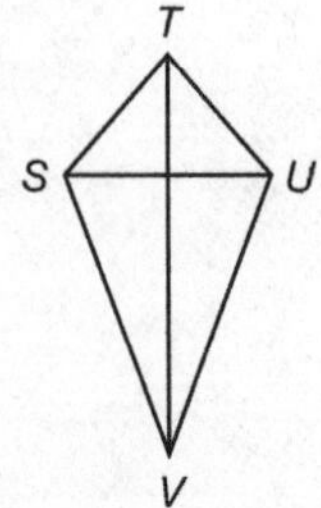


Since $\overline{TV} \cong \overline{TV}$, by the Reflexive Property, and we are given that $\overline{ST} \cong \overline{TU}$, $\Delta STV$ and $\Delta UTV$ are congruent, by the SAS Congruence Theorem, if he finds that angles $STV$ and $UTV$ are congruent.

3. She should place the fountain at the incenter because it is equidistant from each side of the triangle.

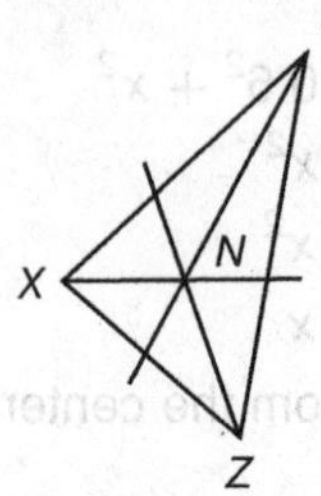


4. The sum of the squares of the lengths of the two sides of the frame should be equal to the square of the diagonal that runs between two opposite corners.

5. Diagonals of a parallelogram bisect each other. Opposite sides of a parallelogram are congruent.

6. $\frac{8}{16} = \frac{1}{2}$

1 : 2

7. **a.** The $y$-intercept, $b$, is 3.

$m = \frac{\text{rise}}{\text{run}} = \frac{-3}{3} = -1$

**b.** $y = -x + 3$

8. $\frac{1}{2} = \frac{10}{x}$

$(1)(x) = (2)(10)$

$1x = 20$

$x = 20$

The perimeter is 20 inches.

9. He is correct. $\Delta ABC \cong \Delta XYZ$ by the ASA Theorem. So, $XY = AB = 5$ by CPCTC.

10. $P = 8 + 3 + 4 + 8 + \frac{2\pi(2.5)}{2}$

$= (23 + 2.5\pi)$ inches

11. 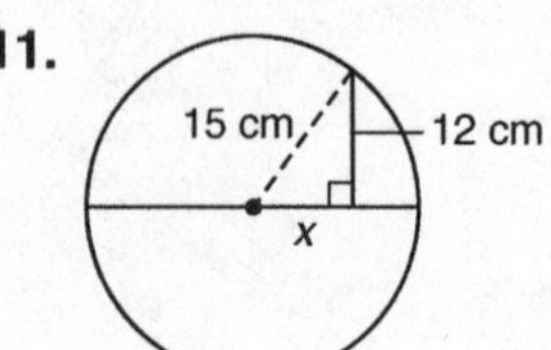

$$15^2 = 12^2 + x^2$$
$$225 - 144 = x^2$$
$$81 = x^2$$
$$9 \text{ cm} = x$$

The other part of the radius is 15 − 9 = 6 cm.

**12.** The $y$-intercept has no effect on the slope of the line.

**13.** $\frac{12}{15} = \frac{4}{5}$

4 : 5

**14.** Since 11 + 15 = 26, which is more than the largest side length given, the triangle can be created.

**15.** The slope of the line perpendicular is $-\frac{3}{2}$.

$$y = -\frac{3}{2}x + b$$
$$3 = -\frac{3}{2}(1) + b$$
$$\frac{9}{2} = b$$
$$y = -\frac{3}{2}x + \frac{9}{2}$$
$$-\frac{3}{2}x + \frac{9}{2} = \frac{2}{3}x - 2$$
$$\frac{13}{6}x = \frac{13}{2}$$
$$x = 3$$
$$y = \frac{2}{3}(3) - 2 = 2 - 2 = 0$$

The point is at (3, 0).

**16. a.** $(9x + 7)° + (42.5)° = 180°$

$$9x + 49.5 = 180$$
$$9x = 130.5$$
$$x = 14.5$$

**b.** $m\widehat{AB} = 137.5°$

$$\frac{137.5°}{360°}(2\pi(10)) \approx 24.0 \text{ cm}$$
$$\frac{222.5°}{360°}(2\pi(10)) \approx 38.8 \text{ cm}$$

**17.** $\frac{42.5°}{360°}(\pi 25^2) \approx 231.8 \text{ in.}^2$

**18.** The slope of the line perpendicular is $-\frac{2}{3}$.

$$y = -\frac{2}{3}x + b$$
$$2 = -\frac{2}{3}(-1) + b$$
$$\frac{4}{3} = b$$
$$y = -\frac{2}{3}x + \frac{4}{3}$$
$$\frac{3}{2}x - 3 = -\frac{2}{3}x + \frac{4}{3}$$
$$\frac{13}{6}x = \frac{13}{3};\ x = 2$$
$$y = -\frac{2}{3}(2) + \frac{4}{3} = -\frac{4}{3} + \frac{4}{3} = 0$$

Find the distance between (2, 0) and (−1, 2).

$$d = \sqrt{(x_2 - x_1)^2 + (y_2 - y_1)^2}$$
$$= \sqrt{(2 - -1)^2 + (0 - 2)^2}$$
$$= \sqrt{3^2 + (-2)^2}$$
$$= \sqrt{13}$$
$$\approx 3.61 \text{ units}$$

**19.** $(n - 2)180° = 1710°$

$$n - 2 = 9.5;\ n = 11.5$$

The polygon would need 11.5 sides, which is impossible.

**20.** $6.2^2 = 3.6^2 + 4.8^2$

$$38.44 = 12.96 + 23.04$$
$$38.44 > 36$$

The triangle is obtuse.

**21.** The chords are congruent. Therefore, $x$ is half of 12 or 6 units.

**22.** Draw a triangle with each school at a vertex. Find the perpendicular bisectors of all three sides of the triangle to find the circumcenter of the triangle. Since it is equidistant from all three vertices, the circumcenter is the optimal location for the emergency siren.

**23.** $\frac{2.5}{9} = \frac{BC}{12.8}$

$$(9)(BC) = (2.5)(12.8)$$
$$9BC = 32$$
$$BC \approx 3.6 \text{ centimeters}$$

Choice **D** is correct.

**24.** $(n-2)180° = 1260°$
$n-2 = 7$
$n = 9$ sides

**25.** $x^2 = 140^2 + 90^2$
$x^2 = 19{,}600 + 8100$
$x^2 = 27{,}700$
$x \approx 166$ yds
The length of the diagonal is approximately 166 yards.
The distance around the edge of the field is 140 + 90 = 230 yards. This is about 230 − 166 = 64 yards longer than the diagonal.

**26.** $\frac{3}{1} = \frac{45}{x}$
$(3)(x) = (1)(45)$
$3x = 45$
$x = 15$
The perimeter of $\triangle VWX$ is 15 inches. Therefore, each side is 5 inches long.

**27. a.** $x^2 = 15^2 + 8^2$
$x^2 = 225 + 64$
$x^2 = 289$
$x = 17$ cm

**b.** $P = 3(17) + 3(15) + 3(8)$
$= 51 + 45 + 24$
$= 120$ cm

**c.** $A = lw + lw + lw + \frac{1}{2}bh$
$= (15)(15) + (17)(17) + (8)(8) + \frac{1}{2}(8)(15)$
$= 225 + 289 + 64 + 60$
$= 638 \text{ cm}^2$

**28.** $m_p = \frac{3-7}{4-4} = \frac{-4}{0}$; undefined
$m_q = \frac{1-1}{5--2} = \frac{0}{7} = 0$
Since one line is horizontal and the other is vertical, the lines are perpendicular.

**29.** $m\angle P = 180° - 70° - 80° = 30°$

**30.** $\overline{JI}$ is a chord. $\overline{FD}$, $\overline{FI}$, and $\overline{FJ}$ are radii. $\overline{JI}$ is a diameter. $\overline{GH}$ is a chord. The lines through $\overline{GH}$ and $\overline{JI}$ are secants, and $D$ is a point of tangency with the tangent line $\overleftrightarrow{DE}$.

## LESSON 45

### Warm Up 45

1. distance
2. Find the distance between (1, 3) and (4, 2).
$d = \sqrt{(x_2 - x_1)^2 + (y_2 - y_1)^2}$
$= \sqrt{(1-4)^2 + (3-2)^2}$
$= \sqrt{(-3)^2 + 1^2}$
$= \sqrt{10}$
$\approx 3.2$
3. midpoint
$= \left(\frac{x_1 + x_2}{2}, \frac{y_1 + y_2}{2}\right)$
$= \left(\frac{3+5}{2}, \frac{-1+7}{2}\right)$
$= \left(\frac{8}{2}, \frac{6}{2}\right) = (4, 3)$
4. $m = \frac{-3-4}{2--1} = \frac{-7}{3}$
5. Find the distance between (0, 0) and (3, 4).
$d = \sqrt{(x_2 - x_1)^2 + (y_2 - y_1)^2}$
$= \sqrt{(3-0)^2 + (4-0)^2}$
$= \sqrt{3^2 + 4^2}$
$= \sqrt{25}$
$= 5$ units

### Lesson Practice 45

**a.**

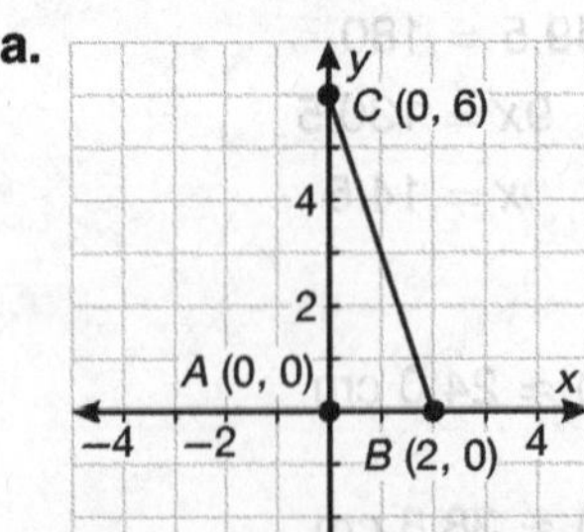


**b.** Proofs will vary, but should show that $JK = KL$, so the triangle is isosceles. For example, find the length of $JK$ and $KL$.
$d_{JK} = \sqrt{(1-0)^2 + (1-0)^2}$

$= \sqrt{1^2 + 1^2}$

$= \sqrt{2}$

$d_{KL} = \sqrt{(1 - 2)^2 + (1 - 0)^2}$

$= \sqrt{(-1)^2 + 1^2}$

$= \sqrt{2}$

**c.**

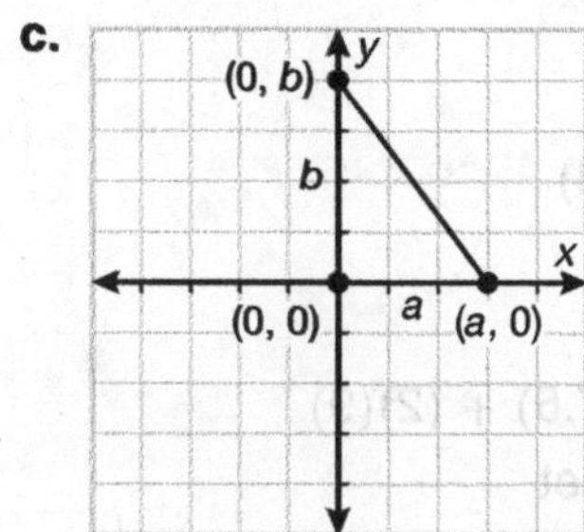


**d.** Proofs will vary, but should show that opposite sides are of equal length or parallel. For example,

$d_{UV} = \sqrt{(-3 - 3)^2 + (5 - 5)^2}$

$= \sqrt{(-6)^2 + 0^2}$

$= \sqrt{36}$

$= 6$

$d_{TW} = \sqrt{(0 - 6)^2 + (0 - 0)^2}$

$= \sqrt{(-6)^2 + 0^2}$

$= \sqrt{36}$

$= 6$

$d_{UT} = \sqrt{(-3 - 0)^2 + (5 - 0)^2}$

$= \sqrt{(-3)^2 + 5^2}$

$= \sqrt{34}$

$d_{VW} = \sqrt{(3 - 6)^2 + (5 - 0)^2}$

$= \sqrt{(-3)^2 + 5^2}$

$= \sqrt{34}$

Since $UV = TW$ and $UT = VW$, $TUVW$ is a parallelogram.

**e.**

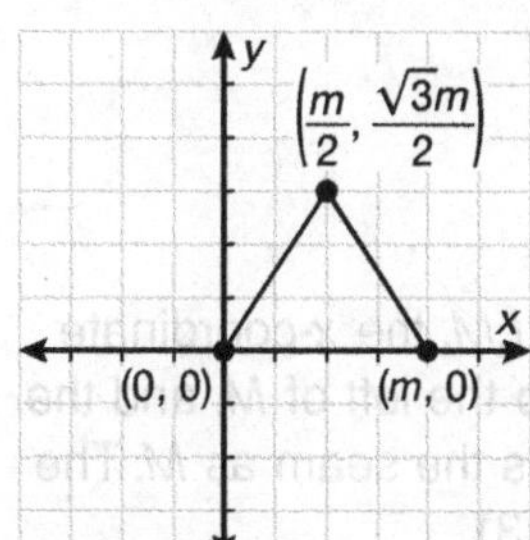


## Practice 45

**1.** Possible answers: (2, 2), (0, 4), (−4, 0), or (−2, −2)

**2.** $\frac{5}{3} = \frac{30}{x - 11}$

$(5)(x - 11) = (3)(30)$

$5x - 55 = 90$

$5x = 145$

$x = 29$

**3.** $7x + 3.2 = 3x + 10$

$4x = 6.8$

$x = 1.7$

**4.** $10y - 4.9 = (0.5)(30.2)$

$10y - 4.9 = 15.1$

$10y = 20$

$y = 2$

**5.** The slope of the line perpendicular is $-\frac{4}{5}$.

$y = -\frac{4}{5}x + b$

$5 = -\frac{4}{5}(-1) + b$

$\frac{21}{5} = b$

$y = -\frac{4}{5}x + \frac{21}{5}$

$-\frac{4}{5}x + \frac{21}{5} = \frac{5}{4}x - 4$

$-\frac{41}{20}x = -\frac{41}{5}$

$x = 4$

$y = \frac{5}{4}(4) - 4 = 5 - 4 = 1$

Find the distance between (4, 1) and (−1, 5).

$d = \sqrt{(x_2 - x_1)^2 + (y_2 - y_1)^2}$

$= \sqrt{(4 - -1)^2 + (1 - 5)^2}$

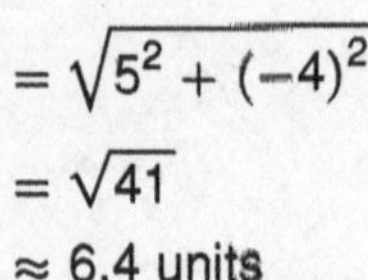



$= \sqrt{5^2 + (-4)^2}$
$= \sqrt{41}$
$\approx 6.4$ units

6. In order for $KN = LM$, the $x$-coordinate of $L$ is four units to the left of $M$, and the $y$-coordinate of $L$ is the seam as $M$. The coordinate is $L(2, 3)$.

7. $\frac{60°}{360°}(2(3.14)(30)) = 31.4$ cm

8. Yes, diagonals of parallelograms bisect each other. No, not enough is known about the shape's angle measures, so more information is needed to classify the shape as a rectangle.

9.

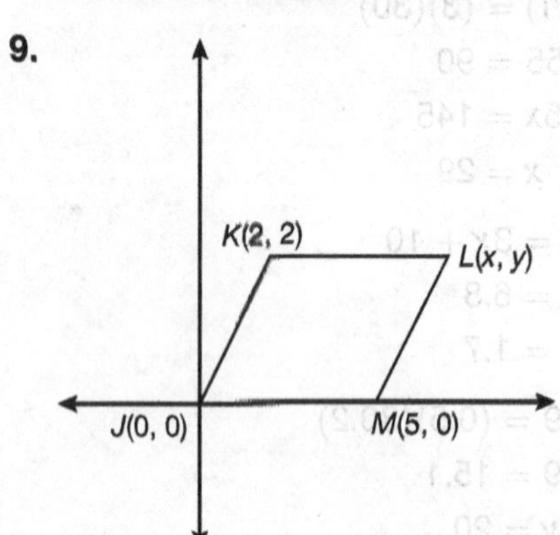


$L(7, 2)$

10. $m\angle A = m\angle X = 77°$
$m\angle Y = m\angle B = 53°$

11. $\frac{16.4}{10.8} = \frac{10.25}{6.75}$
$(16.4)(6.75) = (10.8)(10.25)$
$110.7 = 110.7$
They are similar.
$\frac{10.25}{16.4} = \frac{5}{8}$ or $\frac{16.4}{10.25} = \frac{8}{5}$
The similarity ratio is $\frac{5}{8}$ or $\frac{8}{5}$.

12. $A = ((16)(22) + \frac{1}{2}(22)(5)) - (3(6)(3) + (3)(7))$
$= 407 - 75$
$= 332 \text{ ft}^2$

13. a. $A = 2\left(\left(\frac{1}{2}\right)(14 + 8)(6)\right) + (9)(21)$
$= 321 \text{ cm}^2$

b. Wasted $= (21)(21) - 321$
$= 120 \text{ cm}^2$

14. Width: $\frac{5}{w} = \frac{2}{3}$
$(2)(w) = (5)(3)$
$2w = 15$
$w = 7.5$
Length: $\frac{6}{l} = \frac{2}{3}$
$(2)(l) = (6)(3)$
$2l = 18$
$l = 9$
$P = (2)(7.5) + (2)(9)$
$= 33$ feet

15. Since the remaining angle of this triangle is 60°, the smallest angle is 48° and the 5.5-ft length is the smallest. The 7-ft side is opposite the largest angle, so the piece of wood needed for the unknown side should be somewhere between 5.5 ft and 7 ft.

16. $\frac{10}{4} = \frac{5}{2}$
5:2

17. $(n-2)(180°) = (7-2)(180°)$
$5(180°) = 900°$
$\frac{900°}{7} \approx 128.57°$

18. $2y + 4 = 6x - 5$
$2y = 6x - 9$
$y = 3x - \frac{9}{2}$
The slope of the line parallel to this line is 3 and the $y$-intercept is zero since it passes through the origin.
$y = 3x$

19. $k$ can be any real number (except 3, which would make it the same line). Changing the $y$-intercept only shifts the entire line vertically. It does not change the slope of the line, so the lines will remain parallel.

20. For each pair of right triangles, hypotenuses and one acute angle pair are congruent, because the other acute

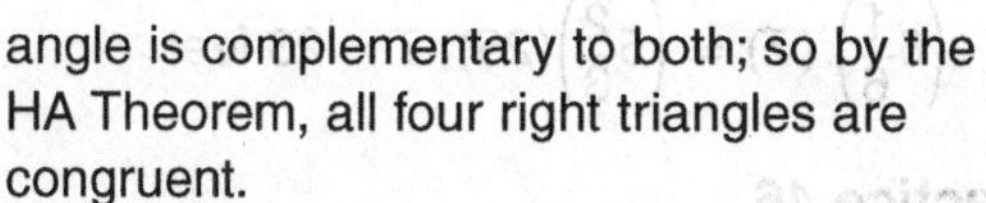



angle is complementary to both; so by the HA Theorem, all four right triangles are congruent.

**21.** No, the possible values of $x$ do not make the measures of the SAS shown equal. For example,

$x + 3 = 2x - 1$

$4 = x$

So, when $x = 4$, check

$16x + 8 = 18x$

$16(4) + 8 = 18(4)$

$72 = 72$

and,

$4x - 8 = 3x - 6$

$4(4) - 8 = 3(4) - 6$

$8 \neq 6$

**22.** By side length, the triangle is scalene because none of the sides are congruent. By angles, the triangle is obtuse.

$265^2 = 240^2 + 100^2$

$70{,}225 = 57{,}600 + 10{,}000$

$70{,}225 > 67{,}600$

**23.**

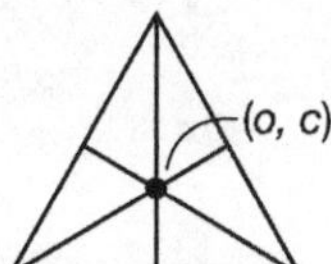


They are in the same location.

**24.** $(n - 2)180° = (8 - 2)180° = 1080°$

**25.**

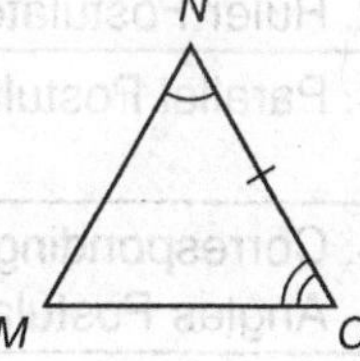


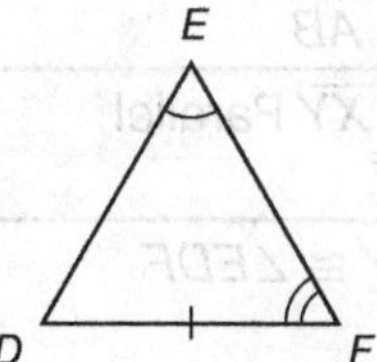


No, $\overline{NO}$ and $\overline{DF}$ are not corresponding sides for the angles given to be equal.

**26.**

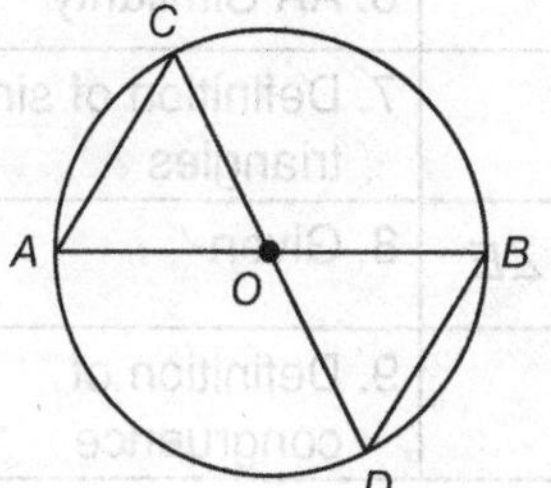


| Statements | Reasons |
|---|---|
| 1. $\overline{AB}$ and $\overline{CD}$ are diameters. | 1. Given |
| 2. $\overline{AO}$, $\overline{BO}$, $\overline{CO}$, and $\overline{DO}$ are all radii. | 2. Definition of radii |
| 3. $\overline{AO} \cong \overline{BO} \cong \overline{CO} \cong \overline{DO}$ | 3. Definition of radii |
| 4 $\angle AOC \cong \angle BOD$ | 4. Vertical Angles Theorem |
| 5. $\Delta AOC \cong \Delta BOD$ | 5. SAS Congruence Theorem |

**27.** $\angle IFG = 180° - 76° = 104°$

$\angle FGH = \angle HIF = 76°$

$\angle HGE = 180° - 76° = 104°$

**28.** Proofs will vary but should show that the distance between the midpoint of the hypotenuse and each vertex is equal. For example,

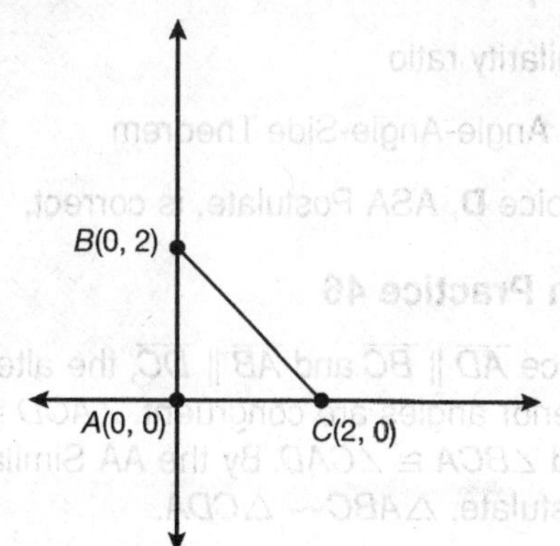


The midpoint, $m$, of the hypotenuse is

$\left(\frac{x_1 + x_2}{2}, \frac{y_1 + y_2}{2}\right)$

$= \left(\frac{2 + 0}{2}, \frac{0 + 2}{2}\right)$

$= \left(\frac{2}{2}, \frac{2}{2}\right) = (1, 1)$

$d_{mA} = \sqrt{(1 - 0)^2 + (1 - 0)^2}$

$= \sqrt{1^2 + 1^2}$

$= \sqrt{2}$

$d_{mB} = \sqrt{(1 - 0)^2 + (1 - 2)^2}$

$= \sqrt{1^2 + (-1)^2}$

$= \sqrt{2}$

$$d_{mC} = \sqrt{(1-2)^2 + (1-0)^2}$$
$$= \sqrt{(-1)^2 + 1^2} = \sqrt{2}$$

**29.** $(2x+10) + (4x+5) = (x+19) + (2x+11)$
$$6x + 15 = 3x + 30$$
$$3x = 15$$
$$x = 5$$
$m\widehat{AB} = 2(5) + 10 = 20°$
$m\widehat{BC} = 4(5) + 5 = 25°$
$m\widehat{AC} = 20° + 25° = 45°$
$m\widehat{XY} = 5 + 19 = 24°$
$m\widehat{YZ} = 2(5) + 11 = 21°$
$m\widehat{XZ} = 24° + 21° = 45°$

**30.** Choice **C** is correct.

## LESSON 46

### Warm Up 46

1. similarity ratio
2. the Angle-Angle-Side Theorem
3. Choice **D**, ASA Postulate, is correct.

### Lesson Practice 46

**a.** Since $\overline{AD} \parallel \overline{BC}$ and $\overline{AB} \parallel \overline{DC}$, the alternate interior angles are congruent. $\angle ACD \cong \angle CAB$ and $\angle BCA \cong \angle CAD$. By the AA Similarity Postulate, $\triangle ABC \sim \triangle CDA$.

**b.** Since $\frac{5}{8} = \frac{16}{25.6} = \frac{9}{14.4}$, the triangles are similar by SSS.

**c.** Since $\frac{4}{8} = \frac{5}{10}$, the triangles have two pairs of proportional sides. $\angle ACB \cong \angle DCE$ since they are vertical angles, so the two triangles are congruent by SAS similarity.
$$\frac{4}{8} = \frac{2x+3}{13}$$
$$(8)(2x+3) = (4)(13)$$
$$16x + 24 = 52$$
$$16x = 28$$
$$x = 1.75$$

**d.** $$\frac{5\frac{2}{3}}{6\frac{1}{6}} = \frac{T}{25}$$
$$\left(6\frac{1}{6}\right)(T) = \left(5\frac{2}{3}\right)(25);\ T \approx 23 \text{ feet}$$

### Practice 46

1. Since $x = 3$ is a vertical line, the distance is 4.
2. Find the distance between $(-220, 80)$ and $(100, -400)$.
$$d = \sqrt{(x_2 - x_1)^2 + (y_2 - y_1)^2}$$
$$= \sqrt{(100 - -220)^2 + (-400 - 80)^2}$$
$$= \sqrt{320^2 + (-480)^2}$$
$$= \sqrt{332{,}800} \approx 577 \text{ miles}$$
3. $$\frac{18.3}{24.6} = \frac{24.4}{32.8}$$
$$(18.3)(32.8) = (24.6)(24.4)$$
$$600.24 = 600.24$$
They are similar.
$$\frac{18.3}{24.4} = \frac{3}{4}$$
The similarity ratio is $\frac{3}{4}$ or $\frac{4}{3}$.
4. $y = 7$ is a horizontal line. When Choice C is simplified to $y = -7$, it is also a horizontal line. Choice **C** is correct.
5. $\frac{360°}{8} = 45°$
6.

| Statements | Reasons |
|---|---|
| 1. $AB < DE$ | 1. Assumed |
| 2. $\overline{XE} \cong \overline{AB}$ | 2. Ruler Postulate |
| 3. Draw $\overline{XY}$ Parallel to $\overline{DF}$. | 3. Parallel Postulate |
| 4. $\angle EXY \cong \angle EDF$ | 4. Corresponding Angles Postulate |
| 5. $\angle E \cong \angle E$ | 5. Reflexive Property of Congruence |
| 6. $\triangle XEY \sim \triangle DEF$ | 6. AA Similarity |
| 7. $\frac{XE}{DE} = \frac{EY}{EF}$ | 7. Definition of similar triangles |
| 8. $\frac{AB}{DE} = \frac{BC}{EF}$, $\angle B \cong \angle E$ | 8. Given |
| 9. $XE = AB$ | 9. Definition of congruence |

| 10. $\frac{XE}{DE} = \frac{BC}{EF}$ | 10. Substitute |
|---|---|
| 11. $\frac{BC}{EF} = \frac{EY}{EF}$ | 11. Trans. Prop. Equality |
| 12. $BC = EY$ | 12. Mult. Prop. Equality |
| 13. $\overline{BC} \cong \overline{EY}$ | 13. Def. of congruence |
| 14. $\triangle ABC \cong \triangle XEY$ | 14. SAS Congruence Postulate |
| 15. $\triangle ABC \sim \triangle XEY$ | 15. Definition of similarity |
| 16. $\triangle ABC \sim \triangle DEF$ | 16. Transitive Property of Equality |

**7.** It is a trapezoid since it has exactly one pair of parallel sides.

**8.** $\frac{3}{12} = \frac{6}{x}$

$(3)(x) = (12)(6)$

$3x = 72$; $x = 24$ feet

**9.** $\frac{25}{15} = \frac{5}{3}$; 5:3

**10.** $x^2 = 120^2 - 119^2$

$x^2 = 14{,}400 - 14{,}161$

$x^2 = 239$; $x \approx 15.5$ meters

**11.** $-3 < x < -2$ or $2 < x < 3$

**12.** $(3x)^2 = 15^2 - 12^2$

$(3x)^2 = 225 - 144$

$(3x)^2 = 81$

$3x = 9$

$x = 3$

**13.** Sample: (0, 0), (6, 0), (6, 6), (0, 6)

**14.** A tangent line intersects the circle at only one point. A secant intersects the circle at two points.

**15.** $x^2 = 9^2 + 12^2$

$x^2 = 81 + 144$

$x^2 = 225$; $x = 15$ inches

**16.** $\triangle HJK$ and $\triangle LMN$ are right triangles. $\overline{HJ} \cong \overline{LM}$ and $\overline{HK} \cong \overline{LN}$. By the LL Congruence Theorem, $\triangle HJK \cong \triangle LMN$.

**17.** $\frac{12}{16} = \frac{x}{20}$

$(16)(x) = (12)(20)$

$16x = 240$

$x = 15$

**18.** Sample: (0, 3), (−4, 0), (4, 0)

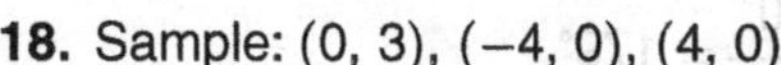

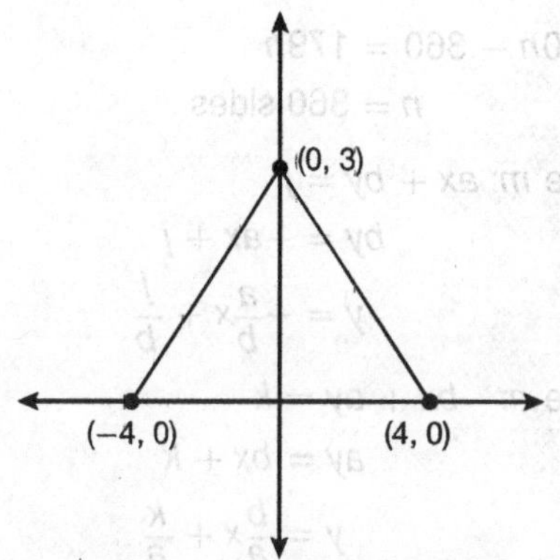


$d_1 = \sqrt{(-4-0)^2 + (0-3)^2}$

$= \sqrt{(-4)^2 + (-3)^2}$

$= \sqrt{25}$

$= 5$

$d_2 = \sqrt{(4-0)^2 + (0-3)^2}$

$= \sqrt{4^2 + (-3)^2}$

$= \sqrt{25}$

$= 5$

**19.** Since $x$ is opposite the longer side, with the other two sides being congruent, $x$ is larger.

**20.** $\frac{25}{40} = \frac{5}{8}$

**21.** $\angle JGK \cong \angle HGF$ by the Vertical Angle Theorem. $\angle J \cong \angle H$ because they are alternate interior angles. So, $\triangle GKJ \sim \triangle GFH$ by AA Similarity.

$\frac{8}{12} = \frac{x}{11}$

$(12)(x) = (8)(11)$

$12x = 88$

$x \approx 7.3$

**22.** This is a list of palindromes (words that spell the same word forwards and backwards) that increase by one letter each entry.

**23.** $(RV)^2 = 10^2 - 6^2$
$(RV)^2 = 100 - 36$
$(RV)^2 = 64$
$RV = 8$

**24.** $\frac{(n-2)180^\circ}{n} = 179^\circ$
$180n - 360 = 179n$
$n = 360$ sides

**25.** Line $m$: $ax + by = j$
$by = -ax + j$
$y = -\frac{a}{b}x + \frac{j}{b}$
Line $n$: $-bx + ay = k$
$ay = bx + k$
$y = \frac{b}{a}x + \frac{k}{a}$
The slopes of the lines are the negative reciprocal of each other. They are perpendicular.

**26.** $\frac{88^\circ}{360^\circ}(2\pi(6.2)) \approx 9.52$ cm

**27.** $\frac{11^\circ}{360^\circ}(2\pi(122)) \approx 23.42$ cm

**28.** $\frac{4x+3}{11} = \frac{\frac{2}{3}}{\frac{1}{3}}$
$\frac{4}{3}x + 1 = \frac{22}{3}$
$\frac{4}{3}x = \frac{19}{3}$
$x = \frac{19}{4} = 4.75$
$3x + 14 = \frac{2}{3}(CY)$
$3(4.75) + 14 = \frac{2}{3}(CY)$
$28.25 = \frac{2}{3}(CY)$
$42.375 = CY$

**29.** Since $\angle T$ and $\angle W$ are right angles, $\triangle RST$ and $\triangle UVW$ are right triangles. $\overline{RT} \cong \overline{UW}$ and $\overline{ST} \cong \overline{VW}$. By the LL Congruence Theorem, $\triangle RST \cong \triangle UVW$.

**30.** $\frac{AB}{DE} = \frac{BC}{EF} = \frac{CA}{FD}$ = similarity ratio
Cross-multiply to find the values of the unknown sides.

## LESSON 47

### Warm Up 47

1. interior
2. Choice **B** is correct.
3. semicircle

### Lesson Practice 47

**a.** Proofs may vary. Sample: It is given that $\angle ADB$ and $\angle ACB$ are inscribed angles. Call the measure of $\widehat{AB}$ $x^\circ$. By Theorem 47-1, both m$\angle ADB$ and m$\angle ACB$ must equal one-half of $x$. By the Transitive Property, m$\angle ADB$ = m$\angle ACB$. Therefore, $\angle ADB \cong \angle ACB$ by the definition of congruence.

**b.** $2y + 90 = 180$
$2y = 90$
$y = 45^\circ$

**c.** $2x + 10 = 3x - 7$
$x = 17$

**d.** $(x + 16) + (x - 18) = 180$
$2x - 2 = 180$
$2x = 182$
$x = 91$
$\angle A = 91 + 16 = 107^\circ$

**e.** $m\angle LMP = m\angle LON = 27^\circ$
$m\angle MPO = \frac{1}{2}(m\widehat{MO})$
$= \frac{1}{2}(94^\circ)$
$= 47^\circ$
$m\angle MLP = 180^\circ - 27^\circ - 47^\circ$
$= 106^\circ$

## Practice 47

1.

| Statements | Reasons |
|---|---|
| 1. *ABCD* is inscribed in a circle. | 1. Given |
| 2. $m\angle A = \frac{1}{2}m\widehat{BCD}$, $m\angle C = \frac{1}{2}m\widehat{DAB}$ | 2. The measure of an inscribed angle is equal to half the measure of its intercepted arc. |
| 3. $m\angle A + m\angle C = \frac{1}{2}m\widehat{BCD} + \frac{1}{2}m\widehat{DAB}$ | 3. Addition Property of Equality |
| 4. $m\angle A + m\angle C = \frac{1}{2}(m\widehat{BCD} + m\widehat{DAB})$ | 4. Factor |
| 5. $m\widehat{BCD} + m\widehat{DAB} = 360°$ | 5. Arc Addition Postulate |
| 6. $m\angle A + m\angle C = \frac{1}{2}(360°)$ | 6. Substitution |
| 7. $m\angle A + m\angle C = 180°$ | 7. Simplify |
| 8. $\angle A$ is supplementary to $\angle C$ | 8. Definition of supplementary angles |

2. $\frac{2}{9} = \frac{x}{45}$

$(9)(x) = (2)(45)$

$9x = 90; x = 10$

$\frac{3}{9} = \frac{x}{45}$

$(9)(x) = (3)(45)$

$9x = 135; x = 15$

$\frac{4}{9} = \frac{x}{45}$

$(9)(x) = (4)(45)$

$9x = 180; x = 20$

The cable lengths are 10 inches, 15 inches, and 20 inches, respectively.

3. Since opposite angles are supplementary, $\angle A + \angle C = 180°$ and $\angle B + \angle D = 180°$.

4. No; This will only be enough tape if the third side is less than or equal to 4 feet. However, if the third side is 4 feet long, then by Triangle Inequality Theorem, the side lengths 4, 14, 22 cannot form a triangle.

5.

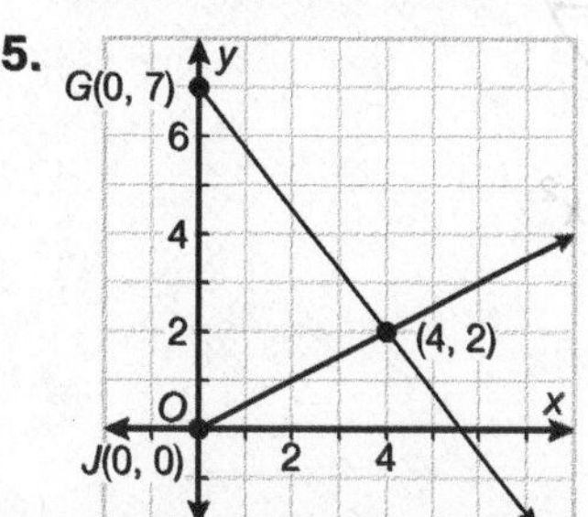


6. $P = 5s$. Since the figure has only 5 sides, the equilateral triangle and the square must fit exactly along one side. So, the triangle's side length must also be *s*. Hence each of the 5 sides has a length of *s*.

7. $\frac{8}{x-4} = \frac{20}{x+3.5}$

$(8)(x + 3.5) = (20)(x - 4)$

$8x + 28 = 20x - 80$

$108 = 12x$

$x = 9$

8. $\frac{\frac{3}{4}}{\frac{5}{8}} = \frac{3}{4} \times \frac{8}{5} = \frac{6}{5}$

6:5

9. No, the corresponding parts are not congruent.

10. a. $P = 34 + 48 + 34 + 24 + 24 + \frac{2\pi(24)}{4}$

$= (164 + 12\pi)$ mm

b. $A = (34)(48) + (24)(24) + \frac{\pi(24)^2}{4}$

$= (2208 + 144\pi)$ mm$^2$

11. The measure of one of the angles is 90°.

12. Sample: 8, 15, 17

$17^2 = 15^2 + 8^2$

$289 = 225 + 64$

$289 = 289$

13. Converse of the Corresponding Angles Postulate, Converse of the Alternate Exterior Angles Theorem; Vertical Angles are congruent.

14.

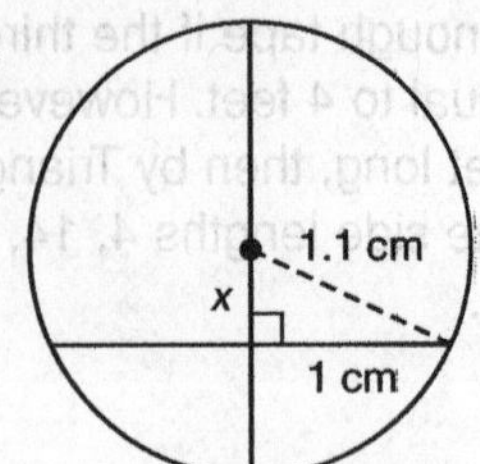


$$1.1^2 = 1^2 + x^2$$
$$1.21 - 1 = x^2$$
$$0.21 = x^2$$
$$0.46 \text{ cm} \approx x$$

15. $\frac{(7-2)180°}{7} \approx 129°$

16.

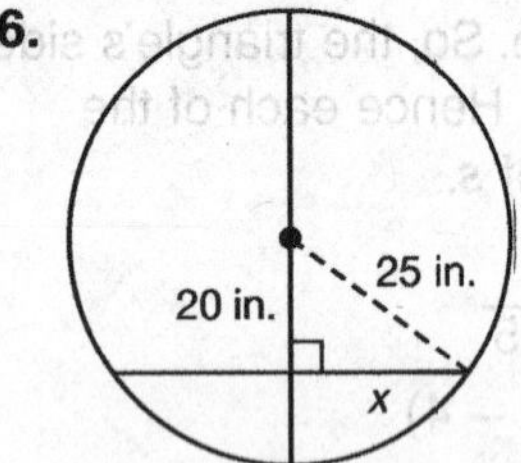


$$x^2 = 25^2 - 20^2$$
$$x^2 = 625 - 400$$
$$x^2 = 225$$
$$x = 15$$
$$CE = 2x = 2(15) = 30 \text{ inches}$$

17. a. The month is not April.
b. It is not spring in the Northern Hemisphere.
c. If it is no spring in the Northern Hemisphere, then the month is not April.

18. $\angle E$ is equal to 77°, which is smaller than the 79° in $\Delta ABC$, so $\overline{DF}$ is shorter than $\overline{AC}$. Therefore, Rosalba is incorrect.

19. They are perpendicular because their slopes are negative reciprocals of each other.

20. $8a - 9 = 7a + 1$
$$a = 10$$
$$m\angle ZWY = 8(10) - 9 = 71°$$

21. $\frac{2}{y-3} = \frac{4}{y}$
$$(4)(y-3) = (2)(y)$$
$$4y - 12 = 2y$$
$$-12 = -2y$$
$$6 = y$$

22. $\left(\frac{k}{2}, \frac{k}{2}\right), \left(-\frac{k}{2}, -\frac{k}{2}\right), \left(-\frac{k}{2}, \frac{k}{2}\right), \left(\frac{k}{2}, -\frac{k}{2}\right)$

23. $x^2 = 40^2 + 30^2$
$$x^2 = 1600 + 900$$
$$x^2 = 2500$$
$$x = 50$$

24.

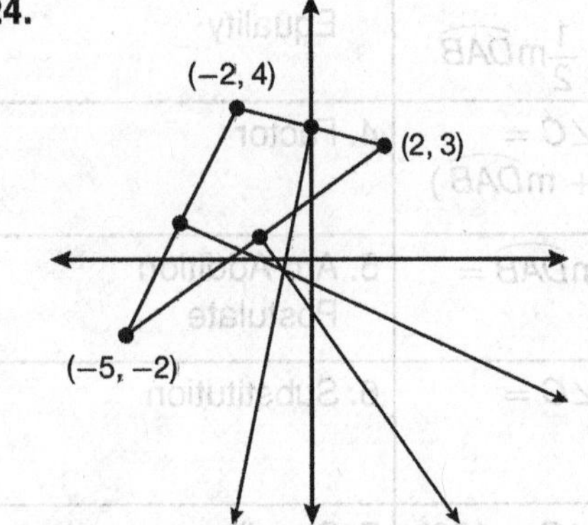


The circumcenter appears to be approximately (−1, −0.25).

25. No, because $\angle XYZ$ is not the included angle in $\Delta XYZ$.

26. $\angle A \cong \angle D$ and $\angle B \cong \angle E$, so $\Delta ABC \sim \Delta DEF$ by AA Similarity.
$$\frac{6}{12} = \frac{6.97}{EF}$$
$$(6)(EF) = (12)(6.97)$$
$$6EF = 83.64$$
$$EF = 13.94$$

27. $\frac{3}{18} = \frac{x}{180}$
$$(18)(x) = (3)(180)$$
$$18x = 540$$
$$x = 30$$
$$\frac{5}{18} = \frac{x}{180}$$
$$(18)(x) = (5)(180)$$
$$18x = 900$$
$$x = 50$$

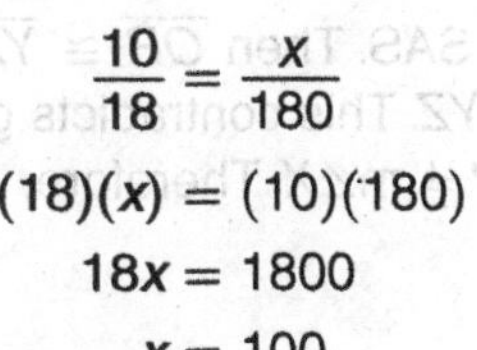

$$\frac{10}{18} = \frac{x}{180}$$
$$(18)(x) = (10)(180)$$
$$18x = 1800$$
$$x = 100$$

The measures of the angles are 30°, 50°, and 100°, respectively.

**28.** The HL Congruence Theorem applies because we know that the hypotenuses and one leg are congruent.

**29.** Choice **A,** half, is correct.

**30.**
$$\frac{1.25}{5} = \frac{3.25}{3.25 + x}$$
$$(1.25)(3.25 + x) = (5)(3.25)$$
$$4.0625 + 1.25x = 16.25$$
$$1.25x = 12.1875$$
$$DE = x = 9.75$$

## LESSON 48

### Warm Up 48

1. flowchart proof
2. False; A counterexample helps to prove a statement false.
3. All of these are types of proofs except for Choice D, a flow proof. Choice **D** is correct.

### Lesson Practice 48

**a.** Assume $m\angle X \neq m\angle Y$.

**b.** $\overleftrightarrow{AB}$ is not perpendicular to $\overleftrightarrow{CB}$.

**c.** Case I: An isosceles triangle has all side lengths equal.
Case II: An isosceles triangle has no sides of equal length.

**d.** Assume that a triangle has more than one right angle. If, in $\triangle ABC$, $\angle A$ and $\angle B$ are right angles, then they each measure 90°. By the Triangle Angle Sum Theorem, $\angle A + \angle B + \angle C = 180°$. By substitution, $90° + 90° + \angle C = 180°$ or $\angle C = 0°$. This contradicts the definition of an angle, so a triangle cannot have more than one right angle.

**e.** Assume that $\angle 4$ is not congruent to $\angle 6$. Since $m \parallel n$ and the corresponding angles formed by a transversal are congruent, $\angle 1 \cong \angle 5$. From the diagram, $\angle 1$ is a linear pair with $\angle 4$, and $\angle 5$ is a linear pair with $\angle 6$. Therefore, $\angle 1$ and $\angle 4$ are supplementary and $\angle 5$ and $\angle 6$ are supplementary. Since $\angle 1 \cong \angle 5$, both $\angle 4$ and $\angle 6$ are supplementary to $\angle 1$. This contradicts the assumption, because angles that are supplementary to the same angle are congruent to each other.

### Practice 48

**1.** See student work. For example, points (0, −4) and (1, −1)

$$m = \frac{-4 - -1}{0 - 1} = \frac{-3}{-1} = 3$$

**2.**

| Statements | Reasons |
|---|---|
| 1. $AD \parallel BC$, $AB \parallel DC$ | 1. Given |
| 2. $\angle ADB \cong \angle CBD$ | 2. Alternate Interior Angles Theorem |
| 3. $\overline{DB} \cong \overline{BD}$ | 3. Symmetric Property of Congruence |
| 4. $\angle ABD \cong \angle CDB$ | 4. Alternate Interior Angles Theorem |
| 5. $\triangle ADB \cong \triangle CBD$ | 5. ASA Postulate |
| 6. $\overline{AD} \cong \overline{CB}$ | 6. CPCTC |
| 7. $AD = CB$ | 7. Def. ≅ segments |

**3.** The slope of the perpendicular line is −1.

$$y = -1x + b$$
$$4 = 6 + b; -2 = b$$
$$y = -x - 2$$
$$x = -x - 2$$
$$2x = -2$$
$$x = -1$$
$$y = -1$$

Find the distance between (−1, −1) and (−6, 4).

$$d = \sqrt{(x_2 - x_1)^2 + (y_2 - y_1)^2}$$
$$= \sqrt{(-6 - -1)^2 + (4 - -1)^2}$$
$$= \sqrt{(-5)^2 + 5^2} = \sqrt{50} \approx 7.07$$

4. 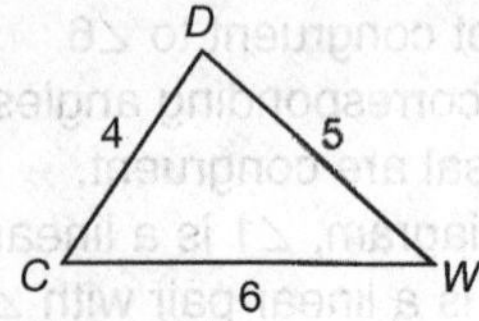


$\angle W, \angle C, \angle D$

5. Yes, since the opposite angles are supplementary.

6. The student found a perpendicular bisector and a median instead of three altitudes.

7. $\frac{3}{66} = \frac{1}{22}$

1:22

8. $A = ((9)(5) - \pi(2.5)^2) + \frac{1}{2}(9)(2)$
$\approx 25 + 9$
$\approx 34 \text{ m}^2$

9. $\frac{6}{16} = \frac{g}{12}$
$(16)(g) = (6)(12)$
$16g = 72$
$g = 4.5$

10. 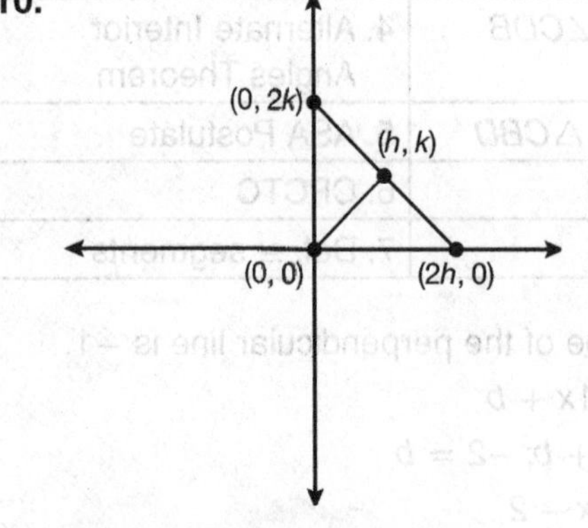


Sample: $(2h, 0)$ or $(0, 2k)$

11. $\frac{100°}{360°}(\pi(6)^2) \approx 31.4 \text{ ft}^2$

12. If $BC = DF$, the triangles will be congruent by SAS.

13. Assume $m\angle P \not> m\angle X$. So, either $m\angle P < m\angle X$ or $m\angle P = m\angle X$.

Case 1: If $m\angle P < m\angle X$, then $QR < YZ$ by the Hinge Theorem. This contradicts the given information, so $m\angle P \not> m\angle X$.

Case 2: If $m\angle P = m\angle X$, then $\angle P \cong \angle X$. So $\triangle PQR \cong \triangle XYZ$ by SAS. Then $\overline{QR} \cong \overline{YZ}$ by CPCTC, and $QR = YZ$. This contradicts given information, so $m\angle P \neq m\angle X$. Therefore, $m\angle P > m\angle X$.

14. 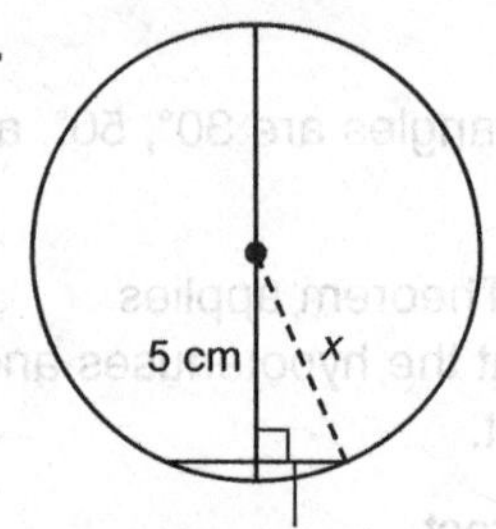


$x^2 = 5^2 + 6^2$
$x^2 = 25 + 36$
$x^2 = 61$
$x \approx 7.8 \text{ cm}$

15. $AB : MN = AC : MP$, $\angle A \cong \angle M$, so $\triangle ABC \sim \triangle MNP$ by SAS Similarity.

16. Since the diagonals bisect each other, choice **D** is correct.

17. 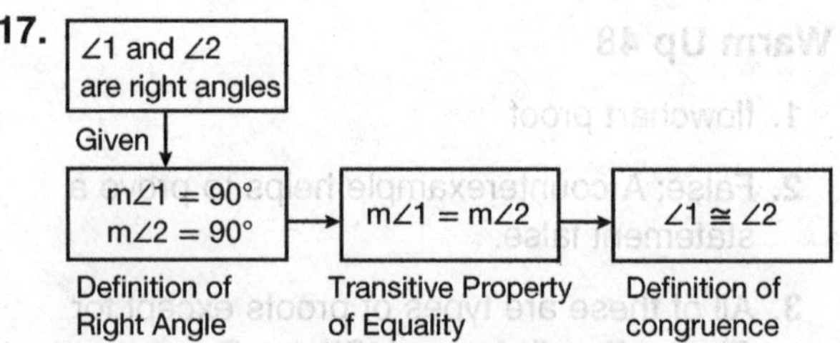


18. Assume that two lines can intersect in two different planes. By the definition of intersecting lines, this means that the points of both lines are contained in both planes. This means that the points in common to both planes form at least these two lines. This contradicts the postulate that if two planes intersect then their intersection is a line, so the assumption was false and exactly one plane contains two intersecting lines.

19. Since the tongs are to be the same length, the triangles they create when open would have two congruent side pairs. The Hinge Theorem can be used to determine which should have the larger spread angle. The tong that needs to pick up larger items needs to be able to open through a longer length, so this needs to open through the greatest angle.

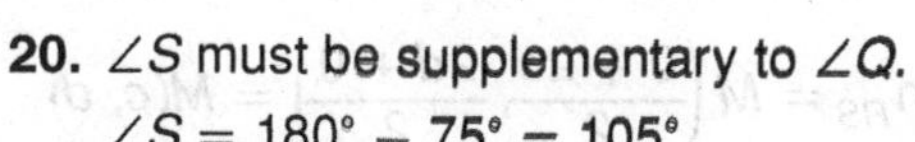



**20.** $\angle S$ must be supplementary to $\angle Q$.
$\angle S = 180° - 75° = 105°$

**21.** The diameter divides the chord into two equal halves. The length of each chord segment is 4 units.

**22.** $P = 5 + 5 + 5 + 2.5 + 6 + 6.5 = 30$ ft

$A = (5)(5) + \frac{1}{2}(2.5)(6) = 32.5 \text{ ft}^2$

**23.** $\begin{cases}(n-2)180 = 2x + 80 \\ (2n-2)180 = 5x + 20\end{cases}$

$180n - 360 = 2x + 80$
$360n - 360 = 5x + 20$
$-2(180n - 2x = 440)$
$360n - 5x = 380$

$-360 + 4x = -880$
$\underline{360n - 5x = 380}$
$-x = -500$
$x = 500$
$(n-2)180 = 2(500) + 80$
$180n - 360 = 1080$
$180n = 1440$
$n = 8$

**24.** Assume that $\angle KJL$ is not congruent to $\angle MIN$. $\angle MIN \cong \angle HIJ$ by the Vertical Angles Theorem. Since $\Delta HIJ \cong \Delta KJL$, by CPCTC, $\angle HIJ \cong \angle KJL$ and by the transitive property of congruence, $\angle KJL \cong \angle MIN$. This contradicts the assumption we made, so $\angle KJL \cong \angle MIN$.

**25.** $(AB)^2 = 25^2 - 7^2$
$(AB)^2 = 625 - 49$
$(AB)^2 = 576$
$AB = 24$

**26.** $5x + 16 = 7x - 8$
$24 = 2x$
$12 = x$
$\overset{\frown}{AB} = 2(m\angle ADB) = 2(7(12) - 8)$
$= 152°$

**27.** Finding arc length applies an angle-measure-to-360° ratio to the formula for circumference.

**28.** $\angle U \cong \angle U$ by the Reflexive Property of Equality, $\angle TSU \cong \angle WVU$, so $\Delta STU \sim \Delta VWU$ by AA Similarity.

$\frac{26}{y + 26} = \frac{28}{42}$
$(28)(y + 26) = (26)(42)$
$28y + 728 = 1092$
$28y = 364$
$y = 13$
$x = 13 + 26 = 39$

**29.** The triangles are right triangles, and each triangle has an 8-inch leg and an 11-inch leg. By the definition of congruent segments, the triangles have two pairs of congruent legs. Therefore the hypothesis of the LL Congruence Theorem is met.

**30.** Assume there are distinct points $X$ and $Y$ such that $\overline{PX}$ and $\overline{PY}$ are both perpendicular to $\overleftrightarrow{AB}$. Then by definition of perpendicularity, $\angle AXP$ and $\angle BYP$ are both right angles. Since $\angle YXP$ and $\angle XYP$ are both complementary to right angles, they are both right angles. But then $\Delta PXY$ has two right angles in it, which implies by the Triangle Sum Theorem that $m\angle XPY = 0°$, which contradicts the assumption that both $\overline{PX}$ and $\overline{PY}$ are perpendicular. So there is only one point on $\overleftrightarrow{AB}$ through which there is a perpendicular through $P$.

## LESSON 49

### Warm Up 49

1. equilateral polygon
2. heptagon
3. decagon
4. Congruent; Choice **A** is correct.

### Lesson Practice 49

**a.** The cone has a vertex at $P$, no edges, and a circular base with center $X$.

**b.** The triangular pyramid has 6 edges, 4 faces, and 4 vertices.

c. The hexagonal pyramid is a regular pyramid, but not a regular polyhedron.

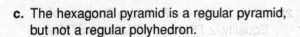

d. The pentagonal prism is not a regular polyhedron.

e. $V - E + F = 2$
$14 - E + 9 = 2$
$-E + 23 = 2$
$-E = -21$
$E = 21$ edges

f. After the first four vertices have been removed, there are 10 faces, 24 edges, and 16 vertices.
$V - E + F = 2$
$16 - 24 + 10 = 2$
$2 = 2$

**Practice 49**

1. Since $\angle D \cong \angle M$ and $\angle F \cong \angle P$, $\triangle DEF \sim \triangle MNP$ by AA Similarity.

2. If a polygon is a hexagon, then the sum of the interior angles is not 720°.

3. All choices are true for an equilateral triangle except choice **B**.

4. $\frac{ON}{28} = \frac{x}{x+3}$
$(ON)(x + 3) = (28)(x)$
$ON = \frac{28x}{x+3}$

5. The same prism results.

6. The triangles are congruent by ASA.
$A = \frac{1}{2}(4)(11.5) = 23 \text{ units}^2$

7.

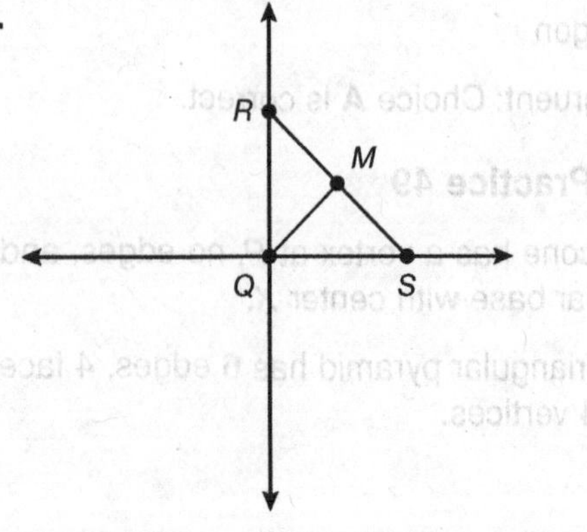


$\text{Median}_{RS} = M\left(\frac{0 + 2c}{2}, \frac{2d + 0}{2}\right) = M(c, d)$

$d_{QM} = \sqrt{(x_2 - x_1)^2 + (y_2 - y_1)^2}$
$= \sqrt{(c - 0)^2 + (d + 0)^2}$
$= \sqrt{c^2 + d^2}$

8. Midpoint $= \left(\frac{7 + 1}{2}, \frac{5 + 2}{2}\right)$
$= \left(\frac{8}{2}, \frac{7}{2}\right) = (4, 3.5)$

9.

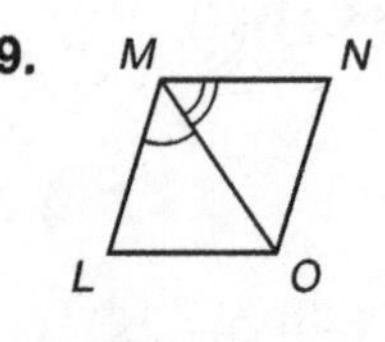


$\overline{OM}$

10. 9 fiberboards (faces), 17 metal strips (edges), and 10 connector pipes (vertices)

11. $3 \times 2 = 6$ units

12. The altitude of any equilateral triangle is not a median.

13. $1.5 \times 10 = 15$ feet wide
$1.5 \times 12 = 18$ feet long
$P = 2(15) + 2(18) = 30 + 36 = 66$ feet

14. $\frac{50}{90} = \frac{x}{70}$
$(90)(x) = (50)(70)$
$90x = 3500$
$x \approx 39$ m

15. $180° - 76° = 104°$
$104° \div 2 = 52°$
Since similar triangles have congruent angles, the angles in the other triangle will measure 76°, 52°, and 52°.

16. All three triangles have pairs of congruent sides, so the angles can be ordered according to the length of the third sides using the Hinge Theorem. Therefore, Camera A pivots through the largest angle, and Camera B pivots through the smallest angle.

**17.** It is necessary to know at least 4 sides, so that the scale factor can be found by comparing corresponding sides.

**18. a.** $P = 2.5 + 1.5 + 2 + 2.5 + 3 + 2.5$
$= 14$ ft

**b.** $A = (2.5)(3) + (2)(1.5) + \frac{1}{2}(2)(1.5)$
$= 12 \text{ ft}^2$

**19.** The slope of the line perpendicular is 1.
$y = x + b$
$4 = 4 + b$
$0 = b$
$y = x$
$x = -x - 4$
$2x = -4$
$x = -2$
$y = -2$
The point closest to the line is $(-2, -2)$.

**20.** No, since $10 - 12 + 7 = 5$, the hypothetical solid does not fit Euler's Theorem.

**21.** Leonardo's solution is incorrect because it does not correctly square the $(x + 5)$ term.

**22.** A cube is the only prism with congruent faces so the probability of the cube landing on each face is the same.

**23.** tangent: line $\ell$; chord: $\overline{BC}$; secant: $\overleftrightarrow{BC}$

**24.** Sample answer: All three angles have the same measure.

**25.** Midpoint $= \left(\frac{2 + -7}{2}, \frac{-2 + 3}{2}\right)$
$= \left(\frac{-5}{2}, \frac{1}{2}\right) = (-2.5, 0.5)$

**26.** $x^2 - 3 = 2x$
$x^2 - 2x - 3 = 0$
$(x + 1)(x - 3) = 0$
$x = 3$ (because the length cannot be negative)
$y^2 + 2y - 1 = 4y - 1$
$y^2 - 2y = 0$
$y(y - 2) = 0$
$y = 2$ (because the length cannot be negative and $y = 0$ would lead to a negative length)

**a.** $UW = (3^2 - 3) + ((2)(3)) = 12$
**b.** $VP = 4(2) - 1 = 7$
**c.** $WP = 2(3) = 6$
**d.** $ZV = (2^2 + 2(2) - 1) + 7 = 14$

**27.** $d = \sqrt{(x_2 - x_1)^2 + (y_2 - y_1)^2}$
Choice A: (3, 2) and (−1, −2)
$= \sqrt{(3 - -1)^2 + (2 - -2)^2}$
$= \sqrt{4^2 + 4^2}$
$= \sqrt{32}$
$\approx 5.66$
Choice B: (4, −1) and (0, 3)
$= \sqrt{(4 - 0)^2 + (-1 - 3)^2}$
$= \sqrt{4^2 + (-4)^2}$
$= \sqrt{32}$
$\approx 5.66$
Choice C: (−1, −2) and (4, −1)
$= \sqrt{(-1 - 4)^2 + (-2 - -1)^2}$
$= \sqrt{(-5)^2 + (-1)^2}$
$= \sqrt{26}$
$\approx 5.1$
Choice D: (3, 2) and (0, 3)
$= \sqrt{(3 - 0)^2 + (2 - 3)^2}$
$= \sqrt{3^2 + (-1)^2}$
$= \sqrt{10} \approx 3.16$
Choice **C**

**28.** Distance between (3, 2) and (−1, −2)
$= \sqrt{(3 - -1)^2 + (2 - -2)^2}$
$= \sqrt{4^2 + 4^2}$
$= \sqrt{32}$
$\approx 5.66$
Choice C is correct.

**29.** $m\angle ABC = \frac{1}{2}\widehat{AC} = \frac{1}{2}(60°) = 30°$

**30.** Since the length of a side of a triangle cannot exceed the sum of the other two sides, the sink is between 1 foot and $8 + 9 = 17$ feet from the fridge.

## LESSON 50

### Warm Up 50

1. means
2. legs
3. 8; 10
4. extremes

### Lesson Practice 50

a. $\triangle DEF \sim \triangle DGE \sim \triangle FGE$

b. $y^2 = 30^2 - 18^2$
$y^2 = 900 - 324$
$y^2 = 576$
$y = 24$
$\frac{x}{24} = \frac{18}{30}$
$(30)(x) = (24)(18)$
$30x = 432$
$x = 14.4$

c. $\frac{4}{x} = \frac{x}{11}$
$(x)(x) = (4)(11)$
$x^2 = 44$
$x \approx 6.6$

d. $\frac{2}{x} = \frac{x}{16}$
$(x)(x) = (2)(16)$
$x^2 = 32$
$x = \sqrt{32} = \sqrt{16 \cdot 2} = 4\sqrt{2}$

e. $\frac{x}{3} = \frac{3}{5}$
$(5)(x) = (3)(3)$
$5x = 9$
$x = 1.8$

f. $\frac{a}{5} = \frac{5}{13}$
$(13)(a) = (5)(5)$
$13a = 25$
$a \approx 1.9$
$\frac{b}{12} = \frac{12}{13}$
$(13)(b) = (12)(12)$
$13b = 144$
$b \approx 11.1$

g. $\frac{5}{b} = \frac{b}{2}$
$(b)(b) = (2)(5)$
$b^2 = 10$
$b \approx 3.2$

The brace is about 3.2 feet.

### Practice 50

1.

A rectangular pyramid has 5 vertices and 5 faces.

2. $m\widehat{AC} = 2(17°) = 34°$
$m\widehat{AE} = 34° + 42° = 76°$
$m\angle ABE = \frac{1}{2}m\widehat{AE} = 38°$

3.

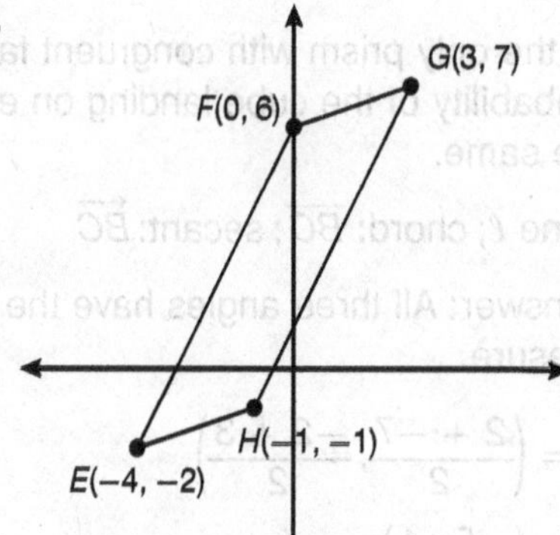


The coordinates of point $H$ are $(-1, -1)$.

4.

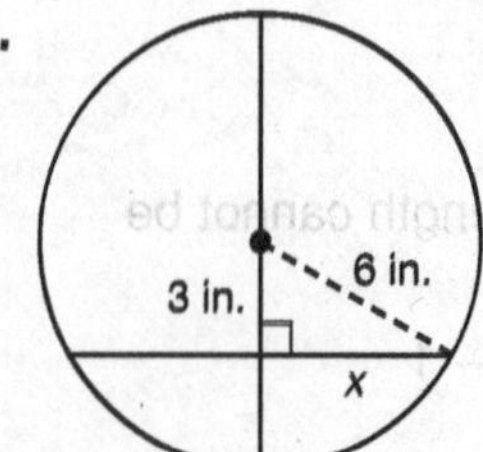


$x^2 = 6^2 - 3^2$
$x^2 = 36 - 9$

$x^2 = 27$

$x \approx 5.2$

The length of the chord is about $2(5.2) = 10.4$ inches.

5. (4, 0)

6. Sample: The geometric mean is the value that is between two numbers so that the mean squared equals the product of the two numbers. The mean is simply the average of the two numbers.

7. Proof: Assume $\overline{XA}$ is an altitude. Then $\overline{XA}$ is perpendicular to $\overline{YZ}$. Since perpendicular segments form four right angles, then $m\angle 1 = m\angle 2$, but it is given that $m\angle 1 \neq m\angle 2$. So, we have a contradiction. Thus, $\overline{XA}$ is not an altitude of $\triangle XYZ$.

8. $$\frac{x}{m} = \frac{m}{y}$$
$$(m)(m) = (x)(y)$$
$$m^2 = xy$$
$$m = \sqrt{xy}$$

9.

| Statements | Reasons |
|---|---|
| 1. $m\angle ADB = 90°$, $m\angle BDC = 90°$, $m\angle ABC = 90°$, $AD = DB$ | 1. Given |
| 2. $m\angle DAB + m\angle ABD = 90°$ | 2. Acute angles in a right triangle |
| 3. $m\angle ABD + m\angle DBC = 90°$ | 3. Angle Addition Postulate |
| 4. $m\angle DAB + m\angle ABD = m\angle ABD + m\angle DBC$ | 4. Substitution Property of Equality |
| 5. $m\angle DAB + m\angle ABD - m\angle ABD = m\angle ABD + m\angle DBC - m\angle ABD$ | 5. Subtraction Property of Equality |
| 6. $m\angle DAB = m\angle DBC$ | 6. Simplify |
| 7. $\angle DAB \cong \angle DBC$ | 7. Definition of congruent angles |
| 8. $\angle ADB \cong \angle BDC$ | 8. All right angles are congruent |
| 9. $\overline{AD} \cong \overline{DB}$ | 9. Def. $\cong$ segments |
| 10. $\triangle ABD \cong \triangle BCD$ | 10. ASA Theorem |

10. $\angle T \cong \angle D$, $\angle V \cong \angle F$, $\triangle TUV \sim \triangle DEF$ by AA Similarity.

11. $(n - 2)180° = 5400°$
$$n - 2 = 30$$
$$n = 32 \text{ sides}$$

12. It is necessary to know only two sides, one on each triangle.

13. $$10m + 8m = 180°$$
$$18m = 180°$$
$$m = 10°$$
$$\angle G = 10(10) = 100°$$

14. The slope of the line perpendicular is $\frac{5}{2}$.
$$y = \frac{5}{2}x + b$$
$$-3 = \frac{5}{2}(3) + b$$
$$-3 = \frac{15}{2} + b$$
$$-\frac{21}{2} = b$$
$$y = \frac{5}{2}x - \frac{21}{2}$$
$$\frac{5}{2}x - \frac{21}{2} = -\frac{2}{5}x + 4$$
$$\frac{29}{10}x = \frac{29}{2}$$
$$x = 5$$
$$y = -\frac{2}{5}(5) + 4 = 2$$

The point closest to the line is (5, 2).

15.

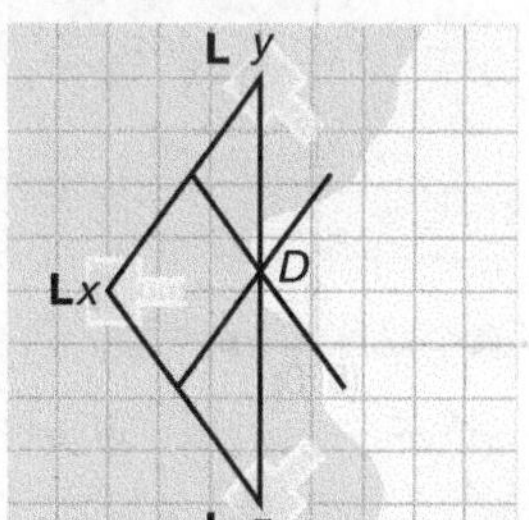


16. Since $13 + 31 = 44$, and this is less than the largest side length given, these side lengths cannot form a triangle.

17. $\frac{x}{3.21} = \frac{3.21}{x}$
$x^2 = (3.21)^2$
$x = 3.21$ in.

18. Using Euler's Formula: $V - E + F = 2$
Choice A: $6 - 9 + 5 = 2$
Choice B: $6 - 10 + 6 = 2$
Choice C: $8 - 10 + 6 = 4$
Choice D: $8 - 12 + 6 = 2$
Choice **C** is not a polyhedron.

19. $z^2 = 10z - 24$
$z^2 - 10z + 24 = 0$
$(z - 4)(z - 6) = 0$
$z = 4, 6; z = \{4, 6\}$

20. $s^2 = 12^2 + 5^2$
$s^2 = 144 + 25$
$s^2 = 169$
$s = 13$ feet

21. Only when the two lines are parallel

22. Answers will vary. Any value for $x$ that is between 0° and 52° is a valid answer. This is due to the fact that the angle at $J$ is 52° (because angles $L$ and $K$ are both 64°) and the opposite side to this third angle is longer than the corresponding third side of the other triangle. This means that the angle at $C$ must be smaller than 52°.

23.
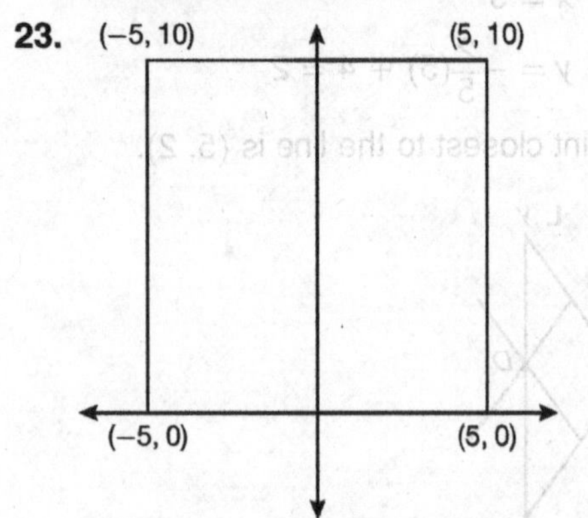


(−5, 10), (−5, 0), (5, 0), and (5, 10)

24. Change each equation into slope-intercept form:
i) $y = -x + 1$
ii) $y = -2x - 3$
iii) $y = \frac{1}{2}x + \frac{5}{2}$

Since equations ii) and iii) have slopes that are negative reciprocals of each other, they are perpendicular. Choice **C** is correct.

25. $x^2 = 90^2 + 90^2$
$x^2 = 8100 + 8100$
$x^2 = 16{,}200$
$x \approx 127.3$ feet

26. $\frac{1}{10} = \frac{x}{360°}$
$(10)(x) = (1)(360)$
$x = 36°$

27. No, because $24 - 48 + 22 = -2$, it does not hold because of Euler's Formula.

28. $\frac{x}{7} = \frac{3}{x}$
$(x)(x) = (7)(3)$
$x^2 = 21$
$x \approx 4.6$

29. $20x - 10 = 15x + 15$
$5x = 25$
$x = 5$

30. In order for the triangles to be similar, corresponding angles must be congruent. Choice **D** contradicts the fact.

## INVESTIGATION 5

1.
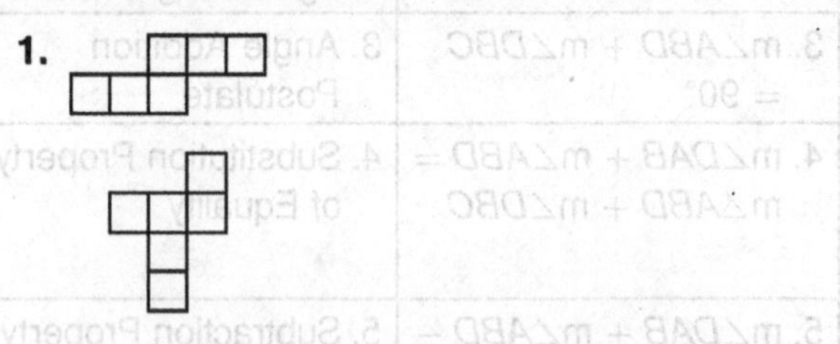

The net is comprised of 6 squares.

2. The first net has too few faces, and the second and third nets would have overlapping parts.

3.
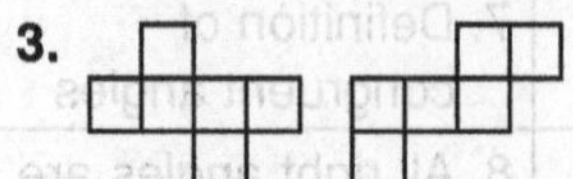

4. It is a pyramid. It is a triangular pyramid.

5. yes

6. Yes, the cube is a prism.
7. yes
8. yes
9. Sample: Draw the base, then construct a congruent triangle extending from each edge of the base.
10. Sample: Construct $n$ congruent rectangles, where $n$ is the number of sides of the base. Then construct the two bases extending from opposite ends of one rectangle.
11. No, a regular polyhedron must have all congruent sides. None of the figures listed have faces that are all of the same shape.

### Investigation 5 Practice

a. 3 nets; One possible pattern is to choose a face to hold fixed, and the other faces can disassemble from it in one, two, or three directions.

b. Sample:

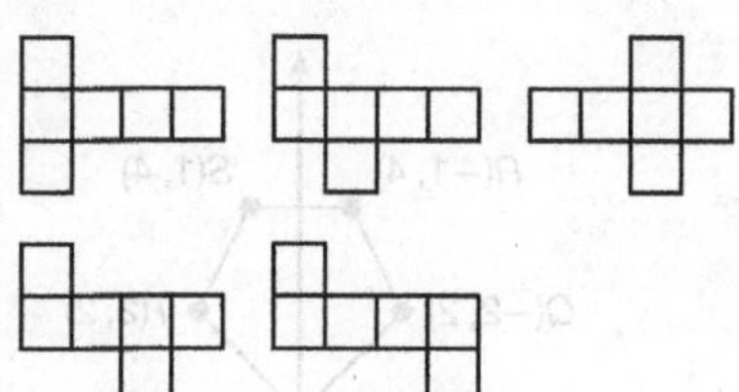

c. Sample:

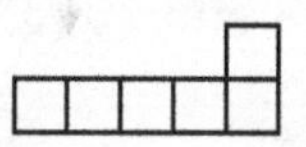

d.

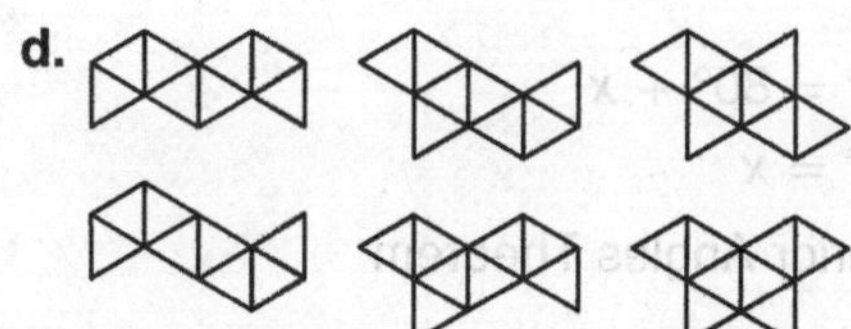

e.

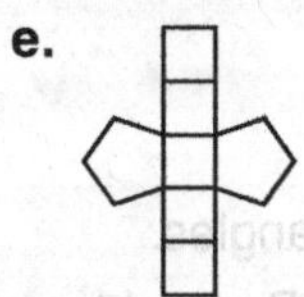

## LESSON 51

### Warm Up 51

1. isosceles triangle
2. $180° - 80° = 100°$

   $m\angle R = m\angle S = \frac{1}{2}(100°) = 50°$
3. Choice B is the only true statement.

### Lesson Practice 51

a. The other base angle is 72° because the base angles are congruent in this triangle.

$180° - 72° - 72° = 36°$

The vertex measures 36°.

b. $YZ$ is congruent to $XY$ and has a measure of 6.3 cm.

$15.2 = 6.3 + 6.3 + XZ$

$2.6 = XZ$; $XZ$ is 2.6 cm

c. The base angles, $b$, are congruent.

$b + b + 20° = 180°$

$2b = 160°$

$b = 80°$

d. $P = s + s + s$

$7 = 3s$

$\frac{7}{3} = s$

The length of each side is $2\frac{1}{3}$ feet or 2 ft 4 in.

e. $180° - 158° = 22°$

$\frac{1}{2}(22°) = 11°$

The angle with the horizontal measures 11°.

### Practice 51

1. $x$ must be greater than 0.25 because the length must be greater than 0.

   $4x - 1 < x + 8$

   $3x < 9$

   $x < 3$

   So, $0.25 < x < 3$
2. Fabian's socks will be in the dresser.
3. a. Use the Pythagorean Theorem to find the lengths of the leftmost sides.

$x^2 = 8^2 + 8^2$
$x^2 = 64 + 64$
$x^2 = 128$
$x = \sqrt{128} = \sqrt{64 \cdot 2} = 8\sqrt{2}$
$P = 8\sqrt{2} + 8\sqrt{2} + 12 + 17 + 17 + 12$
$= 58 + 16\sqrt{2}$ in.

**b.** $A = \frac{1}{2}(16)(8) + (12)(16) + \frac{1}{2}(16)(15)$
$= 376$ in.$^2$

**4.** If $x$ is the geometric mean, then write $\frac{4}{x} = \frac{x}{7}$ and solve for $x$.
$\frac{4}{x} = \frac{x}{7}$
$(x)(x) = (4)(7)$
$x^2 = 28$
$x \approx 5.3$

**5.** $\frac{360°}{6} = 60°$

**6.** $\frac{42°}{360°}[2\pi(6)] \approx 4.40$ cm

**7. a.** $\angle R$ is the vertex angle.

**b.** $m\angle P = \frac{1}{2}(180° - 118°) = 31°$

**8.**
$V - E + F = 2$
$E = V + 10$
$V - (V + 10) + F = 2$
$-10 + F = 2$
$F = 12$

The polyhedron has 12 faces.

**9.** $x^2 = 13^2 - 12^2$
$x^2 = 169 - 144$
$x^2 = 25$
$x = 5$

**10.** By a corollary to the Isosceles Triangle Theorem, an equilateral triangle is equiangular, so by a corollary to the Triangle Angle Sum Theorem, its angles measure 60°.

**11.** If Teresa makes sure both pairs of sides are parallel, her figure will be a parallelogram, which has supplementary consecutive interior angles.

**12.** See student work. $\frac{n}{36} = \frac{-m}{12}$, $n = -3m$
Sample: $m = 3$ and $n = -9$.

$y = \frac{12}{3}x - 2$ $\quad 4y = -\frac{9}{9}x + 5$

$y = 4x - 2$ $\quad y = -\frac{1}{4}x + \frac{5}{4}$

The slopes are negative reciprocals of each other.

**13.** $\frac{3}{x} = \frac{x}{2}$
$(x)(x) = (3)(2)$
$x^2 = 6; x \approx 2.4$

**14.** $\angle EAD \cong \angle CAB$ by the Reflexive Property of Congruence, $AD : AB = 3 : 6 = 1 : 2$, $AE : AC = 2 : 4 = 1 : 2$; therefore $\triangle ADE \sim \triangle ABC$ by the SAS Postulate.

$\frac{3}{3.5} = \frac{6}{BC}$
$(3)(BC) = (3.5)(6)$
$3BC = 21$
$BC = 7$

**15.**

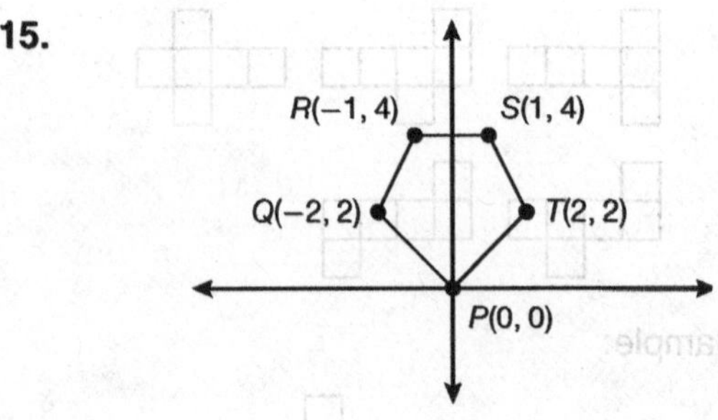


$S(1, 4)$

**16. a.** $122° = 80° + x$
$42° = x$

**b.** Exterior Angles Theorem

**17.** If $FE = 5$, the triangles will be congruent by AAS.

**18.** Sample: $(a, 0)$ or $(0, b)$

**19.** $\triangle OPQ$ and $\triangle RST$ are right triangles. Legs $\overline{OP} \cong \overline{RS}$ and $\overline{PQ} \cong \overline{ST}$. By the LL Congruence Theorem, $\triangle OPQ \cong \triangle RST$.

**20.** The slopes will be negative reciprocals of each other.

$y = \frac{1}{4}x$

**21.** $M = K - 10$

$M = L - 1$

So, the largest angle is $\angle K$ because it is 10 degrees larger than M. $\angle L$ is the next largest angle because it is 1 degree larger than $M$. Therefore, $\angle M$ is the smallest angle. Since towers $K$ and $L$ are across from $\angle M$, they are the closest together.

**22.**

| Statements | Reasons |
|---|---|
| 1. $\triangle ABC$ with $\angle B \cong \angle C$ | 1. Given |
| 2. Construct altitude $\overline{AD}$ | 2. Through a line and a point not on the line, there exists exactly one perpendicular line to the given line. |
| 3. $\angle BDA$ and $\angle CDA$ are right angles | 3. Definition of altitude |
| 4. $\angle BDA \cong \angle CDA$ | 4. All right angles are congruent |
| 5. $\overline{AD} \cong \overline{AD}$ | 5. Reflexive Property of Congruence |
| 6. $\triangle BDA \cong \triangle CDA$ | 6. AAS Theorem |
| 7. $\overline{AB} \cong \overline{AC}$ | 7. CPCTC |
| 8. $\triangle ABC$ is isosceles | 8. Definition of isosceles triangle |

**23.** $\frac{12.1}{11.2} = \frac{y}{12.1}$

$(11.2)(y) = (12.1)(12.1)$

$11.2y = 146.41$

$y \approx 13.1$

$y = x + 11.2$

$13.1 \approx x + 11.2$

$x \approx 1.9$

**24. a.** $\sqrt{99} + 3\sqrt{13} < 21$, which means it is not a triangle.

**b.** $3^2 = (\sqrt{7})^2 + (\sqrt{8})^2$

$9 = 7 + 8$

$9 < 15$

It is an acute triangle.

**c.** $14^2 = 8^2 + 7^2$

$196 = 64 + 49$

$196 > 113$

It is an obtuse triangle.

**25.** Use the Pythagorean Theorem to find the legs of the triangles.

$x^2 + x^2 = 5^2$

$2x^2 = 25$

$x^2 = \frac{25}{2}$

$x = \sqrt{\frac{25}{2}} = \frac{5}{\sqrt{2}} = \frac{5\sqrt{2}}{2}$

$P = 4(10) + 4\left(\frac{5\sqrt{2}}{2}\right)$

$= (40 + 10\sqrt{2})$ cm

$A = [(15)(10)] - 2\left[\frac{1}{2}\left(\frac{5\sqrt{2}}{2}\right)\left(\frac{5\sqrt{2}}{2}\right)\right]$

$= 150 - 12.5$

$= 137.5$ cm$^2$

**26.** $\overline{DF}$

**27.** $(PY)^2 = x^2 + 3^2$

$PY = \sqrt{x^2 + 9}$

**28.** Since the arc of a semicircle measures 180° and the measure of the inscribed angle is one-half the measure of the intercepted arc, the angle must be 90°. Choice **B** is correct.

**29.** $6 - x = \frac{2}{3}x$

$6 = \frac{5}{3}x$

$\frac{18}{5} = x$

**30.** Assume that $QR$ is not greater than $QP$. This means that either $QR < QP$ or $QR = QP$.

**Case 1:** If $QR < QP$, then m$\angle P <$ m$\angle R$ because we know that the larger angle in a triangle is always opposite the longer side. This contradicts the given information, so $QR$ is not less than $QP$.

**Case 2:** If $QR = QP$, then m$\angle P =$ m$\angle R$ because the larger angle in a triangle is always opposite the longer side. If the sides are equal, then their respective opposite angles must be equal. This contradicts the given information, so $QR$ does not equal $QP$. This shows that the assumption that $QR$ is not greater than $QP$ is false. Therefore, $QR > QP$.

## LESSON 52

### Warm Up 52

1. $A = (12.5)^2 = 156.25 \text{ cm}^2$
   The quadrilateral is a square because all four angles are 90° and all four sides are congruent.
2. parallelogram
3. $P = 6(8.7) = 52.2$ m
   The top figure is a rhombus because it has four congruent sides. The bottom figure is a square because it has four congruent sides and four 90° angles.

### Lesson Practice 52

a. Since the diagonals of a rectangle are congruent, $NP$ is 5.4 inches long.

b. $(6x - 12)° + (4x + 2)° = 90°$
$$10x - 10 = 90$$
$$10x = 100$$
$$x = 10$$
$$m\angle OXY = 6(10°) - 12° = 48°$$

c. $m\angle OYZ = 4(10°) + 2° = 42°$

d. $RSTU$ is a square because the diagonals are congruent and perpendicular to each other.

e. $s^2 = 25^2 + 20^2$
$s^2 = 625 + 400$
$s^2 = 1025$
$s \approx 32$ feet per side
$P = 4(32) = 128$ feet

### Practice 52

1.

2. Find the equation of $\overline{KL}$:
$y = -\frac{1}{2}x - \frac{15}{2}$
Now, find the line perpendicular to $\overline{KL}$ that runs through $J$:
$y = 2x + b$
$6 = 2(3) + b$
$0 = b$
$y = 2x$
Next, find the equation of $\overline{JL}$:
$y = \frac{11}{8}x + \frac{15}{8}$
Now, find the line perpendicular to $\overline{JL}$ that runs through $K$:
$y = -\frac{8}{11}x + b$
$-9 = -\frac{8}{11}(3) + b$
$-\frac{75}{11} = b$
$y = -\frac{8}{11}x - \frac{75}{11}$
Find the point of intersection by setting the equations equal to each other.
$2x = -\frac{8}{11}x - \frac{75}{11}$
$\frac{30}{11}x = -\frac{75}{11}$
$x = -\frac{5}{2}$ or $-2.5$
$y = 2(-2.5) = -5$
The orthocenter is located at $(-2.5, -5)$.

3. Answers may vary, but should mention that each figure has congruent parallel bases—the bases of the prism are octagonal, the bases of the cylinder are circular. As the number of sides of the base of a prism increases, the solid becomes more like a cylinder.

4. $h^2 = 7^2 + 4^2$
$h^2 = 49 + 16$
$h^2 = 65$
$h \approx 8.1$
$\frac{4}{x} = \frac{8.1}{7}$

$(8.1)(x) = (4)(7)$
$8.1x = 28$
$x \approx 3.5$

**5.** Joni could fold the paper on a diagonal. This would determine whether the side lengths are equal. If it does not fold perfectly into isosceles triangles, then it is not a square.

**6.** $C = 2\pi r$
$113 = 2\pi r$
$r \approx 18$ ft

$A_{sector} = \frac{x°}{360°}(\pi r^2)$
$12 = \frac{x°}{360°}[\pi(18)^2]$
$4320 = (324\pi)(x°)$
$4° \approx x$

**7.** No, because she took the reciprocal instead of the negative reciprocal of the slope.

**8.** $\triangle PQR \sim \triangle STU$ by SAS Similarity

**9.** A parallelogram can only be similar to a rectangle if the parallelogram is also a rectangle with sides that are proportional in length.

**10.** $(9x + 1)° + (20x + 5)° = 180°$
$29x + 6 = 180$
$29x = 174$
$x = 6$
$9(6) + 1 = 54 + 1 = 55$
$20(6) + 5 = 120 + 5 = 125$
The angles are 55°, 125°, 55°, and 125°.

**11.** $\frac{\sqrt{11}}{x} = \frac{x}{\sqrt{5}}$
$(x)(x) = (\sqrt{11})(\sqrt{5})$
$x^2 = \sqrt{55}$
$x \approx \sqrt{7.416}$
$x \approx 2.7$

**12.** $180° - 104.5° = 75.5°$
$\frac{1}{2}(75.5°) \approx 37.8°$
The measure of each angle is 37.8°.

**13.** Choice A: Converse: If the sum of two angles is 180°, then they are supplementary. This is true.
Choice B: Converse: If a triangle is isosceles, then it has two congruent angles. This is true.
Choice C: Converse: If the number is 2, then it is an even prime. This is true.
Choice D: Converse: If two angles are acute, then they are complementary. This is not necessarily true. A counterexample is 30° and 45°.
Choice **D** is correct.

**14.** $d_{LM} = \sqrt{(6 - 0)^2 + (0 - 0)^2} = \sqrt{36} = 6$
For the triangle to be equilateral, $d_{MN} = 6$.
$\sqrt{(6 - 3)^2 + (0 - y)^2} = 6$
$3^2 + (-y)^2 = 36$
$(-y)^2 = 27$
$y = \pm\sqrt{27} = \pm 3\sqrt{3}$

**15.** $d_{KM} = \sqrt{(0 - 1)^2 + (1 + 6)^2} = \sqrt{50}$
$d_{LN} = \sqrt{(4 + 3)^2 + (-2 + 3)^2} = \sqrt{50}$
$m_{KM} = \frac{-6 - 1}{1 - 0} = \frac{-7}{1} = -7$
$m_{LN} = \frac{-3 - -2}{-3 - 4} = \frac{-1}{-7} = \frac{1}{7}$

**16.** Circumference: $6x = 2\pi r$
$x = \frac{1}{6}(2\pi r)$
Arc: $x = \frac{a°}{360°}(2\pi r)$
Now substitute for $x$:
$\frac{1}{6}\cancel{(2\pi r)} = \frac{a°}{360°}\cancel{(2\pi r)}$
$\frac{1}{6}(360°) = a$
$60° = a$

**17.** $8m + 10m = 180°$
$18m = 180°$
$m = 10°$
$m\angle l = 8(10°) = 80°$

**18.** **a.** $\angle Q$
**b.** $180° - 86° = 94°$
$\angle R = \frac{1}{2}(94°) = 47°$

**19.** They are congruent.

20. Assume m∠$RQS \le$ m∠$S$. The side opposite a smaller angle is smaller, so $RS$ must be less than or equal to $RQ$. This contradicts the given information, so the assumption is false. Therefore, m∠$RQS >$ m∠$S$

21. m∠$B = 180° - 40° - 40° = 100°$

22.
$$9^2 > 6^2 + x^2$$
$$81 - 36 > x^2$$
$$45 > x^2$$
$$\sqrt{45} > x$$
$$3\sqrt{5} > x$$

23.
$$x^2 = 39^2 - 36^2$$
$$x^2 = 1521 - 1296$$
$$x^2 = 225$$
$$x = 15 \text{ feet}$$

24. He can measure the diagonals to verify that their lengths are equal.

25. a. $P = 6(2) + 2(3) + 4 = 22$ cm
b. $20 + 2 + 3 + 2 + 1 = 28$ cm
c. $(6n + 4)$ cm

26.
$$\frac{20}{EF} = \frac{24}{54}$$
$$(24)(EF) = (20)(54)$$
$$24EF = 1080$$
$$EF = 45 \text{ feet}$$

27. Find the perpendicular bisectors of two of the sides of the triangle. Their intersection will be the center of the circle and the distance from the center to the vertices of the triangle will be the radius of the circle.

28.
$$AB = 3AD$$
$$P = 2(AB) + 2(AD)$$
$$P = 2(3AD) + 2AD$$
$$P = 8AD$$
$$12 = 8AD$$
$$1.5 = AD = BC$$
$$AB = CD = 3(1.5) = 4.5$$

29. $\overline{AB}$ is not congruent to $\overline{CD}$.

30. The radius of the circle is 50 m. Use the Pythagorean Theorem to find the length of the direct route:
$$x^2 = 50^2 + 50^2$$
$$x^2 = 2500 + 2500$$
$$x^2 = 5000$$
$$x \approx 70.7 \text{ meters}$$
Now, find the length of the arc:
$$\frac{90°}{360°}(2\pi r) = \frac{90°}{360°}[2\pi(50)] \approx 78.5 \text{ m}$$
$$78.5 - 70.7 = 7.8$$
The direct path is about 8 meters shorter.

## LESSON 53

### Warm Up 53

1. right triangle
2. $A = \frac{1}{2}bh = \frac{1}{2}(11)(17) = 93.5 \text{ in.}^2$
3.
$$h^2 = 8^2 + 2^2$$
$$h^2 = 64 + 4$$
$$h^2 = 68$$
$$h = \sqrt{68}$$
$$h = 2\sqrt{17}$$
The ratio is $2\sqrt{17} : 2$ or $\sqrt{17} : 1$.

### Lesson Practice 53

a. The length of the hypotenuse is equal to the length of a leg times $\sqrt{2}$. Since the leg is 31 yards long, the hypotenuse has a length of $31\sqrt{2}$ yards.

b. To find the length of a leg when given the hypotenuse, divide by $\sqrt{2}$ instead.
$$\frac{63}{\sqrt{2}} = \frac{63\sqrt{2}}{2}$$

c.
$$P = 18 + 18 + 18\sqrt{2}$$
$$= 36 + 18\sqrt{2}$$
$$\approx 61.5 \text{ in.}$$

d.
$$x^2 + x^2 = 48^2$$
$$2x^2 = 2304$$
$$x^2 = 1152$$
$$x \approx 34 \text{ mi}$$

e.

$150 = \sqrt{2}x$

$\frac{150}{\sqrt{2}} = \frac{150\sqrt{2}}{2} = x$

$x = 75\sqrt{2}$

$A = s^2 = (75\sqrt{2})^2 = (5625)(2) = 11{,}250 \text{ ft}^2$

## Practice 53

1. $180° - 48° = 132°$
   The sum of the two unknown angles is 132°. Since the 48° angle is the smallest angle and the mislabeled angle is the largest, the other angle must be greater than 48°. This means that the greatest the mislabeled angle can be is $180° - 48° - 48° = 84°$. Also, the mislabeled angle must be greater than the unknown angle. So, it must be greater then $\frac{1}{2}(180° - 48°) = \frac{1}{2}(132°) = 66°$.
   Therefore the mislabeled angle must be greater than 66° and less than 84°.

2. $V - E + F = 2$
   $8 - 12 + F = 2$
   $F = 6$
   The figure is a cube.

3. To find the length of a leg when given the hypotenuse, divide the hypotenuse by $\sqrt{2}$.
   $\frac{5}{\sqrt{2}} = \frac{5\sqrt{2}}{2}$

4. No, only the centroid is a center of gravity.

5. sometimes

6. $x^2 = 7^2 + 5^2$
   $x^2 = 49 + 25$
   $x^2 = 74$
   $x \approx 8.6$
   $\frac{8.6}{7} = \frac{y}{8.6}$
   $(7)(y) = (8.6)(8.6)$
   $7y = 73.96$
   $y \approx 10.6$

7. **a.** $P = 6.5 + 5 + 3 + 3.5 + 3.5 + 1.5$
   $= 23$ in.
   **b.** $A = (6.5)(5) - (3.5)(3.5)$
   $= 32.5 - 12.25$
   $= 20.25 \text{ in.}^2$ or $20\frac{1}{4} \text{ in.}^2$

8. Yes, since an isosceles triangle has two equal angles at the base of the common side, and the Triangle Sum Theorem states that $x + x + 90° = 180°$, which generates $x = 45°$.

9. $\overline{NM}$ is a radius, $\overline{LM}$ is a chord, $\overline{KM}$ is a tangent, and the line through $L$ is a tangent.

10. The length of the hypotenuse is equal to the length of a leg times $\sqrt{2}$. Since the leg is $x$ yards long, the hypotenuse has a length of $x\sqrt{2}$ inches.

11. We are given that $\angle B \cong \angle D$, and $\angle ACB \cong \angle DCE$ because they are vertical angles. So, $\triangle ABC \sim \triangle EDC$ by Angle-Angle Similarity.

12. A pair of corresponding side lengths, or the perimeter of each of the triangles

13. 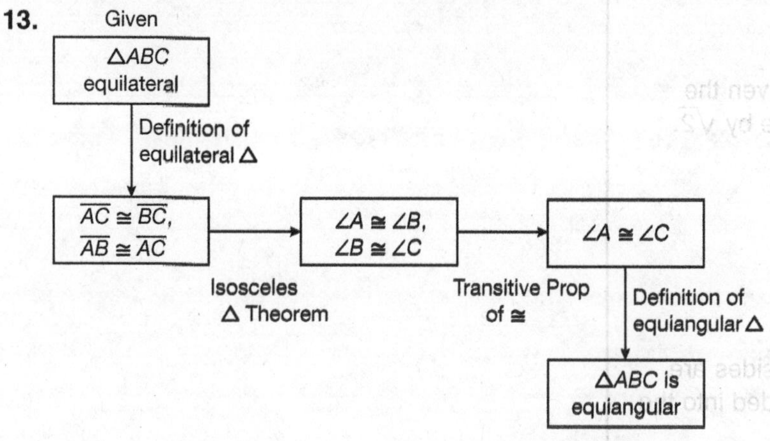

**14.** $r = 4$ m

$A = \frac{1}{2}\pi r^2 = \frac{1}{2}\pi(4)^2 = \frac{1}{2}\pi(16) = 8\pi\ \text{m}^2$

**15.** $(-5, 2)$ is 18 units to the left of the vertical line $x = 13$. The distance is 18 units.

**16.** $12x + 11 = 5x + 18$

$7x = 7$

$x = 1$

**17.** Answers will vary. Any value for $x$ that is between 0 and 26 is valid since the measure of angle $Z$ is smaller than the measure of angle $I$.

**18.** $\frac{2}{5} = \frac{7}{b}$

$(2)(b) = (5)(7)$

$2b = 35$

$b = 17.5$

**19.** Since the $m\angle KLM = 20°$, the intercepted arc, $\widehat{KM}$, is $2(20°) = 40°$. So, $m\widehat{KMP} = 70°$ and $m\angle KNP = \frac{1}{2}m\ \widehat{KMP} = 35°$.

**20.**

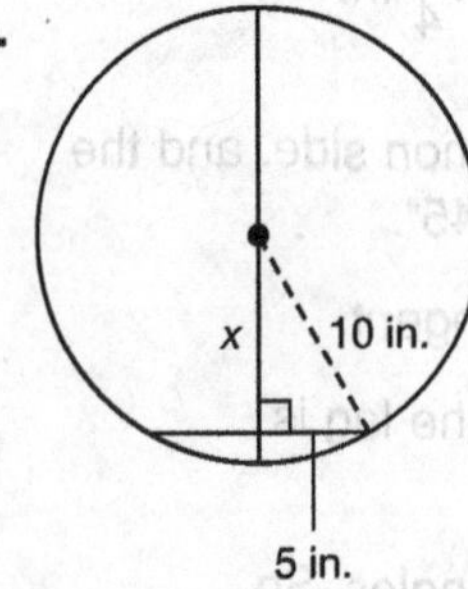


$x^2 = 10^2 - 5^2$

$x^2 = 100 - 25$

$x^2 = 75$

$x \approx 8.7$ inches

**21.** To find the length of a leg when given the hypotenuse, divide the hypotenuse by $\sqrt{2}$.

$\frac{73}{\sqrt{2}} = \frac{73\sqrt{2}}{2}$

$P = 73 + 2\left(\frac{73\sqrt{2}}{2}\right) \approx 176$ feet

Choice **B** is correct.

**22.** In the figure, the four pentagonal sides are congruent, but when the net is folded into the 3D figure, it is not closed.

**23.** $XY = WZ = 10.4$ in.

**24.** $\text{Midpoint}_{DE} = \left(\frac{-3 + 9}{2}, \frac{2 + 8}{2}\right)$

$= \left(\frac{6}{2}, \frac{10}{2}\right) = (3, 5)$

The equation of the median from $F$ to the midpoint of $\overline{DE}$ is the equation of the line through $F(3, -4)$ and $(3, 5)$. The slope is $m = \frac{5-(-4)}{3-3}$, which is undefined, so $x = 3$ is the equation of the median.

$\text{Midpoint}_{EF}$

$= \left(\frac{3 + 9}{2}, \frac{-4 + 8}{2}\right)$

$= \left(\frac{12}{2}, \frac{4}{2}\right) = (6, 2)$

The equation of the median from $D$ to the midpoint of $\overline{EF}$ is the equation of the line through $F(-3,2)$ and $(6, 2)$. The slope is $m = \frac{2-2}{6-(-3)}$, which is zero, so $y = 2$ is the equation of the median.

The centroid is the intersection of these lines. The centroid is at $(3, 2)$.

**25.** $\frac{3}{11} = \frac{12}{DF}$

$(3)(DF) = (11)(12)$

$3DF = 132$

$DF = 44$ units

**26.** SAS Similarity Theorem

27. Since the leg is 16 yards long, the hypotenuse has a length of $16\sqrt{2}$ yards.

28. $\triangle ABC$ and $\triangle DEF$ are right triangles, hypotenuses $\overline{AC} \cong \overline{DF}$, and acute $\angle C \cong \angle F$; so by the HA Congruence Theorem, $\triangle ABC \cong \triangle DEF$.

29. A rhombus is defined by having four congruent sides. A square always has four congruent sides. Therefore, a square is always a rhombus.

30. 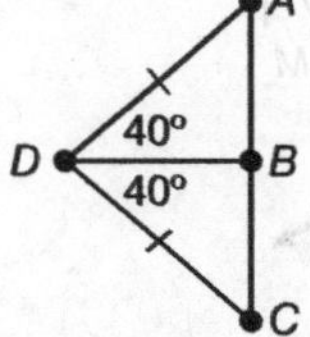


The clock tower is equidistant from the other two. Since $m\angle ADB = 40° = m\angle BDC$, $\overleftrightarrow{DB}$ bisects $\angle ADC$. So, because a line bisecting the vertex angle in an isosceles triangle is the perpendicular bisector of the base (Theorem 51–3), $B$ lies on the perpendicular bisector of $\overline{AC}$ and by the Perpendicular Bisector Equidistance Theorem, $AB = BC$.

## LESSON 54

### Warm Up 54

1. cube
2. cone, rectangular pyramid, sphere
3. $V - E + F = 2$

$10 - E + 7 = 2$

$-E = -15$

$E = 15$

### Lesson Practice 54

a.

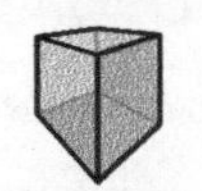

b.

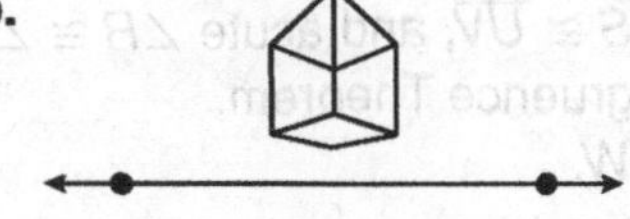

c.

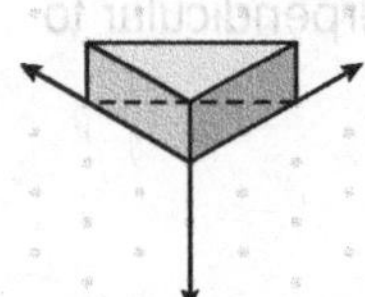

d. one-point perspective;

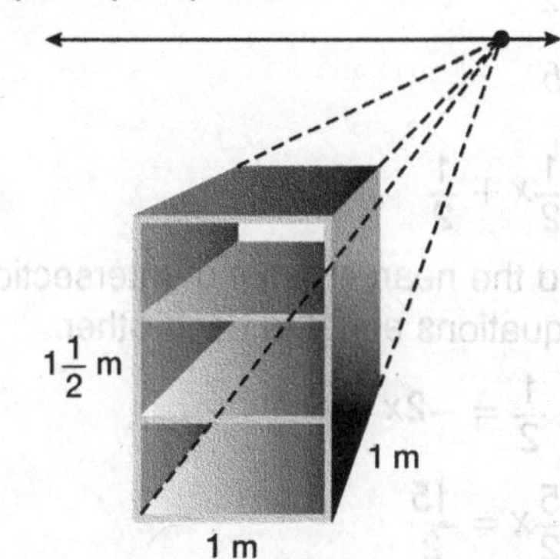


### Practice 54

1.

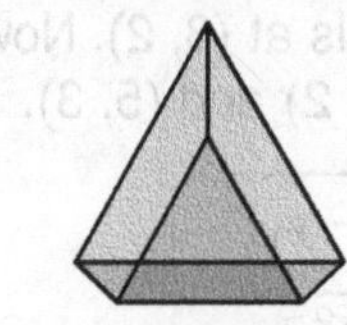

2. A rectangle is a parallelogram with one right angle. A square is a parallelogram and always has four 90° angles, therefore a square is always a rectangle.

3. $11 = \frac{1}{3}(4x + 3 + 11)$

$11 = \frac{4}{3}x + \frac{14}{3}$

$\frac{19}{3} = \frac{4}{3}x$

$\frac{19}{4} = x$

$13\left(\frac{19}{4}\right) - 3 = 58.75$

$ZP = \frac{1}{2}(58.75) = 29.375$

**4.** The slope of the line perpendicular to $y = -2x + 8$ is $\frac{1}{2}$.

$$y = \frac{1}{2}x + b$$
$$3 = \frac{1}{2}(5) + b$$
$$\frac{1}{2} = b$$
$$y = \frac{1}{2}x + \frac{1}{2}$$

To find the nearest point of intersection, set the equations equal to each other.

$$\frac{1}{2}x + \frac{1}{2} = -2x + 8$$
$$\frac{5}{2}x = \frac{15}{2}$$
$$x = 3$$
$$y = -2(3) + 8 = 2$$

The point of intersection is at (3, 2). Now find the distance between (3, 2) and (5, 3).

$$d = \sqrt{(x_2 - x_1)^2 + (y_2 - y_1)^2}$$
$$= \sqrt{(3-5)^2 + (2-3)^2}$$
$$= \sqrt{(-2)^2 + (-1)^2}$$
$$= \sqrt{5}$$
$$\approx 2.24 \text{ units}$$

**5.** one-point perspective;

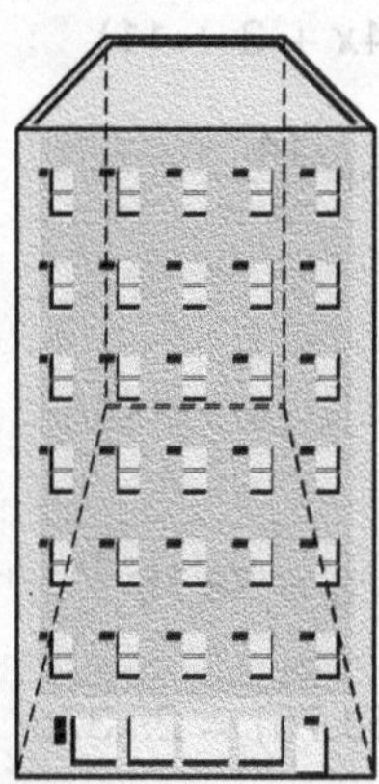

**6.** hexagonal pyramid

**7.** $m_{LM} = \frac{1 - -1}{4 - 3} = \frac{2}{1} = 2$

$$m_{\perp LM} = -\frac{1}{2}$$
$$y = \frac{1}{2}x + b$$
$$-2 = \frac{1}{2}(-2) + b$$
$$-1 = b$$
$$y = \frac{1}{2}x - 1$$

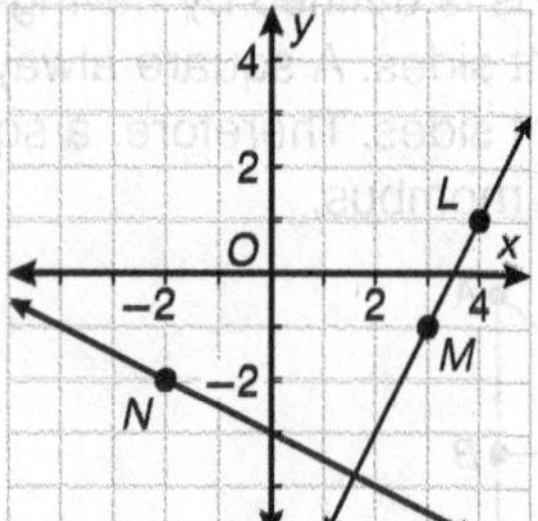


**8.** $\frac{7x}{13} = \frac{13}{x}$

$$(7x)(x) = (13)(13)$$
$$7x^2 = 169$$
$$x^2 \approx 24.14$$
$$x \approx 4.9$$
$$y^2 = [(7)(4.9)]^2 + 13^2$$
$$y^2 = 1176.49 + 169$$
$$y^2 = 1345.49$$
$$y \approx 36.7$$

**9.** The sum of the exterior angles of any convex polygon is 360°.

**10.** sometimes

**11.**

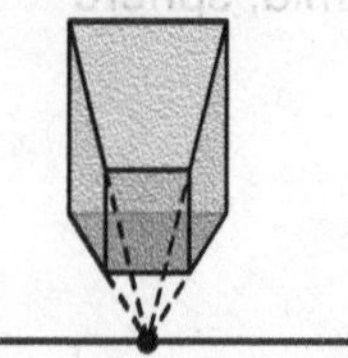

**12.** $3x - 7 = 5x - 17$

$$-2x = -10$$
$$x = 5$$

**13.** point of concurrency

**14.** $\triangle RST$ and $\triangle UVW$ are right triangles, hypotenuses $\overline{RS} \cong \overline{UV}$, and acute $\angle R \cong \angle U$. By the HA Congruence Theorem, $\triangle RST \cong \triangle UVW$.

**15.** The length of the hypotenuse is equal to the length of a leg times $\sqrt{2}$. Since the leg is

57 feet long, the hypotenuse has length $57\sqrt{2}$ feet.

**16.** $A_{shaded} = A_{square} - A_{circles}$
$= s^2 - 4(\pi r^2)$
$= (4r)^2 - 4(\pi r^2)$
$= 16r^2 - 4\pi r^2$

**17.** $2(37°) = 74°$; If a line is the perpendicular bisector of the base of an isosceles triangle, then it bisects the vertex angle.

**18.** Assume that the triangle is not isosceles. We know that the altitudes, $\overline{BX}$ and $\overline{CY}$, are of equal length and are perpendicular to $\overline{AC}$ and $\overline{AB}$, respectively. We know that $\triangle AXB$ and $\triangle AYC$ share $\angle A$ and so by the Angle-Angle-Side Congruence Theorem, $\triangle AXB$ and $\triangle AYC$ are congruent. Thus $\overline{AB} \cong \overline{AC}$, and thus $AB = AC$. This contradicts the assumption that $\triangle ABC$ is not isosceles.

**19.** Both legs are $\frac{17}{\sqrt{2}} = \frac{17\sqrt{2}}{2}$.

$A = \frac{1}{2}bh$

$= \frac{1}{2}\left(\frac{17\sqrt{2}}{2}\right)\left(\frac{17\sqrt{2}}{2}\right)$

$= 72.25 \text{ cm}^2$

**20.**

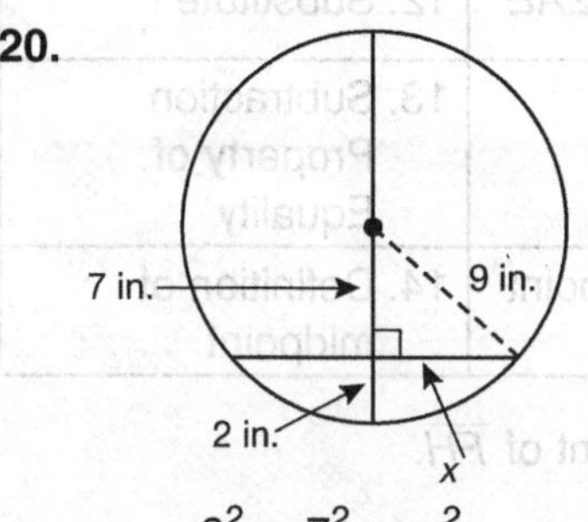


$9^2 = 7^2 + x^2$
$81 - 49 = x^2$
$x^2 = 32$
$x \approx 5.66$
$2(5.66) = 11.3$ inches

or,

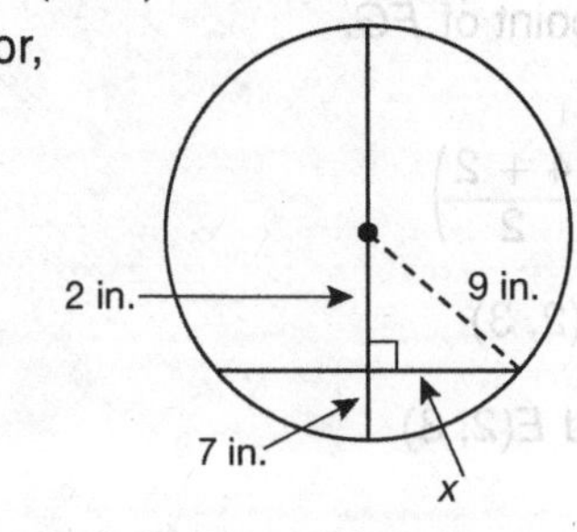


$9^2 = 2^2 + x^2$
$81 - 4 = x^2$
$x^2 = 77$
$x \approx 8.77$
$2(8.77) \approx 17.5$ inches

**21.** When the vanishing points are closer together, the figure becomes narrower. When the vanishing points are farther apart, the figure becomes wider.

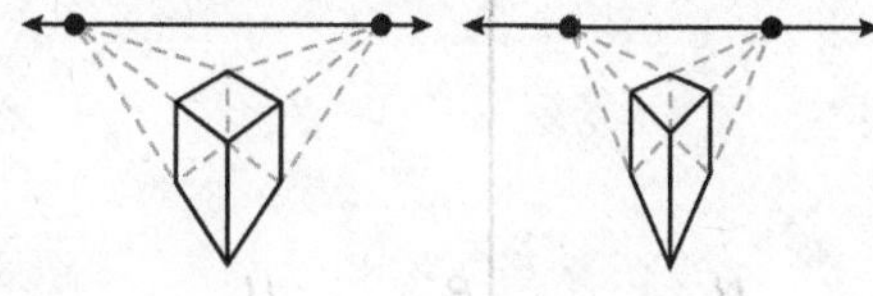

**22.** $\frac{\sqrt{2}}{x} = \frac{x}{5}$
$(x)(x) = (5)(\sqrt{2})$
$x^2 = 5\sqrt{2}$
$x \approx 2.7$

**23.** Since the diagonals of a parallelogram bisect each other, choice **A** is correct.

**24.** The length of the hypotenuse of a 45°–45°–90° triangle is equal to the length of a leg times $\sqrt{2}$. Since the leg is 22 in. long, the hypotenuse has a length of $22\sqrt{2}$ in.

**25.** It is necessary to know at least three sides, two on one triangle and one on the other. If you know these, you can use proportions to find the lengths of the missing sides and the perimeters.

**26.** $\frac{5}{8} = \frac{x}{18}$
$(8)(x) = (5)(18)$
$8x = 90$
$x = 11.25$

**27.**

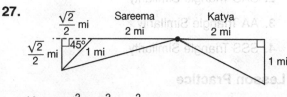

Katya: $d^2 = 2^2 + 1^2$
$d = \sqrt{5}$

Sareema: $d^2 = \left(2 + \frac{\sqrt{2}}{2}\right)^2 + \left(\frac{\sqrt{2}}{2}\right)^2$

$d^2 = \left(4\frac{1}{2} + 2\sqrt{2}\right) + \left(\frac{1}{2}\right)$

$d = \sqrt{5 + 2\sqrt{2}}$

Katya's distance is shorter.

**28.** When the net is folded up, faces 2 and 6 will overlap.

**29.**

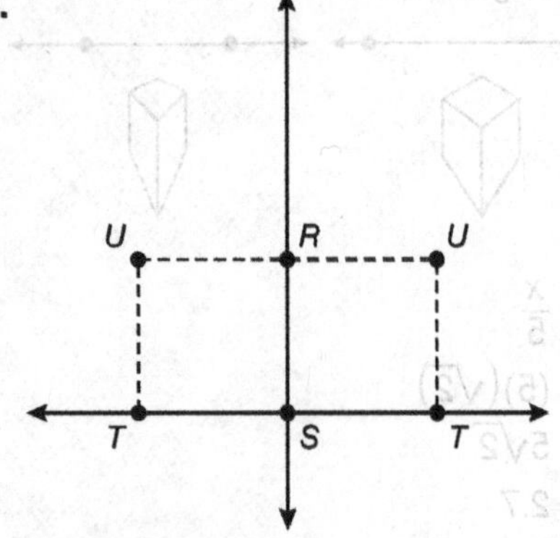


$T(\pm4, 0)$, and $U(0, \pm4)$

**30.** **a.** (2, 0), (2, 2), (0, 2)

**b.** (3, 0), (3,1), (2, 1); (1, 0), (1, 1), (0, 1); (0, 3), (1, 3), (1, 2)

**c.** The smallest blue triangles and smallest white triangles are all congruent. Their angle measures are 45°, 45°, and 90°, so corresponding angles are congruent. Their side measures are 1, 1, and $\sqrt{2}$, so corresponding sides are also congruent.

## LESSON 55

### Warm Up 55

1. similar
2. SAS Triangle Similarity
3. AA Triangle Similarity
4. SSS Triangle Similarity

### Lesson Practice

**a.** $x = 2(12) = 24$

$RT = TQ = y = 8$

**b.**

| Statements | Reasons |
|---|---|
| 1. $\overline{DE} \parallel \overline{BC}$ | 1. Given |
| 2. $\angle ABC \cong \angle ADE$ | 2. Corresponding angles are congruent |
| 3. $\angle A \cong \angle A$ | 3. Reflexive Property of Congruence |
| 4. $\triangle ABC \sim \triangle ADE$ | 4. AA Triangle Similarity Postulate |
| 5. $AD = DB$ | 5. Definition of midpoint |
| 6. $AD + DB = AB$ | 6. Segment Addition Postulate |
| 7. $AD + AD = AB$ | 7. Substitute |
| 8. $AD = \frac{1}{2}AB$ | 8. Solve |
| 9. $AE = \frac{1}{2}AC$ | 9. Corresponding parts of similar triangles are proportional |
| 10. $2AE = AC$ | 10. Multiplication Property of Equality |
| 11. $AE + EC = AC$ | 11. Segment Addition Postulate |
| 12. $AE + EC = 2AE$ | 12. Substitute |
| 13. $EC = AE$ | 13. Subtraction Property of Equality |
| 14. $E$ is the midpoint of $AC$ | 14. Definition of midpoint |

**c.** $D$ is the midpoint of $\overline{FH}$.

$\text{Midpoint}_{FH}$

$= \left(\frac{-2+2}{2}, \frac{4+-1}{2}\right)$

$= \left(\frac{0}{2}, \frac{3}{2}\right) = (0, 1.5)$

$E$ is the midpoint of $\overline{FG}$.

$\text{Midpoint}_{FG}$

$= \left(\frac{-2+6}{2}, \frac{4+2}{2}\right)$

$= \left(\frac{4}{2}, \frac{6}{2}\right) = (2, 3)$

$D(0, 1.5)$ and $E(2, 3)$

**d.** $2x + 4 = 3x + 2$

$-x = -2$

$x = 2$

$BY = YC = 2(2) + 4 = 8$

$XZ = \frac{1}{2}(8 + 8) = 8$

$XY = \frac{1}{2}(14) = 7$

$YZ = \frac{1}{2}(5 + 5) = 5$

$P = 8 + 7 + 5 = 20$

**e.** 5th Street = $2(11) = 22$ m

Distance along Lowery St. = $\frac{1}{2}(10) = 5$ m

Total Distance walked = $22 + 5 = 27$ m

## Practice 55

**1.**

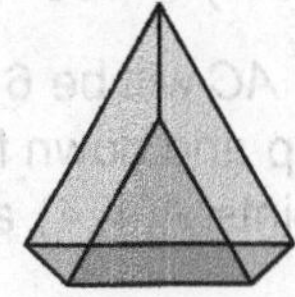

**2.** The diagonals of a rhombus are not necessarily congruent. Choice **C** is correct.

**3.** Sample: Gary could check that the alternate interior angles made by the crossbeams are congruent.

**4.** Ken's form of the theorem would not exclude the possibility that two sides were exactly equal to the third side, a situation that would not produce a triangle. Therefore, he is incorrect.

**5.**

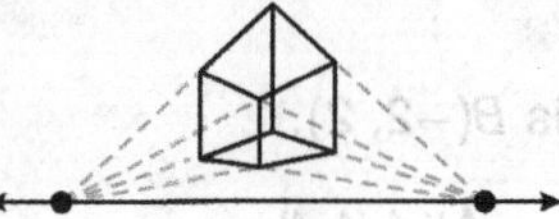

**6.** Each exterior angle of a square is equal to $360° \div 4 = 90°$. By definition, the interior angles of a square are each 90°. The correct answer is a square.

**7.** $V - E + F = 2$

$8 - E + 6 = 2$

$-E = -12$

$E = 12$

**8.** 425 km + 200 km = 625 km

Since the maximum length of the trip back to her starting point would be less than 715 km, she has more than enough fuel to get back.

**9.** Let $\triangle ABC$ be equiangular. By definition, $\angle B \cong \angle C$. By the Converse of the Isosceles Triangle Theorem, $\triangle ABC$ is isosceles with legs $\overline{AB}$ and $\overline{AC}$. By the definition of isosceles triangles, $\overline{AB} \cong \overline{AC}$. Similarly, since $\angle A \cong \angle B$, $\overline{AC} \cong \overline{BC}$. By the Transitive Property of Congruence, $\overline{AB} \cong \overline{BC}$. By definition, $\triangle ABC$ is equilateral.

**10.** Since this is a 45°-45°-90° triangle, the legs are equal to:

$\frac{135}{\sqrt{2}} = \frac{135\sqrt{2}}{2} = 95.5$ yd

**11.**

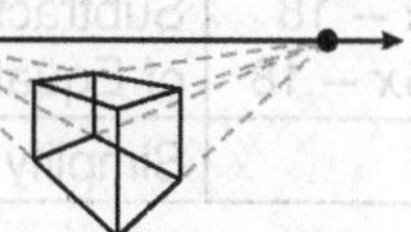

**12.** $D$ is the midpoint of $\overline{AB}$.

$\text{Midpoint}_{\overline{AB}}$

$= \left(\frac{0 + -2}{2}, \frac{-2 + 3}{2}\right)$

$= \left(\frac{-2}{2}, \frac{1}{2}\right) = (-1, 0.5)$

$E$ is the midpoint of $\overline{AC}$.

$\text{Midpoint}_{\overline{AC}}$

$= \left(\frac{0 + 3}{2}, \frac{-2 + 2}{2}\right)$

$= \left(\frac{3}{2}, \frac{0}{2}\right) = (1.5, 0)$

$D(-1, 0.5)$ and $E(1.5, 0)$

**13.** $m\angle S = 39°$, by the Triangle Sum Theorem; $m\angle S = 39°$, so $\angle S \cong \angle V$; so $\triangle QRS \sim \triangle TUV$ by Angle-Angle Similarity.

**14.** $x + 4x + 5x + 6x = 360°$

$16x = 360°$

$x = 22.5°$

$4(22.5) = 90°$

$5(22.5) = 112.5°$

$6(22.5) = 135°$

**15.** $x = \frac{1}{2}(30) = 15$

$XU = UY = y = 21$

16. Since this is a right triangle, the orthocenter is located at the right angle vertex. The orthocenter is located at (−2, −9).

17. $\frac{1}{x} = \frac{x}{5}$

$(x)(x) = (1)(5)$

$x^2 = 5$

$x \approx 2.2$

18.

| Statements | Reasons |
|---|---|
| $2(x+3) = \frac{5x-1}{3}$ | Given |
| $3[2(x+3)] = 3\left(\frac{5x-1}{3}\right)$ | Multiplication Property of Equality |
| $6x + 18 = 5x - 1$ | Simplify |
| $6x + 18 - 5x - 18 = 5x - 1 - 5x - 18$ | Subtraction Property of Equality |
| $x = -19$ | Simplify |

19. $d = \sqrt{(x_2 - x_1)^2 + (y_2 - y_1)^2}$

$d_{LM} = \sqrt{(8-0)^2 + (0-0)^2}$

$= \sqrt{8^2 + 0^2} = \sqrt{64} = 8$ units

$8 = \sqrt{(8-4)^2 + (0-y)^2}$

$8 = \sqrt{4^2 + (-y)^2}$

$64 = 16 + y^2$

$48 = y^2$

$y = \pm\sqrt{48} = \pm 4\sqrt{3}$

20. Sample: On $\triangle ABC$, consider altitude $\overline{AD}$ with $D$ on $\overline{BC}$. By the Isosceles Triangle Theorem, $\angle B \cong \angle C$. Since $\angle BDA$ $\angle CDA$ are right angles, by the HA Theorem, $\triangle ABD \cong \triangle ACD$. By CPCTC, $\overline{BD} \cong \overline{DC}$, so $D$ is the midpoint of $\overline{BC}$. Therefore, $\overline{AD}$ is also the median.

21. $AC + DC = AD$ by the Segment Addition Postulate. So $\angle 1 \cong \angle 2$ by the Isosceles Triangle Theorem, and by the definition of congruent angles, $m\angle 1 = m\angle 2$. $m\angle ABD = m\angle 2 + m\angle 3$ by the Angle Addition Postulate, so by the Comparison Property of Inequality, $m\angle ABD > m\angle 2$. By substitution, $m\angle ABD > m\angle 1$. Since in a triangle the longer side is opposite the larger angle, $AD > AB$. By substitution, $AC + DC > AB$, and by further substitution, $AC + BC > AB$

22.

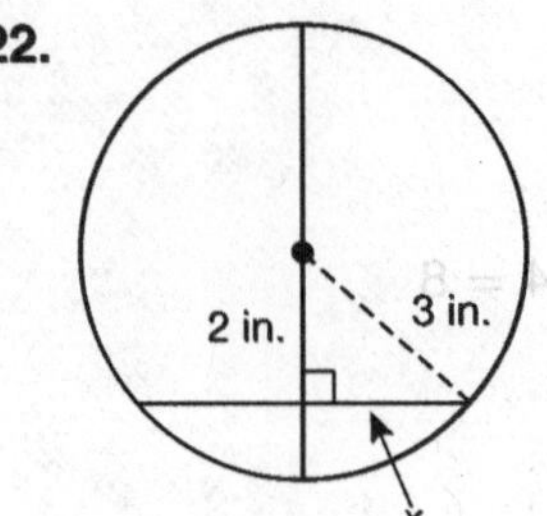


$x^2 = 3^2 - 2^2$

$x^2 = 9 - 4$

$x^2 = 5$

$x \approx 2.2$ inches

23. $7x - 4 = 5x + 20$

$2x = 24$

$x = 12$

$m\angle SVT = 7(12) - 4 = 80°$

$m\overset{\frown}{ST} = 2(m\angle SVT) = 2(80°) = 160°$

24. Since $EF$ is 3 units long, $AC$ will be 6 units long, extending 3 units up and down from point $D$. This gives us points $A(4, 4)$ and $C(4, -2)$.

Since point $E$ is the midpoint of $AB$, we can use the midpoint formula to find the third coordinate.

$(1, 3) = \left(\frac{4+x}{2}, \frac{4+y}{2}\right)$

$\frac{4+x}{2} = 1$

$4 + x = 2$

$x = -2$

$\frac{4+y}{2} = 3$

$4 + y = 6$

$y = 2$

The third point is $B(-2, 2)$.

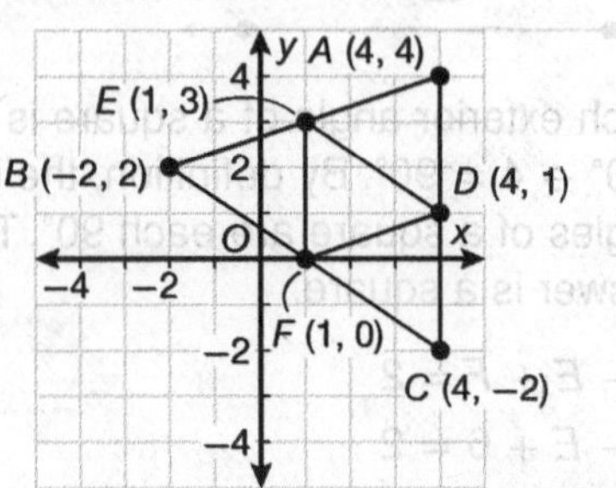


 

25. Since this is a 45°-45°-90° triangle, the hypotenuse is equal to $5\sqrt{2}$. Since each unit on the coordinate plane represents 30 miles, $30(5\sqrt{2}) \approx 212$ miles

26. $x^2 + x^2 = 225^2$
$2x^2 = 50{,}625$
$x^2 = 25{,}312.5$
Since the area of the field is $x^2$, the area is $25{,}312.5 \text{ ft}^2$.

27. $\angle M \cong \angle L$; $KL{:}MN = JL{:}JM$, so $\triangle JKL \sim \triangle JNM$ by SAS Similarity

28. $\frac{11}{x} = \frac{x}{1.5}$
$(x)(x) = (11)(1.5)$
$x^2 = 16.5$
$x \approx 4.1$

29. The situation is impossible because when parallel lines are intersected by a transversal, same-side interior angles are supplementary.

30. $QR = \frac{1}{2}FH$
$2x - 3 = \frac{1}{2}(x + 12)$
$2(2x - 3) = x + 12$
$4x - 6 = x + 12$
$3x = 18$
$x = 6$
$QR = 2(6) - 3 = 9$

## LESSON 56

### Warm Up 56

1. equiangular equilateral

2. $h^2 = 13^2 - 5^2$
$h^2 = 169 - 25$
$h^2 = 144$
$h = 12$

3. $2x + 20° = 180°$
$2x = 160°$
$x = 80°$
Choice **B** is correct.

### Lesson Practice 56

**a.** 7 is the longer leg, and $x$ is the shorter leg. So,
$\sqrt{3}x = 7$
$x = \frac{7}{\sqrt{3}} = \frac{7\sqrt{3}}{3}$
$y$ is the hypotenuse, which is twice the shorter leg. So,
$y = 2\left(\frac{7\sqrt{3}}{3}\right) = \frac{14\sqrt{3}}{3}$

**b.** $y = 2\sqrt{3}$
$x = (\sqrt{3})(\sqrt{3}) = 3$
$P = 2\sqrt{3} + \sqrt{3} + 3 = 3\sqrt{3} + 3$

**c.**

h, 30°, 14 in., 60°, x

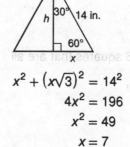

$x^2 + (x\sqrt{3})^2 = 14^2$
$4x^2 = 196$
$x^2 = 49$
$x = 7$
Since $h$ is the longer leg of the right triangle, its length is equal to the length of the shorter leg times $\sqrt{3}$. So, $h = 7\sqrt{3}$
$A = \frac{1}{2}bh$
$= \frac{1}{2}(7)(7\sqrt{3}) = \frac{49\sqrt{3}}{2}$
When we double the area, we get $49\sqrt{3} \text{ in.}^2$.

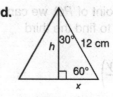

**d.**

h, 30°, 12 cm, 60°, x

$2x = 12$
$x = 6$
$h = 6\sqrt{3}$
$A = \frac{1}{2}bh$
$= \frac{1}{2}(12)(6\sqrt{3}) = 36\sqrt{3}$

When we double the area, we get $36\sqrt{3} \text{ cm}^2$.

## Practice 56

1. $13x + 5x = 180°$
$18x = 180°$
$x = 10°$
$m\angle F = 13(10°) = 130°$

2. A rhombus is defined by having four congruent sides. A square always has four congruent sides. Therefore, a square is always a rhombus.

3. The hypotenuse is twice the length of the shorter leg.
$h = 2(4) = 8$ cm

4. 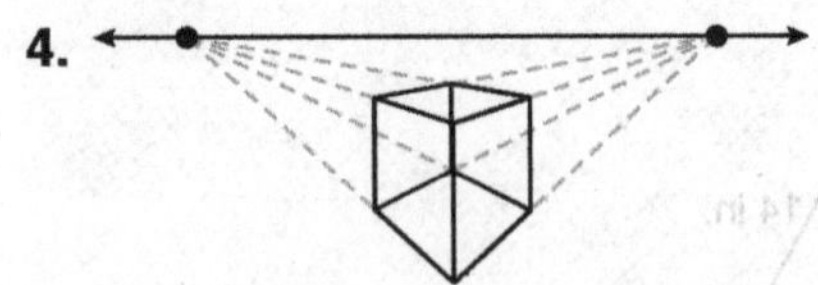

5. The net of a cube is 6 squares that are all 3 cm by 3 cm.
$A = 6(3)(3) = 54$ cm$^2$
Choice **B** is correct.

6. $\frac{9}{12} = \frac{6}{x}$
$(9)(x) = (6)(12)$
$9x = 72$
$x = 8$

7. Since $SU$ is 4 units long, $QR$ will be 8 units long, extending 4 units left and right from point $T$. This gives us points $R(-3, -1)$ and $Q(5, -1)$.
Since point $S$ is the midpoint of $PQ$, we can use the midpoint formula to find the third coordinate.

$(3, 1) = \left(\frac{5 + x}{2}, \frac{-1 + y}{2}\right)$

$\frac{5 + x}{2} = 3$
$5 + x = 6$
$x = 1$

$\frac{-1 + y}{2} = 1$
$-1 + y = 2$
$y = 3$

The third point is $P(1, 3)$.

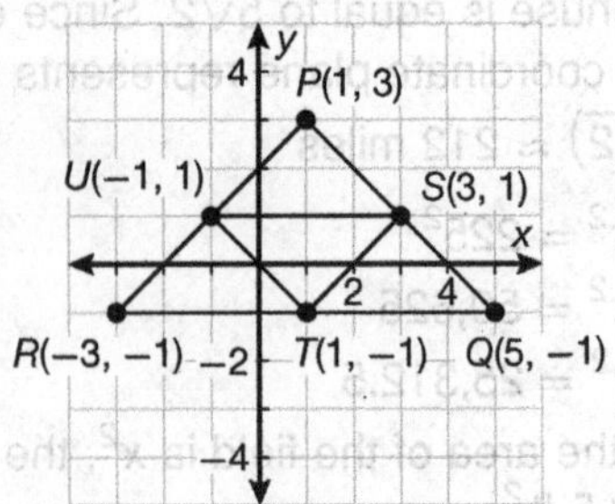


8. $(x + 30)° + (x - 32)° = 180°$
$2x - 2° = 180°$
$2x = 182°$
$x = 91°$
$\angle B = (91 + 30)° = 121°$

9. We can use the Pythagorean Theorem to check each choice.
Choice A: $4^2 + (4\sqrt{3})^2 = 8^2$
$16 + (16)(3) = 64$
$64 = 64$
Choice B: $3^2 + (\sqrt{3})^2 = (2\sqrt{3})^2$
$9 + 3 = (4)(3)$
$12 = 12$
Choice C: $3^2 + (3\sqrt{3})^2 = 6^2$
$9 + (9)(3) = 36$
$36 = 36$
Choice D: $(\sqrt{3})^2 + (2\sqrt{3})^2 = (4\sqrt{3})^2$
$3 + (4)(3) = (16)(3)$
$15 \neq 48$
Choice **D** does not make a 30°-60°-90° triangle.

10. A dodecagon has 12 sides.
$(12 - 2)180° = 1800°$

11. $\angle HJG \cong \angle LJK$ by the Vertical Angles Theorem; $\frac{4}{12} = \frac{3}{9}$, so $\Delta HGJ \sim \Delta LKJ$ by SAS Similarity.

12. $\frac{1.55}{x} = \frac{x}{5.22}$
$(x)(x) = (1.55)(5.22)$
$x^2 = 8.091$
$x \approx 2.8$

13. Since this is a 45°-45°-90° triangle, the legs are equal to:
$\frac{15}{\sqrt{2}} = \frac{15\sqrt{2}}{2}$ miles

14.
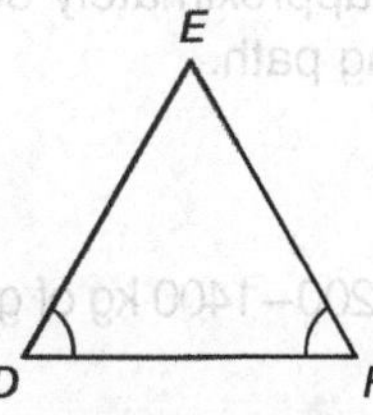


a. $\overline{DE} \cong \overline{EF}$

b. $2x + 14 = 35$
$2x = 21$
$x = 10.5$ millimeters

15. No, because $Q$ could also have any coordinates where $QP = RP$ except (2, −6) or (−2, 6).

16. Current distance $= \frac{1.8\sqrt{2}}{2} + \frac{1.8\sqrt{2}}{2}$
$= \frac{3.6\sqrt{2}}{2}$
$\approx 2.5$
The bridge will reduce the trip by about $2.5 - 1.8 = 0.7$ miles.

17. a. The base angles of an isosceles triangle must be acute.

b. $0 < 2(67 - 3y) < 90$
$0 < 134 - 6y < 90$
$-134 < -6y < -44$
$7.3 < y < 22.3$

18. 

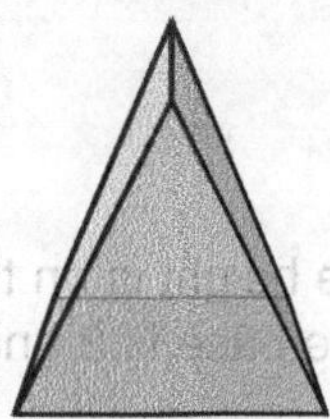

19. $V = \text{Midpoint}_{YZ}$
$= \left(\frac{8 + -1}{2}, \frac{6 + 1}{2}\right)$
$= \left(\frac{7}{2}, \frac{7}{2}\right) = (3.5, 3.5)$
$W = \text{Midpoint}_{XZ}$
$= \left(\frac{5 + -1}{2}, \frac{-4 + 1}{2}\right)$
$= \left(\frac{4}{2}, \frac{-3}{2}\right) = (2, -1.5)$

20. The hypotenuse is 15 ft.
So, the shorter leg is $\frac{15}{2}$ ft.
The longer leg is $\frac{15\sqrt{3}}{2}$.

21. Length of the arc: $\frac{m}{360°}(2\pi r)$
Area of the sector: $\frac{m}{360°}(\pi r^2)$
This is the coefficient because it represents the fractional part of the whole circle the arc or sector covers.

22. No, it is not. There is no 90° angle, so it cannot be a 30°-60°-90° triangle.

23. It is isosceles with the two sides adjacent to the bisected angle congruent.

24. a. Plant $A$ grows taller than Plant $B$.

b. See student work. Sample: Plant $B$ could be slower-growing than Plant $A$ but ultimately taller.

25. $-5x - 4 = 2(-2x + 1)$
$-5x - 4 = -4x + 2$
$-x = 6$
$x = -6$
$DE = -2(-6) + 1 = 13$
$BC = -5(-6) - 4 = 26$

26. The slopes are the negative reciprocal of each other.
$y = -\frac{1}{m}x + c$

27. Since, $14 + 15 > 16$, it is a triangle.
$16^2 = 14^2 + 15^2$
$256 = 196 + 225$
$256 < 421$
The triangle is acute.

28. a. They are similar in shape.

b. 12 in. = 1 ft
The similarity ratio is 108:1.

29. The length of the shorter leg is $\frac{2r}{2} = r$.
The length of the longer leg is $r\sqrt{3}$.

30\. a. $m\angle 1 = 180° - 90° - 37° = 53°$

b. $m\angle 2 = 180° - 90° - 37° = 53°$

## LESSON 57

### Warm Up 57

1\. absolute value

2\. $|6 - -4| = |10| = 10$

3\. $d = \sqrt{(x_2 - x_1)^2 + (y_2 - y_1)^2}$

$= \sqrt{(4 - -2)^2 + (8 - 5)^2}$

$= \sqrt{6^2 + 3^2}$

$= \sqrt{45}$

$\approx 6.71$

### Lesson Practice 57

a. $LO = MN = |-5 - 4| = |-9| = 9$

$LM = ON = |3 - -1| = |4| = 4$

$P = 2(9) + 2(4) = 26$

b. $d = \sqrt{(x_2 - x_1)^2 + (y_2 - y_1)^2}$

$d_{PQ} = \sqrt{(4 - 9)^2 + (-1 - 3)^2}$

$= \sqrt{(-5)^2 + (-4)^2}$

$= \sqrt{41}$

$\approx 6.4$

$d_{PR} = \sqrt{(4 - 6)^2 + (-1 - -4)^2}$

$= \sqrt{(-2)^2 + 3^2}$

$= \sqrt{13}$

$\approx 3.6$

$d_{QR} = \sqrt{(9 - 6)^2 + (3 - -4)^2}$

$= \sqrt{3^2 + 7^2}$

$= \sqrt{58}$

$\approx 7.62$

$P = 6.4 + 3.6 + 7.62 = 17.62$

c. Using $YZ$ as the base, the height can be drawn from points (−3, 1) to (1, 1). The base is 6 units and the height is 4 units.

$A = \frac{1}{2}bh = \frac{1}{2}(6)(4) = 12$

d. It appears that 7 squares are covered completely. There are approximately 4 more squares covered for a total of approximately 11 square units.

e. It appears that there are approximately 33 to 35 squares on the running path.

$33(40) = 1200$

$35(40) = 1400$

They need approximately 1200–1400 kg of gravel.

### Practice 57

1\. shorter leg: hypotenuse $= \frac{1}{2} = 0.500$

longer leg: hypotenuse $= \frac{\sqrt{3}}{2} \approx 0.866$

2\. The ratio of corresponding sides is 1.

3\. $\frac{6\frac{2}{3}}{10} = \frac{x}{6}$

$(10)(x) = \left(6\frac{2}{3}\right)(6)$

$10x = 40$

$x = 4$ inches

$\frac{6\frac{2}{3}}{10} = \frac{x}{8}$

$(10)(x) = \left(6\frac{2}{3}\right)(8)$

$10x = 53\frac{1}{3}$

$x = 5\frac{1}{3}$ inches

4\.

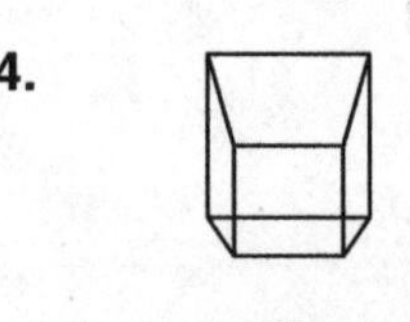

5\. Using $AB$ as the base, the height is on the exterior of the triangle. The base is 3 units and the height is 7 units.

$A = \frac{1}{2}bh = \frac{1}{2}(3)(7) = 10.5$

6.

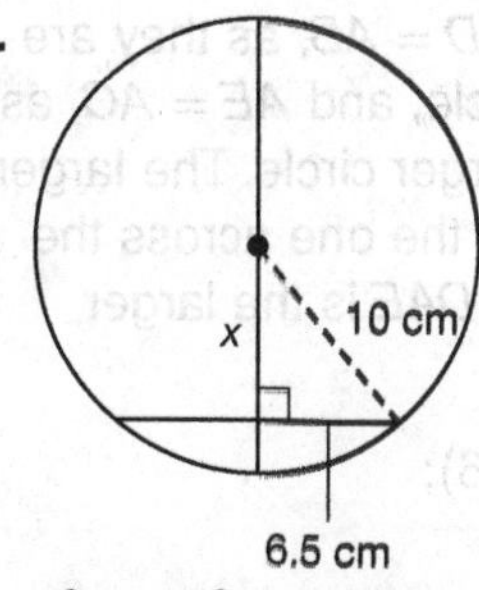


$x^2 = 10^2 - 6.5^2$
$x^2 = 100 - 42.25$
$x^2 = 57.75$
$x \approx 7.6$ centimeters

7. The marked angles are alternate interior angles and are congruent. By the Alternate Interior Angles Theorem, lines *m* and *n* are parallel.

8. $d = \sqrt{(x_2 - x_1)^2 + (y_2 - y_1)^2}$

$d_{WX} = \sqrt{(2 - -2)^2 + (4 - 3)^2}$
$= \sqrt{4^2 + 1^2} = \sqrt{17}$

$d_{XY} = \sqrt{(-2 - -1)^2 + (3 - 7)^2}$
$= \sqrt{(-1)^2 + (-4)^2}$
$= \sqrt{17}$

$d_{YZ} = \sqrt{(-1 - 4)^2 + (7 - 9)^2}$
$= \sqrt{(-5)^2 + (-2)^2}$
$= \sqrt{29}$

$d_{WZ} = \sqrt{(2 - 4)^2 + (4 - 9)^2}$
$= \sqrt{(-2)^2 + (-5)^2}$
$= \sqrt{29}$

$P = \sqrt{17} + \sqrt{17} + \sqrt{29} + \sqrt{29}$
$= 2(\sqrt{17} + \sqrt{29})$

9. $\frac{60^\circ}{360^\circ}(\pi(6)^2) = 6\pi \approx 18.85$

Choice **C** is correct.

10. Since opposite angles in a parallelogram are congruent, their measures are equal. So,

$x - 5 = 3x - 2$
$-2x = 3$
$x = -1.5$

11. $x^2 = 8^2 + 8^2$
$x^2 = 64 + 64$
$x^2 = 128$
$x = \sqrt{128} = 8\sqrt{2}$ inches $\approx 11.3$ inches

12. $10m + 8m = 180^\circ$
$18m = 180^\circ$
$m = 10^\circ$
$m\angle G = 10(10^\circ) = 100^\circ$

13. If two triangles are congruent, then by CPCTC, all corresponding parts are congruent. Therefore, hypotenuses and one pair of acute angles are congruent.

14. $y = 5$ is a horizontal line. So, the distance between the point and the line is the distance between the *y*-coordinates.

$d = |14 - 5| = 9$

15. $J = \text{Midpoint}_{FG}$
$= \left(\frac{-3 + 3}{2}, \frac{5 + 1}{2}\right)$
$= \left(\frac{0}{2}, \frac{6}{2}\right) = (0, 3)$

$K = \text{Midpoint}_{FH}$
$= \left(\frac{-3 + -1}{2}, \frac{5 + -1}{2}\right)$
$= \left(\frac{-4}{2}, \frac{4}{2}\right) = (-2, 2)$

$d_{JK} = \sqrt{(0 - -2)^2 + (3 - 2)^2}$
$= \sqrt{2^2 + 1^2}$
$= \sqrt{5}$

$d_{GH} = \sqrt{(3 - -1)^2 + (1 - -1)^2}$
$= \sqrt{4^2 + 2^2}$
$= \sqrt{20} = 2\sqrt{5}$

So, $JK = \frac{1}{2}GH$

16. $\frac{4}{18} = \frac{x}{21}$

$(18)(x) = (4)(21)$
$18x = 84$
$x = \frac{14}{3}$ inches

$\frac{4}{18} = \frac{x}{24}$

$(18)(x) = (4)(24)$
$18x = 96$
$x = \frac{16}{3}$ inches

**17.** shorter leg = 3.2
hypotenuse = 2(3.2) = 6.4
longer leg = $3.2\sqrt{3}$
$P = 3.2 + 6.4 + 3.2\sqrt{3}$
$= 9.6 + 3.2\sqrt{3}$ inches

**18.** ~*p* and *q*

**19.** First, find the coordinates *D*(1, −2) and *E* (0, 2). Then use the slope formula to find that the slope of $\overline{AC} = -4$ and the slope of $\overline{DE} = -4$. $\overline{AC} \parallel \overline{DE}$.

**20.**

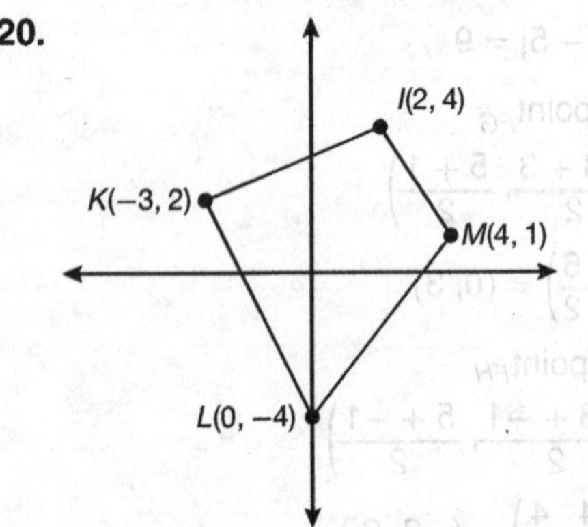


This is an irregular polygon that appears to cover approximately 29 squares.

**21.** $x^2 = 9^2 - 7.5^2$
$x^2 = 81 - 56.25$
$x^2 = 24.75$
$x \approx 4.97$ units

**22.** In order for triangles to be similar, the corresponding angles must be congruent. Choice **D** contradicts this.

**23.** Instead of finding all three medians, Carina found only two medians and one altitude.

**24.** base: longer side = $30\sqrt{3}$
height: shorter side = 30
$A = \frac{1}{2}(30\sqrt{3})(30) \approx 779.42 \text{ ft}^2$
$779.42 \div 4 \approx 195$ minutes

**25.** In the two triangles, *AD* = *AB*, as they are radii of the smaller circle, and *AE* = *AC*, as they are radii of the larger circle. The larger angle will therefore be the one across the longer third side, so ∠*DAE* is the larger angle.

**26.** (2, 6), (2, 0), and (9, 6);
$P = 2(7) + 2(6) = 26$
The perimeter is 26 units.

**27.** Four triangles form a triangular pyramid.

**28.** Since all radii in a circle are congruent, $\overline{PA}$, $\overline{PB}$, $\overline{PC}$, and $\overline{PD}$ are all congruent to each other. By definition of congruent segments, *PA* = *PD*. Since *PX* = *PY*, $\overline{PX}$ and $\overline{PY}$ are congruent. Since △*PAX* and △*PYD* are right triangles with one equal leg and equal hypotenuses, by the HL Congruence Theorem, *AX* = *DY*. By CPCTC, $\overline{AX} \cong \overline{DY}$. Similarly, $\overline{AX}$, $\overline{BX}$, $\overline{DY}$, and $\overline{CY}$ are all congruent, and so all have the same measure. So *AX* + *XB* = *CY* + *YD*, and by the Segment Addition Postulate and by substitution, *AB* = *CD*. By the definition of congruent line segments, $\overline{AB} \cong \overline{CD}$.

**29.** Since m∠1 + m∠2 = 180°, ∠1 and ∠2 are supplementary; they are also same-side interior angles. Converse of the Same-Side Interior Angles Theorem implies lines *d* and *e* are parallel.

**30.** Solving the Pythagorean Theorem for the first triangle gives a third side length of $16\sqrt{3}$, so the first triangle has the proportions of a 30°-60°-90° triangle. By the Triangle Sum Theorem, since the second triangle has a 90° and a 60° angle, the third angle is 30°, so these triangles have the same angles and are similar. But without a side length for the second triangle or a proportionality ratio, it cannot be determined whether they are congruent.

## LESSON 58

### Warm Up 58

**1.** chord

2. Since $\overline{CA} \cong \overline{CB}$ because they are both radii of the same circle, the triangle is isosceles.

3. Line $n$ is tangent to the circle. Lines $p$ and $m$ are both secants to the circle.

## Lesson Practice 58

a.

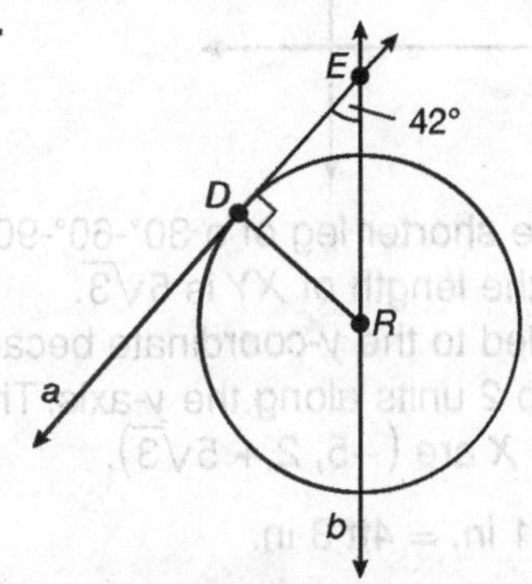


By Theorem 58-1, $\overline{DR}$ is perpendicular to $a$, making $\triangle RED$ a right triangle. So, $\angle DRE = 180° - 90° - 42° = 48°$

b. No, if $\overleftrightarrow{AB}$ was tangent to $\odot C$, then $\angle BAC$ would be a right angle by Theorem 58-1.

c. Draw auxiliary line segments $\overline{PA}$, $\overline{PB}$, and $\overline{PC}$. Since $\overline{AB}$ and $\overline{AC}$ are tangents to $\odot P$, $\overline{AB} \perp \overline{PB}$ and $\overline{AC} \perp \overline{PC}$, so $\triangle ABP$ and $\triangle ACP$ are right triangles. $\overline{PB} \cong \overline{PC}$ since they are both radii of the circle, and $\overline{PA} \cong \overline{PA}$ by the Reflexive Property of Congruence. Therefore, $\triangle ABP \cong \triangle ACP$ by the HL Right Triangle Congruence Theorem, and $\overline{AB} \cong \overline{AC}$ by CPCTC.

d.

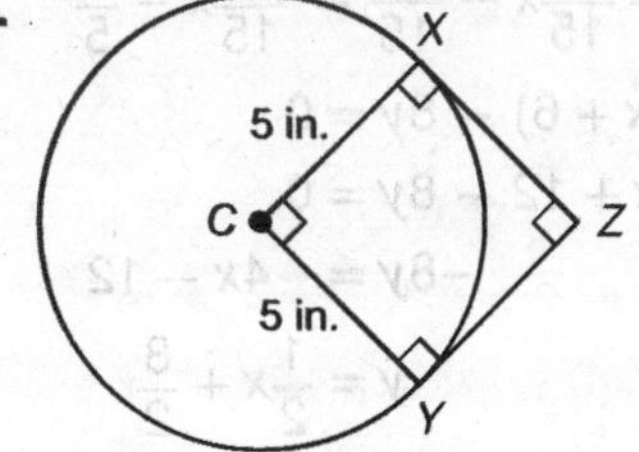


By Theorem 58-1, angles $X$ and $Y$ are right angles. We are given that $\angle C$ is a right angle, therefore, $\angle Z$ is also a right angle. So, quadrilateral $CXZY$ is a square with sides that measure 5 inches.

$A = s^2 = 5^2 = 25 \text{ in.}^2$

e. By Theorem 58-1, $\angle CBQ$ is a right angle.

$(BQ)^2 = (CQ)^2 - (CB)^2$

$(BQ)^2 = 6^2 - 3^2$

$(BQ)^2 = 36 - 9$

$(BQ)^2 = 27$

$BQ = \sqrt{27} = 3\sqrt{3}$

$P = 6\,(3\sqrt{3}) = 18\sqrt{3} \text{ ft}$

## Practice 58

1. $\overline{PQ}$ is tangent to both. $\overline{AP} \perp \overline{PQ}$. If a line in the plane of a circle is perpendicular to a radius at its endpoint on the circle, then the line is tangent to the circle. So, $\overline{PQ}$ is tangent to $\odot A$. $\overline{QZ} \parallel \overline{AP} \perp \overline{PQ} \rightarrow \overline{QZ} \perp \overline{PQ}$. Since if a line in the plane of a circle is perpendicular to a radius at its endpoint on the circle, then the line is tangent to the circle, $\overline{PQ}$ is tangent to $\odot Z$.

2. If you draw line $RG$, it forms a 30°-60°-90° right triangle.

$\frac{\sqrt{3}}{36} = \frac{1}{ER}$

$(\sqrt{3})\,(ER) = (1)(36)$

$\sqrt{3}ER = 36$

$ER = \frac{36}{\sqrt{3}} = \frac{36\sqrt{3}}{3} = 12\sqrt{3}$

3. There are 7 complete squares shaded plus approximately 2.5 partial squares shaded. The area is approximately 9.5 squares.

4. Shorter leg = 72 ft

Hypotenuse = 2(72) = 144 ft

Longer leg = $72\sqrt{3}$ ft

$P = 72 + 144 + 72\sqrt{3}$

$= (216 + 72\sqrt{3}) \text{ ft}$

5. $(x + 20)° + (x - 5)° + x° = 180°$

$3x + 15 = 180$

$3x = 165$

$x = 55$

$m\angle 3 = 55°$

$m\angle 1 = 55° + 20° = 75°$

$m\angle 2 = 55° - 5° = 50°$

Since $\angle 1$ is the largest angle, stations 2 and 3 are the farthest apart.

6. $XY$ and either $m\angle U$ or $m\angle W$. If $XY =$ 3.5 inches and either angle measure is either 33° or 57°, the hypotenuses and one pair of acute angles are congruent.

7. Total Area = (10)(24) = 240 in.$^2$
   Shaded Area = (2)(8) + (2)(16) = 48 in.$^2$
   $$\frac{48}{240} = \frac{1}{5}$$
   $$\frac{1}{5} \times \$10 = \$2$$

8. You will always get a rhombus. If the segments were the same length, you would get a square.

9. She can stretch a rope across the pool to form a short chord and move a second rope until it bisects the first, at which point the second rope would be a diameter of the pool.

10. For $x = 4$, the sides are 14, 16, and 8, which can be used to create a triangle. For $x = 6$, the sides would be 20, 36, and 8. Since 20 + 8 is less than the side length of 36, these three could not form a triangle.

11. $2(3x - 2) = 5x + 2$
    $6x - 4 = 5x + 2$
    $x = 6$
    $GH = 5(6) + 2 = 32$

12. No, it is not a square because the diagonals are not equal. His measurements are off by 0.26 in. and 0.22 in. If he subtracts 0.26 in. from the 17.26 in. diagonal and added 0.22 in. to the 16.78 in. diagonal, the frame would be a square.

13. a.

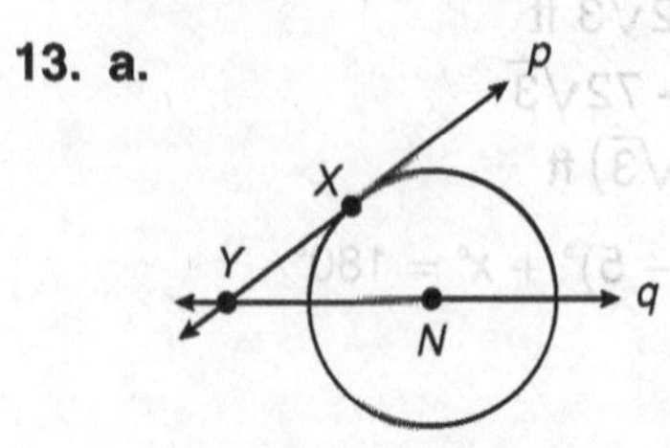


b. By Theorem 58-1, $m\angle NXY = 90°$
   $m\angle NYX = 180° - 90° - 13° = 77°$

14.

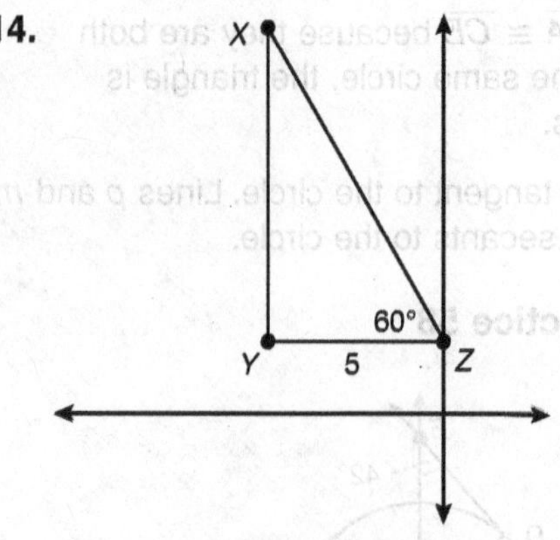


Since $YZ$ is the shorter leg of a 30°-60°-90° right triangle, the length of $XY$ is $5\sqrt{3}$.
2 must be added to the $y$-coordinate because $Y$ is already up 2 units along the $y$-axis. The coordinates of $X$ are $\left(-5, 2 + 5\sqrt{3}\right)$.

15. $P = 3(17) = 51$ in. = 4ft 3 in.

16.

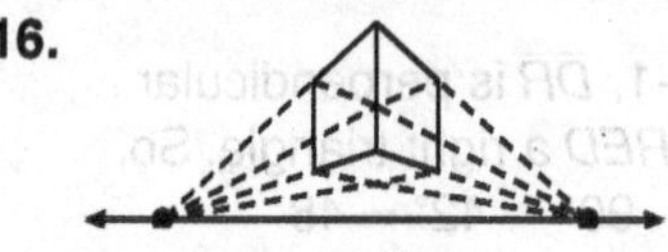

17. $2x + y = 6$
    $y = -2x + 3$
    The slope of line perpendicular to this line will be $\frac{1}{2}$.
    Choice A: $2x + 4y + 7 = 0$
    $4y = -2x - 7$
    $y = -\frac{1}{2}x - \frac{7}{4}$
    Choice B: $7x = 15y + 6$
    $-15y = -7x + 6$
    $y = \frac{7}{15}x - \frac{6}{15} = \frac{7}{15}x - \frac{2}{5}$
    Choice C: $2(2x + 6) - 8y = 0$
    $4x + 12 - 8y = 0$
    $-8y = -4x - 12$
    $y = \frac{1}{2}x + \frac{3}{2}$
    Choice D: $2x - y = 4$
    $-y = -2x + 4$
    $y = 2x - 4$
    Choice **C** is correct because its slope is $\frac{1}{2}$.

18. $P = 73 + 73 + 22 + 22 = 190$ mm

19. $d = \sqrt{(x_2 - x_1)^2 + (y_2 - y_1)^2}$

$d_{HP} = \sqrt{(4 - 0)^2 + (2 - 0)^2}$
$= \sqrt{4^2 + 2^2}$
$= \sqrt{20}$
$\approx 4.47$ units

$d_{PF} = \sqrt{(4 - 8)^2 + (2 - 0)^2}$
$= \sqrt{(-4)^2 + 2^2}$
$= \sqrt{20}$
$\approx 4.47$ units

$d_{FH} = \sqrt{(8 - 0)^2 + (0 - 0)^2}$
$= \sqrt{8^2 + 0^2}$
$= \sqrt{64}$
$= 8$ units

Total distance $= 50(4.47 + 4.47 + 8)$
$= 847$

Jose walked 847 feet.

20. If a quadrilateral has the properties of both a rectangle and a rhombus, then it is a square. Because a rectangle has 90° angles and congruent diagonals and a rhombus has perpendicular diagonals and congruent sides, all of those features together can only make one shape—a square. Therefore, Noyemi is incorrect. Her statement is always true.

21. Since $m\angle AMB = 74°$, $m\widehat{AB} = 74°$. Since $AC$ is a diameter of circle $M$, $\widehat{ABC}$ is a semicircle and measures 180°. So, $m\widehat{BC} = 180° - 74° = 106°$

$m\angle CDB = \frac{1}{2}(106°) = 53°$

22.

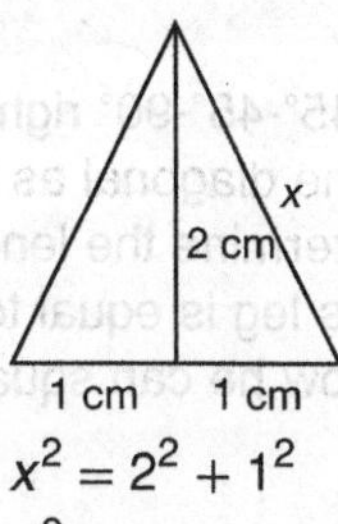


$x^2 = 2^2 + 1^2$
$x^2 = 4 + 1$
$x^2 = 5$
$x = \sqrt{5}$ cm

Choice **C** is correct.

23. $x^2 + x^2 = 72^2$
$2x^2 = 5184$
$x^2 = 2592$
$x \approx 51$

So, the total perimeter of the shed is
$4 \times 51 = 204$ feet
$204 \div 6 = 34$ pieces of lumber

24. $18x + 90° = 180°$
$18x = 90°$
$x = 5°$

25.

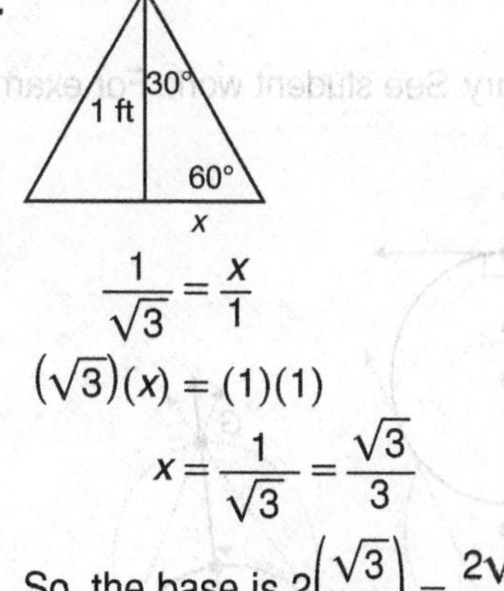


$\frac{1}{\sqrt{3}} = \frac{x}{1}$

$(\sqrt{3})(x) = (1)(1)$

$x = \frac{1}{\sqrt{3}} = \frac{\sqrt{3}}{3}$

So, the base is $2\left(\frac{\sqrt{3}}{3}\right) = \frac{2\sqrt{3}}{3}$

$A = \frac{1}{2}(1)\left(\frac{2\sqrt{3}}{3}\right) = \frac{\sqrt{3}}{3}$ ft$^2$

26.

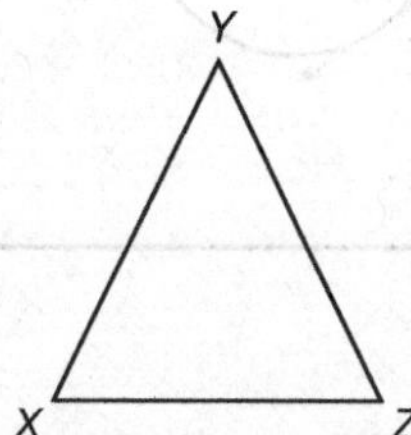


The included angle is $\angle YXZ$.

27. There are 33 complete squares plus approximately 10 partial squares. The area is approximately 43 squares.

28. The triangles are congruent since $\overline{AB} \cong \overline{CD}$ and $\overline{BC} \cong \overline{DA}$ because $ABCD$ is a parallelogram. The last side in both triangles is $\overline{CA}$, so, by SSS, the triangles are congruent.

29. The resulting shape is a septagonal prism.

30. $2x - 4 > 0$
$2x > 4$
$x > 2$
$x$ must be greater than 2 so that $m\angle TQS$ is greater than 0. The larger angle must be less than 180°.
$5x - 8 < 180$
$5x < 188$
$x < \frac{188}{5}$
Yes, if $2 < x < \frac{188}{5}$, $RT > TS$

## LAB 8

### Lab 8 Practice

Answers may vary. See student work. For example, a–d.

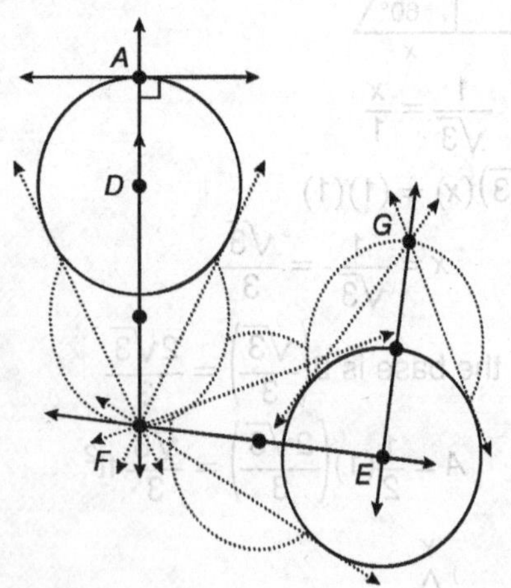


## LESSON 59

### Warm Up 59

1. prism
2. $A = \frac{1}{2}bh = \frac{1}{2}(8)(10) = 40 \text{ in.}^2$
3. $A = lw = (12)(7) = 84 \text{ ft}^2$

### Lesson Practice 59

a. $P_{base} = 2(7) + 2(9) = 32$ yd
$L = (P_{base})(h)$
$= (32)(15)$
$= 480 \text{ yd}^2$

b. $S = L + 2B$
$= 480 + 2(7)(9)$
$= 480 + 126$
$= 606 \text{ yd}^2$

c. $V = Bh$
$B = 5\left[\frac{1}{2}(14)(10)\right] = 350 \text{ cm}^2$
$V = (350)(22) = 7700 \text{ cm}^3$

d. $V = Bh$
$B = \frac{1}{2}(5)(3) = 7.5 \text{ ft}^2$
$V = (7.5)(12) = 90 \text{ ft}^3$

e. $V = lwh = (8)(15)(2) = 240 \text{ m}^3$

### Practice 59

1. There are 5 complete squares shaded plus approximately 4 partial squares shaded. The area is approximately 9 squares.

2. $\frac{9}{p} = \frac{36}{28}$
$(36)(p) = (9)(28)$
$36p = 252$
$p = 7$

3. $\frac{2y}{7} = \frac{7}{y}$
$(2y)(y) = (7)(7)$
$2y^2 = 49$
$y^2 = 24.5$
$y \approx 4.9$

4. 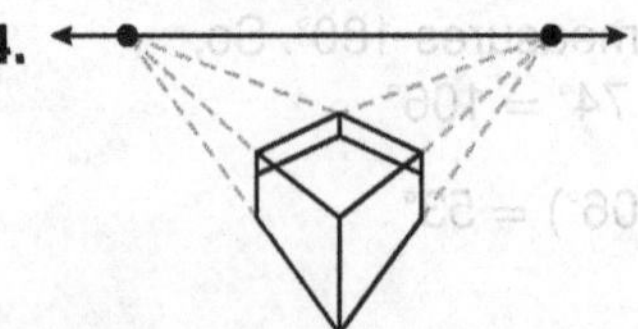

5. Using the properties of a 45°-45°-90° right triangle, Armine can use the diagonal as the hypotenuse length and determine the length of a leg of the triangle. This leg is equal to the length and the width, so now he can square the value for the area.

6. There are 18 complete squares shaded plus approximately 10 partial squares shaded. The area is approximately 28 square inches.

7. The perpendicular segment from a point to a line is the shortest segment from the point to the line; $G$; line $q \perp \overline{FG}$

8. Marina found the centroid (the point of concurrency of the three medians) instead of the orthocenter (the point of concurrency of the three altitudes).

9. The diagonals of a square form right angles. The interior triangles formed by the diagonals are, therefore, all right triangles. Choice **D** is correct.

10. $m\angle DAZ = 180° - 90° - 58° = 32°$

11. Conjunction: The triangle is acute and has exactly two acute angles.
This is false because an acute triangle has three acute angles.

12. Shorter leg: $x = \frac{1}{2}(6) = 3$
Longer leg: $y = x\sqrt{3} = 3\sqrt{3}$

13. a.

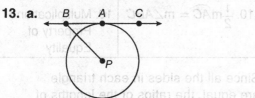

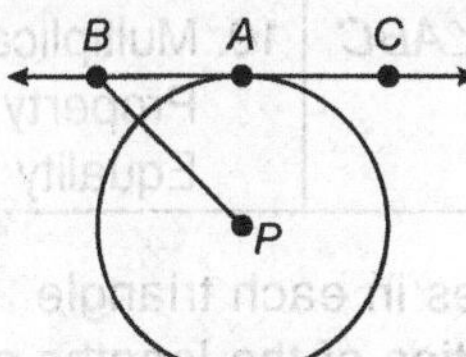


$\angle PBC$ is acute.

b.

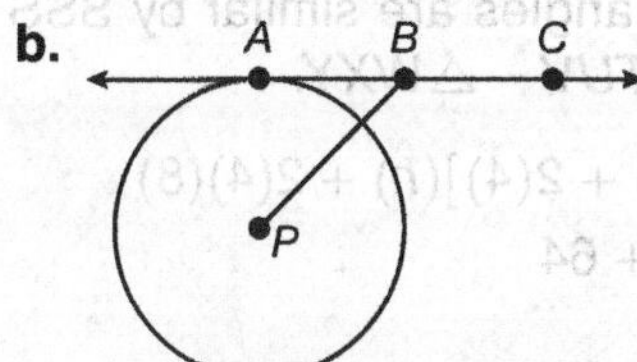


$\angle PBC$ is obtuse.

c. No; If it were, $\overline{PB}$ would be parallel to $\overline{PA}$ because they are both perpendicular to $m$. This is impossible because parallel lines never meet.

14. $L = ph$
$p = 2(36) + 2(38) = 148$ cm
$L = (148)(15) = 2220 \text{ cm}^2$

15. $8.25^2 = 5.25^2 + 6.33^2$
$68.0625 = 25.5625 + 40.0689$
$68.0625 \neq 65.6314$
Because the square of 8.25 is more than the sum of the squares of the other two side lengths, Kai's hypotenuse is too long, so he must cut it down.

16. $V = Bh = (15)(15)(25) = 5625 \text{ ft}^3$

17. Students' polygons will vary but should have corresponding sides with a ratio of 1:4. For example,

4 ft, 1 ft; 8 ft, 2 ft

18. $(PU)^2 = 8^2 - x^2$
$(PU)^2 = 64 - x^2$
$PU = \sqrt{64 - x^2}$

19. The height is the shorter leg.
hypotenuse: 2(shorter leg) = 2(3) = 6 ft

20. $x^2 = 5^2 + 12^2$
$x^2 = 25 + 144$
$x^2 = 169$
$x = 13$
$S = L + 2B$
$L = (5)(6) + (12)(6) + (13)(6)$
$= 180 \text{ in.}^2$
$B = \frac{1}{2}(5)(12) = 30$
$S = 180 + 2(30) = 240 \text{ in.}^2$

21.

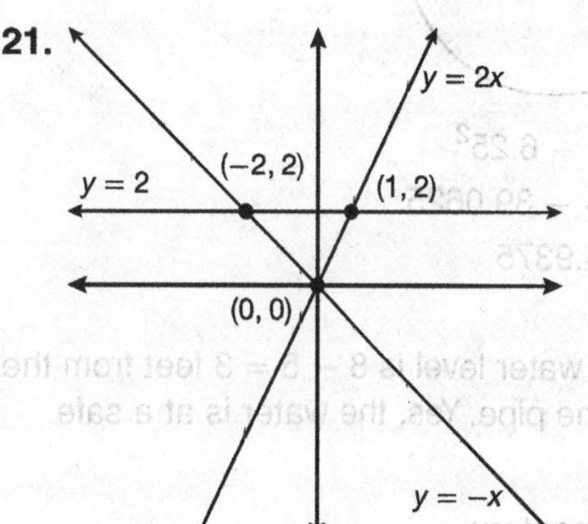


$d = \sqrt{(2-0)^2 + (1-0)^2}$
$= \sqrt{2^2 + 1^2}$
$= \sqrt{5}$

$d = \sqrt{(-2 - 0)^2 + (2 - 0)^2}$
$= \sqrt{(-2)^2 + 2^2}$
$= \sqrt{8}$
$= 2\sqrt{2}$

$d = \sqrt{(1 - -2)^2 + (2 - 2)^2}$
$= \sqrt{3^2 + 0^2}$
$= \sqrt{9}$
$= 3$ units

Perimeter $= 3 + \sqrt{5} + 2\sqrt{2}$

Area $= \frac{1}{2}bh = \frac{1}{2}(3)(2) = 3$

**22.** 1 foot 7 in. = 19 in.

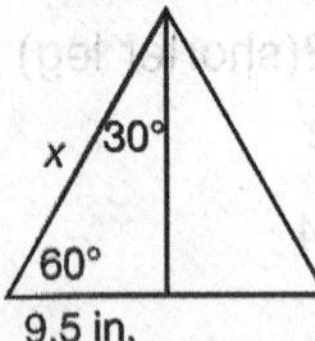


$x = 2(9.5) = 19$ in.
$P = 3(19) = 57$ in. or 4 ft 9 in.

**23.**

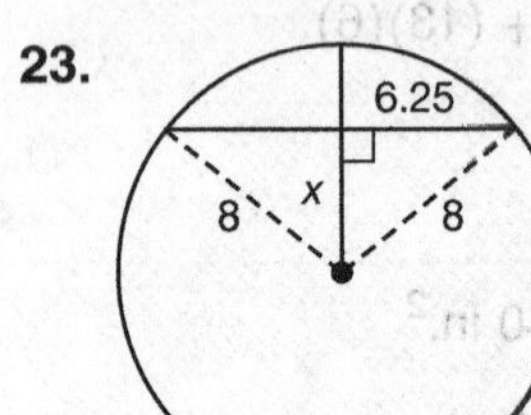


$x^2 = 8^2 - 6.25^2$
$x^2 = 64 - 39.0625$
$x^2 = 24.9375$
$x \approx 5$

So, the water level is $8 - 5 = 3$ feet from the top of the pipe. Yes, the water is at a safe level.

**24.** supplementary

**25.**

| Statements | Reasons |
|---|---|
| 1. $\angle ABX$ is inscribed in $\odot X$ with $X$ on $\overline{BC}$. | 1. Given |
| 2. $m\widehat{AC} = m\angle AXC$ | 2. Def. of arc measure |
| 3. $m\angle AXC = m\angle ABX + m\angle BAX$ | 3. Exterior Angle Theorem |
| 4. $\overline{XA} \cong \overline{XB}$ | 4. Radii of a circle are congruent |
| 5. $\triangle AXB$ is isosceles | 5. Def. of isosceles $\triangle$ |
| 6. $\angle ABC \cong \angle BAX$ | 6. Isosceles Triangle Theorem |
| 7. $m\angle ABC = m\angle BAX$ | 7. Def. of congruent angles |
| 8. $m\angle AXC = 2(m\angle ABC)$ | 8. Substitution |
| 9. $m\widehat{AC} = 2(m\angle ABC)$ | 9. Substitution |
| 10. $\frac{1}{2}m\widehat{AC} = m\angle ABC$ | 10. Multiplication Property of Equality |

**26.** Since all the sides in each triangle are equal, the ratios of the lengths of corresponding sides are equal. So, all equilateral triangles are similar by SSS Similarity. $\triangle TUV \sim \triangle WXY$.

**27.** $352 = [2(8) + 2(4)](h) + 2(4)(8)$
$352 = 24h + 64$
$288 = 24h$
$12 \text{ in.} = h$

**28.** $A_{grass} = (25)(50) - [(8)(16) + (6)(17)]$
$= 1250 - 230$
$= 1020 \text{ ft}^2$
$1020 \times \$0.015 = \$15.30$

**29.** **a.** $\angle T \cong \angle X$; If two angles of one triangle are congruent to two angles of another triangle, then the third angles are congruent.

**b.** $\angle S \cong \angle W$; If two angles of one triangle are congruent to two angles of another triangle, then the third angles are congruent.

**30.** line $n$ only

## LESSON 60

### Warm Up 60

1. parallel
2. Parallel lines have equal slopes. The slopes of perpendicular lines are opposite reciprocals.
3. Choice **A** is correct because alternate interior angles are congruent, not supplementary.

### Lesson Practice 60

**a.** $\frac{AD}{DC} = \frac{AE}{EB}$

$\frac{6}{10} = \frac{4}{EB}$

$(6)(AB) = (10)(4)$

$6AB = 40$

$AB = 6\frac{2}{3}$

**b.** $\frac{x}{2x-1} = \frac{3}{5}$

$(x)(5) = (2x-1)(3)$

$5x = 6x - 3$

$-x = -3$

$x = 3$

$PQ = (2x - 1) + x$

$= 2(3) - 1 + 3$

$= 8$

**c.** Since $\overline{DE} \parallel \overline{BC}$, $\angle ADE \cong \angle ABC$ and $\angle AED \cong \angle ACB$ because they are corresponding angles. Therefore, $\triangle ADE \sim \triangle ABC$ by the AA Similarity Theorem. Since the two triangles are similar, the proportion $\frac{AD}{AB} = \frac{AE}{AC}$ is true. By the Segment Addition Postulate, this is equivalent to $\frac{AD}{AD+DB} = \frac{AE}{AE+EC}$. Taking the cross product and simplifying yields $AD \times EC = AE \times DB$. Dividing both sides of the equation by $DB$ and $EC$ results in $\frac{AD}{DB} = \frac{AE}{EC}$.

**d.** $\frac{3}{4} = \frac{AB}{2}$

$(4)(AB) = (3)(2)$

$4AB = 6$

$AB = 1.5$

$AC = 1.5 + 3 = 4.5$

**e.** If they are parallel, the segments will be proportional.

$\frac{12}{9} = \frac{13}{9.75}$

$(12)(9.75) = (9)(13)$

$117 = 117$

Yes, they are parallel.

**f.** $\frac{10}{8} = \frac{AE}{20}$

$(8)(AE) = (10)(20)$

$8AE = 200$

$AE = 25$

### Practice 60

**1.**

| Statements | Reasons |
|---|---|
| 1. $\overline{KN} \cong \overline{LM}$ | 1. Opposite sides of a parallelogram are ≅. |
| 2. $\overline{KM} \cong \overline{KM}$ | 2. Reflexive Property of Congruence |
| 3. $\overline{KN} \parallel \overline{LM}$ | 3. Definition of a parallelogram |
| 4. $\angle LMK \cong \angle NKM$ | 4. Alternate Interior Angles Theorem |
| 5. $\triangle LKM \cong \triangle NMK$ | 5. SAS |

**2.** $\frac{WV}{15} = \frac{28x}{25x}$

$(25x)(WV) = (15)(28x)$

$(25x)(WV) = 420x$; $WV = 16.8$

**3.** Find the slope of the line perpendicular to $y = \frac{3}{2}x - 3$. The slope is $-\frac{2}{3}$.

$y = -\frac{2}{3}x + b$

$2 = -\frac{2}{3}(-1) + b$

$\frac{4}{3} = b$; $y = -\frac{2}{3}x + \frac{4}{3}$

Now, find the point of intersection by setting the equations equal to each other.

$$\frac{3}{2}x - 3 = -\frac{2}{3}x + \frac{4}{3}$$

$$\frac{13}{6}x = \frac{13}{3}$$

$$x = 2$$

$$y = \frac{3}{2}(2) - 3 = 0$$

The point of intersection is (2, 0). Find the distance between (2, 0) and (−1, 2).

$$d = \sqrt{(2 - -1)^2 + (0 - 2)^2}$$

$$= \sqrt{3^2 + (-2)^2}$$

$$= \sqrt{13}$$

$$\approx 3.61$$

**4.** Reflexive; SAS Similarity; Congruence; Converse of Corresponding Angles Postulate.

**5.** $\frac{4}{6} = \frac{5}{PY}$

$$(4)(PY) = (6)(5)$$

$$4PY = 30$$

$$PY = 7.5$$

$$(RQ)^2 = (5 + 4)^2 + (7.5 + 6)^2$$

$$(RQ)^2 = 9^2 + 13.5^2$$

$$(RQ)^2 = 81 + 182.25$$

$$(RQ)^2 = 263.25$$

$$RQ \approx 16.2$$

$$P = 16.2 + 9 + 13.5 = 38.7$$

**6.** $l = w = h$

$$V = lwh$$

$$343 = l^3$$

$$l = w = h = 7$$

$$S = L + 2B$$

$$= (4)(7)(7) + 2(7)(7) = 294 \text{ m}^2$$

**7.** It is given that $\overline{AD}$ bisects $\angle A$. Draw $\overline{BX}$ parallel to $\overline{AD}$ and extend $\overline{BX}$ to $X$. By the Triangle Proportionality Theorem, $\frac{BD}{DC} = \frac{AX}{AC}$. By the Corresponding Angles Postulate, $\angle CAD \cong \angle AXB$, and by the definition of angle bisector, $\angle CAD \cong \angle DAB$. So by the Alternate Interior Angles Theorem, $\angle DAB \cong \angle ABX$. By the Transitive Property of Congruence, $\angle DAB \cong \angle AXB$ and $\angle ABX \cong \angle AXB$. By the Converse of the Isosceles Triangle Theorem, $\overline{AX} \cong \overline{AB}$, which also implies by the definition of congruence that $AX = AB$. By substitution, $\frac{BD}{DC} = \frac{AB}{AC}$.

**8.** $7y + 11y = 180$

$$18y = 180$$

$$y = 10°$$

$$m\angle M = 7(10°) = 70°$$

$$m\angle N = 8(10°) + 8 = 88°$$

$$m\angle Q = 11(10°) = 110°$$

$$m\angle P = 180° - 88° = 92°$$

**9.** Cedrick will be tired all day.

**10.** Find the equation of $\overline{RT}$:

$$y = -x + 4$$

Now, find the line perpendicular to $\overline{RT}$ that runs through $V$:

$$y = x + b$$

$$3 = (7) + b$$

$$-4 = b$$

$$y = x - 4$$

Next, find the equation of $\overline{RV}$:

$$y = -\frac{1}{3}x + \frac{16}{3}$$

Now, find the line perpendicular to $\overline{RV}$ that runs through $T$:

$$y = 3x + b$$

$$3 = 3(1) + b$$

$$0 = b$$

$$y = 3x$$

Find the point of intersection by setting the equations equal to each other.

$$3x = x - 4$$

$$2x = -4$$

$$x = -2$$

$$y = 3(-2) = -6$$

The orthocenter is located at (−2, −6).

**11.** Mariah has assumed that $\triangle ABD$ is a right triangle, but since $\overleftrightarrow{BD}$ is not given to be a tangent, it cannot be assumed that it is perpendicular to $\overline{AB}$.

**12.** $\frac{33}{x} = \frac{x}{27}$

$$(x)(x) = (33)(27)$$

$$x^2 = 891$$

$$x = \sqrt{891} = 9\sqrt{11}$$

**13.** Choice A: $4 + 5 < 10$

Choice B: $1 + 2 > 2$

Choice C: $11 + 15 > 20$

Choice D: $41 + 37 > 55$

Choice **A** is correct because it is the option where the sum of the shorter two sides is not greater than the third side.

**14.**
$$S = L + 2B$$
$$= (8 + 5 + 8 + 5)(11) + 2(8)(5)$$
$$= 286 + 80$$
$$= 366 \text{ in.}^2$$

**15.**
$$x^2 + x^2 = 175^2$$
$$2x^2 = 30{,}625$$
$$x^2 = 15{,}312.5$$

The area of each floor is 15,312.5 square feet. There are 4 floors for a total of $4(15{,}312.5) = 61{,}250$ square feet.

$61{,}250 \div 8000 \approx 7.65$

8 cans will be needed.

**16.**
$$\frac{8}{7} = \frac{7}{6}$$
$$(8)(6) = (7)(7)$$
$$48 \neq 49$$

No, they are not parallel because they do not divide the transversals proportionally.

**17.** The endpoints of $\overline{DE}$ are located at (3, 2) and (0, 1).

$$d_{DE} = \sqrt{(3 - 0)^2 + (2 - 1)^2}$$
$$= \sqrt{3^2 + 1^2}$$
$$= \sqrt{10}$$
$$d_{GH} = \sqrt{(4 - -2)^2 + (-2 - -4)^2}$$
$$= \sqrt{6^2 + 2^2}$$
$$= \sqrt{40}$$
$$= 2\sqrt{10}$$

So, $DE = \frac{1}{2}GH$.

**18.**
$$\frac{PS}{QT} = \frac{SR}{TR}$$

Choice A: $\frac{7}{10} = \frac{14}{19}$
$$(7)(19) = (10)(14)$$
$$133 \neq 140$$

Choice B: $\frac{7}{10} = \frac{10}{13.3}$
$$(7)(13.3) = (10)(10)$$
$$93.1 \neq 100$$

Choice C: $\frac{7}{10} = \frac{17.5}{25}$
$$(7)(25) = (10)(17.5)$$
$$175 = 175$$

Choice D: $\frac{7}{10} = \frac{13}{20}$
$$(7)(20) = (10)(13)$$
$$140 \neq 130$$

Choice **C** is correct because the segments are proportional.

**19.** $V = Bh = (10)(8)(16) = 1280 \text{ m}^3$

**20. a.**

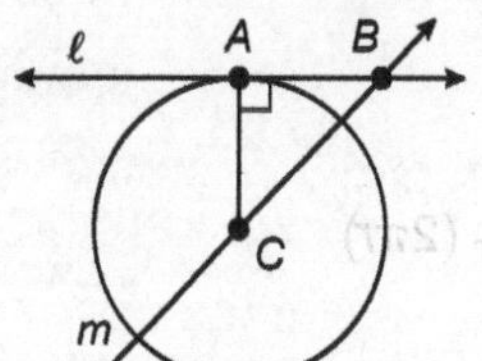


$\triangle ACB$ is a right triangle.

**b.** $m\angle CBA = 180° - 90° - 53° = 37°$

**21.** No, solids with curved surfaces are not polyhedra.

**22.** The dodecahedron has congruent regular pentagons as its faces.

**23.** Assume that $\overline{AX}$ is not a median of $\overline{BC}$. We know that an equilateral triangle has all sides equal and all angles are equal. The altitude $\overline{AX}$ is perpendicular to $\overline{BC}$ and this means that $\triangle AXB$ is congruent to $\triangle AXC$ by AAS Congruence. Thus $\overline{BX} \cong \overline{XC}$ by CPCTC. So, $BX = XC$ by the definition of congruent line segments. This contradicts the assumption that $\overline{AX}$ is not a median of $\overline{BC}$.

**24.** The line goes through the points (0, 0) and (2, 7)
$$m = \frac{7 - 0}{2 - 0} = \frac{7}{2} = 3.5$$

The equation of the line is $y = 3.5x$ since the $y$-intercept is 0. The correct units are newtons per kilogram or N/kg.

25.

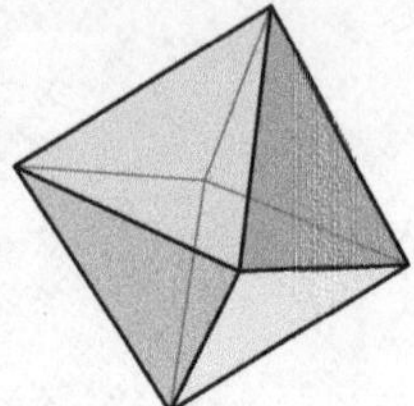

The faces are equilateral triangles. There are 8 faces, 6 vertices, and 12 edges.

26.
$$\frac{15}{7} = \frac{7}{y}$$
$$(15)(y) = (7)(7)$$
$$15y = 49$$
$$y \approx 3.3$$
$$\frac{15 - 3.3}{x} = \frac{x}{3.3}$$
$$(x)(x) = (11.7)(3.3)$$
$$x^2 = 38.61$$
$$x \approx 6.2$$

27.
$$5280 = \frac{85°}{360°}(2\pi r)$$
$$22{,}362.35 \approx 2\pi r$$
$$3559 \text{ ft} \approx r$$

28. Since $\triangle ABC$ and $\triangle DEF$ have two congruent angles, the triangles are similar by AA Similarity. By inspection of the sides adjacent to $\angle A$ and $\angle D$, the proportionality constant is 2. So $x$ is twice $BC$, or 20.

29. $A = \frac{1}{2}bh = \frac{1}{2}$(shorter leg)(longer leg)

shorter leg = $x$
longer leg = $x\sqrt{3}$
$$A = \frac{1}{2}(x)(x\sqrt{3}) = \frac{x^2\sqrt{3}}{2}$$

30. First, find the length of the slanted sides:
$$s^2 = 2^2 + 2^2$$
$$s^2 = 4 + 4$$
$$s^2 = 8$$
$$s = \sqrt{8} = 2\sqrt{2}$$
$$P = 4(2) + 4(2\sqrt{2})$$
$$= 8 + 8\sqrt{2}$$
This is not a regular octagon because the sides are not all congruent.

## INVESTIGATION 6

1. 180°, 72°, and 108° respectively

2. $\frac{180°}{360°} = 0.5 = 50\%$; The spinner will land on red 50% of the time. This is because it makes up exactly half the area of the spinner.

3. Blue: $\frac{72°}{360°} = 20\%$

Yellow: $\frac{108°}{360°} = 30\%$

Red: $\frac{180°}{360°} = 50\%$

4. See student work.

5. Students should observe that experimental probabilities trend toward theoretical probabilities as the number of trials increases.

6. See student work. Sample: The geometric probability approaches the theoretical probability of drawing any one color as the number of draws increases.

7. Total Area = (5)(7) = 35 squares

Area of Shape 1 = $\frac{1}{2}(4)(4)$ = 8 squares

Area of Shape 2 = $(\sqrt{2})(3\sqrt{2})$
= 6 squares

Theoretical Probability = $\frac{14}{35}$ = 40%

8. They tend to become closer and closer together.

### Investigation 6 Practice

a. See student work. Sample:

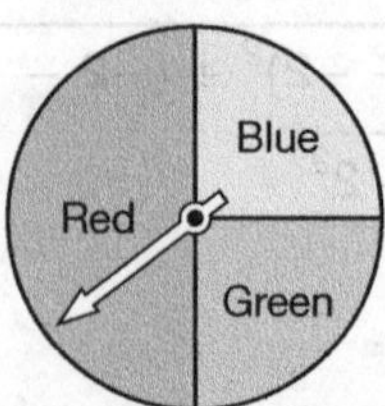


b. Experimental probabilities should approach $\frac{1}{2}$, $\frac{1}{4}$, and $\frac{1}{4}$.

**c.** See student work. Sample:

**d.** See student work.

**e.** The probability was proportional in both. Experimental probabilities trend toward theoretical probabilities. In both experiments, theoretical probabilities were proportional to area.

## LESSON 61

### Warm Up 61

1. rhombus; square
2. true
3. Choice **C** is correct.

### Lesson Practice 61

**a.**

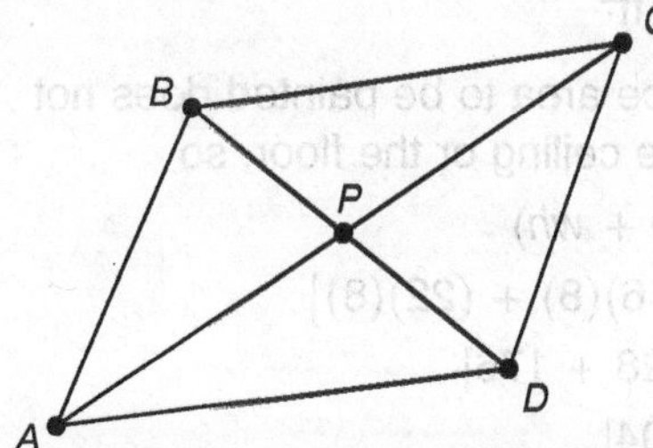


Since the opposite sides of *ABCD* are congruent, *ABCD* is a parallelogram. In a parallelogram, the diagonals bisect each other.

**b.** Since both pairs of opposite angles are given as being congruent, the quadrilateral is a parallelogram, so opposite sides are congruent.

**c.** Since $\triangle WXY \cong \triangle YZW$, $\overline{WX} \cong \overline{ZY}$ and $\angle XWY \cong \angle ZYW$. By the Converse of the Alternate Interior Angles Theorem, therefore $\overline{WX} \parallel \overline{ZY}$. Since one pair of sides is both parallel and congruent, *WXYZ* is a parallelogram.

**d.** By CPCTC, the corresponding sides $\overline{AE}$ and $\overline{EC}$ are congruent. Corresponding sides $\overline{DE}$ and $\overline{EB}$ are also congruent, so the diagonals of *ABCD* bisect each other, which proves that *ABCD* is a parallelogram.

**e.** Since both pairs of opposite angles of the quadrilateral are congruent, the quadrilateral is a parallelogram. Therefore, the top and bottom rail are parallel.

### Practice 61

**1.**

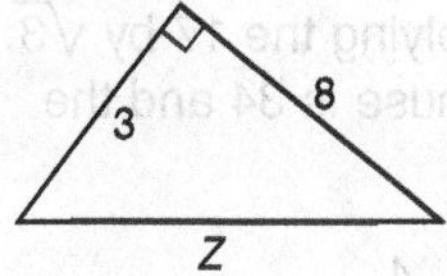


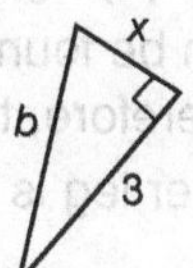


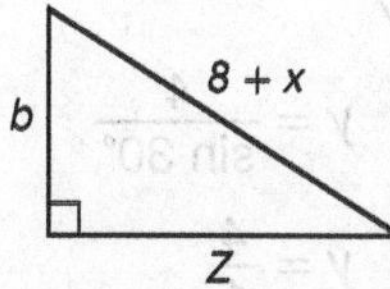


In the right triangle with 3, 8 and z

$z^2 = 3^2 + 8^2$

$z^2 = 9 + 64$

$z^2 = 73$

$z = \sqrt{73}$

In the right triangle with *b*, *x*, and 3:

$b^2 = x^2 + 3^2$

$b^2 = x^2 + 9$

The right triangle with *b*, *x* + 8, and *z*:

$$(8 + x)^2 = b^2 + \sqrt{73}^2$$

$$64 + 16x + x^2 = b^2 + 73$$

$$\text{But } b^2 = x^2 + 9$$

So, $64 + 16x + x^2 = x^2 + 9 + 73$

$$14x = 18$$

$$x = 1.1$$

$$\text{And since } y = x + 8$$

$$y = 1.1 + 8$$

$$y = 9.1$$

**2.** The diagonal *d* of the square is given by

$d^2 = 1^2 + 1^2$

$d^2 = 1 + 1$

$d^2 = 2$

$d = \sqrt{2}$

$d \approx 141\text{cm}$ [Note: 1 m = 100 cm]

Dividing the table down the middle, the length of tape needed would be 100 cm.

141 cm − 100 cm = 41 cm

Approximately 41 cm more tape would be needed to divide the table diagonally.

3. A 30°-60°-90° triangle has side lengths of 1, $\sqrt{3}$, 2 respectively. The shorter leg corresponds to the shorter side of the triangle, which means the side length of 1 unit. The hypotenuse can be found by multiplying the 17 by 2 and the other leg can be found by multiplying the 17 by $\sqrt{3}$. Therefore, the hypotenuse is 34 and the other leg is $17\sqrt{3}$.

4. $\tan 30° = \frac{4}{x}$ $\quad \sin 30° = \frac{4}{y}$

$x = \frac{4}{\tan 30°}$ $\quad y = \frac{4}{\sin 30°}$

$x = \frac{4}{\frac{1}{\sqrt{3}}}$ $\quad y = \frac{4}{\frac{1}{2}}$

$x = 4\sqrt{3}$ $\quad y = 8$

5. Take a circle and divide it in half. One-half of this circle will make up one sector. Take the remaining half and divide it into thirds to make up the remaining sectors.

6. For $\overline{EF}$ and $\overline{XY}$ to be parallel,

$\frac{\overline{DX}}{\overline{DE}} = \frac{\overline{DY}}{\overline{DF}}$

$\frac{\overline{DX}}{\overline{DE}} = \frac{9}{17}$ and $\frac{\overline{DY}}{\overline{DF}} = \frac{16}{30}$ or $\frac{8}{15}$

But $\frac{9}{17} \neq \frac{8}{15}$

Therefore, the two line segments are not parallel.

7. Since the city block forms a parallelogram, opposite sides must be equal in length. Therefore, the fourth side would need to be 156 meters in length.

8. proportional

9. Midpoint $= \left(\frac{x_1 + x_2}{2}, \frac{y_1 + y_2}{2}\right)$

$Q\left(\frac{1 + (-2)}{2}, \frac{1 + 8}{2}\right)$ $\quad R\left(\frac{6 + (-2)}{2}, \frac{4 + 1}{2}\right)$

$Q(-0.5, 4.5)$ $\quad R(2, 2.5)$

10. $c^2 = 1^2 + 1^2$

$c^2 = 2$

$c = \sqrt{2}$ or 1.41 miles

Since the range is only 1.35 miles, the communicators will not work.

11. Counting full squares, there are approximately 28 full squares. Counting half squares, there are approximately 12 half squares that make up an additional 6 full squares. Therefore, the approximate area will be (28 + 6) 34 square units.

12. Midpoint $= \left(\frac{x_1 + x_2}{2}, \frac{y_1 + y_2}{2}\right)$

$\left(\frac{-7 + 0}{2}, \frac{3 + 8}{2}\right) = (-3.5, 5.5)$

Choice **A** is correct.

13. $SA = 2(lw + lh + wh)$

$SA = 2[(6)(5) + (5)(13) + (6)(13)]$

$= 2[30 + 65 + 78]$

$= 2[173]$

$= 346 \text{ ft}^2$

14. The surface area to be painted does not include the ceiling or the floor, so

$SA = 2(lh + wh)$

$SA = 2[(16)(8) + (22)(8)]$

$= 2[128 + 176]$

$= 2[304]$

$= 608 \text{ ft}^2$

15. Since $\triangle XYZ$ is equiangular, all angles are 60°. In $\triangle XCZ$, $\angle XZC = 30°$, due to the fact that the line through $\overline{ZC}$ bisects the 60° angle. $\tan 30° = \frac{5}{\overline{XZ}}$, so $\overline{XZ} = \frac{5}{\tan 30°}$ or $5\sqrt{3}$ This is also the length of $\overline{YX}$. $\overline{XC}$ and $\overline{YC}$ are both 5 cm, the radius of the circle. To find the perimeter of the quadrilateral, add the lengths of all four sides:

$P = 5 + 5 + 5\sqrt{3} + 5\sqrt{3} = (10 + 10\sqrt{3})$ cm

16. Applying the scale factor of the sides to the perimeter, we obtain

$4 : 5 = x : 30$

$\frac{4}{5} = \frac{x}{30}$

$5x = 120$

$x = 24$ inches

**17.** If the triangle were right angled:

$$12^2 = x^2 + (2x)^2$$
$$144 = x^2 + 4x^2$$
$$144 = 5x^2$$
$$\frac{144}{5} = x^2$$
$$\sqrt{\frac{144}{5}} = x$$
$$5.4 = x$$

Therefore, for there to be an obtuse angle, $x > 5.4$, and for the angles to all be acute, $0 < x < 5.4$.

**18.** Use the area of the circle to find the radius of the circle:

$$A = \pi r^2$$
$$40.6 = \pi r^2$$
$$\frac{40.6}{\pi} = r^2$$
$$\sqrt{\frac{40.6}{\pi}} = r$$
$$3.595 = r$$

Arc length $= r\theta$

$$2.8 = (3.595)\theta$$
$$\frac{2.8}{3.595} = \theta \text{ so } \theta = 0.7789 \text{ rad}$$

Converting this to degrees:

$$0.7789 \text{ rad} \times \frac{180°}{\pi \text{ rad}} = 44.6° \approx 45°$$

**19.** In the tangram, pieces A and B represent the same amount of area of the full square. This area is $\frac{1}{4}$ of the whole shape each. Pieces E and G are each $\frac{1}{16}$ of the total area, leaving pieces C, D, and F each representing $\frac{1}{8}$ of the total area.

**20.** There are two possible locations of the fourth point to form a parallelogram. One is 4 units to the right and 3 units up from the point (–2, 1), which would be point (2, 4) or 4 units to the left and 3 units down from the point (–2, 1), which would be point (–6, –2). Choice **D** is correct.

**21.** $\triangle AYB \sim \triangle XYZ$ by AA Similarity
Therefore,

$$\frac{AY}{XY} = \frac{BY}{ZY}$$
$$\frac{9}{9 + y} = \frac{5}{9}$$
$$5(9 + y) = 81$$
$$45 + 5y = 81$$
$$5y = 81 - 45$$
$$5y = 36$$
$$y = \frac{36}{5}$$
$$y = 7.2$$

**22.** **a.** Since line $l$ is tangent to the circle, $\angle CAB = 90°$. Therefore, $\triangle ABC$ is a right triangle.

**b.** By the Angle Sum of a Triangle Theorem,

$$m\angle ACB + m\angle CBA + m\angle BAC = 180°$$
$$53° + m\angle CBA + 90° = 180°$$
$$143° + m\angle CBA = 180°$$
$$m\angle CBA = 180° - 143°$$
$$m\angle CBA = 37°$$

**23.** By the Linear Pair Theorem, $\angle 1$ and $\angle 4$ are supplementary, as are $\angle 2$ and $\angle 3$. It is given that $\angle 4 \cong \angle 3$, so by the Congruent Supplements Theorem, $\angle 1 \cong \angle 2$. By the definition of congruent angles, $m\angle 1 = m\angle 2$.

**24.** By definition, a rectangle is a quadrilateral with 4 equal angles. If all angles of a rhombus are equal in measure, the rhombus is a rectangle. Therefore, sometimes a rhombus is a rectangle.

**25.** No, the side on the bottom could either make it a parallelogram or it could be longer and make the shape a trapezoid.

**26.** By the Triangle Midsegment Theorem, when the midpoints of two sides are connected, they form a line that is always parallel to the third side.

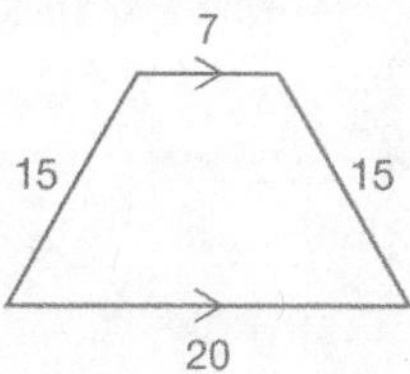


**27.** Midpoint $= \left(\frac{x_1 + x_2}{2}, \frac{y_1 + y_2}{2}\right)$

$$\left(\frac{0 + 0}{2}, \frac{0 + 2w}{2}\right) = (0, w)$$

28. The shortest side is always opposite the smallest angle. To find the shortest side, we need to find the smallest angle. In the diagram,

$\angle J = 2\angle F$
$= 2(70°)$
$= 140°$

This means that in $\triangle JHG$,

$\angle HGJ + \angle J + \angle JHG = 180°$
$\angle HGJ + 140° + 30° = 180°$
$\angle HGJ + 170° = 180°$
$\angle HGJ = 180° - 170°$
$\angle HGJ = 10°$

The shortest side is $\overline{JH}$.

29. Equilateral triangles will form a parallelogram when joined. This parallelogram will have all sides of equal length, since the triangles were equilateral. Therefore the parallelogram will be a rhombus.

30. If the plane contacts the sphere at one point, then the intersection will simply be a point. If the plane intersects the sphere, then the intersection will be a cross section of the sphere, which will always be a circle.

## LESSON 62

### Warm Up 62

1. surface area

2. $SA = 2(lw + lh + wh)$
$SA = 2[(3)(4) + (3)(8) + (4)(8)]$
$= 2[12 + 24 + 32]$
$= 2[68]$
$= 136 \text{ in.}^2$

3. $V = lwh$
$V = (3)(4)(8)$
$= 96 \text{ in.}^3$

### Lesson Practice 62

a. $S = 2\pi rh$
$= 2\pi(12)(22)$
$= 528\pi \text{ in.}^2$

b. $S = 2\pi rh + 2\pi r^2$
$= 2(\pi)(35)(50) + 2(\pi)(35)^2$
$\approx 1{,}8692 \text{ cm}^2$

c. $V = \pi r^2 h$
$= (\pi)(9)^2(17)$
$= 1377\pi \approx 4326 \text{ ft}^3$

d. $V = \pi r^2 h$
$= (\pi)(75)^2(150)$
$= 843{,}750\pi \approx 2{,}650{,}719 \text{ ft}^3$

### Practice 62

1. $\frac{AC}{CE} = \frac{BD}{DF}$

2. 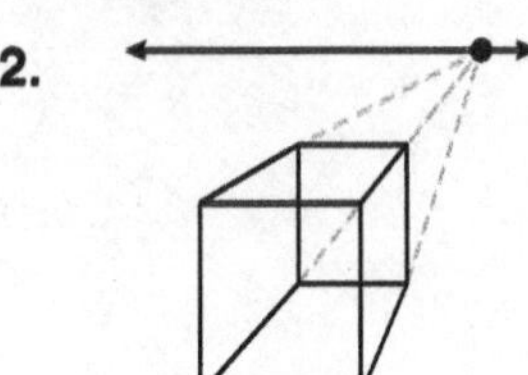

3. Since the two triangles are congruent,

$BC = DE$

So, $5x - 7 = 4x + 13$
$5x - 4x = 13 + 7$
$x = 20$

Substituting,

$AB = 3x + 2$ becomes
$AB = 3(20) + 2$
$= 62$

4. $V = \pi r^2 h$
$= (\pi)(13.5)^2(43)$
$= 7836.75\pi \approx 24{,}619.9 \text{ yd}^3$

5. $r^2 = (4.3)^2 + (4.6)^2$
$r^2 = 39.65$
$r \approx 6.3$ inches

6. A basketball resembles a sphere.

7. $A = \frac{60}{360}$ or $\frac{1}{6}$ $= 0.17$; $B = \frac{120}{360}$ or $\frac{1}{3}$ $= 0.33$; $C = \frac{180}{360}$ or $\frac{1}{2}$ $= 0.5$

8. Another name for an equiangular quadrilateral is a rectangle.

9. Alicia drew altitudes; therefore, she found the orthocenter, not the centroid.

**10.** Choice **D** is correct. None of the given theorems proves that the two triangles are congruent.

**11.** $1 : 2 : \sqrt{3} = x : y : 6$

Therefore,

$$\frac{x}{6} = \frac{1}{\sqrt{3}} \quad \text{and} \quad \frac{y}{6} = \frac{2}{\sqrt{3}}$$

$$\sqrt{3}x = 6 \qquad \sqrt{3}y = 12$$

$$x = \frac{6}{\sqrt{3}} \qquad y = \frac{12}{\sqrt{3}}$$

$$x = \frac{6}{\sqrt{3}} \times \frac{\sqrt{3}}{\sqrt{3}} \qquad y = \frac{12}{\sqrt{3}} \times \frac{\sqrt{3}}{\sqrt{3}}$$

$$x = 2\sqrt{3} \qquad y = 4\sqrt{3}$$

$$P = 6 + 2\sqrt{3} + 4\sqrt{3}$$
$$= 6 + 6\sqrt{3}$$
$$= 6(1 + \sqrt{3})$$

**12. a.** $\angle B \cong \angle C$; Isosceles Triangle Theorem

**b.** $m\angle A + m\angle B + m\angle C = 180°$

$$3x + x + x = 180°$$
$$5x = 180°$$
$$x = 36°$$

Therefore,

$m\angle B = m\angle C = 36°$ and $m\angle A = 108°$

**13.** Her statement is false; the shape could also be a rhombus.

**14.** $V = \pi r^2 h$

$$\approx (3.14)(25)^2(32)$$
$$\approx 62{,}800 \text{ in.}^3$$

**15.** A 12-inch chord is bisected by the line from the center to the chord, along the perpendicular to the chord. Therefore, the distance from this intersection to the circle is 6 inches. The line from the center of the circle to the chord is $x$ inches long, and completing the triangle, the line from the center to the point where the chord contacts the circle is the radius of the circle, which is 10 inches (half of the diameter).

Using the Pythagorean Theorem:

$$10^2 = x^2 + 6^2$$
$$100 = x^2 + 36$$
$$100 - 36 = x^2$$
$$64 = x^2$$
$$8 \text{ in.ches} = x$$

**16.** $L = 2\pi rh$

$$= 2\pi(1.5)(4) \approx 2(3.14)(1.5)(4)$$
$$= 37.68 \text{ in.}^2$$

Since 1092 of these are needed, we can multiply this result by 1092 to get the answer: $37.68 \text{ in.}^2 \times 1092 = 41{,}146.56 \text{ in.}^2$

**17.**

With the altitude as a geometric means:

$$\frac{x}{20} = \frac{20}{5x}$$
$$5x^2 = 400$$
$$x^2 = 80; x \approx 8.9$$

With the short leg as a geometric means:

$$\frac{6x}{y} = \frac{y}{x}$$
$$6x^2 = y^2$$

Since $x^2 = 80$, $6x^2 = 6(80) = y^2$, so $y^2 = 480$ and $y \approx 21.9$.

**18.** No, it cannot be proven that $ABCD$ is a parallelogram. It could be a trapezoid.

**19.** If $x = 12$, $x^2 - 16 = 144 - 16$ or $128°$ and $4x + 4 = 4(12) + 4$ or $52°$. Since these two angles add to $180°$, $\overline{AB}$ is parallel to $\overline{DC}$ by the Converse of the Same-Side Interior Angles Theorem. Since we are also given that $\overline{DA}$ is parallel to $\overline{CB}$, $ABCD$ is a parallelogram.

**20.** Theorem 60-3 states that parallel lines divide transversals proportionally, which is exactly what the Triangle Proportionality Theorem states. It is just that the Triangle Proportionality Theorem states Theorem 60-3 is true for both sides of the triangle. Theorem 60-3, however, does not necessarily apply to a triangle.

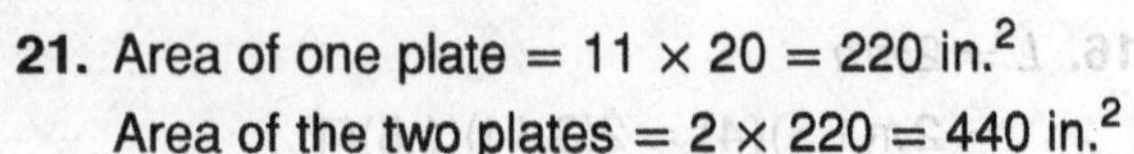



**21.** Area of one plate $= 11 \times 20 = 220$ in.$^2$
Area of the two plates $= 2 \times 220 = 440$ in.$^2$

**22.** Geometric mean $= \sqrt{13 \times 17} \approx 14.9$.

**23.** To find $x$, we can use the Opposite Angle Theorem and set the two expressions equal to each other.

$$\frac{x+2}{3} = 3x - 3$$
$$x + 2 = 9x - 9$$
$$-8x = -11$$
$$x = \frac{-11}{-8}$$
$$x = 1.375$$

**24.** Purple: $\frac{45}{360} = 0.125$ or 12.5% Yellow:

$$\frac{105}{360} \approx 0.292 \text{ or } 29.2\%$$

Orange: $\frac{210}{360} \approx 0.583$ or 58.3%

**25.** Since $ABCD$ is a cyclic quadrilateral,

$$m\angle Q + m\angle S = 180°$$
$$(4x + 12)° + (10x)° = 180°$$
$$14x = 180 - 12$$
$$14x = 168$$
$$x = 12$$
$$m\angle S = (10(12))° = 120°$$
$$m\angle T = (6(12) + 3)° = 75°$$
$$m\angle Q = (4(12) + 12)° = 60°$$
$$m\angle T + m\angle R = 180°$$
$$75° + m\angle R = 180°$$
$$m\angle R = 180° - 75°$$
$$m\angle R = 105°$$

**26.** For one box, $V = (2)(3)(5) = 30$ in.$^3$
Mrs. Jenkins has 360 in.$^3$ to place in boxes, so: $\frac{360}{30} = 12$ boxes

**27.** The slope of the given line is $\frac{1}{2}$. The slope of a line perpendicular to the given line would be $-2$. The line that has a slope of $-2$, and includes the point $(-6, 2)$ is $y = -2x - 10$.
This line intersects the given line along the shortest distance to the given point. To find their point of intersection:

$$\frac{1}{2}x = -2x - 10$$
$$x = -4x - 20$$
$$5x = -20$$
$$x = -4$$

To find the corresponding $y$-value:

$$y = \frac{1}{2}(-4) = -2$$

The point on the line closest to $(-6, 2)$ is $(-4, -2)$.

**28.** $S = 2\pi rh + 2\pi r^2$
$\approx 2(3.14)(13)(30) + 2(3.14)(13)^2$
$= 3510.52$ ft$^2$

**29.** The statement is never true. A trapezoid has one pair of opposite sides that are not parallel, so it can never be a parallelogram.

**30.** Choose two sides of the triangle, and by the ITT, their base angles must be equal. Choose one of these two sides and the side that was not originally chosen, and again by the ITT, their base angles must be equal. The only way that these angles can all be equal is for them all to have the same measure. Therefore, the triangle must be equiangular.

## LESSON 63

### Warm Up 63

1. segment
2. $c^2 = 12^2 + 5^2$
   $c^2 = 169$
   $c = 13$ cm
3. Malia ends up 22 meters north and 24 meters east of her house. To find the distance, use the Pythagorean Theorem:
   $r^2 = 22^2 + 24^2$
   $r^2 = 1060$
   $r \approx 32.6$ meters
   Choice **B** is correct.
4. A line extends in both directions forever, whereas a line segment has a defined length.

## Lesson Practice 63

**a.** $\vec{x}$ has initial point $A$, $\vec{y}$ has initial point $C$, $\vec{z}$ has initial point $F$.

**b.** Magnitude of $\langle 5, 3\rangle = \sqrt{5^2 + 3^2} = \sqrt{34}$

**c.** $\vec{a} + \vec{b} = \langle 3, 2\rangle + \langle 3, 2\rangle = \langle 6, 4\rangle$

**d.** In component form,
$\vec{a} = \langle 3, 2\rangle$ and $\vec{c} = \langle -3, -2\rangle$, so
$\vec{a} + \vec{b} = \langle 3, 2\rangle + \langle -3, -2\rangle = \langle 0, 0\rangle$

**e.** In component form, all four vectors are $\langle 5, 2\rangle$, so to find the resultant, multiply the component form by the scalar 4. The resultant is $\langle 4 \times 5, 4 \times 2\rangle = \langle 20, 8\rangle$.

**f.** canoe vector: $\langle 2, 0\rangle$; river vector: $\langle 1.5, 0\rangle$
$\langle 2 + 1.5, 0 + 0\rangle = \langle 3.5, 0\rangle$; 3.5 miles per hour

## Practice 63

**1.** Since $KLMN$ is a rhombus, $\overline{XK}$ bisects the angle at $K$. Therefore,
$m\angle NKL = 2 \times m\angle XKL$
$= 2 \times 57°; = 114°$

**2.**
$$V = \pi r^2 h$$
$$75.36 \approx (3.14)r^2(6)$$
$$4 \approx r^2;\ 2 \text{ inches} = r$$

**3.** The opposite vector to $\langle 4, 6\rangle$ is $\langle -4, -6\rangle$,
so $-4 = 2x + 2$ check $2x = -6$
$-6 = 2x$ $\quad x = -3$
$-3 = x$

**4.** 5 of 16 squares are white.
$\frac{5}{16} = 0.3125$
4 of the 16 squares are blue.
$\frac{1}{4} = 0.25$

**5.** To swim at 4 miles per hour assisted by a current of 2 miles per hour, solve
$v + 2 = 4$
$v = 2$ miles per hour; Choice **C** is correct.

**6.** always true

**7.** For $\angle P > \angle S$ $\qquad$ For $\angle P < \angle S$
$3x - 6 > 9$ $\qquad$ $0 < 3x - 6 < 9$
$3x > 15$ $\qquad$ $6 < 3x < 15$
$x > 5$ $\qquad$ $2 < x < 5$

**8.** For $\triangle ABD$ to be congruent to $\triangle ACD$, $\frac{AB}{BD} = \frac{AC}{DC}$. But for this to be true $BD$ would need to be equal to $DC$, as the triangle is isosceles, and $AB = BD$. But since $D$ is not the midpoint of $BC$, the two triangles are not congruent.

**9.** $\text{Base}_{\text{upper triangle}} = \text{Midsegment}_{\text{larger triangle}}$
$= \frac{1}{2}(150) = 75$
$A = \frac{1}{2}bh = \frac{1}{2}(90)(75) = 3375 \text{ m}^2$
Whole triangle:
$A = \frac{1}{2}bh = \frac{1}{2}(180)(150) = 13{,}500 \text{ m}^2$
Trapezoidal area:
$13{,}500 - 3375 = 10{,}125 \text{ m}^2$

**10.** Choice **B** is correct. A trapezoid is not a parallelogram, since only one opposite pair of sides is parallel.

**11.**

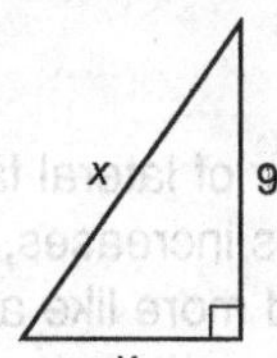


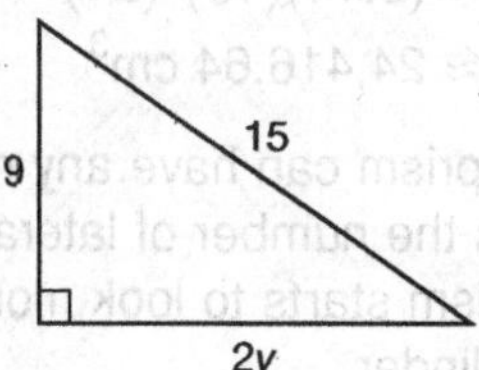


$15^2 = 9^2 + (2y)^2$
$225 = 81 + 4y^2$
$144 = 4y^2$
$36 = y^2$
and
$x^2 = y^2 + 9^2$
$x^2 = 36 + 81$
$x^2 = 117$
$x = \sqrt{117} = 3\sqrt{13}$

**12.** If the points of tangency of the two lines can be connected with a line that passes through the center of the circle, the two tangent lines will be parallel to each other.

**13.** Rafael was thinking that the line segment $BD$ created an isosceles triangle with vertex $C$, which is not the case.

**14.** $\langle 3, 2\rangle + \langle 3.7, -8.2\rangle + \langle 3, 2\rangle + \langle -3.7, 8.2\rangle = \langle 6, 4\rangle$

15. $L = 2\pi rh$
$= 2\pi(15)(25) \approx 2(3.14)(15)(25)$
$= 2355 \text{ yd}^2$

16. $6 : 1 = x : 12$
$\frac{6}{1} = \frac{x}{12}$; $x = 72$ inches

17. $24 + 6z + 3z - 15 = 180$
$9z + 9 = 180$
$9z = 171$
$z = 19$

18. 120 mph + 30 mph = 150 mph

19. $P = 8.6 + 8.6 + 5.3 + 5.3 = 27.8$ cm
*ABCD* is a kite.

20. In the triangle, if the short leg is $x$, the longer leg will be equal to $\sqrt{3}x$. The area will be:
$A_{\text{triangle}} = \frac{1}{2}bh = \frac{1}{2}(x)(\sqrt{3}x) = \frac{\sqrt{3}x^2}{2}$

21. $V = \pi r^2 h$
$V \approx (3.14)(18)^2(24)$
$V \approx 24{,}416.64 \text{ cm}^3$

22. A prism can have any number of lateral faces. As the number of lateral faces increases, the prism starts to look more and more like a cylinder.

23. $\frac{360°}{n} = 60°$, which means that $n = 6$.

24. Drawing a line from where the top of the pyramid was to the base will cut the base in half, so the base of this right triangle will be 30 ft. As well, this right triangle will be a 45°-45°-90° triangle, so the height will be 30 ft.

25. a. $2^2 = 1^2 + h^2$
$4 = 1 + h^2$
$3 = h^2$
$\sqrt{3}$ in. $= h$

b. $A_{\text{triangle}} = \frac{1}{2}bh = \frac{1}{2}(2)(\sqrt{3}) = \sqrt{3} \text{ in.}^2$

26. Yes. Because the opposite sides are parallel, the associated alternate interior angles are congruent. Along with the congruent sides shown and vertical angles congruent, this proves that one pair of interior triangles are congruent. By CPCTC, the parallel sides of the quadrilateral are also congruent, so this is a parallelogram.

27. $V = lwh = (20)(12)(0.5) = 120 \text{ ft}^3$

28. Counting whole squares and estimating the others, there are approximately 40 full squares within the shape.

29. The side length from $L$ to $M$:
$\sqrt{(0 - 0)^2 + (6 - 0)^2} = 6$
For the triangle to be equilateral, all sides must be 6 in. So, between $L$ and $N$:
$6 = \sqrt{(3 - 0)^2 + (y - 0)^2}$
$6 = \sqrt{9 + y^2}$
$36 = 9 + y^2$
$27 = y^2$
$3\sqrt{3} = y$

30. $C = 2\pi r \approx 2(3.14)(500) = 3140$ meters
For Henrietta to cover one-third of this distance (approximately1047 meters) at 2 meters per second, she will need $\frac{1047}{2} \approx 524$ seconds.

## LESSON 64

### Warm Up 64

1. inscribed angle
2. $x = 18°$
3. Since $\overline{CB}$ is a diameter of the cyclic triangle, the angle at $A$ must be a right angle, therefore, $x = 90°$.

### Lesson Practice 64

a. The measure of the angle formed by the tangent and the chord is equal to half of the measure of the arc that subtends it.
Therefore, $m\angle x = 102°$

b. The measure of the arc subtended by the chord and the tangent is twice the measure of the angle made by the chord and the tangent. Therefore, $m\widehat{MNO} = 184°$.

**c.** Case 1: Assume $\overline{AB}$ is a diameter of the circle. Then $m\widehat{AB} = 180°$, and $\angle ABC$ is a right triangle. Thus $m\angle ABC = \frac{1}{2}m\widehat{AB}$.

Case 2: Assume $\overline{AB}$ is not a diameter of the circle. Let $X$ be the center of the circle and draw radii $\overline{XA}$ and $\overline{XB}$. Since they are radii, $\overline{XA} \cong \overline{XB}$, so $\triangle AXB$ is isosceles. Thus $\angle XAB \cong \angle XBA$ and $2m\angle XBA + m\angle AXB = 180°$. This means that $m\angle XBA = 90° - \frac{1}{2}m\angle AXB$. Since tangents are perpendicular to radii drawn to the point of tangency, $\angle XBC$ is a right angle. Therefore, $m\angle XBA + m\angle ABC = 90°$ or $m\angle ABC = 90° - (90° - \frac{1}{2}m\angle AXB)$. Simplifying gives $m\angle ABC = \frac{1}{2}m\angle AXB$. $m\angle AXB = m\widehat{AB}$ because $\angle AXB$ is a central angle. Thus $m\angle ABC = \frac{1}{2}m\widehat{AB}$.

**d.** $x = \dfrac{115° + 59°}{2} = 87°$

**e.** The measure of the angle formed by the tangent and the chord is equal to half of the measure of the angle that subtends it. Therefore, $x = 120°$

## Practice 64

**1. a.** Since each has an area of 5 unit squares, and there are 12 of them, the total area will be $5 \times 12 = 60$ square units.

**b.** $\frac{1}{12}$ or 0.083 each

**c.** The V piece is one of the 4 pieces used, so $\frac{1}{4}$ or 0.25. The T piece was not used, so 0.

**2. a.** To be a polygon, the shape must have at least 3 sides.

**b.** To be a polyhedron, the shape must have at least 4 faces.

**3.** Since the stain covers just under half of the pillow, just over half, or approximately 53% of the pillow is not stained.

**4.** Choice **C** is correct. To be supplementary, the two vertices must be consecutive.

**5.** $\angle B \cong \angle Y$ and $\angle C \cong \angle Z$; Also, by AA Similarity, $\triangle ABC \sim \triangle XYZ$

**6.** You can always find the coordinates of a fourth point that will make a parallelogram with three given points, as long as these given points are not collinear.

**7.**

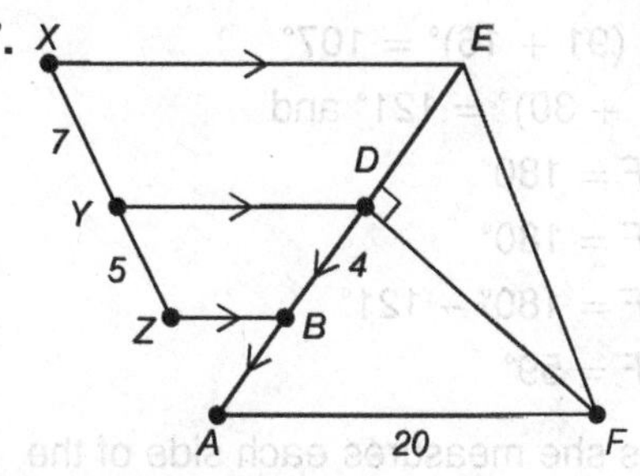


$$\frac{XY}{YZ} = \frac{ED}{DB}$$

$$\frac{7}{5} = \frac{ED}{4}$$

$5ED = 28$

$ED = 5.6$

And

$DF^2 + 8^2 = 20^2$

$DF^2 = 400 - 64$

$DF = 18.3$

Also,

$EF^2 = ED^2 + DF^2$

$EF^2 = (5.6)^2 + (18.3)^2$

$EF^2 = 366.25$

$EF = 19.1$

**8.** $\sqrt{4\sqrt{3} \times 5\sqrt{2}} \approx 7$

**9.** $m\angle ABC = 2 \times 117° = 234°$

**10.** These vectors are opposite vectors that add to $\langle 0,0 \rangle$.

**11.**

$$1^2 = \left(\frac{1}{2}\right)^2 + x^2$$

$$1 = \frac{1}{4} + x^2$$

$$1 - \frac{1}{4} = x^2$$

$$\frac{3}{4} = x^2$$

$$\frac{\sqrt{3}}{2} \text{ inches} = x$$

**12.** See student work, but be sure that the congruent angle is between the sides that are proportional.

**13.** $x + 16 + x - 18 = 180$

$2x - 2 = 180$

$2x = 182$

$x = 91$

So, $\angle C = (91 + 16)° = 107°$
$\angle D = (91 + 30)° = 121°$ and
$\angle D + \angle F = 180°$
$121° + \angle F = 180°$
$\angle F = 180° - 121°$
$\angle F = 59°$

**14.** As long as she measures each side of the table to be one-third of the perimeter (or 3 feet, the triangle will be equilateral.

**15.** $x = \frac{33° + 129°}{2}$
$x = 81°$

**16.** They are both correct; $34\sqrt{2} \approx 48$

**17.** $S = 2\pi rh + 2\pi r^2$
$\approx 2(3.14)(6)(9) + 2(3.14)(6)^2$
$= 565.2 \text{ in.}^2$

**18.** Any values for $p$ and $q$ such that $pq = -8$ will be a possible set of values. For example, $p = -4$ and $q = 2$

**19.** Choice **A** is correct.

**20.** $3 : 1 = 6 : x; x = 2$

**21.** $A \approx 6 \times 8 + \frac{1}{2}(3.14)(4)^2$
$= 73.12 \text{ ft}^2 \times 144$
$= 10{,}529.28 \text{ in.}^2$
A pane of glass covers 80 in.$^2$.
The number of panes is:
$\frac{10{,}529.28}{80} = 131.616$
132 panes would be needed.

**22.** $S = 2\pi rh + 2\pi r^2$
$\approx 2(3.14)(6)(27) + 2(3.14)(6)^2$
$= 1243.44 \text{ cm}^2$

**23.** Since $\overline{DE}$ is the midsegment, it bisects each side, therefore $y = 9$. As well, the midsegment is half the length of the base side of the shape, so $x = 2(17) = 34$.

**24.** Magnitude $= \sqrt{1^2 + (-2)^2} = 2.2$

**25.** Centroid $= \left(\frac{-2 + 1 + 4}{3}, \frac{4 - 6 - 4}{3}\right)$
$= (1, -2)$

**26.** $x = \frac{240°}{2}$
$= 120°$

**27.** When a prism is cut parallel to its base to form two prisms, the sum of the two prisms' volumes will be equal to the volume of the original prism. The sum of the two prisms' lateral surface areas will be equal to the lateral surface area of the original prism, and the sum of the total surface areas of the two prisms will be greater than the surface area of the original prism.

**28.** $x = \frac{155° + 20°}{2} = \frac{175°}{2} = 87.5°$

**29.** **a.** In 1980 there were 5 million species.
**b.** In 2100, $x = 120$. $y = 5 - 0.025(120) = 2$. Therefore, in 2100 there will be 2 million species.
**c.** The extinction portion of the function is $0.025x$, so when $x = 10$, $0.025(10) = 0.25$ million or 250,000 species are expected to become extinct in a 10-year period.

**30.** The vector in component form is $\langle 5, -3 \rangle$.

## LESSON 65

### Warm Up 65

1. quadrilateral
2. sometimes true
3. Choice **B** is correct.

### Lesson Practice 65

**a.** Yes, it is a rectangle. Opposite sides are parallel. Checking the angles,
$6x + 12 = 7x - 1$
$x = 13$
Substituting in the angle expressions:
$6(13) + 12 = 90°$
$7(13) - 1 = 90°$
The two angles are 90°.
Since the other two angles are their supplements, they will also measure 90°.

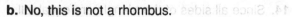

**b.** No, this is not a rhombus.

$4x + 7 = \frac{81}{5}$ and $9x - 5 = \frac{81}{5}$

$x = 2.30 \quad x = 2.36.$

Since the values of $x$ are not equal, the sides are not of the same length.

**c.** Yes, this is a rectangle.

$AO = OC = 5$, and when

$x - 3 = \frac{1}{2}x + 1$

$2x - 6 = x + 2$ When $x = 8$, $x - 3 = 5$ and

$x = 8$

$\frac{1}{2}x + 1 = 5$

Both diagonals are 10 units long.

**d.** No, this is not a rhombus.

$4x + 13 + 6x - 13 = 180$

$x = 18$

Substituting into the two expressions for the angles,

$(4(18) + 13)° \quad (6(18) - 13)°$

$= 85° \quad = 95°$

These are not right angles.

**e.** Yes, the shape is a rhombus.

$3x + 4 = 5x - 10$

$x = 7$

and

$2x + 11 = 4x - 3$

$x = 7$

This means that all the angles in the diagram are equal, so the diagonal bisects the opposite angles.

**f.** The triangle on the right side of the sign is also an equilateral triangle through SSS congruency. This means that the diagonals are congruent, proving that the sign is a perfect rectangle.

## Practice 65

**1.** For the shape to be a rhombus,

$x^2 - 2x + 2x^2 - 190 = 90$

$3x^2 - 2x - 280 = 0$

$(x - 10)(3x + 28) = 0$

$x = 10$ (ignore the solution $x = -\frac{28}{3}$, since angle's measures must be positive)

**2.** $V = \pi r^2 h$

$V = \pi(5)^2(3) \approx (3.14)(75)$

$V = 235.5 \text{ in.}^3$

Dividing this into 8 equal pieces means that each piece would have a volume of 29.4375 in.$^3$.

Multiplying this by the 5 remaining pieces gives a remaining volume of about 147 in.$^3$.

**3.** The conclusion does not show what was asked. The conclusion should be that $\angle 2$ and $\angle 3$ are supplementary. The second step should have the reason as the Linear Pair Theorem, not the definition of supplementary angles.

**4.** Two vertices of the triangle are (0, 1) and (0, −1), since $x = 0$ is one of the lines. The third vertex can be found by finding the point of intersection of the other two lines.

So $\frac{1}{2}x + 1 = x - 1$

$x + 2 = 2x - 2$

$x = 4$

This gives a $y$-value of $y = 3$. To find the area of the triangle:

$A = \frac{1}{2}bh$

$= \frac{1}{2}(2)(3)$

$= 3$

To find the perimeter, add the length of each side. The base length is 2 units. The other two side lengths can be found using the Pythagorean Theorem:

Short side $= \sqrt{16 + 16} = 4\sqrt{2}$

Long side $= \sqrt{16 + 4} = 2\sqrt{5}$

$P = 2 + 2\sqrt{5} + 4\sqrt{2}$

**5.** Area of the base:

$A = \frac{1}{2}$(perimeter)(apothem)

$A = \frac{1}{2}(5 \times 14)(9.63)$

$= 337.05 \text{ in.}^2$

$V = 32 \times A_{base}$
$= 32 \times 337.05 = 10{,}785.6 \text{ in.}^3$

6. $12 - 3 = 9$ miles per hour

7. The diagonals of a rhombus bisect each other and meet at a right angle, so the lengths of the legs for the right triangle are 6 cm and 2.5 cm. Use the Pythagorean Theorem:
$c^2 = 6^2 + 2.5^2$
$c^2 = 42.25$
$c = 6.5$ cm
Since the shape is a rhombus, all sides are equal.
$P = 4(6.5) = 26$ cm

8. $LM = \sqrt{(-6)^2 + 1^2} = \sqrt{37}$
$MN = \sqrt{1^2 + (-6)^2} = \sqrt{37}$
$NP = \sqrt{6^2 + 1^2} = \sqrt{37}$
$PL = \sqrt{1^2 + (-6)^2} = \sqrt{37}$
Slopes: $\overline{MN} = \frac{1}{6}$ and $\overline{LP} = -6$. Since these are negative reciprocals of each other, the angle is 90°, so the shape is a square.

9. $d^2 = 3^2 + \left(\frac{50}{12}\right)^2$
$d^2 \approx 26.36$
$d \approx 5.13$ ft

10. $x = \dfrac{22° + 19°}{2} = 20.5°$

11. $r = \sqrt{3^2 + 5^2}$
$r = \sqrt{34}$
$A = \pi r^2 = 34\pi$
Choice **A** is correct.

12. Since the base angles are all given to be equal, the triangle is isosceles. Therefore, the missing side is $3\frac{1}{4}$ in.
$P = 3\frac{1}{4} + 3\frac{1}{4} + 4\frac{1}{2} = 11$ in.

13. $12 : 8 = 9 : x$, so $12x = 72$ and $x = 6$.
$c^2 = 9^2 + 6^2$
$c^2 = 117$
$c \approx 10.82$ ft

14. Since all sides of the triangle are equal, all the angles have the same measure.

15. Since $9 + 40 > 41$, the three sides can form a triangle. As well, since $9^2 + 40^2 = 41^2$, the triangle is a right triangle.

16. By the Exterior Angle Theorem, the exterior angle at $P = 35° + 113° = 148°$.
Choice **B** is correct.

17. $S = 2\pi rh + \pi r^2$
$\approx 2(3.14)(12.5)(75) + (3.14)(12.5)^2$
$\approx 6378 \text{ ft}^2$

18. In component form,
$\langle -3, -1\rangle + \langle 2, 6\rangle = \langle -1, 5\rangle$

19. $c^2 = 12^2 + 16^2$
$c^2 = 400$
$c = 20$ in.

20. If the opposite angles are supplementary, $m\angle 1 + m\angle 3 = 180°$ and $m\angle 2 + m\angle 4 = 180°$.
Since the shape is a parallelogram, the opposite angles must be equal. So $m\angle 1 = m\angle 3$ and $m\angle 2 = m\angle 4$. This means that each angle must measure 90°, making the parallelogram a rectangle.

21. Using similar triangles,
$\dfrac{x}{16} = \dfrac{5.6}{3}$
$3x = 89.6$
$x \approx 30$ ft

22. $110° = \frac{1}{2}(37 + 5x + 3)°$
$220 = 5x + 40$
$220 - 40 = 5x$
$180 = 5x$
$x = 36$

23. $6^3 = \pi r^2(3) = (3.14)\, r^2\, (3)$
$r^2 \approx 22.9299$
$r \approx 4.79$ mm

24. The two lines are parallel as the transversals are divided proportionally. This can only happen if the lines are parallel.

25. There are three possible positions for $H$. One would be located 4 units to the left

and 6 units up from $E$ (this is the pattern of movement from $H$ to $F$), which is the point (−4, 6). A second is 4 units down and 4 units to the left of $H$ (this is the pattern of movement from $F$ to $E$), which is the point (6, −4). The final possible location is 4 units to the right and 4 units up from $H$ (this is the pattern from $E$ to $F$), which is the point (14, 4).

**26.** Since the shape is a rhombus,

$$2x + 3x = 180°$$
$$x = 36°$$

$m\angle 1 = 2x$, so $m\angle 1 = 2(36)° = 72°$

**27.** The circumcenter of an isosceles right triangle will lie on the midpoint of the hypotenuse.

**28.** The measure of $\overparen{AC}$ is twice the given angle of **35°**, therefore the arc is **70°**.

**29.**

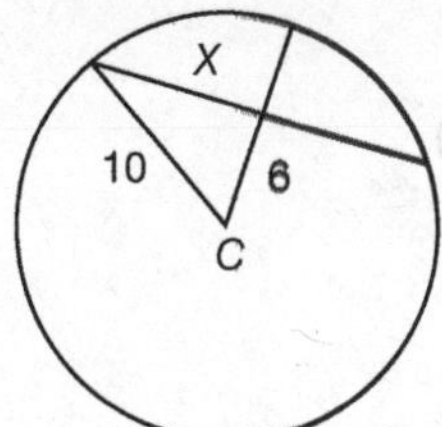


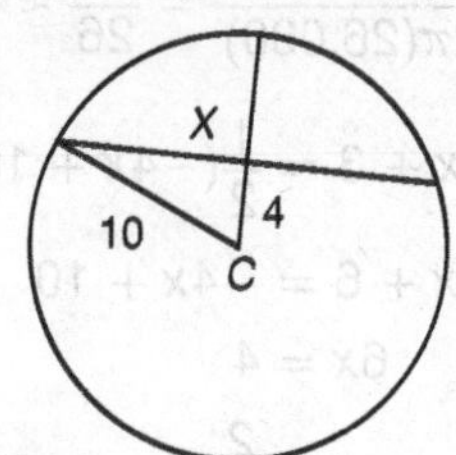


There are two possibilities here, pictured in the diagram.

In possibility 1:

$$10^2 = 6^2 + x^2$$
$$100 = 36 + x^2$$
$$64 = x^2$$
$$x = 8 \text{ inches}$$

The length of the chord is 16 inches.

In possibility 2:

$$10^2 = 4^2 + x^2$$
$$100 = 16 + x^2$$
$$84 = x^2$$
$$x \approx 9.2 \text{ inches}$$

The length of the chord is about 18.4 inches.

**30.** $\overleftrightarrow{HJ}$ is not a tangent to the circle. For it to be a tangent to the circle, the Pythagorean Theorem would need to hold, since a tangent to the circle and the radius of the circle are at right angles to each other. Here,

$14^2 \neq 6^2 + 12^2$

## LESSON 66

### Warm Up 66

1. altitude

2. $h^2 = 5^2 - 3^2$
$h^2 = 25 - 9$
$h^2 = 16$
$h = 4$
$A = \frac{1}{2}bh = \frac{1}{2}(14)(4) = 28 \text{ in.}^2$

3. Choice **A** is regular because it is equilateral.

4. $h^2 = 15^2 - 12^2$
$h^2 = 225 - 144$
$h^2 = 81$
$h = 9$
$A = lw + \frac{1}{2}bh$
$= (24)(8) + \frac{1}{2}(24)(9) = 300 \text{ cm}^2$
$P = 24 + 8 + 15 + 15 + 8 = 70 \text{ cm}$

### Lesson Practice 66

**a.** $P = 8(32) = 256 \text{ yd}$

**b.** $A = \frac{1}{2}aP$
$= \frac{1}{2}(13)(5)(19) = 617.5 \text{ ft}^2$

**c.** $A = \frac{1}{2}aP$
$P = (6)(24) = 144 \text{ ft}$
$a = 12\sqrt{3}$
$A = \frac{1}{2}(12\sqrt{3})(144)$
$= 864\sqrt{3} \text{ ft}^2$

**d.** $A = \frac{1}{2}aP$
$\frac{a}{6} = \frac{1}{\sqrt{3}}$
$(\sqrt{3})(a) = (1)(6)$
$a = \frac{6}{\sqrt{3}} = \frac{6\sqrt{3}}{3} = 2\sqrt{3}$
$P = 3(12) = 36$

$A = \frac{1}{2}(2\sqrt{3})(36) = 36\sqrt{3}\text{ m}^2$

**e.** $A = \frac{1}{2}aP$

$P = (6)(78) = 468\text{ ft}$

$a = 39\sqrt{3}$

$A = \frac{1}{2}(39\sqrt{3})(468)$

$= 9126\sqrt{3}\text{ ft}^2$

$9126\sqrt{3}\text{ ft}^2 \times \frac{1\text{ yd}^2}{9\text{ ft}^2} = 1014\sqrt{3}\text{ yd}^2$

## Practice 66

**1.** Assume $\overline{XA}$ is an altitude. Then $\overline{XA}$ is perpendicular to $\overline{YZ}$. Since perpendicular segments form four right angles, then $m\angle 1 = m\angle 2$, but it is given that $m\angle 1 \neq m\angle 2$, so we have a contradiction. Thus, $\overline{XA}$ is not an altitude of $\triangle XYZ$.

**2.** $A = \frac{1}{2}aP$

$P = (6)(14) = 84\text{ ft}$

$a = 7\sqrt{3}$

$A = \frac{1}{2}(7\sqrt{3})(84)$

$= 294\sqrt{3}\text{ ft}^2$

$40{,}000(294\sqrt{3}) \approx 20{,}000{,}000\text{ in.}^2$

**3.** sometimes

**4.** $y = 2(110) = 220$

$x = 110\sqrt{3}$

**5.** They meet at a right angle.

**6.** $\frac{\pi 2^2}{\pi 18^2} = \frac{4}{324} = \frac{1}{81}$

$\frac{1}{81} \cdot \frac{1}{2} = \frac{1}{162}$ or about 0.00617 or about 0.617%

**7.** $V - E + F = 2$

$10 - E + 10 = 2$

$-E = -18$

$E = 18$

**8.** The incenter of a triangle is equidistant from all sides of the triangle. So, if $S$ is the incenter,

$2x = 20$

$x = 10$

**9.**

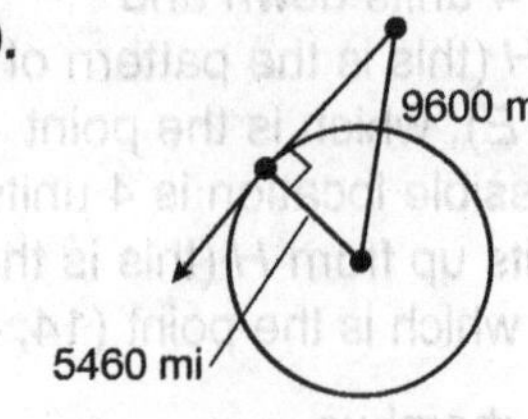


$x^2 = 9600^2 - 5460^2$

$x^2 = 62{,}348{,}400$

$x \approx 7900\text{ miles}$

**10.** The vector moves points over 2 and up 3, so the vector will move any point on the line.

**11.** $x = \frac{1}{2}(46° + 98°) = 72°$

**12.** $\frac{2\pi(17{,}000)}{2\pi(26{,}000)} = \frac{17}{26} \approx 0.65$

**13.** $x + 3 = \frac{1}{2}(-4x + 10)$

$2x + 6 = -4x + 10$

$6x = 4$

$x = \frac{2}{3}$

$JK = \frac{2}{3} + 3 = 3\frac{2}{3}$ or $\frac{11}{3}$

$FG = -4\left(\frac{2}{3}\right) + 10 = \frac{22}{3}$ or $7\frac{1}{3}$

**14.** $\frac{8}{14} = \frac{4}{7}$ or 4 : 7

**15.** In the two triangles, $KL = KP$, as they are radii of the smaller circle, and $KM = KN$, as they are radii of the larger circle. The longer side will therefore be the one across from the larger contained angle, so $\overline{LM}$ is the longer side.

**16.** $P = 7(77) = 539\text{ ft}$

**17.** $v = 2v - 1$ and $u = 4 - u$

$v = 1$ and $u = 2$

or

$v = 4 - u$ and $u = 2v - 1$

$v = 4 - (2v - 1)$

$v = 5 - 2v$

$3v = 5$

$v = \frac{5}{3}$

$u = 2\left(\frac{5}{3}\right) - 1$

$u = \frac{7}{3}$

**18.** Since the sides are congruent and the diagonals are not congruent, it is a rhombus.

**19.** rectangle

**20.** $A = \frac{1}{2}aP$

$2A = aP$

$\frac{2A}{P} = a$

Choice **D** is correct.

**21.** "Midpoint Theorem" should be "Definition of Midpoint" and "Corresponding Segments Postulate" should be "Segment Addition Postulate."

**22.**

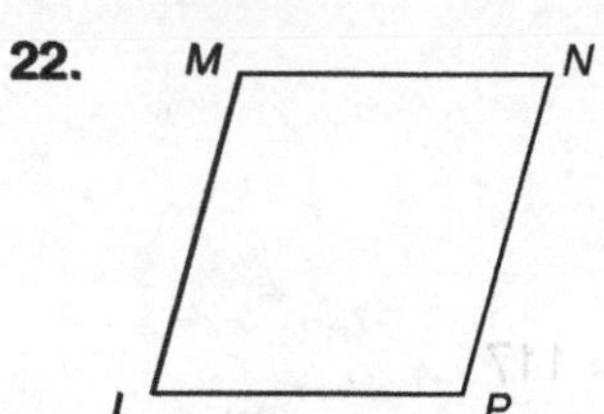


$\angle L$ and $\angle P$ are supplementary.

Choice **B** is correct.

**23.** $x = \frac{1}{2}(146) = 73°$

**24.** $5x + 12 = 2x + 24$

$3x = 12$

$x = 4$

$2y - 4 = 4 + y$

$y = 8$

**25.** Though $\angle AYF$ and $\angle AXH$ are both right angles, it is not known that $Y$, $A$, and $X$ are collinear.

**26.** Since the triangle is equilateral, the angles measure 60°. This is also the measure of the smaller angles in the parallelogram and the central angle of the circle.

$A = \frac{60°}{360°}\left(\pi(3^2)\right) = 1.5\pi$

**27.** $V = (\pi 6^2)(6) \approx 678.58 \text{ in.}^3$

$678.58 \times 8 \approx 5400$ mints

**28.** The slope of the line perpendicular to $y = 2x - 7$ is $-\frac{1}{2}$.

$y = -\frac{1}{2}x + b$

$6 = -\frac{1}{2}(-1) + b$

$\frac{11}{2} = b$

$y = -\frac{1}{2}x + \frac{11}{2}$

To find the point of intersection, set the equations equal to each other.

$-\frac{1}{2}x + \frac{11}{2} = 2x - 7$

$\frac{25}{2} = \frac{5}{2}x$

$x = 5$

$y = 2(5) - 7 = 3$

The point of intersection is (5, 3).

Find the distance between (5, 3) and (−1, 6).

$d = \sqrt{(5 - -1)^2 + (3 - 6)^2}$

$= \sqrt{6^2 + (-3)^2}$

$= \sqrt{45}$

$\approx 6.71$

**29.** Since $DE$ and $JK$ are parallel, $\frac{LD}{DJ} = \frac{LE}{EK}$.

$\frac{6}{DJ} = \frac{8}{6}$

$(8)(DJ) = (6)(6)$

$8DJ = 36$

$DJ = 4.5$

$17.5^2 = 10.5^2 + 14^2$

$306.25 = 110.25 + 196$

$306.25 = 306.25$

$\Delta JKL$ is a right triangle.

**30.**

34 ft

x

 

$$x = \frac{34}{\sqrt{3}} = \frac{34\sqrt{3}}{3}$$

$$P = 12\left(\frac{34\sqrt{3}}{3}\right) = 136\sqrt{3}\text{ ft}$$

$$A = \frac{1}{2}aP$$

$$= \frac{1}{2}(34)(136\sqrt{3})$$

$$= 2312\sqrt{3}\text{ ft}^2$$

## LAB 9

### Lab Practice 9

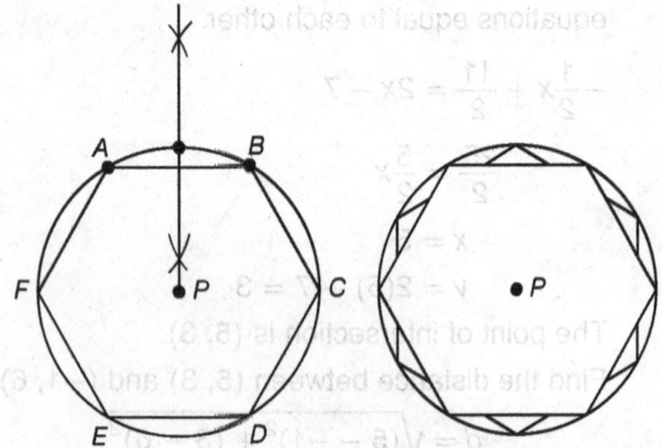


Students should bisect $\overline{AB}$ to find the point on the circle where the point of the dodecagon will go. They should repeat this process for each side of the hexagon.

## LESSON 67

### Warm Up 67

1. congruent
2. The perpendicular bisector divides the segment into two equal parts. So, $AP = A'P$.
3. Choice **A**, magnitude and direction, is correct.

### Lesson Practice 67

**a.** It is a translation since each point is shifted the same distance.

**b.**

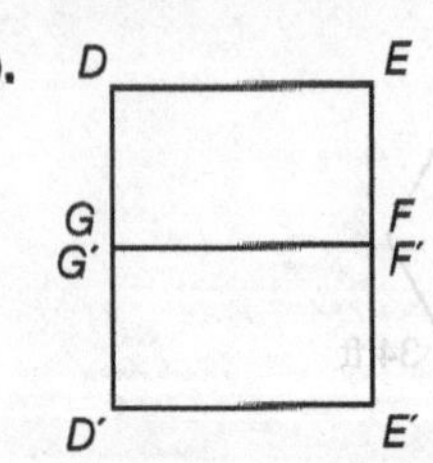


**c.**

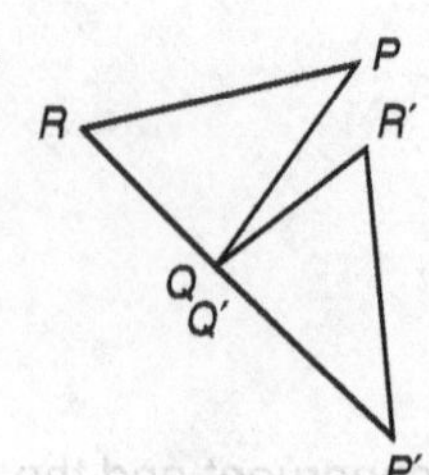


**d.**

### Practice 67

1. $A = \frac{1}{2}aP = \frac{1}{2}(36.5)[(5)(53)] \approx 4836.3\text{ cm}^2$

2. $x^2 = 6^2 + 6^2$
   $x^2 = 36 + 36$
   $x^2 = 72$
   $x \approx 8.5$ in.

3. $\frac{1}{2}(4x + 8 + 186) = 117$
   $4x + 194 = 234$
   $4x = 40$
   $x = 10$

4. The slope of the line perpendicular to $y = \frac{-4}{3}x + 3$ is $\frac{3}{4}$.
   $y = \frac{3}{4}x + b$
   $6 = \frac{3}{4}(4) + b$
   $3 = b$
   $y = \frac{3}{4}x + 3$
   To find the point of intersection, set the equations equal to each other.
   $\frac{3}{4}x + 3 = \frac{-4}{3}x + 3$
   $x = 0$
   $y = \frac{3}{4}(0) + 3 = 3$
   The point of intersection is (0, 3).

Find the distance between (0, 3) and (4, 6).

$d = \sqrt{(0 - 4)^2 + (3 - 6)^2}$

$= \sqrt{(-4)^2 + (-3)^2}$

$= \sqrt{25}$

$= 5$

5. $P = 8(30) = 240$ feet

$A = \frac{1}{2}aP$

$= \frac{1}{2}(36.2)(240)$

$= 4344$ square feet

6. This is a translation because all the points are shifted the same distance.

7. $26 - 8 = 18$ feet per second

8. No, we do not know if the corners are right angles.

9. Sample: $2x^2 - 8 = 0$

$2x^2 = 8$

$x^2 = 4$

$x = 2$

But 8 is not a perfect square.

10. $\frac{5}{3} = \frac{3}{DE}$

$(5)(DE) = (3)(3)$

$5DE = 9$

$DE = 1.8$

11. $m\angle Z = m\angle Y = 68°$

$m\angle X = 180° - 2(68°) = 44°$

12. $A = 2(Ph)$

$= 2(14 + 14 + 9 + 9)(8)$

$= 736 \text{ ft}^2$

13. 5 inches

14. Choice **A** is correct. The transformation is a reflection because it flips across a line of reflection.

15. Geometric probability does not apply to part a, because the player does not have an equally likely chance of hitting any area. The player is aiming for a specific location. Geometric probability does apply to part b, because meteors are equally likely to occur in any given portion of the sky.

16. $A = \frac{1}{2}(b_1 + b_2)h$

$= \frac{1}{2}(b + \frac{1}{2}b)h$

$= \left(\frac{1}{2}b + \frac{1}{4}b\right)h$

$= \frac{3}{4}bh$

17. $S = L + 2B$

$= 2\pi rh + 2\pi r^2$

$= 2\pi(40)(115) + 2\pi(40^2)$

$\approx 38{,}956 \text{ ft}^2$

18. Only line $m$ appears to be tangent to $\odot C$. Choice **B** is correct.

19. $7x + 7y = 49$

$7y = -7x + 49$

$y = -1x + 7$

The slope of the line perpendicular to this is 1.

$y = x + b$

$3 = 1(4) + b$

$-1 = b$

$y = x - 1$

20.

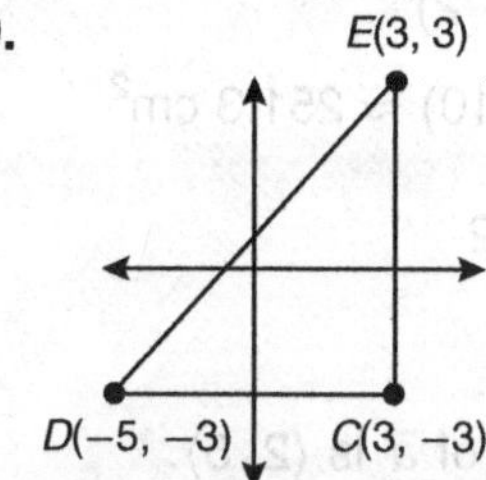


The polygon is a right triangle.

$DC = 8$

$CE = 6$

$DE^2 = 8^2 + 6^2$

$DE^2 = 64 + 36$

$DE^2 = 100$

$DE = 10$

$P = 10 + 8 + 6 = 24$

21. He has incorrectly used the $1 : 2 : \sqrt{3}$ ratio for the sides of a 30°-60°-90° triangle. Since the length of the shorter leg of the triangle is

2, The length of $k$, the hypotenuse, is $2(2) = 4$.

**22.** This transformation could be a reflection or a rotation (by 180°). It could not be a translation.

**23.**

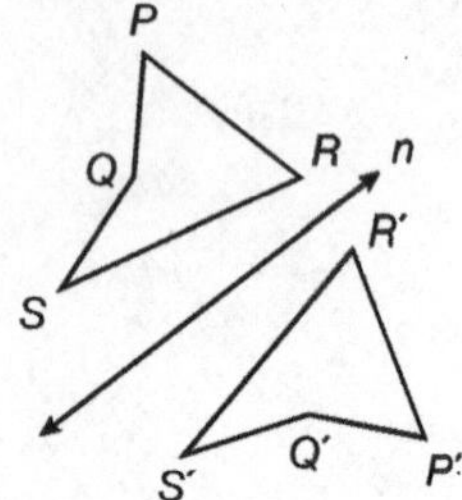


**24.** Given: $\triangle ABC$ where $\angle A \neq \angle B \neq \angle C$
Prove: $AB \neq BC \neq CA$
Proof: Assume that $AB = BC$.
Since we know that if two sides of a triangle are congruent then the two angles opposite those sides are congruent, that means $\angle A \cong \angle C$. However, this contradicts the original given statement. Therefore, the assumption is incorrect. Thus, if a triangle has no two angles congruent then it has no two sides congruent.

**25.** Since angles $L$ and $M$ are supplementary in a rhombus,
$m\angle L = 180° - 2(x + 2)°$

**26.** $L = 2\pi rh = [2\pi(4)](10) \approx 251.3 \text{ cm}^2$

**27.** $\frac{48°}{360°}[2\pi(8.5)] \approx 7.12$
Choice **C** is correct.

**28.** The component form of $\vec{a}$ is $\langle 2, 5\rangle$.
The component form of $\vec{b}$ is $\langle 2, -3\rangle$.
Therefore, the resultant vector is
$\langle 2 + 2, 5 - 3\rangle = \langle 4, 2\rangle$.

**29.** $P = 3(32) = 96$ ft

$$A = \frac{1}{2}aP$$

$$a = \frac{16}{\sqrt{3}} = \frac{16\sqrt{3}}{3}$$

$$A = \frac{1}{2}\left(\frac{16\sqrt{3}}{3}\right)(96) \approx 443.4 \text{ ft}^2$$

**30.** Yes, the centroid is always in the interior of the triangle.

Yes, the orthocenter is outside the triangle when the triangle is obtuse.

## LESSON 68

### Warm Up 68

**1.** ratio

**2.** The shorter leg $a$ is opposite the 30° angle. So, $a = \frac{1}{2}(12) = 6$.

**3.** Both shorter legs $= x + 2$
hypotenuse $= (x + 2)\sqrt{2}$
$P = 2(x + 2) + \sqrt{2}(x + 2)$
$= 2x + 4 + \sqrt{2}(x + 2)$
Choice **B** is correct.

### Lesson Practice 68

**a.** $\sin T = \frac{12}{13}$

**b.** $\tan U = \frac{5}{12}$

**c.** $\sin 39° = \frac{x}{41}$
$x = 41 \sin 39°$
$x \approx 25.80$

**d.** $\sin 30° = 0.5$

**e.** $\cos 90° = 0$

**f.** $\tan 45° = 1$

**g.** $\sin 38° = \frac{h}{16}$
$h = 16 \sin 38°$
$h \approx 9.85$ ft

### Practice 68

**1.** with the current: 1 mile per hour against the current: 5 miles per hour

**2.**
$h^2 = 8^2 + 5^2$
$h^2 = 64 + 25$
$h^2 = 89$
$h = \sqrt{89}$
$(\sqrt{89})^2 = x^2 + 6^2$

$89 - 36 = x^2$

$53 = x^2$

$x = \sqrt{53}$

**3.** 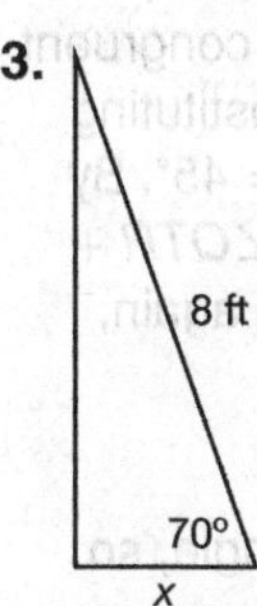


$\cos 70° = \frac{x}{8}$

$x = 8 \cos 70°$

$x \approx 2.74$ ft

**4.** 5 is the shorter leg of a 30°-60°-90° triangle. So, $h = 2(5) = 10$

**5.** $m_{DE} = \frac{3-0}{3-0} = \frac{3}{3} = 1$

$m_{EF} = \frac{0-3}{6-3} = \frac{-3}{3} = -1$

Since these slopes are negative reciprocals of each other, it is a right triangle. Choice **D** is correct.

**6.** $\angle W = \frac{2}{3}\angle X$

$\angle W + \angle X = 180°$

$\frac{2}{3}\angle X + \angle X = 180°$

$\frac{5}{3}\angle X = 180°$

$\angle X = 108°$

$m\angle Y = 180° - 108° = 72°$

**7.** $\sin Q = \frac{a}{c}$; $\cos Q = \frac{b}{c}$; $\tan Q = \frac{a}{b}$

**8.** For *ABCD* to be a rhombus, the diagonals must be perpendicular. Therefore, $m\angle AOD$ must be 90°.

**9.** $\frac{1}{8}(1000) = 125$ spins

**10.** $x^2 + x^2 = 8^2$

$2x^2 = 64$

$x^2 = 32$

$x = \sqrt{32} = 4\sqrt{2}$

$P = 4(4\sqrt{2}) = 16\sqrt{2}$ in.

$A = (4\sqrt{2})^2 = (16)(2) = 32$ in.$^2$

**11.** $S = L + 2B$

$= [2(14) + 2(13)](7) + 2(13)(14)$

$= (54)(7) + 364$

$= 742$ m$^2$

**12.** No, the vertices of the square do not shift to the same places in a rotation and a reflection.

**13.** Total Area = $(8)(10) = 80$ ft$^2$

Area foot from wall = $80 - (6)(8) = 32$ ft$^2$

$\frac{32}{80} = \frac{2}{5} = 0.4$

**14.** $(EG)^2 = 5^2 - 4^2$

$(EG)^2 = 9$

$EG = 3$

**15.** Marilou counted the diagonal sections as having a length of 1.

Starting from the bottom left corner and working counterclockwise:

$P = 3 + 1 + \sqrt{2} + \sqrt{5} + 5 + 2 + \sqrt{2} + \sqrt{5} + 2\sqrt{2}$

$= 12 + 4\sqrt{2} + 2\sqrt{5}$

**16.** Since $\overline{EM}$ and $\overline{BA}$ are parallel, $\angle MEB \cong \angle ABK$. Since $\angle ABK \cong \angle KAR$ and $\angle BKR \cong \angle BAR$, *BARK* is a parallelogram.

**17.** No. While it is true that whales do not have feathers, it does not follow from the given statements, since the first statement does not say that birds exclusively have feathers.

**18.** $P = 8(6) = 48$ inches

**19.** 575 mL = 575 cm$^3$

$r = 3.75$ cm

$V = Bh$

$575 = (\pi 3.75^2)(h)$

$h \approx 13$ cm

**20.** Both triangles are isosceles because $MQ = M'Q$ and $PQ = P'Q$. Since their vertex angles both measure 72°, their base angles each measure 54°. So, by definition of angles and AA similarity, $\triangle MM'Q \sim \triangle PP'Q$.

**21.** 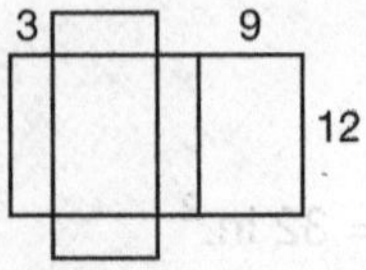


**22.** Yes, but only if the side length is 4 units.

$4^2 = 4(4)$

$16 = 16$

**23.** $\triangle LMN$ and $\triangle OPQ$ are right triangles, $\overline{LM} \cong \overline{QP}$, and $\overline{MN} \cong \overline{PO}$. By the LL Congruence Theorem, $\triangle LMN \cong \triangle QPO$.

**24.** 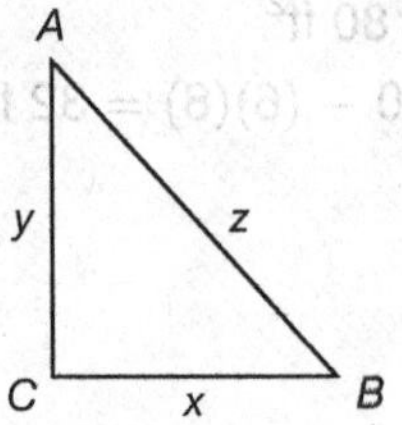


Choice A:

$\sin A = \frac{x}{z}$

$\tan B = \frac{y}{x}$

Choice B:

$\sin A = \frac{x}{z}$

$\cos B = \frac{x}{z}$

Choice C:

$\tan A = \frac{x}{y}$

$\frac{1}{\tan B} = \frac{x}{y}$

Choice D:

$\sin B = \frac{y}{z}$

$\cos A = \frac{y}{z}$

Choice **A** is correct.

**25.** $m\angle YXZ = \frac{1}{2} m\widehat{XY} = \frac{1}{2}(100°) = 50°$

**26.** $\frac{5}{x} = \frac{10}{5}$

$(10)(x) = (5)(5)$

$10x = 25$

$x = 2.5$

$y + 2.5 = 10$

$y = 7.5$

**27.** By the definition of an angle bisector, $\angle QTR \cong \angle RTS$. By definition of congruent angles, $m\angle QTR = m\angle RTS$. Substituting the given information, $m\angle RTS = 45°$. By the Angle Addition Postulate, $m\angle QTR + m\angle RTS = m\angle QTS$. Substituting again,

$45° + 45° = m\angle QTS$

$90° = m\angle QTS$

This is the definition of a right angle, so $\angle QTS$ is a right angle.

**28.** $\frac{33}{45} \approx 0.73$

**29.** Yes, they are parallel because the transversals divide the lines proportionately.

**30.** This transformation is a reflection across the line shown. Choice **C** is correct.

## LESSON 69

### Warm Up 69

**1.** kite

**2.** $A = \frac{1}{2}(b_1 + b_2)h$

$= \frac{1}{2}(12 + 7)(4)$

$= 38$ square units

**3.** $A = \frac{1}{2}(b_1 + b_2)h$

$24 = \frac{1}{2}(12 + b)(3)$

$48 = 36 + 3b$

$12 = 3b$

$4 = b$

The other base is 4 inches.

### Lesson Practice 69

**a.** $EF = \frac{1}{2}(AB + CD)$

$38 = \frac{1}{2}(22 + CD)$

$76 = 22 + CD$

$54 \text{ in.} = CD$

**b.** $m\angle S = m\angle R = 48°$
$m\angle Q = m\angle T = 180° - 48° = 132°$

**c.** $MQ = NQ = 17.5 - 9.6 = 7.9$ yards

**d.** $(FG)^2 = 4^2 + 2^2$
$(FG)^2 = 16 + 4$
$(FG)^2 = 20$
$FG = FJ \approx 4.5$
$(GH)^2 = 7^2 + 2^2$
$(GH)^2 = 49 + 4$
$(GH)^2 = 53$
$GH = HJ \approx 7.3$

**e.** $65 = \frac{1}{2}(80 + R)$
$130 = 80 + R$
$50 \text{ m} = R$

## Practice 69

**1.** $GK = \frac{1}{2}(HJ + FL)$
$28 = \frac{1}{2}(16 + FL)$
$56 = 16 + FL$
$40 \text{ ft} = FL$

**2.** $d_{WX} = \sqrt{(4-5)^2 + (-9 - -1)^2}$
$= \sqrt{(-1)^2 + (-8)^2}$
$= \sqrt{65}$
$d_{YZ} = \sqrt{(0 - -1)^2 + (2 - -6)^2}$
$= \sqrt{1^2 + 8^2}$
$= \sqrt{65}$
$d_{XY} = \sqrt{(5-0)^2 + (-1-2)^2}$
$= \sqrt{5^2 + (-3)^2}$
$= \sqrt{34}$
$d_{ZW} = \sqrt{(4 - -1)^2 + (-9 - -6)^2}$
$= \sqrt{5^2 + (-3)^2}$
$= \sqrt{34}$

The distances from $W$ to $X$ and from $Y$ to $Z$ are equal, as are the distances from $X$ to $Y$ and from $Z$ to $W$.

**3.** $x > 180 - 140$
$x > 40$

**4.** $21 - 7 = 14$ miles per hour

**5.** Since $\overline{AP}$, $\overline{BP}$, $\overline{EP}$, and $\overline{FP}$ are all radii of the circle, there are pairs of congruent sides, so the Hinge Theorem can be used to find the largest angle. With $\overline{AB}$ longer than $\overline{EF}$, $\angle APB$ is the larger angle.

**6.** Hypothesis: $x^2 + 16 = 25$
Conclusion: $x = 3$

**7.** The length of the side opposite a 30° is half the length of the hypotenuse in a right triangle. This is also the side adjacent to the 60° angle.
$\sin 30° = \frac{5}{10} = \frac{1}{2}$
$\cos 30° = \frac{5}{10} = \frac{1}{2}$

**8.** $V_{cylinder} = Bh = (\pi)(2.5^2)(4) \approx 78.5 \text{ in.}^3$
$V_{rectangular} = lwh = (5)(2)(8) = 80 \text{ in.}^3$
There is more fluid in the rectangular container.

**9.** 2 reflections must be preformed—one across the line of reflection and then one back to the original position. 4 rotations by 90° will return the figure to its original position.

**10.** $m\angle ACB = m\angle ACK = m\angle CAK$
$= 180° - 90° - 37° = 53°$
$m\angle K = 180° - 53° - 53° = 74°$

**11.** $\frac{288°}{360°}(2\pi(6)) \approx 30.16$
Choice **A** is correct.

**12.** 12 in. = 1 foot
$A = \frac{1}{2}aP$
$P = 6(1) = 6 \text{ ft}$
$a = 0.5\sqrt{3}$
$A = \frac{1}{2}(0.5\sqrt{3})(6)$
$\approx 2.6 \text{ ft}^2$

$A_{floor} = (25)(32) = 800 \text{ ft}^2$
$800 \div 2.6 \approx 308$ tiles

13. No, because a calendar either has 365 or 366 days, neither of which is divisible by 7, so there will never be an equal number of each day of the week represented on a calendar.

14. $(RS)^2 = 6^2 + 6^2$
$(RS)^2 = 36 + 36$
$(RS)^2 = 72$
$RS = ST \approx 8.5$
$(UR)^2 = 10^2 + 6^2$
$(UR)^2 = 100 + 36$
$(UR)^2 = 136$
$UR = TU \approx 11.7$

15. He counted the diagonal lines as 1. Starting from the lower left corner and going counterclockwise:
$P = 3\sqrt{2} + 1 + \sqrt{5} + 4 + \sqrt{2} + 5 + \sqrt{2} + 4 + 2\sqrt{2} + 7$
$= 21 + 7\sqrt{2} + \sqrt{5}$

16. $V - E + F = 2$
$V - 12 + 6 = 2$
$V = 8$

17. $x = \frac{1}{2}(76°) = 38°$

18.
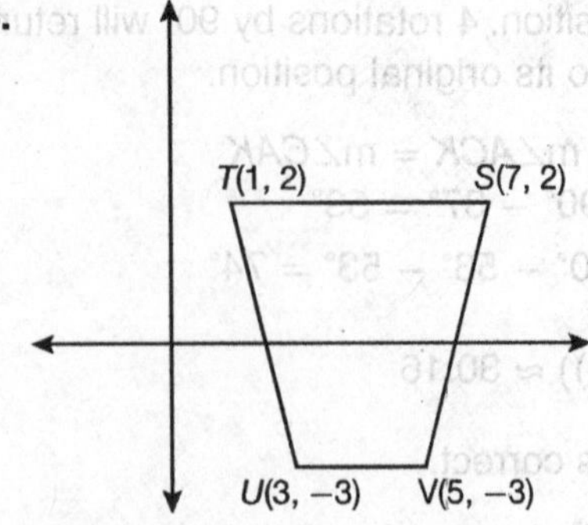


It is an isosceles trapezoid.
$d_{TS} = 6$
$d_{UV} = 2$
$h = 5$
$A = \frac{1}{2}(6 + 2)(5) = 20$ square units

19. $UW = TV = TX + VX = 23 + 28.7 = 51.7$ in.

20. Answers will vary. Sample: 35°, 85°, and 60°. The triangle is acute.

21. $\frac{15}{6} = \frac{AD}{4}$
$(6)(AD) = (15)(4)$
$6AD = 60$
$AD = 10$

22. $V = (\pi)(1.5^2)(6) = 42.4 \text{ in.}^3$
$\frac{1}{8} = \frac{42.4}{w}$
$(1)(w) = (8)(42.4)$
$w \approx 340 \text{ in.}^3$

23. $PZ = PM = y$

24. $-2(60 = x + y)$
$5 = 2x - 3y$
$-120 = -2x - 2y$
$5 = 2x - 3y$
$-115 = -5y$
$23 = y$
$37 = x$

25. $m\angle B = m\angle C = 93°$
$m\angle A = m\angle D = 180° - 93° = 87°$

26. $\sin b = \frac{8}{17}$; $\cos b = \frac{15}{17}$; $\tan b = \frac{8}{15}$

27. perpendicular

28. No, you do not, because the sine and cosine depend only the ratio of side lengths, not the actual lengths.

29. $x = \frac{1}{2}(33° + 97°) = 65°$

30. Choice **D** is correct. The transformations are isometries, which do not change the size or the shape of the figure.

## LESSON 70

### Warm Up 70

1. apothem
2. $n$ is the number of sides and $s$ is the side length.
3. Choice B, $V = Bh$, is correct.

## Lesson Practice 70

**a.** $L = \frac{1}{2}Pl$

$P = 8(5) = 40$ cm

$L = \frac{1}{2}(40)(7) = 140 \text{ cm}^2$

**b.** $S = L + B$

$B = \frac{1}{2}aP$

$= \frac{1}{2}(2\sqrt{3})(24)$

$\approx 41.57 \text{ in.}^2$

$S = L + B$

$S = \frac{1}{2}Pl + B$

$S = \frac{1}{2}(24)(8) + 41.57$

$= 137.57 \text{ in.}^2$

**c.** $V = \frac{1}{3}Bh = \frac{1}{3}(5)(5)(10) \approx 83.3 \text{ ft}^3$

**d.** $S = L + B$

$B = 600^2 = 360{,}000 \text{ ft}^2$

$S = L + B$

$S = \frac{1}{2}Pl + B$

$l = \sqrt{321^2 + 300^2} = \sqrt{193{,}041} \approx 439.36$ ft

$S = \frac{1}{2}(2400)(\sqrt{193{,}041}) + 360{,}000$

$\approx 887{,}237 \text{ ft}^2$

## Practice 70

**1.** $m\angle R = m\angle P = \frac{1}{2}(360° - 100° - 38°) = 111°$

**2.** $V = \frac{1}{3}Bh$

$B = \frac{1}{2}aP$

$= \frac{1}{2}(3.5\sqrt{3})(42)$

$\approx 127.31 \text{ ft}^2$

$V = \frac{1}{3}(127.31)(10)$

$\approx 424 \text{ ft}^3$

**3.** $P = 10 + 4 + 6 + 2 + 4 + 2 = 28$ cm

**4.** $m\angle 1 = 26°$

$m\angle 2 = 90° - 26° = 64°$

$m\angle 3 = 180° - 2(64°) = 52°$

**5.** $P = 521 + 482.5 + 519 = 1522.5$ miles

It is half the perimeter of the Bermuda Triangle.

**6.** $A = \frac{1}{2}bh = \frac{1}{2}(8)(4\sqrt{3}) = 16\sqrt{3} \text{ in.}^2$

**7.** $V = Bh = \left(\frac{1}{2}\right)(3)(1.5\sqrt{3})(8) \approx 31.177 \text{ cm}^2$

$34 \times 31.177 \approx 1060.02$ g

**8.** sine; cosine

**9.** Both are special because their angles are the largest whole number divisors of 90° (and associated complements); 45°-45°-90° triangles are isosceles, whereas 30°-60°-90° triangles are not.

**10.** $\frac{x}{5} = \frac{5}{2}$

$(2)(x) = (5)(5)$

$2x = 25$

$x = 12.5$

**11.** $L = \frac{1}{2}Pl$

$= \frac{1}{2}(32)(10)$

$= 160 \text{ in.}^2$

**12.** A disjunction is an "or" statement. So, it is true when either *p* is true, or *q* is true, or both are true. Choice **B** is correct.

**13.** Choice **B** is correct. The other options can all be simplified to *x* equals a constant, making all of these options vertical lines parallel to $x = 2$.

**14.**

| Statements | Reasons |
|---|---|
| 1. $\angle 1 \cong \angle 2$ | 1. Given |
| 2. $\angle 1 \cong \angle 3$ | 2. Vertical Angles Theorem |
| 3. $\angle 2 \cong \angle 3$ | 3. Transitive Property of Congruence |
| 4. $j \parallel k$ | 4. Converse of Corresponding Angles Postulate |

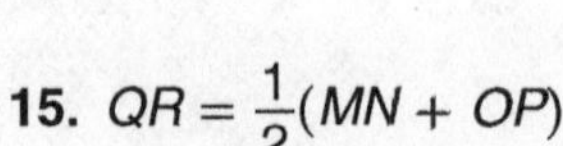



15. $QR = \frac{1}{2}(MN + OP)$

$3x = \frac{1}{2}(x + 3 + 2x + 6)$

$6x = 3x + 9$

$3x = 9$

$x = 3$

$QR = 3(3) = 9$

$MN = 3 + 3 = 6$

$OP = 2(3) + 6 = 12$

16. $A_{Total} = (24)(14) = 336 \text{ in.}^2$

$A_{Blue} = (6)(2) + (5)(4) = 32 \text{ in.}^2$

$\frac{32}{336} = \frac{2}{21}$ or about 9.5%

17. $7\sqrt{3} = \frac{21\sqrt{3}}{3} = \frac{21}{\sqrt{3}}$

The sides are each 42 ft.

$A = \frac{1}{2}aP = \frac{1}{2}(7\sqrt{3})(126) = 441\sqrt{3}$

18. $\angle HJG \cong \angle LJK$ by the Vertical Angles Theorem, and $18 : 27 = 16 : 24$, so $\angle HGJ \sim \angle LKJ$ by SAS Similarity.

19. $S = L + B$

$B = \frac{1}{2}aP$

$= \frac{1}{2}(\sqrt{3})(12)$

$\approx 10 \text{ cm}^2$

$S = L + B$

$S = \frac{1}{2}Pl + B$

$S = \frac{1}{2}(12)(8) + 10$

$= 58 \text{ cm}^2$

20. Raquel is correct; the vertices of the image are labeled in a different orientation than the vertices of the preimage. By looking at the relationships between $A$ and $A'$, $B$ and $B'$, and $C$ and $C'$, you can determine that the image was rotated.

21. $d_{ST} = 10$

If $ST$ is the shorter leg, then $R$ would be located at $\left(-1, 10\sqrt{3} - 4\right)$.

If $ST$ is the longer leg, then $R$ would be located at $\left(-1, \frac{10\sqrt{3}}{3} - 4\right)$.

22. $m\widehat{MNO} = 2(118°) = 236°$

23. $L = \frac{1}{2}Pl$

$l = \sqrt{115.5^2 + 147^2} = \sqrt{34{,}949.25} \approx 187 \text{ m}$

$L = \frac{1}{2}(924)(187) \approx 86{,}400 \text{ m}^2$

24. $m\angle J = m\angle H = 97°$

$m\angle F = m\angle G = \frac{1}{2}[360° - 2(97°)] = 83°$

25. $\frac{12}{x} = \frac{x}{300}$

$(x)(x) = (12)(300)$

$x^2 = 3600$

$x = 60$

26. See student work. This should form a 30°-60°-90° triangle. So, $l = w\sqrt{3}$.

27. $\cos 56° = \frac{14}{MN}$

$MN = \frac{14}{\cos 56°}$

$MN \approx 25.04$

28. $AB = 3BC$

$AB + BC + AB + BC = 84$

$3BC + BC + 3BC + BC = 84$

$8BC = 84$

$BC = AD = 10.5$

$AB = CD = 3(10.5) = 31.5$

29.

| $V$ is the midpoint of $\overline{SW}$. (Given) | $W$ is the midpoint of $\overline{VT}$. (Given) | |
|---|---|---|
| $\overline{SV} \cong \overline{VW}$ (Definition of midpoint) → | $\overline{VW} \cong \overline{WT}$ (Definition of midpoint) → | $\overline{SV} \cong \overline{WT}$ (Transitive Property of Equality) |

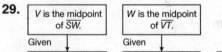

30. $h = 40$ cm

base length $= 5$ cm

$V = \frac{1}{3}Bh = \frac{1}{3}(25)(40) \approx 333 \text{ cm}^3$

## INVESTIGATION 7

**1–4.**

| $x$ | $\sin x$ | $\cos x$ | $\tan x$ |
|---|---|---|---|
| 0° | 0 | 1 | 0 |
| 15° | $\approx 0.26$ | $\approx 0.97$ | $\approx 0.27$ |
| 30° | $\frac{1}{2} = 0.5$ | $\frac{\sqrt{3}}{2} \approx 0.87$ | $\frac{\sqrt{3}}{3} \approx 0.58$ |
| 45° | $\frac{\sqrt{2}}{2} \approx 0.71$ | $\frac{\sqrt{2}}{2} \approx 0.71$ | 1 |
| 60° | $\frac{\sqrt{3}}{2} \approx 0.87$ | $\frac{1}{2} = 0.5$ | $\sqrt{3} \approx 1.73$ |
| 75° | $\approx 0.97$ | $\approx 0.26$ | $\approx 3.73$ |
| 90° | 1 | 0 | undefined |

**5.** The sine and the cosine of the 30° and 60° rows are switched.

**6.** They are equal. If $x$ and $y$ are complementary angles, then $\sin x = \cos y$.

**7.** $0 \leq \sin x \leq 1$,
$0 \leq \cos x \leq 1$

**8.** $\sin x + \cos x$ equals 1 for $x = 0°$ and 90°. This is not true for the rest of the table.

**9.** $\sin^2 (60°) + \cos^2 (60°)$

$= \left(\frac{\sqrt{3}}{2}\right)^2 + \left(\frac{1}{2}\right)^2$

$= \frac{3}{4} + \frac{1}{4} = 1$

$\sin^2 (45°) + \cos^2 (45°)$

$= \left(\frac{\sqrt{2}}{2}\right)^2 + \left(\frac{\sqrt{2}}{2}\right)^2$

$= \frac{1}{2} + \frac{1}{2} = 1$

It is always 1.

**10.** $\tan x \geq 0$; The two legs can have any positive measures, so the ratio of their lengths can be any value greater than 0.

### Investigation Practice 7

**a.** $m\angle F = 90° - 45° = 45°$

$DE = EF = 1; DF = \sqrt{2}$

$\sin 45° = \frac{1}{\sqrt{2}}$; $\cos 45° = \frac{1}{\sqrt{2}}$; $\tan 45° = 1$

**b.** $HJ = 2GH; GH = \sqrt{3}; HJ = 2\sqrt{3}$

$\sin 60° = \frac{\sqrt{3}}{2}$; $\cos 60° = \frac{1}{2}$; $\tan 60° = \sqrt{3}$

**c.**

$\sqrt{2}$, 45°, 1, 45°, 1

**d.**

$2\sqrt{3}$, 60°, $\sqrt{3}$, 30°, 3

## LESSON 71

### Warm Up 71

**1.** preimage; image

**2.** translation

**3. a.** $m = \frac{13 - 7}{7 - 4} = \frac{6}{3} = 2$

The slope of $\overline{RS} = 2$

**b.** length = distance =

$\sqrt{(x_2 - x_1)^2 + (y_2 - y_1)^2}$

$= \sqrt{(4 - 7)^2 + (7 - 13)^2}$

$= \sqrt{(-3)^2 + (-6)^2}$

$= \sqrt{45} = 3\sqrt{5}$

The length of $\overline{RS} = 3\sqrt{5}$

### Lesson Practice 71

**a.** $A'(11, 5 + 5) = A'(11, 10)$

$B'(4, 9 + 5) = B'(4, 14)$

**b.** $K'(2 - 2, 5 + 1) = K'(0, 6)$

$L'(1 - 2, 11 + 1) = L'(-1, 12)$

$M'(5 - 2, 7 + 1) = M'(3, 8)$

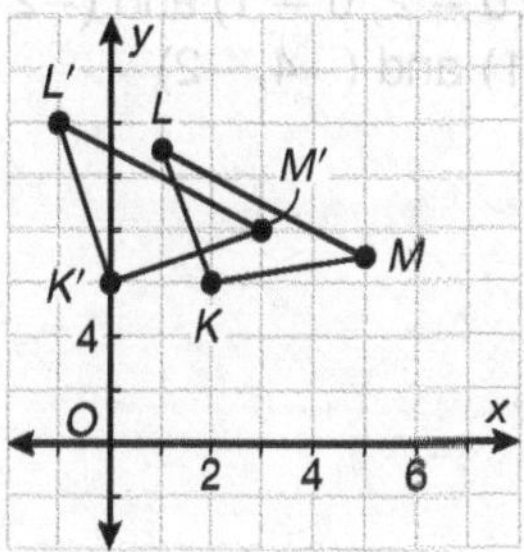

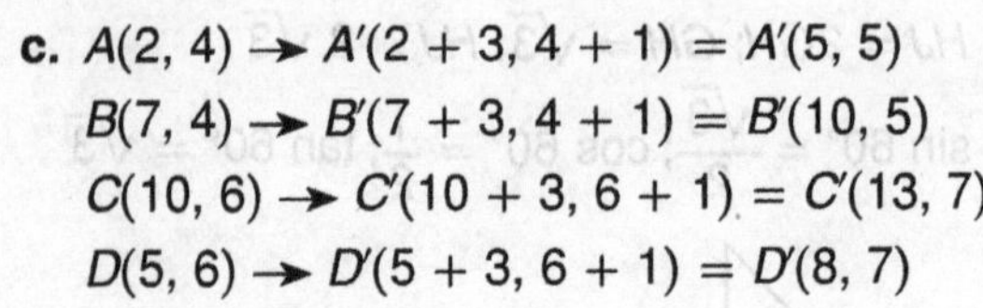

**c.** $A(2, 4) \rightarrow A'(2 + 3, 4 + 1) = A'(5, 5)$
$B(7, 4) \rightarrow B'(7 + 3, 4 + 1) = B'(10, 5)$
$C(10, 6) \rightarrow C'(10 + 3, 6 + 1) = C'(13, 7)$
$D(5, 6) \rightarrow D'(5 + 3, 6 + 1) = D'(8, 7)$

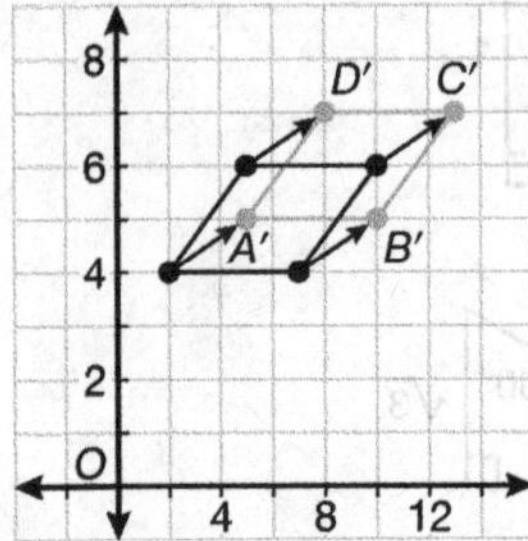


**d.** In both translations, the change in the $x$-values is 8, and the change in the $y$-values is 1, so the vector is $\langle 8, 1\rangle$.

## Practice 71

**1.** If $X$ is connected to $Y$, then the result is a rhombus, because the diagonals of a rhombus bisect the opposite angles and also meet at a right angle.

**2.** $V = \frac{1}{3}Bh = \frac{1}{3}(15)(10) = 50 \text{ cm}^3$

**3.** $1.6 + 1.8 = 3.4$
Since the sum of the shorter legs is equal to the longest leg, this is not a triangle.

**4.** $0.5 \cancel{\text{liters}} \times \left(\frac{1000 \text{ mL}}{1 \cancel{\text{liter}}}\right) = 500 \text{ mL}$

$$V = (\pi r^2)(h)$$
$$500 = (\pi r^2)(20)$$
$$7.96 \approx r^2$$
$$2.82 \text{ cm} \approx r$$

**5.** $(1, 2) \rightarrow (1 - 2, 2 - 1)$ and $(-1 - 2, 1 - 1)$
$= (-1, 1)$ and $(-3, 0)$
$(2, 1) \rightarrow (2 - 2, 1 - 1)$ and $(0 - 2, 0 - 1)$
$= (0, 0)$ and $(-2, -1)$
$(0, 0) \rightarrow (0 - 2, 0 - 1)$ and $(-2 - 2, -1 - 1)$
$= (-2, -1)$ and $(-4, -2)$

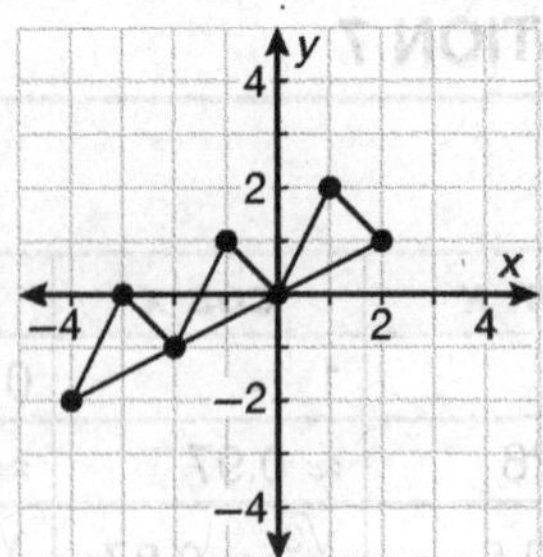


**6.** $5 + x = 1$
$x = -4$
$y + 11 = -6$
$y = -17$

**7.** $P'(5 - 3, 5 + 4) = P'(2, 9)$
$Q'(-5 - 3, -5 + 4) = Q'(-8, -1)$

**8.** It is a rhombus because it has equal sides and perpendicular diagonals.

**9.** $d_{EF} = \sqrt{(2 - 3)^2 + (3 - 1)^2}$
$= \sqrt{(-1)^2 + 2^2}$
$= \sqrt{5}$
$d_{HG} = \sqrt{(-1 - 2)^2 + (4 - -2)^2}$
$= \sqrt{(-3)^2 + 6^2}$
$= \sqrt{45}$
$= 3\sqrt{5}$
Midsegment $= \frac{1}{2}(\sqrt{5} + 3\sqrt{5})$
$= \frac{1}{2}(4\sqrt{5})$
$= 2\sqrt{5}$

**10.** $S = L + B = 10 + 5 = 15 \text{ ft}^2$

**11.** $\frac{6}{9} = \frac{5}{GH}$
$(6)(GH) = (9)(5)$
$6GH = 45$
$GH = 7.5$ in.

**12.** $\frac{1}{2}y = -3x + 4$
$y = -6x + 8$
The slope of the line perpendicular to this line is $\frac{1}{6}$.
$y = \frac{1}{6}x + b$

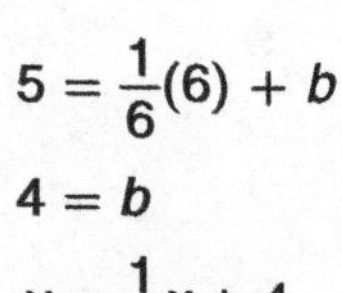

$$5 = \frac{1}{6}(6) + b$$

$$4 = b$$

$$y = \frac{1}{6}x + 4$$

**13.** If a triangle is not equilateral, then the sides are not congruent.

**14.** Reflect the figure in the horizontal line. Reflect the figure in the vertical line. Rotate the figure 180° about the intersection of the two lines.

**15.** $V = \frac{1}{3}Bh$

$$= \frac{1}{3}(115)(115)(70) = 308{,}583 \text{ ft}^3$$

**16.** The $x$-value was moved 3 units to the left and the $y$-value was moved 2 units up. So, the translation of $F(1, -4)$ is $F'(1 - 3, -4 + 2) = F'(-2, -2)$.
Choice **C** is correct.

**17.** longer leg = 1

$$\text{shorter leg} = \frac{1}{\sqrt{3}} = \frac{\sqrt{3}}{3}$$

$$\text{hypotenuse} = 2\left(\frac{\sqrt{3}}{3}\right) = \frac{2\sqrt{3}}{3}$$

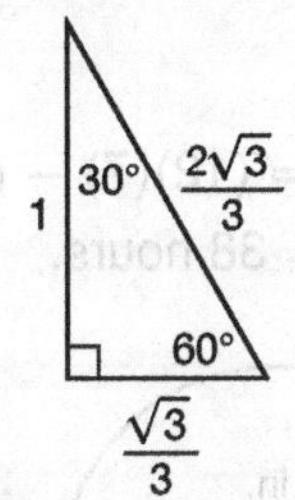


**18.** For angles between 0° and 45°, the tangent ratio is less than 1. For angles between 45° and 90°, the tangent ratio is greater than 1.

**19.** Let $SU = ST = x$

$$x^2 + x^2 = (3.5)^2$$

$$2x^2 = 12.25$$

$$x^2 = 6.125$$

$$x = \sqrt{6.125} \approx 2.47$$

**20.**

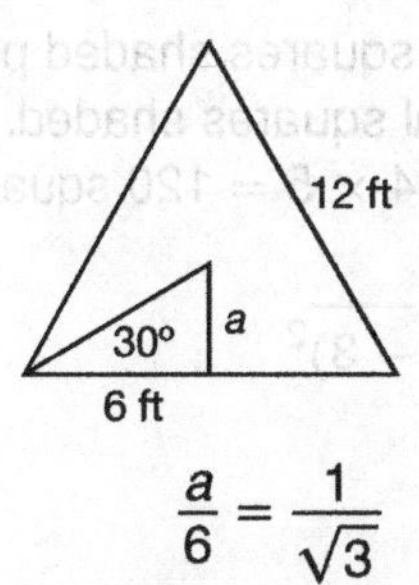


$$\frac{a}{6} = \frac{1}{\sqrt{3}}$$

$$(\sqrt{3})(a) = (6)(1)$$

$$a = \frac{6}{\sqrt{3}} = \frac{6\sqrt{3}}{3} = 2\sqrt{3}$$

$$A = \frac{1}{2}aP = \frac{1}{2}(2\sqrt{3})(36) = 36\sqrt{3}$$

**21.** $AC$ is the greatest side length of $\triangle ABC$. Since $\overline{AB}$ and $\overline{BC}$ are congruent, $\angle A$ and $\angle C$ must also be congruent at 40° each. Therefore, by the Triangle Angle Sum Theorem, $\angle B$ is 100°. So, $\overline{AC}$ is the longest since it is across from the longest side, while $\overline{AB}$ and $\overline{BC}$ are shorter but equal.

**22.** Since alternate angles are on opposite sides of the transversal, choice **A** is correct.

**23.** $VY = \frac{1}{2}(UZ + WX)$

$$11 = \frac{1}{2}(16 + WX)$$

$$22 = 16 + WX$$

$$WX = 6 \text{ cm}$$

**24.** A reflection would change the order of the vertices. Therefore, choice **C** is correct.

**25.** The component form of $\vec{c}$ is $\langle 4, 2\rangle$.
The component form of $\vec{d}$ is $\langle -6, -4\rangle$.
Therefore, the resultant vector is $\langle -2, -2\rangle$.

**26. a.**

E
3 cm
45°
D F

**b.** $$\frac{3}{\sqrt{2}} = \frac{DF}{1}$$

$$(\sqrt{2})(DF) = (1)(3)$$

$$DF = \frac{3}{\sqrt{2}} = \frac{3\sqrt{2}}{2} \approx 2.12$$

27. There are 10 complete squares shaded plus approximately 14 partial squares shaded. The area is approximately $24 \times 5 = 120$ square meters.

28. $d_{KL} = \sqrt{(7-3)^2 + (0-3)^2}$
$= \sqrt{4^2 + (-3)^2}$
$= \sqrt{25}$
$= 5$
$d_{LM} = \sqrt{(7-3)^2 + (0--3)^2}$
$= \sqrt{4^2 + 3^2}$
$= \sqrt{25}$
$= 5$
$d_{MN} = \sqrt{(3--1)^2 + (-3-0)^2}$
$= \sqrt{4^2 + (-3)^2}$
$= \sqrt{25}$
$= 5$
$d_{KN} = \sqrt{(3--1)^2 + (0-3)^2}$
$= \sqrt{4^2 + (-3)^2}$
$= \sqrt{25} = 5$
Since the lengths of the sides are all equal, the quadrilateral is a rhombus.

29. $x$ is across from a 51° angle, $y$ is across from a 42° angle, and $z$ is across from a 48° angle. So, the order of the sides from least to greatest is $y$, $z$, and $x$.

30. a. $\frac{60°}{360°} = \frac{1}{6}$
b. $\frac{180°}{360°} = \frac{1}{2} = 0.5$

## LESSON 72

### Warm Up 72

1. tangent
2. $4x + 1 = 3x + 6$
$x = 5$
$RS = 4(5) + 1 = 21$
$RT = 3(5) + 6 = 21$

3. 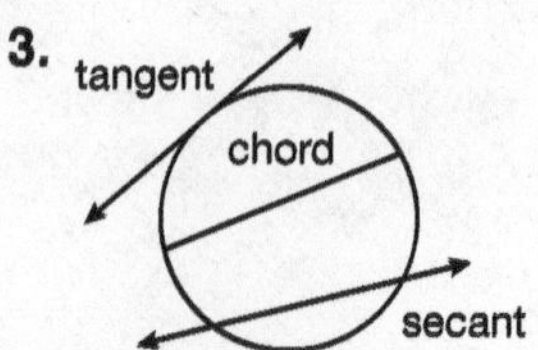


### Lesson Practice 72

a. $x + 3 = 8$
$x = 5$
$RS = 5 + 3 = 8$
$ST = SU = 5 + 8 = 13$

b. $PR = 6$ in.
$PQ = 2(6) = 12$ in.
$(RQ)^2 = 12^2 - 6^2$
$(RQ)^2 = 144 - 36$
$(RQ)^2 = 108$
$RQ = \sqrt{108} \approx 10.39$ in.
$A = \frac{1}{2}bh = \frac{1}{2}(6)(10.39) \approx 31 \text{ in.}^2$

c. $5x - 6 = 19$
$5x = 25$
$x = 5$

### Practice 72

1. $\frac{0.5 \text{ hr}}{1 \text{ ft}^2} = \frac{1 \text{ hr}}{2 \text{ ft}^2}$;
Area to paint $= (12)(7) - (1)(8) = 76 \text{ ft}^2$
$76 \text{ ft}^2 \times \frac{1 \text{ hr}}{2 \text{ ft}^2} = 38$ hours.

2. 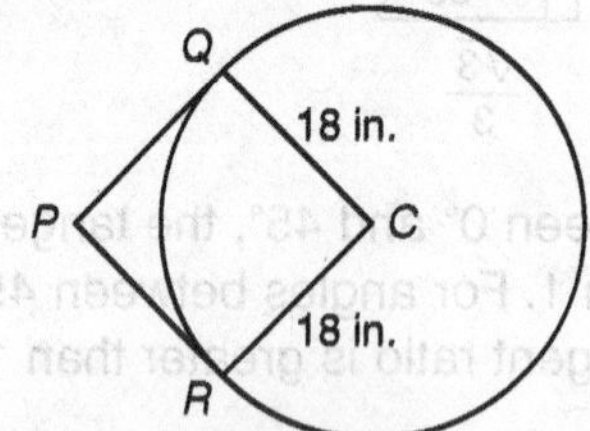


Since $CQ = 2PQ$,
$PQ = PR = 9$ in.
$P = 18 + 18 + 9 + 9 = 54$ in. = 4 ft 6 in.

3. The image has a different shape and orientation, so the transformation was not an isometry and, therefore, not a translation.

4. Negation of the hypothesis: A polygon does not have six sides;
Negation of the conclusion: The polygon is not a hexagon.

**5.** $2x - 3 = 17$

$2x = 20$

$x = 10$

$BE = 2(10) - 3 = 17$

$CE = DE = 10 + 5 = 15$

**6.** hypotenuse = 6 in.
shorter leg = $6 \div 2 = 3$ in.
longer leg = $3\sqrt{3}$

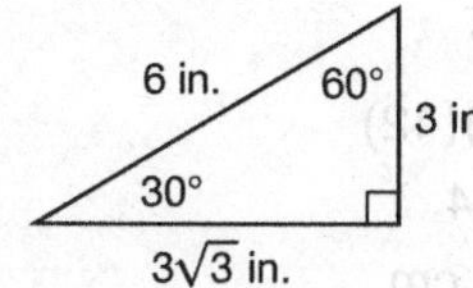


**7.** $(5 - 2, 4 - 1) = (3, 3)$

**8.** $S = L + 2B$

$= (2\pi)(40)(50) + 2(\pi)(40)^2$

$\approx 22{,}620 \text{ m}^2$

**9.** Since we know that the hypotenuses and one leg are congruent, the HL Congruence Theorem applies to these triangles. Choice **A** is correct.

**10.** $m_1 = \frac{2-2}{3-5} = \frac{0}{-2} = 0$

$m_2 = \frac{1-1}{-2 - -8} = \frac{0}{6} = 0$

The lines are parallel because the slopes are equal.

**11.** The point of tangency is (0, −1). The tangent line is the horizontal line $y = -1$. The radius of ⊙ $A$ is 2 and the radius of ⊙ $B$ is 1.

**12.**

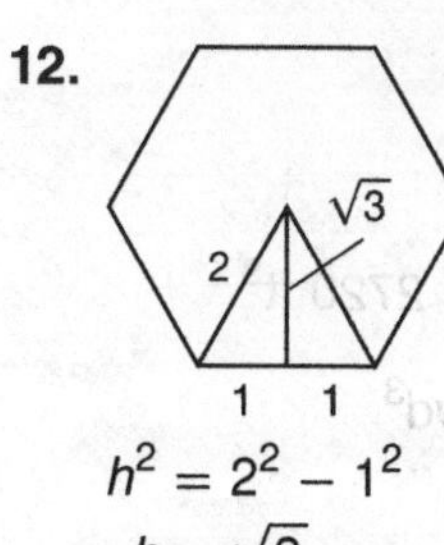


$h^2 = 2^2 - 1^2$

$h = \sqrt{3}$

Therefore, the sides of the hexagon are 2.

$L = \frac{1}{2}Pl$

$= \frac{1}{2}(12)(2) = 12 \text{ in.}^2$

**13.** $BD = \frac{1}{2}AE = \frac{1}{2}(4) = 2$ mi

$AB = BC = 1.7$ mi

$DE = DC = 1.5$ mi

distance $= 4 + 1.7 + 2 + 1.5 = 9.2$ mi

**14.** $K'(4 - 5, 11) = K'(-1, 11)$

**15.** Label the points $A(0, 0)$, $B(10, 0)$, and $C(5, 4)$.
The midpoint of $AB$ is (5, 0).
The midpoint of $AC$ is (2.5, 2).
The line perpendicular to $AB$ through (5, 0) is $x = 5$.
To find the line perpendicular to $AC$:

$m_{AC} = \frac{4}{5} \quad m_{\perp AC} = -\frac{5}{4}$

$y = -\frac{5}{4}x + b$

$2 = -\frac{5}{4}(2.5) + b$

$\frac{41}{8} = b$

$y = -\frac{5}{4}x + \frac{41}{8}$

The line perpendicular to $AC$ through (2.5, 2) is $y = -\frac{5}{4}x + \frac{41}{8}$.
To find the circumcenter, solve the system of equations.

$x = 5$

$y = -\frac{5}{4}x + \frac{41}{8}$

$y = -\frac{5}{4}(5) + \frac{41}{8}$

$y = -1.125$

The circumcenter is located at (5, −1.125).

**16.** The point of tangency is (4, −1). The tangent line is the vertical line $x = 4$. The radius of ⊙ $X$ is 4 and the radius of ⊙ $Y$ is 3.

**17.** $H'(3 - 3, -5 + 3) = H'(0, -2)$

$T: (x, y) \rightarrow (x - 3, y + 3)$

**18.** $x = \frac{1}{2}(222°) = 111°$

**19.** The apothem is half the side length of the square.

20. $EF = \frac{1}{2}(AB + DC)$

$EF = \frac{1}{2}(13 + 28)$

$EF = 20.5$ m

21. polyhedron

22. The slope of the line perpendicular to $y = -\frac{3}{2}x - 1$ is $\frac{2}{3}$.

$y = \frac{2}{3}x + b$

$4 = \frac{2}{3}(1) + b$

$\frac{10}{3} = b$

$y = \frac{2}{3}x + \frac{10}{3}$

To find the point of intersection, set the equations equal to each other.

$\frac{-3}{2}x - 1 = \frac{2}{3}x + \frac{10}{3}$

$-\frac{13}{6}x = \frac{13}{3}$

$x = -2$

$y = \frac{-3}{2}(-2) - 1 = 2$

The point of intersection is (−2, 2). Find the distance between (−2, 2) and (1, 4).

$d = \sqrt{(-2 - 1)^2 + (2 - 4)^2}$

$= \sqrt{(-3)^2 + (-2)^2}$

$= \sqrt{13}$

$\approx 3.61$

23. Based on the given information, $\overline{PN}$ is congruent to $\overline{NM}$ by the definition of midpoint. By the Transitive Property of Congruence, $\overline{PN}$ is congruent to $\overline{PQ}$. By the definition of midpoint, $\overline{PQ}$ is congruent to $\overline{QR}$. By the Transitive Property of Congruence, $\overline{PN}$ is congruent to $\overline{QR}$.

24. To find the height of the base, use the Pythagorean Theorem.

$h^2 = 10^2 - 5^2$

$h^2 = 100 - 25$

$h^2 = 75$

$h \approx 8.66$ in.

$S = L + B$

$\approx 3\left(\frac{1}{2}\right)(10)(5) + \frac{1}{2}(10)(8.66)$

$\approx 118 \text{ in.}^2$

25. The parallelogram is a rectangle because its angles are right, and it is a rhombus because the diagonals are perpendicular to each other. So, it is both.

26. $\frac{7}{3} = \frac{l}{42}$

$(3)(l) = (7)(42)$

$3l = 294$

$l = 98$ cm

27. $6y - 24 > 4y + 9$

$2y > 33$

$y > 16.5$

$6y - 24 < 180°$

$6y < 204$

$y < 34$

So, $16.5 < y < 34$

28. 7 ft 8 in. = 92 in.

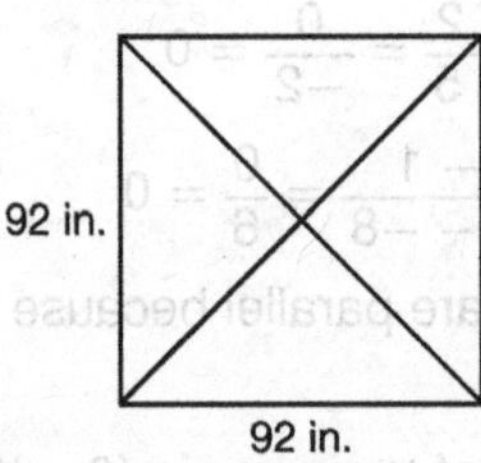


$d^2 = 92^2 + 92^2$

$d^2 = 8464 + 8464$

$d^2 = 16{,}928$

$d \approx 130$ in.

130 in. = 10 ft 10 in.

29. $V = lwh = (40)(8)(8.5) = 2720 \text{ ft}^3$

$2720 \text{ ft}^3 \times \frac{1 \text{ yd}^3}{27 \text{ ft}^3} \approx 101 \text{ yd}^3$

$101 \times \$25 = \$2525$

30. Sample:

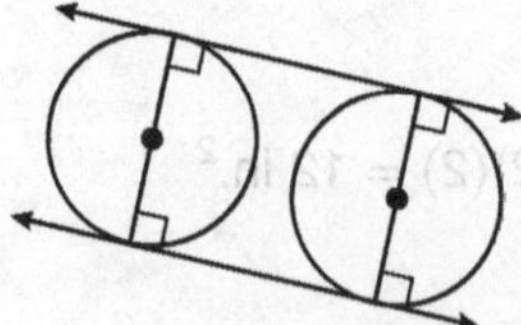

## LESSON 73

### Warm Up 73

1. cosine

2. $\tan 72° = \frac{41}{x}$

$x = \frac{41}{\tan 72°}$

$x \approx 13.32$

3. leg: 1

hypotenuse: $\sqrt{2}$

ratio: $\frac{1}{\sqrt{2}} = \frac{\sqrt{2}}{2}$

Choice **C** is correct.

### Lesson Practice 73

a.

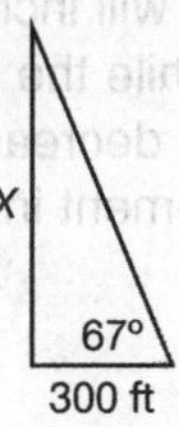


$\tan 67° = \frac{x}{300}$

$x = 300 \tan 67°$

$x \approx 707$ feet

b. $\sin 55° = \frac{160}{x}$

$x = \frac{160}{\sin 55°}$

$x \approx 195$ meters

c.

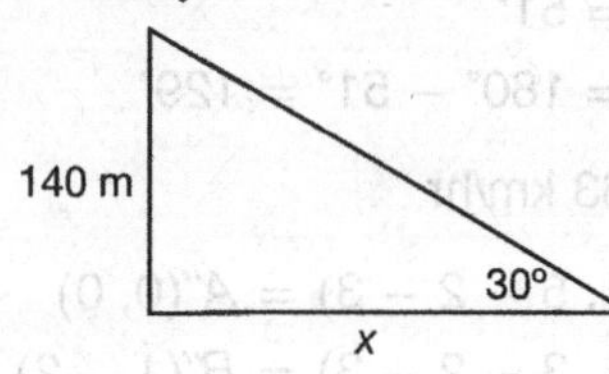


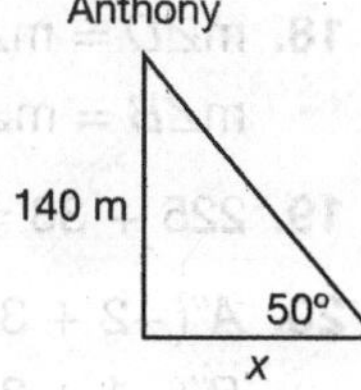


Jocelyn:

$\tan 30° = \frac{140}{x}$

$x = \frac{140}{\tan 30°}$

$x \approx 242.5$ m

Anthony:

$\tan 50° = \frac{140}{x}$

$x = \frac{140}{\tan 50°}$

$x \approx 117.5$ m

Jocelyn is $242.5 - 117.5 = 125$ meters farther from the balloon than Anthony.

d.

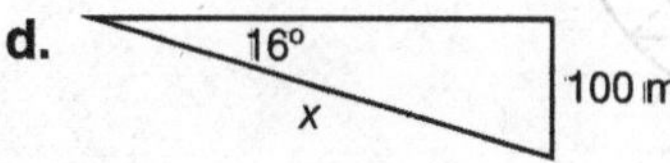


$\sin 16° = \frac{100}{x}$

$x = \frac{100}{\sin 16°}$

$x \approx 363$ meters

### Practice 73

1. $\sin 45° = \frac{22}{h}$

$h = \frac{22}{\sin 45°}$

$h \approx 31.11$ ft

2. Since $11.6 > 2\sqrt{33}$, $m\angle Y > m\angle M$.

Choice **B** is correct.

3. Sample:

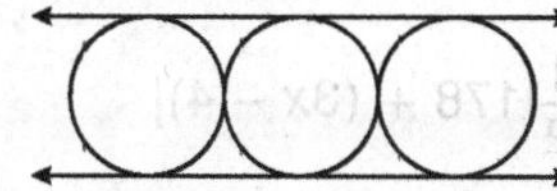

4. Since sectors 2 and 5 have the greatest area, the geometric probability is greatest for these sectors.

5. $L = \frac{1}{2}Pl = \frac{1}{2}(n)(1)(2) = n\text{ m}^2$

6. Yes, it is a right triangle. Since $\overleftrightarrow{AB}$ is parallel to the base $\overline{DE}$, it divides the other sides of the triangle proportionately. So, $AF = 6$. Therefore, the side lengths of $\triangle DEF$ are 4, 8, and $4\sqrt{3}$.

$4^2 + (4\sqrt{3})^2 = 8^2$

$16 + (16)(3) = 64$

$16 + 48 = 64$

$64 = 64$

So, by the Converse of the Pythagorean Theorem, $\triangle DEF$ is a right triangle.

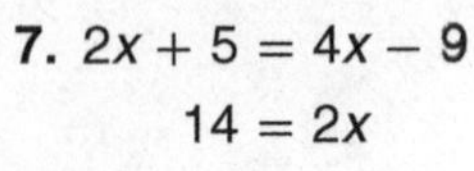



**7.** $2x + 5 = 4x - 9$

$14 = 2x$

$7 = x$

**8.**

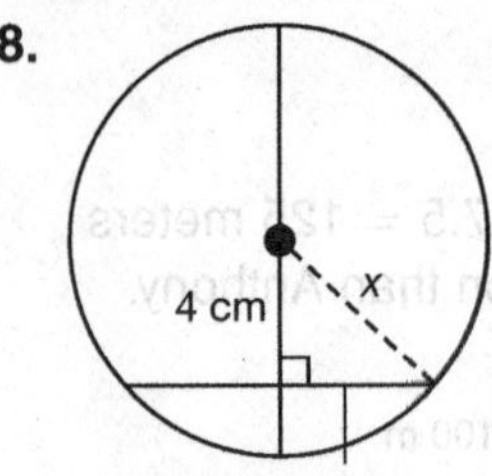


$x^2 = 4^2 + 4^2$

$x^2 = 16 + 16$

$x^2 = 32$

$x \approx 5.7$ cm

**9.** $\frac{360°}{8} = 45°$

**10.** $A = (12)(12) - 4(3)(3) = 108 \text{ ft}^2$

$108 \text{ ft}^2 \times \frac{144 \text{ in.}^2}{1 \text{ ft}^2} = 15{,}552 \text{ in.}^2$

$15{,}552 \div 18 = 864$ bricks

**11.** $\tan 60° = \frac{x}{136}$

$\sqrt{3} = \frac{x}{136}$

$x = 136\sqrt{3}$ meters

**12.** $101° = \frac{1}{2}[178 + (3x - 4)]$

$202 = 3x + 174$

$28 = 3x$

$9\frac{1}{3} = x$

**13.** $\cos 8° \approx 0.99$

$\cos 10° \approx 0.98$

$\cos 25° \approx 0.91$

$\cos 30° \approx 0.87$

$\cos 60° \approx 0.5$

$\cos 70° \approx 0.34$

$\cos 90° \approx 0$

The cosine cannot be greater than 1 because that would mean that the hypotenuse would be shorter than one leg.

**14. a.**

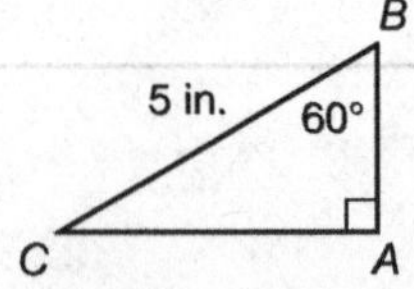


**b.** $\cos 60° = \frac{AB}{5}$

$AB = 5 \cos 60°$

$AB = 2.5$ in.

**c.** $\sin 60° = \frac{AC}{5}$

$AC = 5 \sin 60°$

$AC = 5\left(\frac{\sqrt{3}}{2}\right) = 2.5\sqrt{3}$ in. $\approx 4.33$ in.

**15.** $\frac{112°}{360°}[2\pi(4)] \approx 7.82$ in.

**16.** Quinton is correct. The $x$-values will increase by 3 and then decrease by 3, while the $y$-values will increase by 8, then decrease by 8.The net result shows no movement in the image based on the preimage.

**17.**

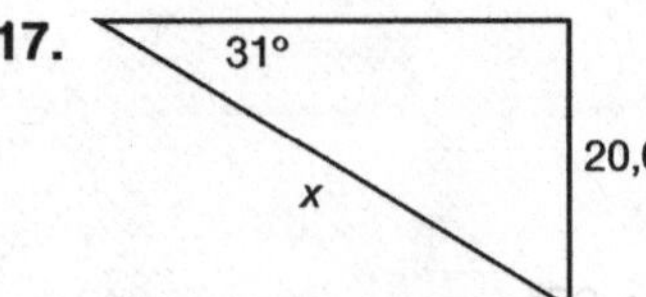


$\sin 31° = \frac{20{,}000}{x}$

$x = \frac{20{,}000}{\sin 31°}$

$x \approx 38{,}832$ ft

Choice **D** is correct.

**18.** $m\angle D = m\angle A = 51°$

$m\angle B = m\angle C = 180° - 51° = 129°$

**19.** $225 + 38 = 263$ km/hr

**20.** $A''(-2 + 3 - 1, 5 - 2 - 3) = A''(0, 0)$

$B''(-1 + 3 - 1, 3 - 2 - 3) = B''(1, -2)$

$C''(1 + 3 - 1, 5 - 2 - 3) = C''(3, 0)$

**21.** $m\angle K = 180° - 42° - 53° = 85°$

So, from shortest to longest, the segments are $KL$, $JK$, and $JL$ based on the size of the angles they are across from.

22. 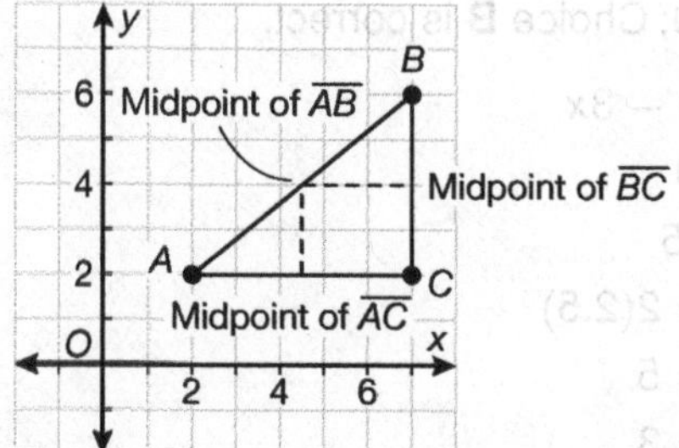


23. 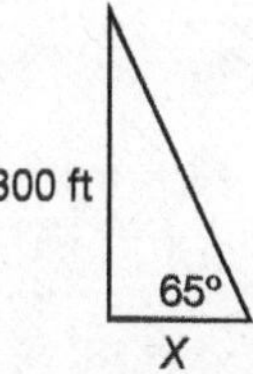


$$\tan 65^\circ = \frac{800}{x}$$

$$x = \frac{800}{\tan 65^\circ}$$

$$x \approx 373 \text{ ft}$$

24. $DP = \frac{2}{3}(AP) = \frac{2}{3}(123) = 82$

25. $BD = \frac{1}{3}(BT)$

$$63 = \frac{1}{3}(BT)$$

$$189 = BT$$

26. No; The fly is more likely to land in the section with the largest area.

27. Midpoint =

$$\left(\frac{(5x-3)+(2x+3)}{2}, \frac{(2-6y)+(2y+1)}{2}\right)$$

$$= \left(\frac{7x}{2}, \frac{3-4y}{2}\right) = (3.5x, 1.5-2y)$$

28. Yes, it is a parallelogram because diagonals of a parallelogram bisect each other.

29. $CD = AC = 5$

$$4x - 12 = 3x - 7$$

$$x = 5$$

$$CE = BC = 3(5) - 7 = 8$$

30. $\overline{KJ}$ is a radius. $\overline{LM}$ is a chord. $\overleftrightarrow{MN}$ is a tangent.

## LESSON 74

### Warm Up 74

1. isometries

2. P Q P′

S R S′

3. The line of reflection must be identified to describe a reflection. Choice **C** is correct.

### Lesson Practice 74

a. $T: (x, y) \to (-x, y)$

$T: A(1, 1) \to A'(-1, 1)$

$T: B(5.5, 1) \to B'(-5.5, 1)$

$T: C(5.5, 3.5) \to C'(-5.5, 3.5)$

$T: D(1, 3.5) \to D'(-1, 3.5)$

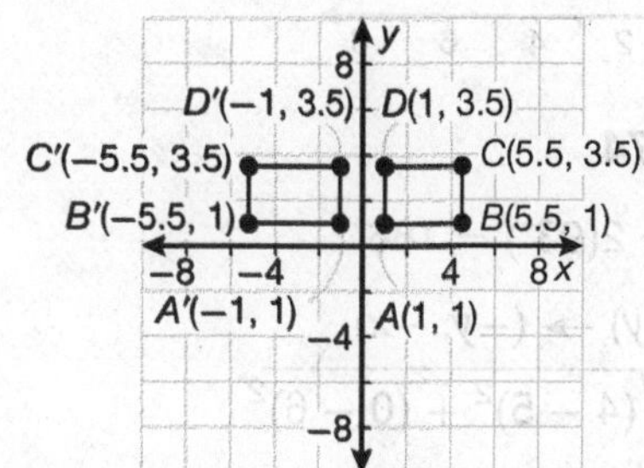


b. $T: (x, y) \to (x, -y + 4)$

$T: A(1, 1) \to A'(1, 3)$

$T: B(5.5, 1) \to B'(5.5, 3)$

$T: C(5.5, 3.5) \to C'(5.5, 0.5)$

$T: D(1, 3.5) \to D'(1, 0.5)$

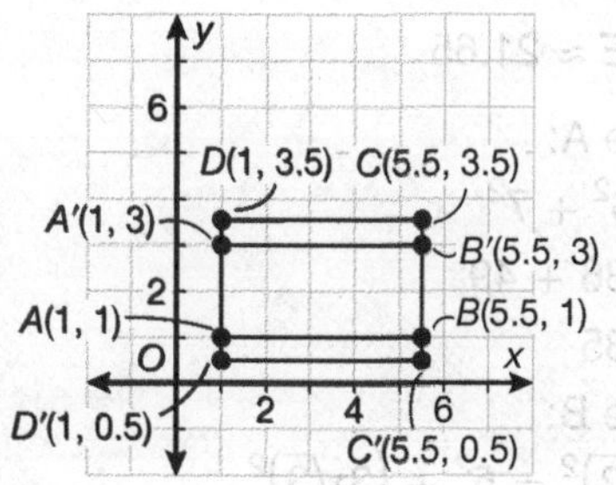


c. $T: (x, y) \to (y, x)$

$T: A(1, 1) \to A'(1, 1)$

$T: B(5.5, 1) \to B'(1, 5.5)$

$T: C(5.5, 3.5) \to C'(3.5, 5.5)$

$T: D(1, 3.5) \to D'(3.5, 1)$

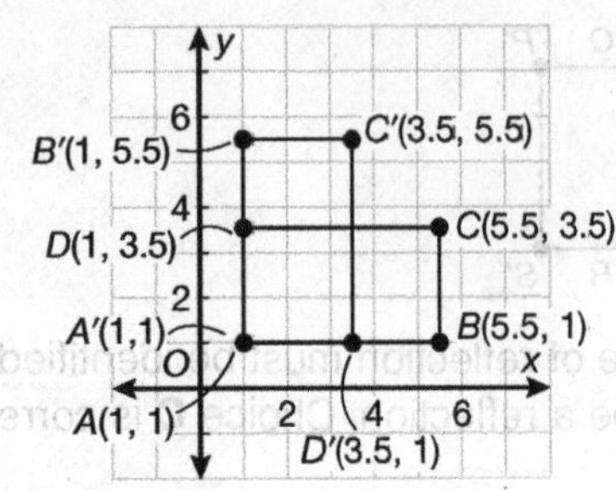


d. 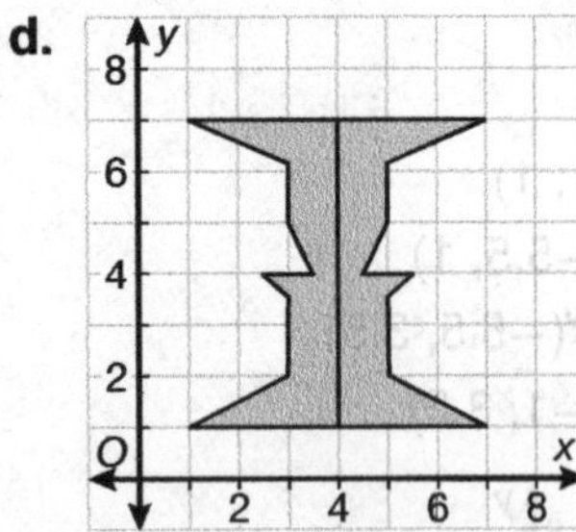


## Practice 74

1. $\widehat{JKL} = 2(93°) = 186°$
2. $T: (x, y) \rightarrow (-y, -x)$
3. $d = \sqrt{(4-5)^2 + (0-6)^2}$
   $= \sqrt{(-1)^2 + (-6)^2}$
   $= \sqrt{37}$
   $\approx 6.08$
4. $\tan 61° = \dfrac{DE}{12}$
   $DE = 12 \tan 61°$
   $DE \approx 21.65$
5. Choice A:
   $8^2 = 6^2 + 7^2$
   $64 = 36 + 49$
   $64 \neq 85$
   Choice B:
   $(2\sqrt{13})^2 = 5^2 + (3\sqrt{3})^2$
   $(4)(13) = 25 + (9)(3)$
   $52 = 52$
   Choice C:
   $(\sqrt{89})^2 = 6^2 + 7^2$
   $89 = 36 + 49$
   $89 \neq 85$
   Choice D:
   $9^2 = 5^2 + 5^2$
   $81 = 25 + 25$
   $81 \neq 50$; Choice **B** is correct.
6. $x = 10 - 3x$
   $4x = 10$
   $x = 2.5$
   $y + 2 = 2(2.5)$
   $y + 2 = 5$
   $y = 3$
7. $\dfrac{3}{12} = \dfrac{6}{a}$
   $(3)(a) = (6)(12)$
   $3a = 72$
   $a = 24$
8. $\dfrac{4}{1} = \dfrac{12}{XW}$
   $(4)(XW) = (1)(12)$
   $XW = 3$
9. $V = Bh = (\pi)(1.5^2)(4) \approx 28.27 \text{ ft}^3$
   Since 9 rainy days would fill 27 $\text{ft}^3$, it would take 10 rainy days to fill the rain barrel.
10. No, since $\overleftrightarrow{BD}$ is a tangent, $m\angle ABD = 90°$ and $m\angle A = 50°$.
11. $(0, 0) \rightarrow (0 + 4, 0 + 6) = (4, 6)$
    $(2, 5) \rightarrow (2 + 4, 5 + 6) = (6, 11)$
    $(4, 0) \rightarrow (4 + 4, 0 + 6) = (8, 6)$

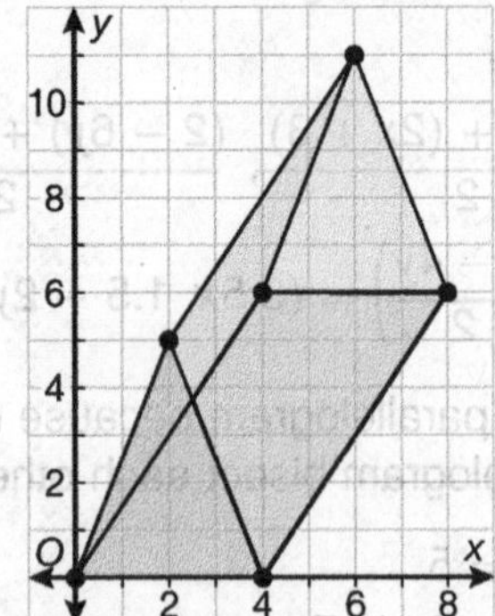


12. 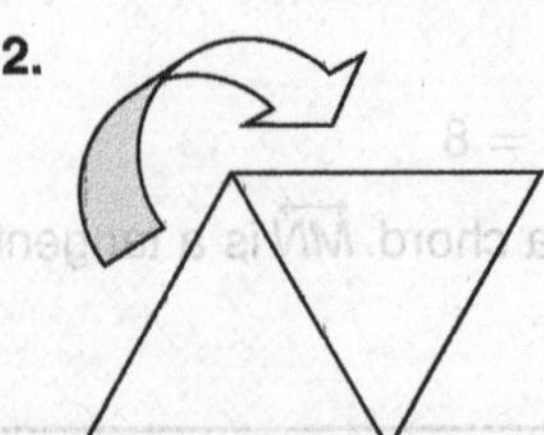

The figure formed is a parallelogram.

13. $\tan 37^\circ = \frac{200}{x}$

14. 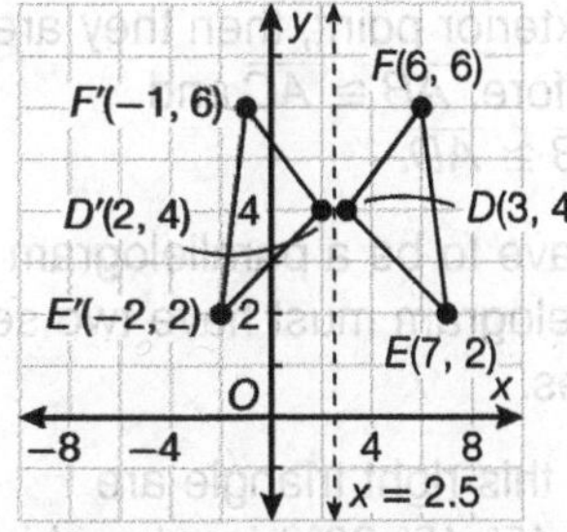


15. The slope of the line perpendicular to $y = 3x - 1$ is $-\frac{1}{3}$.

$$y = -\frac{1}{3}x + b$$

$$4 = -\frac{1}{3}(5) + b$$

$$\frac{17}{3} = b$$

$$y = -\frac{1}{3}x + \frac{17}{3}$$

To find the point of intersection, set the two equations equal to each other.

$$3x - 1 = -\frac{1}{3}x + \frac{17}{3}$$

$$\frac{10}{3}x = \frac{20}{3}$$

$$x = 2$$

$$y = 3(2) - 1 = 5$$

The point of intersection is (2, 5). Find the distance between (2, 5) and (5, 4).

$$d = \sqrt{(2-5)^2 + (5-4)^2}$$

$$= \sqrt{(-3)^2 + 1^2}$$

$$= \sqrt{10}$$

$$\approx 3.16$$

16. $\cos 15^\circ = \frac{PQ}{8}$

$PQ = 8 \cos 15^\circ$

$PQ \approx 7.73$

$\sin 15^\circ = \frac{QR}{8}$

$QR = 8 \sin 15^\circ$

$QR \approx 2.07$

17. The third side of the triangle must be greater than 6 because:

$15 + x > 21$

$x > 6$

This means the perimeter must be greater than $6 + 15 + 21 = 42$.

The third side must be shorter than $15 + 21 = 36$. So, the perimeter must be less than $15 + 21 + 36 = 72$.

$42 \text{ ft} < P < 72 \text{ ft}$

18.

| | |
|---|---|
| $x + (2x + 5) + (8x + 10) = 180$ | Triangle Sum Theorem |
| $11x + 15 = 180$ | Simplify |
| $11x + 15 - 15 = 180 - 15$ | Subtraction Property of Equality |
| $11x = 165$ | Simplify |
| $\frac{11x}{11} = \frac{165}{11}$ | Division Property of Equality |
| $x = 15$ | Simplify |

19. 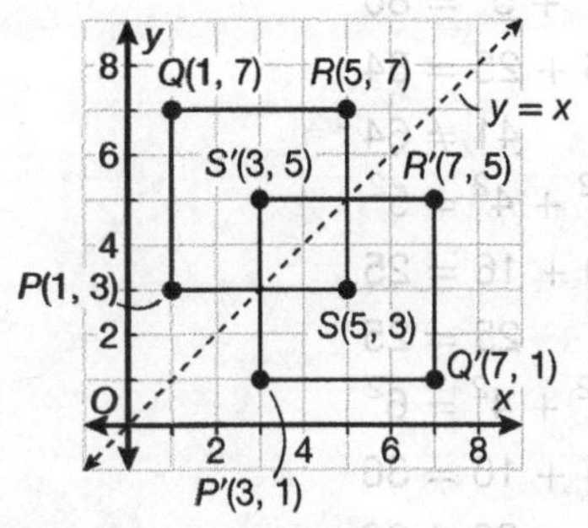


20. 0.12, 0.24, 0.39, 0.83, 0.98, and 1. The sine cannot be greater than 1 because that would mean that the hypotenuse would be shorter than one leg, which cannot be.

21. 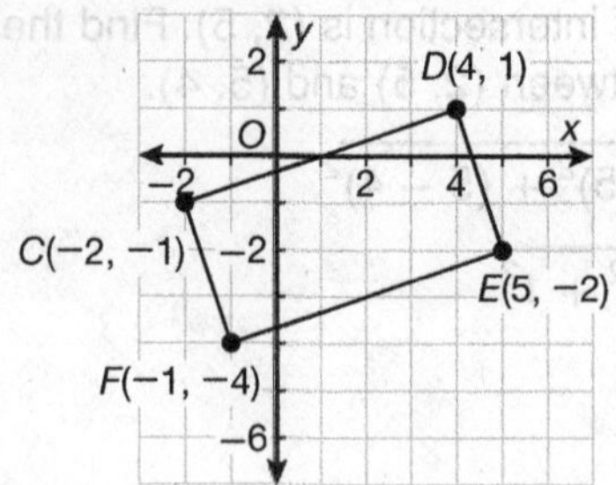


$m_{CD} = \frac{-1-1}{-2-4} = \frac{-2}{-6} = \frac{1}{3}$

$m_{FE} = \frac{-4--2}{-1-5} = \frac{-2}{-6} = \frac{1}{3}$

$m_{CF} = \frac{-1--4}{-2--1} = \frac{3}{-1} = -3$

$m_{DE} = \frac{1--2}{4-5} = \frac{3}{-1} = -3$

The polygon is a rectangle.

$d_{CD} = \sqrt{(-2-4)^2 + (-1-1)^2}$

$= \sqrt{(-6)^2 + (-2)^2}$

$= \sqrt{40}$

$d_{CF} = \sqrt{(-2--1)^2 + (-1--4)^2}$

$= \sqrt{(-1)^2 + (3)^2} = \sqrt{10}$

$A = (\sqrt{40})(\sqrt{10}) = \sqrt{400} = 20$

22. $P = 340 + (2\pi)(32) + 340$

$\approx 680 + 201 \approx 881$ yd

23. $m_g = \frac{-2-7}{3-4} = \frac{-9}{-1} = 9$

The slope of $h$ is $-\frac{1}{9}$.

$\frac{5-4}{1--x} = \frac{1}{-9}$

$1 + x = -9$

$x = -10$

24. a. $x = 3y + 2$

$-3y = -x + 2$

$y = \frac{1}{3}x - \frac{2}{3}$

b. $-x = 3(-y) + 2$

$3y = x + 2$

$y = \frac{1}{3}x + \frac{2}{3}$

25. $\overline{AB} \cong \overline{AD}$ because Theorem 58-3 says that if two tangent segments are drawn to a circle from the same exterior point, then they are congruent. Therefore, $\overline{AB} \cong \overline{AC}$ and $\overline{AC} \cong \overline{AD}$. So, $\overline{AB} \cong \overline{AD}$.

26. No, it does not have to be a parallelogram because a parallelogram must have two sets of congruent sides.

27. Since the legs of this right triangle are congruent, it is a 45°-45°-90° triangle, which makes the angle 45°.

28. 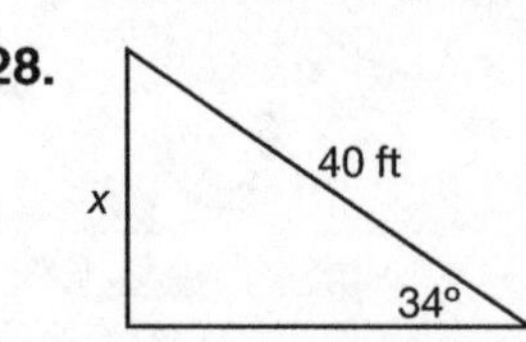


$\sin 34° = \frac{x}{40}$

$x = 40 \sin 34°$

$x \approx 22$ ft

29. The point of tangency is (2, 0). The tangent line is the horizontal line $y = 0$. The radius of ⊙ $A$ is 1 and the radius of ⊙ $B$ is 2.

30. height $= \frac{1}{2}(13) = 6.5$ yd

base $= 2(6.5\sqrt{3}) \approx 22.5$ yd

## LESSON 75

### Warm Up 75

1. radius

2. $(0 + 2, 0) \rightarrow (2, 0)$

$(0 - 2, 0) \rightarrow (-2, 0)$

$(0, 0 + 2) \rightarrow (0, 2)$

$(0, 0 - 2) \rightarrow (0, -2)$

3. Choice A: $4^2 + 5^2 = 80$

$16 + 25 = 64$

$41 \neq 64$

Choice B: $3^2 + 4^2 = 5^2$

$9 + 16 = 25$

$25 = 25$

Choice C: $2^2 + 4^2 = 6^2$

$4 + 16 = 36$

$20 \neq 36$

Choice D: $5^2 + 8^2 = 13^2$

$25 + 64 = 169$

$89 \neq 169$

Choice **B** is correct.

## Lesson Practice 75

**a.**

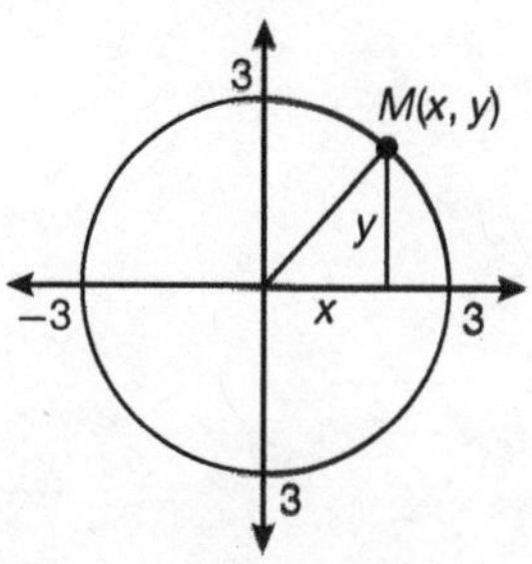


Since $PM$ is a radius of the circle, $PM = 3$. The equation of the circle is

$x^2 + y^2 = 3^2$

$x^2 + y^2 = 9$

**b.** $x^2 + y^2 = (\sqrt{2})^2$

$x^2 + y^2 = 2$

**c.** The center of ⊙ $B$ is at (2, 0) and the radius is 4.

$(x - h)^2 + (y - k)^2 = r^2$

$(x - 2)^2 + (y - 0)^2 = 4^2$

$(x - 2)^2 + y^2 = 16$

**d.** Circle $C$ has the same radius as ⊙ $B$, (2, 0). The radius is 3.5. The equation of the circle is:

$(x - 2)^2 + (y - 0)^2 = 3.5^2$

$(x - 2)^2 + y^2 = 12.25$

**e.** Circle $D$ is centered at (0, 0) and has a radius of $\sqrt{6.25} = 2.5$.

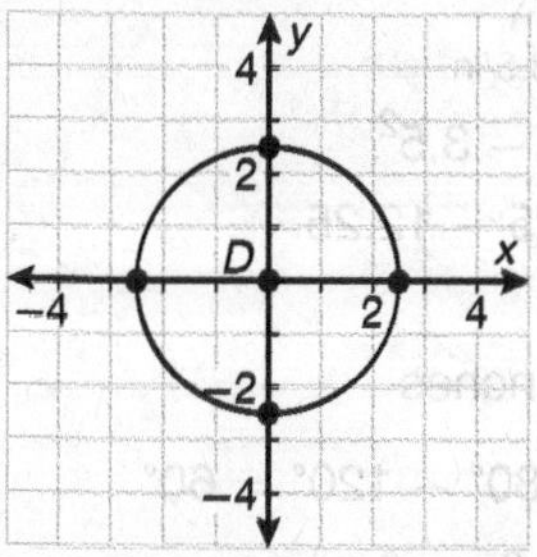


**f.** Circle $E$ is centered at (−1, 3) and has a radius of $\sqrt{4} = 2$.

**g.** The length of the diameter $AB$ is $31 - 19 = 12$. So, the radius is 6. The center is at $\left(47, \frac{31 + 19}{2}\right)$ or (47, 25).

$(x - 47)^2 + (y - 25)^2 = 6^2$

$(x - 47)^2 + (y - 25)^2 = 36$

## Practice 75

**1.** The center of ⊙ $A$ is at (0, 0) and the radius is 4.

$(x - h)^2 + (y - k)^2 = r^2$

$(x - 0)^2 + (y - 0)^2 = 4^2$

$x^2 + y^2 = 16$

**2.**

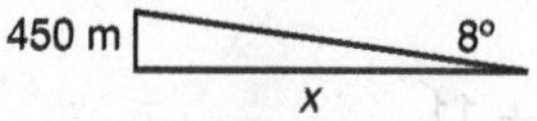


$\tan 8° = \frac{450}{x}$

$x = \frac{450}{\tan 8°}$

$x \approx 3202$ meters

**3.** $m\angle X = 180° - 50° - 58° = 72°$

So, Choice A is correct because the angle across from $YZ$ is larger than the angle across from $ED$. Choice B is also correct because $72° > 68°$. Choice **C** is the correct answer.

**4.** $\frac{7}{x} = \frac{x}{5}$

$(x)(x) = (5)(7)$

$x^2 = 35$

$x \approx 5.9$

**5.** $\angle N$ and $\angle P$ are not a pair of base angles. They are supplementary angles. $m\angle N$ is 82°.

**6.**

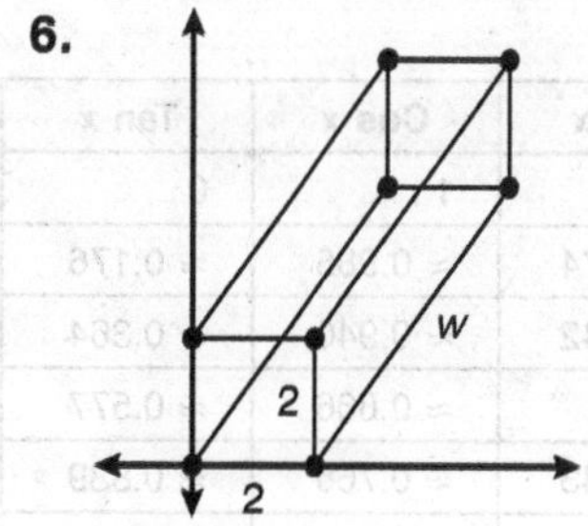


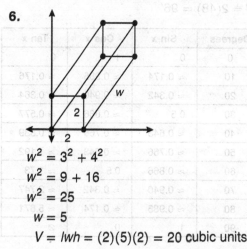

$w^2 = 3^2 + 4^2$

$w^2 = 9 + 16$

$w^2 = 25$

$w = 5$

$V = lwh = (2)(5)(2) = 20$ cubic units

7. 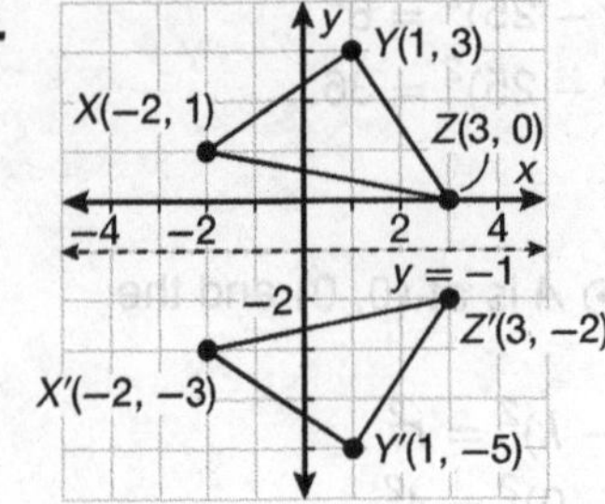


8. $l = 2h$

$L = V + 11$

$\frac{1}{2}Pl = \frac{1}{3}Bh + 11$

$\frac{1}{2}(4)(2h) = \frac{1}{3}(1)(h) + 11$

$4h = \frac{1}{3}h + 11$

$\frac{11}{3}h = 11$

$h = 3$

He should make his pyramid 3 units tall.

9. 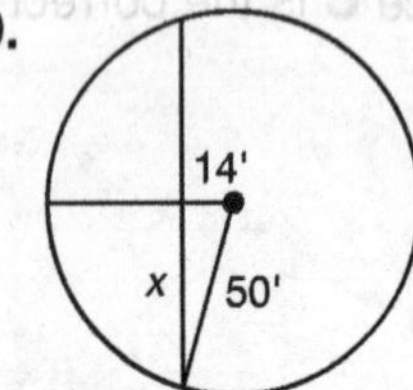


$x^2 = 50^2 - 14^2$

$x^2 = 2304$

$x = 48$

$LN = 2(48) = 96'$

10.

| Degrees | Sin $x$ | Cos $x$ | Tan $x$ |
|---|---|---|---|
| 0 | 0 | 1 | 0 |
| 10 | ≈ 0.174 | ≈ 0.985 | ≈ 0.176 |
| 20 | ≈ 0.342 | ≈ 0.940 | ≈ 0.364 |
| 30 | 0.5 | ≈ 0.866 | ≈ 0.577 |
| 40 | ≈ 0.643 | ≈ 0.766 | ≈ 0.839 |
| 50 | ≈ 0.766 | ≈ 0.643 | ≈ 1.192 |
| 60 | ≈ 0.866 | 0.5 | ≈ 1.73 |
| 70 | ≈ 0.940 | ≈ 0.342 | ≈ 2.747 |
| 80 | ≈ 0.985 | ≈ 0.174 | ≈ 5.671 |
| 90 | 1 | 0 | ∅ |

**a.** increases; 0; 1

**b.** Cos $x$ decreases from 1 to 0 as $x$ increases from 0° to 90°.

Tan $x$ increases from 0 to undefined (extremely large) as $x$ increases from 0° to 90°.

11. $\frac{12}{144} = \frac{x}{360}$

$(144)(x) = (12)(360)$

$144x = 4320$

$x = 30°$

12. 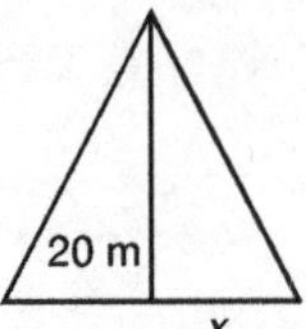


$x = \frac{20}{\sqrt{3}} = \frac{20\sqrt{3}}{3}$

$P = 12\left(\frac{20\sqrt{3}}{3}\right) \approx 138.564$

$a = 20$

$A = \frac{1}{2}aP$

$A = \frac{1}{2}(20)(138.564)$

$A \approx 1386 \text{ m}^2$

13. $(x - h)^2 + (y - k)^2 = r^2$

$(x - 2)^2 + (y - 4)^2 = 3^2$

$(x - 2)^2 + (y - 4)^2 = 9$

14. 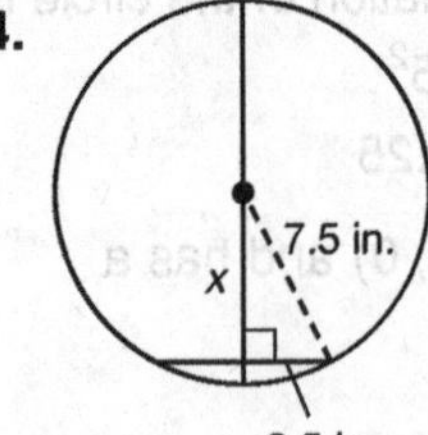


$x^2 = 7.5^2 - 3.5^2$

$x^2 = 56.25 - 12.25$

$x^2 = 44$

$x \approx 6.6$ inches

15. $m\angle D = 180° - 120° = 60°$

16. $x^2 = (-3)^2 + 5^2$

$x^2 = 9 + 25$

$x^2 = 34$

$x \approx 5.8$

17. There are 4 common tangents.

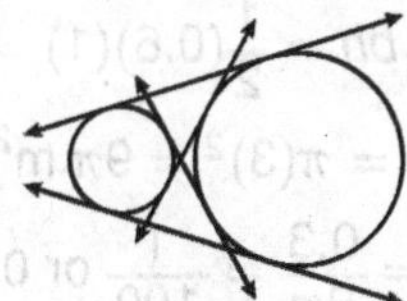

18. The center of $\odot B$ is at (0, 0) and the radius is 3.

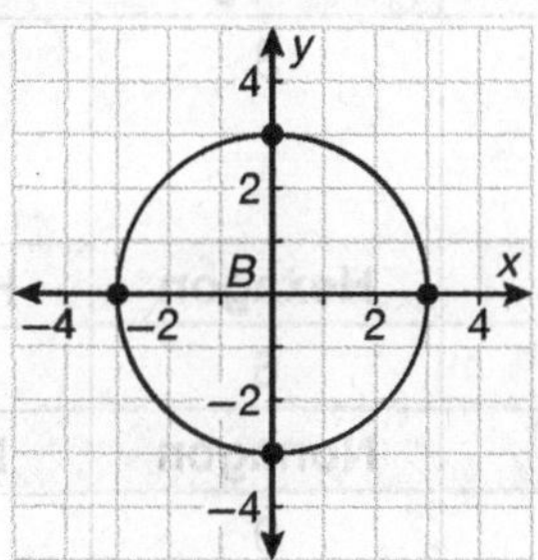


19. slope of $f = \frac{\text{rise}}{\text{run}} = \frac{1}{4}$

parallel to $f = \frac{1}{4}$

perpendicular to $f = -4$

20. (4, 0) is 3 units away from $y = 3$. The reflection across $y = 3$ will take the point 3 units past $y = 3$ to where the $y$-coordinate is 6. The $x$-coordinate remains unchanged. Choice A, (4, 6), is correct.

21. $\tan 33° = \frac{28}{XY}$

$XY = \frac{28}{\tan 33°}$

$XY \approx 43.12$

22.

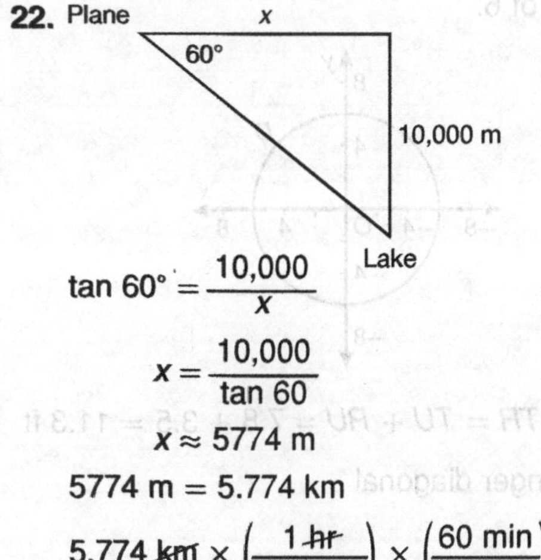


$\tan 60° = \frac{10{,}000}{x}$

$x = \frac{10{,}000}{\tan 60}$

$x \approx 5774$ m

5774 m = 5.774 km

$5.774 \text{ km} \times \left(\frac{1 \text{ hr}}{300 \text{ km}}\right) \times \left(\frac{60 \text{ min}}{1 \text{ hr}}\right) \approx 1 \text{ min}$

23.

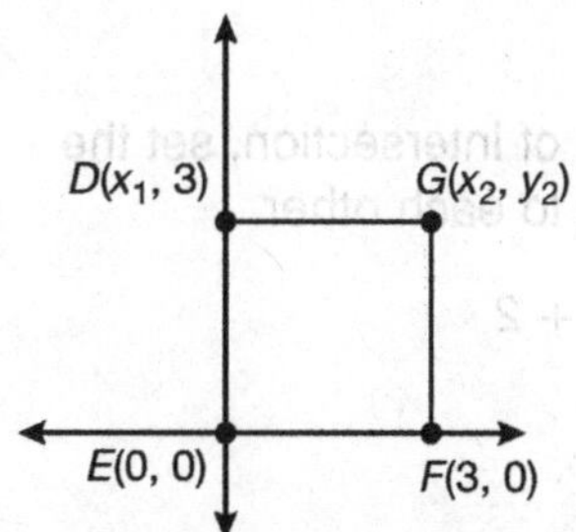


$x_1 = 0,\ x_2 = 3,\ y_2 = 3$

24. It is a rhombus because its sides are congruent.

25. The two possibilities for circles $C$ and $D$ are as follows:

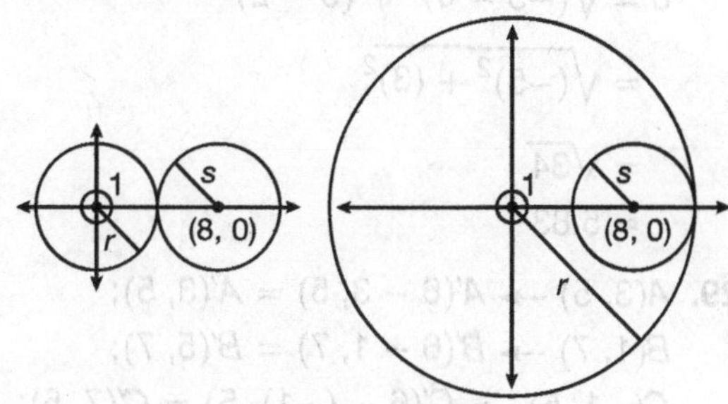


Either $r + s = 8$ or $|r - s| = 8$

26. Since $\overline{FD}$ bisects $\angle EFC$, and $\overline{FC}$ bisects $\angle DFB$, by the definition of angle bisector, $\angle EFD \cong \angle DFC$ and $\angle DFC \cong \angle CFB$. By the definition of congruent angles, $m\angle EFD = m\angle DFC$ and $m\angle DFC = m\angle CFB$. By the Transitive Property of Equality, $m\angle EFD = m\angle CFB$. By the definition of congruent angles, $\angle EFD \cong \angle CFB$.

27. $x + x + 1 + x + 2 = 54$

$3x + 3 = 54$

$3x = 51$

$x = 17$

So, the side lengths of $\triangle ABC$ are 17, 18, and 19. The side lengths of $\triangle PQR$ are 2(17), 2(18), and 2(19) or 34 inches, 36 inches, and 38 inches.

28. The slope of the line perpendicular to $y = \frac{5}{3}x + 2$ is $-\frac{3}{5}$.

$y = -\frac{3}{5}x + b$

$5 = -\frac{3}{5}(-5) + b$

$2 = b$

$y = -\frac{3}{5}x + 2$

To find the point of intersection, set the equations equal to each other.

$-\frac{3}{5}x + 2 = \frac{5}{3}x + 2$

$-\frac{34}{15}x = 0$

$x = 0$

$y = -\frac{3}{5}(0) + 2 = 2$

The point of intersection is (0, 2). Find the distance between (0, 2) and (−5, 5).

$d = \sqrt{(-5-0)^2 + (5-2)^2}$

$= \sqrt{(-5)^2 + (3)^2}$

$= \sqrt{34}$

$\approx 5.83$

**29.** $A(3, 5) \rightarrow A'(6 - 3, 5) = A'(3, 5)$;
$B(1, 7) \rightarrow B'(6 - 1, 7) = B'(5, 7)$;
$C(-1, 5) \rightarrow C'(6 - (-1), 5) = C'(7, 5)$;
$D(1, 3) \rightarrow D'(6 - 1, 3) = D'(5, 3)$

**30.** Since $0.5 + 0.3 > 0.7$, by the Triangle Inequality Theorem, these three side lengths can form a triangle.

## LESSON 76

### Warm Up 76

1. translation
2. This is a translation 5 units to the left and 3 units up.
3. Choice **A** is correct because $(-x)^2 = x^2$.

### Lesson Practice 76

a. Yes, it has five lines of symmetry.

b. The order of rotational symmetry is 5. The angle of rotational symmetry is $\frac{360°}{5} = 72°$.

c. Yes, the figure composed of the triangles would have a line of symmetry on the x-axis.

d. A 50-sided regular polygon would have 50 lines of symmetry.

### Practice 76

**1.** $A_{triangle} = \frac{1}{2}bh = \frac{1}{2}(0.6)(1) = 0.3 \text{ m}^2$

$A_{circle} = \pi r^2 = \pi(3)^2 = 9\pi \text{ m}^2$

$\text{Probability} = \frac{0.3}{9\pi} \approx \frac{1}{100}$ or 0.01

**2.**

| Polygon | Triangle | Quadrilateral |
|---|---|---|
| Order of rotational symmetry | 3 | 4 |
| **Pentagon** | **Hexagon** | **Heptagon** |
| 5 | 6 | 7 |
| **Octagon** | **Nonagon** | **Decagon** |
| 8 | 9 | 10 |

Rotational symmetry in regular polygons resembles lines of symmetry: the order is equal to the number of sides in the polygon.

**3.** The triangle ends up in the original location. So, $J''(-2, 3)$, $K''(-2, 5)$, $L''(-4, 4)$.

**4.** $12y = 4x - 6$

$y = \frac{1}{3}x - \frac{1}{2}$

The slope of the line perpendicular to this is −3.

Choices A, C, and D all have slopes of −3 and are perpendicular to the line given. Choice B has a slope of 3, which is not perpendicular. Choice **B** is correct.

**5.** The center of the circle is at (0, 0) and has a radius of 6.

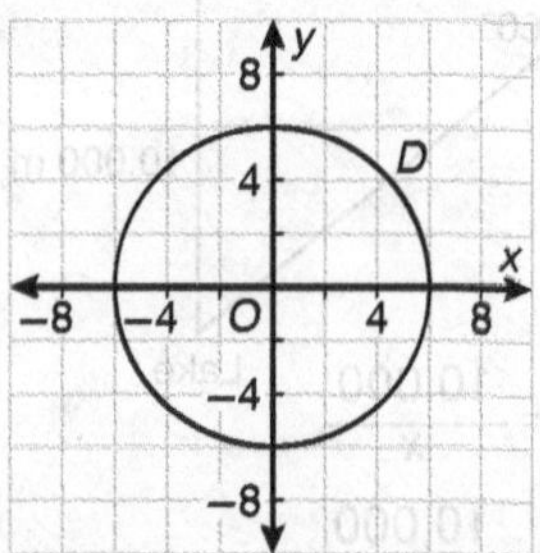


**6.** $QS = TR = TU + RU = 7.8 + 3.5 = 11.3$ ft

**7.** The longer diagonal

**8.** If $LM = LN$, then $m\angle N = m\angle M$ by the Isosceles Triangle Theorem. That expression contradicts the given information, so $LM \neq LN$.

**9.** There is no rotational symmetry in this symbol because when you rotate it 180°, the blue and white sides have switched.

**10.** 6 ft/s − 2 ft/s = 4 ft/s

**11.** $L = \frac{1}{2}Pl$

$P = 4(5) = 20$ cm

$L = \frac{1}{2}(20)(10) = 100 \text{ cm}^2$

**12.** Area of one triangle $= \frac{1}{2}as$

Area of six triangles $= 6\left(\frac{1}{2}as\right) = 3as$

**13.** Angle-Angle Similarity Postulate

**14.** Yes, $x = 0$ is the line of symmetry because $(-x)^2 + 7 = x^2 + 7$.

**15.** $x = 2(13) = 26$

Since $QN = QM$, $y = 16$

**16.** Since ∠1 and ∠5 are corresponding angles, choice **A** is correct.

**17.** Equation of $\odot C$ is $(x - 1)^2 + (y - 1)^2 = 25$.

For point $P(6, 1)$,

$(6 - 1)^2 + (1 - 1)^2 = 25$

$5^2 + 0^2 = 25$

$25 = 25$

For point $Q(4, 5)$,

$(4 - 1)^2 + (5 - 1)^2 = 25$

$3^2 + 4^2 = 25$

$9 + 16 = 25$

$25 = 25$

**18.** $z^2 - 2 = z$

$z^2 - z - 2 = 0$

$(z + 1)(z - 2) = 0$

Since $z$ must be positive, $z = 2$.

**19.** $A = \frac{1}{2}aP$

$P = 10(14) = 140$ cm

$A = \frac{1}{2}(21.5)(140) = 1505 \text{ cm}^2$

**20.**

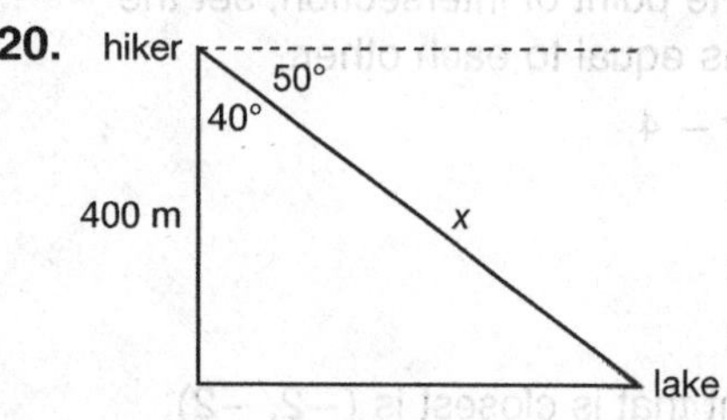


$\cos 40° = \frac{400}{x}$

$x = \frac{400}{\cos 40°}$

$x \approx 522$ meters

**21.** no; yes, $\frac{360°}{4} = 90°$, order 4; no

**22.** Midpoint $= \left(\frac{6+0}{2}, \frac{0+0}{2}\right) = \left(\frac{6}{2}, \frac{0}{2}\right) = (3,0)$

**23.** $GE = 2(8) = 16$

$GF = DE = 15$

$m\angle GDE = m\angle EFG = 130°$

$m\angle DFG = \frac{1}{2}(m\angle EFG) = \frac{1}{2}(130°) = 65°$

**24.** $(x - h)^2 + (y - k)^2 = r^2$

$(x + 3)^2 + (y - 4)^2 = 6^2$

$(x + 3)^2 + (y - 4)^2 = 36$

Choice **B** is correct.

**25.** Sample: Since tangent is equal to $\frac{\sin}{\cos}$, and cos 90° is 0, the denominator of tangent is 0 at 90°. Another degree measure for which the tangent is undefined is 270°.

**26.** $(15)(y) = (6)(8)$

$15y = 48$

$y = 3.2$

**27.** $\frac{0.4}{0.5} = \frac{x}{0.3}$

$(0.5)(x) = (0.3)(0.4)$

$0.5x = 0.12$

$x = 0.24$ km

**28.** The slope of the line perpendicular to $y = -x - 4$ is 1.

$y = 1x + b$

$4 = 1(4) + b$

$0 = b$

$y = 1x + 0$

To find the point of intersection, set the equations equal to each other.

$x = -x - 4$

$2x = -4$

$x = -2$

$y = -2$

The point that is closest is (−2, −2).

**29.** No; Magnitude is an absolute value, so it is impossible for magnitude to have an opposite value.

**30.**

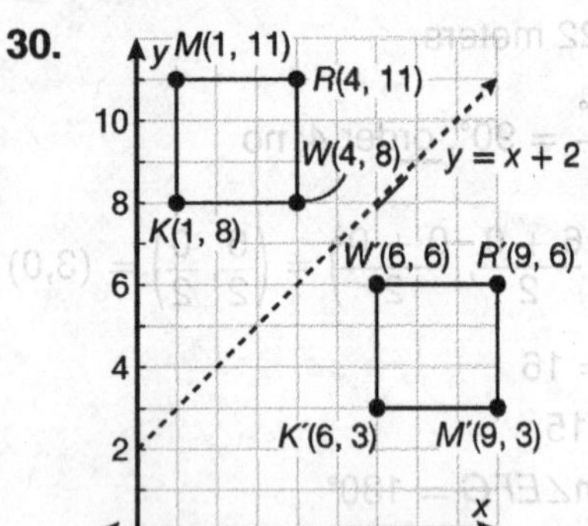


## LESSON 77

### Warm Up 77

1. base
2. $V = \frac{1}{3}Bh = \frac{1}{3}(12)(5) = 20 \text{ cm}^3$
3. Choice **D**, slant height, is correct.

### Lesson Practice 77

**a.** $L = \pi rl = \pi(2)(7) \approx 43.98 \text{ ft}^2$

**b.** $l^2 = 8^2 + 3^2$

$l^2 = 64 + 9$

$l^2 = 73$

$l \approx 8.544$

$S = L + B$

$= \pi rl + \pi r^2$

$= \pi(3)(8.544) + \pi(3^2) \approx 108.80 \text{ m}^2$

**c.** $V = \frac{1}{3}Bh$

$B = 36\pi$

$V = \frac{1}{3}(36\pi)(10) \approx 377.0 \text{ in.}^3$

**d.** $V = \frac{1}{3}Bh$

$B = 100\pi$

$V = \frac{1}{3}(100\pi)(70) \approx 7330.4 \text{ cm}^3$

### Practice 77

1. $L = \pi rl = \pi(3)(5) \approx 47.1 \text{ cm}^2$
2. The range of the cosine function is $0 \leq y \leq 1$. Choice **C** is correct.
3. $V = Bh$

   $B = \pi(1^2) = \pi \text{ ft}^2$

   $V = (\pi)(3) \approx 9.425 \text{ ft}^3$

   $9.425 \text{ ft}^3 \times \left(\frac{7.5 \text{ gal}}{1 \text{ ft}^3}\right) \approx 70.69 \text{ gal}$
4. The side must be greater than 266 − 115 = 151 feet and no more than 266 + 115 = 381 feet.
5. Choice A: These angles would be supplementary if the lines were parallel.

   Choice B: These are vertical angles and do not indicate parallel lines.

   Choice C: If these angles are congruent, they are corresponding angles, which makes the lines parallel.

   Choice D: These angles would be supplementary if the lines were parallel.

   Choice **C** is correct.
6. The house is located 5 miles from the fire station. The radius of the circle is $\sqrt{10} \approx$ 3.16 miles. The siren can be heard 3.16 miles from the station which means someone at the house cannot hear it.
7. 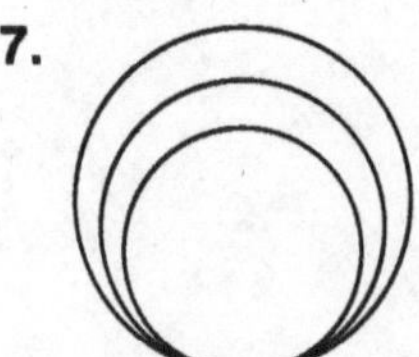
8. $\frac{x-2}{9} = \frac{6}{18}$

   $(18)(x - 2) = (6)(9)$

   $18x - 36 = 54$

   $18x = 90$

   $x = 5$

$PQ = 5 - 2 = 3$

$\frac{y^2}{12} = \frac{6}{18}$

$(18)(y^2) = (6)(12)$

$18y^2 = 72$

$y^2 = 4$

$y = 2$

$QR = 2^2 = 4$

$P = 4 + 3 + 6 = 13$

9. $\frac{60°}{360°}(\pi r^2) = 6\pi$

$r^2 = 36$

$r = 6$

10. $PQ > PS$ because $PQ$ is across from a larger angle than $PS$.

11. $S = L + B$

$= \pi rl + \pi r^2$

$= \pi(7)(10) + \pi(7^2)$

$\approx 374 \text{ in.}^2$

12. $P(-2, 1) \rightarrow P'(1 + 3, 1) = P'(4, 1)$;
$Q(2, 2) \rightarrow Q'(1 - 1, 2) = Q'(0, 2)$;
$R(0, 5) \rightarrow R'(1 + 1, 5) = R'(2, 5)$

13.

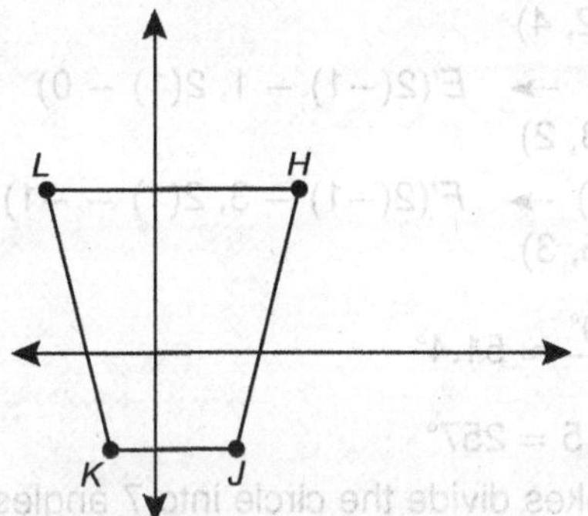


Yes, it has line symmetry but not rotational symmetry.

14. HL Congruence Theorem

15.

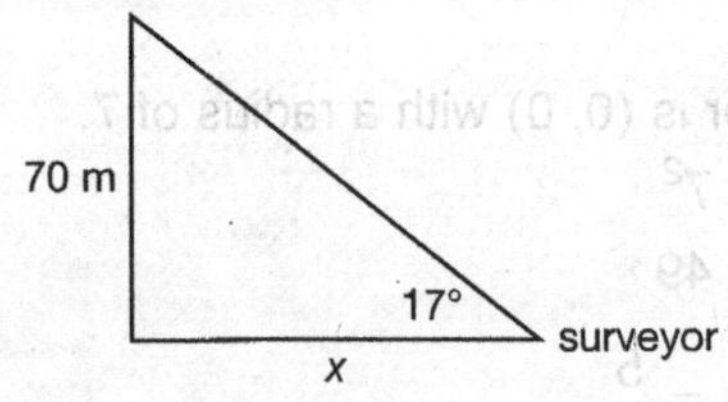


$\tan 17° = \frac{70}{x}$

$x = \frac{70}{\tan 17°}$

$x \approx 229$ meters

16. Pegs along the hypotenuse: $15(2) = 30$ pegs
length of the legs: $\frac{15}{\sqrt{2}}$

$2(4)\left(\frac{15}{\sqrt{2}}\right) \approx 85$ pegs

$85 + 30 = 115$

There are approximately 115 pegs.

17. No; The diagonals of a kite are always perpendicular, but it is possible for other quadrilaterals to have perpendicular diagonals.

18. $l^2 = 3.5^2 + 14^2$

$l \approx 14.43$

$L = \pi rl = \pi(3.5)(14.43) \approx 159 \text{ cm}^2$

19. m∠ that intercepts $\overset{\frown}{JKL} = 180° - 78° = 102°$

$m\overset{\frown}{JKL} = 2(102°) = 204°$

20. $(x - h)^2 + (y - k)^2 = r^2$

$(x - 0)^2 + (y - 3)^2 = 2^2$

$x^2 + (y - 3)^2 = 4$

21. $6f = 21$

$f = 3.5$; The factor is 3.5.

22. It has no line of symmetry and it has rotational symmetry of 180°.

23. $m_{LN} = \frac{-3.5 - -1.5}{-4.5 - 1.5} = \frac{-2}{-6} = \frac{1}{3}$

$m_{MP} = \frac{-1 - -4}{-2 - -1} = \frac{3}{-1} = -3$

The diagonals are perpendicular.

$m_{LM} = \frac{-3.5 - -1}{-4.5 - -2} = \frac{-2.5}{-2.5} = 1$

$m_{LP} = \frac{-3.5 - -4}{-4.5 - -1} = \frac{0.5}{-3.5}$

The adjacent sides are not perpendicular.
It is a rhombus.

24. $x$ must be less than $15 + 8 = 23$ to be a triangle.

$x^2 > 15^2 + 8^2$

$x^2 > 225 + 64$

$x^2 > 289$

$x > 17$

$17 < x < 23$

25. isosceles

26. If two angles are known, then the third is given by the Triangle Angle Sum Theorem.

27. $V = \frac{1}{3}Bh = \frac{1}{3}(\pi)(1^2)(2) \approx 2.1 \text{ m}^3$

28. They are congruent.

29.

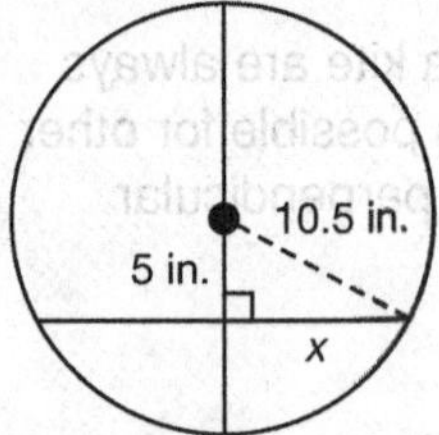


$x^2 = 10.5^2 - 5^2$

$x^2 = 110.25 - 25$

$x^2 = 85.25$

$x = \sqrt{85.25}$

Chord Length $= 2\sqrt{85.25} \approx 18.5$ inches

30. Since $\angle JKL$ is a right angle, $m\angle JKL = 90°$ by the definition of a right angle. By the Angle Addition Postulate, $m\angle JKL = m\angle 1 + m\angle 2$. Using substitution, $90° = m\angle 1 + m\angle 2$. Thus, by the definition of complementary angles, $\angle 1$ and $\angle 2$ are complementary angles.

## LESSON 78

### Warm Up 78

1. transformation

2. $D(1, 3) \rightarrow D'(1 - 3, 3 - 4) = D'(-2, -1)$

$E(3, 6) \rightarrow E'(3 - 3, 6 - 4) = E'(0, 2)$

$F(5, 1) \rightarrow F'(5 - 3, 1 - 4) = F'(2, -3)$

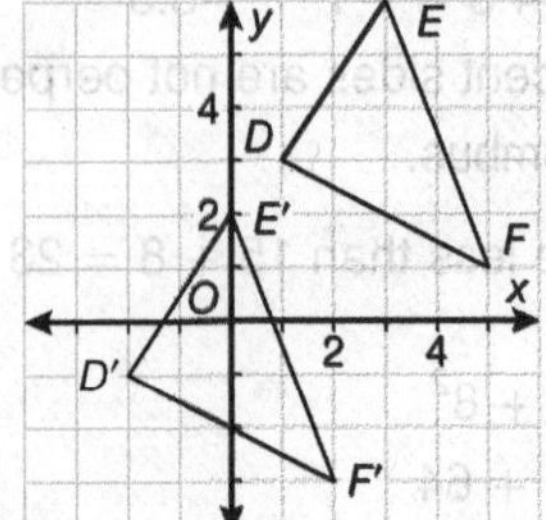


3.

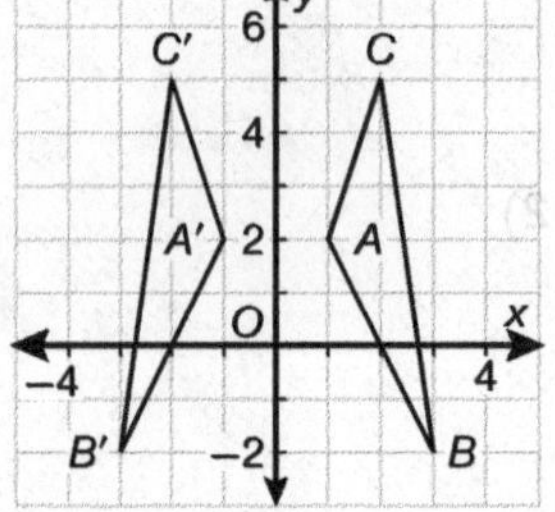


### Lesson Practice 78

a. $(x, y) \rightarrow (-y, x)$

$A(-2, -3) \rightarrow A'(3, -2)$

$B(1, 1) \rightarrow B'(-1, 1)$

$C(2, -1) \rightarrow C'(1, 2)$

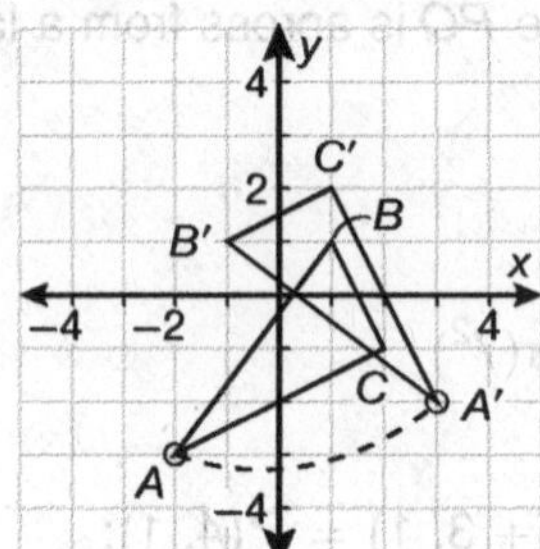


b. $(x, y) \rightarrow (2a - x, 2b - y)$

$D(0, -2) \rightarrow D'(2(-1) - 0, 2(1) - -2)$
$= D'(-2, 4)$

$E(1, 0) \rightarrow E'(2(-1) - 1, 2(1) - 0)$
$= E'(-3, 2)$

$F(3, -1) \rightarrow F'(2(-1) - 3, 2(1) - -1)$
$= F'(-5, 3)$

c. $\frac{360°}{7} \approx 51.4°$

$51.4° \times 5 = 257°$

The spokes divide the circle into 7 angles, each measuring 51.4°. The spoke moves 5 places counterclockwise, so the angle of rotation is $5 \times 51.4°$, or 257°.

### Practice 78

1. The center is (0, 0) with a radius of 7.

$x^2 + y^2 = 7^2$

$x^2 + y^2 = 49$

2. $\frac{1}{0.8} = \frac{10}{8} = \frac{5}{4}$

Choice **C** is correct.

**3.** $8x - 15 = 3x + 5$
$5x = 20$
$x = 4$

**4.** Robin is correct. Gustavo forgot that the 30°-60°-90° triangle only represents one half of each of the six equilateral triangles.

**5.** Choice **D** is correct because the net would form a square based pyramid without a base.

**6.** $(x, y) \rightarrow (y, -x)$
$F(4, 5) \rightarrow F'(5, -4)$
$G(1, 2) \rightarrow G'(2, -1)$
$H(5, 1) \rightarrow H'(1, -5)$

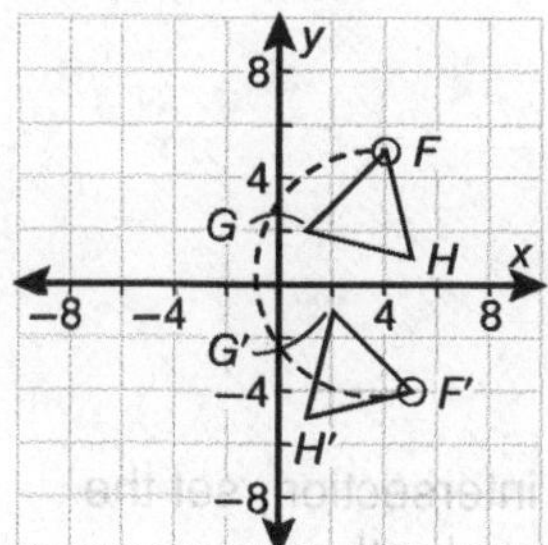


**7.** It has no lines of symmetry and no rotational symmetry.

**8.** $y - 7 = 3(x + 4)$
The slope is 3. So, the slope of the line parallel to this is also 3.
$y = 3x + b$
$3 = 3(2) + b$
$-3 = b$
$y = 3x - 3$

**9.** Sample:

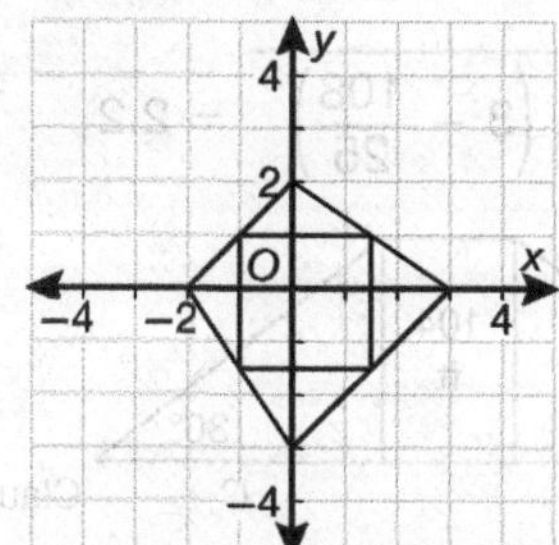


**10.**

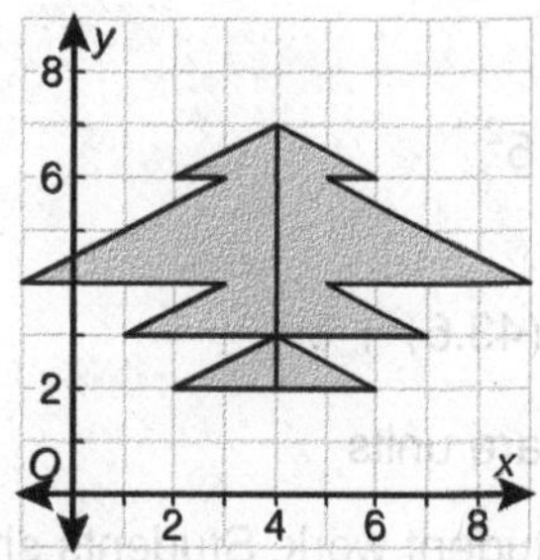


**11.** $(x, y) \rightarrow (-y, x)$
$A(-2, 4) \rightarrow A'(-4, -2)$
$B(3, 6) \rightarrow B'(-6, 3)$
$C(1, 3) \rightarrow C'(-3, 1)$

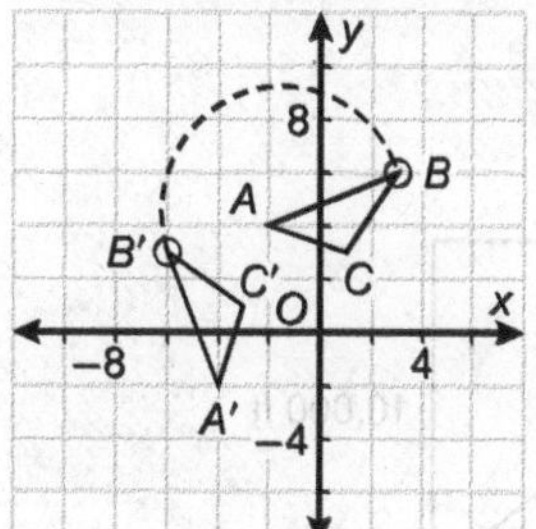


**12.** $z = 39$
$y = 180 - 39 - 90 = 51$
$x = y = 51$ (because they are alternate interior angles)

**13.** $V = \frac{1}{3}Bh = \frac{1}{3}(\pi r^2)(r) = \frac{1}{3}\pi r^3$

**14.** $2\frac{1}{2}$ feet =30 in.; $1\frac{1}{2}$ feet = 18 in.
$r = 9$ in.
$V = Bh = (\pi(9^2))(30) \approx 7634 \text{ in.}^3$
$7634 \times \frac{3}{4} = 5725.5 \text{ in.}^3$
$5725.5 \text{ in.}^3 \times \left(\frac{1 \text{ gal}}{231 \text{ in.}^3}\right) \approx 25$ gallons

**15.** $h = s$
$3x - 17.5 = 6y - 3$
$3x - 17.5 = 6(7) - 3$
$3x = 56.5$
$x = 18.8\overline{3}$
$h = s = 39$
$V = \frac{1}{3}Bh = \frac{1}{3}(39^2)(39) = 19{,}773$ cubic units
$S = L + B$

$S = \frac{1}{2}Pl + s^2$

$l^2 = 39^2 + 19.5^2$

$l \approx 43.6$

$S = \frac{1}{2}(4)(39)(43.6) + 39^2$

$\approx 4922$ square units

**16.** obtuse; See student work. Students should sketch an obtuse triangle with the orthocenter shown. Sample:

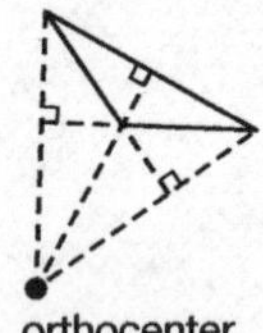

orthocenter

**17.**

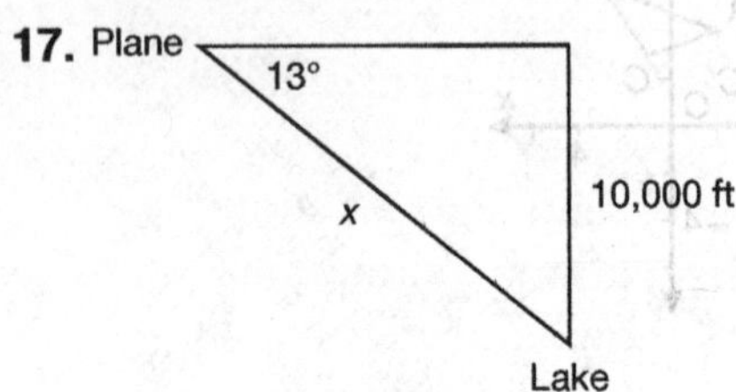


$\sin 13° = \frac{10,000}{x}$

$x = \frac{10,000}{\sin 13°}$

$x \approx 44,454$ ft

**18.** $m\angle L > m\angle l$ because $\angle L$ is across from a longer side than $\angle l$.

**19.** $S = L + B$

$S = \frac{1}{2}Pl + \pi r^2$

$l^2 = 12^2 + 5^2$

$l = 13$

$S = \frac{1}{2}[2\pi(5)](13) + \pi(5^2) \approx 282.7 \text{ cm}^2$

**20.** $AC = CD$

$4x - 3 = x + 6$

$3x = 9$

$x = 3$

$AC = CD = 3 + 6 = 9$

$CE = BC = 2(3) + 5 = 11$

**21.**

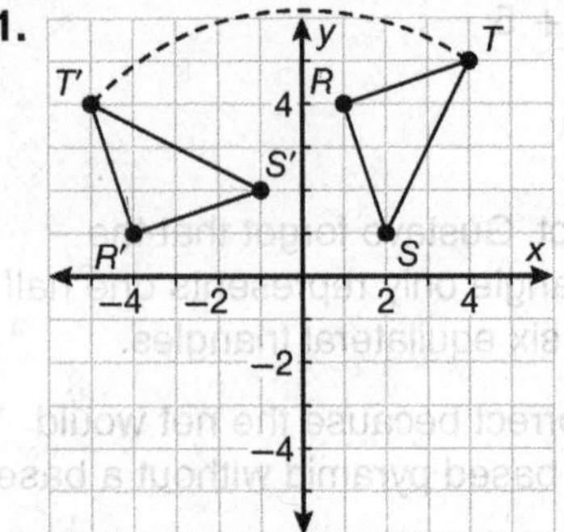


**22.** The slope of the line perpendicular to $y = \frac{4}{3}x$ is $-\frac{3}{4}$.

$y = -\frac{3}{4}x + b$

$3 = -\frac{3}{4}(5) + b$

$\frac{27}{4} = b$

$y = -\frac{3}{4}x + \frac{27}{4}$

To find the point of intersection, set the equations equal to each other.

$-\frac{3}{4}x + \frac{27}{4} = \frac{4}{3}x$

$-\frac{25}{12}x = -\frac{27}{4}$

$x = \frac{81}{25}$

$y = \frac{4}{3}\left(\frac{81}{25}\right) = \frac{108}{25}$

The point of intersection is $\left(\frac{81}{25}, \frac{108}{25}\right)$.

Find the distance between $\left(\frac{81}{25}, \frac{108}{25}\right)$ and (5, 3).

$d = \sqrt{\left(5 - \frac{81}{25}\right)^2 + \left(3 - \frac{108}{25}\right)^2} = 2.2$

**23.**

104 ft

45°

30°

Maribeth M C Claudia

$\tan 45° = \frac{104}{M}$

$M = \frac{104}{\tan 45°}$

$M = 104$ ft

$\tan 30° = \frac{104}{C}$

$C = \frac{104}{\tan 30°}$

$C \approx 180$ ft

Maribeth is 104 feet away, and Claudia is approximately 180 feet away.

**24.** $A = \frac{1}{2}(b_1 + b_2)h = \frac{1}{2}(9 + 11)(9) = 90 \text{ ft}^2$

$90 \text{ ft}^2 \times \left(\frac{144 \text{ in.}^2}{1 \text{ ft}^2}\right) = 12{,}960 \text{ in.}^2$

$12{,}960 \text{ in.}^2 \div 24 \text{ in.}^2 = 540$ bricks

**25.** Therefore, the mail will not be delivered today. Law of Detachment

**26.** There is a line of symmetry for all even values of *n* because positive and negative values of *x* will result in the same *y*.

**27.** $25x - 44 = 22x - 11$

$3x = 33$

$x = 11$

**28.** $m\angle FGI = \frac{1}{2} m\overset{\frown}{FI} = \frac{1}{2}(18°) = 9°$

**29.**

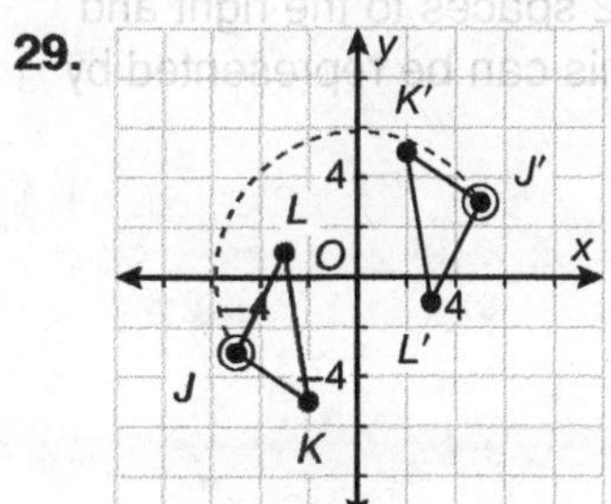


**30.** The slant height, the height, and the radius of a cone form a right triangle with the slant height as the hypotenuse. Since the hypotenuse of a right triangle is always longer than the legs of the triangle, the slant height is always longer than the height of the cone.

## LAB 10

### Lab Practice 10

Reflecting over the *y*-axis: $(x, y) \rightarrow (-x, y)$

$(3, 2) \rightarrow (-3, 2)$

$(7, 5) \rightarrow (-7, 5)$

$(1, 8) \rightarrow (-1, 8)$

Reflecting over $y = x$: $(x, y) \rightarrow (y, x)$

$(3, 2) \rightarrow (2, 3)$

$(7, 5) \rightarrow (5, 7)$

$(1, 8) \rightarrow (8, 1)$

## LESSON 79

### Warm Up 79

**1.** secant

**2.** $C = 2\pi r = 2\pi(3.5) = 7\pi$ inches

**3.** $\frac{137°}{360°}[2\pi(12)] \approx 28.7$ in.

Choice **A** is correct.

### Lesson Practice 79

**a.** Draw $\overline{EG}$. By the Exterior Angle Theorem, $m\angle DEG = m\angle EFG + m\angle EGF$, so $m\angle EFG = m\angle DEG - m\angle EGF$. The measure of an angle formed by a tangent and a chord is equal to half the measure of the intercepted arc, so $m\angle DEG = \frac{1}{2}m\overset{\frown}{EHG}$ and $m\angle EGF = \frac{1}{2}m\overset{\frown}{EG}$. By substitution, $m\angle EFG = \frac{1}{2}m\overset{\frown}{EHG} - \frac{1}{2}m\overset{\frown}{EG}$. By the Distributive Property of Equality, $m\angle EFG = \frac{1}{2}(m\overset{\frown}{EHG} - m\overset{\frown}{EG})$.

**b.** $m\angle P = \frac{1}{2}(265° - 95°) = 85°$

**c.** $m\angle 1 = \frac{1}{2}(154° - 88°) = 33°$

**d.** $m\overset{\frown}{AD} = 360° - 88° - 154° - 64° = 54°$

$m\angle 2 = \frac{1}{2}[(154° + 64°) - (54° + 88°)] = 38°$

**e.**

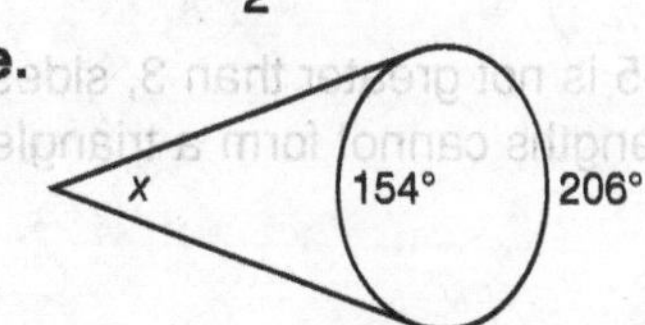


$m\angle x = \frac{1}{2}(206° - 154°) = 26°$

### Practice 79

**1.** Choice A: $m\angle X = \frac{1}{2}(m\overset{\frown}{VZ} - m\overset{\frown}{WY})$

Choice B: $m\angle X > m\overset{\frown}{WY}$

Choice C: $m\angle X < m\overset{\frown}{VZ}$

Choice D: $m\angle X < m\overset{\frown}{VZ}$

Choice **C** is correct.

**2.** 80 km/hr + 20 km/hr = 100 km/hr north

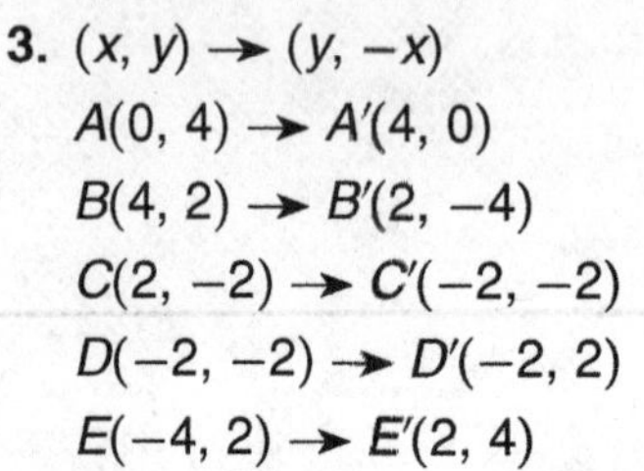

**3.** $(x, y) \rightarrow (y, -x)$

$A(0, 4) \rightarrow A'(4, 0)$

$B(4, 2) \rightarrow B'(2, -4)$

$C(2, -2) \rightarrow C'(-2, -2)$

$D(-2, -2) \rightarrow D'(-2, 2)$

$E(-4, 2) \rightarrow E'(2, 4)$

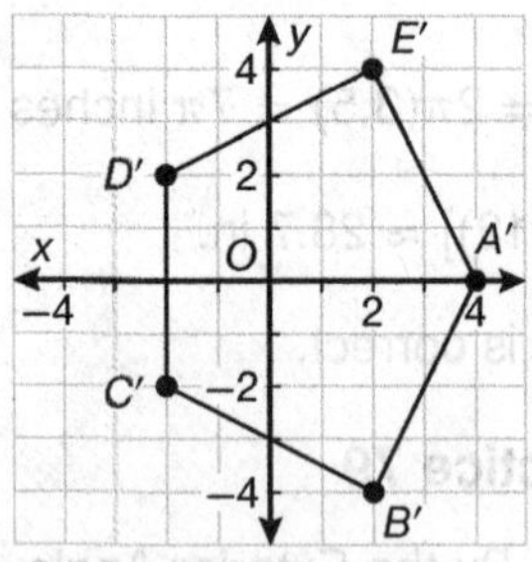


**4.** Choice A: $3^2 + 4^2 = 4.5^2$

$9 + 16 = 20.25$

$25 > 20.25$

This is a scalene acute triangle.

Choice B: $3^2 + 4^2 = 6^2$

$9 + 16 = 36$

$25 < 36$

This is a scalene obtuse triangle.

Choice C: This is a scalene obtuse triangle.

Choice D: This is a right triangle.

Choice **A** is the counterexample.

**5.** The center is at (0, 0) with a radius of 1.5.

$x^2 + y^2 = 1.5^2$

$x^2 + y^2 = 2.25$

**6.** Since 2.4 + 0.55 is not greater than 3, sides of these three lengths cannot form a triangle.

**7.** $S = L + B$

$S = \frac{1}{2}Pl + B$

$S = \frac{1}{2}(2\pi r)(l) + \pi r^2$

$l^2 = r^2 + r^2$

$l^2 = 2r^2$

$l = \sqrt{2r^2} = r^1\sqrt{2}$

$S = \frac{1}{2}(2\pi r)(r\sqrt{2}) + \pi r^2$

$= \sqrt{2}\pi r^2 + \pi r^2$

$= (\sqrt{2} + 1)\pi r^2$

**8.** $m\angle BAC = \frac{1}{2}(260° - 100°) = 80°$

**9.** $d = \sqrt{(2 - 2)^2 + (4 - 2)^2}$

$= \sqrt{(0)^2 + (2)^2}$

$= \sqrt{4}$

$= 2$

$P = 6(2) = 12$

**10.** $2x - 6 < 108$

$2x < 114$

$x < 57$

$2x - 6 > 0$

$2x > 6$

$x > 3$

$3 < x < 57$

**11.** It has one line of symmetry and no rotational symmetry.

**12.** Since cos 0° = 1, cos 60° = 0.5, and cos 90° = 0 choice **D** is correct.

**13.** The piece moves 2 spaces to the right and 4 spaces down. This can be represented by $\langle 2, -4 \rangle$.

**14.** $h^2 = l^2 - r^2$

$h^2 = 17^2 - 8^2$

$h^2 = 289 - 64$

$h^2 = 225$

$h = 15$

$V = \frac{1}{3}Bh = \frac{1}{3}[\pi(8^2)](15) \approx 1005.3 \text{ mm}^3$

**15.** $\angle E \cong \angle C$ and $\angle ADE \cong \angle B$ because corresponding angles are congruent, and $\frac{3}{9} = \frac{7}{21}$, so both SAS Similarity and AA Similarity can be used. Note that $\angle A \cong \angle A$ can also be used to show AA Similarity.

**16.** The slope of the line perpendicular to $y = x$ is −1.

$y = -1x + b$

$8 = -1(2) + b$

$10 = b$

$y = -1x + 10$

To find the point of intersection, set the equations equal to each other.

$-1x + 10 = x$

$-2x = -10$

$x = 5$

$y = 5$

The point of intersection is (5, 5). Find the distance between (5, 5) and (2, 8).

$d = \sqrt{(5-2)^2 + (5-8)^2}$

$\approx 4.24$

**17.** $(x, y) \rightarrow (-x, -y)$

$D(3, -3) \rightarrow D'(-3, 3)$

$E(0, -1) \rightarrow E'(0, 1)$

$F(-2, -4) \rightarrow F'(2, 4)$

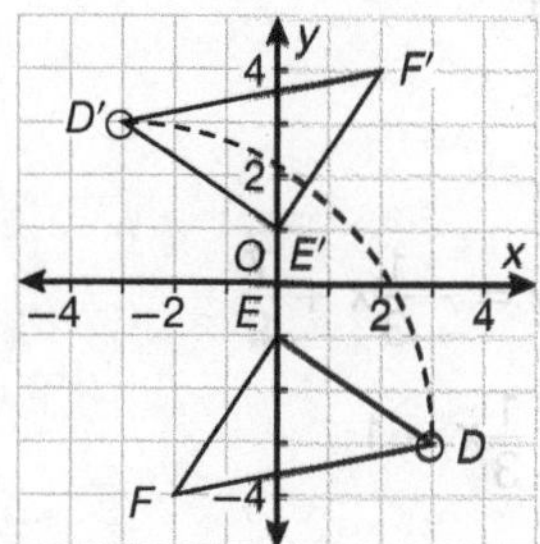


**18.** $A = \frac{1}{2}(3 + 9)(3) = 18 \text{ ft}^2$

He needs $18 \div 9 = 2$ ounces of paint.

**19.** The point of tangency is (2, −1). The tangent line is the vertical line $x = 2$. The radius of $\odot A$ is 3 and the radius of $\odot B$ is 2.

**20. a.** Since $B$ is the tangent point between circle $O$ and $AC$, $\angle ABO$ is a right angle, so $\triangle AOB$ and $\triangle BOC$ are right triangles. Also, $\angle AOC$ is a right angle (property of a rhombus); $\angle BAO$ and $\angle BOA$ are complementary, and $\angle BOC$ and $\angle BOA$ are also complementary. So, $\angle BAO \cong \angle BOC$. Since $\angle ABO$ and $\angle CBO$ are congruent, by the AA Similarity Postulate, $\triangle AOB$ and $\triangle BOC$ are similar.

**b.** $x^2 = 78^2 + 30^2$

$x^2 = 6084 + 900$

$x^2 = 6984$

$x = \sqrt{6984}$

$P = 4(\sqrt{6984}) \approx 334$ mm

**21.** $m\angle Q = \frac{1}{2}(206 - 66) = 70°$

**22.** $(x, y) \rightarrow (-x, -y)$

$A(-4, -2) \rightarrow A'(4, 2)$

$B(-1, 5) \rightarrow B'(1, -5)$

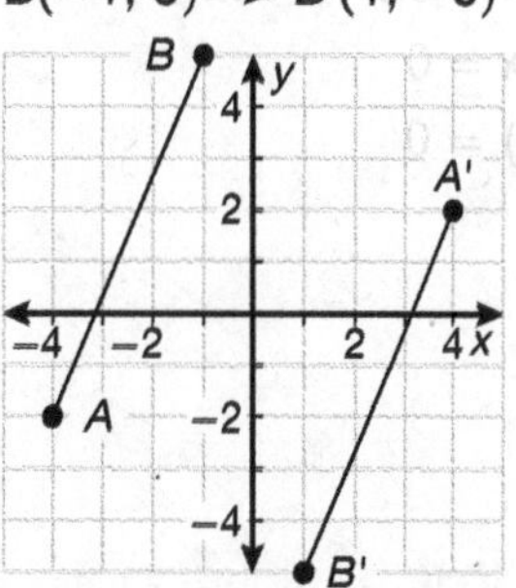


**23.** $\triangle BCD$ and $\triangle EFG$ are right triangles. $\overline{CD} \cong \overline{FG}$. By the Triangle Angle Sum Theorem, $\angle D$ is congruent to $\angle G$. By the LA Congruence Theorem, $\triangle BCD \cong \triangle EFG$.

**24.** $(x - h)^2 + (y - k)^2 = r^2$

$(x - 5.2)^2 + (y - -3.4)^2 = 3.5^2$

$(x - 5.2)^2 + (y + 3.4)^2 = 12.25$

**25.** Since two points determine a line, draw $\overline{JM}$. By the Exterior Angle Theorem, $m\angle JMN = m\angle JLN + m\angle KJM$, so $m\angle JLN = m\angle JMN - m\angle KJM$. By the Inscribed Angle Theorem, $m\angle JMN = \frac{1}{2}m\overset{\frown}{JN}$ and $m\angle KJM = \frac{1}{2}m\overset{\frown}{KM}$. By substitution, $m\angle JLN = \frac{1}{2}m\overset{\frown}{JN} - \frac{1}{2}m\overset{\frown}{KM}$. Thus, by the Distributive Property, $m\angle JLN = \frac{1}{2}(m\overset{\frown}{JN} - m\overset{\frown}{KM})$.

**26.** To find the length of the hypotenuse, multiply the shorter side length by 2. To find the length of the longer leg, multiply the shorter leg length by $\sqrt{3}$.

**27.** $m\angle 1 = \frac{1}{2}(90° - 70°) = 10°$

**28.** $L = \frac{1}{2}Pl$

$s = \sqrt{64} = 8$

$l^2 = 4^2 + 3^2$

$l^2 = 25$

$l = 5$

$L = \frac{1}{2}(4)(8)(5) = 80 \text{ in.}^2$

**29.** faces: 14; vertices: 24; edges: 36;

$F - E + V = 2$

$14 - 36 + 24 = 2$

So, the answers fit Euler's Formula.

30. $x^2 + (2x+2)^2 = (3x-2)^2$
$x^2 + 4x^2 + 8x + 4 = 9x^2 - 12x + 4$
$5x^2 + 8x = 9x^2 - 12x$
$-4x^2 + 20x = 0$
$x(-4x + 20) = 0$
Since $x \neq 0$,
$-4x + 20 = 0$
$-4x = -20$
$x = 5$

## LESSON 80

### Warm Up 80

1. solid
2. $S = L + 2B$
$S = Ph + 2lw$
$S = (4)(7)(7) + 2(7)(7)$
$S = 294\ \text{ft}^2$
$V = Bh = lwh = (7)(7)(7) = 343\ \text{ft}^3$
3. $S = L + 2B$
$S = Ph + 2\pi r^2$
$S = 2\pi(4)(15) + 2\pi(4^2)$
$S \approx 477.52\ \text{in.}^2$
$V = Bh = \pi r^2 h = \pi(4^2)(15) \approx 753.98\ \text{in.}^3$

### Lesson Practice 80

a. $S = 4\pi r^2 = 4\pi(4^2) \approx 201.06\ \text{m}^2$

b. $V = \frac{4}{3}\pi r^3 = \frac{4}{3}\pi(11^3) \approx 5575.28\ \text{in.}^3$

c. $S = \frac{1}{2}(4\pi r^2) + \pi r^2$
$= \frac{1}{2}[4\pi(16^2)] + \pi(16^2)$
$\approx 2412.74\ \text{ft}^2$
$V = \frac{1}{2}\left(\frac{4}{3}\pi r^3\right)$
$= \frac{1}{2}\left(\frac{4}{3}\pi(16)^3\right)$
$\approx 8578.64\ \text{ft}^3$

d. $2\pi r = 20$ cm
$r \approx 3.18$
$V = \frac{4}{3}\pi r^3 = \frac{4}{3}\pi(3.18^3) \approx 134.70\ \text{cm}^3$

### Practice 80

1. $\frac{5}{x} = \frac{11}{5}$
$(11)(x) = (5)(5)$
$11x = 25$
$x \approx 2.3$

2. $S = 4\pi r^2 = 4\pi(25^2) \approx 7854.0\ \text{in.}^2$

3. $x = 180° - 33° = 147°$
$m\widehat{AB} = \frac{1}{7}(147) + 23 = 44$
$147 = \frac{1}{2}(m\widehat{CD} + 44)$
$294 = m\widehat{CD} + 44$
$m\widehat{CD} = 250°$

4. $y = 3x + 4$
$9y = -3x + 7 \rightarrow y = -\frac{1}{3}x + \frac{7}{9}$
$3y = x - 3 \rightarrow y = \frac{1}{3}x - 1$
$y = \frac{1}{3}x - 6$
Parallel: $3y = x - 3$ and $y = \frac{1}{3}x - 6$
Perpendicular: $y = 3x + 4$ and $9y = -3x + 7$

5. $360° - 238° = 122°$
$\frac{1}{2}(238° - 122°) = 58°$

6. Between two objects, the angle of depression looking downward is the same as the angle of elevation looking upward.

7. Yes. It has two pairs of congruent opposite sides.

8. $S = \frac{1}{2}(4\pi r^2) + \pi r^2$
$= \frac{1}{2}[4\pi(11.5^2)] + \pi(11.5^2)$
$\approx 1246.43$ square yards
$V = \frac{1}{2}\left(\frac{4}{3}\pi r^3\right)$
$= \frac{1}{2}\left[\frac{4}{3}\pi(11.5^3)\right]$
$\approx 3185.31$ cubic yards

**9.** $A = lw - lw - lw$

$= (30)(20) - (7)(4) - (3)(6) = 554 \text{ ft}^2$

$554 \text{ ft}^2 \times \left(\frac{1 \text{ min}}{60 \text{ ft}^2}\right) \approx 9.23$ minutes

**10.** $(x, y) \rightarrow (y, -x)$

$M(-3, 3) \rightarrow M'(3, 3)$

$N(4, -1) \rightarrow N'(-1, -4)$

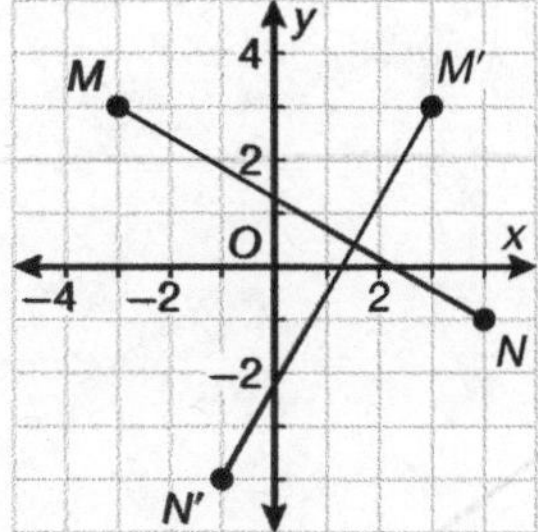


**11.** $A = \frac{1}{2}b_1h + \frac{1}{2}b_2h$

$(b_1)^2 = 8^2 - 5^2$

$(b_1)^2 = 64 - 25$

$b_1 \approx 6.24$

$(b_2)^2 = 18^2 - 5^2$

$(b_2)^2 = 324 - 25$

$b_2 \approx 17.29$

$A \approx \frac{1}{2}(6.24)(5) + \frac{1}{2}(17.29)(5)$

$\approx 59$ square inches

**12.** $4x + 5 + 3x + 7 = 180°$

$7x + 12 = 180$

$7x = 168$

$x = 24°$

$m\angle M = 4(24°) + 5° = 101°$

$m\angle N = 4(24°) - 10° = 86°$

$m\angle P = 3(24°) + 7° = 79°$

$m\angle Q = 360° - 101° - 86° - 79° = 94°$

**13.** Inverse: If $3x + 2 \neq 11$, then $x - 6 \neq -3$. The inverse is true.

**14.** $x^2 = 6^2 + (-10)^2$

$x^2 = 36 + 100$

$x^2 = 136$

$x \approx 11.7$

**15.** $360° - 94° - 30° - 160° - 20° = 56°$

$m\angle TPR = \frac{1}{2}(94° - 56°) = 19°$

**16.** Yes, but not a unique solution. Yes. Three non-collinear points define a triangle with a unique circumcenter, which is the center of the unique circle to pass through the points.

**17.** $2\pi r = 3$

$r = \frac{3}{2\pi}$

$V = \frac{4}{3}\pi r^3 = \frac{4}{3}\pi\left(\frac{3}{2\pi}\right)^3 \approx 0.46 \text{ ft}^3$

**18.** Sample: It would have to be known that the four triangles shown are congruent to one another.

**19.**

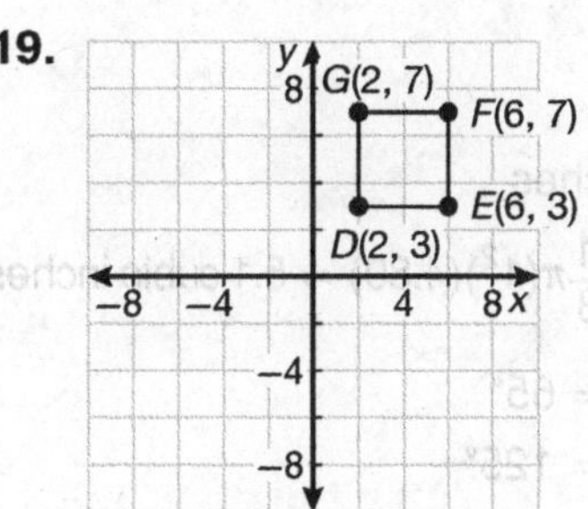


$x_1 = 2, x_2 = 2, y_2 = 7$

**20.**

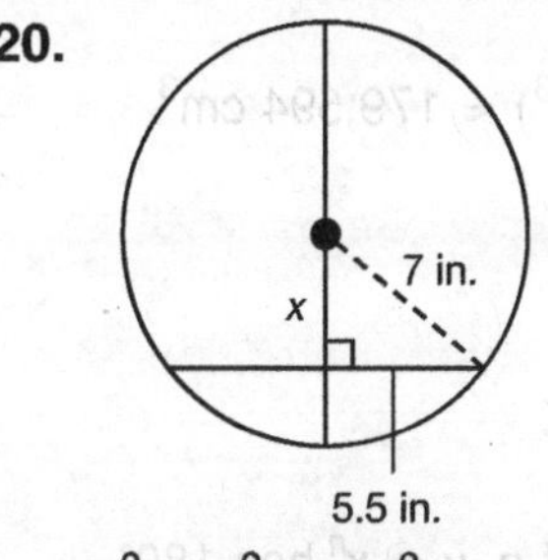


$x^2 = 7^2 - 5.5^2$

$x^2 = 49 - 30.25$

$x^2 = 18.75$

$x \approx 4.3$ inches

**21.** $360° - 50° - 140° - 130° = 40°$

$m\angle 1 = \frac{1}{2}(130° - 40°) = 45°$

**22.** $\frac{1}{6} = \frac{2}{QS}$

$QS = (2)(6)$

$QS = 12$

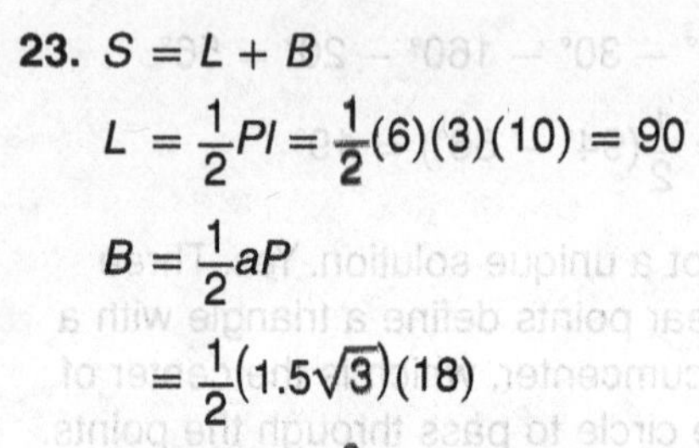

23. $S = L + B$

$L = \frac{1}{2}Pl = \frac{1}{2}(6)(3)(10) = 90 \text{ in.}^2$

$B = \frac{1}{2}aP$

$= \frac{1}{2}(1.5\sqrt{3})(18)$

$\approx 23.4 \text{ in.}^2$

$S = 23.4 + 90 = 113.4 \text{ in.}^2$

24. The hypothesis of the converse is the conclusion of the original statement. Choice **C** is correct.

25. $15.7 = \pi(1)(l)$

$l \approx 5$ inches

$h^2 = 5^2 - 1^2$

$h^2 = 25 - 1$

$h^2 = 24$

$h = 4.89$ inches

$V = \frac{1}{3}Bh = \frac{1}{3}\pi(1^2)(4.89) \approx 5.1$ cubic inches

26. $m\angle L = m\angle B = 65°$

$m\angle M = m\angle C = 125°$

$m\angle N = m\angle D = 50°$

$m\angle O = m\angle E = 120°$

27. $V = \frac{4}{3}\pi r^3 = \frac{4}{3}\pi(35^3) \approx 179{,}594 \text{ cm}^3$

28. $\frac{45°}{360°}[\pi(r^2)] = 2\pi$

$r^2 = 16$

$r = 4$

29. For all odd values of $n$, $y = x^n$ has 180° rotational symmetry.

30. $(x, y) \rightarrow (-x, -y)$

$J(1, 1) \rightarrow J'(-1, -1)$

$K(2, 6) \rightarrow K'(-2, -6)$

$L(5, 4) \rightarrow L'(-5, -4)$

$M(4, 0) \rightarrow M'(-4, 0)$

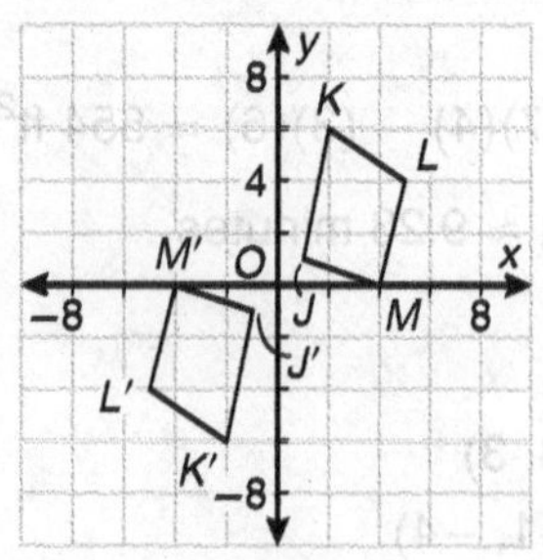


## INVESTIGATION 8

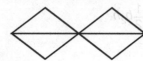

1. 4
2. no
3. 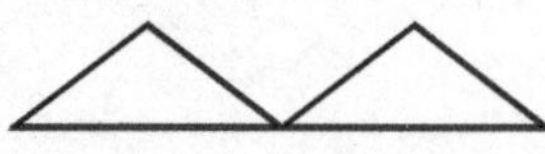
4. 
5. yes; 2
6. yes; 2
7. reflection
8. no
9. yes; 1
10. 

6 segments

11. 10; 15; 21
12. $L_n = L_{n-1} + (n - 1)$
13. For $n = 50$, $\frac{50(51)}{2} = 1275$

For $n = 100$, $\frac{100(101)}{2} = 5050$

## Investigation Practice 8

**a.**

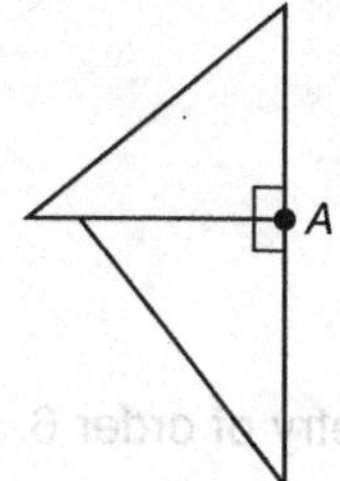


**b.** 4; no

**c.**

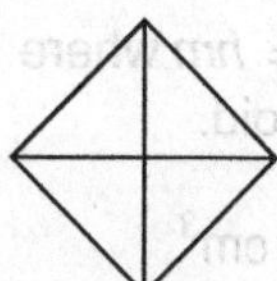

rhombus

**d.** yes; yes

**e.** $x = n^2$

**f.** For $n = 30$, $x = 30^2 = 900$

## LESSON 81

### Warm Up 81

1. Perpendicular lines

2. $b = 3$

$$m = \frac{3 - 0}{0 - -\frac{3}{2}} = \frac{3}{\frac{3}{2}} = 2$$

$y = 2x + 3$

3. The slope of the line perpendicular to $y = -x + 1$ is 1.

$y = 1x + b$

$2 = 1(3) + b$

$-1 = b$

$y = 1x - 1$

To find the point of intersection, set the equations equal to each other.

$1x - 1 = -x + 1$

$2x = 2$

$x = 1$

$y = 1(1) - 1 = 0$

The point of intersection is (1, 0). Find the distance between (1, 0) and (3, 2).

$$d = \sqrt{(3-1)^2 + (2-0)^2}$$

$$= \sqrt{(2)^2 + (2)^2}$$

$$= \sqrt{8}$$

$$= 2\sqrt{2}$$

### Lesson Practice 81

**a.** $\frac{2}{3}x - 8 = \frac{1}{4}x + 2$

$\frac{5}{12}x = 10$

$x = 24$

$y = \frac{1}{4}(24) + 2 = 8$

(24, 8)

**b.** $-\frac{2}{3}x - 3 = \frac{1}{2}x + 2$

$-\frac{7}{6}x = 5$

$x = -\frac{30}{7}$

$y = \frac{1}{2}\left(-\frac{30}{7}\right) + 2 = -\frac{1}{7}$

$\left(-\frac{30}{7}, -\frac{1}{7}\right)$

**c.**

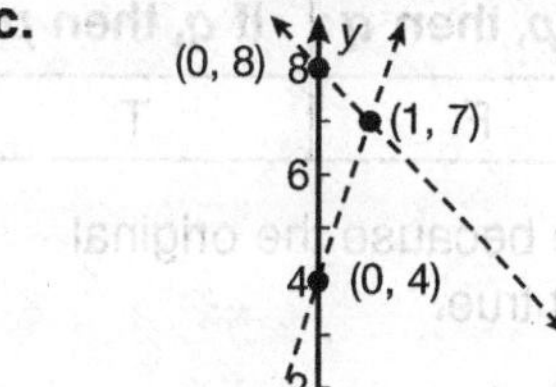


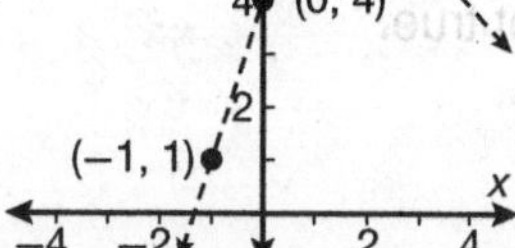

The solution is (1, 7).

Check:

| | |
|---|---|
| $y = 3x + 4$ | $y = -x + 8$ |
| $7 = 3(1) + 4$ | $7 = -(1) + 8$ |
| $7 = 7$ | $7 = 7$ |

The solution is correct.

**d.** The lines are parallel. Each has a slope of −2. So, therefore, there is no solution.

e. $2x + 20 = -\frac{1}{2}x + 80$

$\frac{5}{2}x = 60$

$x = 24$ units

$y = 2(24) + 20 = \$68$

## Practice 81

1. $m\angle UZY = \frac{1}{2}(m\widehat{UY} + m\widehat{VX})$ and

$m\angle VWX = \frac{1}{2}(m\widehat{UY} - m\widehat{VX})$.

Since $m\widehat{VX} > 0$, $m\angle UZY > m\angle VWX$.

2. $5x - 4 = \frac{2}{3}x + 1$

$\frac{13}{3}x = 5$

$x = \frac{15}{13}$

$y = 5\left(\frac{15}{13}\right) - 4 = \frac{23}{13}$

$\left(\frac{15}{13}, \frac{23}{13}\right)$

3. a. Only the converse is true.

| $p$ | $q$ | Statement: If $p$, then $q$ | Converse: If $q$, then $p$ |
|---|---|---|---|
| T | F | F | T |

b. No, it is not true because the original statement is not true.

4. $y = \frac{1}{2}(16) = 8$

$x = 10$

5. Since $\tan 45° = 1$, choice **B** is correct.

6. $V = \frac{1}{3}Bh = \frac{1}{3}(\pi r^2)(h)$

$45\pi = \frac{1}{3}(\pi r^2)(15)$

$9 = r^2$

$r = 3$ cm

7. a. 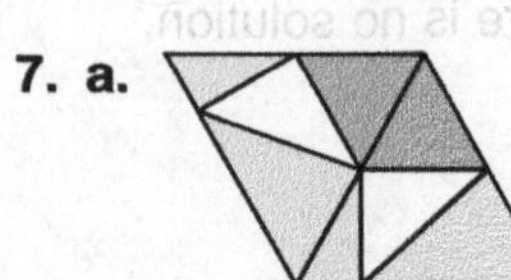

b. 

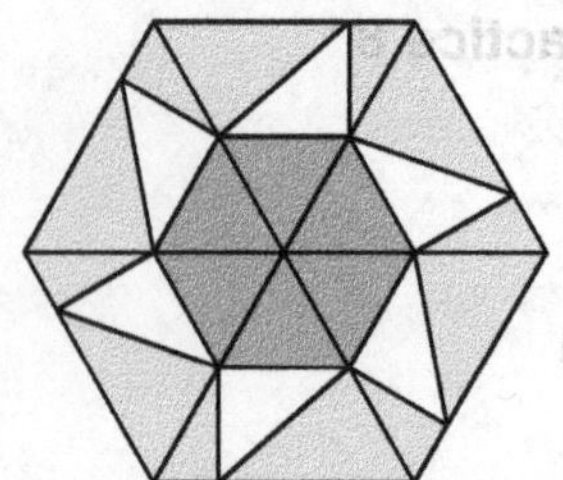

c. It has rotational symmetry of order 6.

8. Yes, since the midsegment $= \frac{1}{2}(b_1 + b_2)$ and the area of a trapezoid $= \frac{1}{2}(b_1 + b_2)h$, the formula can be written as $A = hm$ where $m$ is the midsegment of the trapezoid.

9. $V = \frac{1}{3}Bh = \frac{1}{3}(6\pi)(7) = 14\pi \text{ cm}^3$

10. $\pi r^2 = 121\pi$

$r^2 = 121$

$r = 11$

$V = \frac{4}{3}\pi r^3 = \frac{4}{3}\pi(11^3) \approx 5575 \text{ in.}^3$

11. $\sin 30° = \frac{5}{JL}$

$JL = \frac{5}{\sin 30°}$

$JL = 10$ cm

$\tan 30° = \frac{5}{JK}$

$JK = \frac{5}{\tan 30°}$

$JK \approx 8.7$ cm

12. $1.5T + 6 = 0.5T + 8$

$1T = 2$

$1.5(2) + 6 = 9$

2 toppings; \$9

13. Yes, since an equilateral triangle has three congruent sides, it has at least two congruent sides.
No, because some isosceles triangles have only two congruent sides.

14. $L = \pi rl$

$l^2 = 18^2 + 4^2$

$l^2 = 324 + 16$

$l^2 = 340$

$l \approx 18.44$ in.

$L = \pi(4)(18.44) \approx 232$ in.$^2$

**15.** $100° = \frac{1}{2}(m\widehat{AB} + 102°)$

$m\widehat{AB} = 98°$

$m\widehat{BD} = 360° - 98° - 102° - 108° = 52°$

$m\angle C = \frac{1}{2}(m\widehat{AE} - m\widehat{BD})$

$= \frac{1}{2}(108° - 52°) = 28°$

**16.** $V - E + F = 2$

$5 - 8 + F = 2$

$F = 5$

**17.** The orthocenter of a right triangle is located at the vertex of the right angle.

**18.** Hypothesis: A pair of corresponding angles formed by a transversal $l$ are congruent. Choice **D** is correct.

**19.** $1 = \frac{2}{3}(-1) + b$

$\frac{5}{3} = b$

**20.** $\frac{21}{28} = \frac{KL}{48}$

$(28)(KL) = (21)(48)$

$28KL = 1008$

$KL = 36$

**21.** The surface area is the number of square units it would take to cover, or wrap, the sphere. The volume is the number of cubic units it would take to fill the sphere.

**22.** $2x - 4 > x + 6$

$x - 4 > 6$

$x > 10$

**23.**

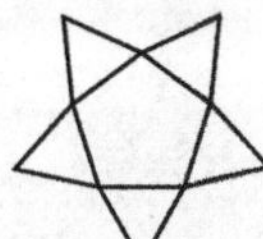

**24.** The slope of the line perpendicular to $y = x + 6$ is $-1$.

$y = -1x + b$

$0 = -1(0) + b$

$0 = b$

$y = -1x$

To find the point of intersection, set the equations equal to each other.

$-x = x + 6$

$-2x = 6$

$x = -3$

$y = -(-3) = 3$

The point of intersection is $(-3, 3)$. Find the distance between $(-3, 3)$ and $(0, 0)$.

$d = \sqrt{(-3 - 0)^2 + (3 - 0)^2}$

$= \sqrt{(-3)^2 + (3)^2}$

$= \sqrt{18}$

$\approx 4.24$

**25.** Hector forgot to multiply the negative sign through the second equation. He left $-3$ as $-3$ instead of changing it to $+3$.

$-\frac{7}{2}x = 4$

$x = -\frac{8}{7}$

$y = \frac{5}{2}\left(-\frac{8}{7}\right) + 1 \qquad y = -\left(-\frac{8}{7}\right) - 3$

$y = -\frac{13}{7} \qquad y = -\frac{13}{7}$

The correct solution is $\left(-\frac{8}{7}, -\frac{13}{7}\right)$.

**26.**

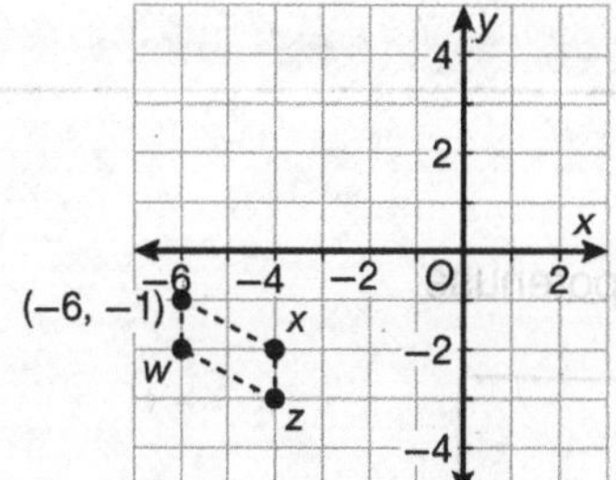


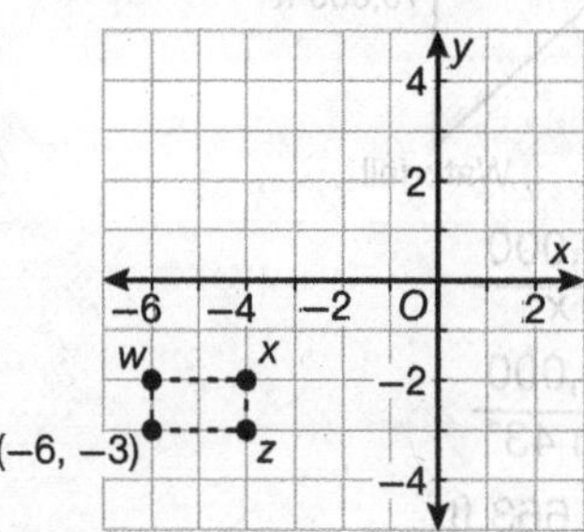

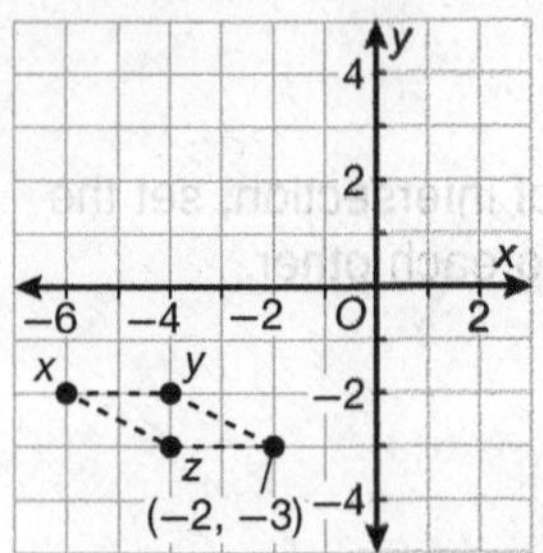


The other vertex could be at (−6, −1); (−6, −3); or (−2, −3).

27. Since ∠$B$ and ∠$E$ are right angles, $\triangle ABC$ and $\triangle DEF$ are right triangles. Therefore, since $\overline{BC} \cong \overline{EF}$, by the HL Congruence Theorem, $\triangle ABC \cong \triangle DEF$.

28. $V = \frac{4}{3}\pi r^3 = \frac{4}{3}\pi(7^3) \approx 1437 \text{ m}^3$

29. 270°; The blades divide the circle into 4 angles, each measuring 90°. Because the blade moves 3 places counterclockwise, the angle of rotation is 90° times 3.

30. $14 + s > 22$

$s > 8$

$s < 22 + 14$

$s < 36$

The length of the third side must be between 8 cm and 36 cm.

## LESSON 82

### Warm Up 82

1. adjacent; hypotenuse

2. 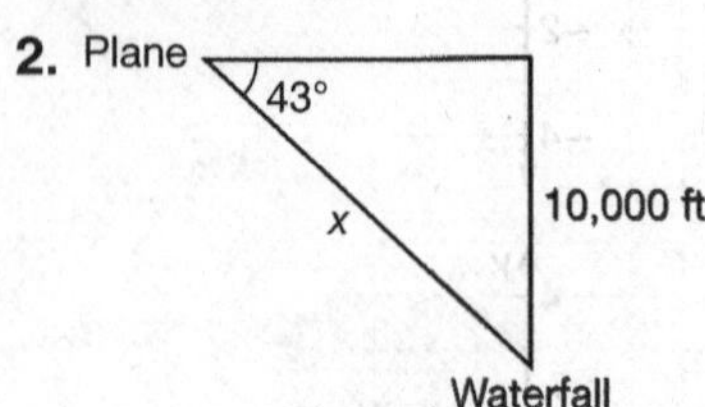


$\sin 43° = \frac{10{,}000}{x}$

$x = \frac{10{,}000}{\sin 43°}$

$x \approx 14{,}663 \text{ ft}$

3. Since the triangle is a 30°-60°-90° triangle, the ratio of the shorter leg to the longer leg is $1 : \sqrt{3}$.

### Lesson Practice 82

a. $\theta_1 = \sin^{-1}\frac{18}{25} \approx 46°$

b. $\theta_2 = \cos^{-1}\frac{18}{25} \approx 44°$

c. $\theta = \tan^{-1}\frac{72}{90} \approx 39°$

d. $\theta = \cos^{-1}\frac{18}{24} \approx 41°$

### Practice 82

1. $\theta_1 = \cos^{-1}\frac{25}{40} \approx 51°$

$\theta_2 = \sin^{-1}\frac{25}{40} \approx 39°$

2. $m_{PQ} = \frac{6-3}{4-1} = \frac{3}{3} = 1$

$m_{RS} = \frac{6-0}{6-0} = \frac{6}{6} = 1$

$\overline{PQ}$ and $\overline{RS}$ are the bases because they both have a slope of 1, making them parallel.

3. $A_{\text{large rectangle}} = lw = (10)(25) = 250 \text{ cm}^2$

$A_{\text{square}} = lw = (5)(5) = 25 \text{ cm}^2$

$A_{\text{trapezoid}} = \frac{1}{2}(b_1 + b_2)h$

$= \frac{1}{2}(7 + 5)(5) = 30 \text{ cm}^2$

$P(\text{prize}) = \frac{25}{250} = \frac{1}{10}$

$P(\text{token}) = \frac{30}{250} = \frac{3}{25}$

$P(\text{nothing}) = \frac{250 - 25 - 30}{250} = \frac{195}{250} = \frac{39}{50}$

4. $1 = m(-3) - \frac{7}{2}$

$-3m = \frac{9}{2}$

$m = -\frac{3}{2}$

5. $m\angle PLK = 180° - 90° - 57° = 33°$

6. Solve the equation $\tan\theta = \frac{2.2}{4.5}$ for $\theta$.

$\theta = \tan^{-1}\frac{2.2}{4.5} \approx 26°$

Then substitute into $\sin 26° = \frac{2.2}{r}$.

$r = \frac{2.2}{\sin 26°} \approx 5$ inches

**7.** $\pi r^2 = 85.2$

$r \approx 5.2$ cm

$S = 4\pi r^2 = 4\pi(5.2^2) \approx 339.79$ cm$^2$

**8.** The m$\angle SRT$ = m$\angle SQT$ because they share the intercepted arc. So, m$\angle SRT = 77°$.

**9.** $J(0, 1) \rightarrow J'(0 - 4, 1 + 2) = J'(-4, 3)$

$K(4, 2) \rightarrow K'(4 - 4, 2 + 2) = K'(0, 4)$

$L(3, -1) \rightarrow L'(3 - 4, -1 + 2) = L'(-1, 1)$

**10.** Choice A: $\angle B \neq \angle A$

Choice B: $\angle B = \angle B$

Choice C: $\angle B = \angle B$

Choice D: $\angle A = \angle A$

Choice **A** is correct.

**11.** 5 lines of symmetry

**12.** No, they are not parallel because the proportion $\frac{LN}{NP} = \frac{MO}{OQ}$ does not hold.

$\frac{7}{8} = \frac{6}{7}$

$(7)(7) = (8)(6)$

$49 \neq 48$

**13.** A rectangle has diagonals that are equal in length. Choice **D** is correct.

**14.** $\frac{n(n + 1)}{2}$

For $n = 8$, $\frac{8(9)}{2} = 36$ cans of soup

**15.** $\tan\theta = \frac{600}{400}$

$\theta = \tan^{-1}\frac{600}{400} \approx 56°$

**16. a.**

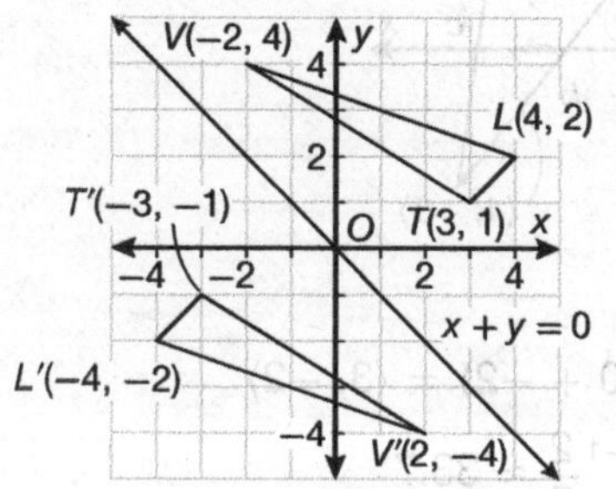


Rueben forgot to reverse the $x$- and $y$-coordinates after taking their opposites.

**b.**

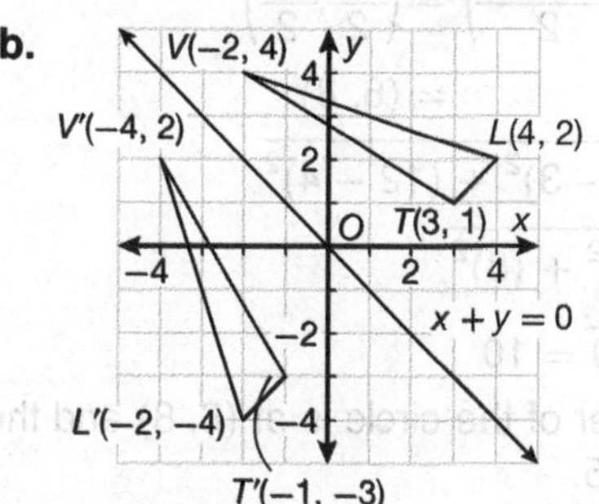


**17. a.** m$\angle N = 180° - 140° - 20° = 20°$

Since the triangle has two congruent angles, it is isosceles. Since it has an obtuse angle, it is obtuse.

**b.** The vertex angle is $\angle L$ because $\angle M$ and $\angle N$ have the same measure.

**18.**

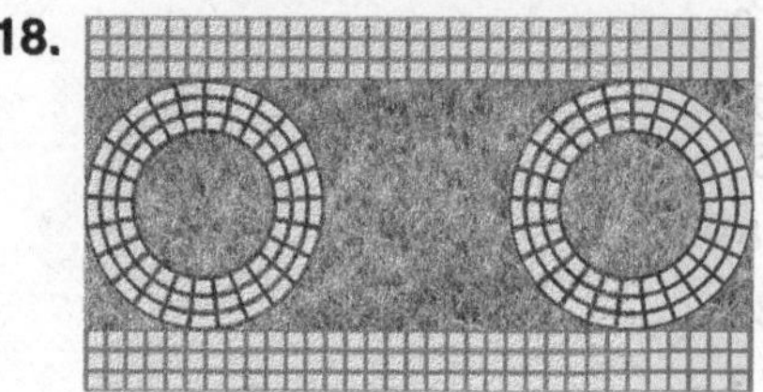

**19.** $-2x - 5 = x + 1$

$-3x = 6$

$x = -2$

$y = -2 + 1 = -1$

$(-2, -1)$

**20.** m$\angle 2 = \frac{1}{2}(73° - 50°) = 11.5°$

**21.** $\frac{y - y_1}{x - x_1} = m$

$y - y_1 = m(x - x_1)$

This is the equation of a line through $(x_1, y_1)$ with slope $m$. Substitute $(0, b)$ for $(x_1, y_1)$ and isolate $y$ to find the slope-intercept form.

**22.** $\frac{3}{2}x + 4 = -\frac{1}{3}x - \frac{10}{3}$

$\frac{11}{6}x = -\frac{22}{3}$

$x = -4$

$y = \frac{3}{2}(-4) + 4 = -2$

$(-4, -2)$

23. Midpoint =

$\left(\frac{3+9}{2}, \frac{12+4}{2}\right) = \left(\frac{12}{2}, \frac{16}{2}\right)$

$= (6, 8)$

$d = \sqrt{(9-3)^2 + (12-4)^2}$

$= \sqrt{(6)^2 + (8)^2}$

$= \sqrt{100} = 10$

The center of the circle is at (6, 8) and the radius is 5.

$(x-h)^2 + (y-k)^2 = r^2$

$(x-6)^2 + (y-8)^2 = 5^2$

$(x-6)^2 + (y-8)^2 = 25$

24. $h^2 = 8^2 + 6^2$

$h^2 = 64 + 36$

$h^2 = 100$

$h = 10$

$\frac{x}{10} = \frac{8}{6}$

$(6)(x) = (8)(10)$

$6x = 80$

$x \approx 13.3$

$\frac{13.3}{8} = \frac{y}{10}$

$(8)(y) = (10)(13.3)$

$8y = 133$

$y \approx 16.6$

25. $S = \frac{1}{2}(4\pi r^2) + \pi r^2$

$= \frac{1}{2}[4\pi(20^2)] + \pi(20^2)$

$\approx 3770 \text{ in.}^2$

$V = \frac{1}{2}\left(\frac{4}{3}\pi r^3\right)$

$= \frac{1}{2}\left(\frac{4}{3}\pi(20)^3\right) \approx 16{,}755 \text{ in.}^3$

26. $(14-x)^2 + (2\sqrt{14})^2 = x^2$

$196 - 28x + x^2 + 56 = x^2$

$252 = 28x$

$9 = x$

27. Reason 1: Given

Reason 2: Definition of supplementary angles

Reason 3: Linear Pair Theorem

Reason 5: Subtraction Property of Equality

28. $x + 1 + x + 2 + x + 3 = 12$

$3x + 6 = 12$

$3x = 6$

$x = 2$

The lengths of the legs are 3 and 4. The length of the hypotenuse is 5.

$\theta = \tan^{-1}\frac{3}{4} \approx 37°$

$\theta = \tan^{-1}\frac{4}{3} \approx 53°$

29. $P = 5.5 + 4 + 4 + 5 + 5.5 + 7 = 31$ yd

30. Each side of $\Delta WXY = 24 \div 3 = 8$ in.

Each side of $\Delta RST = 8 \div 4 = 2$ in.

## LESSON 83

### Warm Up 83

1. parallelogram
2. never
3. Choice **B** is correct.

### Lesson Practice 83

a.

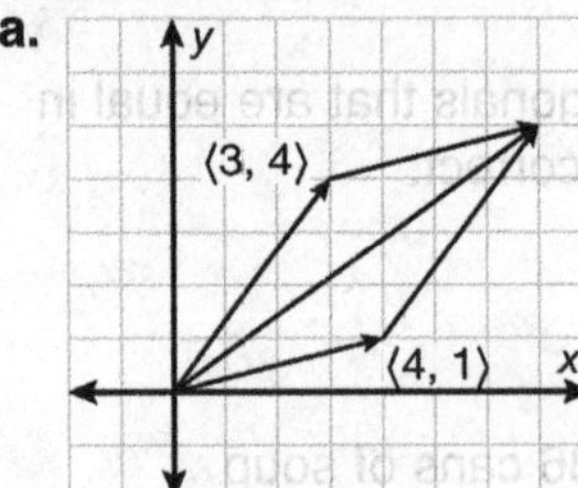


$\langle 7, 5\rangle$

b.

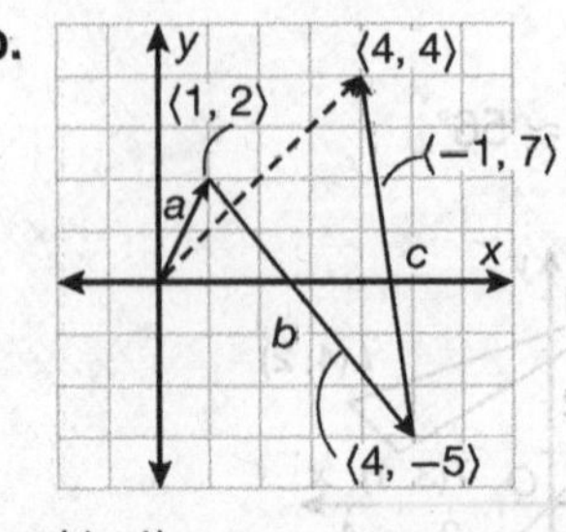


$\langle 4, 4\rangle$

c. $\langle 3+0, 0+-2\rangle = \langle 3, -2\rangle$

$\theta = \tan^{-1}\frac{2}{3} \approx 33.7°$

The direction will be $-33.7°$ or $360° - 33.7° = 326.3°$.

$$|\vec{a}|^2 + |\vec{b}|^2 = |\vec{a} + \vec{b}|^2$$
$$|3|^2 + |-2|^2 = |\vec{a} + \vec{b}|^2$$
$$|\vec{a} + \vec{b}| = 3.6$$

magnitude: 3.6

**d.** $\langle 2000, 0\rangle$ and $\langle 0, 3000\rangle$
$$|\langle 2000, 0\rangle|^2 + |\langle 0, 3000\rangle|^2 = |\vec{x}|^2$$
$$2000^2 + 3000^2 = |\vec{x}|^2$$
$x \approx 3605.55$ meters

## Practice 83

**1.** Since the side opposite must be 10 and adjacent 8, $\theta_2$ is the angle being used.

**2.** The side length of the hexagon is $2(28) = 56$.
$P = 6(56) = 336$ m

**3.** semicircle: 1
circle: infinitely many

**4.**

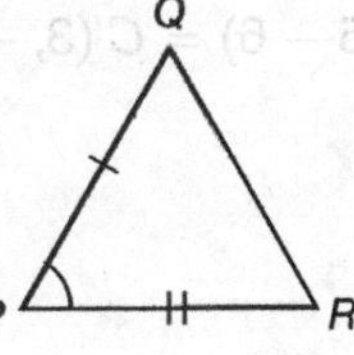


$\triangle PQR \cong \triangle TUS$

**5.** $m\angle ADB < m\angle DBC$ because $\angle ADB$ is across from a shorter side.

**6.** $\langle 4 - 2, 5 + 2\rangle = \langle 2, 7\rangle$
$$2^2 + 7^2 = x^2$$
$$x \approx 7.28$$

**7.** $\frac{1}{\sqrt{2}} = \frac{5}{x}$
$x = 5\sqrt{2}$ inches

**8.** $V = \frac{1}{3}Bh = \frac{1}{3}\pi(1^2)(7) \approx 7.33$ cubic inches

**9.** concave octagonal prism

**10.** $d^2 = 80^2 + 50^2$
$d^2 = 8900$
$d \approx 94$ meters
$\theta = \tan^{-1}\frac{80}{50} \approx 58°$ from the east

**11.** The radius is still 5, but the center is at $(4 + 2, 2)$ or $(6, 2)$.

**12.** $V = Bh = \pi(33^2)(68) \approx 232{,}641\text{ cm}^3$

**13.** Choice A: $\theta = \tan^{-1}\frac{4}{3} \approx 53°$

Choice B: $\theta = \tan^{-1}\frac{2}{7} \approx 16°$

Choice C: $\theta = \tan^{-1}\frac{7}{4} \approx 60°$ not $30°$

Choice D: $\theta = \tan^{-1}\frac{5}{2} \approx 68°$

Choice **C** is the correct answer.

**14.** Corresponding Angles Postulate

**15.** The lines are parallel. The slopes of parallel lines are equal.
$6 = \frac{a}{2}$
$a = 12$

**16.** $A = (8)(14) - (4)(4) - (4)(4) = 80\text{ in.}^2$

**17.** $\langle 2 + 2(2) - 2, 3 + 2(3) - 3\rangle = \langle 4, 6\rangle$

**18.** Sample: $(b, 0)$ and $(b, b)$

**19.**

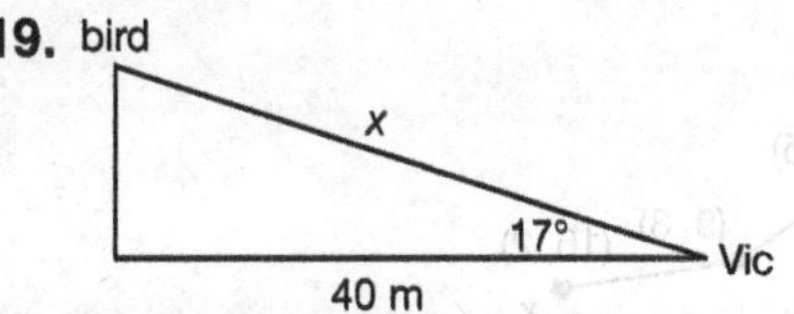


$\cos 17° = \frac{40}{x}$
$x = \frac{40}{\cos 17°}$
$x \approx 42$ meters

**20.** Because they are related in part by a factor of $\pi$.

**21.** Choice **B** is correct because a cube only has 6 sides and this net has 7.

**22.** 15

**23.** $d = |-4 + 0| = 4$

**24.**

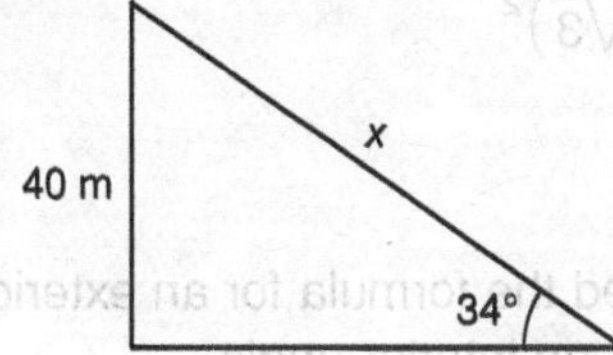

$$\sin 34^\circ = \frac{40}{x}$$
$$x = \frac{40}{\sin 34^\circ}$$
$$x \approx 72 \text{ meters}$$

**25.** $\theta_1 = \cos^{-1}\frac{10}{15} \approx 48^\circ$

$\theta_2 = \sin^{-1}\frac{10}{15} \approx 42^\circ$

**26.** It will have no solutions because the lines are parallel.

**27.** $rx + 3y = 4$
$$3y = -rx + 4$$
$$y = -\frac{1}{3}rx + \frac{4}{3}$$
$$y = -\frac{2}{s}x + 6$$
So, $-\frac{1}{3}r = \frac{s}{2}$
$$r = -\frac{3}{2}s$$

**28.**

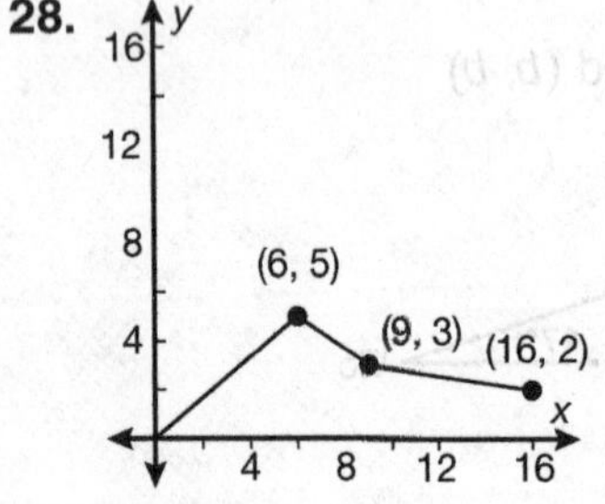


$\langle 16, 2\rangle$
$$x^2 = 16^2 + 2^2$$
$$x \approx 16.12$$

**29.** $V = lwh$
$$= (4\sqrt{3})(4\sqrt{3})(4\sqrt{3})$$
$$= 192\sqrt{3} \text{ in.}^3$$
$L = Ph$
$$= 4(4\sqrt{3})(4\sqrt{3})$$
$$= 192 \text{ in.}^2$$
$S = L + 2B$
$$= 192 + 2(4\sqrt{3})^2$$
$$= 192 + 96$$
$$= 288 \text{ in.}^2$$

**30.** The student used the formula for an exterior angle instead of an interior angle.

$$m\angle DHE = \frac{1}{2}(m\widehat{DE} + m\widehat{FG})$$
$$98^\circ = \frac{1}{2}(108^\circ + m\widehat{FG})$$
$$44^\circ = \frac{1}{2}m\widehat{FG}$$
$$88^\circ = m\widehat{FG}$$
$$m\widehat{DF} = 360^\circ - 108^\circ - 92^\circ - 88^\circ = 72^\circ$$
$$m\angle C = \frac{1}{2}(m\widehat{EG} - m\widehat{DF})$$
$$= \frac{1}{2}(92^\circ - 72^\circ)$$
$$= 10^\circ$$

## LESSON 84

### Warm Up 84

1. transformation
2. $B(-1, 2) \rightarrow B'(-1 + 3, 2 - 6) = B'(2, -4)$
   $A(3, 4) \rightarrow A'(3 + 3, 4 - 6) = A'(6, -2)$
   $C(0, -5) \rightarrow C'(0 + 3, -5 - 6) = C'(3, -11)$
3. $$\frac{9}{24} = \frac{DF}{16}$$
   $$(24)(DF) = (9)(16)$$
   $$24DF = 144$$
   $$DF = 6$$

### Lesson Practice 84

**a.**

C Q Q′ R S S′ R′

**b.**

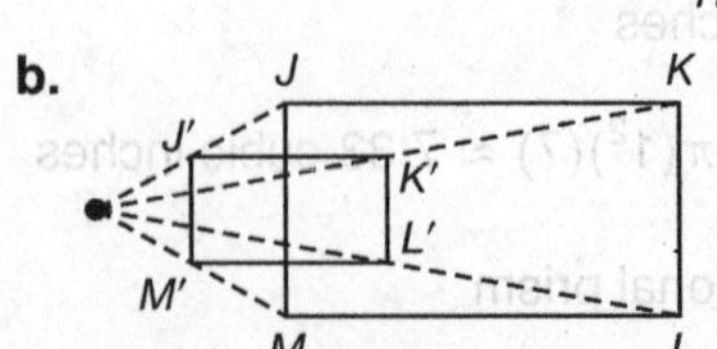


**c.** $M(-2, 1) \rightarrow M'(3(-2), 3(1)) = M'(-6, 3)$
$N(-1, -2) \rightarrow N'(3(-1), 3(-2)) = N'(-3, -6)$
$P(-3, -2) \rightarrow P'(3(-3), 3(-2)) = P'(-9, -6)$

 

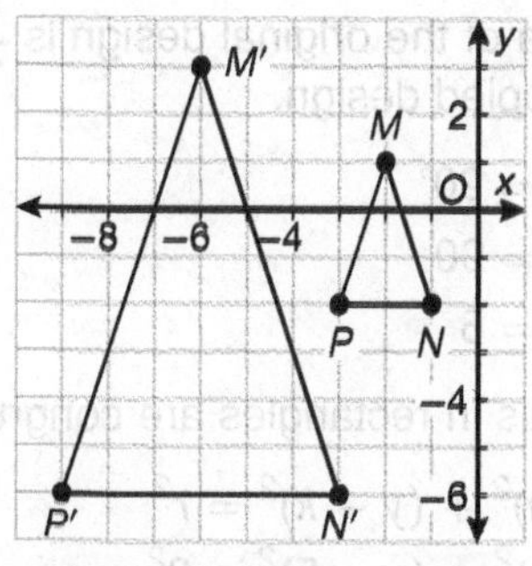


d. 4 ft × 20 by 2.5 ft × 20 = 80 ft by 50 ft

$A_{building} = (80)(50) = 4000 \text{ ft}^2$

$A_{drawing} = (4)(2.5) = 10 \text{ ft}^2$

$\frac{10 \text{ ft}^2}{4000 \text{ ft}^2} = \frac{1}{400}$

## Practice 84

**1.**

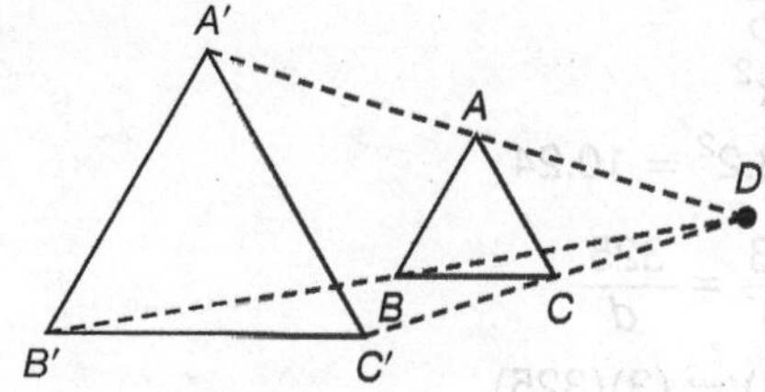


**2.** $2x + 6 = 2$

$2x = -4$

$x = -2$

$(-2, 2)$

**3.** $14.44 = \pi(1.75^2)(h)$

$h \approx 1.5$ inches

**4.** It will remain tangent until ⊙ $B$ and ⊙ $C$ are the same size. Then, it will be tangent again as it becomes larger than ⊙ $C$.

**5.** $V = \frac{4}{3}\pi r^3 + \frac{4}{3}\pi r^3 + \frac{4}{3}\pi r^3$

$= \frac{4}{3}\pi(1^3) + \frac{4}{3}\pi(2^3) + \frac{4}{3}\pi(3^3)$

$\approx 4 + 34 + 113$

$\approx 151 \text{ ft}^3$

**6.** Since $\langle 6 - 3, a + 0\rangle = \langle 3, a\rangle$, the other vector is $\langle -3, 0\rangle$.

**7.** $m\angle ABD = 48°$

$m\angle CBD = 46°$

Choice **A** is correct because $\angle ABD$ is the larger angle and the longest walk must include a hypotenuse and a leg rather than 2 legs of the triangle.

**8.** Sample: A parallelogram is a rectangle if any one angle is a right angle.

**9.** $M(6, 6) \rightarrow M'\left(\frac{1}{3}(6), \frac{1}{3}(6)\right) = M'(2, 2)$

$N(6, 3) \rightarrow N'\left(\frac{1}{3}(6), \frac{1}{3}(3)\right) = N'(2, 1)$

$P(-3, 3) \rightarrow P'\left(\frac{1}{3}(-3), \frac{1}{3}(3)\right) = P'(-1, 1)$

$Q(-3, 6) \rightarrow Q'\left(\frac{1}{3}(-3), \frac{1}{3}(6)\right) = Q'(-1, 2)$

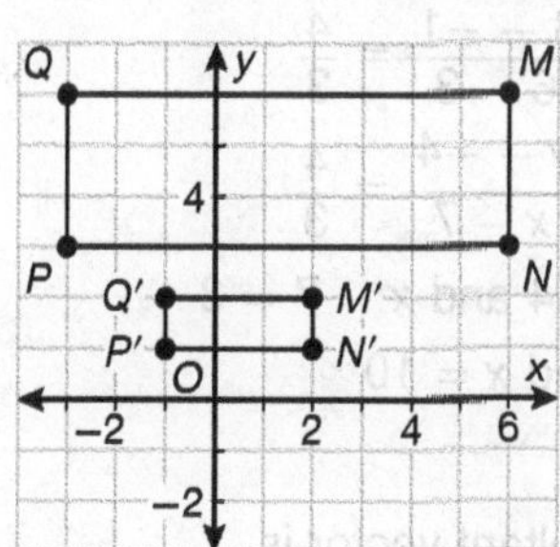


**10.** 15 is the length of the hypotenuse and 9 is the length of the side adjacent because $\frac{9}{15} = \frac{3}{5}$. So, $\cos\theta_2 = \frac{3}{5}$.

**11.** Let $a$ be the apothem and let $P$ be the perimeter of the regular polygon base, and let $l$ be the slant height of the pyramid. If the base area and the lateral area are equal, then $\frac{1}{2}aP = \frac{1}{2}Pl$. So $a = l$. However, this would mean that the height of the pyramid is 0. Hence this is not possible.

**12.** $V - E + F = 2$

$10 - 15 + F = 2$

$-5 + F = 2$

$F = 7$

**13.**

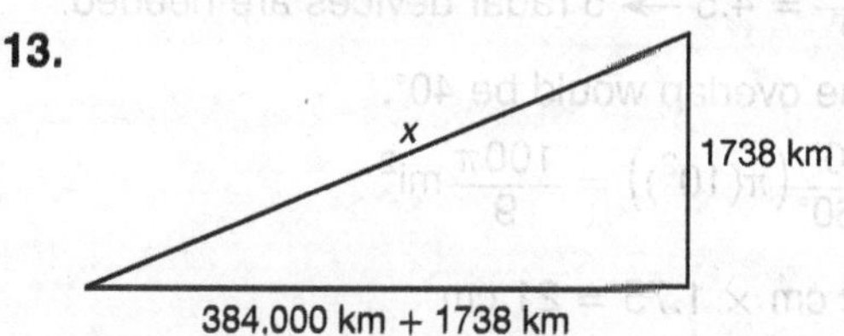


$x^2 = 385{,}738^2 + 1738^2$

$x \approx 385{,}742$ km

**14.** $(x, y) \rightarrow (y, -x)$

$M(6, 1) \rightarrow M'(1, -6)$

$N(2, 1) \rightarrow N'(1, -2)$

$P(1, 4) \rightarrow P'(4, -1)$

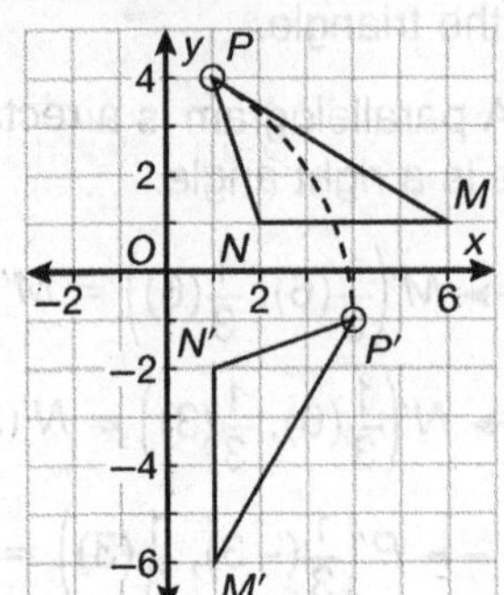


**15.** $m_{ST} = m_{VU}$

$m_{ST} = \dfrac{3 - -1}{6 - 3} = \dfrac{4}{3}$

$m_{VU} = \dfrac{y - -4}{x - 7} = \dfrac{4}{3}$

$y + 4 = 4$ and $x - 7 = 3$

$y = 0$ and $x = 10$

$(10, 0)$

**16.** The resultant vector is

$\langle 4 - 2, 3 + 3\rangle = \langle 2, 6\rangle$.

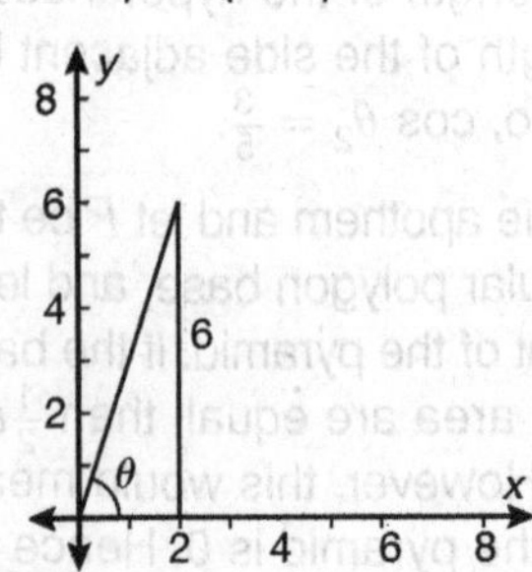


$\tan\theta = \dfrac{6}{2}$

$\theta = \tan^{-1}(3) \approx 72°$

**17.** If an animal is a dog, then it has four legs.

**18.** $\frac{360°}{80°} = 4.5 \rightarrow 5$ radar devices are needed.

The overlap would be 40°.

$\dfrac{40°}{360°}\left(\pi(10^2)\right) = \dfrac{100\pi}{9}\text{mi}^2$

**19.** $12 \text{ cm} \times 1.75 = 21 \text{ cm}$

$8 \text{ cm} \times 1.75 = 14 \text{ cm}$

The enlarged design is 21 cm by 14 cm.

$A_{\text{original}} = (12)(8) = 96 \text{ cm}^2$

$A_{\text{copy}} = (21)(14) = 294 \text{ cm}^2$

$\dfrac{96}{294} = \dfrac{16}{49}$

The area of the original design is $\frac{16}{49}$ the area of the copied design.

**20.** $m\angle JKL = 90°$

$15a = 90$

$a = 6$

**21.** Diagonals in rectangles are congruent.

**22.** $(x - h)^2 + (y - k)^2 = r^2$

$(x - -1)^2 + (y - 5)^2 = 8^2$

$(x + 1)^2 + (y - 5)^2 = 64$

**23.** $\theta_1 = \tan^{-1}\dfrac{20}{14} \approx 55°$

$\theta_2 = \tan^{-1}\dfrac{14}{20} \approx 35°$

**24.** If $a$ and $b$ are the two numbers,

$\dfrac{a}{x} = \dfrac{x}{b}$

$ab = x^2$

$ab = 3.2^2 = 10.24$

**25.** $\dfrac{13}{3} = \dfrac{325}{d}$

$(13)(d) = (3)(325)$

$13d = 975$

$d = 75$ dimes

$\dfrac{13}{1} = \dfrac{325}{q}$

$(13)(q) = (1)(325)$

$13q = 325$

$q = 25$ quarters

**26.**

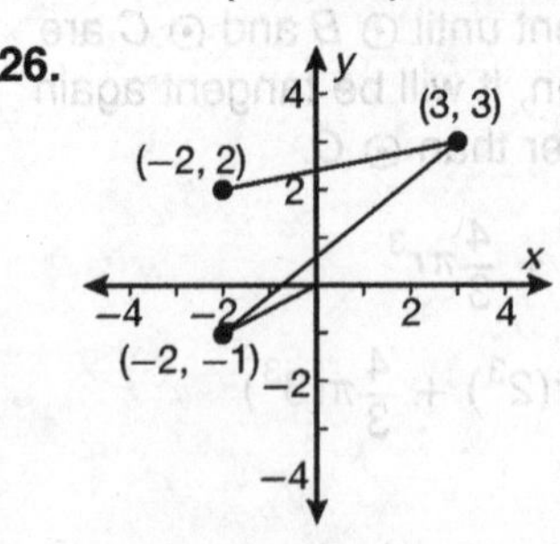


$\langle -2, 2\rangle$

**27. a.** $\angle 3$ and $\angle 5$, $\angle 4$ and $\angle 6$

**b.** $\angle 3$ and $\angle 8$ are given to be supplementary angles, and $\angle 8 \cong \angle 5$ because they are vertical angles. Therefore, $\angle S$ and $\angle Z$ are supplementary. The Converse of the Same-Side Interior Angles Theorem implies that lines $a$ and $b$ are parallel.

**28. a.** $2^5 = 32$

**b.** In addition to the 6 that are shown in the hint, there are:

10 monostrips

**c.** $2^n$ monostrips; $\frac{n(n-1)}{2}$

**29.**

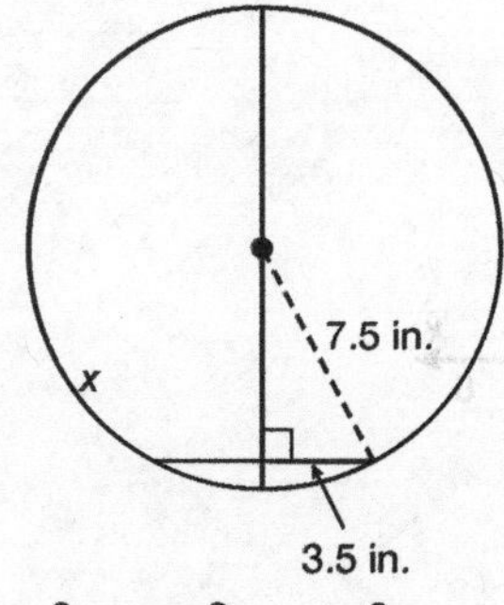


$x^2 = 7.5^2 - 3.5^2$

$x^2 = 56.25 - 12.25$

$x^2 = 44$

$x = 2\sqrt{11}$ inches

**30.**

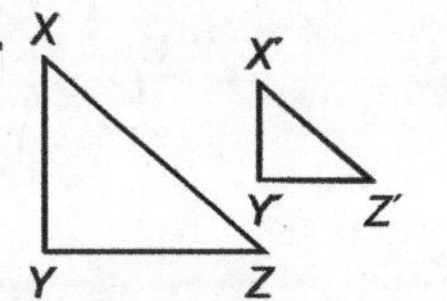


## LESSON 85

### Warm Up 85

1. isometric drawing
2. $S = 4\pi r^2 = 4\pi(12^2) = 576\pi\text{ cm}^2$

   $V = \frac{4}{3}\pi r^3 = \frac{4}{3}\pi(12^3) \approx 2304\pi\text{ cm}^3$
3. A circle is not a solid. Choice **C** is correct.

### Lesson Practice 85

**a.** The cross section is a hexagon.

**b.** $P = 4s = 4(4) = 16$ inches

**c.**

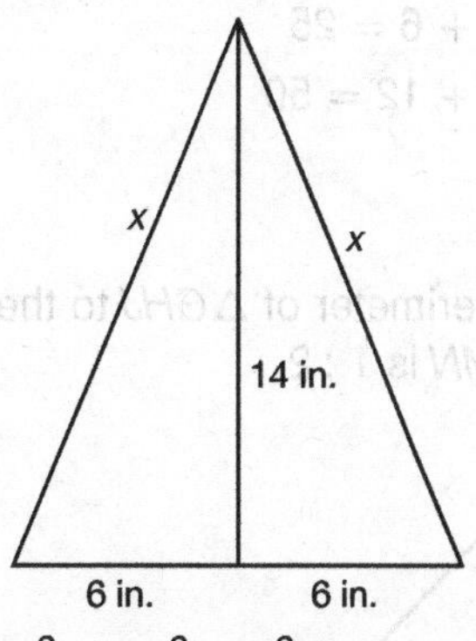


$x^2 = 14^2 + 6^2$

$x \approx 15.23$ inches

$P \approx 15.23 + 15.23 + 12 \approx 42.46$ inches

**d.** $d^2 = 4^2 + 4^2$

$d \approx 5.66$ cm

$A \approx (5.66)(4) \approx 22.64$ square centimeters

**e.** $h^2 = 13^2 - 5^2$

$h = 12$

$V = \frac{1}{3}(\pi)(2.5^2)(12) = 25\pi\text{ cm}^3$

### Practice 85

1. $\theta = \tan^{-1}\frac{15}{16} \approx 43°$
2. A cylinder could not have a triangular cross section. Choice **D** is correct.
3. $A(3, 4) \rightarrow A'(3 - 2, 4 + 4) = A'(1, 8)$

   $B(4, 7) \rightarrow B'(4 - 2, 7 + 4) = B'(2, 11)$

   $C(5, -2) \rightarrow C'(5 - 2, -2 + 4) = C'(3, 2)$

   The vector $\langle -2, 4\rangle$ translates $\triangle ABC$ to $\triangle A'B'C'$.
4. $\frac{x^2 + 2}{36} = \frac{6}{12}$

   $(12)(x^2 + 2) = (6)(36)$

   $12x^2 + 24 = 216$

   $12x^2 = 192$

   $x^2 = 16$

   $x = 4$

   $\frac{y - 4}{2} = \frac{6}{12}$

   $(12)(y - 4) = (2)(6)$

   $12y - 48 = 12$

   $12y = 60$

   $y = 5$

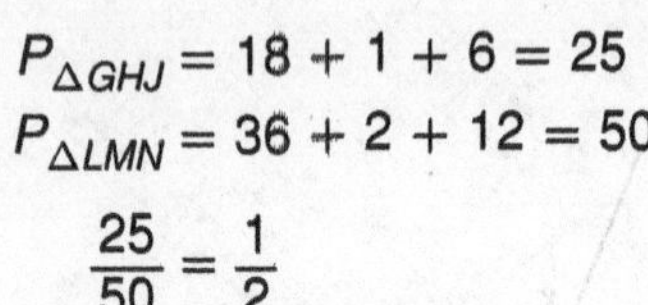

$P_{\triangle GHJ} = 18 + 1 + 6 = 25$

$P_{\triangle LMN} = 36 + 2 + 12 = 50$

$\frac{25}{50} = \frac{1}{2}$

The ratio of the perimeter of $\triangle GHJ$ to the perimeter of $\triangle LMN$ is 1 : 2.

**5.**

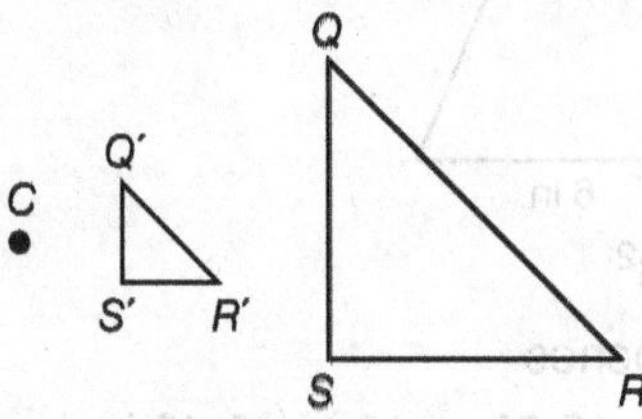


**6.** $0.883 = \frac{1}{3}(\pi r^2)(1.5)$

$0.56 \approx r^2$

$r \approx 0.75$ in.

**7. a.** $26 = 7.5 + 7.5 + JL$

$JL = 11$ in.

**b.** $JM = \frac{1}{2}(JL) = \frac{1}{2}(11) = 5.5$ in.

**8.** $D = \text{Midpoint}_{BC}$

$= \left(\frac{6 + -1}{2}, \frac{1 + 1}{2}\right) = \left(\frac{5}{2}, \frac{2}{2}\right) = (2.5, 1)$

$E = \text{Midpoint}_{AB}$

$= \left(\frac{6 + 1}{2}, \frac{1 + 6}{2}\right) = \left(\frac{7}{2}, \frac{7}{2}\right) = (3.5, 3.5)$

**9.** Choice A: $2^2 + (3\sqrt{5})^2 = 7^2$

$4 + 45 = 49$

$49 = 49$

This is a right triangle.

Choice B: $4^2 + (\sqrt{17})^2 > (3\sqrt{2})^2$

$16 + 17 > 18$

$33 > 49$

This is an acute triangle.

Choice C: $11^2 + 17^2 > 19^2$

$121 + 289 > 361$

$410 > 361$

This is an acute triangle.

Choice D: $8^2 + (4\sqrt{5})^2 < 16^2$

$64 + 80 < 256$

$144 < 256$

This is an obtuse triangle.

Choice **D** is correct.

**10.** a circle:

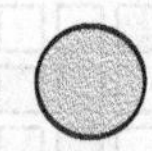

**11.** No, only pairs of right triangles with side lengths that are proportional Pythagorean Triples are similar. For example, (3, 4, 5) and (6, 8, 10)

**12.** Since $ZY$ is across from a larger angle, $ZY > WZ$.

**13.**

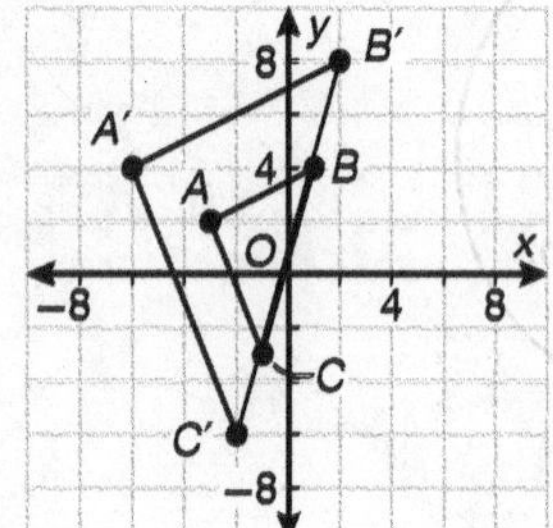


**14.** triangular prism: 9 edges

rectangular prism: 12 edges

pentagonal prism: 15 edges

$E = 3n$ for $n$ sides

**15.**

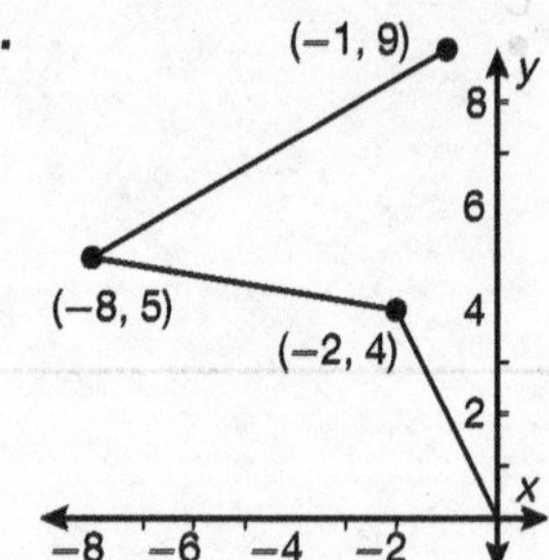


$\langle -1, 9 \rangle$

$x^2 = (-1)^2 + 9^2$

$x \approx 9.06$

**16. a.**

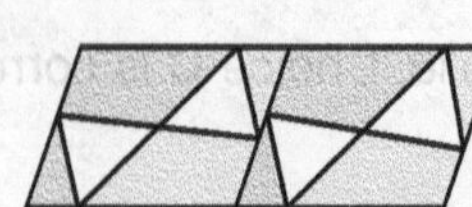

**b.**

frieze pattern; translation symmetry

17. Theorem 64-1 states that the angle is half the arc, not the arc is half the angle, as Todd wrote. The answer should be 74°.

18. $\Delta ABC$ and $\Delta DEF$ are right triangles, it is given that $\overline{AC} \cong \overline{DF}$, and $\overline{AB} \cong \overline{DE}$, Therefore, by the *HL* Congruence Theorem, $\Delta ABC \cong \Delta DEF$.

19.

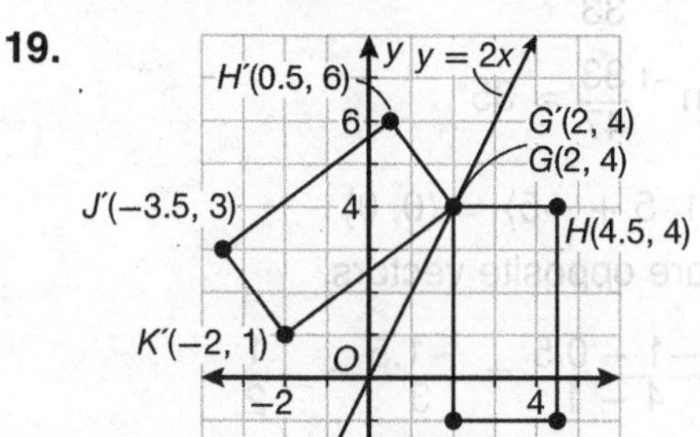


20. $P = 4(2) = 8$ inches

21. $V = Bh = (\pi(3.5^2))(13) \approx 500 \text{ cm}^3$

22. $XY = WZ = 10.4$ in.
$WY = 2(XO) = 2(12.6) = 25.2$ in.

23. They have a pair of congruent sides. $\angle PRQ \cong \angle TRS$ by the Vertical Angles Theorem, and $\angle RPQ \cong \angle RST$ because alternate interior angles are congruent. Therefore, $\Delta PQR \cong \Delta SRT$ by AAS Triangle Congruence.

24. $\theta = \tan^{-1}\frac{8}{15} \approx 28°$

25. $7x + 2x = 360$
$9x = 360$
$x = 40$
$7(40) = 280$
$2(40) = 80$
$m\angle A = \frac{1}{2}(280° - 80°) = 100°$

26. A circle has an infinite order and infinitely many lines of symmetry.

27. The cross section is a circle with a circular hole.

28. $m\angle A = m\angle E = 75°$
$m\angle C = 360° - 75° - 100° - 120° = 65°$

29. The dilation is an enlargement or expansion.
$M(-3, -2) \rightarrow M'(3(-3), 3(-2)) = M'(-9, -6)$
$N(1, 1) \rightarrow N'(3(1), 3(1)) = N'(3, 3)$
$P(-2, 4) \rightarrow P'(3(-2), 3(4)) = P'(-6, 12)$
The scale factor is 3.

30. $190° - 120° = 70°$ clockwise rotation

## LESSON 86

### Warm Up 86

1. line segment; endpoints

2. $\angle E$ is a right angle.

3.

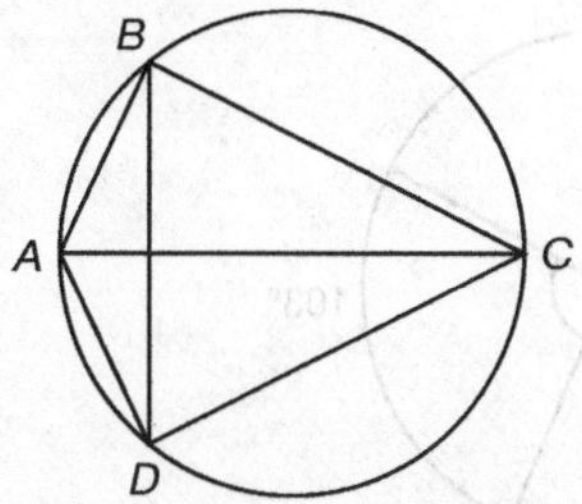


The quadrilateral *ABCD* is a kite.
Choice **B** is correct.

### Lesson Practice 86

a. $(9)(DE) = (3)(16)$
$9DE = 48$
$DE = \frac{16}{3}$ or $5\frac{1}{3}$

b. $7y = 2(4 - y)$
$7y = 8 - 2y$
$9y = 8$
$y = \frac{8}{9}$

c. $7(2x + 4) = 6(3x - 1)$
$14x + 28 = 18x - 6$
$-4x = -34$
$x = 8.5$

d.

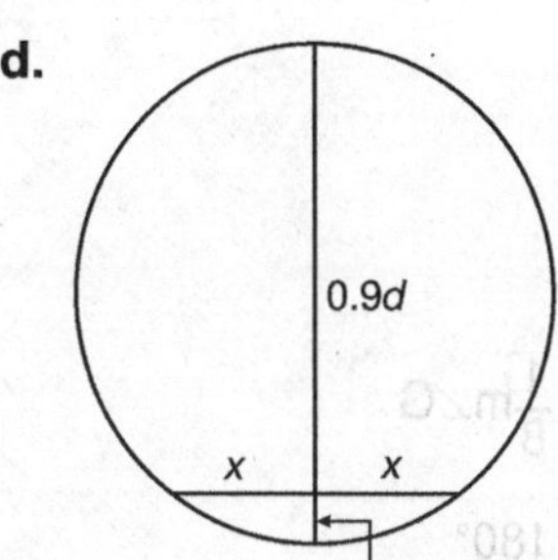

$(x)(x) = (0.1d)(0.9d)$

$x^2 = 0.09d^2$

$x = 0.3d$

4 ft 9 in. = 57 in.

$0.3(57) \approx 17$ in.

$2(17) = 34$ in. = 2 ft 10 in.

## Practice 86

1. $(6)(VZ) = (4)(4.5)$

   $6VZ = 18$

   $VZ = 3$

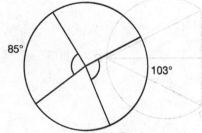

2. $\frac{1}{2}(103° + 85°) = 94°$

3. Yes. If you just consider the areas of the bases, the cone has only one base and the cylinder has two bases, all three having equal areas. The lateral surface area for the cone is also less than the lateral surface area for the cylinder. If you imagine taking the lateral surface of the cylinder and "wrapping" it to create a cone, there would be areas of overlap.

4. $d = |-2 - 5| = |-7| = 7$

5. Sample: Subtract the angle measure of that sector from 360° and divide by 360°.

6. 

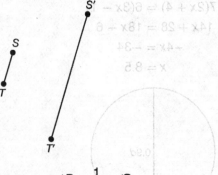

7. $m\angle D = \frac{1}{8}m\angle G$

   $\frac{1}{8}m\angle G + m\angle G = 180°$

   $\frac{9}{8}m\angle G = 180°$

   $m\angle G = m\angle E = 160°$

   $m\angle D = m\angle F = \frac{1}{8}(160°) = 20°$

8. $\theta_1 = \tan^{-1}\frac{47}{33} \approx 55°$

   $\theta_2 = \tan^{-1}\frac{33}{47} \approx 35°$

9. $\langle 1 + -1, 5 + -5\rangle = \langle 0, 0\rangle$

   These are opposite vectors.

10. $m_{AB} = \frac{-1 - 0.5}{4 - 1} = \frac{-1.5}{3} = -\frac{1}{2}$

    $m_{AC} = \frac{-1 - 2}{4 - -2} = \frac{-3}{6} = -\frac{1}{2}$

    $m_{BC} = \frac{2 - 0.5}{-2 - 1} = \frac{1.5}{-3} = -\frac{1}{2}$

    The slope between $A$ and $B$ is $-\frac{1}{2}$, which is equal to the slope between $B$ and $C$ and the slope between $A$ and $C$.

11. $P = 2(10) + 2(18) = 56$ cm

12. $V = \frac{1}{2}\left(\frac{4}{3}\pi r^3\right)$

    $= \frac{1}{2}\left(\frac{4}{3}\pi(6)^3\right) \approx 452$ cubic inches

13. $47^2 = x^2 + x^2$

    $2209 = 2x^2$

    $1104.5 = x^2$

    $x \approx 33.23$

    $P = 4(33.23) \approx 133$ ft

14. They are congruent.

15. The best description for $\angle S$ is remote interior angle. Choice **B** is correct.

16. $(6)(x) = (2)(3 + 2x)$

    $6x = 6 + 4x$

    $2x = 6$

    $x = 3$

17. The resultant vector is

    $\langle -3 + 6, 5 + 4\rangle = \langle 3, 9\rangle$.

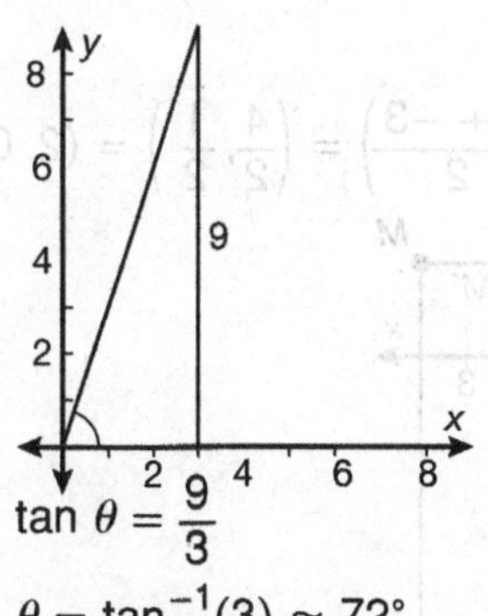


$\tan\theta = \frac{9}{3}$

$\theta = \tan^{-1}(3) \approx 72°$

**18.** $4x - 2 + 7x - 30 + 150 = 360$

$11x + 118 = 360$

$11x = 242$

$x = 22$

$m\angle Y = \frac{1}{2}[(7(22) - 30] - [4(22) - 2)] = 19°$

$m\angle X = \frac{1}{2}[(4(22) - 2) + 150] = 118°$

$m\angle Z = \frac{1}{2}(4(22) - 2) = 43°$

**19.**

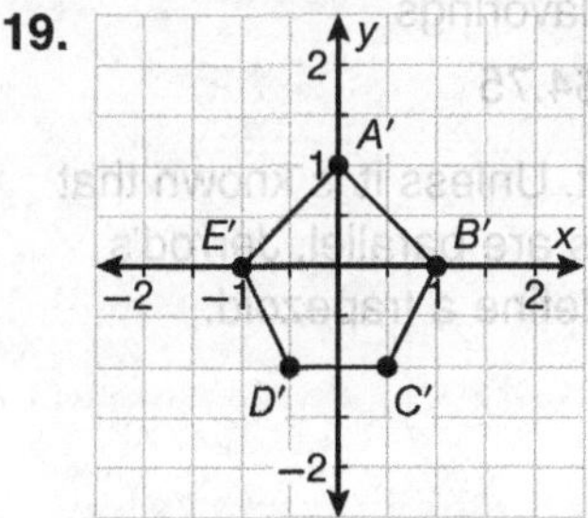


**20.** $x = \frac{13}{\sqrt{3}} = \frac{13\sqrt{3}}{3}$

$y = 2\left(\frac{13\sqrt{3}}{3}\right) = 26\frac{\sqrt{3}}{3}$

**21.** By the Reflexive Property of Congruence, $\overset{\frown}{CD} \cong \overset{\frown}{CD}$. The measure of an angle that is outside a circle is equal to half the difference of the intercepted arcs, so $m\angle A = \frac{1}{2}(m\overset{\frown}{CD} - m\overset{\frown}{FE})$ and $m\angle B = \frac{1}{2}(m\overset{\frown}{CD} - m\overset{\frown}{HG})$. Solve for $m\overset{\frown}{FE}$ and $m\overset{\frown}{HG}$ to get $m\overset{\frown}{FE} = m\overset{\frown}{CD} - 2(m\angle A)$ and $m\overset{\frown}{HG} = m\overset{\frown}{CD} - 2(m\angle B)$. Since $\angle A \cong \angle B$, substitute to find that $m\overset{\frown}{HG} = m\overset{\frown}{CD} - 2(m\angle A)$. Therefore, by the Transitive Property of Equality, $m\overset{\frown}{FE} = m\overset{\frown}{HG}$.

**22.**

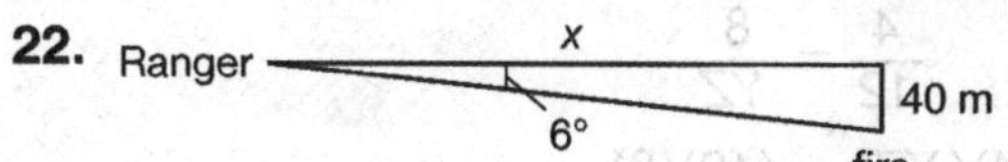


$\tan 6° = \frac{40}{x}$

$x = \frac{40}{\tan 6°}$

$x \approx 380.6$ meters

**23.** $P = 3(8) = 24$ centimeters

**24.** $V = \frac{1}{3}Bh = \frac{1}{3}(200)(18) = 1200 \text{ cm}^3$

**25.** Today sandwiches are 25% off.

**26.** $5(3 - 2y) = 4(y - 4)$

$15 - 10y = 4y - 16$

$-14y = -31$

$y = \frac{31}{14}$

**27.** $A = \frac{1}{2}\pi r^2 = \frac{1}{2}\pi(5^2) \approx 39 \text{ m}^2$

**28.** If folded, the pentagons will overlap. It could be fixed by moving one of the pentagons to the opposite edge of the rectangle it is attached to.

**29.** $\frac{1}{13\sqrt{2}} = \frac{\sqrt{2}}{x}$

$x = (\sqrt{2})(13\sqrt{2})$

$x = 26$ cm

**30.** A sphere could not have a square cross section. Choice **B** is correct.

## LAB 11

### Lab 11 Practice

Yes. Sample: If you call the unknown segment *x*, multiply the segments of each chord together. These values will be equal. Solve for *x*.

## LESSON 87

### Warm Up 87

**1.** composite

**2.** $P = 43 + 28 + 43 + 28 = 142$ in.

$A = (43)(20) = 860 \text{ in.}^2$

3. $\dfrac{4}{12} = \dfrac{8}{YZ}$

$(4)(YZ) = (12)(8)$

$4YZ = 96$

$YZ = 24$

Choice **D** is correct.

## Lesson Practice 87

**a.** By the definition of similar polygons $\frac{PQ}{WX} = \frac{QR}{XY} = \frac{PR}{WY}$ and $\angle P \cong \angle W$. In $\Delta PQS$ and $\Delta WXZ$, $\angle PSQ \cong \angle WZX$. Therefore $\Delta PQS \sim \Delta WXZ$ by the AA Similarity Postulate. By the definition of similar polygons, $\frac{PQ}{WX} = \frac{QS}{XZ} = \frac{SP}{ZW}$. By substitution, $\frac{PR}{WY} = \frac{QS}{XZ}$. By the formula for the area of a triangle, $\frac{\text{Area } \Delta PQR}{\text{Area } \Delta WXY} = \left(\frac{PR}{WY}\right)\left(\frac{QS}{XZ}\right)$. By substitution, $\frac{QS}{XZ}\frac{PR}{WY} = \frac{PR^2}{WY^2}$.

Therefore, $\frac{\text{Area } \Delta PQR}{\text{Area } \Delta WXY} = \frac{PR^2}{WY^2}$.

**b.** $\dfrac{1}{1.5} = \dfrac{P_s}{120}$

$(1.5)(P_s) = (1)(120)$

$P_s = 80$ ft

**c.** Ratio of Areas: $2^2 : 5^2 = 4 : 25$

$A_L = (25)(15) = 375 \text{ cm}^2$

**d.** Ratio of Areas: $1^2 : 10^2 = 1 : 100$

$\dfrac{1}{100} = \dfrac{1.5}{A_T}$

$(1)(A_T) = (100)(1.5)$

$A_T = 150 \text{ ft}^2$

## Practice 87

1. 4 m-by-5 m becomes (4)(7) m-by-(5)(7) m or 28 m-by-35 m.
   $A = (28)(35) = 980 \text{ m}^2$

2. $S = L + B$
   $S = \pi rl + \pi r^2$
   $S = \pi(5.21)(13.78) + \pi(5.21^2)$
   $S \approx 311 \text{ cm}^2$

3. $D = \text{Midpoint}_{AB}$
   $= \left(\frac{-2 + -4}{2}, \frac{5 + -3}{2}\right) = \left(\frac{-6}{2}, \frac{2}{2}\right)$
   $= (-3, 1)$

   $E = \text{Midpoint}_{BC}$
   $= \left(\frac{8 + -4}{2}, \frac{4 + -3}{2}\right) = \left(\frac{4}{2}, \frac{1}{2}\right) = (2, 0.5)$

4. 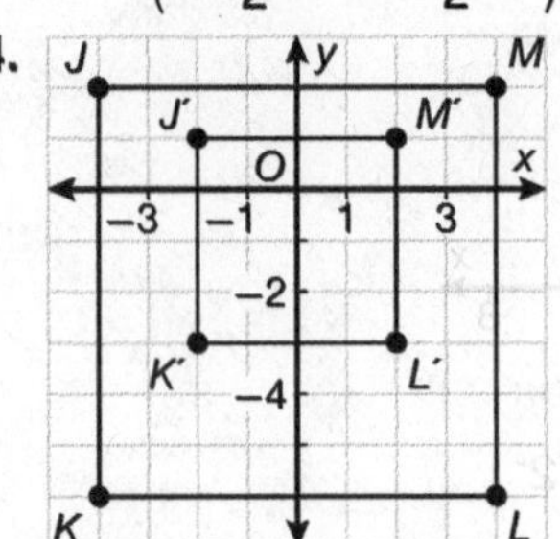


5. $a + b > c$, $b + c > a$, and $c + a > b$

6. $(8)(DE) = (6)(6)$
   $8DE = 36$
   $DE = 4.5$

7. $V = \frac{1}{3}Bh = \frac{1}{3}(6)(6)(8) = 96 \text{ ft}^3$

8. $2.5 + 0.75F = 3.25 + 0.50F$
   $0.25F = 0.75$
   $F = 3$ additional flavorings
   $2.5 + 0.75(3) = \$4.75$

9. Anthony is correct. Unless it is known that both pairs of sides are parallel, Jerrod's statement could define a trapezoid.

10. $\dfrac{1}{5} = \dfrac{32}{P_L}$
    $P_L = 160$ inches

11. $10m + 8m = 180°$
    $18m = 180$
    $m = 10$
    $m\angle H = 5(10) = 50°$

12. $S = 4\pi r^2 = 4\pi(4^2) \approx 201.1 \text{ cm}^2$

13. Cut the cross section just below one of the corners and through three edges.

14. Shorter leg: $4 \div 2 = 2$
    Longer leg: $2\sqrt{3}$

15. The ratio of the perimeters is 1 : 2. So, the ratio of the areas is $1^2 : 2^2$ or 1 : 4. The area is four times as large. Choice **C** is correct.

16. $s^2 = 300^2 + 300^2$
    $s^2 = 180{,}000$
    $s \approx 424$ feet

**17.** $x + 2y = 8$

$2y = -x + 8$

$y = -\frac{1}{2}x + 4$

The slope is $-\frac{1}{2}$ and the $y$-intercept is at $y = 4$.

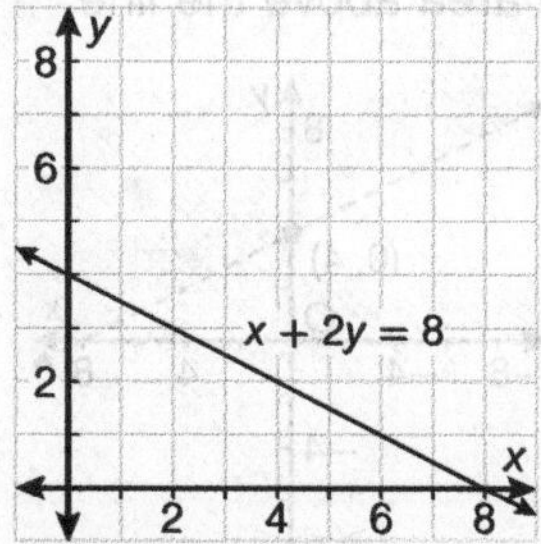


**18.** $(8)(QT) = (3)(16)$

$8QT = 48$

$QT = 6$

**19.** $\frac{1}{3}(16.5) \approx 5.83$

**20.**

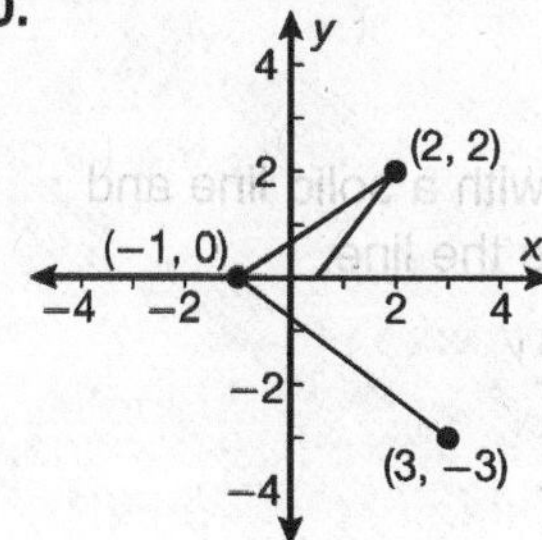


resultant vector $= \langle 3, -3 \rangle$

$x^2 = 3^2 + (-3)^2$

$x \approx 4.24$

magnitude $\approx 4.24$

**21.** $m_y = \frac{7-4}{4-2} = \frac{3}{2}$

$m_x = \frac{k - -3}{3-1} = \frac{3}{2}$

$k + 3 = 3$

$k = 0$

**22.**

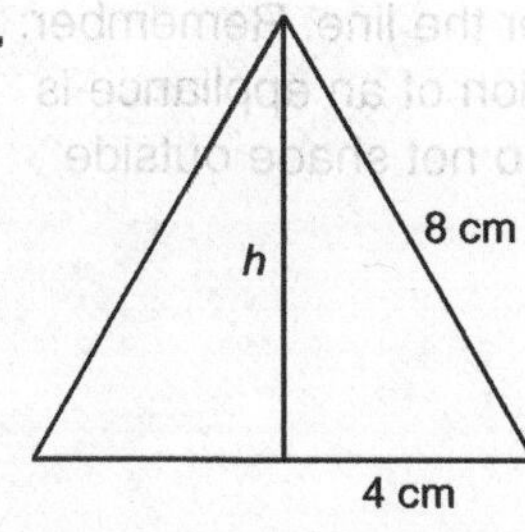


$h^2 = 8^2 - 4^2$

$h \approx 6.93$

$A = \frac{1}{2}bh = \frac{1}{2}(8)(6.93) \approx 27.71 \text{ cm}^2$

**23.** No. The ratio of the legs of the two new trapezoids will be 1 : 1, but the corresponding bases need not be in this ratio.

**24.** The similarity ratio is 3 : 7. So, the ratio of the areas is $3^2 : 7^2$ or 9 : 49.

Perimeter: $\frac{3}{7} = \frac{36}{P}$

$(3)(P) = (7)(36)$

$3P = 252$

$P = 84 \text{ cm}$

Area: $\frac{9}{49} = \frac{93.5}{A}$

$(9)(A) = (49)(93.5)$

$9A = 4581.5$

$A \approx 509 \text{ cm}^2$

**25.** The sum of the areas of each plane figure in the net is equal to the surface area of the completed solid.

**26.** The two circles do not have any common tangents and they are not tangent circles.

**27.** First find the distances between adjacent vertices using the distance formula. Then add the distances together to find the perimeter.

**28.** sine; cosine

**29.** $(15)(x) = (6)(10)$

$15x = 60$

$x = 4$

Choice **C** is correct.

**30.** Let $s$ represent the length of the sides and $h$ the height. Since it is a cube, $s = h$.

$S = L + 2B$

$54 = 4sh + 2s^2$

$54 = 4s^2 + 2s^2$

$54 = 6s^2$

$9 = s^2$

$3 = s$

$V = lwh = (3)(3)(3) = 27 \text{ in.}^3$

## LESSON 88

### Warm Up 88

1. Inequality
2. Graph each line on the coordinate grid. The lines intersect at (–6, –11).

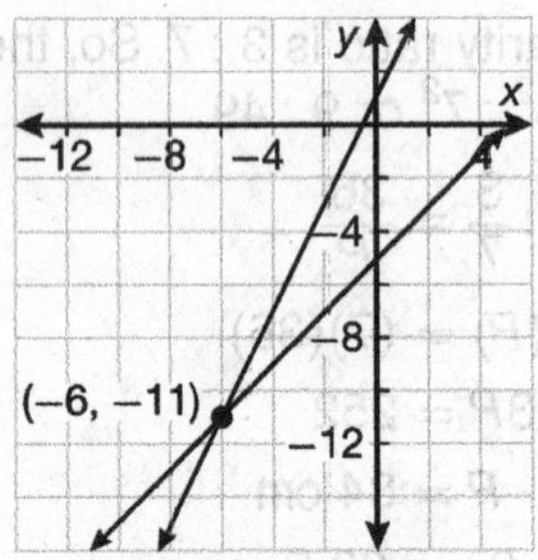


3. Choice **B** is correct. Nonparallel lines intersect at exactly one point.

### Lesson Practice 88

**a.** Rearrange the linear inequality as if it were a linear equation.

$-2x - 4y < -8$

$-2x + 2x - 4y < -8 + 2x$

$-4y < 2x - 8$

$y > \frac{2x - 8}{-4}$

$y > -\frac{1}{2}x + 2$

**b.** Graph $y = 2x - 6$ using a solid line because the inequality includes the line itself. Since $y \geq 2x - 6$, shade the area above the linear equation.

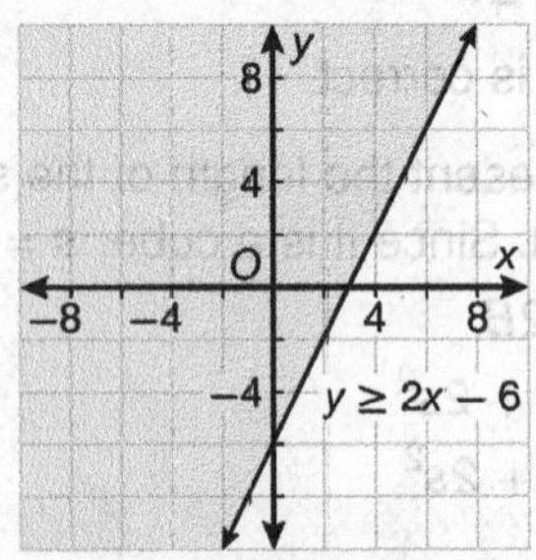


**c.** Solve the inequality for *y*.

$2y - 3 > 5 - x$

$2y > 5 - x + 3$

$y > \frac{8 - x}{2}$

$y > -\frac{1}{2}x + 4$

Graph $y = -\frac{1}{2}x + 4$ with a dotted line and shade the area above the line.

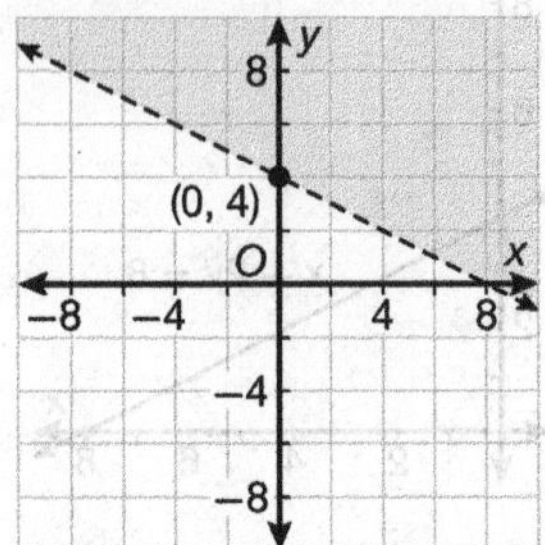


**d.** Solve the inequality for *y*.

$x - 4y \leq 7x + 8$

$-4y \leq 6x + 8$

$y \geq \frac{6x + 8}{-4}$

$y \geq -\frac{3}{2}x - 2$

Graph $y = -\frac{3}{2}x - 2$ with a solid line and shade the area above the line.

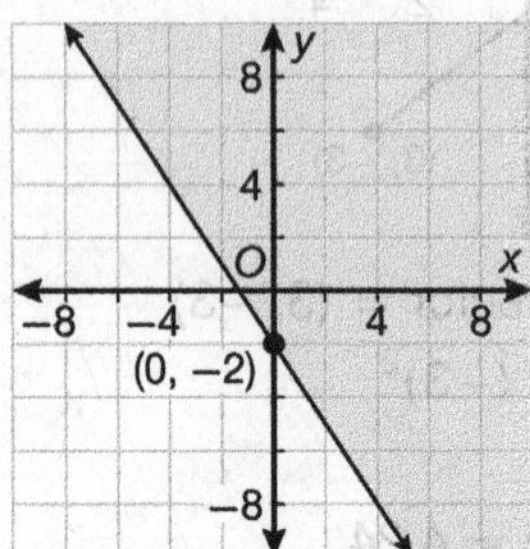


**e.** The sum of the power consumption must be equal to or less than 15, so $x + y \leq 15$.

Solve the inequality for *y*.

$x + y \leq 15$

$y \leq -x + 15$

Graph $y = -x + 15$ using a solid line and shade the area under the line. Remember: the power consumption of an appliance is always positive, so do not shade outside Quadrant I.

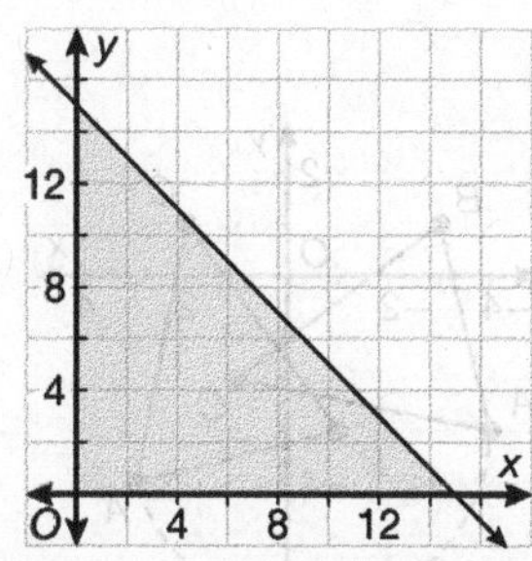


He can send 7 J/s to the first appliance and 6 J/s to the second appliance since the point (7, 6) lies in the solution region.

## Practice 88

1. From Theorem 87-1, the ratio of their areas is $3^2 : 11^2$

$$\frac{\text{Area}}{22^2} = \frac{3^2}{11^2}$$

$$\text{Area} = \frac{9(484)}{121}$$

$$\text{Area} = 36 \text{ cm}^2$$

2. First, use the formula for the lateral surface area of a cone.

$L = \pi r l$

$L = \pi r \sqrt{r^2 + h^2}$

$L = \pi(0.5)\sqrt{0.5^2 + 2.25^2}$

$L \approx 3.62$

Now, substitute the lateral surface area and the formula for the area of a circle into the formula for total surface area.

$S = L + B$

$S = L + \pi r^2$

$S \approx 3.62 + 0.5^2\pi$

$S \approx 4.41 \text{ in.}^2$

3. Rearrange the linear inequality as if it were a linear equation.

$$6x + 3y > 9$$

$$6x - 6x + 3y > -6x + 9$$

$$y > \frac{-6x + 9}{3}$$

$$y > -2x + 3$$

4. The cross section is an isosceles triangle that has the same height as the pyramid, and its base is the diagonal of the pyramid.

$A = \frac{1}{2}bh, b = \sqrt{2s^2}$

$A = \frac{1}{2}h\sqrt{2s^2}$

$A = \frac{1}{2}(70)\sqrt{2(50)^2}$

$A \approx 2474.87 \text{ cm}^2$

5. If $x > y$, then $\frac{x}{y} > 1$; Both the statement and its converse are true.

6. They are not equal.
Counterexample:

$$x = 30°. \sin^{-1}\left(\frac{1}{2}\right) = 30°, \frac{1}{\sin\left(\frac{1}{2}\right)} \approx 114.59$$

7. Using Theorem 86-1,

$2(7 - a) = 5a$

$14 - 2a = 5a$

$-2a - 5a = -14$

$-7a = -14$

$a = 2$

8. Any line with a slope that is the opposite reciprocal of $\frac{2}{5}$ will be perpendicular to $y = \frac{2}{5}x + 7$. Sample: $y = -\frac{5}{2}x - 3$

9. Using the Heron Formula,

$A = \frac{1}{2}aP$

$a = 5\sqrt{3}$ and $P = 90$

$A = \frac{1}{2}(5\sqrt{3})(90)$

$A = 225\sqrt{3} \text{ cm}^2$

The correct answer is B.

10. Opposite angles are congruent.

$m\angle y = 57°$

Same side interior angles are supplementary.

$m\angle x + m\angle y = 180°$

$m\angle x = 180° - 57°$

$m\angle x = 123°$

Opposite angles are congruent.

$m\angle z = m\angle x$

$m\angle z = 123°$

**11.** Graph each line on the coordinate grid. It appears that the lines intersect at (36, 87).

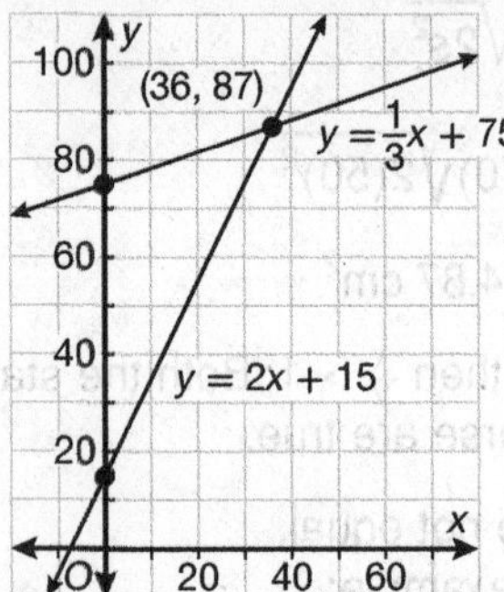


The optimum number of units and the price for Brand A is 36 units and $87.

**12.** Solve the inequality for $y$.

$4 + 2y > 8x - 4$

$2y > 8x - 4 - 4$

$y > \frac{8x - 8}{2}$

$y > 4x - 4$

Graph $y = 4x - 4$ with a dotted line and shade the area above the line.

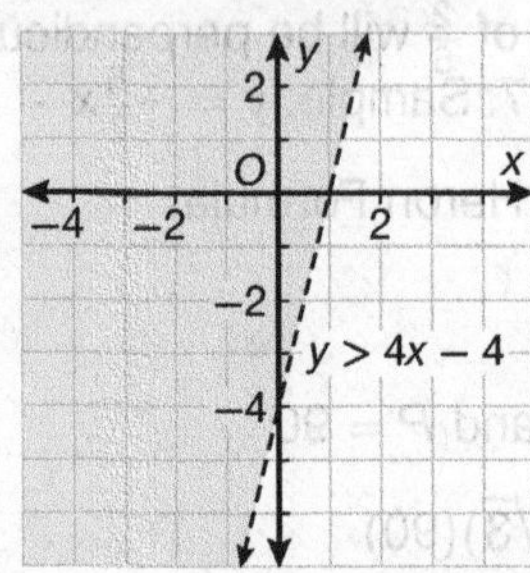


**13.** First, solve for the total exterior area of the barn.

$S = 4(bh)$

$S = 4(24)(12)$

$S = 1152 \text{ ft}^2$

From Theorem 87-1, the ratio of their areas is $1^2 : 16^2$

$\frac{\text{Area of the model}}{1152 \text{ ft}^2} = \frac{1^2}{16^2}$

Area of the model $= 4.5 \text{ ft}^2$

**14.**

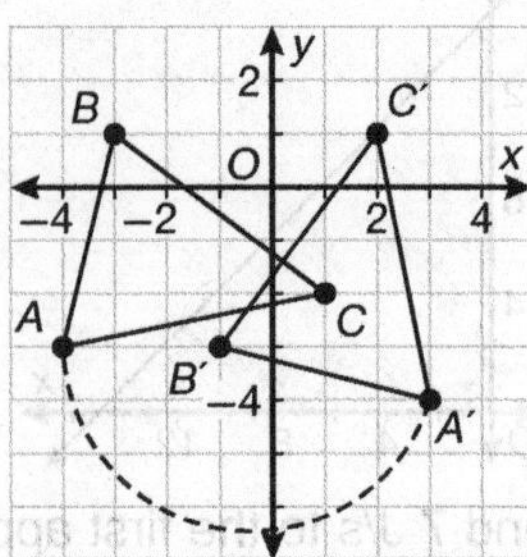


$A'(3, -4)$, $B'(-1, -3)$, $C'(2, 1)$

**15.** By Theorem 87-1, 1 : 8

**16.** The cross section is a rectangle with the base length of $2r$, and the height equal to the height of the cylinder.

$A = bh, b = 2r$

$A = 2rh$

$A = 2(5)(18)$

$A = 180 \text{ cm}^2$

**17.** Find the distance of each of the line segments.

$d_{RS} = \sqrt{(-2 - 1)^2 + (5 - 2)^2}$

$d_{RS} = \sqrt{(-3)^2 + 3^2}$

$d_{RS} = 3\sqrt{2}$

$d_{ST} = \sqrt{(9 - (-2))^2 + (4 - 5)^2}$

$d_{ST} = \sqrt{11^2 + (-1)^2}$

$d_{ST} = \sqrt{122}$

$d_{TR} = \sqrt{(1 - 9)^2 + (2 - 4)^2}$

$d_{TR} = \sqrt{(-8)^2 + (-2)^2}$

$d_{TR} = 2\sqrt{17}$

Since all sides have different lengths, it is a scalene triangle.

$P = d_{RS} + d_{ST} + d_{TR}$

$= 3\sqrt{2} + \sqrt{122} + 2\sqrt{17}$

$\approx 23.53$

**18.** Solve for the side length.

$s\sqrt{2} = 14$

$s = \frac{14\sqrt{2}}{2}$

$s = 7\sqrt{2}$

Calculate the area.

$A = \frac{bh}{2}$

$A = \frac{s^2}{2}$

$A = \frac{(7\sqrt{2})^2}{2}$

$A = 49 \text{ m}^2$

**19.** The angle of depression will not increase at a steady rate. As Jin travels up the building, the angle will get incrementally larger. Also, the distance does not increase at a steady rate; it changes according to the Pythagorean Theorem, which uses the square and the square root of numbers.

**20.** Solve the inequality for $y$.

$-3y \geq 2x - 6$

$y \leq -\frac{2}{3}x + 2$

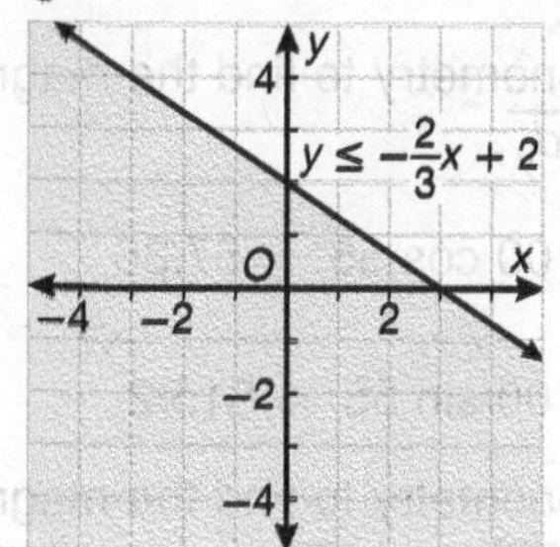


**21.** Solve the proportion for $x$.

$\frac{6}{x+2} = \frac{3}{5}$

$6(5) = 3(x + 2)$

$30 = 3x + 6$

$3x = 24$

$x = 8$

**22.** Corresponding angles in two congruent triangles are equal in measure.

$3x + 80 = 4x + 70$

$3x - 4x = 70 - 80$

$-x = -10$

$x = 10$

**23.** Using Theorem 86-1, solve for the missing measurement.

$7x = 6 \times 14$

$x = 12$

So the length of the horizontal cross piece is $7 + 12 = 19$ in.

**24.** Raquel is incorrect. The ratio of the perimeters is 2 : 3, not 4 : 9.

**25.** Expand the equation.

$$(x - h)^2 + (y - k)^2 = r^2$$

$$x^2 + y^2 - 2hx - 2ky + h^2 + y^2 - r^2 = 0$$

Complete the squares for the equation.

$$x^2 + y^2 + 2x - 6y - 15 = 0$$

$$x^2 + y^2 + 2x - 6y = 15$$

$$(x^2 + 2x + 2) + (y^2 - 6y + 9) - 2 - 9 = 15$$

$$(x + 1)^2 + (y - 3)^2 = 26$$

$$(x + 1)^2 + (y - 3)^2 = (\sqrt{26})^2$$

So, the center of the circle is$(h, k) = (-1, 3)$, and it has a radius of $\sqrt{26}$.

**26.** Using the Pythagorean Theorem,

$x^2 + 3.2^2 = (12x)^2 - (11x)^2 - 3.2^2$

$x^2 + 3.2^2 = 144x^2 - 121x^2 - 3.2^2$

$22x^2 = 2(3.2)^2$

$11x^2 = 3.2^2$

$x = \frac{3.2\sqrt{11}}{11}$

$x \approx 0.96$

Substitute $x$ into $x^2 + 3.2^2 = y^2$ and solve for $y$.

$(0.96)^2 + 3.2^2 = y^2$

$y = 11.1616$

**27.** The angle across from the 5-meter side.

**28.** The sum of the lengths is equal to or less than 20, so $2(x + y) \leq 20$.

Solve the inequality for $y$.

$2(x + y) \leq 20$

$y \leq -x + 10$

Graph $y = -x + 10$ using a solid line and shade the area under the line. Remember: lengths are always positive, so do not shade outside of Quadrant I.

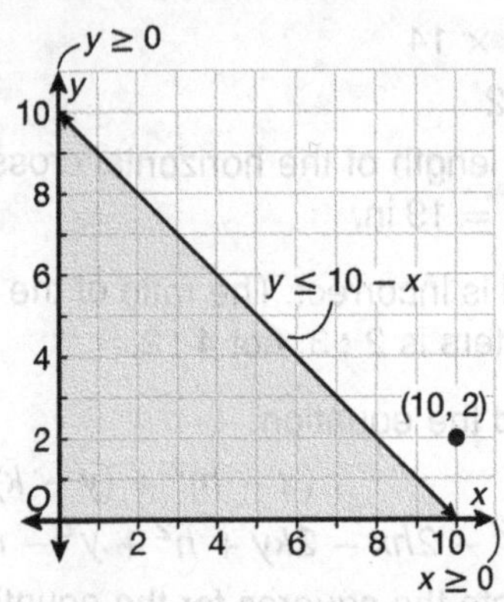


Veruka cannot build such a fence since the point (10, 2) lies outside the solution region.

**29.** First, solve for $x$.

$$(10x - 18) + (6x) + (7x + 9) + 70 = 360$$
$$23x = 299$$
$$x = 13$$

By Theorem 79-1,

$$m\angle E = \frac{(6x) + (7x + 9) - (70)}{2} = \frac{13x - 61}{2} = 54°$$

$$m\angle G = \frac{(10x - 18) + (70) - (7x + 9)}{2} = \frac{3x + 43}{2} = 41°$$

By Theorem 18-1,

$$m\angle E + m\angle F + m\angle G = 180°$$
$$m\angle F = 180° - m\angle E - m\angle G = 85°$$

**30.** Use the midpoint formula.

$$(x_M, y_M) = \left(\frac{x_P + x_Q}{2}, \frac{y_P + y_Q}{2}\right) = \left(\frac{-5 + 10}{2}, \frac{4 + 0}{2}\right) = (2.5, 2)$$

## LESSON 89

### Warm Up 89

**1.** resultant vector

**2.** $\langle 5, -3\rangle + \langle -2, 4\rangle + \langle -1, -6\rangle$
$= \langle 5 - 2 - 1, -3 + 4 - 6\rangle$
$= \langle 2, -5\rangle$

**3.** By Theorem 18-1,

$$m\angle D + m\angle E + m\angle F = 180°$$
$$m\angle D = 180° - m\angle E - m\angle F = 50°$$

Using trigonometry ratios,

$$a = \frac{6}{\tan 40°} \approx 7.15$$

Using the Pythagorean Theorem,

$$a^2 + b^2 = c^2$$
$$c = \sqrt{a^2 + b^2}$$
$$c \approx 9.33$$

### Lesson Practice 89

**a.** Use trigonometry to find the magnitude of $\overrightarrow{d_x}$ and $\overrightarrow{d_y}$.

$$\left|\overrightarrow{d_x}\right| = 100 \cos 55° \approx 57.36$$

$$\left|\overrightarrow{d_y}\right| = 100 \sin 55° \approx 81.92$$

**b.** Use trigonometry to find the magnitude of $\overrightarrow{p_x}$, $\overrightarrow{p_y}$, $\overrightarrow{q_x}$, and $\overrightarrow{q_y}$.

$$\left|\overrightarrow{p_x}\right| = 30 \cos 35° \approx 24.57$$

$$\left|\overrightarrow{p_y}\right| = 30 \sin 35° \approx 17.21$$

$$\left|\overrightarrow{q_x}\right| = 40 \cos 40° \approx 30.64$$

$$\left|\overrightarrow{q_y}\right| = 40 \sin 40° \approx 25.71$$

$$\left|\overrightarrow{p_x}\right| + \left|\overrightarrow{q_x}\right| \approx 24.57 + 30.64 \approx 55.21$$

$$\left|\overrightarrow{p_y}\right| + \left|\overrightarrow{q_y}\right| \approx 17.21 + 25.71 \approx 42.92$$

Now that we know the magnitudes of the legs of the right triangle, we can use the Pythagorean Theorem to find the magnitude of the resultant vector.

$$a^2 + b^2 = c^2$$
$$(55.21)^2 + (42.92)^2 = c^2$$
$$\sqrt{4890.27} \approx c$$
$$c = 69.93$$

Finally, use the tangent ratio to find the angle measure of the resultant vector.

$$\tan\theta = \frac{42.92}{55.21}$$

$$\tan^{-1}\frac{42.92}{55.21} = \theta$$

$$\theta \approx 38°$$

The resultant vector has a magnitude of 69.93 and makes a 38° angle with the horizontal.

**c.** Use trigonometry to find the magnitude of $\overrightarrow{u_x}$, $\overrightarrow{u_y}$, $\overrightarrow{t_x}$, $\overrightarrow{t_y}$, $\overrightarrow{v_x}$, and $\overrightarrow{v_y}$.

$$\left|\overrightarrow{u_x}\right| = 16\cos 0° = 16$$

$$\left|\overrightarrow{u_y}\right| = 16\sin 0° = 16$$

$$\left|\overrightarrow{t_x}\right| = 12\cos 80° \approx 2.08$$

$$\left|\overrightarrow{t_y}\right| = 12\sin 80° \approx 11.82$$

$$\left|\overrightarrow{v_x}\right| = 8\cos 64° \approx 3.51$$

$$\left|\overrightarrow{v_y}\right| = 8\sin 64° \approx 7.19$$

$$\left|\overrightarrow{t_x}\right| + \left|\overrightarrow{u_x}\right| + \left|\overrightarrow{v_x}\right| \approx 2.08 + 16.00 + 3.51 \approx 21.59$$

$$\left|\overrightarrow{t_y}\right| + \left|\overrightarrow{u_y}\right| + \left|\overrightarrow{v_y}\right| \approx 11.82 + 0.00 + 7.19 \approx 19.01$$

Now that we know the magnitudes of the legs of the right triangle, we can use the Pythagorean Theorem to find the magnitude of the resultant vector.

$$a^2 + b^2 = c^2$$

$$(21.59)^2 + (19.01)^2 = c^2$$

$$\sqrt{827.51} \approx c$$

$$c \approx 28.77$$

Finally, use the tangent ratio to find the angle measure of the resultant vector.

$$\tan\theta = \frac{19.01}{21.59}$$

$$\tan^{-1}\frac{19.01}{21.59} = \theta$$

$$\theta \approx 41°$$

The resultant vector has a magnitude of 28.77 and makes a 41° angle with the horizontal.

**d.** Use trigonometry to find the magnitude of $\overrightarrow{F_x}$ and $\overrightarrow{F_y}$.

$$|\overrightarrow{F_x}| = 25\cos 86° \approx 1.74 \text{ lbs}$$

$$|\overrightarrow{F_y}| = 25\sin 86° \approx 24.94 \text{ lbs}$$

## Practice 89

**1. a.** By Theorem 58-1, $m\angle B = 90°$. By the Pythagorean Theorem,

$$OD^2 = OB^2 + BD^2$$

$$OD = \sqrt{4^2 + 3^2}$$

$$OD = \sqrt{25} = 5 \text{ in.}$$

**b.** $OD = OA + AD$

$$AD = OD - OA$$

$$= 5 - 4 = 1 \text{ in.}$$

**2.** Use trigonometry to find the magnitude of $\overrightarrow{v_x}$ and $\overrightarrow{v_y}$.

$$\left|\overrightarrow{v_x}\right| = 4\cos 35° \approx 3.28$$

$$\left|\overrightarrow{v_y}\right| = 4\sin 35° \approx 2.29$$

So, $\overrightarrow{v_y} = \langle 3.28, 2.29\rangle$.

**3.** Let the chords' intersection be at $E$; By Theorem 86-1, $(AE)(BE) = (CE)(DE)$; Since $\overline{CD}$ bisects $\overline{AB}$, $AE = BE = \frac{1}{2}(AB)$, so $(CE)(DE) = \left(\frac{1}{2}AB\right)^2 = \frac{1}{4}(AB)^2$.

**4.** Choice **A** is correct.
The translation vector is $\langle 4, 1\rangle$.
So $C' = (0 + 4, 0 + 1) = (4, 1)$

**5.** Use the Pythagorean Theorem.

$$v = \sqrt{5^2 + 2^2}$$

$$v = \sqrt{29} \approx 5.39$$

So the actual speed of the kayaker is 5.39 km/h.

**6.** $(4, 5) - (0, 4) = (4, 1)$

**7.** Write the proportion.

$$\frac{KL}{CD} = \frac{JL}{BD}$$

$$KL = \frac{(CD)(JL)}{BD}$$

$$KL = \frac{(8)(9)}{6} = 12$$

**8.** $\frac{360°}{6°} = 60$ sides

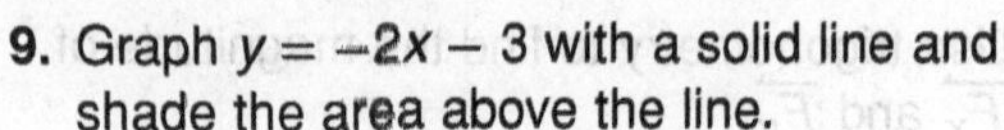



9. Graph $y = -2x - 3$ with a solid line and shade the area above the line.

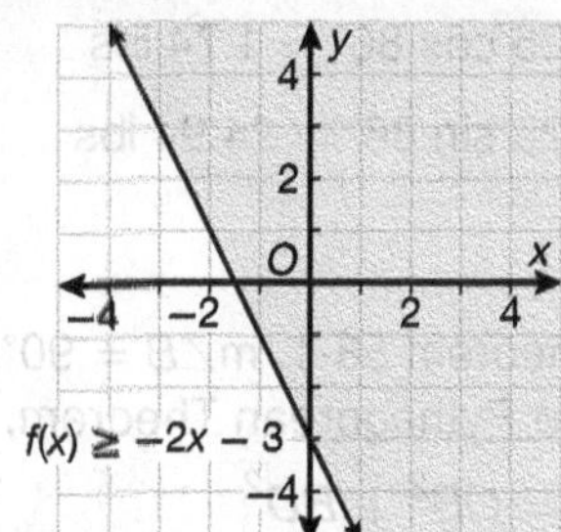


10. a. The surface area will be the total surface area of the cube minus the surface area of the hole on two of its faces.
$S = 6s^2 - 2(\pi r^2)$
$S = 6(8)^2 - 2(1^2\pi)$
$S = 384 - 2\pi \text{ in.}^2$

b. Use the formula for the lateral surface of a cylinder.
$L = 2r\pi \cdot l$
$L = 2(1)\pi \cdot 8$
$L = 16\pi \approx 50.3 \text{ in.}^2$

11. The cross section is a rectangle.
$P = 2(l + h)$
$= 2(5 + 12)$
$= 2(17) = 34$ inches

12. By Theorem 87-1, choice **B** is true.

13. By Theorem 50-1,
$\frac{x}{2} = \frac{9}{x}$
$x^2 = 18$
$x \approx 4.2$

14. The perpendicular bisector of each segment needs to be found. The midpoints of the segments are (2, −5), (−4, −5), and (0, −2). Perpendicular lines can be found through the midpoints using the method learned in Lesson 37.
The line perpendicular to the segment with midpoint (0, −2) is $x = 0$.
The line perpendicular to the segment with midpoint (2, −5) is $y = -\frac{1}{3}(4x + 7)$.

To find the circumcenter, solve the system of equations.
$x = 0$
$y = -\frac{1}{3}(4x + 7)$
$y = -\frac{7}{3}$
Finally, substitute this value of $y$ into one of the equations above to find $x$.
The coordinate of the circumcenter is $(0, 2.\overline{3})$.

15. $3x$, $(\theta + 180°)$

16. The sum if the vector is the opposite vertex of the origin in the parallelogram:

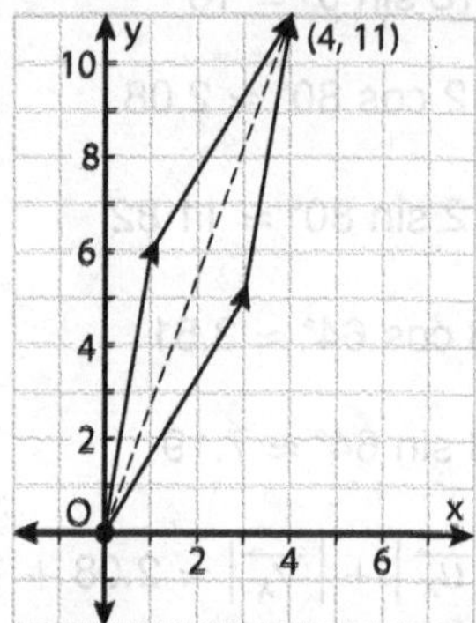


$\langle 3, 5\rangle + \langle 1, 6\rangle = \langle 4, 11\rangle$

17. The pattern for triangular number seems to be $t_n = \frac{n(n+1)}{2}$.
$t_{15} = \frac{15(15+1)}{2} = \frac{15(16)}{2} = 120$ $\quad t_{20} = \frac{20(20+1)}{2} = \frac{20(21)}{2} = 210$

18. The cargo ship can carry at most 120,000 kilograms of items. The total weight of rice and flour is $782x + 528y$, so the inequality for the total weight of items that the cargo ship can carry is $782x + 528y \leq 120{,}000$.

19. When the hour hand points to 7, it makes a 60° angle with the horizontal. Using trigonometry ratios, $|\overrightarrow{h_x}| = 5 \cos 60° = 2.5$.

20. The hypotenuse of the triangle is 20 inches, so each leg is $\frac{20}{\sqrt{2}} = 10\sqrt{2}$ inches
$A = \frac{1}{2}bh$
$= \frac{1}{2}(10\sqrt{2})^2$

$= 100 \text{ in.}^2$

The perimeter is

$P = 2(10\sqrt{2}) + 20$

$= 20(1 + \sqrt{2})$

$\approx 48.28$ in.

21. By Theorem 79-1, the measure of the exterior to a circle made by one tangent and one secant is half of the difference between the two arc measures.

$m\angle E = \frac{1}{2}(112° - 54°)$

$= \frac{1}{2}(58°) = 29°$

22. Since $AB$ is the diameter, 100 cm is half the circle's circumference, so the total circumference is 200 cm.

23. By Theorem 87-1, the ratio of the perimeters is the square root of the ratio of their areas.

$\sqrt{76} : \sqrt{931}$

$\sqrt{4}\sqrt{19} : \sqrt{49}\sqrt{19}$

$2 : 7$

24. No; One pair of opposite sides is not congruent.

25. reduction or contraction; scale factor of $\frac{1}{3}$.

26. Using tangent ratios,

$\tan^{-1} \theta = \frac{1}{16}$ $\quad$ $\tan^{-1} \theta = \frac{1}{12}$

$\theta \approx 4°$ $\quad$ $\theta \approx 5°$

27. The student reversed the components. The correct answer is $\langle a \cos \theta, a \sin \theta \rangle$.

28. By the properties of a 30°-60°-90° triangle from Lesson 56, the lengths of the two legs are $\frac{125}{2}$ and $\frac{125\sqrt{3}}{2}$.

29. By Theorem 40-1, since $9 < 10 < 11$, $m\angle z < m\angle y < m\angle x$.

30. Solve the inequality for $y$.

$4x + 3 < 2y - 5$

$2y > 4x + 3 + 5$

$y > \frac{4x + 8}{2}$

$y > 2x + 4$

Graph $y = 2x + 4$ with a dotted line, and shade the area above the line.

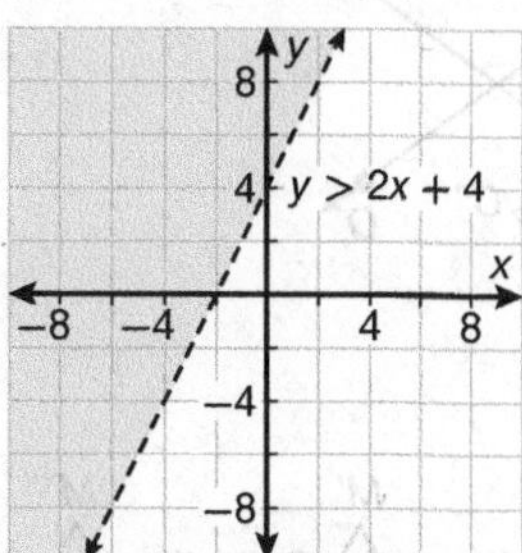


## LESSON 90

### Warm Up 90

1. dilation
2. 

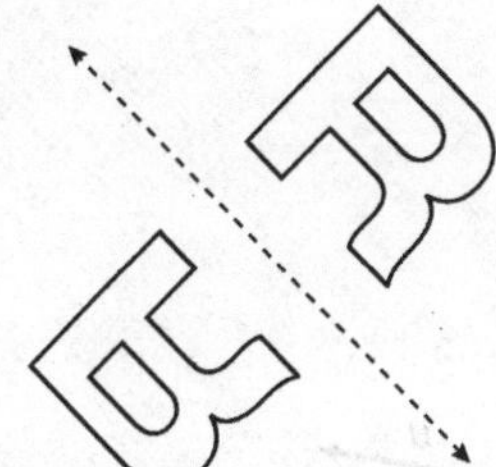

3. the original figure

### Lesson Practice 90

a. 

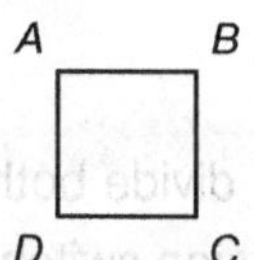


D″ C″ D′ C′

A″ B″ A′ B′

$\vec{v}$

b. 

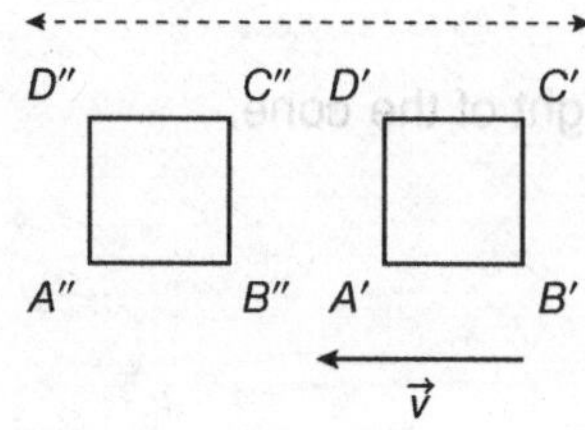

c.

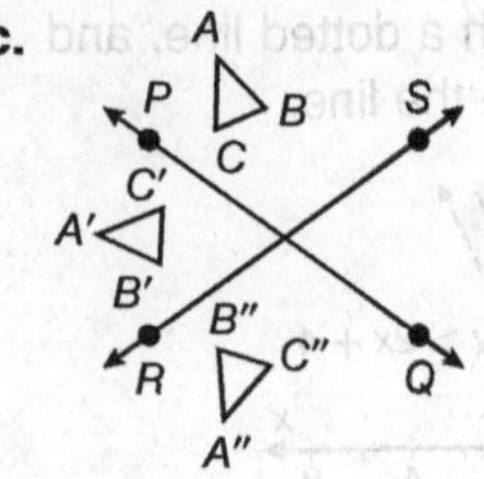


d.

e. a rotation of 220°

## Practice 90

1. Choice **A** is correct.

2.

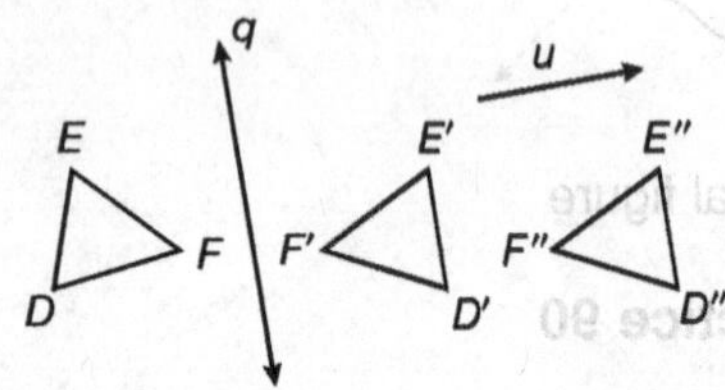


3. $27x - 3y < 9$

$-3y < 9 - 27x$, divide both sides by $-3$

$y > 9x - 3$, the sign switches because of the division by $-3$

4. Let $h$ be the height of the cone.

$$5^2 + h^2 = 13^2$$
$$25 + h^2 = 169$$
$$h^2 = 144$$
$$h = 12$$
$$V = \frac{1}{3}\pi r^2 h$$
$$V = \frac{1}{3}\pi(5^2)(12) = 100\pi = 314.16 \text{ cm}^2$$

5. $(x - a)^2 + (y - b)^2 = r^2$

$$(2 - 4)^2 + (1 - 6)^2 = r^2$$
$$4 + 25 = r^2$$
$$r = \sqrt{29}$$
$$A = \pi r^2 = \pi(\sqrt{29})^2 = 29\pi$$

6. $MQ = NQ = NP - PQ$

$$= 51.7 - 24.8$$
$$= 26.9 \text{ cm}$$

7. $\sin\theta = \frac{60}{120}$

$$\theta = 30°$$

8. $A = (5 \times 5) + \frac{6\left(\frac{5}{2}\right)}{2} = 25 + \frac{30}{4} = 32.5 \text{ ft}^2$

9. Sample: $n = 4$

$4(4) - 1 = 15$

10. Represent the resultant vector with $v$.

$$|\langle 0,60\rangle|^2 + |\langle 22,0\rangle|^2 = |\vec{x}|^2$$
$$60^2 + 22^2 = |\vec{x}|^2$$
$$3600 + 484 = |\vec{x}|^2$$
$$63.91 = x$$

The magnitude of the sailboat's speed is 63.91 ft/sec.

Represent the angle of the sailboat's course with $\theta$.

$$\theta = \tan^{-1}\left(\frac{60}{22}\right)$$
$$\theta = 69.86$$

The angle of the sailboat's course is 69.86° north of east.

11. $AC(1 + \sqrt{3}) = (3\sqrt{3} - 5)(3 + \sqrt{3})$

$$AC(1 + \sqrt{3}) = 9\sqrt{3} + 9 - 15 - 5\sqrt{3}$$
$$AC(1 + \sqrt{3}) = 4\sqrt{3} - 6$$
$$AC(1 + \sqrt{3}) = 4\sqrt{3} - 6$$
$$AC = \frac{4\sqrt{3} - 6}{1 + \sqrt{3}}$$
$$AC = \frac{4\sqrt{3} - 6}{1 + \sqrt{3}} \cdot \frac{1 - \sqrt{3}}{1 - \sqrt{3}}$$
$$AC = \frac{4\sqrt{3} - 12 - 6 + 6\sqrt{3}}{1 - 3}$$
$$AC = \frac{10\sqrt{3} - 18}{-2}$$
$$AC = 9 - 5\sqrt{3}$$

12. $V = \frac{4}{3}\pi r^3 = \frac{4}{3}\pi\left(\frac{d}{2}\right)^3 = \frac{4}{3}\pi\left(\frac{d^3}{8}\right) = \frac{1}{6}\pi d^3$

**13.** $\frac{AB}{DE} = \frac{BC}{EF}$

$\frac{15}{20} = \frac{BC}{16}$

$BC = \frac{15 \cdot 16}{20}$

$BC = 12$

**14.** $\angle JKL = 180° - 114° = 66°$

The other two interior angles must add up to 180° because all interior angles of a triangle add up to 180°. If either of the other angles was 114°, the remaining angle would be 0°. Thus, the measure of the external angle at vertex *K* must be larger than either of the two internal angles.

**15.** By the Triangle Midsegment Theorem,

$MP = \frac{1}{2}GH$

$GH = 2(15)$

$GH = 30$

$30 = 4x - 6$

$36 = 4x$

$x = 9$

**16.** $8 + 8 + 8 = 24$

$\frac{2}{5} = \frac{24}{P}$

$P = \frac{(24)(5)}{2}$

$P = 60$ inches

Let *s* be the side length of the larger triangle.

$\frac{2}{5} = \frac{8}{s}$

$s = \frac{(8)(5)}{2}$

$s = 20$

Let *h* be the height of the larger triangle.

$10^2 + h^2 = 20^2$

$100 + h^2 = 400$

$h^2 = 300$

$h = 17.3$

$A = \frac{(20)(17.3)}{2} = 173.2 \text{ in.}^2$

**17.** No, instead of reflecting across *x*, Quan translated along *y*. Then instead of reflecting across *y*, a translation along *x* was performed.

**18.** $7 - a = a - 2$

$7 = 2a - 2$

$a = 4.5$

**19.**



**20.** $\cos(180° - \theta) = \frac{x_1}{x}$

$x_1 = x\cos(180° - \theta)$

$\sin(180° - \theta) = \frac{y_1}{x}$

$y_1 = x\sin(180° - \theta)$

$\langle x\cos(180° - \theta), x\sin(180° - \theta)\rangle$

**21.** reflection and translation

**22.** $\sqrt{5 \cdot 8} = \sqrt{40} = \sqrt{4}\sqrt{10} = 2\sqrt{10}$

**23.** **a.** If it is evening, then the time is 9 p.m.

**b.** The statement is true; the converse is not true.

**24.** Since the quadrilateral *WXYZ* is a rectangle, the diagonals bisect each other. The diagonals are also equal, so $WK = KX = 12.6$ in.

**25.** They share two common tangents.

**26.** $x = \frac{1}{2}(12° + 189°) = 100.5°$

**27.** The components −3 and 4 create a right triangle with its hypotenuse $= \sqrt{(-3)^2 + 4^2} = 5$.

$\cos\theta = \frac{4}{5}$

$\theta \approx 37°$

$\cos\theta = \frac{-3}{5}$

$\theta = 127°$

The possible angle measures are 127°, for the vector ⟨−3,4⟩, and 32°, for the vector ⟨4,−3⟩ since the vector is in Q IV and $360° - 37° = 323°$.

28. Yes, they are parallel, since the transversals divide the segments proportionally.

29. $1.00x + 1.50y \geq 650$

$1.50y \geq 650 - 1.00x$

$y \geq 650 \div \frac{3}{2} - x \div \frac{3}{2}$

$y \geq -\frac{2}{3}x + \frac{1300}{3}$

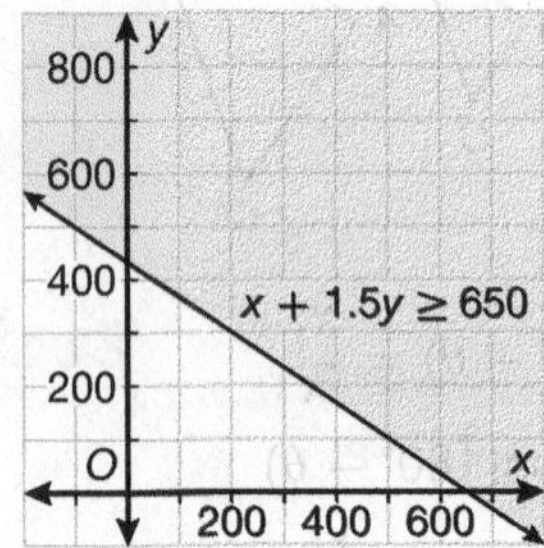


30.

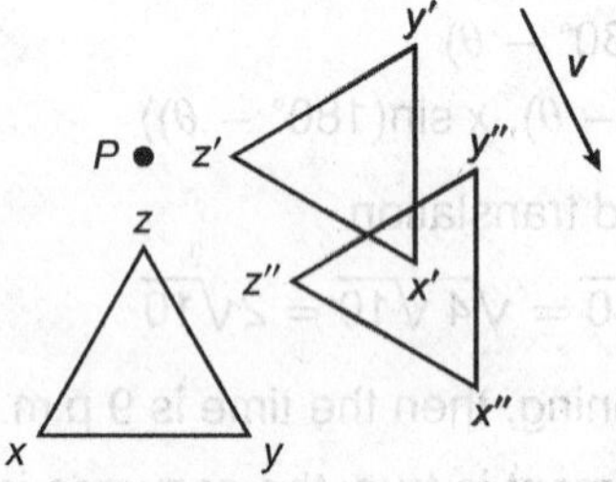


## INVESTIGATION 9

1. yes;

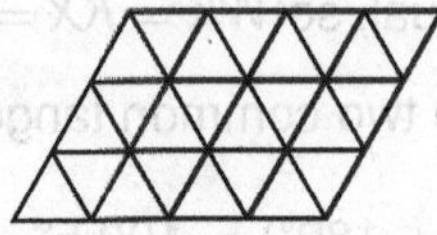

2. 6 triangles; each angle measure = 60°; total angle measure = 360°.

3. It will tessellate if its interior angle measure is a divisor of 360°.

4. $\frac{180(4-2)^\circ}{4} = 90^\circ; \frac{180(5-2)^\circ}{5} = 108^\circ;$

$\frac{180(6-2)^\circ}{6} = 120^\circ; \frac{180(7-2)^\circ}{7} = 128.57^\circ$

5. The square and the hexagon can tessellate.

6. square tessellation:

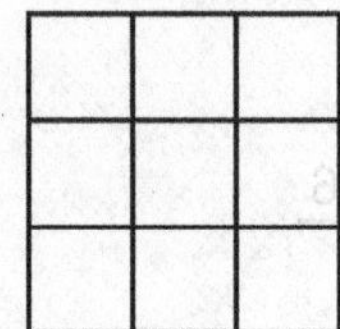

regular hexagonal tessellation:

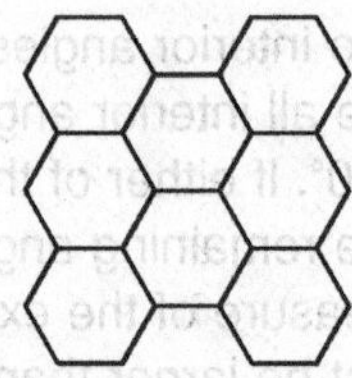

7. No; Polygons with more than 8 sides have interior angle measures greater than 120°. The only other divisor of 360° is 180° but a polygon cannot have interior angles that measure180°.

8. tessellation of regular/equiangular triangles; tessellation of regular quadrilaterals (squares); tessellation of regular hexagons

9. 3; 360°

10.

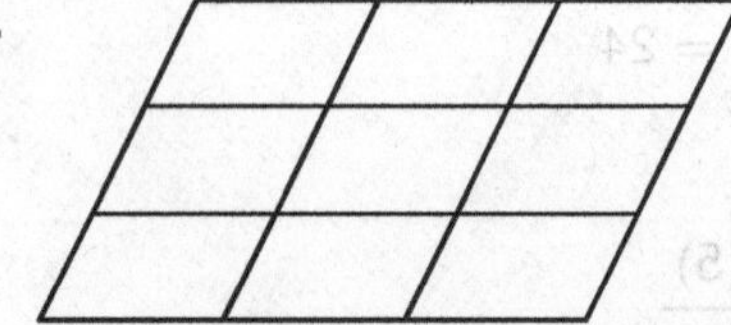

11. Yes; The vertex of the tessellation contains one of each of the parallelogram's angles. Since the parallelogram is equilateral, its angles sum to 360°.

12. Yes; The sum of the angles of any quadrilateral is 360°.

13. Tesselation C; The tessellation consists of congruent regular hexagons and congruent equilateral triangles, and there are two hexagons and two triangles at each vertex.

14. Tesselations B and C; 90° and 180°

15. Tesselations A and C

## Investigation 9 Practice

**a.** Yes, since the sum of its angles is 360°.

**b.**

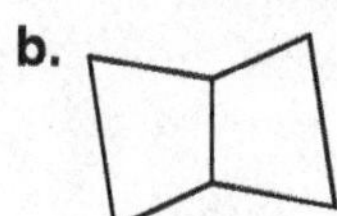

**c.**

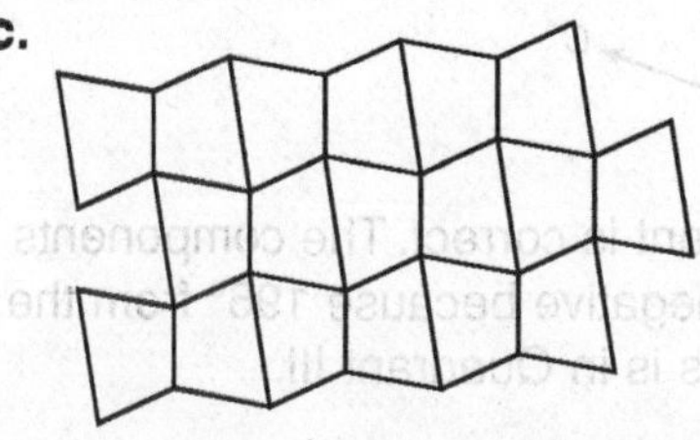

**d.** Yes, it has rotational symmetry at 180° rotation.

**e.** no

## LESSON 91

### Warm Up 91

**1.** Parallel vectors

**2.** $\cos \theta = \frac{8}{14}$

$\theta = \cos^{-1} \frac{8}{14} \approx 55°$

**3.**

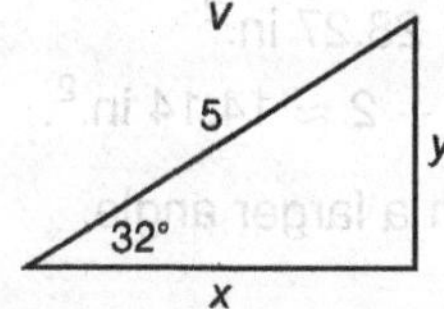


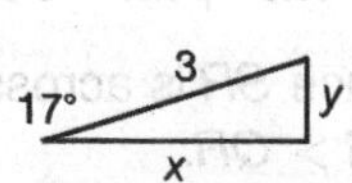


$x = 5 \cos 32°$ $\quad$ $x = 3 \cos 17°$

$x \approx 4.24$ $\quad$ $x \approx 2.87$

$R_x \approx 4.24 + 2.87 \approx 7.11$

$y = 5 \sin 32°$ $\quad$ $y = 3 \sin 17°$

$y \approx 2.65$ $\quad$ $y \approx 0.88$

$R_y \approx 2.65 + 0.877 \approx 3.53$

### Lesson Practice 91

**a.** $\sin^2 \theta + \cos^2 \theta = 1$

$0.67 + \cos^2 \theta = 1$

$\cos^2 \theta = 0.33$

$\cos \theta = \sqrt{0.33}$

$\cos \theta \approx 0.57$

**b.** $\tan \theta = \frac{\sin \theta}{\cos \theta}$

$\tan \theta = \frac{\sqrt{1 - \cos^2 \theta}}{\cos \theta}$

$(\tan \theta)^2 = \left(\frac{\sqrt{1 - \cos^2 \theta}}{\cos \theta}\right)^2$

$\tan^2 \theta = \frac{1 - \cos^2 \theta}{\cos^2 \theta}$

$\tan^2 \theta \cos^2 \theta = 1 - \cos^2 \theta$

$\tan^2 \theta \cos^2 \theta + \cos^2 \theta = 1$

$\cos^2 \theta (\tan^2 \theta + 1) = 1$

$\cos^2 \theta = \frac{1}{\tan^2 \theta + 1}$

$\cos \theta = \frac{1}{\sqrt{1 + \tan^2 \theta}}$

**c.** $\sin \theta = \frac{1}{2}$

$\left(\frac{1}{2}\right)^2 + \cos^2 \theta = 1$

$\cos^2 \theta = \frac{3}{4}$

$\cos \theta = \frac{\sqrt{3}}{2} \approx 0.87$

### Practice 91

**1.**

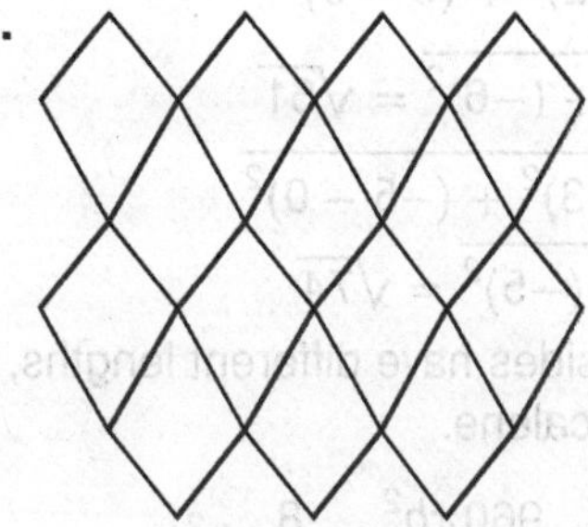

**2.** Graph both functions and determine where they intersect. 0°, 180°, ...

**3.**

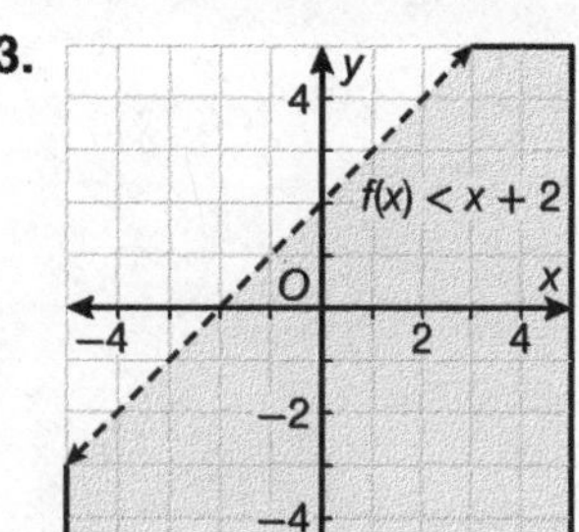

**4.** $16 - 4 = 12$ ft/s

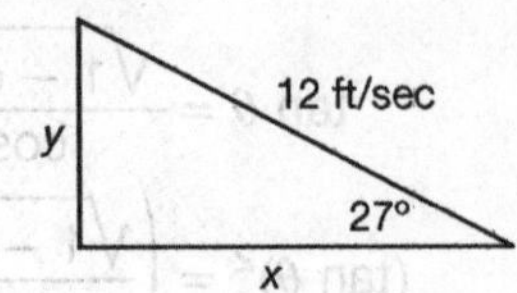


Vertical: $y = 12 \sin 27° \approx 5.45$ ft/s
Horizontal: $x = 12 \cos 27° \approx 10.69$ ft/s

**5.**

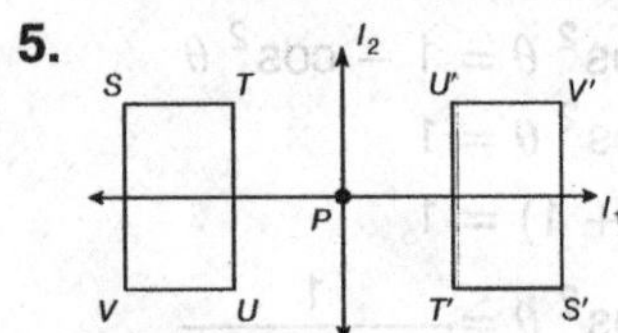


**6.** $\frac{360°}{15°} = 24$ sides

**7.** $S = 4\pi r^2 = 4\pi\left(\frac{4}{\sqrt{\pi}}\right)^2$

$= 4\pi\left(\frac{16}{\pi}\right) = 4(16) = 64 \text{ cm}^2$

**8.** Label points $A(2, 6)$, $B(4, -5)$, and $C(-3, 0)$.

$d_{AB} = \sqrt{(4-2)^2 + (-5-6)^2}$
$= \sqrt{(2)^2 + (-11)^2}$
$= \sqrt{125}$

$d_{AC} = \sqrt{(-3-2)^2 + (0-6)^2}$
$= \sqrt{(-5)^2 + (-6)^2} = \sqrt{61}$

$d_{BC} = \sqrt{(4 - -3)^2 + (-5-0)^2}$
$= \sqrt{(7)^2 + (-5)^2} = \sqrt{74}$

Since all three sides have different lengths, the triangle is scalene.

**9.** $\frac{60°}{360°}(\pi(4b)^2) = \frac{960\pi b^2}{360} = \frac{8}{3}\pi b^2$

**10.** Hypotenuse: $2(68) = 136$
Longer leg: $68\sqrt{3}$

**11.**

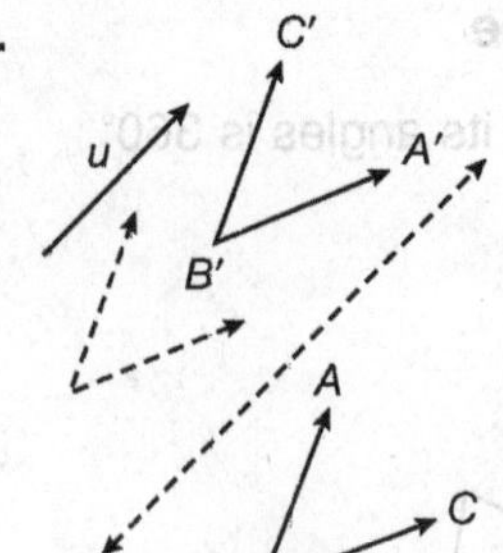


**12.** Yes, the student is correct. The components will both be negative because 196° from the positive *x*-axis is in Quadrant III.

**13.** The point is made when the plane cuts through the outermost tip of the solid. On a sphere, this is any tangent plane. On a cube, this is at one of the eight vertices. On a cylinder, this is a tipped plane tangent to the edge of one circular base.

**14.** $(3 - x)(6 - x) = 2(6 - 2x)$
$18 - 9x + x^2 = 12 - 4x$
$x^2 - 5x + 6 = 0$
$(x - 3)(x - 2) = 0$
$x = 2$; $x \neq 3$ because $3 - 3 = 0$ and the side length cannot be 0.

**15.** 2 : 1

**16.** $S = 4\pi r^2 = 4\pi(1.5)^2 \approx 28.27 \text{ in.}^2$
So each patch is $28.27 \div 2 \approx 14.14 \text{ in.}^2$.

**17.** Since $SR$ is across from a larger angle, $SR > QR$.

**18.** $S = L + B$
$B = 6^2 = 36 \text{ ft}^2$
$S = \frac{1}{2}Pl + 36$
$l^2 = 3^2 + 4^2$
$l = 5$
$S = \frac{1}{2}(4)(6)(5) + 36$
$S = 96 \text{ ft}^2$

19. Sample:

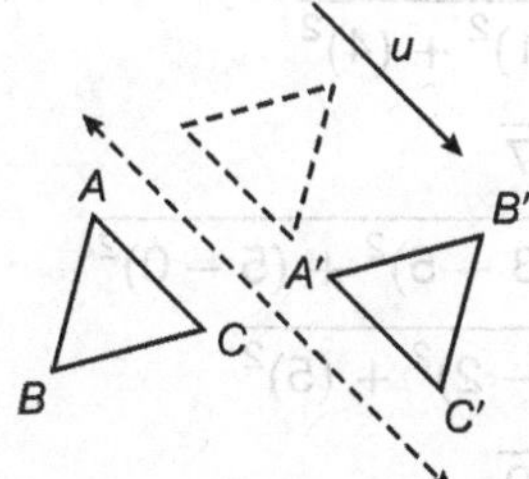


20. Choice **C** is not true, so it is the correct choice.

21. $V = Bh = \pi(3^2)(12) \approx 339 \text{ in.}^3$

22. $\pi r^2 = lw$

$\pi r^2 = (31.4)(2r)$

$r \approx 20 \text{ cm}$

23.

| | |
|---|---|
| $A = 2x + 28$, $l = 3x - 2$, $w = 2x + 1$ | Given |
| $lw = A$ | Area of rectangles |
| $(3x - 2)(2x + 1) = 2x + 28$ | Substitution Property of Equality |
| $6x^2 - x - 2 = 2x + 28$ | Simplify |
| $6x^2 - 3x - 30 = 0$ | Subtraction Property of Equality |
| $(3x + 6)(2x - 5) = 0$ | Factor |
| $x = \frac{5}{2}, x = -2$ | Solve for $x$ |
| $x = \frac{5}{2}$ | $x = -2$ gives a negative length |

24. Since $\tan\theta = \frac{\sqrt{1 - \cos^2\theta}}{\cos\theta}$,

$$\tan^2\theta = \left(\frac{\sqrt{1 - \cos^2\theta}}{\cos\theta}\right)^2 = \frac{1 - \cos^2\theta}{\cos^2\theta}$$

25. The diagonals of the square are 20 inches in length.

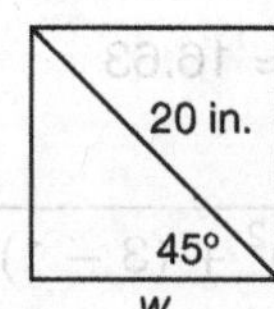


$\frac{w}{1} = \frac{20}{\sqrt{2}}$

$\sqrt{2}w = 20$

$w \approx 14.1 \text{ inches}$

26. $d = |6 - -5| = 11$

27. $\cos^2\theta = 3\sin^2\theta$

$1 = \frac{3\sin^2\theta}{\cos^2\theta}$

$\frac{1}{3} = \frac{\sin^2\theta}{\cos^2\theta}$

$\frac{1}{3} = \tan^2\theta$

$\tan\theta = \frac{1}{\sqrt{3}}$

$\theta = 30°$

28. $\frac{2.25}{6} = \frac{20.25}{x}$

$(2.25)(x) = (6)(20.25)$

$2.25x = 121.5$

$x = 54 \text{ ft}$

29. $200^2 + 500^2 = x^2$

$290{,}000 = x^2$

$x = 538.5 \text{ lb}$

$\tan x = \frac{200}{500}$

$x = \tan^{-1}\frac{200}{500} \approx 21.8°$

30. Desi made an error in step 3. He needed to use a common denominator and incorrectly multiplied with a binomial.

## LESSON 92

### Warm Up 92

1. sides; angles
2. rectangle
3. A trapezoid has exactly one pair of parallel sides. Choice **D** is correct.

### Lesson Practice 92

a. $m_{CD} = \frac{0 - 4}{1 - -1} = \frac{-4}{2} = -2$

$m_{DE} = \frac{4 - 1}{-1 - 3} = \frac{3}{-4} = -\frac{3}{4}$

$m_{EF} = \frac{1 - -3}{3 - 5} = \frac{4}{-2} = -2$

$m_{CF} = \frac{-3 - 0}{5 - 1} = \frac{-3}{4}$

The slope of $\overline{CD} = -2$, of $\overline{DE} = -\frac{3}{4}$, of $\overline{EF} = -2$, and of $\overline{CF} = -\frac{3}{4}$; $\overline{CD} \parallel \overline{EF}$ and $\overline{DE} \parallel \overline{CF}$, so *CDEF* is a parallelogram.

**b.** $m_{PQ} = \frac{7-1}{-4-5} = \frac{6}{-9} = -\frac{2}{3}$

$m_{QR} = \frac{-1-1}{2-5} = \frac{-2}{-3} = \frac{2}{3}$

$m_{RS} = \frac{-1-3}{2--4} = \frac{-4}{6} = -\frac{2}{3}$

$m_{PS} = \frac{3-7}{-4--4} = \frac{-4}{0} = \varnothing$

The slope of $\overline{PQ} = -\frac{2}{3}$, of $\overline{QR} = \frac{2}{3}$, of $\overline{RS} = -\frac{2}{3}$, and of $\overline{PS}$ is undefined; $\overline{PQ} \parallel \overline{RS}$ but $\overline{QR} \nparallel \overline{QS}$, so *PQRS* is a trapezoid.

**c.** $d_{JK} = \sqrt{(5-3)^2 + (4-5)^2}$

$= \sqrt{(2)^2 + (-1)^2}$

$= \sqrt{5}$

$d_{ST} = \sqrt{(7-5)^2 + (2-3)^2}$

$= \sqrt{(2)^2 + (-1)^2}$

$= \sqrt{5}$

$d_{KL} = \sqrt{(5-5)^2 + (4-0)^2}$

$= \sqrt{(0)^2 + (4)^2}$

$= 4$

$d_{TU} = \sqrt{(7-7)^2 + (2--2)^2}$

$= \sqrt{(0)^2 + (4)^2}$

$= 4$

$d_{LM} = \sqrt{(5-2)^2 + (0-1)^2}$

$= \sqrt{(3)^2 + (-1)^2}$

$= \sqrt{10}$

$d_{UV} = \sqrt{(7-4)^2 + (-2--1)^2}$

$= \sqrt{(3)^2 + (-1)^2}$

$= \sqrt{10}$

$d_{JM} = \sqrt{(3-2)^2 + (5-1)^2}$

$= \sqrt{(1)^2 + (4)^2}$

$= \sqrt{17}$

$d_{SV} = \sqrt{(5-4)^2 + (3--1)^2}$

$= \sqrt{(1)^2 + (4)^2}$

$= \sqrt{17}$

$d_{JL} = \sqrt{(3-5)^2 + (5-0)^2}$

$= \sqrt{(-2)^2 + (5)^2}$

$= \sqrt{29}$

$d_{SU} = \sqrt{(5-7)^2 + (3--2)^2}$

$= \sqrt{(-2)^2 + (5)^2}$

$= \sqrt{29}$

$JK = \sqrt{5}$, $ST = \sqrt{5}$, $KL = 4$, $TU = 4$, $LM = \sqrt{10}$, $UV = \sqrt{10}$, and $JM = \sqrt{17}$, $SV = \sqrt{17}$, $JL = \sqrt{29}$, and $SU = \sqrt{29}$, so $JKLM \cong STUV$

**d.** $m_{GH} = \frac{5-2}{8-7} = \frac{3}{1} = 3$

$m_{HJ} = \frac{2-2}{7-2} = \frac{0}{5} = 0$

$m_{JK} = \frac{8-2}{4-2} = \frac{6}{2} = 3$

$m_{GK} = \frac{5-8}{8-4} = \frac{-3}{4}$

The slope of $\overline{GH} = 3$, of $\overline{HJ} = 0$, of $\overline{JK} = 3$, and of $\overline{GK} = -\frac{3}{4}$; $\overline{GH} \parallel \overline{JK}$ but $\overline{HJ} \nparallel \overline{GK}$, so *GHJK* is a trapezoid.

## Practice 92

**1.** $E(1, 5) \longrightarrow E'(1-3, 5-3) = E'(-2, 2)$
$F(4, 3) \longrightarrow F'(4-3, 3-3) = F'(1, 0)$
Choice **C** is correct.

**2.**

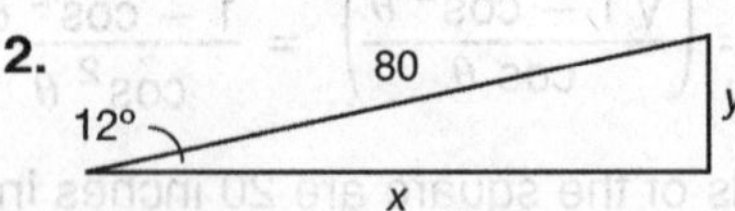


$x = 80 \cos 12° \approx 78.25$
$y = 80 \sin 12° \approx 16.63$
$\langle 78.25, 16.63 \rangle$

**3.** $d_{AB} = \sqrt{(5-3)^2 + (3-1)^2}$

$= \sqrt{(2)^2 + (2)^2}$

$= \sqrt{8} = 2\sqrt{2}$

$d_{EF} = \sqrt{(-3 - -1)^2 + (5 - 3)^2}$
$= \sqrt{(-2)^2 + (2)^2}$
$= \sqrt{8} = 2\sqrt{2}$

$d_{BC} = \sqrt{(5 - 2)^2 + (3 - 3)^2}$
$= \sqrt{(3)^2 + (0)^2}$
$= 3$

$d_{FG} = \sqrt{(-3 - -3)^2 + (5 - 2)^2}$
$= \sqrt{(0)^2 + (3)^2}$
$= 3$

$d_{CD} = \sqrt{(2 - 1)^2 + (3 - 2)^2}$
$= \sqrt{(1)^2 + (1)^2}$
$= \sqrt{2}$

$d_{GH} = \sqrt{(-3 - -2)^2 + (2 - 1)^2}$
$= \sqrt{(-1)^2 + (1)^2}$
$= \sqrt{2}$

$d_{AD} = \sqrt{(3 - 1)^2 + (1 - 2)^2}$
$= \sqrt{(2)^2 + (-1)^2}$
$= \sqrt{5}$

$d_{EH} = \sqrt{(-1 - -2)^2 + (3 - 1)^2}$
$= \sqrt{(1)^2 + (2)^2}$
$= \sqrt{5}$

$m_{AB} = \frac{3 - 1}{5 - 3} = \frac{2}{2} = 1$

$m_{BC} = \frac{3 - 3}{5 - 2} = \frac{0}{3} = 0$

$m_{CD} = \frac{3 - 2}{2 - 1} = \frac{1}{1} = 1$

$m_{AD} = \frac{1 - 2}{3 - 1} = \frac{-1}{2}$

$m_{EF} = \frac{3 - 5}{-1 - -3} = \frac{-2}{2} = -1$

$m_{FG} = \frac{5 - 2}{-3 - -3} = \frac{3}{0} = \varnothing$

$m_{GH} = \frac{2 - 1}{-3 - -2} = \frac{1}{-1} = -1$

$m_{EH} = \frac{3 - 1}{-1 - -2} = \frac{2}{1} = 2$

$AB = 2\sqrt{2} = EF$, $BC = 3 = FG$, $CD = \sqrt{2} = GH$, and $AD = \sqrt{5} = EH$. Slopes of $\overline{AB}$, $\overline{BC}$, $\overline{CD}$, and $\overline{AD}$ are 1, 0, 1, and $-\frac{1}{2}$, while slopes of $\overline{EF}$, $\overline{FG}$, $\overline{GH}$, and $\overline{EH}$ are $-1$, undefined, $-1$, and 2. Therefore, $ABCD \cong EFGH$

4. $\overline{AE}$ is opposite a 60° angle, $\overline{CD}$ is opposite a 26° angle, and $\overline{ED}$ is opposite a 94° angle. Side $\overline{AB}$ is opposite a 60° angle and side $\overline{BC}$ is opposite a 44° angle; $60 + 44 = 104$. $104 > 94 > 60 > 26$. So, $\overline{AC}$ is the longest side.

5. $y = 0.2x - 4$ is the same as $y = \frac{1}{5}x - 4$. Answers may vary, but the slopes should be $-5$ for the line perpendicular or 0.2 for the line parallel.

   Sample: $y = -5x + 3$ and $y = 0.2x$

6. For $n = 3$, the line is divided into 2 segments.

   For $n = 4$, the line is divided into 3 segments.

   The pattern is $n - 1$.

7. $33° = \frac{1}{2}(112° - m\widehat{BF})$

   $66° = 112° - m\widehat{BF}$; $m\widehat{BF} = 46°$

   $33° = \frac{1}{2}(86° - m\widehat{CE})$

   $66° = 86° - m\widehat{CE}$; $m\widehat{CE} = 20°$

8. $m_{WX} = \frac{3 - 2}{0 - 3} = \frac{1}{-3}$

   $m_{XY} = \frac{2 - -3}{3 - -2} = \frac{5}{5} = 1$

   $m_{YZ} = \frac{-3 - -2}{-2 - -5} = \frac{-1}{3}$

   $m_{WZ} = \frac{3 - -2}{0 - -5} = \frac{5}{5} = 1$

   The slopes of $WX$, $XY$, $YZ$, and $WZ$ are $-\frac{1}{3}$, 1, $-\frac{1}{3}$, and 1; $\overline{WX} \parallel \overline{YZ}$ and $\overline{XY} \parallel \overline{WZ}$, so $WXYZ$ is a parallelogram.

9. Line $l$ is not a tangent, because this would contradict Theorem 58-2. Since it does intersect $\odot C$, it does so at two points, one of which is $P$. So, the other is $Q$. Since $\overline{CP} \cong \overline{CQ}$, $\triangle CPQ$ is isosceles with base angles $\angle CPQ$ and $\angle CQP$. These angles are

congruent by the Isosceles Triangle Theorem, and since a triangle can have at most one right or one obtuse angle, $\angle CPQ$ and $\angle CQP$ are congruent acute angles.

**10.** $m_{PQ} = \frac{6-1}{-3-(-4)} = \frac{5}{1} = 5$

$m_{QR} = \frac{1-1}{-4-1} = \frac{0}{-5} = 0$

$m_{RS} = \frac{6-1}{3-1} = \frac{5}{2}$

$m_{PS} = \frac{6-6}{-3-3} = \frac{0}{-6} = 0$

The slopes of $\overline{PQ}$, $\overline{QR}$, $\overline{RS}$, and $\overline{PS}$ are 5, 0, $\frac{5}{2}$, and 0. $\overline{QR} \parallel \overline{PS}$ but $\overline{PQ} \nparallel \overline{RS}$, so $PQRS$ is a trapezoid.

**11.** The boat sailed out to $\langle 3+1, 4+5\rangle = \langle 4, 9\rangle$. To go directly back to its starting point, it would follow the vector $\langle -4, -9\rangle$.

**12.** Sample:

**13.**

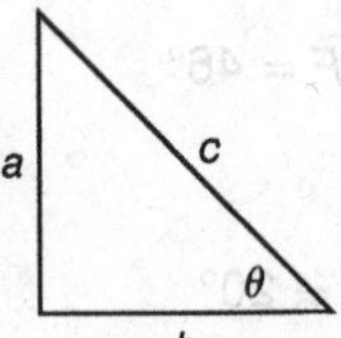


$$\frac{b}{c} = \frac{1}{\sqrt{1+\left(\frac{a}{b}\right)^2}} = \frac{1}{\sqrt{\frac{b^2}{b^2}+\frac{a^2}{b^2}}}$$

$$= \frac{1}{\sqrt{\frac{c^2}{b^2}}} = \frac{1}{\frac{c}{b}} = \frac{b}{c}$$

**14.** $10 = \frac{2}{3}AF$

$AF = 15$

$GF = 15 - 10 = 5$

$BG = \frac{2}{3}(16) = \frac{32}{3} \approx 10.7$

**15. a.** $A_{\text{dartboard}} = \pi 10^2 = 100\pi$

$A_{\text{center circle}} = \pi 2.5^2 = 6.25\pi$

$P(\text{center circle}) = \frac{6.25\pi}{100\pi} = \frac{1}{16}$ or 0.0625

**b.** Sample answer: Yes; since a person would be aiming for the center, it would not be the same probability as a random event.

**16.** C

F′ —— G′

F ———— G

**17.**

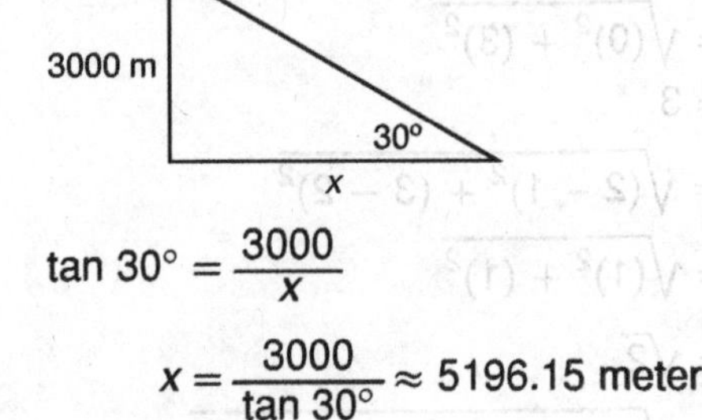


$\tan 30° = \frac{3000}{x}$

$x = \frac{3000}{\tan 30°} \approx 5196.15$ meters

**18.** $L = Ph$

$31.4 = (2\pi r)(5)$

$r \approx 1$

$C_{\log} = 2\pi(1) \approx 6.28$

The log will revolve $62.8\pi \div 2\pi = 31.4$ times.

**19.** $\frac{2\pi}{x} = \frac{120}{360}$

$x = 2\pi$ yards

**20.** $d_{JK} = \sqrt{(4-1)^2 + (1-1)^2}$

$= \sqrt{(3)^2 + (0)^2}$

$= 3$

$d_{NO} = \sqrt{(8-5)^2 + (7-7)^2}$

$= \sqrt{(3)^2 + (0)^2}$

$= 3$

$d_{KL} = \sqrt{(5-4)^2 + (4-1)^2}$

$= \sqrt{(1)^2 + (3)^2}$

$= \sqrt{10}$

$d_{OP} = \sqrt{(8-9)^2 + (7-4)^2}$

$= \sqrt{(-1)^2 + (3)^2}$

$= \sqrt{10}$

$$d_{LM} = \sqrt{(5-2)^2 + (4-5)^2}$$
$$= \sqrt{(3)^2 + (-1)^2} = \sqrt{10}$$
$$d_{PQ} = \sqrt{(9-6)^2 + (4-3)^2}$$
$$= \sqrt{(3)^2 + (1)^2}$$
$$= \sqrt{10}$$
$$d_{JM} = \sqrt{(1-2)^2 + (1-5)^2}$$
$$= \sqrt{(-1)^2 + (-4)^2}$$
$$= \sqrt{17}$$
$$d_{NQ} = \sqrt{(5-6)^2 + (7-3)^2}$$
$$= \sqrt{(-1)^2 + (4)^2}$$
$$= \sqrt{17}$$
$$m_{JK} = \frac{1-1}{4-1} = \frac{0}{3} = 0$$
$$m_{KL} = \frac{4-1}{5-4} = \frac{3}{1} = 3$$
$$m_{LM} = \frac{4-5}{5-2} = \frac{-1}{3}$$
$$m_{JM} = \frac{1-5}{1-2} = \frac{-4}{-1} = 4$$
$$m_{NO} = \frac{7-7}{5-8} = \frac{0}{-3} = 0$$
$$m_{OP} = \frac{4-7}{9-8} = \frac{-3}{1} = -3$$
$$m_{PQ} = \frac{4-3}{9-6} = \frac{1}{3}$$
$$m_{NQ} = \frac{7-3}{5-6} = \frac{4}{-1} = -4$$

$JK = 3 = NO$, $KL = \sqrt{10} = OP$, $LM = \sqrt{10} = PQ$, and $JM = \sqrt{17} = NQ$; The slopes of $\overline{JK}$, $\overline{KL}$, $\overline{LM}$, and $\overline{JM}$ are 0, 3, $-\frac{1}{3}$, and 4, while the slopes of $\overline{NO}$, $\overline{OP}$, $\overline{PQ}$, and $\overline{NQ}$ are 0, −3, $\frac{1}{3}$, and −4, so $\angle J \cong \angle N$, $\angle K \cong \angle O$, $\angle L \cong \angle P$, and $\angle M \cong \angle Q$; Therefore, $JKLM \cong NOPQ$.

**21.**

$\tan x = \frac{6}{2}$

$\tan x = 3$

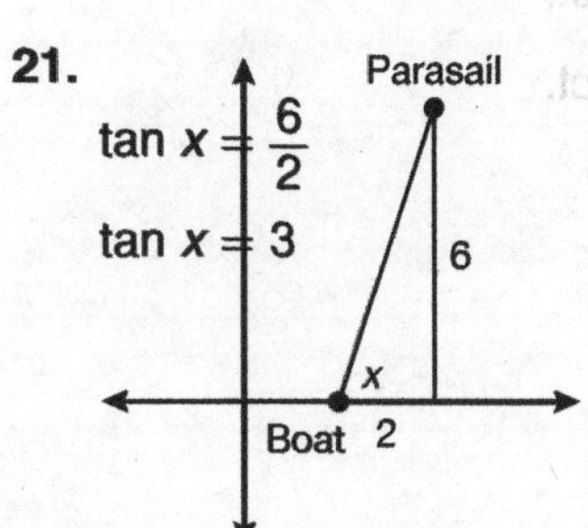


**22.**

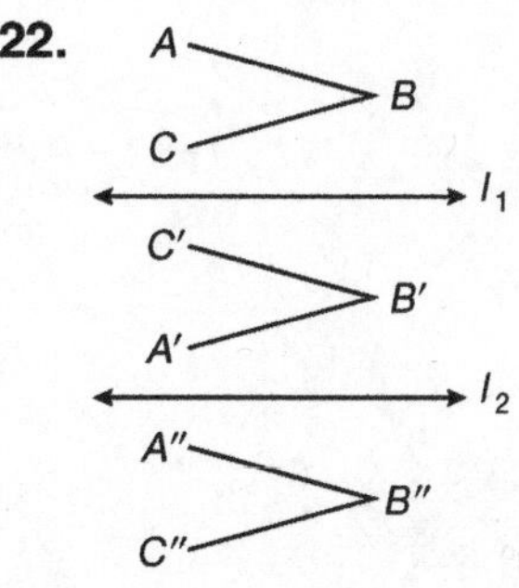


**23.** $\cos\theta \cdot \tan\theta = \cos\theta \cdot \frac{\sin\theta}{\cos\theta}$
$= \sin\theta$

**24.**

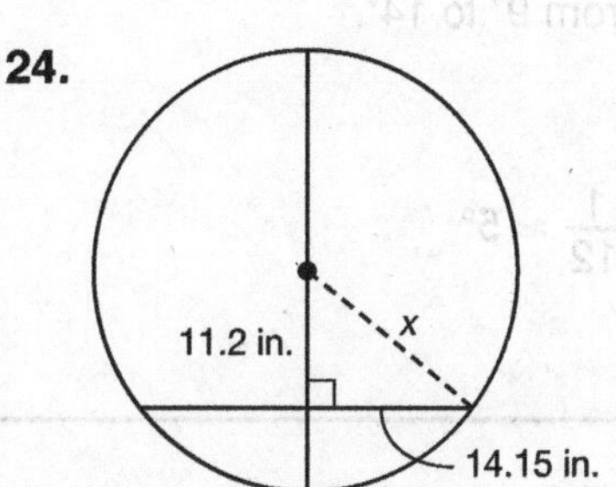


$$x^2 = 11.2^2 + 14.15^2$$
$$x^2 = 125.44 + 200.2225$$
$$x^2 = 325.6625$$
$$x \approx 18 \text{ inches}$$

**25.** $V = \frac{1}{3}Bh = \frac{1}{3}(3)(3)(5) = 15 \text{ in.}^3$

**26.** Law of Detachment

**27.** The sides of the final image will lie on the sides of the original triangle, but the vertices will be different. $E''$ will coincide with $F$, $F''$ with $G$, and $G''$ with $E$.

**28. a.**

**b.**

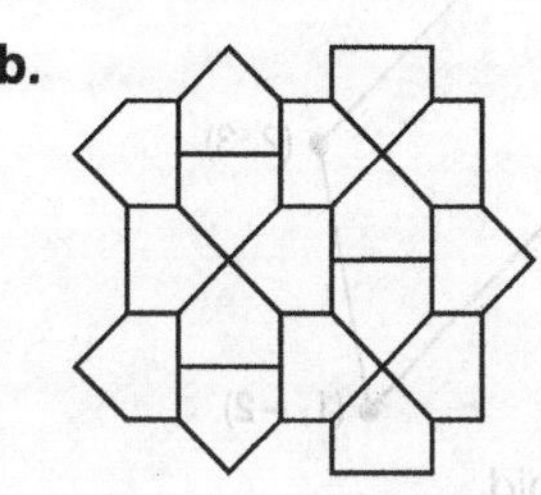

29. 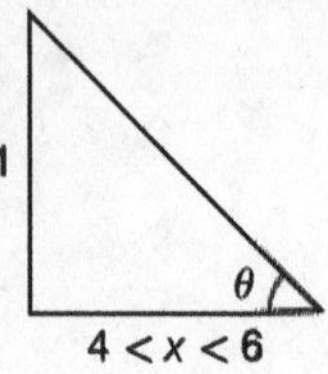


$\tan\theta = \frac{1}{6}$

$\theta = \tan^{-1}\frac{1}{6} \approx 9°$

$\theta = \tan^{-1}\frac{1}{4} \approx 14°$

The range is from 9° to 14°.

30. $\tan\theta = \frac{1}{12}$

$\theta = \tan^{-1}\frac{1}{12} \approx 5°$

## LAB 12

a. 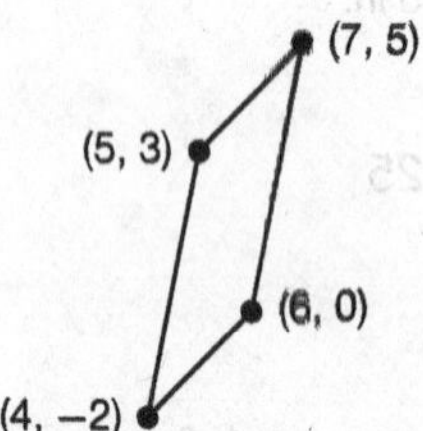


parallelogram

b. 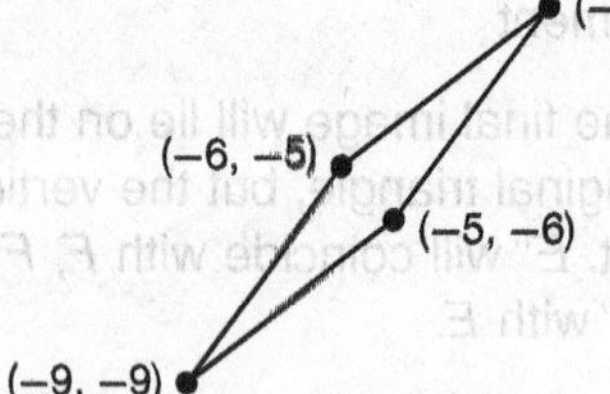


rhombus, parallelogram

c. 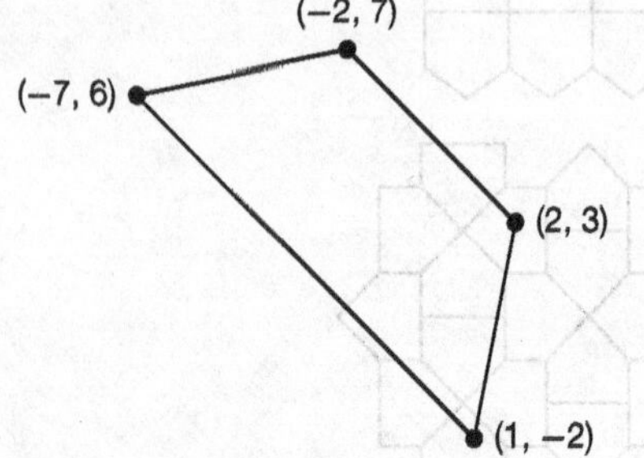


isosceles trapezoid

d. 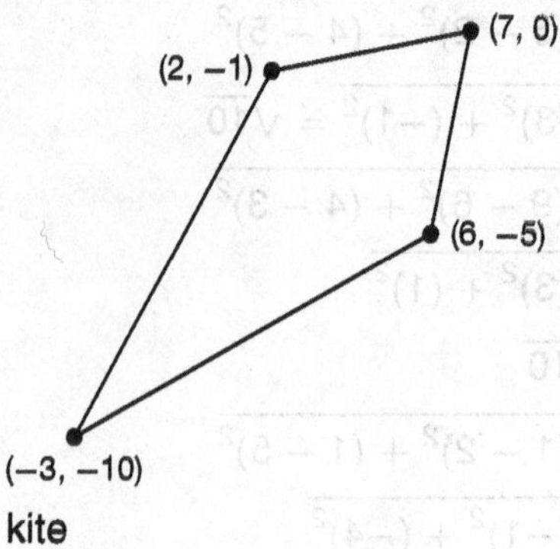


kite

e. 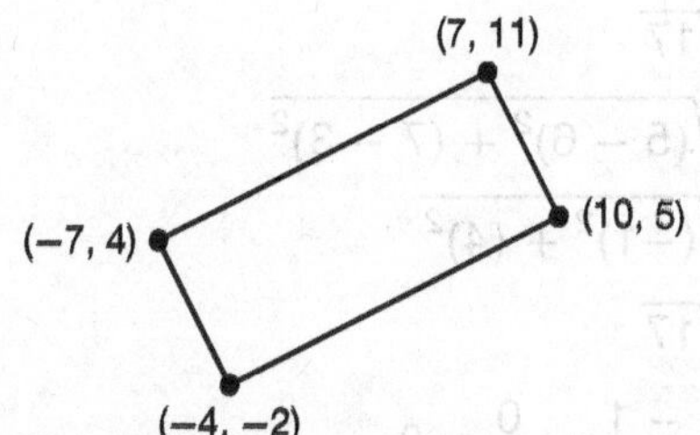


rectangle, parallelogram

## LESSON 93

### Warm Up 93

1. cube
2. 12 edges, 8 vertices, and 6 faces
3. 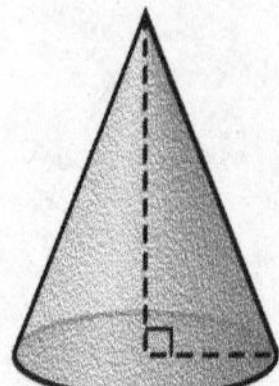
4. right rectangular pyramid

### Lesson Practice 93

a. 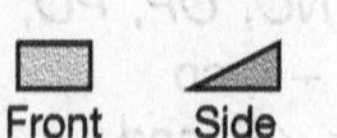


b. Choice **A** is correct.

c. Choice **B** is correct.

### Practice 93

1. 

2. 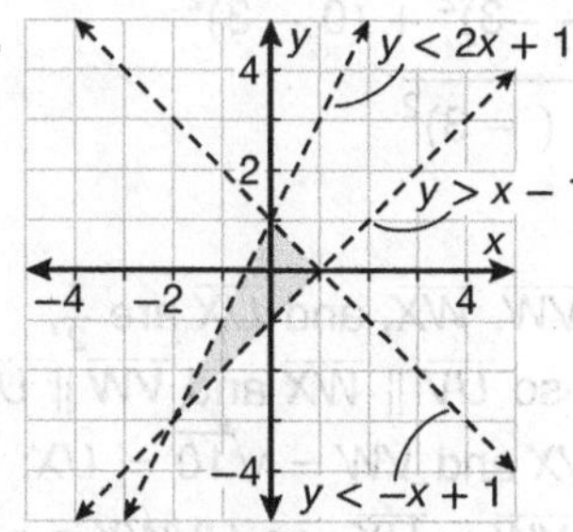


3. $\tan\theta = \sqrt{3.2}$

$\tan\theta = \frac{\sqrt{3.2}}{1}$

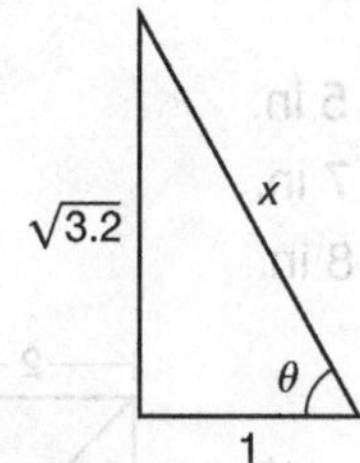


$x^2 = 1^2 + (\sqrt{3.2})^2$

$x \approx 2.05$

$\cos\theta = \frac{1}{2.05}$

$\cos\theta \approx 0.49$

4. 1 mm = 0.1 cm

$V = Bh - Bh$

$= (\pi)(5.25^2)(0.1) - (\pi)(0.75^2)(0.1)$

$\approx 8.48 \text{ cm}^3$

The total volume of 25 discs is $25 \times 8.48 = 212.1 \text{ cm}^3$.

5. $S = \frac{1}{2}(4\pi r^2) = \frac{1}{2}(4\pi 6^2) \approx 226 \text{ in.}^2$

6. This is a translation along *w* and then a reflection across *l*. Choice **D** is correct.

7. $\frac{76}{931} = \frac{4}{49}$

$\frac{\sqrt{4}}{\sqrt{49}} = \frac{2}{7}$

The ratio of the perimeters is 2 : 7.

8. Any point could be moved to make a parallelogram. Three points define two lines of the parallelogram, and the fourth point will define the other 2 lines, so it determines whether or not there are two parallel pairs.

9. Choice **D** is correct.

10. $d_{KL} = \sqrt{(-2-1)^2 + (-2--3)^2}$

$= \sqrt{(-3)^2 + (1)^2}$

$= \sqrt{10}$

$\approx 3.2$

$d_{KM} = \sqrt{(-2-3)^2 + (-2-3)^2}$

$= \sqrt{(-5)^2 + (-5)^2}$

$= \sqrt{50}$

$\approx 7.1$

$d_{LM} = \sqrt{(1-3)^2 + (-3-3)^2}$

$= \sqrt{(-2)^2 + (-6)^2}$

$= \sqrt{40}$

$\approx 6.3$

$m_{LM} = \frac{-3-3}{1-3} = \frac{-6}{-2} = 3$

$m_{KL} = \frac{-2--3}{-2-1} = \frac{1}{-3}$

Sides *LM* and *KL* are perpendicular. So, $m\angle L = 90°$.

$\cos K = \frac{3.2}{7.1}$

$K \approx 63°$

$\sin M = \frac{3.2}{7.1}$

$M \approx 27°$

11. Since the diagonals of a rhombus intersect at 90°, $m\angle KSL = 90°$.

12. **i)** $y = -x + 1$

**ii)** $y = x - 3$

**iii)** $y = x + 5$

i is perpendicular to both ii and iii. Choice **D** is correct.

13. $\triangle AGK \cong \triangle OJV$

14. The distances *PQ* and *BR* are equal, as are the distances *PB* and *QR*. Sarita will be traveling the same distance.

15. The slope of the line perpendicular to $y = 3x - 4$ is $-\frac{1}{3}$.

$y = -\frac{1}{3}x + b$

$6 = -\frac{1}{3}(0) + b$

$6 = b$

$y = -\frac{1}{3}x + 6$

To find the point of intersection, set the equations equal to each other.

$-\frac{1}{3}x + 6 = 3x - 4$

$-\frac{10}{3}x = -10$

$x = 3$

$y = 3(3) - 4 = 5$

The point of intersection is (3, 5). This is the point on the line closest to $C$.

**16.** $A = (6)(5) + \frac{1}{2}(1)(1) + (1)(5) + (1)(1) + \frac{1}{2}(1)(1)$

$A = 30 + 0.5 + 5 + 1 + 0.5$

$A = 37 \text{ m}^2$

**17.** $S = 4\pi r^2 = 4\pi(5.5^2) \approx 380.13 \text{ m}^2$

**18.** equilateral triangle

**19.** $m_{UV} = \frac{2 - 0}{2 - -2} = \frac{2}{4} = \frac{1}{2}$

$m_{VW} = \frac{2 - 5}{2 - 1} = \frac{-3}{1} = -3$

$m_{WX} = \frac{5 - 3}{1 - -3} = \frac{2}{4} = \frac{1}{2}$

$m_{UX} = \frac{3 - 0}{-3 - -2} = \frac{3}{-1} = -3$

$d_{UV} = \sqrt{(-2 - 2)^2 + (0 - 2)^2}$

$= \sqrt{(-4)^2 + (-2)^2}$

$= \sqrt{20} = 2\sqrt{5}$

$d_{WX} = \sqrt{(1 - -3)^2 + (5 - 3)^2}$

$= \sqrt{(4)^2 + (2)^2}$

$= \sqrt{20} = 2\sqrt{5}$

$d_{VW} = \sqrt{(2 - 1)^2 + (2 - 5)^2}$

$= \sqrt{(1)^2 + (-3)^2}$

$= \sqrt{10}$

$d_{UX} = \sqrt{(-2 - -3)^2 + (0 - 3)^2}$

$= \sqrt{(1)^2 + (-3)^2}$

$= \sqrt{10}$

Slopes of $\overline{UV}$, $\overline{VW}$, $\overline{WX}$, and $\overline{UX}$ are $\frac{1}{2}$, $-3$, $\frac{1}{2}$, and $-3$, so $\overline{UV} \parallel \overline{WX}$ and $\overline{VW} \parallel \overline{UX}$. $UV = 2\sqrt{5} = WX$ and $VW = \sqrt{10} = UX$; $\overline{UV} \cong \overline{WX}$ and $\overline{VW} \cong \overline{UX}$, so $UVWX$ is a parallelogram.

**20.** $2 = 3(3) + b$

$-7 = b$

**21.** $DE = QP = 5$ in.

$EF = PR = 7$ in.

$QR = DF = 8$ in.

**22.**

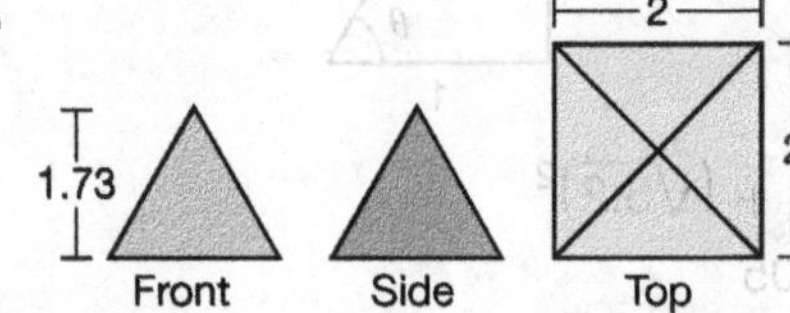


**23.** 6 m/s$^2$ down and 8 m/s$^2$ to the left, or $\langle -6, 8 \rangle$ with positive $y$ as up and positive $x$ as right.

**24.** $3(x + 2) = (6 - x)(5)$

$3x + 6 = 30 - 5x$

$8x = 24$

$x = 3$

**25.** $RT = 2(UV) = 2(12) = 24$

**26.** $d_{MP} = \sqrt{(2 - 5)^2 + (2 - 6)^2}$

$= \sqrt{(-3)^2 + (-4)^2}$

$= \sqrt{25} = 5$

$d_{NO} = \sqrt{(3 - 6)^2 + (0 - 4)^2}$

$= \sqrt{(-3)^2 + (-4)^2}$

$= \sqrt{25} = 5$

$d_{NM} = \sqrt{(3 - 2)^2 + (0 - 2)^2}$

$= \sqrt{(1)^2 + (-2)^2}$

$= \sqrt{5}$

$$d_{OP} = \sqrt{(6-5)^2 + (4-6)^2}$$
$$= \sqrt{(1)^2 + (-2)^2}$$
$$= \sqrt{5}$$

$MP$ and $NO$ are 5 and $NM$ and $OP$ are $\sqrt{5}$; $\overline{MN} \cong \overline{OP}$ and $\overline{NO} \cong \overline{MP}$, so $MNOP$ is a parallelogram.

**27.** $\cos\theta = \dfrac{1}{\sqrt{1 + \tan^2\theta}}$

**28.**

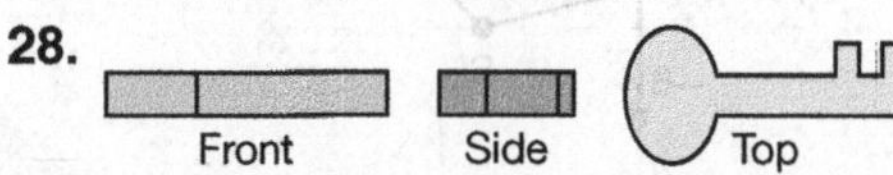


**29.**

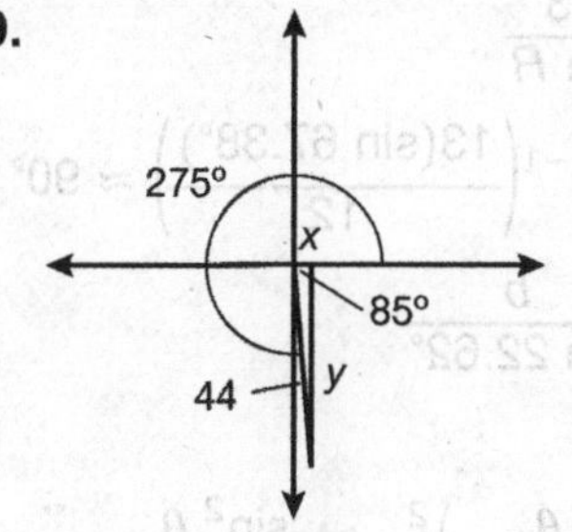


$$\cos 85° = \frac{x}{44}$$
$$x \approx 3.83$$
$$\sin 85° = \frac{y}{44}$$
$$y \approx 43.83$$
$$\langle 3.83, -43.83 \rangle$$

**30.** $\dfrac{4}{5} = \dfrac{6}{x}$

$(4)(x) = (5)(6)$

$4x = 30$

$x = 7.5$

## LESSON 94

### Warm Up 94

1. tangent
2. This is false; $\sin\theta = \dfrac{\tan\theta}{\sqrt{1 + \tan\theta}}$.
3. Plane 38° x 11,000 ft Lake

$$\sin 38° = \frac{11{,}000}{x}$$
$$x = \frac{11{,}000}{\sin 38°} \approx 17{,}867 \text{ feet}$$

### Lesson Practice 94

**a.** $\dfrac{TU}{\sin V} = \dfrac{TV}{\sin U}$

$$\frac{TU}{\sin 31°} = \frac{110}{\sin 108°}$$
$$TU \approx 59.57$$

**b.** $\dfrac{DE}{\sin F} = \dfrac{DF}{\sin E}$

$$\frac{6}{\sin 20°} = \frac{13}{\sin E}$$
$$6(\sin E) = 13(\sin 20°)$$
$$\sin E = \frac{13(\sin 20°)}{6}$$
$$m\angle E = \sin^{-1}\left(\frac{13(\sin 20°)}{6}\right)$$
$$m\angle E \approx 48°$$
$$m\angle D = 180° - 48° - 20° \approx 112°$$

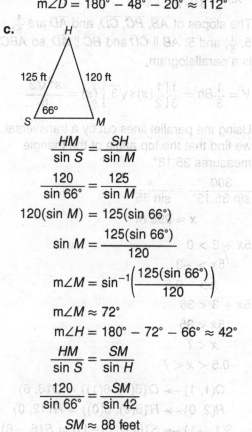

**c.** H, 125 ft, 120 ft, 66°, S, M

$$\frac{HM}{\sin S} = \frac{SH}{\sin M}$$
$$\frac{120}{\sin 66°} = \frac{125}{\sin M}$$
$$120(\sin M) = 125(\sin 66°)$$
$$\sin M = \frac{125(\sin 66°)}{120}$$
$$m\angle M = \sin^{-1}\left(\frac{125(\sin 66°)}{120}\right)$$
$$m\angle M \approx 72°$$
$$m\angle H = 180° - 72° - 66° \approx 42°$$
$$\frac{HM}{\sin S} = \frac{SM}{\sin H}$$
$$\frac{120}{\sin 66°} = \frac{SM}{\sin 42}$$
$$SM \approx 88 \text{ feet}$$

## Practice 94

1. $\frac{2h}{4p} = \frac{h}{2p}$ or $h : 2p$

2. Humberto only found the magnitude of the velocity, but did not specify the direction of 53.13° $\left(\text{found by } \tan\theta = \frac{24}{18}\right)$.

3. Since the diagonal from the top to the bottom of the square is 90°, the angle is half of that or 45°.

4. $d^2 = 90^2 + 90^2$
   $d^2 = 16{,}200$
   $d \approx 127.3$ ft

5. $m_{AB} = \frac{8-7}{8-3} = \frac{1}{5}$
   $m_{BC} = \frac{8-3}{8-7} = \frac{5}{1} = 5$
   $m_{CD} = \frac{3-2}{7-2} = \frac{1}{5}$
   $m_{AD} = \frac{7-2}{3-2} = \frac{5}{1} = 5$
   The slopes of $\overline{AB}$, $\overline{BC}$, $\overline{CD}$, and $\overline{AD}$ are $\frac{1}{5}$, 5, $\frac{1}{5}$, and 5. $\overline{AB} \parallel \overline{CD}$ and $\overline{BC} \parallel \overline{AD}$, so $ABCD$ is a parallelogram.

6. $V = \frac{1}{3}Bh = \frac{1}{3}\left[\frac{1}{2}(s)s\sqrt{3}\right](s) = \frac{s^3\sqrt{3}}{6}$

7. Using the parallel lines cut by a transversal, we find that the top angle of the triangle measures 35.13°.
   $\frac{300}{\sin 35.13°} = \frac{x}{\sin 35°}$
   $x \approx 299$ m

8. $5x + 3 > 0$
   $5x > -3$
   $x > -0.6$
   $5x + 3 < 38$
   $5x < 35$
   $x < 7$
   $-0.6 < x < 7$

9. $Q(1, 1) \rightarrow Q'(6(1), 6(1)) = Q'(6, 6)$
   $R(2, 0) \rightarrow R'(6(2), 6(0)) = R'(12, 0)$
   $S(1, -1) \rightarrow S'(6(1), 6(-1)) = S'(6, -6)$
   $T\left(-1, -\frac{1}{2}\right) \rightarrow T'\left[6(-1), 6\left(-\frac{1}{2}\right)\right] = T'(-6, -3)$
   $U\left(-1, \frac{1}{2}\right) \rightarrow U'\left[6(-1), 6\left(\frac{1}{2}\right)\right] = U'(-6, 3)$

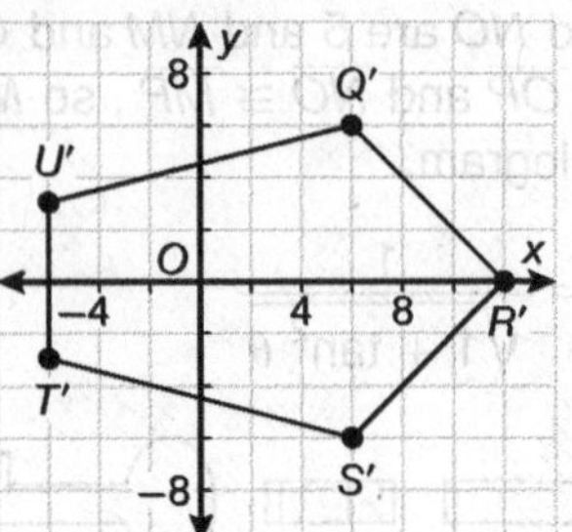


10. $\frac{12}{\sin 67.38°} = \frac{13}{\sin R}$
    $R = \sin^{-1}\left(\frac{13(\sin 67.38°)}{12}\right) \approx 90°$
    $\frac{12}{\sin 67.38°} = \frac{b}{\sin 22.62°}$
    $PR = b \approx 5$

11. $\tan^2\theta = \left(\frac{\sin\theta}{\sqrt{1 - \sin^2\theta}}\right)^2 = \frac{\sin^2\theta}{1 - \sin^2\theta}$

12. 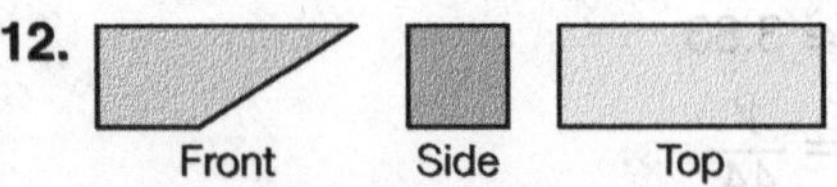


13. Choice **A** is correct because a pair of opposite sides is parallel.

14. $6x = 90°$
    $x = 15$

15. $96\pi = \frac{1}{3}(\pi)(6^2)(h)$
    $8 = h$
    $l = 8^2 + 6^2$
    $l = 10$
    $S = \pi(6)(10) + \pi(6^2)$
    $S = 60\pi + 36\pi$
    $S \approx 301.6 \text{ cm}^2$

16. $P = 5(45) = 225$ in.
    $A = \frac{1}{2}aP = \frac{1}{2}(31)(225) = 3487.5 \text{ in.}^2$

17. Since $\sin\theta = \sqrt{1-\cos^2\theta}$

$$\frac{a}{\sqrt{1-\cos^2 A}} = \frac{b}{\sqrt{1-\cos^2 B}} = \frac{c}{\sqrt{1-\cos^2 C}}$$

18.

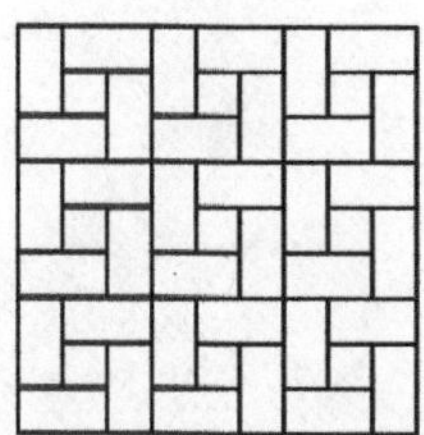

19. $(x-1)^2 + (y+1)^2 = 1^2$

$(x-1)^2 + (y+1)^2 = 1$

20. Yes, Nadim can get two potentially correct answers. Because a measure for a second angle in the triangle is not known, the angle between sides $a$ and $b$ can be $\theta_1$ or $180° - \theta_1$.

21. Using the formulas for the surface area and volume of a sphere, if $V = S$, then $\frac{4}{3}\pi r^3 = 4\pi r^2$. Simplifying, $r = 3$.

22. 3 common tangents;

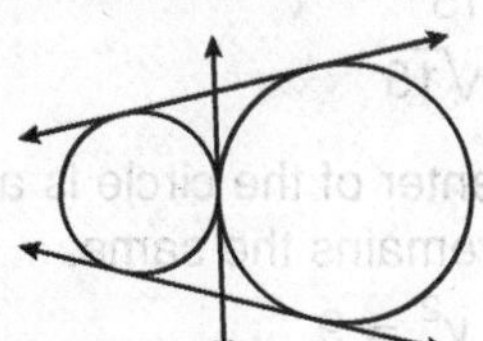

23. $7x - 36 = 3x + 16$

$4x = 52$

$x = 13$

24. Sample: Divide the circle in half. Then divide one half into thirds.

25. LA Congruence Theorem

26. Choice A: $3^2 + 4^2 = 5^2$

$9 + 16 = 25$

$25 = 25$

Choice B: $(2\sqrt{2})^2 + (2\sqrt{2})^2 = (\sqrt{8})^2$

$8 + 8 = 8$

$16 \neq 8$

Choice C: $2^2 + 2^2 = (2\sqrt{2})^2$

$4 + 4 = 8$

$8 = 8$

Choice D: $7^2 + (6\sqrt{2})^2 = 11^2$

$49 + 72 = 121$

$121 = 121$

Choice **B** is correct.

27. about 14 basalt rocks

28. $(13 - c)(5) = 7(c - 1)$

$65 - 5c = 7c - 7$

$72 = 12c$

$c = 6$

29.

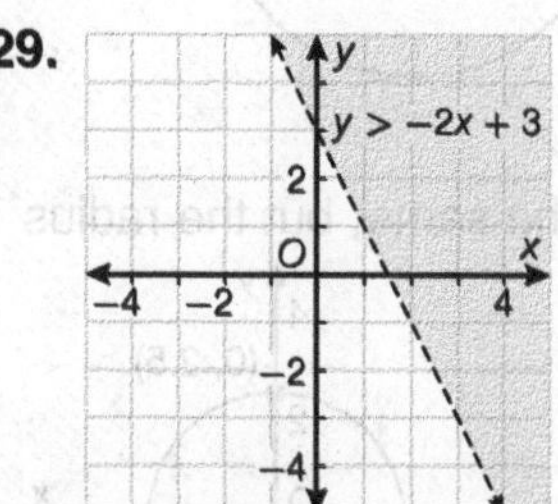


30.

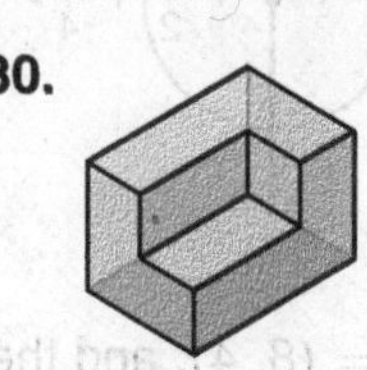

## LESSON 95

### Warm Up 95

1. center

2. $(x-0)^2 + (y-0)^2 = 2^2$

center = (0, 0); radius = 2 units

3. The center is (0, 0) and the radius is 3.

$x^2 + y^2 = 3^2$

$x^2 + y^2 = 9$

4. $(x-1)^2 + (y+1)^2 = 3^2$

$(x-1)^2 + (y+1)^2 = 9$

Choice **B** is correct.

**Lesson Practice 95**

**a.** The new center of the circle is at (4, 1) and the radius remains the same.
$(x-4)^2 + (y-1)^2 = 16$

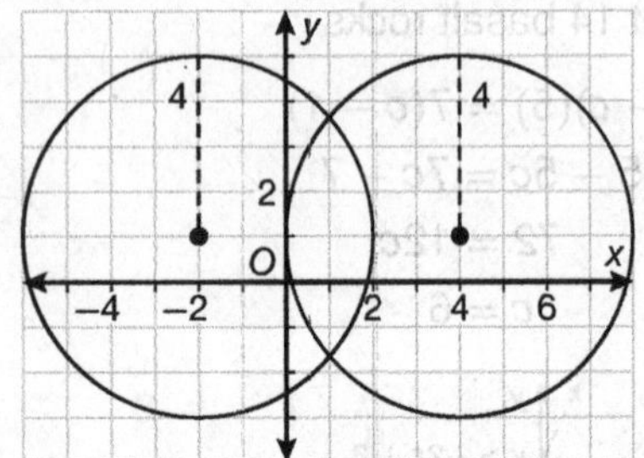


**b.** The center remains the same, but the radius is now $\frac{1}{2}(5) = \frac{5}{2}$.
$x^2 + y^2 = \left(\frac{5}{2}\right)^2$
$x^2 + y^2 = \frac{25}{4}$

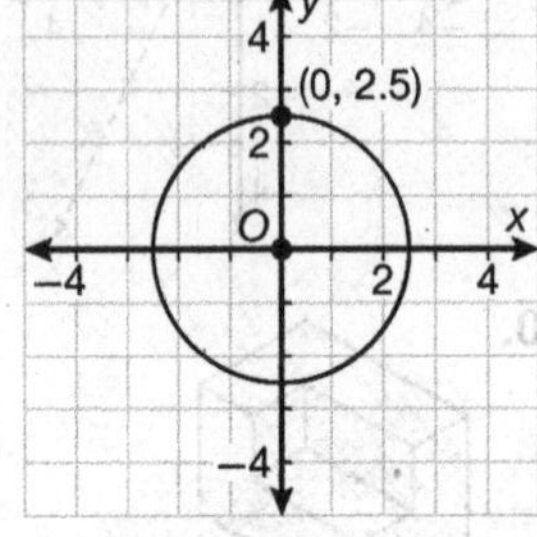


**c.** The center is at (4(2), 4(1)) = (8, 4), and the radius is now 4(1) = 4.
$(x-8)^2 + (y-4)^2 = 4^2$
$(x-8)^2 + (y-4)^2 = 16$

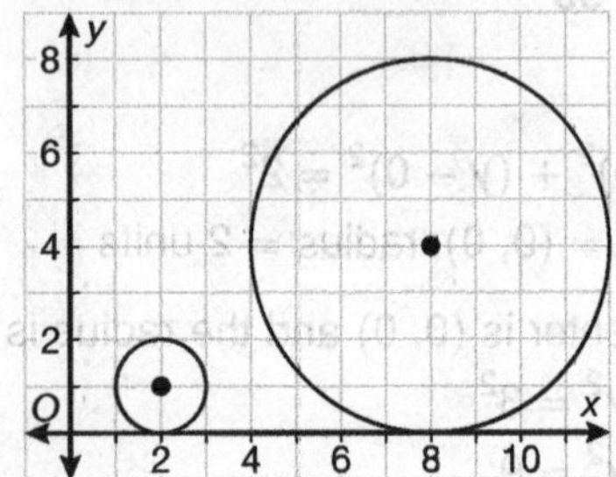


**d.** Let (0,0) be the location of the siren. So the equation is $x^2 + y^2 = 9$. For any ordered pair that satisfies the inequality $x^2 + y^2 \leq 9$, the siren is audible. So at (−2, 2), where June lives, the siren is audible because $(-2)^2 + (2)^2 + \leq 9$.
If the siren moves, its new equation will be $x^2 + (y-2)^2 = 20.25$. The siren will still be audible because $(-2)^2 + (2-2)^2 \leq 20.25$.

**Practice 95**

**1.**

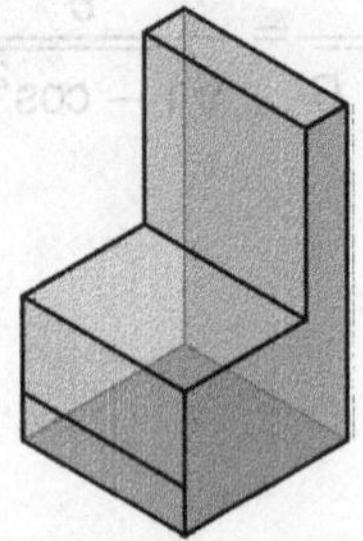

**2.** $\frac{1}{2}(150° - 60°) = 45°$

**3.**

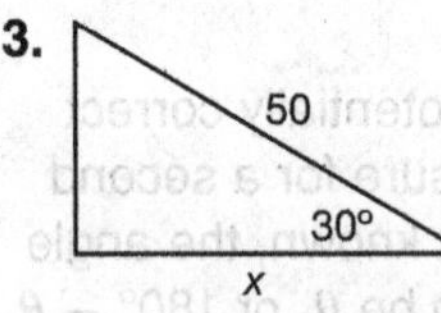


$\cos 30° = \frac{x}{50}$
$x = 50 \cos 30° \approx 43.3$ miles per hour

**4.** $x^2 + 7^2 > 8^2$
$x^2 > 15$
$x > \sqrt{15}$

**5.** The new center of the circle is at (8, 0) and the radius remains the same.
$(x-8)^2 + y^2 = 9$

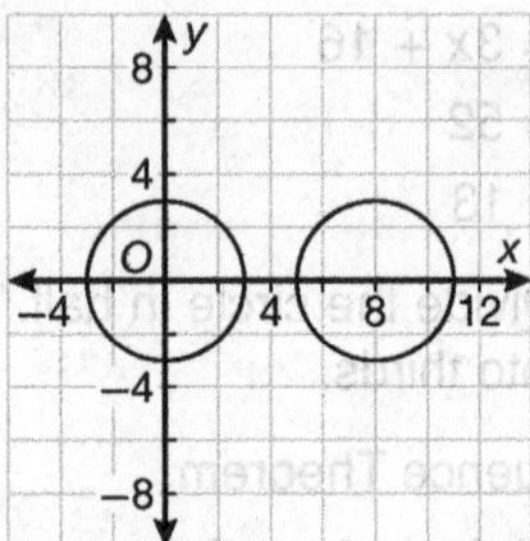


**6.** $\sqrt{\frac{1}{2} \times \frac{1}{32}} = \sqrt{\frac{1}{64}} = \frac{1}{8}$

**7.**

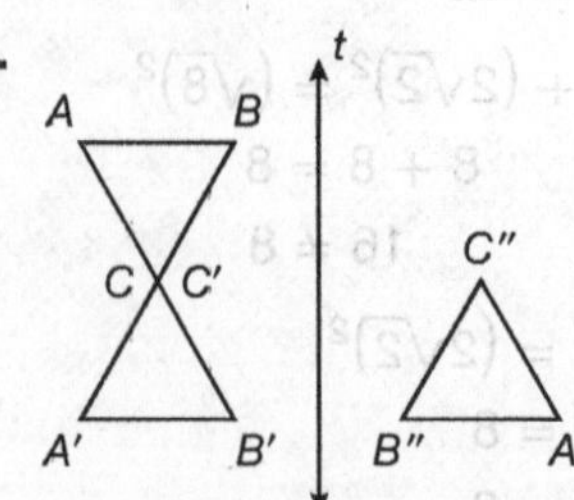

**8.** The center remains the same, but the radius is now $\frac{1}{4}(12) = 3$.

$(x - 1)^2 + (y + 4)^2 = 9$

**9.** $\frac{25}{\sin 108°} = \frac{20}{\sin A}$

$\sin A \approx 0.76$

$A \approx 49.54$

$m\angle B = 22.46°$

$\frac{25}{\sin 108°} = \frac{AC}{\sin 22.46°}$

$AC \approx 10.04$

**10.** $14 - 2 = 12$ m/s

$14 + 2 = 16$ m/s

**11.** $\frac{6}{x} = \frac{4}{9}$

$(4)(x) = (6)(9)$

$4x = 54$

$x = 13.5$

**12.** The new center of the circle is at (0, 4) and the radius remains the same.

$x^2 + (y - 4)^2 = 36$

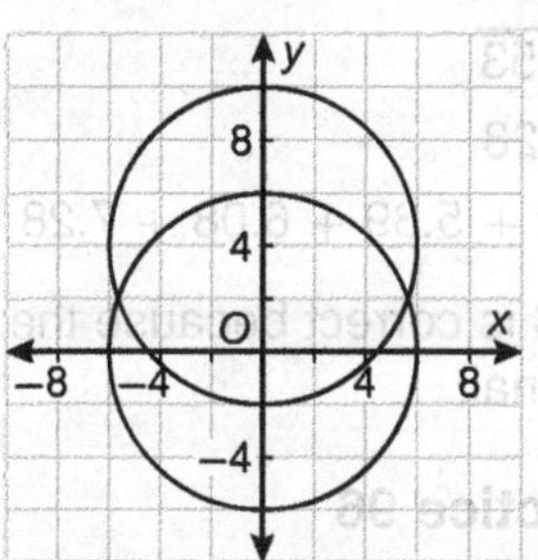


**13.** $y + 62 = 180$; $y = 118$; If $y = 118$, then the two angles are supplementary same-side interior angles.

**14.** 90°; Cosine is 0 at 90°. Since $\tan\theta = \frac{\sin\theta}{\cos\theta}$, it is undefined.

**15.** $m\angle L = 180° - 98° - 35° = 47°$

$\frac{50}{\sin 47°} = \frac{LM}{\sin 35°}$

$LM \approx 39.21$

**16.** The equations in i and ii have slopes of 2 whereas iii has a slope of 1. i and ii are parallel. Choice **A** is correct.

**17.** $m_{CD} = \frac{7 - 4}{3 - 5} = \frac{3}{-2}$

$m_{DE} = \frac{4 - 1}{5 - -3} = \frac{3}{8}$

$m_{EF} = \frac{4 - 1}{-4 - -3} = \frac{3}{-1} = -3$

$m_{CF} = \frac{7 - 4}{3 - -4} = \frac{3}{7}$

The slopes are all different, so no two sides are parallel, meaning *CDEF* cannot be a trapezoid.

**18.** $\frac{1}{\sqrt{2}} = \frac{x}{31}$

$x = \frac{31}{\sqrt{2}} = \frac{31\sqrt{2}}{2}$ cm

**19.** Since $\sin\theta = \frac{\tan\theta}{\sqrt{1 + \tan\theta}}$,

$$\frac{a\sqrt{1+\tan^2 A}}{\tan A} = \frac{b\sqrt{1+\tan^2 B}}{\tan B} = \frac{c\sqrt{1+\tan^2 C}}{\tan C}$$

**20.** Since $12 - 3 \neq 2(3) + 5$ and the angles are right angles, it is a rectangle.

**21.** $3x - 10 = -x + 60$

$4x = 70$

$x = 17.5$

**22.** a circle

**23.** yes; $\frac{360°}{90°} = 4$

**24.** The center remains the same, but the radius is now $3(4) = 12$.

$x^2 + y^2 = (12)^2$

$x^2 + y^2 = 144$

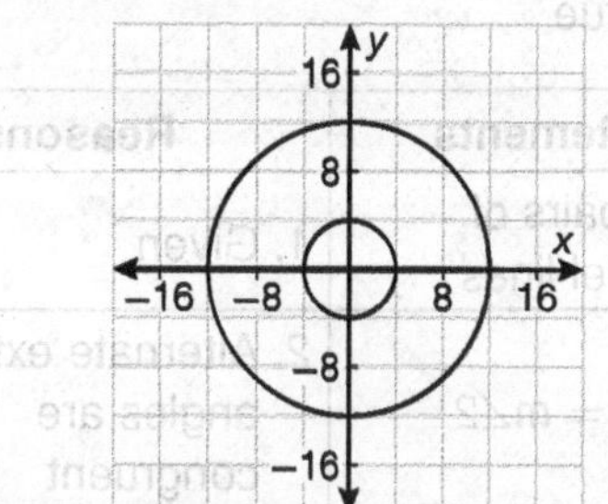


**25.**

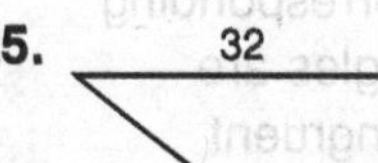

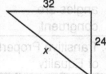

$x^2 = 32^2 + 24^2$

$x = 40$ in.

**26.** $(x, y) \longrightarrow (-y, x)$

$Q(5, -6) \longrightarrow Q'(6, 5)$

$R(6, -4) \longrightarrow R'(4, 6)$

$S(3, -1) \longrightarrow S'(1, 3)$

$T(1, -3) \longrightarrow T'(3, 1)$

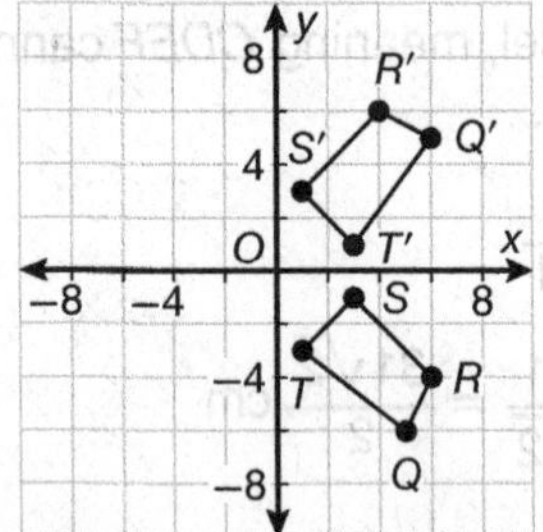


**27.**

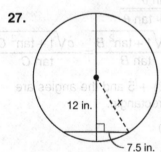

$x^2 = 7.5^2 + 12^2$

$x^2 = 56.25 + 144$

$x^2 = 200.25$

$x \approx 14.2$ inches

**28.**

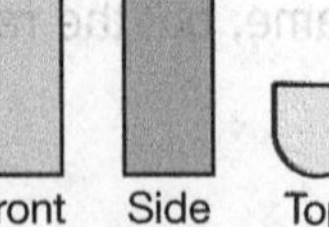


**29.** always true

**30.**

| Statements | Reasons |
|---|---|
| 1. Two pairs of parallel lines | 1. Given |
| 2. m∠1 = m∠2 | 2. Alternate exterior angles are congruent |
| 3. m∠2 = m∠3 | 3. Corresponding angles are congruent |
| 4. m∠1 = m∠3 | 4. Transitive Property of Equality |

## LESSON 96

### Warm Up 96

1. tessellation

2. $d_{MN} = \sqrt{(7-3)^2 + (1-2)^2}$

$= \sqrt{(4)^2 + (-1)^2}$

$= \sqrt{17}$

$\approx 4.12$

$d_{NO} = \sqrt{(7-2)^2 + (1--1)^2}$

$= \sqrt{(5)^2 + (2)^2}$

$= \sqrt{29}$

$\approx 5.39$

$d_{OP} = \sqrt{(2--4)^2 + (-1--2)^2}$

$= \sqrt{(6)^2 + (1)^2}$

$= \sqrt{37}$

$\approx 6.08$

$d_{MP} = \sqrt{(3--4)^2 + (2--2)^2}$

$= \sqrt{(7)^2 + (4)^2}$

$= \sqrt{53}$

$\approx 7.28$

$P \approx 4.12 + 5.39 + 6.08 + 7.28 \approx 22.87$

3. Choice **C** is correct because the lengths are proportional.

### Lesson Practice 96

**a.** Original Perimeter $= x + x + x + x = 4x$

New Perimeter $= x + x + 4x + 4x = 10x$

$\frac{10x}{4x} = \frac{5}{2}$ or 5 : 2

**b.** Original Area $= \frac{1}{2}(3x + x)\left(\frac{1}{2}x\right) = x^2$

New Area $= \frac{1}{2}\left(2x + \frac{1}{2}x\right)\left(\frac{3}{2}x\right) = \frac{15}{8}x^2$

The ratio of the trapezoids' areas is 8 : 15.

**c.** Original Area $= \pi x^2$

New Area $= \pi\left(\frac{1}{2}x\right)^2 = \frac{1}{4}\pi x^2$

The ratio of the areas is 4 : 1.

Original Circumference $= 2\pi x$

New Circumference $= 2\pi\left(\frac{1}{2}x\right) = \pi x$

The ratio of the areas is 2 : 1.

**d.** Original Area $= s^2$

New Area $= \left(\frac{9}{10}s\right)^2 = \frac{81}{100}s^2$

The ratio of the areas is 81 : 100.

## Practice 96

**1.** $m\angle F = 180° - 112° - 27° = 41°$

$\frac{16}{\sin 27°} = \frac{DE}{\sin 41°}$

$DE \approx 23.12$

**2. a.**

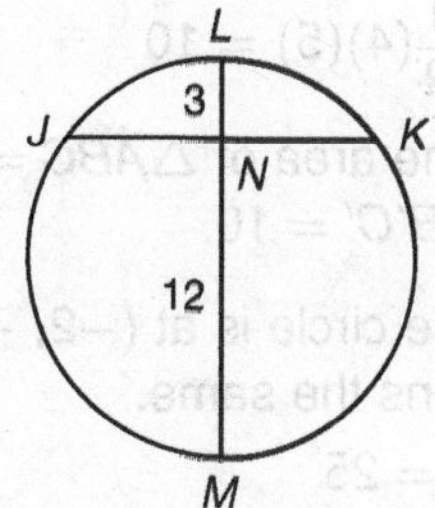


**b.** $(x)(x) = (12)(3)$

$x^2 = 36$

$x = 6 = JN$

**3.** $m_m = \frac{-6 - -3}{2 - 5} = \frac{-3}{-3} = 1$

$m_n = -1$

$\frac{3 - y}{-2 - 4} = \frac{3 - y}{-6} = -1$

$3 - y = 6$

$y = -3$

**4.** The new center of the circle is at (0, 3) and the radius remains the same.

$x^2 + (y - 3)^2 = 100$

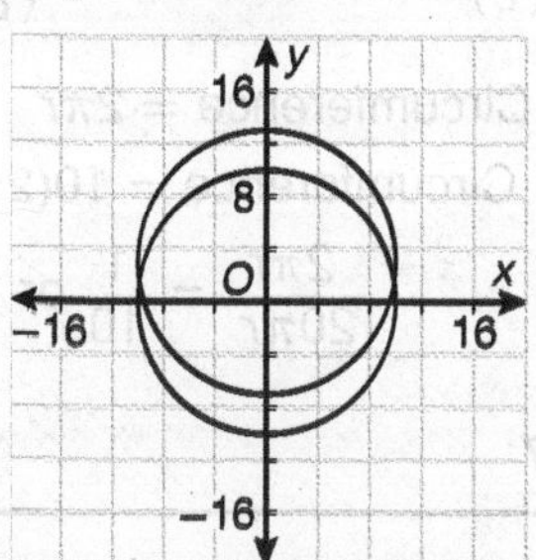


**5.** The length of the sides of the original square was 4 cm. So, the area was 16 cm$^2$, and the new area will be 32 cm$^2$.

The new side length will be $\sqrt{32} = 4\sqrt{2}$ centimeters.

**6.** Sample: No, because when the net is folded up, the two "hanging" squares overlap.

**7.** $h = 14 + 2 = 16$ in.

$V = Bh$

$452 = (\pi r^2)(16)$

$r^2 \approx 9$

$r \approx 3$ inches

**8.** $A = lw + lw + \pi r^2$

$A = (3)(3) + (3)(3) + \pi(3^2)$

$A = 18 + 9\pi$ ft$^2$ or 46.3 ft$^2$

**9.** $(x, y) \longrightarrow (y, -x)$

This is a 270° rotation.

**10.** No, the Law of Sines cannot be used because it requires that at least one angle and its opposite side are both known.

**11.** $2\pi r = \pi x$

$r = \frac{1}{2}x$

New radius $= 2\left(\frac{1}{2}x\right) = x$

$A = \pi x^2$

**12.** $\frac{8}{9.6} = \frac{10}{2k}$

$(8)(2k) = (10)(9.6)$

$16k = 96$

$k = 6$

**13.** The new center of the circle is at (1, 0) and the radius remains the same.

$(x - 1)^2 + y^2 = 64$

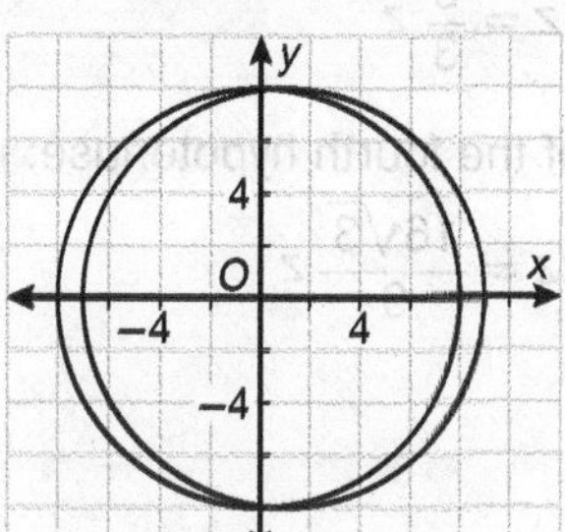

14. He translated twice instead of reflecting and translating.

15. $A = \frac{1}{2}aP$

$P = 5(44) = 220$ ft

$A = \frac{1}{2}(50.5)(220) = 5555 \text{ ft}^2$

Choice **D** is correct.

16. $\frac{15}{6} = \frac{40 + x}{x}$

$240 + 6x = 15x$

$240 = 9x$

$x \approx 26.7$ ft

17.

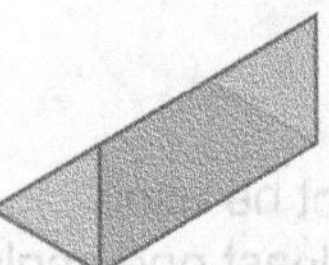

This is a triangular prism.

18. The slanted cross section will have the larger area than the circular parallel cross section, because the cross section stretches in the direction it slants, while the width remains the same, forming an oval.

19. $m\angle DFE = 70°$

20. 90 square feet; There are 9 $\text{ft}^2$ in 1 $\text{yd}^2$. Therefore, multiply 10 by 9.

21. Length of the first hypotenuse: $z \cdot 2 = 2z$

Length of the second hypotenuse:

$\frac{2}{\sqrt{3}} \cdot 2z = \frac{4\sqrt{3}}{3}z$

Length of the third hypotenuse:

$\frac{4\sqrt{3}}{3\sqrt{3}} \cdot 2z = \frac{8}{3}z$

Length of the fourth hypotenuse:

$\frac{8}{3\sqrt{3}} \cdot 2z = \frac{16\sqrt{3}}{9}z$

22. $\frac{2}{41} = \frac{3}{b}$

$b = 61.5$ ft

$\frac{2}{41} = \frac{4}{h}$

$h = 82$ ft

$A = \frac{1}{2}(61.5)(82) = 2521.5 \text{ ft}^2$

23. It is a hexagonal prism with 12 vertices, 18 edges, and 2 bases.

24. $S = 4\pi r^2 = 4\pi(12^2) \approx 1810 \text{ in.}^2$

25. $\frac{60°}{360°} = \frac{12}{x}$

$60x = 4320$

$x = 72$ ft

26. Area of $\triangle ABC = \frac{1}{2}(4)(5) = 10$

Area of $\triangle A'B'C' = \frac{1}{2}(4)(5) = 10$

See student work. The area of $\triangle ABC = 10$ and the area of $\triangle A'B'C' = 10$.

27. The new center of the circle is at $(-2, -1)$ and the radius remains the same.

$(x + 2)^2 + (y + 1)^2 = 25$

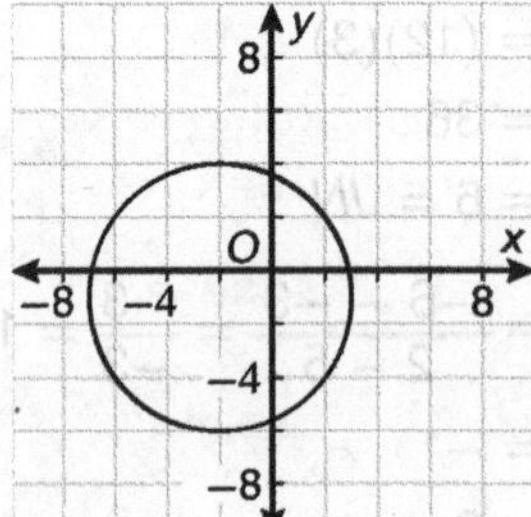


28. $\frac{360°}{x} = 10°$

$x = 36$

29. $\frac{\tan\theta}{\sin\theta} = \frac{\left(\frac{a}{b}\right)}{\left(\frac{a}{c}\right)} = \left(\frac{a}{b}\right)\left(\frac{c}{a}\right) = \frac{c}{b} = \frac{1}{\left(\frac{b}{c}\right)} = \frac{1}{\cos\theta}$

30. Replica's Circumference $= 2\pi r$

Actual Circumference $= 10(2\pi r) = 20\pi r$

$\frac{2\pi r}{20\pi r} = \frac{1}{10}$ or 1 : 10

## LESSON 97

### Warm Up 97

1. dilation

2. 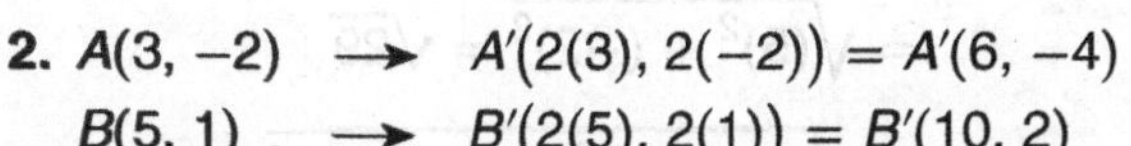

$A(3, -2) \rightarrow A'(2(3), 2(-2)) = A'(6, -4)$
$B(5, 1) \rightarrow B'(2(5), 2(1)) = B'(10, 2)$
$C(1, 3) \rightarrow C'(2(1), 2(3)) = C'(2, 6)$

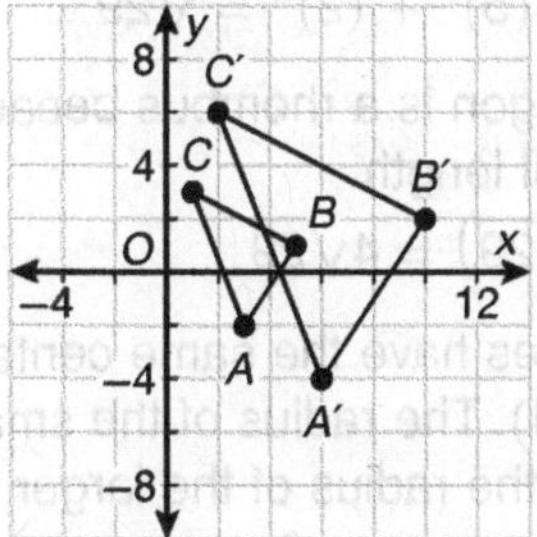


3. The new center of the circle is at (3, −5) and the radius remains the same.
$(x - 3)^2 + (y + 5)^2 = 64$

## Lesson Practice 97

a. No, they are coplanar, but they do not share the same center.

b. $(x - 3)^2 + (y - 4)^2 = 4$
$(x - 3)^2 + (y - 4)^2 = 25$
Both circles are coplanar and have the same center, but different radii. The larger circle is the smaller circle dilated by a scale factor of $\frac{5}{2}$.

c. Area of the annulus $= \pi(11^2) - \pi(7^2)$
$= 72\pi \text{ ft}^2$

d. $P = \dfrac{\text{Area of the annulus}}{\text{Area of the target}}$
$= \dfrac{49\pi - 25\pi}{49\pi} = \dfrac{24}{49}$

## Practice 97

1. Julius thought that the sine of an angle was the ratio of the lengths of the hypotenuse to the opposite side, instead of the other way around. The correct sine is $\frac{5}{13}$.

2. 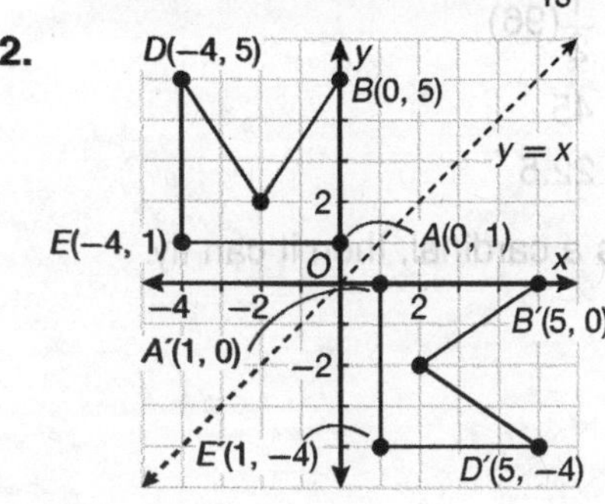


3. $A = \pi(15^2) - \pi(2^2)$
$= 221\pi \text{ in.}^2$

4. $(x + 4)^2 + (y - 3)^2 = 1{,}000{,}000$

5. $\cos 60° = \dfrac{x}{30}$
$x = 30 \cos 60° = 15$ lbs

6. 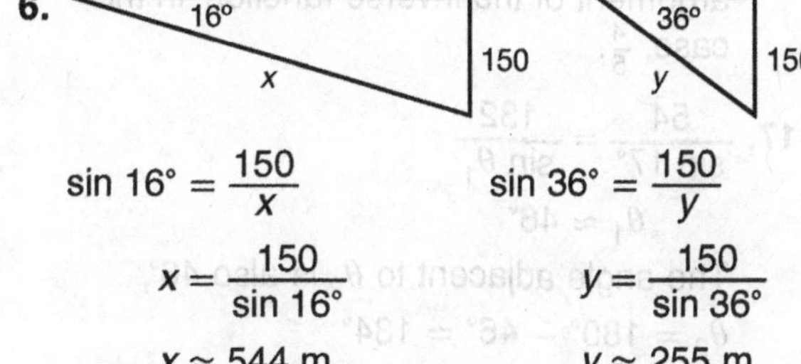


$\sin 16° = \dfrac{150}{x}$ $\quad$ $\sin 36° = \dfrac{150}{y}$

$x = \dfrac{150}{\sin 16°}$ $\quad$ $y = \dfrac{150}{\sin 36°}$

$x \approx 544$ m $\quad$ $y \approx 255$ m

They are $544 - 255 = 289$ meters closer.

7. $P = \dfrac{\text{Area of the annulus}}{\text{Area of the figure}}$
$= \dfrac{484\pi - 144\pi}{484\pi} = \dfrac{85}{121}$

8. $M(3, 3) \rightarrow M'(2(3) - 1, 2(3) - 2) = M'(5, 4)$
$N(5, 1) \rightarrow N'(2(5) - 1, 2(1) - 2) = N'(9, 0)$
$P(1, 1) \rightarrow P'(2(1) - 1, 2(1) - 2) = P'(1, 0)$

9. $P = 9(13) = 117$ mm
Choice **B** is correct.

10. 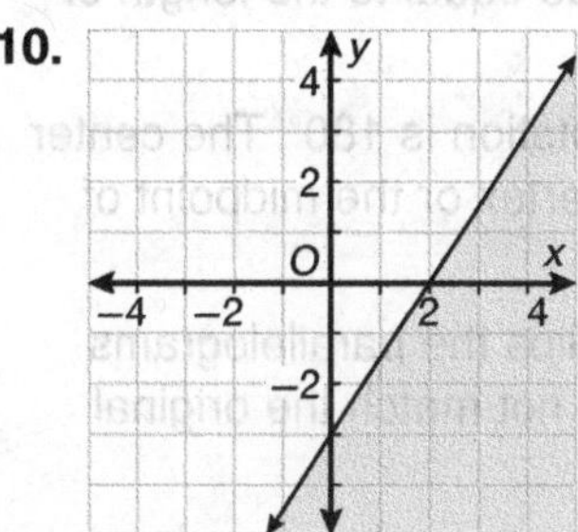


11. $L = 2\pi rh = 2\pi(1.5)(4.375) \approx 41.23 \text{ in.}^2$
$41.23 \text{ in.}^2 \times \left(\dfrac{1 \text{ ft}^2}{144 \text{ in.}^2}\right) \approx 0.286 \text{ ft}^2$
$A = lw = (8)(6) = 48 \text{ ft}^2$
$48 \text{ ft}^2 \div 0.286 \text{ ft}^2 \approx 167.83$
167 lateral surfaces

12. For four points not to form a quadrilateral, at least three must be collinear, so one point must lie on the line segment connecting two of the other points.

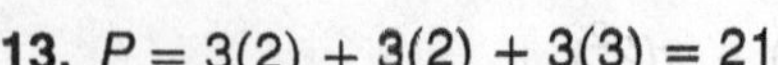



13. $P = 3(2) + 3(2) + 3(3) = 21$

14. Multiply the height by 3.

15. $A = \pi(18^2) - \pi(10^2)$
$= 224\pi \text{ in.}^2$

16. Taking the inverse of any function as the argument of that function will result in the argument of the inverse function; in this case, $\frac{4}{5}$.

17. $\frac{54}{\sin 17°} = \frac{132}{\sin \theta_1}$
$\theta_1 \approx 46°$
The angle adjacent to $\theta_2$ is also 46°,
$\theta_2 = 180° - 46° = 134°$

18. A rhombus has all side lengths equal. A rectangle has slopes of consecutive sides with a product −1. A trapezium has different slopes of all sides.

19. The boundary is a regular hexagon.
$P = 6(700) = 4200$ m

20. $w^2 = 13^2 - 5^2$
$w = 12$
$A = lw = (5)(12) = 60$ square units

21. **a.** Each is parallel to one pair of sides and has a magnitude equal to the length of those sides.
**b.** The angle of rotation is 180°. The center could be any vertex or the midpoint of any side.
**c.** Any reflection flips the parallelograms so that they do not match the original parallelogram.

22. $\frac{0.01}{x} = \frac{1}{2500}$
$x = 25$
$A = (25)(25) = 625 \text{ m}^2$

23. $d_{PQ} = \sqrt{(7-2)^2 + (-1-1)^2}$
$= \sqrt{(5)^2 + (-2)^2} = \sqrt{29}$
$d_{QR} = \sqrt{(7-2)^2 + (-1 - -3)^2}$
$= \sqrt{(5)^2 + (2)^2} = \sqrt{29}$
$d_{RS} = \sqrt{(2 - -3)^2 + (-3 - -1)^2}$
$= \sqrt{(5)^2 + (-2)^2} = \sqrt{29}$
$d_{PS} = \sqrt{(2 - -3)^2 + (1 - -1)^2}$
$= \sqrt{(5)^2 + (2)^2} = \sqrt{29}$
The polygon is a rhombus because the sides are equal length.
$P = 4(\sqrt{29}) = 4\sqrt{29}$

24. The circles have the same center, located at (5, −4). The radius of the smaller circle is 4 and the radius of the larger circle is 6.
$(x-5)^2 + (y+4)^2 = 16$
$(x-5)^2 + (y+4)^2 = 36$

25. The new center of the circle is at (0, −6) and the radius remains the same.
$x^2 + (y+6)^2 = 169$

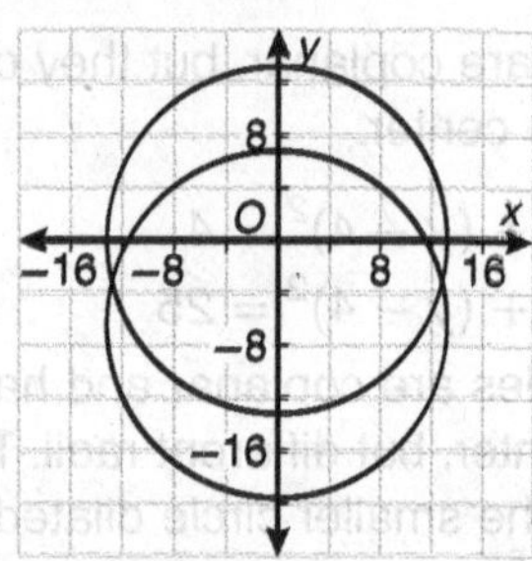


26. Since the angle formed by the intersection of the diagonals of a rhombus measures 90°, $m\angle NSM = 90°$.

27. Converse: If Noel cannot find her shoes, she did not clean her room.
This is false.

28. $\frac{5w}{35} = \frac{40}{20}$
$(20)(5w) = (35)(40)$
$100w = 1400$
$w = 14$

29. $2x + 3 = \frac{1}{2}(96)$
$2x = 45$
$x = 22.5$

30. If a bird is a cardinal, then it can fly.

## LESSON 98

### Warm Up 98

1. component

2. $\sin 36° = \frac{\text{vertical}}{7}$

$7 \sin 36° = \text{vertical}$

$\text{vertical} = 4.11$

$\cos 36° = \frac{\text{horizontal}}{7}$

$7 \cos 36° = \text{horizontal}$

$\text{horizontal} = 5.66$

3. $\cos \theta = \frac{30}{45}$

$\theta = \cos^{-1}\left(\frac{30}{45}\right)$

$\theta = 48°$

### Lesson Practice 98

a. $c^2 = a^2 + b^2 - 2ab \cos C$

$c^2 = 40^2 + 48^2 - 2(40)(48) \cos 92°$

$c^2 = 4038$

$c = 63.54$

$c \approx 64$

b. $\cos X = \frac{y^2 + z^2 - x^2}{2yz}$

$\cos X = \frac{14^2 + 12^2 - 7^2}{2(14)(12)}$

$\cos X = 0.86607$

$m\angle X = 30°$

c. $a^2 = b^2 + c^2 - 2bc \cos A$

$a^2 = 27^2 + 14^2 - 2(27)(14) \cos 90°$

$a \approx 30.4$

You could use the Pythagorean Theorem to find *a*.

d. $x^2 = 45^2 + 38^2 - 2(45)(38)\cos 66°$

$x^2 = 2077.96$

$x \approx 45.58$ yards

### Practice 98

1. $\cos \theta = \frac{(2x)^2 + \left(\frac{4}{3}x\right)^2 - (3x)^2}{2(2x)\left(\frac{4}{3}x\right)}$

$\cos \theta = \frac{4x^2 + \frac{16}{9}x^2 - 9x^2}{\frac{16}{3}x^2}$

$\cos \theta = \frac{x^2\left(\frac{36}{9} + \frac{16}{9} - \frac{81}{9}\right)}{x^2\left(\frac{16}{3}\right)}$

$\cos \theta = \frac{(36 + 16 - 81) \cdot 3}{9 \cdot 16}$

$\cos \theta = \frac{-29}{48}$

$\cos \theta = -0.604$

$\theta \approx 127°$

2. Both students would have the same equation of the circle after the dilation and the translation in either order:

$(x + 3)^2 + (y + 2)^2 = 36$

For Franklin:

Dilation first: $x^2 + y^2 = 36$ as radius goes from 2 to 6.

Then the translation:

$(x + 3)^2 + (y + 2)^2 = 36$

For Benjamin:

Translation first: $(x + 3)^2 + (y + 2)^2 = 4$

Then the dilation (which increases the radius from 2 to 6):

$(x + 3)^2 + (y + 2)^2 = 36$

3. $A = (3.14)(50)^2 - (3.14)(45)^2$

$A = 1491.5$

$A \approx 1492 \text{ m}^2$

4. Since congruent chords are the same distance from the center of the circle, the distance must be 3 inches.

5. magnitude $= \sqrt{3^2 + (-4)^2} = \sqrt{25}$ or 5

6. A midsegment divides sides of the triangle into two equal segments, and is exactly one-half of the length of the parallel side.

Therefore, $x = 58$ and $y = \frac{112}{2} = 56$

7. $\dfrac{\sin\theta}{\tan\theta} = 0.6$

$\dfrac{\sin\theta}{\frac{\sin\theta}{\cos\theta}} = 0.6$

$\cos\theta = 0.6$

$\theta \approx 53°$

8. In $\Delta SXY$, $SX = SY$ because they are radii of the circle. Therefore, $\Delta SXY$ is isosceles. This means $m\angle SXY = m\angle SYX$ and $m\angle SXY = m\angle 1$ by the Opposite Angle Theorem. Also $m\angle SXY = m\angle 2$ by the Opposite Angle Theorem. Therefore, $m\angle 1 = m\angle 2$

9. Area of the base of the pyramid $= (200)^2 = 40{,}000 \text{ ft}^2$

Half way up the height of the pyramid, the area of the floor will be $\left(\frac{1}{2}\right)^2 = \frac{1}{4}$ of the base of the full pyramid. Therefore, $\frac{1}{4}(40{,}000) = 10{,}000 \text{ ft}^2$

10. There would be two such unique vectors, one at an angle of 120° above the positive $x$-axis and the second at an angle of 60° below the positive $x$-axis. These both make a 90° angle to the given line.

11. $\cos\theta = \dfrac{10^2 + 6^2 - 12^2}{2(10)(6)}$

$\cos\theta = -0.0666$

$\theta \approx 94°$

12. In $\Delta JKL$ and $\Delta PQR$, $m\angle J = m\angle P$, $KJ = QP$, and $m\angle K = m\angle Q$ are all given. Therefore, by the ASA Congruence Theorem, $\Delta JKL \cong \Delta PQR$

13. The factor of $\frac{1}{6}$ applied to a side length of 6 gives a new height of 1. So $P = 2(h + l)$ becomes $P = 2(1 + 6) = 14$.

An expression for the new perimeter, based on the original perimeter:

Originally: $\frac{P}{2}$ between the two lengths and $\frac{P}{2}$ between the two heights.

Now, the new heights become $\frac{1}{6}\left(\frac{P}{2}\right)$.

This gives the new perimeter as

$P_{new} = \frac{P}{2} + \frac{1}{6}\left(\frac{P}{2}\right)$

14. Since the segment moves to the left by 7 units, only the $x$-coordinate is affected. So, $(-1, -3)$ becomes $(-1 - 7, -3) = (-8, -3)$

15. Since $\overline{AB} \cong \overline{CD}$, $\overline{AC} \cong \overline{BD}$, and $BC = AD$, the frame is a rectangle.

16. $\sin 60° = \cos 30°$

17. Inner circle: $r = 5$, so $(x + 1)^2 + y^2 = 25$

Outer circle: $r = 10$, so $(x + 1)^2 + y^2 = 100$

Similarities: They both are centered at the origin and they both have points that are a fixed distance from the center.

Differences: Their radii are not the same, so they have different circumferences and different areas.

18. When one angle within the triangle is a right angle, the law of cosines $c^2 = a^2 + b^2 - 2ab\cos C$ becomes the Pythagorean Theorem. This is because $\cos 90° = 0$.

19. As can be seen in the two diagrams, the angles opposite the 18-unit side can either be acute (diagram to the right) or obtuse (diagram to the left). Therefore, with the given information, it is not possible to conclude that the triangles are congruent.

20.

| Statements | Reasons |
|---|---|
| 1. $\overline{JK} \parallel \overline{HL}$; $m\angle KML > m\angle HML$ | 1. Given |
| 2. $\angle JMK \cong \angle LMH$ | 2. Vertical angles |
| 3. $\angle JHK \cong \angle LHK$ | 3. Alternate interior angles |
| 4. $\overline{JK} \cong \overline{HL}$ | 4. Given |
| 5. $\Delta JKM \cong \Delta LHM$ | 5. AAS |
| 6. $\overline{MK} \cong \overline{MH}$ | 6. CPCTC |
| 7. $\overline{ML} \cong \overline{ML}$ | 7. Reflexive Property |
| 8. $KL > HL$ | 8. Hinge Theorem |

21. In the isosceles triangle, use $x$ for the measure of the two legs:

$x^2 + x^2 = 75^2$

$2x^2 = 75^2$

$x^2 = \dfrac{75^2}{2}$

$x = \dfrac{75}{\sqrt{2}}$ or $\dfrac{75\sqrt{2}}{2}$ inches

22. $c^2 = a^2 + b^2 - 2ab \cos C$
$x^2 = 35^2 + 55^2 - 2(35)(55)\cos 95°$
$x^2 = 4585.5$
$x = 67.7$
$x \approx 68$ feet

23. The square root of $\sin^2 \theta + \cos^2 \theta$ is not $\sin \theta + \cos \theta$. If we square $\sin \theta + \cos \theta$,
$(\sin \theta + \cos \theta)^2$
$= \sin^2 \theta + 2 \sin \theta \cos \theta + \cos^2 \theta$
The sum of radicals is not the same as the radical of a sum.

24. $\frac{(2x + 6) + 76}{2} = 87$
$2x + 6 + 76 = 174$
$2x = 92$
$x = 46$

25. For green: 25% × 360° = 90°
Looking for green at this value, choice **B** is correct.

26. The two diagonal lines and the top and bottom sides of the box as drawn here all touch both circles at a tangent. Therefore, there are 4 common tangents. The right and left sides, or ends, of the box are tangent to only one circle each, so there are 2 tangents.

27. When the base dilates by a factor of 3, the square becomes a rectangle. The current square has side lengths of 2 units. When the base dilates by a factor of 3, the two opposite sides dilate to 6 units.

| | |
|---|---|
| $P = 2(l + w)$ | $A = lw$ |
| $P = 2(6 + 2)$ | $A = (6)(2)$ |
| $P = 16$ units | $A = 12$ square units |

28. Total area: $\pi(31)^2 = 961\pi$ cm$^2$
Area of small white circle:
$\pi(5)^2 = 25\pi$ cm$^2$
Area of larger white circular band:
$\pi(19)^2 - \pi(10)^2 = 261\pi$ cm$^2$
Total white area:
$(25\pi + 261\pi)$ cm$^2 = 286\pi$ cm$^2$
Area that is shaded:
$(961\pi - 286\pi)$ cm$^2 = 675\pi$ cm$^2$
Therefore, the probability of landing on the shaded area is $\frac{675\pi}{961\pi} = \frac{675}{961}$.

29. The larger circle will have a radius in the ratio of 7 : 4 or $\frac{7}{4}$ times the radius of the smaller circle. As a result, the ratio of their circumferences will be $\frac{7}{4}$. The ratio of their areas will be $\left(\frac{7}{4}\right)^2 = \frac{49}{16}$.

30.

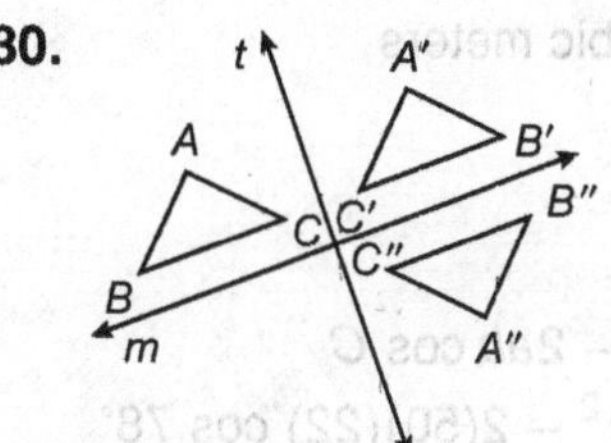


## LESSON 99

### Warm Up 99

1. rectangular pyramid

2. $V = \frac{1}{3}b^2h$

$V = \frac{1}{3}(3.5)^2(2.7) = 11.025$ cm$^3$

3. Choice **B** is correct.

### Lesson Practice 99

a. The perimeter of the smaller base $= 8 + 15 + 17 = 40$ in. So:
$3 : 4 = 40 : x$
$\frac{3}{4} = \frac{40}{x}$
$3x = 160$
$x = 53.33$ inches

b. $\left(\frac{3}{4}\right)^2 = \frac{182}{y}$
$\frac{9}{16} = \frac{182}{y}$
$9y = 2912$
$y = 323.56$ in.$^2$

c. $\left(\frac{3}{4}\right)^3 = \frac{323}{z}$
$\frac{27}{64} = \frac{323}{z}$

$27z = 20{,}672$
$z = 765.63 \text{ in.}^3$

**d.** $V = \pi r^2 h$
$V = (3.14)(0.10)^2(0.59)$
$V = 0.018526 \text{ m}^3$
$\left(\frac{1}{50}\right)^3 = \frac{0.018526}{x}$
$x = 50^3 \times 0.018526$
$x \approx 2316$ cubic meters

## Practice 99

**1.** Let $x = c$
$c^2 = a^2 + b^2 - 2ab\cos C$
$c^2 = 50^2 + 22^2 - 2(50)(22)\cos 78°$
$c^2 = 2526.59$
$c = x \approx 50.3$

**2.**

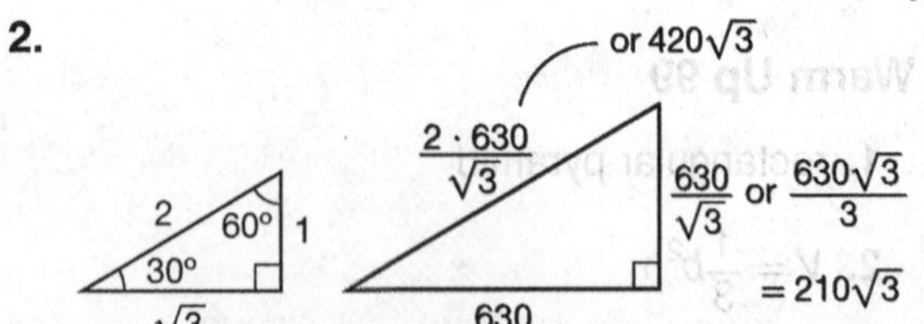


$P = 630 + 420\sqrt{3} + 210\sqrt{3}$
$P = 630 + 630\sqrt{3}$
$P = 630(1 + \sqrt{3})$

**3.**

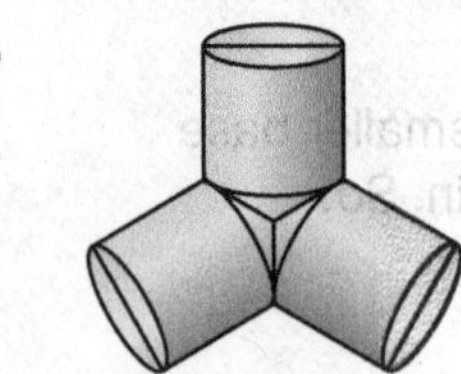

**4.** For prism $R$:
Area of the faces:

| $3 \times 4.5$ | $3 \times 9$ | $4.5 \times 9$ |
|---|---|---|
| $= 13.5$ | $= 27$ | $= 40.5$ |

For prism $S$, we apply the scale factor for area of $4^2 : 3^2$ or $\frac{16}{9}$:

| $13.5 \times \frac{16}{9}$ | $27 \times \frac{16}{9}$ | $40.5 \times \frac{16}{9}$ |
|---|---|---|
| $= 24 \text{ cm}^2$ | $= 48 \text{ cm}^2$ | $= 72 \text{ cm}^2$ |

**5.** $P = 4 \times 10 + 2(6 + 4) = 60$ in.
Applying the scale factor of $\frac{5}{4}$:
Perimeter: $60 \times \frac{5}{4} = 75$ in.
Length $= 6 \times \frac{5}{4} = 7.5$ in.
Width $= 4 \times \frac{5}{4} = 5$ in.
Height $= 10 \times \frac{5}{4} = 12.5$ in.

**6.** For $a = 0$, the relation becomes $x = 1$. Rearranging for $y$, we obtain $y = \frac{1}{a}x + \frac{a^2 - 1}{a}$, with a slope of $\frac{1}{a}$ and a $y$-intercept of $\frac{a^2 - 1}{a}$. So, as $a$ increases, the slope approaches zero (meaning that the line becomes horizontal) and the $y$-intercept becomes larger and larger.

**7.** $\frac{\sin 108°}{25} = \frac{\sin\theta}{20}$
so, $25 \sin\theta = 20 \sin 108°$
$\sin\theta = \frac{20 \sin 108°}{25}$
$\theta = 49.53°$ or $50°$

**8.** Since only one measure of the trapezoid is changing in the ratio 2 : 1, the ratio of the area between the two trapezoids is also changing by the same ratio of 2 : 1.

**9.** At the art museum:
$\cos X = \frac{110^2 + 95^2 - 125^2}{2(110)(95)}$
$\cos X = 0.2631578947$
$\angle X \approx 74.7°$
At the park:
$\cos Y = \frac{110^2 + 125^2 - 95^2}{2(110)(125)}$
$\cos Y = 0.68$
$\angle Y \approx 47.2°$
At the fountain:
$\angle X + \angle Y + \angle Z = 180°$
$74.7° + 47.2° + \angle Z = 180°$
$121.9° + \angle Z = 180°$
$\angle Z \approx 58.1°$

**10.** The perimeter ratio will be equal to 8 : 13. The area ratio will be 64 : 169 or $\frac{64}{169}$.

11. Shaded area:
$= \pi(22.34^2 - 7.5^2) = 442.8256\pi$
Recordable area:
$= \pi(60^2 - 7.5^2) = 3543.75\pi$
Ratio $= \frac{3543.75\pi}{442.8256\pi} \approx 8$, which means 8 times the length of recorded music could be stored on the CD.

10 minutes × 8 = 80 minutes of music could be recorded.

12. $L = 2\pi rh$
$L = 2(3.14)(1.5)(1)$
$L = 9.42 \text{ in.}^2$

13. Since a kite has diagonals that intersect at right angles, the lengths of the missing sides can be found using the Pythagorean Theorem:
$AB^2 = a^2 + b^2$
$AB^2 = 7^2 + 6^2$
$AB^2 = 85$
$AB \approx 9.2$; Therefore, $AD \approx 9.2$
$CD^2 = a^2 + b^2$
$CD^2 = 7^2 + 12^2$
$CD^2 = 193$
$CD \approx 13.9$; Therefore, $BC \approx 13.9$

14. $\cos 1 = \dfrac{(x)^2 + (2x)^2 - \left(\frac{3}{2}x\right)^2}{2(x)(2x)}$
$= \dfrac{x^2 + 4x^2 - \frac{9}{4}x^2}{4x^2}$
$= \dfrac{x^2(4 + 16 - 9)}{16x^2} = \dfrac{11}{16}$
$m\angle 1 \approx 47°$
$\cos 2 = \dfrac{(x)^2 + \left(\frac{3}{2}x\right)^2 - (2x)^2}{2(x)\left(\frac{3}{2}x\right)}$
$= \dfrac{x^2 + \frac{9}{4}x^2 - 4x^2}{3x^2}$
$= \dfrac{x^2(4 + 9 - 16)}{12x^2}$
$= -\frac{1}{4}$; $m\angle 2 \approx 104°$

$m\angle 1 + m\angle 2 + m\angle 3 = 180°$
$m\angle 3 = 180° - (104° + 47°)$
$m\angle 3 = 29°$

15. Geometric mean $= \sqrt{12.1 \times 5.6} = 8.2$

16. a. $P = (15 + 36 + 8 + 39 + 8) = 106$ mm
b. $A_{total} = A_{rectangle} + A_{triangle}$

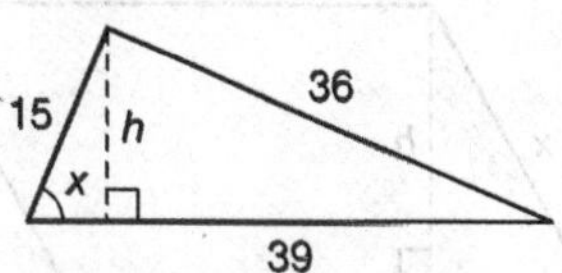


In the triangle:
$\cos X = \dfrac{15^2 + 39^2 - 36^2}{2(15)(39)}$
$\angle X \approx 67.4°$
$\sin 67.4° = \dfrac{h}{15}$
$h = 15 \sin 67.4°$
$h \approx 13.85$
$A = 39 \times 8 + \frac{1}{2}(39)(13.85) = 582 \text{ mm}^2$

17. $\tan\theta = \dfrac{\sin\theta}{\cos\theta}$, and since
$\sin^2\theta + \cos^2\theta = 1$, then
$\sin\theta = \sqrt{1 - \cos^2\theta}$, which means that
$\tan\theta = \dfrac{\sqrt{1 - \cos^2\theta}}{\cos\theta}$

18. For a regular triangular pyramid with side length $s$, slant length $l$, and base altitude $x$, $S = \frac{1}{2}xl + \frac{3}{2}sl$ With a scale factor for all the sides of $\frac{a}{b}$,
$S = \frac{1}{2}xl + \frac{3}{2}sl$ becomes
$S = \frac{1}{2}\frac{a}{b}x\frac{a}{b}l + \frac{3}{2}\frac{a}{b}s\frac{a}{b}l$
$S = \frac{a^2}{b^2}\frac{1}{2}xl + \frac{a^2}{b^2}\frac{3}{2}sl$
$S = \frac{a^2}{b^2} \times \left(\frac{1}{2}xl + \frac{3}{2}sl\right)$
Therefore, the ratio of the surface areas is $\frac{a^2}{b^2}$ or $a^2 : b^2$.

**19.** The smallest side is opposite the smallest angle, so the smallest side is $XZ$. The largest side is opposite the largest angle, so the largest side is $ZC$. Therefore, the order of the sides from smallest to largest is $XZ$, $XC$, $ZC$.

**20.** $A = \pi(6^2 - 1^2) = (3.14)(35) = 109.9$ in.$^2$

**21.**

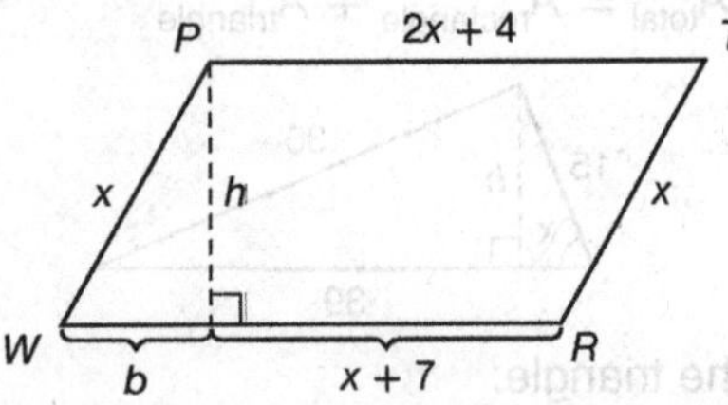


Since $PQRW$ is a parallelogram, $PT = WR$, so $b + x + 7 = 2x + 4$, and $b = x - 3$. Using the Pythagorean Theorem,

$$x^2 = (x - 3)^2 + h^2$$
$$x^2 = x^2 - 6x + 9 + h^2$$
$$6x - 9 = h^2$$
$$h = \sqrt{6x - 9}$$

**22.** Since the shape is a parallelogram, opposite angles are equal. And since the 33° is already paired up, the missing fourth angle must measure 147°.

**23.** In simplifying $\sqrt{4 + 4}$, Luka multiplied the 4s instead of adding them. The result should be $\sqrt{8}$ or $2\sqrt{2}$.

**24.** Let $x$ represent the price of milk and $y$ represent the price of eggs. One less than three times the price of milk can be written as $3x - 1$. If the price of eggs is at least this amount, the inequality can be written as $y \geq 3x - 1$.

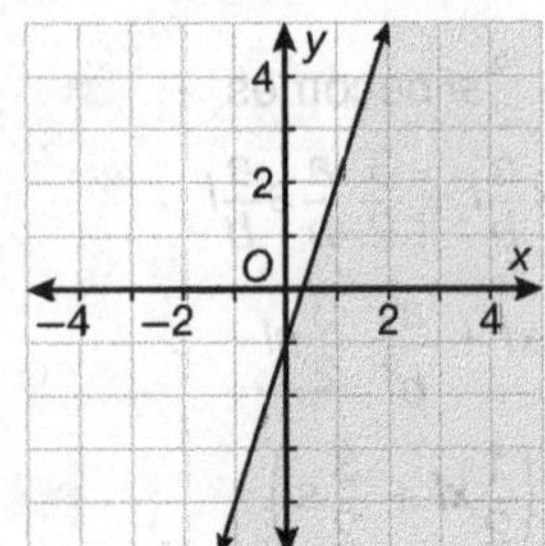


**25.** Calculating surface area $A$:

$$S = \text{base area} + \frac{1}{2}b_1h_1 + \frac{1}{2}b_2h_2 + \frac{1}{2}b_3h_3$$

$$S = \frac{1}{2}(80)(150) + \frac{1}{2}(140)(170) + \frac{1}{2}(120)(80) + \frac{1}{2}(120)(150)$$

$$S = 31{,}700 \text{ mm}^2$$

The ratio for the surface areas is $2^2 : 5^2$ or $4 : 25$. So, the surface area for $B$ is:

$$31{,}700 \times \frac{25}{4} = 198{,}125 \text{ mm}^2$$

**26.** The angle that the radii make with the tangents is a right angle, with the sides being equal to the radius of the circle, making this shape a square. Therefore, the correct choice is **C**.

**27.** Translated 6 units to the left means that the center moves from (0, 0) to (−6, 0). Therefore, the equation is:

$$(x + 6)^2 + y^2 = 121$$

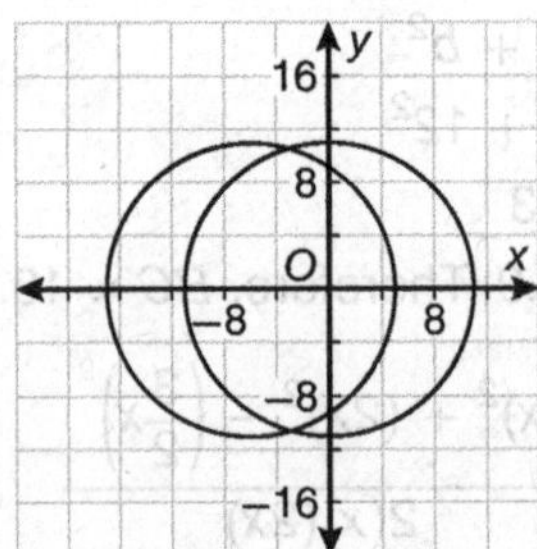


**28.** $\frac{\sin S}{14} = \frac{\sin 102°}{20}$

$m\angle S = 43.2°$

$m\angle T = 180° - (102° + 43.2°)$

$m\angle T = 34.8°$

Now solve for $RS$:

$$\frac{20}{\sin 102°} = \frac{RS}{\sin 34.8°}$$

$RS = 11.7$ or approx. 12

Therefore, choice **C** is correct.

**29.** The measure of the interior angle for each triangle would be $\frac{360°}{6} = 60°$, and since the sides of these triangles joining to the side of the hexagon are all of the same length, the triangles are all equilateral. So, all sides of these triangles would be 40 inches each.

30. The slope of $QR = \frac{1}{2}$, which is the same as the slope of $PS$, so $PS$ and $QR$ are parallel. The slope of $QP = -\frac{2}{3}$ while the slope of $RS = -3$, so these two sides are not parallel; Therefore the shape is a trapezoid.

## LESSON 100

### Warm Up 100

1. composite transformation
2. $\langle 2, 3\rangle + \langle -1, 0\rangle = \langle 2-1, 3+0\rangle$ or $\langle 1, 3\rangle$
3. A reflection through $y = x$ interchanges the coordinates such that the point $(x, y)$ becomes the point $(y, x)$ under the transformation. Choice **D** is correct.

### Lesson Practice 100

a. $\begin{bmatrix} 2+0 & 0+4 \\ -2+3 & 1+(-1) \end{bmatrix} = \begin{bmatrix} 2 & 4 \\ 1 & 0 \end{bmatrix}$

b. $\overrightarrow{AB} = \begin{bmatrix} 2 & 4 \\ 1 & 4 \end{bmatrix}$

$\overrightarrow{AB} + \begin{bmatrix} -1 & -1 \\ -1 & -1 \end{bmatrix} = \begin{bmatrix} 2-1 & 4-1 \\ 1-1 & 4-1 \end{bmatrix} = \begin{bmatrix} 1 & 3 \\ 0 & 3 \end{bmatrix}$

The matrix translates the line down one unit and left one unit.

c. Three units to the left affects the $x$-values by $-3$ and 1 unit down affects the $y$-values by $-1$. Since a line is defined by two points, the translation matrix is a 2 by 2 matrix. Therefore, the matrix is $\begin{bmatrix} -3 & -3 \\ -1 & -1 \end{bmatrix}$

d. Applying a matrix to one point only requires a one-column matrix. 6 meters to the right affects the $x$-values by $+6$ and 5 meters down affects the $y$–values by $-5$. Therefore, the matrix is $\begin{bmatrix} 6 \\ -5 \end{bmatrix}$.

### Practice 100

1. $A = \pi(44)^2 - \pi(25)^2 = 1311\pi \text{ in.}^2$
2. magnitude $= \sqrt{60^2 + 5^2}$
   $= \sqrt{3625}$ or 60.2
3. The shape $ABCDE$ has been reflected through the line $l$ to produce the image.

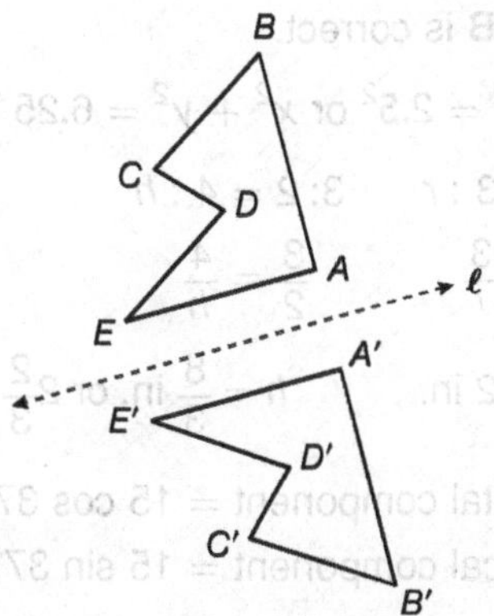


4. The ratio of surface areas is $3^2 : 5^2$ or $9 : 25$. Therefore, $S_B = \frac{25}{9}S_A$, which means that choice **B** is correct.
5. All of the $x$–values decrease by 4, and all of the $y$-values decrease by 1. This is applied to all three points, so the transformation matrix is $\begin{bmatrix} -4 & -4 & -4 \\ -1 & -1 & -1 \end{bmatrix}$
6. $\sin^2\theta + \cos^2\theta = 1$
   $\sin^2\theta = 1 - \cos^2\theta$
   $\sin\theta = \sqrt{1 - \cos^2\theta}$
   $\sin\theta = \sqrt{1 - (0.4)}$
   $\sin\theta \approx 0.77$
7. If $v = 3.2$,
   $(10v - 5)° = [10(3.2) - 5]° = 27°$
   The measure of $\widehat{JK} = 2(27°) = 54°$
8. $12 : 18 : x = y : 9 : 13$
   $12 : 18 = y : 9$ and $18 : x = 9 : 13$
   $\frac{12}{18} = \frac{y}{9}$    $\frac{18}{x} = \frac{9}{13}$
   $18y = 9 \times 12$    $9x = 18 \times 13$
   $y = \frac{9 \times 12}{18}$    $x = \frac{18 \times 13}{9}$
   $y = 6$    $x = 26$
9. The orthocenter is the point of intersection of any two altitudes and since a right triangle has two altitudes that form the right angle, the location of the orthocenter of a right triangle is at the vertex of the right angle.
10. Using a 2 by 1 matrix, 3 steps forward and 3 steps to the right can be represented using $\begin{bmatrix} 3 \\ 3 \end{bmatrix}$.

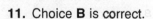

11. Choice **B** is correct.

12. $x^2 + y^2 = 2.5^2$ or $x^2 + y^2 = 6.25$

13. $3:2 = 3:r$  $3:2 = 4:h$

$\frac{3}{2} = \frac{3}{r}$  $\frac{3}{2} = \frac{4}{h}$

$r = 2$ in.  $h = \frac{8}{3}$ in. or $2\frac{2}{3}$ in.

14. Horizontal component $= 15 \cos 37° \approx 11.98$
Vertical component $= 15 \sin 37° \approx 9.03$

15. Sample:

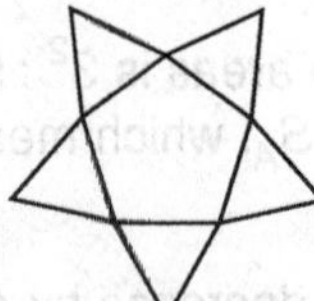

16. $\cos R = \frac{18^2 + 25^2 - 30^2}{2(18)(25)}$

$\cos R = 0.0544$

$m\angle R \approx 87°$

$\frac{\sin 87°}{30} = \frac{\sin Q}{18}$

so $30 \sin Q = 18 \sin 87°$

$\sin Q = \frac{18 \sin 87°}{30}$

$m\angle Q \approx 37°$

$m\angle P + m\angle Q + m\angle R = 180°$

$m\angle P + 37° + 87° = 180°$

$m\angle P + 37° + 87° = 180° - 124°$

$m\angle P = 56°$

17. Since the diagonals of the given shape are not equal in length, the shape is a rhombus or kite.

18. Base area of the smaller pyramid $= (30)^2 = 900 \text{ mm}^2$. The 3 : 8 scale factor becomes a 9 : 64 scale factor for area. Appling this to the smaller area, we obtain $900 \times \frac{64}{9} = 6400 \text{ mm}^2$ for the base area of the larger pyramid.

A lateral face of the smaller pyramid has $A = \frac{1}{2}(30)(36) = 540 \text{ mm}^2$. Again, applying the scale factor for area, we obtain $540 \times \frac{64}{9} = 3840 \text{ mm}^2$

19. Since the two circles contact each other at only one point, there is only one common tangent.

20. Neither. There is not a unique triangle that can be drawn if only the three angles are given. Many similar triangles could be drawn with congruent angles. We would need to know at least the length of one side to be able to create a unique triangle.

21.

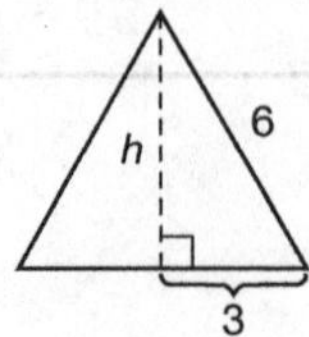


In this diagram,

$6^2 = 3^2 + h^2$

$36 = 9 + h^2$

$27 = h^2$

$3\sqrt{3} = h$

$A = 3 \times (6 \times 4) + 2\left(\frac{1}{2}(6)(3\sqrt{3})\right)$

$A = 72 + 18\sqrt{3} \text{ in.}^2$

22. A square-based pyramid with the area of the bottom as $s^2$ and 4 triangular sides with an area of $\frac{1}{2}sl$ each. The total area will be

$A = s^2 + 4\left(\frac{1}{2}sl\right) = s^2 + 2sl$

23. She confused the columns with the rows. The columns represent each point and the rows represent either the $x$- or $y$-components. The translation matrix should be $\begin{bmatrix} -3 & -3 \\ 1 & 1 \end{bmatrix}$.

24. If $y^2 + 1 = x$ was translated 1 unit up, the equation would be $y^2 = x$, which is symmetric along the $x$-axis.

25. $\frac{QR}{ST} = \frac{JK}{LM}$

$\frac{45}{ST} = \frac{12}{15}$; $12x = 675$; $x = 56.25$

26. The dilation factor of 3 will change the radius from $r = 3$ to $r = 9$. As a result, the equation will be $(x + 3)^2 + (y - 2)^2 = 81$.

27. Translations up or down only affect the $y$-coordinate. Up $2x$ and then down $x - 1$ means that the $y$-coordinates will be changed by $2x - (x - 1) = x + 1$. The translation matrix is therefore $\begin{bmatrix} 0 & 0 \\ x + 1 & x + 1 \end{bmatrix}$.

28. Circumference is 28 inches, so

$$28 = 2\pi r \text{ means } r = \frac{28}{2\pi} = 4.46 \text{ in.}$$

$$S = 4\pi r^2 = 4\pi(4.46^2) \approx 250 \text{ in.}^2$$

29. $\frac{15}{45} = \frac{33}{y}$

$15y = 1485$

$y = 99$

30. $P$ is the center of the circle.

$\overline{BC}$ and $\overline{AD}$ are diameters. Given

| | |
|---|---|
| $\overline{AP} \cong \overline{CP}$ | Radii of the same circle ≅ |
| $\angle APB \cong \angle CPD$ | Vertical Angles Theorem |
| $\overline{BP} \cong \overline{DP}$ | Radii of the same circle ≅ |
| so $\triangle PAB \cong \triangle PCD$ | SAS congruency |

## INVESTIGATION 10

1.

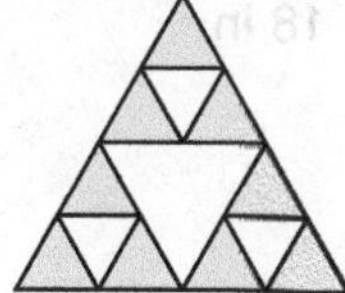

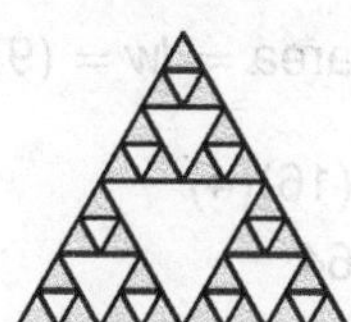

2. From these diagrams, it is clear that the Sierpinski triangle is self-similar.

3. triangle, midpoint, sides, triangle

4. Sample: Dilate the triangle to half its size and translate it so the midpoint of its base is intersected by the original triangle's vertex and is perpendicular to the original triangle's altitude from that vertex.

5. Choice **B** is correct.

6.

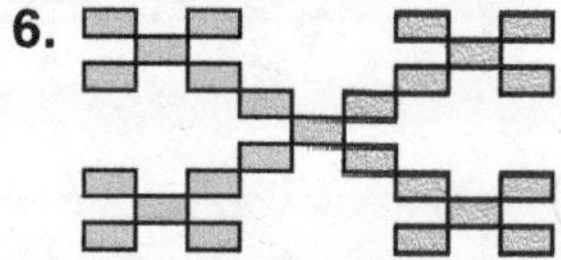

7. Symmetrically add equilateral triangles to all sides of the previous triangle by dividing each side of the larger triangle into three sections, and locate the base of the added triangles in the middle third of section of each side.

8.

9. equilateral triangle, segments, 60°

### Investigation 10 Practice

a.

b. Choice **C** is correct.

c. The segment is dilated by a factor less than 1, then rotated and translated to the ends of the original segment. Two copies of this segment are produced and transformed in this way.

d.

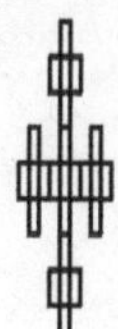

## LESSON 101

### Warm Up 101

1. secant

2. $\frac{6}{8} = \frac{14 - x}{14}$

$8(14 - x) = (6)(14)$

$112 - 8x = 84$

$-8x = -28$

$x = 3.5$ cm

3. $(3x)(2x) = (6)(20 - x)$

$6x^2 = 120 - 6x$

$6x^2 + 6x - 120 = 0$

$6(x^2 + x - 20) = 0$

$6(x + 5)(x - 4) = 0$

$x = 4$ (because the lengths must be positive)

$UW = 3(4) + 2(4) = 20$

Choice **D** is correct.

## Lesson Practice 101

**a.** $(x + 2)(2) = (10)(3)$

$2x + 4 = 30$

$2x = 26$

$x = 13$

**b.** Since 2 points determine a line, draw $\overline{AD}$ and $\overline{BD}$. By the Inscribed Angle Theorem, Theorem 47-1, $m\angle CAD = \frac{1}{2}m\widehat{BD}$. By Theorem 64-1, the measure of an angle formed by an intersecting tangent and chord is half the measure of the intercepted arc, so $m\angle BDC = \frac{1}{2}m\widehat{BD}$. Therefore, $m\angle CAD \cong \angle BDC$. By the Reflexive Property of Congruence, $\angle C \cong \angle C$. Therefore, $\triangle CAD \sim \triangle CDB$ by the AA Similarity Postulate. Corresponding sides are proportional, so $\frac{AC}{DC} = \frac{DC}{BC}$. The cross product is $AC \times BC = DC^2$.

**c.** $x^2 = (10)(5)$

$x = \sqrt{50} = 5\sqrt{2}$

**d.** 200 ft $\approx$ 0.038 mi

$x^2 = (7920.038)(0.038)$

$x^2 = 300.96$

$x \approx 17.3$ mi

## Practice 101

**1.** $17(2x + 17) = 15(x + 24)$

$34x + 289 = 15x + 360$

$19x = 71$

$x \approx 3.73$

$EG = 2(3.73) + 17 = 24.5$

**2.** A square with vertices at (2, 0), (−2, 0), (0, −2), and (0, 2).

**3.** $\langle 3 + 1, 4 - 1\rangle = \langle 4, 3\rangle$

**4.** $\begin{bmatrix} 1 & -2 & 4 \\ 1 & 3 & 4 \end{bmatrix} + \begin{bmatrix} 3 & 3 & 3 \\ 0 & 0 & 0 \end{bmatrix} = \begin{bmatrix} 4 & 1 & 7 \\ 1 & 3 & 4 \end{bmatrix}$

**5.** This would be the same as a counterclockwise rotation of 231° − 99° = 132° or a clockwise rotation of 360° − 132° = 228°.

**6.** $2y = \frac{h}{6}x + 4$

$y = \frac{h}{12}x + 2$

$\frac{2}{k} = \frac{h}{12}$

Sample: If $k = 6$,

$\frac{2}{6} = \frac{h}{12}$

$h = 4$

**7.** $m_{AB} = \left(\frac{-4 + -2}{2}, \frac{5 + -4}{2}\right) = \left(\frac{-6}{2}, \frac{1}{2}\right)$

$= (-3, 0.5)$

**8.** $\tan\theta = \frac{\sin\theta}{\sqrt{1 - \sin^2\theta}}$

**9.** Base area $= \frac{1}{2}bh = \frac{1}{2}\left(1\frac{1}{2}\right)(2) = 1\frac{1}{2}$ in.$^2$

Face area $= lw = (9)\left(1\frac{1}{2}\right) = 13\frac{1}{2}$ in.$^2$

Missing side length: $x^2 = 2^2 + 1.5^2$

$x = 2\frac{1}{2}$

Face area $= lw = (9)\left(2\frac{1}{2}\right) = 22\frac{1}{2}$ in.$^2$

Face area $= lw = (9)(2) = 18$ in.$^2$

**10.** $x^2 = (16)(4)$

$x^2 = 64$

$x = 8$

**11.**

45°, 1, $\sqrt{2}$, 90°, 45°, 1

**12.** $14^2 = 8^2 + 12^2 - 2(8)(12)\cos\theta$

$196 = 64 + 144 - 192\cos\theta$

$0.0625 = \cos\theta$

$\theta = \cos^{-1} 0.0625 \approx 86°$

**13.** $\begin{bmatrix} -5 & -5 \\ 3 & 3 \end{bmatrix}$

**14.** $A = \pi(27^2) - \pi(15^2)$

$= 729\pi - 225\pi$

$= 504\pi$ cm$^2$

**15.** The intersection will be in Quadrant I.

**16.** $16^2 = 8(8 + AB)$

$256 = 64 + 8AB$

$192 = 8AB$

$AB = 24$ cm

Choice **C** is correct.

**17.** No. If $\triangle PQR$ were equiangular, then $\triangle PQR$ would be equilateral. So, $\overline{PQ} \cong \overline{QR}$, which means that $PQ = QR$, which contradicts $PQ > QR$.

**18.** $\begin{bmatrix} 3x & 3x \\ -2x & -2x \end{bmatrix}$

**19.** $\frac{16}{\sin 27°} = \frac{EF}{\sin 112°}$

$EF \approx 32.68$

**20.** Sum of interior angles $= (5 - 2)180°$

$= 3(180°)$

$= 540°$

$540° - 4(100°) = 140°$

**21.** $x^2 = (16)(4)$

$x^2 = 64$

$x = 8$ in.

**22.**

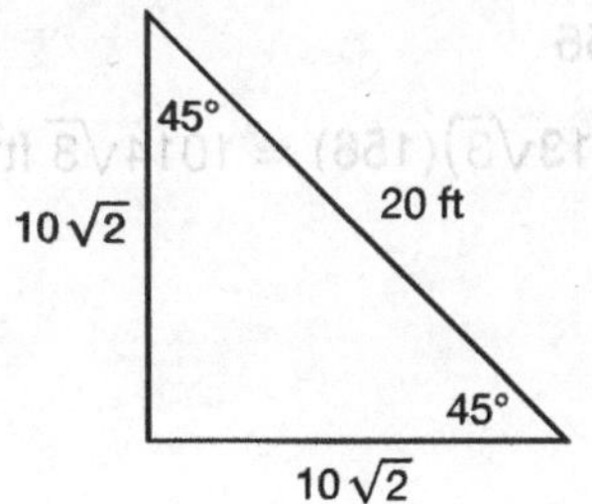


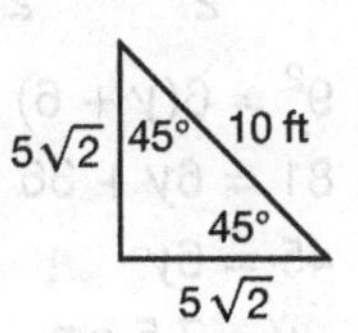


$P_1 - P_2 = [20 + 2(10\sqrt{2})] - [10 + 2(5\sqrt{2})]$

$\approx 24$ ft

**23.** Use proportions to find the dimensions of the larger prism.

$\frac{4}{9} = \frac{16}{h}$

$h = 36$ cm

$\frac{4}{9} = \frac{28}{w}$

$w = 63$ cm

$\frac{4}{9} = \frac{36}{l}$

$l = 81$ cm

$A_{front} = (81)(36) = 2916 \text{ cm}^2$

$A_{back} = (81)(36) = 2916 \text{ cm}^2$

$A_{top} = (81)(63) = 5103 \text{ cm}^2$

$A_{bottom} = (81)(63) = 5103 \text{ cm}^2$

$A_{left} = (63)(36) = 2268 \text{ cm}^2$

$A_{right} = (63)(36) = 2268 \text{ cm}^2$

**24.** $d = |-2 - -5| = |3| = 3$

**25.** $d_{LM} = \sqrt{(-1 - 1)^2 + (2 - -1)^2}$

$= \sqrt{(-2)^2 + (3)^2}$

$= \sqrt{13}$

$m_{LM} = \frac{-1 - 2}{1 - -1} = \frac{-3}{2}$

Choice A: $m_{MN} = \frac{-1 - 3}{1 - 7} = \frac{-4}{-6} = \frac{2}{3}$

This is a right triangle because $LM$ is perpendicular to $MN$.

$d_{MN} = \sqrt{(1 - 7)^2 + (-1 - 3)^2}$

$= \sqrt{(-6)^2 + (-4)^2}$

$= \sqrt{52} = 2\sqrt{13}$

$A = \frac{1}{2}(\sqrt{13})(2\sqrt{13}) = 13$

Choice B: $m_{LN} = \frac{2 - 6}{-1 - 5} = \frac{-4}{-6} = \frac{2}{3}$

This is a right triangle because $LM$ is perpendicular to $LN$.

$d_{LN} = \sqrt{(-1 - 5)^2 + (2 - 6)^2}$

$= \sqrt{(-6)^2 + (-4)^2}$

$= \sqrt{52} = 2\sqrt{13}$

$A = \frac{1}{2}(\sqrt{13})(2\sqrt{13}) = 13$

Since choices A and B result in an area of 13 square units, then choices C and D must not by elimination.

**26.** $H(3, -5) \rightarrow H'(3, -5 - 11) = H'(3, -16)$

$I(-5, -8) \rightarrow I'(-5, -8 - 11) = I'(-5, -19)$

**27.** $r = \frac{2}{3}(3) = 2$ cm

$A = \pi(2^2) = 4\pi \approx 12.57 \text{ cm}^2$

**28.** $\left(\frac{1}{4}\right)^2 = \frac{1}{16}$

The area would be divided by 16.

29. $\text{Midpoint}_{MN}$
$= \left(\frac{1+7}{2}, \frac{2+7}{2}\right)$
$= \left(\frac{8}{2}, \frac{9}{2}\right) = (4, 4.5)$
This is the point located at point $S$. Choice **B** is correct.

30. $2(6) = 12$ feet

## LAB 13

### Lab 13 Practice

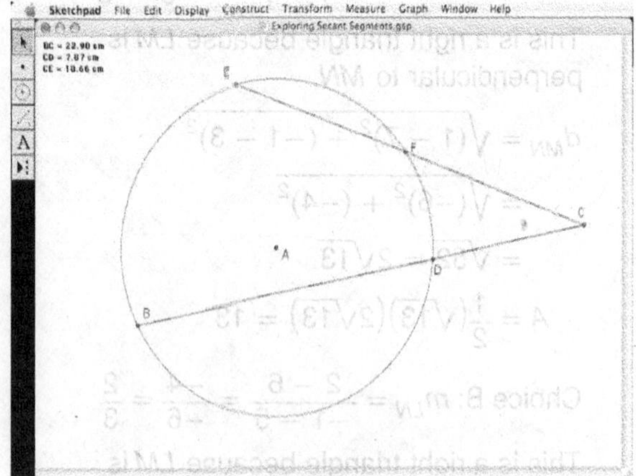


Yes you can determine the length of the fourth segment from the three measurements. We can calculate using the property we discovered in the lab.

$BC \cdot CD = CE \cdot CF$
$22.90 \cdot 7.87 = 18.66 \cdot CF$
$CF = \frac{22.90 \cdot 7.87}{18.66} \approx 9.66$

## LESSON 102

### Warm Up 102

1. translation

2.

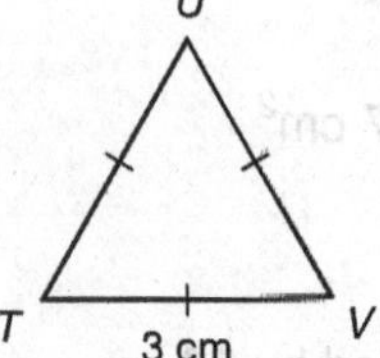


3. A dilation, by definition, does not preserve the size of a figure. Choice **D** is correct.

### Lesson Practice 102

a. $D_{O,\,2.5}(10, -4) \rightarrow (2.5 \times 10, 2.5 \times -4)$
$= (25, -10)$
$D_{O,\,2.5}(0, 8) \rightarrow (2.5 \times 0, 2.5 \times 8) = (0, 20)$

b. $2 \cdot \begin{bmatrix} 2 & 2 & 4 & 4 \\ 2 & 7 & 7 & 2 \end{bmatrix} = \begin{bmatrix} 4 & 4 & 8 & 8 \\ 4 & 14 & 14 & 4 \end{bmatrix}$

c. $50 \cdot \begin{bmatrix} 1 & 1 & 5 & 5 \\ 1 & 4 & 4 & 1 \end{bmatrix} = \begin{bmatrix} 50 & 50 & 250 & 250 \\ 50 & 200 & 200 & 50 \end{bmatrix}$
So, the vertices of the park are (50, 50), (50, 200), (250, 200), and (250, 50).
$A = lw = (150)(200) = 30{,}000 \text{ ft}^2$

### Practice 102

1. $\frac{\text{Area of the annulus}}{\text{Area of the target}} = \frac{196\pi - 64\pi}{196\pi}$
$= \frac{132}{196} = \frac{33}{49}$

2. $D_{O,\,7}(-4, 5) \rightarrow (7 \times -4, 7 \times 5) = (-28, 35)$

3. Each side length is 26 ft.
$P = 6(26) = 156$
$A = \frac{1}{2}aP = \frac{1}{2}(13\sqrt{3})(156) = 1014\sqrt{3} \text{ ft}^2$

4. $9^2 = 6(y + 6)$
$81 = 6y + 36$
$45 = 6y$
$y = 7.5$ cm

5. $\langle 50 + 12, 6 + 75 \rangle = \langle 62, 81 \rangle$

6. $x^2 = 40^2 + 57^2 - 2(40)(57) \cos 70°$
$x^2 = 4849 - 4560 \cos 70°$
$x \approx 57.35$

7. From greatest to least, the angles are 45°, 60°, and 75°. So the lengths are Abilene to Austin, Austin to Fort Worth, and Abilene to Fort Worth from greatest to least.

8. $l = w, h = 2l$
$432 = (l)(l)(2l) = 2l^3$
$216 = l^3$
$l = 6$
$S = L + 2B$
$S = Ph + 2lw$
$S = 4(6)(12) + 2(6)(6)$
$S = 360 \text{ ft}^2$

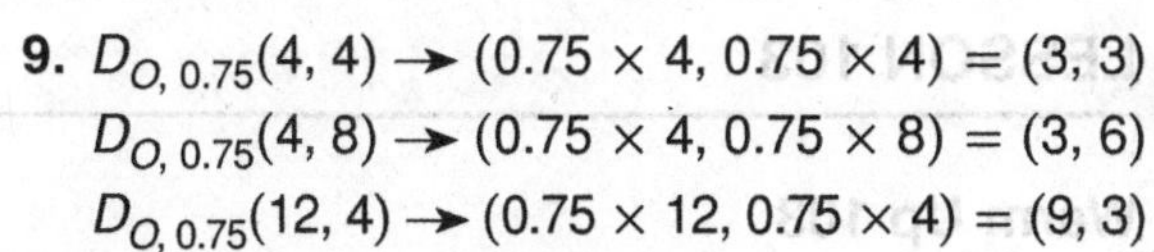



9. $D_{O,\,0.75}(4, 4) \rightarrow (0.75 \times 4, 0.75 \times 4) = (3, 3)$
$D_{O,\,0.75}(4, 8) \rightarrow (0.75 \times 4, 0.75 \times 8) = (3, 6)$
$D_{O,\,0.75}(12, 4) \rightarrow (0.75 \times 12, 0.75 \times 4) = (9, 3)$

10. $576 \div 12^2 = 4$ units$^2$

11. $V = Bh = (\pi 20^2)(56) \approx 70{,}372$ ft$^3$
$70{,}372 \times 7.5 \approx 528{,}000$ gallons

12. $6(6 + x) = (4)(12)$
$36 + 6x = 48$
$6x = 12$
$x = 2$

13.
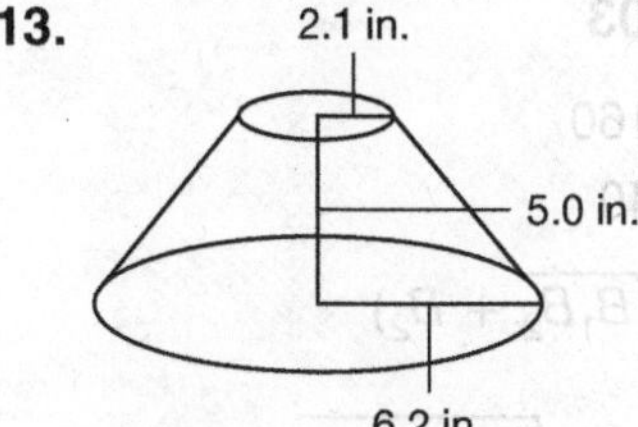


Model:
First, find the surface area of the cone before it was truncated.
$S = \pi rl + \pi r^2$
$l^2 = 6.2^2 + 7.4^2$
$l \approx 9.654$ in.
$S = \pi(6.2)(9.654) + \pi(6.2^2)$
$S \approx 308.8$
The surface area of the truncated cone is the difference of the large surface area and small cone's lateral area plus the top base.
$S = 308.8 - \pi rl + \pi r^2$
$l^2 = 2.1^2 + 2.4^2$
$l \approx 3.189$ in.
$S = 308.8 - \pi(2.1)(3.189) + \pi(2.1^2)$
$S \approx 302$ in.$^2$
To find the volume, subtract the volume of the small cone from the volume of the large cone.
$V = \frac{1}{3}Bh - \frac{1}{3}Bh$
$V = \frac{1}{3}(\pi 6.2^2)(7.4) - \frac{1}{3}(\pi 2.1^2)(2.4)$
$V \approx 287$ in.$^3$

Actual Surface Area:
$\frac{1^2}{16^2} = \frac{302}{S}$
$S = 77{,}312$ in.$^2 \approx 537$ ft$^2$
Actual Volume:
$\frac{1^3}{16^3} = \frac{287}{V}$
$V = 1{,}175{,}552$ in.$^3 \approx 680$ ft$^3$

14. $T(3, -2) \rightarrow (3 \times 3, 3 \times -2) = (9, -6)$
$S(-4, 1) \rightarrow (3 \times -4, 3 \times 1) = (-12, 3)$
Choice **C** is correct.

15. $S = 2\pi rl$
$l^2 = r^2 + (0.5h)^2$
$l^2 = r^2 + 0.25h^2$
$l^2 = \frac{4r^2 + h^2}{4}$
$l = \frac{\sqrt{4r^2 + h^2}}{2}$
$S = \pi r\sqrt{4r^2 + h^2}$

16. First, find the coordinates $D(0, 4)$ and $E(-2, -1)$. Then use the slope formula to find that the slope of $\overline{BC}$ is $\frac{5}{2}$; and the slope of $\overline{DE}$ is $\frac{5}{2}$. So, $\overline{BC} \parallel \overline{DE}$

17. Since the vertical and horizontal components are equal, the vector forms a 45°-45°-90° triangle. The angle of the resultant vector is 45°. The magnitude is the hypotenuse, which is $x\sqrt{2}$.

18. $\begin{bmatrix} 4 & 4 & 4 \\ -3 & -3 & -3 \end{bmatrix}$

19. $\begin{bmatrix} 3 & 1 \\ 4 & 0 \end{bmatrix} + \begin{bmatrix} 0 & 0 \\ -2 & -2 \end{bmatrix} = \begin{bmatrix} 3 & 1 \\ 2 & -2 \end{bmatrix}$

20. $(5.4)(VT) = (3.9)(1.8)$
$5.4VT = 7.02$
$VT = 1.3$

21. By the Vertical Angles Theorem, $\angle 1$ and $\angle 3$ are congruent.

22. $6x - 3 = 4x + 5$
$2x = 8$
$x = 4$
$AC = CD = 5(4) - 2 = 18$
$BC = CE = 6(4) - 3 = 21$

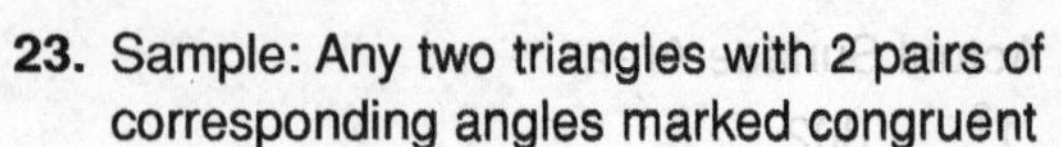



**23.** Sample: Any two triangles with 2 pairs of corresponding angles marked congruent

**24.**
$$A_{\text{screen}} = (8)(13) = 104$$
$$A_{\text{Earth}} = \pi 3^2 \approx 28.27$$
$$A_{\text{black background}} = 104 - 28.27 = 75.73$$
$$P(\text{black background}) = \frac{75.73}{104} = 0.73$$

**25.**

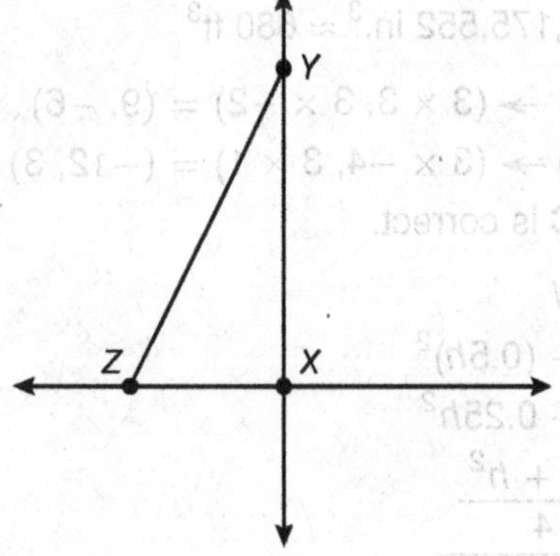


$XY = 4$

$XZ = 2$

$YZ^2 = 4^2 + 2^2$

$YZ \approx 4.5$

$m\angle X = 90°$

$\tan Y = \frac{1}{2}$

$m\angle Y \approx 27°$

$m\angle Z = 180° - 90° - 27° = 63°$

**26.** $3 \cdot \begin{bmatrix} -2 & 2 & 2 & -2 \\ 4 & 4 & -4 & -4 \end{bmatrix} = \begin{bmatrix} -6 & 6 & 6 & -6 \\ 12 & 12 & -12 & -12 \end{bmatrix}$

**27.** $(x^2 - 2x) + (6x + 3) + (12) = 180°$
$$x^2 + 4x - 165 = 0$$
$$(x + 15)(x - 11) = 0$$
$$x = 11 \text{ or } x = -15$$
$$x = 11$$

**28.** $\frac{35}{x} = \frac{x}{57}$

$x^2 = 1995$

$x = 44.7$

**29.** A tangent can be thought of as a secant that intersects the circle at only one point.

**30.** HA Congruence Theorem

## LESSON 103

### Warm Up 103

**1.** volume

**2.** $V = \frac{1}{3}Bh = \frac{1}{3}(\pi x^2)(2x) = \frac{2}{3}\pi x^3$

**3.** $243 = \frac{1}{3}(s^2)(s)$

$729 = s^3$

$s = 9$ cm

### Lesson Practice 103

**a.** $B_1 = (20)(8) = 160$

$B_2 = (10)(4) = 40$

$V = \frac{1}{3}h(B_1 + \sqrt{B_1B_2} + B_2)$

$V = \frac{1}{3}(12)(160 + \sqrt{(160)(40)} + 40)$

$= (4)(280)$

$= 1120 \text{ in.}^3$

**b.** $B_1 = \pi(12^2) \approx 452.39$

$B_2 = \pi(7^2) \approx 153.94$

$V = \frac{1}{3}h(B_1 + \sqrt{B_1B_2} + B_2)$

$V = \frac{1}{3}(7)(452.39 + \sqrt{(452.39)(153.94)} + 153.94)$

$V \approx \frac{1}{3}(7)(870.23)$

$V \approx 2030.52 \text{ in.}^3$

**c.** $B_1 = (231)(231) = 53{,}361$

$B_2 = (42)(42) = 1764$

$V = \frac{1}{3}h(B_1 + \sqrt{B_1B_2} + B_2)$

$V = \frac{1}{3}(120)(53{,}361 + \sqrt{(53{,}361)(1764)} + 1764)$

$= (40)(64{,}827)$

$= 2{,}593{,}080 \text{ m}^3$

### Practice 103

**1.** $1.5 \cdot \begin{bmatrix} -2 & 2 & 3 & -3 \\ 2 & 2 & -3 & -3 \end{bmatrix} = \begin{bmatrix} -3 & 3 & 4.5 & -4.5 \\ 3 & 3 & -4.5 & -4.5 \end{bmatrix}$

$A'(-3,3)$, $B'(3,3)$, $C'(4.5,-4,5)$, and $D'(-4.5,-4.5)$

**2.** 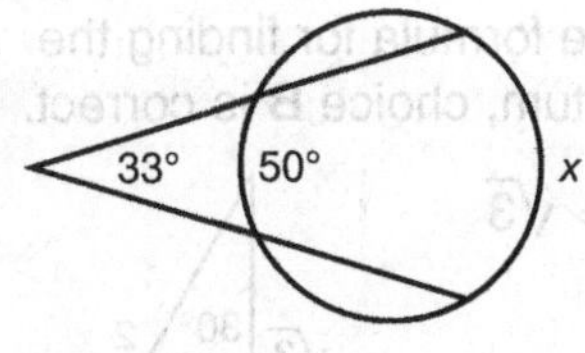


$33° = \frac{1}{2}(x - 50°)$

$66 = x - 50$

$x = 116°$

**3.** Samantha is correct. Farnaz has made an error by using m∠U instead of m∠W.

**4.** $V = \frac{1}{3}h(B_1 + \sqrt{B_1B_2} + B_2)$

$V = \frac{1}{3}\left(\frac{5}{8}y\right)(x^2 + \sqrt{(x^2)(16)} + 16)$

$V = \left(\frac{5}{24}\right)y(x^2 + 4x + 16)$ units$^3$

**5.** $\sin 35° \approx \frac{1.72}{3} \approx 0.573$

$\cos 35° \approx \frac{2.46}{3} \approx 0.82$

$\tan 35° \approx \frac{1.72}{2.46} \approx 0.699$

**6.** You will always get a rectangle because when you fold in the acute angles, you are making a 90° angle.

**7.** Since $FH$ is across from the larger angle, $FH > AB$.

**8.** The $O$ indicates a dilation centered at the origin.

**9.** $(x - 17) + (2x + 2) = 180°$

$3x - 15 = 180$

$3x = 195$

$x = 65$

$m\angle L = 65 - 17 = 48°$

$m\angle K = 65 + 25 = 90°$

$m\angle J = 2(65) + 2 = 132°$

$m\angle M = 360° - 48° - 90° - 132° = 90°$

**10.** The robot will paint it blue and then attach a widget to it.

**11.** See student work. Sample:

**12.** ∠1 and ∠3

**13.** 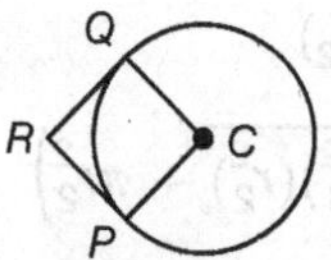


Since $\overline{RP}$ is tangent to ⊙ C, m∠CPR = 90°, so $x^2 - x - 90 = 0$, or $(x - 10)(x + 9) = 0$, so $x = 10$; $(x > 0)$. Since m∠PRQ = (9x)° then m∠PRQ = 90°. Since ∠CQR is also a right angle, ∠PCQ is the fourth right angle of a rectangle. $\overline{CP}$ and $\overline{CQ}$ are radii of ⊙ C, so $\overline{CP} \cong \overline{CQ}$. Since two tangents that intersect at a point exterior to a circle are congruent, $\overline{RP} \cong \overline{RQ}$. Since △QCP ≅ △QRP by ASA, then $\overline{QC} \cong \overline{QR}$ and $\overline{PC} \cong \overline{PR}$ by CPCTC. Then $\overline{PC} \cong \overline{RQ}$ and $\overline{QC} \cong \overline{PR}$ by the Transitive Property of Congruence. So, *CPRQ* is a square.

**14.** 2640 ft = 0.5 mi

$x^2 = 0.5(0.5 + 7920)$

$x^2 = 3690.25$; $x \approx 63$ miles

**15.** $12^2 = 24^2 + 28^2 - 2(24)(28)\cos\theta$

$144 = 1360 - 1344\cos\theta$

$\cos\theta \approx 0.905$; $\theta \approx 25°$

**16.** $d_{WX} = \sqrt{(-3 - 1)^2 + (2 - 0)^2}$

$= \sqrt{(-4)^2 + (2)^2} = \sqrt{20} = 2\sqrt{5}$

$d_{YZ} = \sqrt{(-1 - -3)^2 + (-2 - -1)^2}$

$= \sqrt{(2)^2 + (-1)^2} = \sqrt{5}$

The length of the midsegment is:

$\frac{1}{2}(2\sqrt{5} + \sqrt{5}) = \frac{3\sqrt{5}}{2}$

**17.** 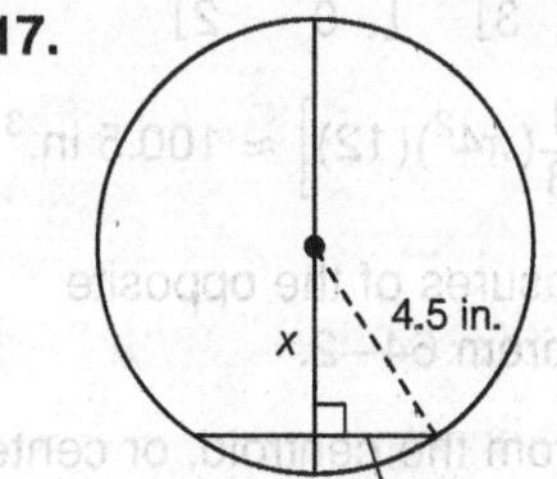


$x^2 = 4.5^2 - 2.5^2$

$x^2 = 20.25 - 6.25$

$x^2 = 14$; $x \approx 3.7$ inches

 

**18.** 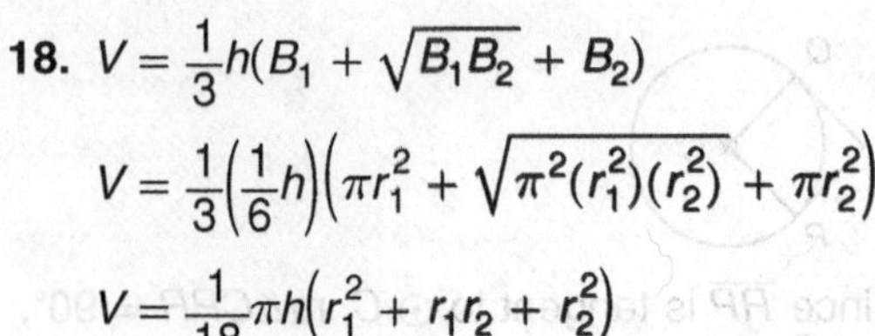

$V = \frac{1}{3}h(B_1 + \sqrt{B_1B_2} + B_2)$

$V = \frac{1}{3}\left(\frac{1}{6}h\right)\left(\pi r_1^2 + \sqrt{\pi^2(r_1^2)(r_2^2)} + \pi r_2^2\right)$

$V = \frac{1}{18}\pi h\left(r_1^2 + r_1r_2 + r_2^2\right)$

**19.** The new dimensions are 27 ft, 54 ft, and 36 ft.

$S = L + 2B = Ph + 2lw$

$S = (2(36) + 2(27))(54) + 2(27)(36)$

$S = 8748 \text{ ft}^2$

$V = lwh = (36)(27)(54) = 52{,}488 \text{ ft}^3$

**20.** A fractal is self-similar because it is composed of copies (or near-copies) of itself; the same relationships among larger sections of the fractal exist among corresponding smaller sections.

**21.** $D_{O,\,3.5}(4, 6) \rightarrow (3.5 \times 4, 3.5 \times 6) = (14, 21)$

$D_{O,\,3.5}(-2, -4) \rightarrow (3.5 \times -2, 3.5 \times -4) = (-7, -14)$

**22.** $(1, 2) \rightarrow 2 > 2(1) + 3$

$2 > 5$

$(2, 9) \rightarrow 9 > 2(2) + 3$

$9 > 7$

$(-2, 3) \rightarrow 3 > 2(-2) + 3$

$3 > -1$

No, (1, 2) is not.

**23.** $52 = 2\pi r$

$r \approx 8.28$

$S = 4\pi r^2 = 4\pi(8.28^2) \approx 861.5 \text{ m}^2$

**24.** $\begin{bmatrix} -6 & -2 \\ -3 & -1 \end{bmatrix} + \begin{bmatrix} -2 & -2 \\ 3 & 3 \end{bmatrix} = \begin{bmatrix} -8 & -4 \\ 0 & 2 \end{bmatrix}$

**25.** $V = \frac{1}{2}\left(\frac{1}{3}Bh\right) = \frac{1}{2}\left[\frac{1}{3}(\pi 4^2)(12)\right] \approx 100.5 \text{ in.}^3$

**26.** The sum of the measures of the opposite arcs is 180° by Theorem 64–2.

**27.** He should hang it from the centroid, or center of gravity.

$\frac{2}{3} \times 2.4 = 1.6$ inches from one vertex

$\frac{2}{3} \times 3.2 \approx 2.1$ inches from another

$\frac{2}{3} \times 3.75 = 2.5$ inches from the third

**28.** By examining the formula for finding the volume of a frustum, choice **B** is correct.

**29.** $\tan 60° = \frac{\sqrt{3}}{1} = \sqrt{3}$

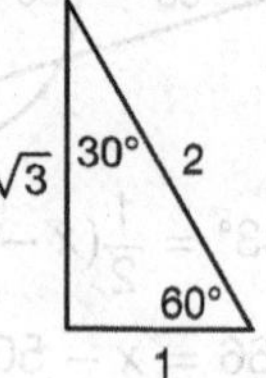


**30.** $x(2x) = (26)(8)$

$2x^2 = 208$

$x^2 = 104$

$x \approx 10.2$ in.

$2x \approx 20.4$ in.

## LESSON 104

### Warm Up 104

**1.** central angle

**2.** arc

**3.** $4x - 5 = 85°$

$4x = 90$

$x = 22.5$

### Lesson Practice 104

**a.** $14x + 28 = 19x + 3$

$-5x = -25$

$x = 5$

$m\widehat{AB} = 14(5) + 28 = 98°$

$m\widehat{DC} = 19(5) + 3 = 98°$

**b.**

| Statements | Reasons |
|---|---|
| 1. $\overline{BC} \cong \overline{DC}$ | 1. Given |
| 2. $\overline{AB} \cong \overline{AC}$, $\overline{AC} \cong \overline{AD}$ | 2. Radii of the same circle are congruent. |
| 3. $\triangle ABC \cong \triangle DAC$ | 3. SSS |
| 4. $\angle BAC \cong \angle DAC$ | 4. CPCTC |
| 5. $m\angle BAC = m\angle DAC$ | 5. Def. of ≅ angles |
| 6. $m\widehat{BC} = m\angle BAC$, $m\widehat{DC} = m\angle DAC$ | 6. The measure of a minor arc is the same as the measure of its central angle |
| 7. $m\widehat{BC} = m\widehat{DC}$ | 7. Transitive Prop. Of Equality |
| 8. $\widehat{BC} \cong \widehat{DC}$ | 8. Def. of ≅ arcs |

c. $4x - 80 = 2x + 20$
$2x = 100$
$x = 50$

## Practice 104

1. $4x + 3 = 6x - 27$
$-2x = -30$
$x = 15$
$m\widehat{AD} = 4(15) + 3 = 63°$

2. Find the circumcenter of $A(0, 0)$, $B(6, 0)$, and $C(0, 2)$.
The midpoint of $AB$ is (3, 0).
The midpoint of $AC$ is (0, 1).
The line perpendicular to $AB$ through (3, 0) is $x = 3$.
The line perpendicular to $AC$ through (0, 1) is $y = 1$.
The circumcenter is located at (3, 1). This is where the stop should be located.

3. Cylinder $C$:
$S = L + 2B = (2\pi r)(h) + 2(\pi r^2)$
$= (2\pi)(42)(69) + 2\pi(42^2)$
$S \approx 29{,}292$
Cylinder $D$: $\frac{29{,}292}{S} = \frac{9^2}{4^2}$
$S \approx 5786 \text{ in.}^2$
$5786 \cancel{\text{in}^2} \times \frac{2.54^2 \cancel{\text{cm}^2}}{1 \cancel{\text{in}^2}} \times \frac{1 \text{ m}^2}{10{,}000 \text{ cm}^2}$
$\approx 3.73 \text{ m}^2$

4.

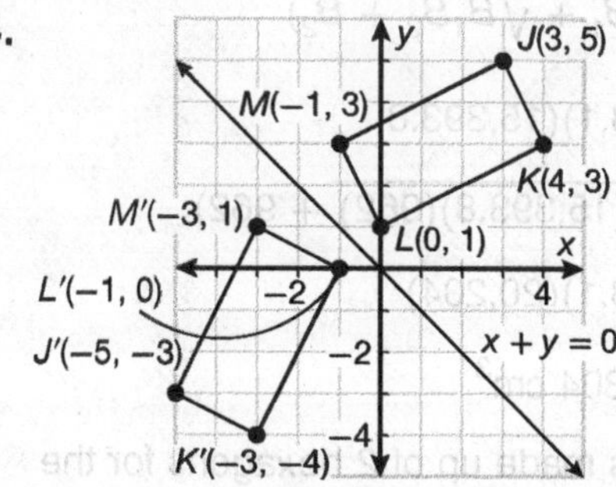


5. $2 \cdot \begin{bmatrix} 3 & 4 & 0 \\ -1 & 0 & 9 \end{bmatrix} = \begin{bmatrix} 6 & 8 & 0 \\ -2 & 0 & 18 \end{bmatrix}$

6.

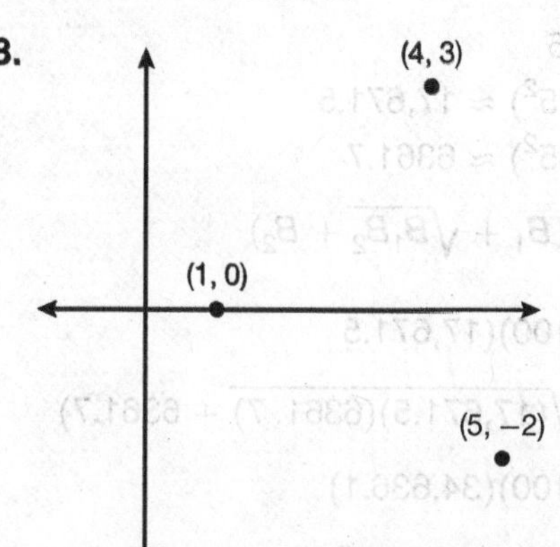


7. Choice **C** is correct.

8.

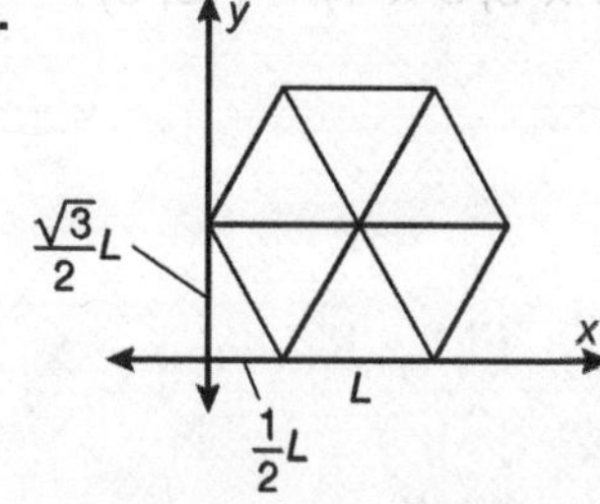


The possible coordinates for the fourth vertex are (0, 5), (2, −5), and (8, 1).

9. $5(5 + x) = 7(15)$
$25 + 5x = 105$
$5x = 80$
$x = 16$

10. Choice **A** is correct. The equations both have slopes equal to −1, so they are parallel.

11. $x^2 + 4x = 96$
$x^2 + 4x - 96 = 0$
$(x + 12)(x - 8) = 0$
$x = -12$ or $8$

12.



The hexagon can be divided into equilateral triangles, and the facts regarding 30°-60°-90° to determine the coordinates of the vertices.

$\left(0, \frac{\sqrt{3}}{2}L\right), \left(\frac{1}{2}L, 0\right), \left(\frac{1}{2}L, 2\left(\frac{\sqrt{3}}{2}L\right)\right) =$
$\left(\frac{1}{2}L, \sqrt{3}L\right), \left(\frac{1}{2}L + L, \sqrt{3}L\right) =$
$\left(\frac{3}{2}L, \sqrt{3}L\right), \left(2L, \frac{\sqrt{3}}{2}L\right), \left(\frac{3}{2}L, 0\right)$

**13.** To find the top radius,

$$\frac{250}{75} = \frac{150}{r}$$
$$r = 45$$
$$B_1 = \pi(75^2) \approx 17{,}671.5$$
$$B_2 = \pi(45^2) \approx 6361.7$$
$$V = \frac{1}{3}h(B_1 + \sqrt{B_1B_2} + B_2)$$
$$V = \frac{1}{3}(100)(17{,}671.5 + \sqrt{(17{,}671.5)(6361.7)} + 6361.7)$$
$$V \approx \frac{1}{3}(100)(34{,}636.1)$$
$$V \approx 1{,}154{,}535.6 \text{ mm}^3$$

**14.** The radius of the original circle is $12 \div 4 = 3$.
$C = 2\pi(3) = 6\pi$

**15.**
$$8x - 35 = 5x + 25$$
$$3x = 60$$
$$x = 20$$
$$m\widehat{MN} = 5(20) + 25 = 125°$$

**16.** The area would increase by a factor of 4.

**17.** $\frac{n(n-1)}{2} = \frac{9(9-1)}{2} = 36$

**18.**
$D_{O,3}(2, 1) \rightarrow (3 \times 2, 3 \times 1) = (6, 3)$
$D_{O,3}(2, 7) \rightarrow (3 \times 2, 3 \times 7) = (6, 21)$
$D_{O,3}(5, 1) \rightarrow (3 \times 5, 3 \times 1) = (15, 3)$

**19.**
$$\frac{36}{24} = \frac{42}{y}$$
$$36y = 1008$$
$$y = 28$$
$$\frac{36}{24} = \frac{x}{30}$$
$$24x = 1080$$
$$x = 45$$

**20.** The graph is translated two units right and four units down. The resulting matrix is $\begin{bmatrix} 2 \\ -4 \end{bmatrix}$.

**21.**
$$\frac{1}{\tan^2 \theta} = 0.6$$
$$1 = 0.6 \tan^2 \theta$$
$$\tan^2 \theta \approx 1.67$$
$$\tan \theta \approx 1.29$$
$$\theta \approx 52.24°$$
$$\sin 52.24° \approx 0.79$$

**22.** To find the top radius,

$$\frac{120}{70} = \frac{30}{r}$$
$$r = 17.5 \text{ cm}$$

To find the height of the frustum, find the height of the large cone minus the height of the small cone.

$$h_L^2 = 120^2 - 70^2$$
$$h_L^2 = 9500$$
$$h_L \approx 97.5 \text{ cm}$$
$$h_S^2 = 30^2 - 17.5^2$$
$$h_S^2 = 593.75$$
$$h_S \approx 24.4 \text{ cm}$$

The height of the frustum is $97.5 - 24.4 = 73.1$.

$$B_1 = \pi(70^2) \approx 15{,}393.8$$
$$B_2 = \pi(17.5^2) \approx 962$$
$$V = \frac{1}{3}h(B_1 + \sqrt{B_1B_2} + B_2)$$
$$V = \frac{1}{3}(73.1)(15{,}393.8 + \sqrt{(15{,}393.8)(962)} + 962)$$
$$V \approx \frac{1}{3}(73.1)(20{,}204)$$
$$V \approx 492{,}304 \text{ cm}^3$$

**23.** The net is made up of 2 hexagons for the bases and 6 rectangles for the lateral sides.

24. $m\angle CED = m\angle BEA = 130°$ because they are vertical angles.
So, $m\widehat{AB} = m\widehat{CD} = 130°$ because the intercepted arcs are equal to their central angles.
$m\angle AED = m\angle BEC = 180° - 130° = 50°$
So, $m\widehat{AD} = m\widehat{BC} = 50°$
$\overline{AD} \cong \overline{BC}$; $\overline{AB} \cong \overline{CD}$
The chords are congruent because the respective arcs and central angles are congruent.

25. $m_{EF} = \frac{-3 - -1}{-3 - 1} = \frac{-2}{-4} = \frac{1}{2}$

$m_{FG} = \frac{5 - -1}{3 - 1} = \frac{6}{2} = 3$

$m_{GH} = \frac{5 - 2}{3 - -3} = \frac{3}{6} = \frac{1}{2}$

$m_{EH} = \frac{-3 - 2}{-3 - -3} = \frac{-5}{0} = \varnothing$

The slopes of $\overline{EF}$, $\overline{FG}$, $\overline{GH}$, and $\overline{EH}$ are $\frac{1}{2}$, 3, $\frac{1}{2}$, and undefined. $\overline{EF} \parallel \overline{GH}$ but $\overline{FG} \nparallel \overline{EH}$, so $EFGH$ is a trapezoid.

26. $16^2 = 8^2 + (x - 4)^2 - 2(8)(x - 4)\cos 60°$
$256 = 64 + (x^2 - 8x + 16) - (8x - 32)$
$x^2 - 16x - 144 = 0$
$x = \frac{16 \pm \sqrt{256 - 4(1)(-144)}}{2(1)}$
$x = 8 \pm \frac{\sqrt{832}}{2}$
$x \approx 22.42$ (because length must be positive)

27.

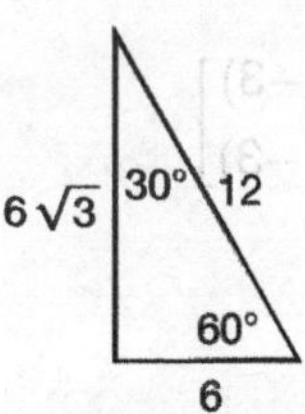


$P = 6\sqrt{3} + 6 + 12$
$= 18 + 6\sqrt{3}$
$= 6(3 + \sqrt{3})$ centimeters

28. To find the top radius,
$\frac{15}{4} = \frac{5}{r}$
$r \approx 1.33$
$B_1 = \pi(4^2) \approx 50.3$
$B_2 = \pi(1.33^2) \approx 5.6$
$V = \frac{1}{3}h(B_1 + \sqrt{B_1B_2} + B_2)$
$V = \frac{1}{3}(10)(50.3 + \sqrt{(50.3)(5.6)} + 5.6)$
$\approx 242$ in.$^3$

29. $d = |3 - 2| = 1$

30. $A = \frac{1}{2}(B_1 + B_2)h + \frac{1}{2}(B_1 + B_2)h$
$= \frac{1}{2}(25 + 10)(6.5) + \frac{1}{2}(25 + 10)(6.5)$
$= 113.75 + 113.75$
$= 227.5$ cm$^2$

## LESSON 105

### Warm Up 105

1. transformation
2. translation
3. $(x, y) \rightarrow (-x, -y)$
$A(3, 2) \rightarrow A'(-3, -2)$
$B(-4, 1) \rightarrow B'(4, -1)$
$C(0, 4) \rightarrow C'(0, -4)$

### Lesson Practice 105

a. $\begin{bmatrix} -2 & 7 \\ 1 & -3 \end{bmatrix}\begin{bmatrix} 2 & 1 \\ 3 & -5 \end{bmatrix}$

$= \begin{bmatrix} (-2)(2) + (7)(3) & (-2)(1) + (7)(-5) \\ (1)(2) + (-3)(3) & (1)(1) + (-3)(-5) \end{bmatrix}$

$= \begin{bmatrix} 17 & -37 \\ -7 & 16 \end{bmatrix}$

**b.** $\begin{bmatrix}-1 & 0\\ 0 & 1\end{bmatrix}\begin{bmatrix}2 & 6 & 4\\ 1 & 1 & 5\end{bmatrix}$

$$=\begin{bmatrix}(-1)(2)+(0)(1) & (-1)(6)+(0)(1) & (-1)(4)+(0)(5)\\ (0)(2)+(1)(1) & (0)(6)+(1)(1) & (0)(4)+(1)(5)\end{bmatrix}$$

$$=\begin{bmatrix}-2 & -6 & -4\\ 1 & 1 & 5\end{bmatrix}$$

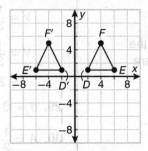

**c.** $\begin{bmatrix}0 & -1\\ 1 & 0\end{bmatrix}\begin{bmatrix}2 & 4 & 1\\ -4 & 1 & 3\end{bmatrix}$

$$=\begin{bmatrix}(0)(2)+(-1)(-4) & (0)(4)+(-1)(1) & (0)(1)+(-1)(3)\\ (1)(2)+(0)(-4) & (1)(4)+(0)(1) & (1)(1)+(0)(3)\end{bmatrix}$$

$$=\begin{bmatrix}4 & -1 & -3\\ 2 & 4 & 1\end{bmatrix}$$

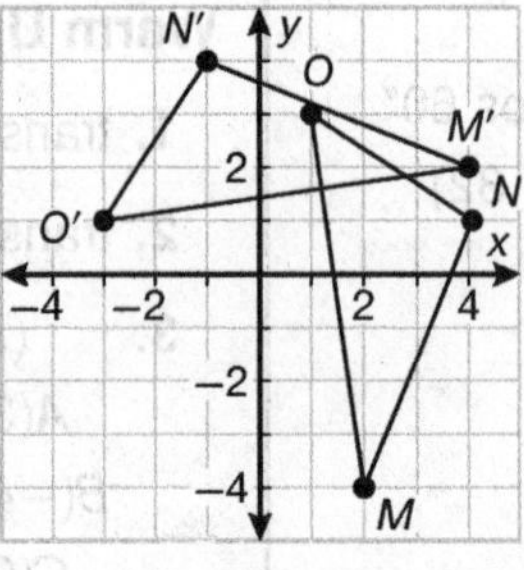


**d.** $\begin{bmatrix}-1 & 0\\ 0 & -1\end{bmatrix}\begin{bmatrix}2 & 4 & 5 & 1\\ -1 & -1 & -3 & -3\end{bmatrix}$

$$=\begin{bmatrix}(-1)(2)+(0)(-1) & (-1)(4)+(0)(-1) & (-1)(5)+(0)(-3) & (-1)(1)+(0)(-3)\\ (0)(2)+(-1)(-1) & (0)(4)+(-1)(-1) & (0)(5)+(-1)(-3) & (0)(1)+(-1)(-3)\end{bmatrix}$$

$$=\begin{bmatrix}-2 & -4 & -5 & -1\\ 1 & 1 & 3 & 3\end{bmatrix}$$

## Practice 105

**1.** $\begin{bmatrix}6 & -1\\ 3 & 2\end{bmatrix}\begin{bmatrix}5 & 2\\ -8 & 4\end{bmatrix}$

$$=\begin{bmatrix}(6)(5)+(-1)(-8) & (6)(2)+(-1)(4)\\ (3)(5)+(2)(-8) & (3)(2)+(2)(4)\end{bmatrix}$$

$$=\begin{bmatrix}38 & 8\\ -1 & 14\end{bmatrix}$$

**2.** $\langle -4, 1\rangle$

**3.** $d_{AB}=\sqrt{(6-3)^2+(1-2)^2}$

$=\sqrt{(3)^2+(-1)^2}$

$=\sqrt{10}$

$\approx 3.2$

$d_{AC}=\sqrt{(3-2)^2+(2--4)^2}$

$= \sqrt{(1)^2 + (6)^2}$
$= \sqrt{37}$
$\approx 6.1$
$d_{BC} = \sqrt{(6-2)^2 + (1 - -4)^2}$
$= \sqrt{(4)^2 + (5)^2}$
$= \sqrt{41} \approx 6.4$
$6.4^2 = 3.2^2 + 6.1^2 - 2(3.2)(6.1)\cos A$
$40.96 = 47.45 - 39.04\cos A$
$m\angle A \approx 80°$
$\frac{6.4}{\sin 80°} = \frac{6.1}{\sin B}$
$m\angle B \approx 70°$
$m\angle C = 180° - 70° - 80° = 30°$

**4.** $\frac{4}{7} = \frac{P}{87.5}$
$7P = 350$
$P = 50$ centimeters

**5.** If the design is to be symmetrical, then $\overline{AB}$ and $\overline{AC}$ must be congruent, which means $\widehat{AB}$ and $\widehat{AC}$ must also be congruent to each other.

**6.** $(x+2)^2 + (y-3)^2 = 5^2$
$(x+2)^2 + (y-3)^2 = 25$

**7.** To find the height of the frustum,
$\frac{9}{20} = \frac{3}{h}$
$h \approx 6.67$
$B_1 = \pi(9^2) \approx 254.5$
$B_2 = \pi(3^2) \approx 28.3$
$V = \frac{1}{3}h(B_1 + \sqrt{B_1B_2} + B_2)$
$V = \frac{1}{3}(6.67)(254.5 + \sqrt{(254.5)(28.3)} + 28.3)$
$V \approx 817 \text{ in.}^3$

**8.** Choice **B** is correct.

**9.** $x = 2$
$y = \frac{3}{2}(2) - 3$
$y = 3 - 3 = 0$
$(2, 0)$

**10.** $V = \frac{1}{12}a^3\sqrt{2}$, where $a$ = edge length
$V = \frac{1}{12}(2m)^3\sqrt{2}$
$V = \frac{1}{12}8m^3\sqrt{2}$
$V = \frac{2\sqrt{2}}{3}m^3$

**11.** $\begin{bmatrix}1 & 0\\0 & -1\end{bmatrix}\begin{bmatrix}-6 & -6 & 1\\2 & -3 & -3\end{bmatrix}$

$= \begin{bmatrix}(1)(-6)+(0)(2) & (1)(-6)+(0)(-3) & (1)(1)+(0)(-3)\\(0)(-6)+(-1)(2) & (0)(-6)+(-1)(-3) & (0)(1)+(-1)(-3)\end{bmatrix} = \begin{bmatrix}-6 & -6 & 1\\-2 & 3 & 3\end{bmatrix}$

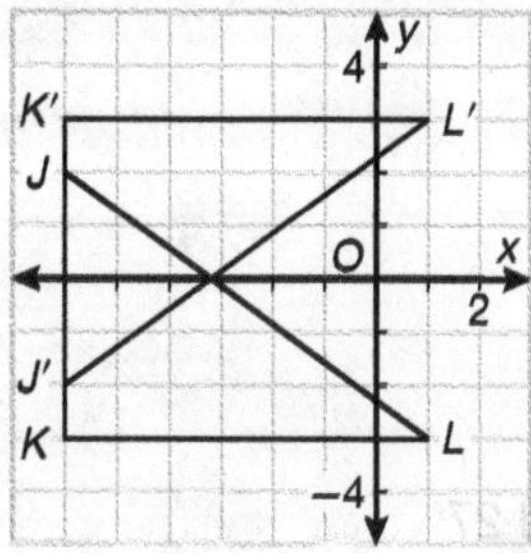

12. $\dfrac{100}{V} = \dfrac{4^3}{9^3}$

$64V = 72{,}900$

$V \approx 1139$ cubic meters

13.

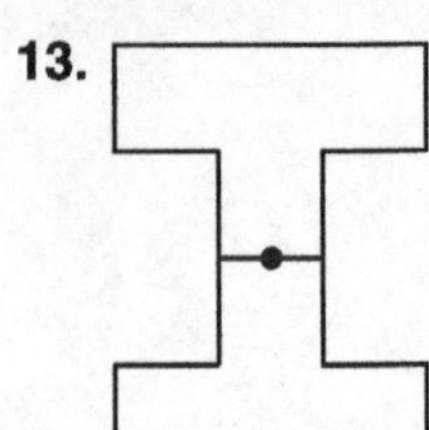

14. The center of the new circle is located at (5, −6) and the radius is 2(7) = 14.

$(x - 5)^2 + (y + 6)^2 = 14^2$

$(x - 5)^2 + (y + 6)^2 = 196$

Choice **A** is correct.

15. A translation of 0.5(3) = 1.5 units to the left and 0.5(4) = 2 units up.

16. rectangular prism

17. If $0 < k < 1$, the dilation is a reduction. For $k > 1$, the dilation is an enlargement.

18. $\begin{bmatrix} -1 & 0 \\ 0 & -1 \end{bmatrix}\begin{bmatrix} -5 & -4 & -1 \\ -1 & 3 & 1 \end{bmatrix}$

$= \begin{bmatrix} (-1)(-5) + (0)(-1) & (-1)(-4) + (0)(3) & (-1)(-1) + (0)(1) \\ (0)(-5) + (-1)(-1) & (0)(-4) + (-1)(3) & (0)(-1) + (-1)(1) \end{bmatrix} = \begin{bmatrix} 5 & 4 & 1 \\ 1 & -3 & -1 \end{bmatrix}$

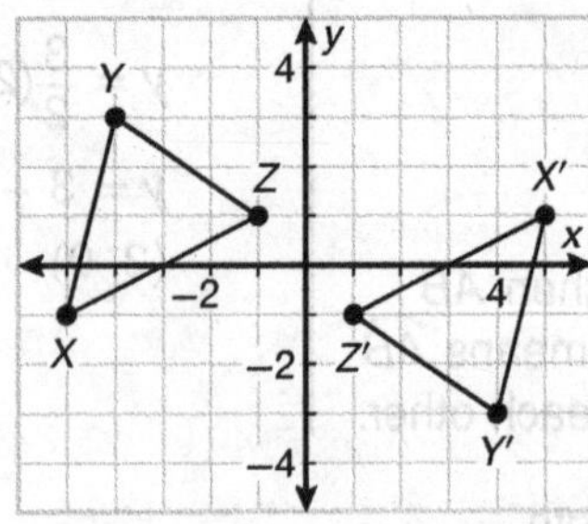


19. $8(8 + z) = 9(18)$

$64 + 8z = 162$

$8z = 98$

$z = 12.25$

20. "A bus is a downtown bus or it is green." true

21. $5x + 2 = 7x - 6$

$-2x = -8$

$x = 4$

$m\widehat{AB} = 5(4) + 2 = 22°$

22. $(10 - 2)180° = 1440°$

23. $3(x + 5) + 2(2x - 47) = 180°$

$3x + 15 + 4x - 94 = 180$

$7x = 259$

$x = 37$

vertex angle = 3(37 + 5) = 126°

base angles = 2(37) − 47 = 27° and 27°

24. $\begin{bmatrix} 0 & -1 \\ 1 & 0 \end{bmatrix}\begin{bmatrix} -2 & -1 & 0 & -3 \\ 2 & 2 & 1 & 1 \end{bmatrix}$

$= \begin{bmatrix} (0)(-2)+(-1)(2) & (0)(-1)+(-1)(2) & (0)(0)+(-1)(1) & (0)(-3)+(-1)(1) \\ (1)(-2)+(0)(2) & (1)(-1)+(0)(2) & (1)(0)+(0)(1) & (1)(-3)+(0)(1) \end{bmatrix}$

$= \begin{bmatrix} -2 & -2 & -1 & -1 \\ -2 & -1 & 0 & -3 \end{bmatrix}$

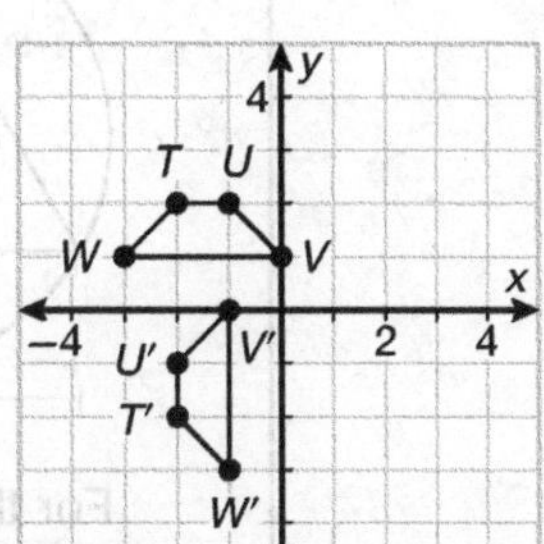


25. The perimeter of the larger triangle is twice the perimeter of the smaller triangle. So, the larger triangle has $2^2$ or four times the area of the smaller.

26. Choice A: $3 + 5 = 8$

Choice B: $5 + 9 < 18$

Choice C: $4 + 7 > 9$

Choice D: $6 + 8 < 16$

By the Triangle Inequality Theorem, choice **C** is correct.

27. $\frac{1}{\sqrt{2}} = \frac{m}{5\sqrt{2}}$

$m = 5$

They both have a magnitude of 5.

28.

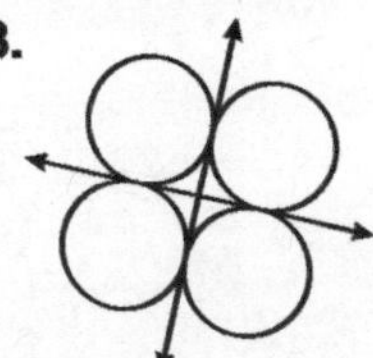

29. To find the height of the cone,

$h^2 = 25^2 - 10^2$

$h \approx 22.9$

The height of the frustum,

$\frac{2}{3}(22.9)$

$h \approx 15.27$

Find the radius of the top base,

$\frac{7.63}{22.9} = \frac{r}{10}$

$r \approx 3.33$

$B_1 = \pi(10^2) \approx 314$

$B_2 = \pi(3.33^2) \approx 35$

$V = \frac{1}{3}h(B_1 + \sqrt{B_1B_2} + B_2)$

$V = \frac{1}{3}(15.27)(314 + \sqrt{(314)(35)} + 35)$

$\approx 2310 \text{ cm}^3$

30.

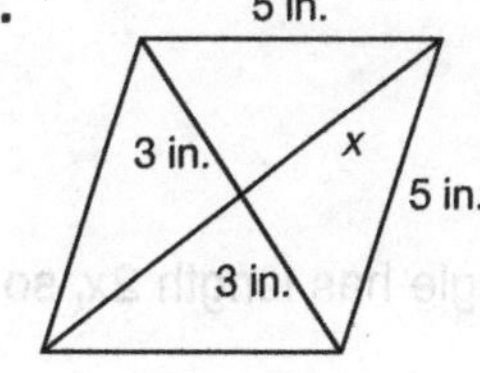


$x^2 = 5^2 - 3^2$

$x = 4$

The other diagonal is $2(4) = 8$ inches.

## LESSON 106

### Warm Up 106

1. concentric circles
2. $(x - 2)^2 + (y - 2)^2 = 36$
3. $A = \frac{\theta}{360°}\pi r^2$

$\theta = 360° - 235° = 125°$

$A = \frac{125}{360}\pi(8)^2 = 69.8 \text{ in.}^2$

Choice **C** is correct.

## Lesson Practice 106

**a.** The central angle of a regular octagon is:

$\frac{360°}{8} = 45°$

With a radius of 6, the side length of the inscribed octagon is:

$c^2 = 6^2 + 6^2 - 2(6)(6) \cos 45°$

$c = 4.59$

$P = 8 \times 4.59 = 36.7$

**b.**

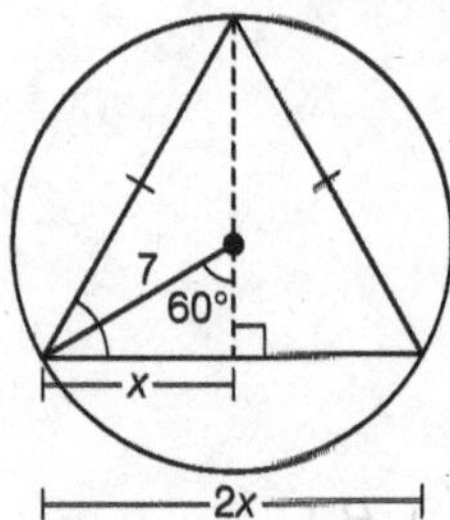


For the equilateral triangle, the central angle is $\frac{360°}{3} = 120°$.

From the diagram,

$\tan 60° = \frac{x}{7}$

$x = 7 \tan 60°$

$= 12.1$

Each side of the triangle has length $2x$, so $2(12.1) = 24.2$.

$P = 3(24.2) = 72.6$ or 73 units

**c.**

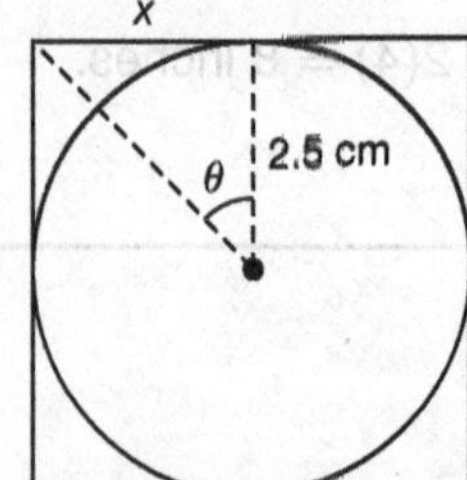


Since the angle $\theta$ is 45°, the triangle is isosceles and $x = 2.5$ cm.

The side length is: $2(2.5) = 5$ cm

$A = 5 \times 5$

$= 25 \text{ cm}^2$

**d.** The central angle is $\frac{360°}{4} = 90°$.

Using the Pythagorean Theorem,

$x^2 = 8^2 + 8^2$

$x^2 = 128$

$x \approx 11.3$ inches

## Practice 106

**1.**

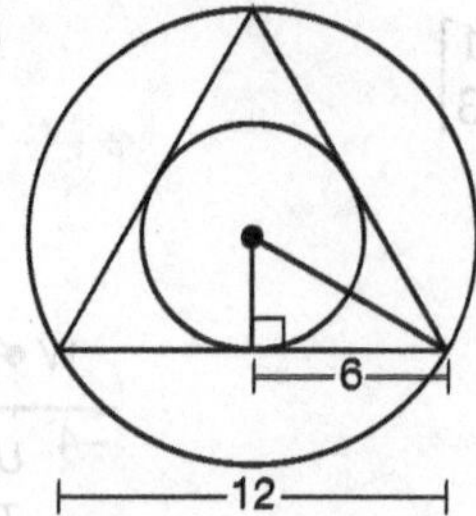


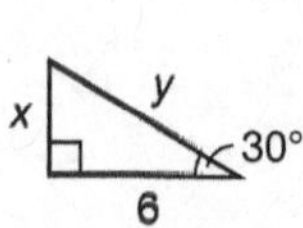


For the smaller circle,

$\tan 30° = \frac{x}{6}$

$x = 6 \tan 30°$

$x = \frac{6}{\sqrt{3}}$

$x = 2\sqrt{3}$

$C = 2\pi r$

$= 2\pi(2\sqrt{3})$

$= 4\pi\sqrt{3}$ cm

For the larger circle,

$\cos 30° = \frac{6}{y}$

$x = \frac{6}{\cos 30°}$

$x = \frac{6}{\frac{\sqrt{3}}{2}}$

$x = \frac{12}{\sqrt{3}}$

$x = 4\sqrt{3}$

$C = 2\pi r$

$C = 2\pi(4\sqrt{3})$

$C = 8\pi\sqrt{3}$ cm

**2.** Choice **C** is correct.

**3.** $M(-6, 5)$ to $M'(-3, -4)$ moves to the right 3 units and down 9 units. The vector that makes this translation is $\langle 3, -9 \rangle$.

**4.** $\sqrt{4 \times 9} = \sqrt{36} = 6$ units

**5.** $V = \pi r^2 h$

$100.48 = \pi x^2(4x)$

$100.48 = 4\pi x^3$

$x = \sqrt[3]{\frac{100.48}{4\pi}} = 2$

Therefore, the radius is 2 cm and the height is 8 cm.

$S = 2\pi r^2 + 2\pi rh = 2\pi(2)^2 + 2\pi(2)(8)$

$SA = 125.6 \approx 126 \text{ cm}^2$

**6.**

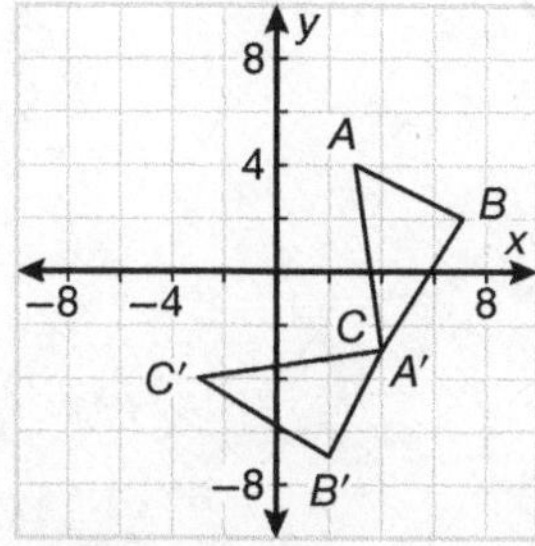


Applying this to the matrix representing the vertices of the triangle:

$$\begin{bmatrix} 0 & 1 \\ -1 & 0 \end{bmatrix}\begin{bmatrix} 3 & 7 & 4 \\ 4 & 2 & -3 \end{bmatrix} = \begin{bmatrix} 4 & 2 & -3 \\ -3 & -7 & -4 \end{bmatrix}$$

**7.** $DE = \sqrt{3^2 + 6^2} \approx 6.7$

$EF = \sqrt{0^2 + 3^2} = 3$

$DF = \sqrt{6^2 + 0^2} = 6$

These three sides form a right angle triangle, so $m\angle F = 90°$.

$\tan D = \frac{3}{6}$

$m\angle D \approx 27°$

$m\angle E \approx 180° - 90° - 27° \approx 63°$

**8.** $5x = 3x + 56$

$2x = 56$

$x = 28°$; And: $5x = 5(28)° = 140°$

**9.**

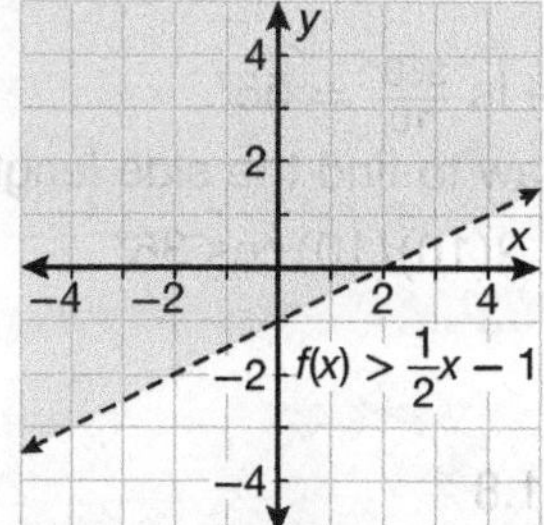


**10.** If a quadrilateral is not a trapezoid, then it does not have exactly one pair of sides. This statement is true.

**11.** For the full pyramid:

$V = \frac{1}{3}b^2h$

$V = \frac{1}{3}(30)^2(40)$

$V = 12{,}000 \text{ m}^3$

For the top piece of the pyramid:

$\frac{40}{15} = \frac{30}{x}$

$40x = 450$

$x = 11.25$

So, the volume of the frustum is:

$= \frac{1}{3}(25)(30^2 + \sqrt{(30^2)(11.25^2)} + 11.25^2)$

$\approx 11{,}367.19 \text{ m}^3$

**12.** There are three locations for the point $D$, as long as the points do not need to be sequentially listed as $ABCD$. The first location can be in Quadrant I, where the point can be found by moving to the right 6 and up 1 from $A$ (this is how to move from point $B$ to $C$). This gives $D$ as (5, 2). The second location is in Quadrant IV, found by moving to the right 4 and down 3 from $B$ (this is how to move from $A$ to $C$). This gives $D$ as (1, −6). Finally, the third location can be found by moving to the left 6 and down 1 from A (this is how to move from $C$ to $B$). This gives $D$ as (−7, 0).

**13.** $V = x^3$

$x^3 = 343$

$x = 7$

$S = L + 2B$

$S = ph + 2B = (28)(7) + 2(7^2)$

$S = 294 \text{ m}^2$

**14.** If $y = x^2$ is rotated either 90° clockwise or counterclockwise around the origin, the result would be symmetric along the $x$-axis.

**15.** $5z = 3(7z - 4)$

$5z = 21z - 12$

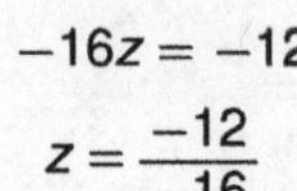



$-16z = -12$

$z = \frac{-12}{-16}$

$z = 0.75$

**16.** For the inscribed square in the circle of radius $r$, the central angle is 90°. Use the Pythagorean Theorem to find the length of the side of the inscribed square:

$x^2 = r^2 + r^2$

$x^2 = 2r^2$

$x = \sqrt{2}r$

The ratio of this side to the radius is $\sqrt{2}r : r$ or $\sqrt{2} : 1$.

**17.** $\frac{180°}{360°}(2\pi(17)) \approx 53.4$ cm.

**18.** The circles are not concentric, because they do not have a common center.

**19.**

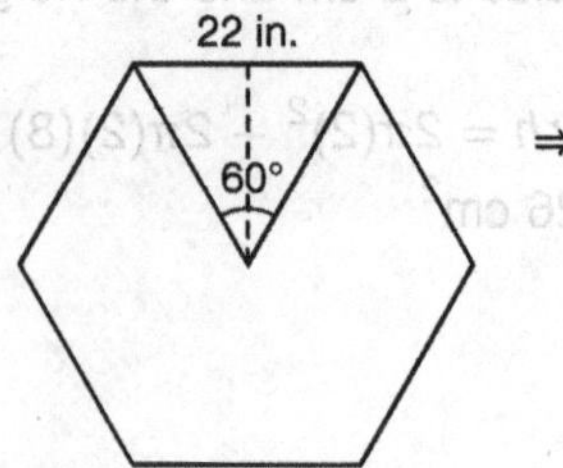


⇒

From the diagram,

$\tan 30° = \frac{11}{h}$

$h = \frac{11}{\tan 30°}$

$h = 11\sqrt{3}$

$A = 6\left(\frac{1}{2}(11\sqrt{3})(22)\right)$

$= 726\sqrt{3}$ in.$^2$

**20.** $\begin{bmatrix} -5 & 0 \\ 2 & -7 \end{bmatrix}\begin{bmatrix} 3 & 1 & -1 \\ -2 & 6 & -3 \end{bmatrix}$

$= \begin{bmatrix} -5 \times 3 + 0 \times -2 & -5 \times 1 + 0 \times 6 & -5 \times -1 + 0 \times -3 \\ 2 \times 3 - 7 \times -2 & 2 \times 1 - 7 \times 6 & 2 \times -1 - 7 \times -3 \end{bmatrix}$

$= \begin{bmatrix} -15 & -5 & 5 \\ 20 & -40 & 19 \end{bmatrix}$

**21.** $(3x + 33)° = (4x - 7)°$

$x = 40°$

$(4x - 7)° = [4(40) - 7]° = 153°$

**22.** The longest side is opposite the largest angle and the shortest side is opposite the smallest angle. Therefore, in order from largest to smallest, the angles are $K$, $L$, and $J$.

**23.**

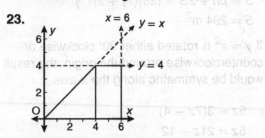

The shape can be split up into a triangle and a rectangle.

Area = $\text{Area}_{\text{triangle}} + \text{Area}_{\text{rectangle}}$

$A = \frac{1}{2}(4)(4) + (2)(4)$

$A = 8 + 8$

$A = 16$ square units

**24.**

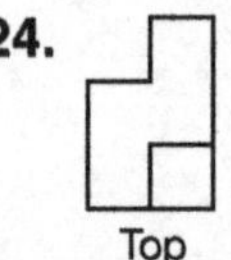


**25.** Each central angle is $\frac{360°}{10} = 36°$.

Using the cosine law to find the side length $x$:

$x^2 = 10^2 + 10^2 - 2(10)(10)\cos 36°$

$x^2 = 38.2$

$x = 6.18$

$P = 10(6.18) = 61.8$

**26.** The matrix for a reflection across the $y$-axis is $\begin{bmatrix} -1 & 0 \\ 0 & 1 \end{bmatrix}$.

Applying this to the vertices,

$$\begin{bmatrix}-1 & 0\\ 0 & 1\end{bmatrix}\begin{bmatrix}3 & 5 & 7\\ -1 & -5 & -1\end{bmatrix} = \begin{bmatrix}-3 & -5 & -7\\ -1 & -5 & -1\end{bmatrix}$$

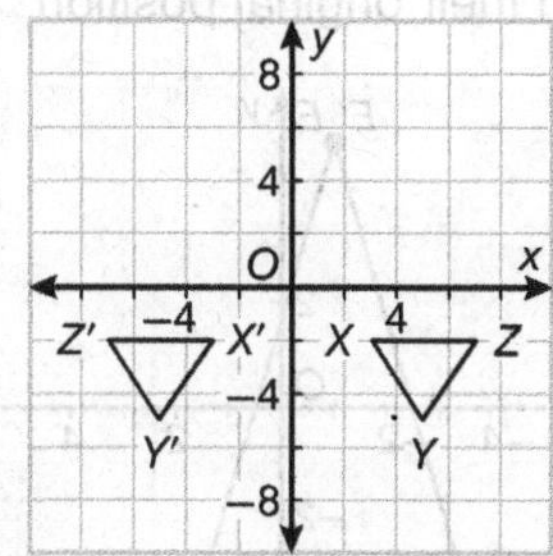


**27.** $2(3x) = 4x + 1$

$6x = 4x + 1$

$2x = 1$

$x = \frac{1}{2}$

$JK = 3\left(\frac{1}{2}\right) = \frac{3}{2}$

$FH = 4\left(\frac{1}{2}\right) + 1 = 3$

**28.** Under the dilation, all values in the points are multiplied by 1.5:

$(-3, 0) \rightarrow (-4.5, 0)$

$(5, 2) \rightarrow (7.5, 3)$

$(2, -4) \rightarrow (3, -6)$

**29.** Answers will vary. Any two triangles with SSS are acceptable.

**30.** Each triangle formed by 2 radii and a side length is an equilateral triangle. In the triangle, all angles measure 60°, including the central angle. So,

$\frac{360}{n} = 60$

$60n = 360$

$n = \frac{360}{60}$

$n = 6$

The shape is a hexagon.

## LESSON 107

### Warm Up 107

**1.** apothem

**2.** $P_{square} = 4 \times 12 = 48$ cm

$P_{rectangle} = 2(b + h)$

$= 2(8 + 18)$

$= 52$ cm

The rectangle has the greater perimeter.

**3.** Choice **A** is correct.

### Lesson Practice 107

**a.** $P = 144$

$2(b + h) = 144$ or $b + h = 72$

When $b = 9$ and $h = 63$:

$A = 9 \times 63$

$A = 567$ in.$^2$

When $b = 12$ and $h = 60$:

$A = 12 \times 60$

$A = 720$ in.$^2$

When $b = 18$ and $h = 54$:

$A = 18 \times 54$

$A = 972$ in.$^2$

**b.** The rectangle with the maximum area is a square. For a square:

$P = 4s$

$s = \frac{144}{4}$

$s = 36$

$A = s^2$

$A = (36)^2$

$A = 1296$ in.$^2$

**c.** Since the triangle with sides 6, 8, and 8 is closer to an equilateral triangle, it will have the larger area.

**d.** The rectangle with the least possible perimeter is a square.

$A = s^2$

$625 = s^2$

$s = 25$

The area is 25 tiles by 25 tiles.

### Practice 107

**1.** $3x° = (5x - 22)°$

$-2x = -22$

$x = 11$

And, $3x° = 3(11)° = 33°$

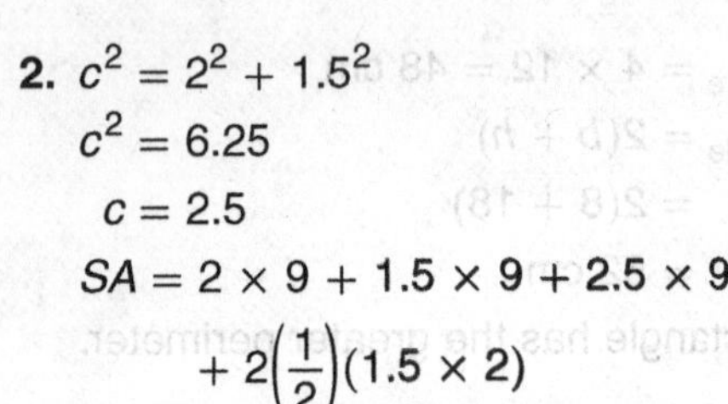

**2.** $c^2 = 2^2 + 1.5^2$

$c^2 = 6.25$

$c = 2.5$

$SA = 2 \times 9 + 1.5 \times 9 + 2.5 \times 9 + 2\left(\frac{1}{2}\right)(1.5 \times 2)$

$SA = 57 \text{ in.}^2$

**3.** For the first triangle:

$P = 3 + 4 + 5 = 12$ in.

For the second triangle:

$P = 4 + 4 + 4 = 12$ in.

The area for the right triangle:

$A = \frac{1}{2}(4)(3)$

$A = 6 \text{ in.}^2$

Prediction: The equilateral triangle will have the greater area because it is a regular polygon.

The area for the equilateral triangle:

$4^2 = h^2 + 2^2$

$16 - 4 = h^2$

$h = 12$

$h = 2\sqrt{3}$

$A = \frac{1}{2}(4)\left(2\sqrt{3}\right)$

$A = 4\sqrt{3}$

$A \approx 6.9 \text{ in.}^2$

**4.** pentagonal prism

**5.**

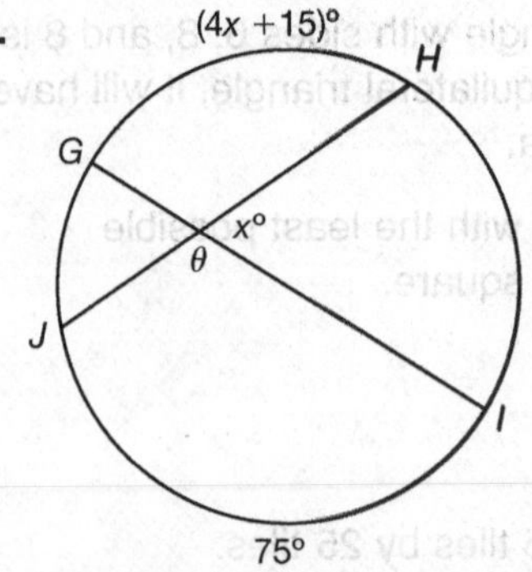


In the diagram, $\theta = 180° - x$, so

$(180 - x)° = \frac{1}{2}(4x + 15 + 75)°$

$360 - 2x = 4x + 90$

$270 = 6x$

$45 = x$

**6.** Answers will vary. Any two negative numbers will be correct. For example: $-1$ and $-2$

**7.** $\begin{bmatrix} 1 & 0 \\ 0 & 1 \end{bmatrix}\begin{bmatrix} -4 & -1 & 2 \\ -5 & 5 & -5 \end{bmatrix} = \begin{bmatrix} -4 & -1 & 2 \\ -5 & 5 & -5 \end{bmatrix}$

Therefore, under a rotation of 360°, the points remain in their original position.

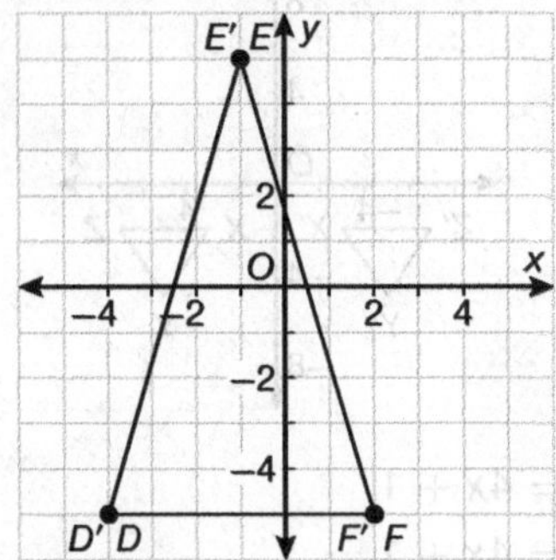


**8.** For a hexagon,

$P = 6s$

$12 = 6s$

$s = 2$

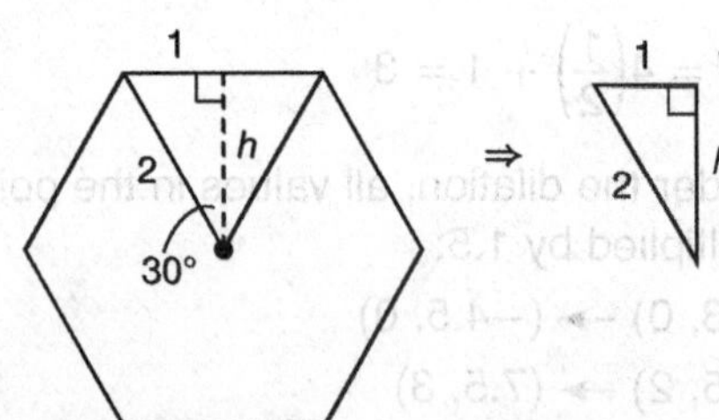


$2^2 = 1^2 + h^2$

$4 = 1 + h^2$

$h^2 = 3$

$h = \sqrt{3}$

$A = 6\left(\frac{1}{2}\right)(2)\left(\sqrt{3}\right)$

$A = 6\sqrt{3}$

$A = 10.4 \text{ cm}^2$

**9.** If $DE = 3(XY)$ then the ratio of the perimeters will be $1 : 3$.

**10.** For the large square $A = 10 \times 10 = 100$. The side length of the smaller square can be found using the Pythagorean Theorem:

$s^2 = 5^2 + 5^2$
$s^2 = 25 + 25$
$s^2 = 50$
$s = 5\sqrt{2}$
$A = 5\sqrt{2} \times 5\sqrt{2} = 50$

The ratio of the two areas:

$$\frac{A_{small}}{A_{large}} = \frac{50}{100} = \frac{1}{2}$$

**11.** This is either a square inscribed in a square of a square circumscribed about a square.

**12.** $s^2 = (3x)^2 + (4x)^2$
$s^2 = 9x^2 + 16x^2$
$s^2 = 25x^2$
$s = 5x$
$\sin P = \frac{3x}{5x} = \frac{3}{5}$

**13.** Under the dilation of 4 about the origin, the $x$- and $y$-coordinates were multiplied by 4. To find the original point, divide each coordinate in the resulting point by 4. Therefore, (20, −4) becomes (5, −1). Choice **B** is correct.

**14.** $\tan\theta = 1$
$\tan^{-1}(1) = \theta$
$\theta = 45°$

**15.** $x(x) = 5(10)$, or $x^2 = 50$, therefore Jeremy is incorrect. The correct answer is $5\sqrt{2}$ in.

**16.** An equilateral triangle will have a minimum perimeter. For an equilateral triangle with a base of $x$, the height is $\frac{\sqrt{3}}{2}x$ (found by using the Pythagorean Theorem). Using this information in the area formula for a triangle:

$$A = \frac{1}{2}(x)\left(\frac{\sqrt{3}}{2}x\right)$$

$$100 = \frac{\sqrt{3}}{4}x^2$$

$$x = \sqrt{\frac{400}{\sqrt{3}}}$$

$x = 15.2$ ft
$P = 3x = 3(15.2) = 45.6$ ft.

**17.** $3(2b) = 9 \times 4$
$6b = 36$
$b = 6$

**18.** For the hexagon,
$P = 6s$
$60 = 6s$
$s = 10$ inches

To find the central angle: $\frac{360°}{6} = 60°$

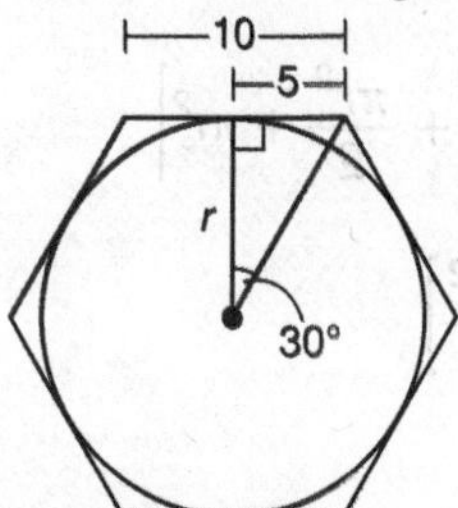


From the diagram:

$\tan 30° = \frac{5}{r}$

$r = \frac{5}{\tan 30°}$

$r = 5\sqrt{3}$ in.

So,
$A = \pi r^2$
$A = \pi(5\sqrt{3})^2$
$A = 75\pi$ in.$^2$

**19.** Since $AB$ is tangent to the circle, the angle made by the tangent and the radius is 90°.
$m\angle ZAB + m\angle AZB = 90°$
$(3x + 72 + 13 - 2x) = 90$
$(x + 85) = 90$
$x = 5$

**20.**

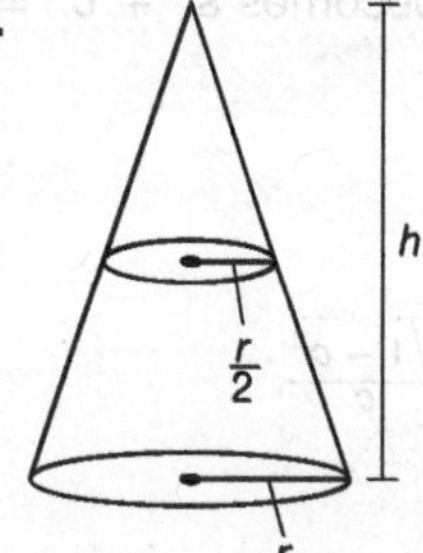


From the diagram and using the volume of a frustum formula:

$V = \frac{1}{3}h\left(B_1 + \sqrt{B_1B_2} + B_2\right)$

$= \frac{1}{3}\left(\frac{h}{2}\right)\left[\pi\left(\frac{r}{2}\right)^2 + \sqrt{\pi\left(\frac{r}{2}\right)^2 \bullet \pi(r)^2} + \pi(r)^2\right]$

$= \left(\frac{h}{6}\right)\left[\frac{\pi r^2}{4} + \sqrt{\left(\frac{\pi r^2}{4}\right) \bullet \pi r^2} + \pi r^2\right]$

$= \left(\frac{h}{6}\right)\left[\frac{\pi r^2}{4} + \sqrt{\left(\frac{\pi^2 r^4}{4}\right)} + \pi r^2\right]$

$= \left(\frac{h}{6}\right)\left[\frac{\pi r^2}{4} + \frac{\pi r^2}{2} + \pi r^2\right]$

$= \left(\frac{h}{6}\right)\left[\frac{7\pi r^2}{4}\right]$

$= \frac{7\pi h r^2}{24}$

But $H = h\left(\frac{r}{R - r}\right)$, so

$V = \frac{\pi}{3}H\left[\frac{R^3 - r^3}{r}\right]$

$V = \frac{\pi}{3}h\left(\frac{r}{R - r}\right)\left(\frac{R^3 - r^3}{r}\right)$

$V = \frac{\pi}{3}h\left(\frac{r}{R - r}\right)\left(\frac{(R - r)(R^2 + Rr + r^2)}{r}\right)$

$V = \frac{\pi}{3}h(R^2 + Rr + r^2)$

**21.**



**22.** $\begin{bmatrix} 4 & 2 & -7 \\ -1 & -3 & 5 \end{bmatrix}\begin{bmatrix} 9 & 6 \\ 3 & 5 \\ 1 & -2 \end{bmatrix}$

$= \begin{bmatrix} 4 \times 9 + 2 \times 3 - 7 \times 1 & 4 \times 6 + 2 \times 5 - 7 \times -2 \\ -1 \times 9 - 3 \times 3 + 5 \times 1 & -1 \times 6 - 3 \times 5 + 5 \times -2 \end{bmatrix} = \begin{bmatrix} 35 & 48 \\ -13 & -31 \end{bmatrix}$

**23.** HA Right Triangle Congruence is derived from AAS congruence. AA in AAS represents the right angle and an acute angle, and S represents the hypotenuse.

**24.** $s = \sin x$, $c = \cos x$ and $t = \tan x$

$\tan x = \frac{\sin x}{\cos x}$ becomes $t = \frac{s}{c}$

and $\sin^2 x + \cos^2 x = 1$ becomes $s^2 + c^2 = 1$.

Solving for $s$:

$s^2 = 1 - c^2$

$s = \sqrt{1 - c^2}$

So, $t = \frac{s}{c}$ becomes $t = \frac{\sqrt{1 - c^2}}{c}$.

Solving for $c$:

$c^2 = 1 - s^2$

$c = \sqrt{1 - s^2}$

So $t = \frac{s}{c}$ becomes $t = \frac{s}{\sqrt{1 - s^2}}$.

**25.** For each central angle, $\frac{360°}{5} = 72°$.
Using the cosine law to find the side length $x$:

$x^2 = 7^2 + 7^2 - 2(7)(7)\cos 72°$

$x^2 = 67.7$

$x = 8.22$

$P = 5(8.22) = 41.1$

**26.** The statement is sometimes true. The diagonals of a rhombus are congruent if the rhombus is a square.

**27.** Under the dilation, the radius increases from 3 to 9. The equation is:

$(x + 3)^2 + (y - 2)^2 = 9^2$

$(x + 3)^2 + (y - 2)^2 = 81$

**28.** The shape with the maximum area is a square.

$P = 4x$

$64 = 4x$

$x = 16$ ft
$A = 16 \times 16$
$A = 256 \text{ ft}^2$

**29.**

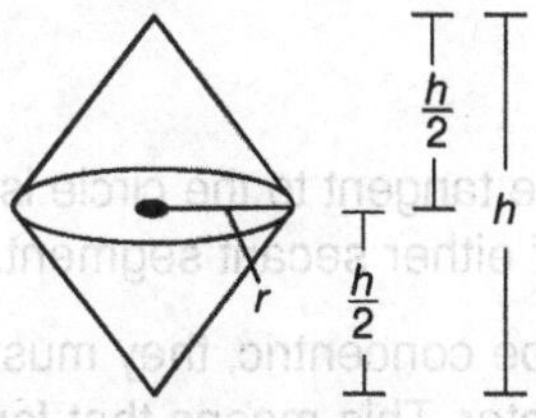


From the diagram:

$$V = \frac{1}{3}\pi r^2\left(\frac{h}{2}\right) + \frac{1}{3}\pi r^2\left(\frac{h}{2}\right)$$

$$V = \frac{1}{3}\pi r^2 h$$

**30.** The circumcenter is the point of concurrency in a triangle where the circle contains all three vertices. It is found by constructing the perpendicular bisector of each side, and locating their point of intersection.

## LAB 14

### Lab 14 Practice

Repeat the steps in the lab for an octagon, a decagon, and a dodecagon, and record its area.

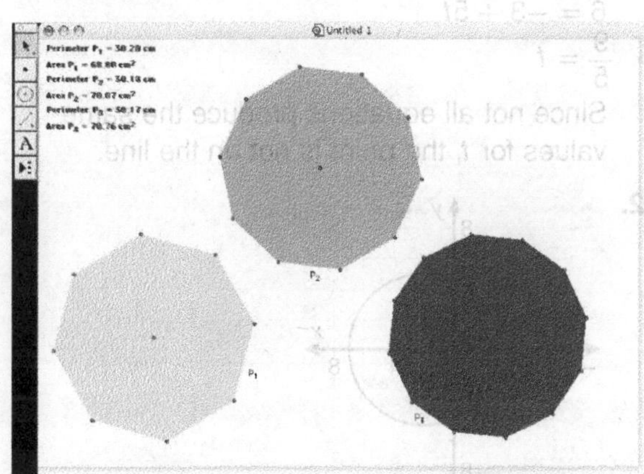

The area of each polygon increases as the number of sides increases while their perimeter stays the same. This result supports the conjecture above.

## LESSON 108

### Warm Up 108

**1.** coordinate (or Cartesian)

**2.** $A(-2, 5)$ and $B(3, -3)$

**3.** Drawing a line through the points $R$ and $S$ will give the required line. Only the point (2, 4) lies on this line.
Choice **C** is correct.

### Lesson Practice 108

**a.** $A(0, 0, 0)$, $B(3, 0, 0)$, $C(3, 3, 0)$, $D(0, 3, 0)$ and $E(0, 0, 5)$, $F(3, 0, 5)$, $G(3, 3, 5)$, $H(0, 3, 5)$

**b.**

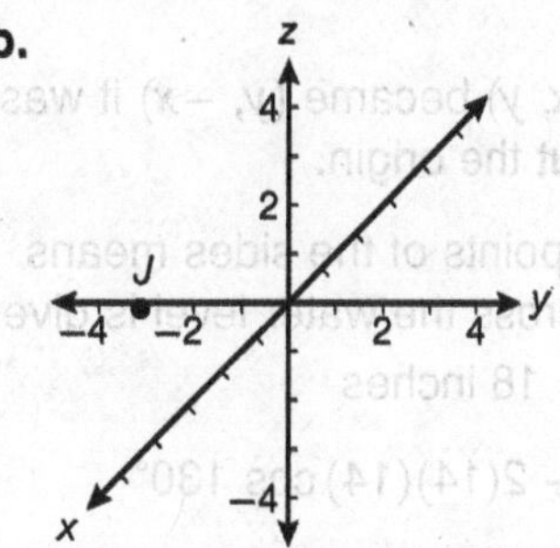


**c.** Answers will vary. Sample answer:
Direction vector:
$(1 - 2, -5 - (-2), 5 - 3) = (-1, -3, 2)$
Therefore,
$(x, y, z) = (2, -2, 3) + t(-1, -3, 2)$
If $t = 2$:
$(x, y, z) = (2, -2, 3) + 2(-1, -3, 2)$
$(x, y, z) = (0, -8, 7)$
If $t = -1$:
$(x, y, z) = (2, -2, 3) - 1(-1, -3, 2)$
$(x, y, z) = (3, 1, 1)$

**d.** Direction vector:
$(4 - 1, 7 - 12, 2 - 13) = (3, -5, -11)$
Therefore,
$(x, y, z) = (4, 7, 2) + t(3, -5, -11)$
For the point $(-11, 32, 60)$ to be on the line:
$-11 = 4 + 3t$
$-15 = 3t$ or $t = -5$
$32 = 7 - 5t$
$25 = -5t$ or $t = -5$

And

$60 = 2 - 11t$

$58 = -11t$ or $t = -\frac{58}{11}$

Since the results for all values of $t$ are not the same, the point is not on the line.

## Practice 108

1. $G(4, 0, 3)$ and $K(-5, 1, 0)$

2. $(AP)(BP) = (CP)(DP)$

$8x = 2(2x + 3)$

$8x = 4x + 6$

$4x = 6$

$x = \frac{6}{4} = 1.5$

3. Since the point $(x, y)$ became $(y, -x)$ it was rotated 270° about the origin.

4. Touching the midpoints of the sides means that the length across the water level is given by $\frac{15 + 21}{2} = \frac{36}{2} = 18$ inches

5. $b^2 = 14^2 + 14^2 - 2(14)(14)\cos 130°$

$b^2 = 643.97$

$b = 25.38$

$h^2 = 14^2 + 14^2 - 2(14)(14)\cos 50°$

$h^2 = 140.02$

$h = 11.83$

Now, the perimeter can be found:

$P = 2l + 2w$

$P = 2(25.38) + 2(11.83)$

$P \approx 74.4$ cm

6. For the points $(3, -1)$ and $(7, 1)$

$m = \frac{1 - (-1)}{7 - 3}$

$m = \frac{2}{4} = \frac{1}{2}$

For the points $(-2, 4)$ and $(0, 0)$

$m = \frac{0 - 4}{0 - (-2)}$

$m = -\frac{4}{2} = -2$

Since the two slopes are negative reciprocals of each other, the two lines are perpendicular.

7. Let the length of the tangent segment = $y$ and each secant segment = $x$. The secant tangent theorem states that:

$y^2 = (x)(2x)$

$y^2 = 2x^2$

$y = \sqrt{2}x$

This means that the tangent to the circle is $\sqrt{2}$ times the length of either secant segment.

8. For two circles to be concentric, they must have the same center. This means that for $(x - p)^2 + (y - q)^2 = r_1^2$ and $(x - a)^2 + (y - b)^2 = r_2^2$, if $(p, q)$ is the same point as $(a, b)$, then the two circles are concentric.

9. Oliver shaded the wrong side of the line on his graph.

10. $\sqrt{\sqrt{3} \times \sqrt{13}} = 2.4989$ or $2.5$

11. If this point is on the line then $5 = 1 + 2t$, $-2 = 0 - t$, and $6 = -3 + 5t$ have to produce the same value for $t$.

In the first equation:

$5 = 1 + 2t$

$4 = 2t$

$t = 2$

In the second equation:

$-2 = -t$

$1 = t$

In the third equation:

$6 = -3 + 5t$

$\frac{9}{5} = t$

Since not all equations produce the same values for $t$, the point is not on the line.

12.

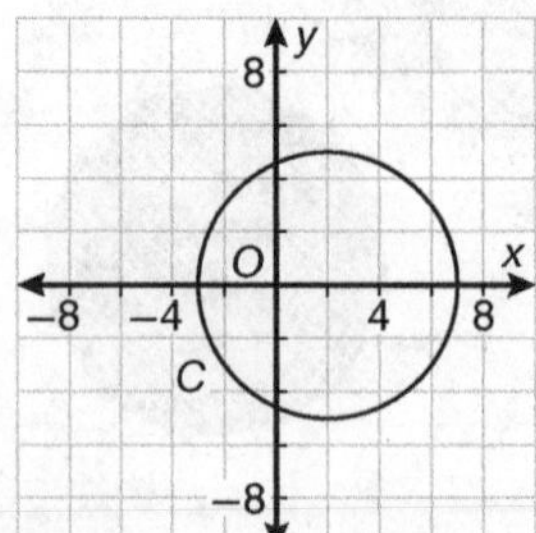


13. The rectangle with the smallest area that encloses a circle is a square with a side length that is equal to the diameter of the circle. This means that the sides of the square are 20 inches in length.

$A = s^2$

$A = (20)^2 = 400 \text{ in}^2$

14. Since congruent arcs have congruent chords, the corresponding chord must be 5 cm in length.

15. $(AP)(BP) = (CP)(DP)$

$(x - 1)\,9 = 6(x + 1)$

$9x - 9 = 6x + 6$

$3x = 15$

$x = 5$

16. $4x - 28 = 2x - 5$

$2x = 23$

$x = \frac{23}{2} = 11.5$

17.

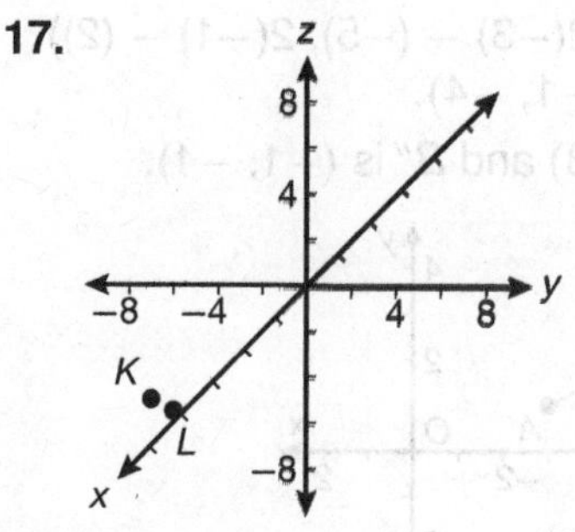


18. $V = \frac{4}{3}\pi r^3$

$V = \frac{4}{3}(3.14)(4)^3$

$V = 267.95 \text{ in.}^3$

19. $P = 16$ in means that each side is $\frac{16}{8} = 2$ in.

The central angle for each triangle is $\frac{360°}{8} = 45°$.

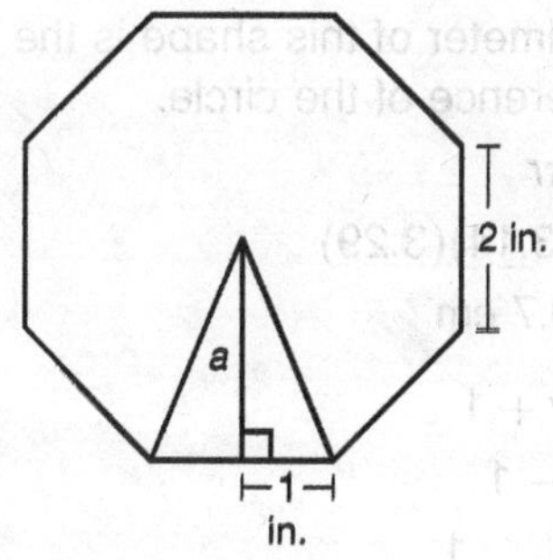


From the diagram:

$\tan 22.5° = \frac{1}{a}$

$a = \frac{1}{\tan 22.5°}$

$a = 2.414$

$A = \frac{1}{2}aP$

$A = \frac{1}{2}(2.414)(16)$

$A = 19.3 \text{ in.}^2$

20. $m\angle Q = 180° - (106° + 18°)$

$m\angle Q = 56°$

Use the Law of Sines to find the lengths of the unknown sides:

$\frac{60}{\sin 56°} = \frac{QR}{\sin 106°}$

$QR = \frac{60 \times \sin 106°}{\sin 56°}$

$QR = 69.6$ units

$\frac{60}{\sin 56°} = \frac{QP}{\sin 18°}$

$QP = \frac{60 \times \sin 18°}{\sin 56°}$

$QP = 22.4$ units

$P = 69.6 + 22.4 + 60 = 152$ units

21. Sample: To prove that a quadrilateral is a parallelogram, it must be proven that both pairs of opposite sides are congruent to each other.

22. $A_{bite} = \frac{1}{2}(\pi r^2)$

$= \frac{1}{2}(3.14)(2.5)^2$

$= 9.8125 \text{ cm}^2$

$A_{sandwich} = b \times h$

$= (12)(9)$

$= 108 \text{ cm}^2$

The number of bites needed to finish the sandwich can be found by dividing:

$\frac{108}{9.8125} = 11.006$

Since this is slightly larger than 11, she will need 12 bites to finish the sandwich.

23.



The central angle for the triangle is:

$\frac{360°}{5} = 72°$

From the diagram,

$\tan 36° = \frac{x}{8}$

$x = 8 \tan 36°$

$x = 5.81$

The side length for the pentagon is $2x$ or 11.62 units.

$P = 5s$

$P = 5(11.62)$

$P = 58.1$ units

**24.** $\sin 18° = \frac{12}{x}$

$x = \frac{12}{\sin 18°}$

$x \approx 139$ ft

**25.** Direction vector

$= (-1 - (-10), 4 - 1, 4 - (-8))$

$= (9, 3, 12)$

$= (3, 1, 4)$

Therefore,

$(x, y, z) = (-1, 4, 4) + t(3, 1, 4)$

For the point (5, 6, 10)

$5 = -1 + 3t$

$6 = 3t$

$t = 2$

$6 = 4 + t$

$t = 2$

$10 = 4 + 4t$

$6 = 4t$

$t = 1.5$

Therefore, choice **A** is incorrect.

For the point (2, 2, 8)

$2 = -1 + 3t$

$3 = 3t$ or $t = 1$

$2 = 4 + t$ or $t = -2$

Therefore, **B** is incorrect.

For the point (−7, 2, −4)

$-7 = -1 + 3t$

$-6 = 3t$ or $t = -2$

$2 = 4 + t$ or $t = -2$

$-4 = 4 + 4t$

$-8 = 4t$ or $t = -2$

Therefore, choice **C** is correct.

**26.** Use the rule for a 90° Counterclockwise rotation about the origin to find $A'$ and $B'$.

$T: (x, Y) \rightarrow (-y, x)$

$A(1, 3) \rightarrow (-3, 1)$

$B(2, 5) \rightarrow (-5, 2)$

So, $A'$ is (−3, 1) and $B'$ is (−5, 2).

Use the transformation mapping $T(x, y) \rightarrow (2a - x, 2b - y)$ to rotate $A'$ and $B'$ about $C(-3, -1)$ to find $A''$ and $B''$.

$T_{A'}: (-3, 1) \rightarrow (2(-3) - (-3), 2(-1) - (1)) \rightarrow (-3, -3)$

$T_{B'}: (-5, 2) \rightarrow (2(-3) - (-5), 2(-1) - (2)) \rightarrow (-1, -4)$

So, $A''$ is (−3, −3) and $B''$ is (−1, −4).

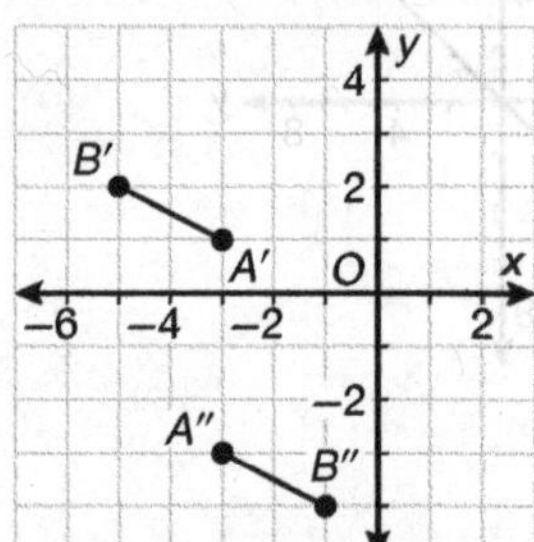


**27.** For the minimum length of wire for a given area, the wire should be shaped into a circle.

$A = \pi r^2$

$34 = (3.14)r^2$

$r = 3.29$ cm

The perimeter of this shape is the circumference of the circle.

$C = 2\pi r$

$= 2(3.14)(3.29)$

$= 20.7$ cm

**28.** $x = by + 1$

$by = x - 1$

$y = \frac{1}{b}x - \frac{1}{b}$

To have no solution means that the two lines are parallel (i.e., have the same slope).

For $y = -\frac{1}{3}x - 4$, the slope is $-\frac{1}{3}$.

This means that $\frac{1}{b} = -\frac{1}{3}$ or $b = -3$.

**29.** $y = x^3$ has been translated 3 units to the right. Therefore, the translation matrix is $\begin{bmatrix} 3 \\ 0 \end{bmatrix}$.

**30.** $\sin\theta + \sin^2\theta + \cos^2\theta = 1.25$

$$\sin\theta + 1 = 1.25$$
$$\sin\theta = 0.25$$
$$\theta = 14.4775°$$

## LESSON 109

### Warm Up 109

**1.** absolute value

**2.** $2x - 2 = -3x + 3$

$$5x = 5$$
$$x = 1$$

When $x = 1$, $y = 2(1) - 2 = 0$

Therefore the solution is (1, 0).

**3.** The slope perpendicular to the given line is $-\frac{4}{3}$. This means that the line through each point must be of the form $y = -\frac{4}{3}x + b$ to be perpendicular.

For choice A:

$$-1 = -\frac{4}{3}(4) + b$$
$$b = -1 + \frac{16}{3}$$
$$b = \frac{13}{3}$$

We can now find the point of intersection of $y = \frac{3}{4}x + 2$ and $y = -\frac{4}{3}x + \frac{13}{3}$. This point is (1.12, 2.84). The distance between (1.12, 2.84) and (4, −1) is

$$d = \sqrt{(2.88)^2 + (-3.84)^2}$$
$$d = 4.8$$

Choice **A** is correct.

### Exploration 109

**1–3.** Answers will vary based on the student's choice of three cities.

**4.** Answers will vary. They should find that the total is not the same as it is when found using trigonometry.

**5.** The angles add to a value greater than 180°.

### Lesson Practice 109

**a.** A great circle is *XW*, a segment is *ZW*, and a triangle is $\triangle XWZ$.

**b.** Since all sides have different lengths, the triangle is scalene.

**c.** $A = \frac{\pi r^2}{180°}(m\angle X + m\angle Y + m\angle Z - 180°)$

$$A = \frac{(3.14)(12)^2}{180°}(65° + 68° + 99° - 180°)$$
$$A = \frac{(3.14)(144)}{180°}(52°)$$
$$A = 130.6 \text{ in.}^2$$

### Practice 109

**1.** Answers will vary. Sample: You could measure the straight line distances from spoke to spoke. If these chords have the same length, the arc lengths are equal.

Or

Measure the central angles that the spokes make. If the central angles are equal, then the arc lengths are equal.

**2.** $A = \frac{(3.14)(10)^2}{180°}(90° + 80° + 45° - 180°)$

$$A = \frac{(3.14)(100)}{180°}(35°)$$
$$A = 61.1 \text{ cm}^2$$

**3.** Choice **C** is correct.

**4.** For the given shape:

$SA = 2(8 \times 20) + 2(4 \times 8) + 2(4 \times 20)$

$SA = 544 \text{ cm}^2$

Applying the scale factor for area of $1^2 : 4^2$, or 1 : 16:

$$\frac{544}{S} = \frac{16}{1}$$
$$16S = 544$$
$$S = \frac{544}{16}$$
$$S = 34 \text{ cm}^2$$

$V = 8 \times 20 \times 4$

$V = 640 \text{ cm}^3$

Applying the scale factor for volume of $1^3 : 4^3$ or 1 : 64:

$$\frac{640}{V} = \frac{64}{1}$$

$$64V = 640$$

$$V = 10 \text{ cm}^3$$

5. $\begin{bmatrix} 0 & -1 \\ 1 & 0 \end{bmatrix}\begin{bmatrix} 1 & 5 & 2 \\ 1 & 3 & -3 \end{bmatrix} = \begin{bmatrix} -1 & -3 & 3 \\ 1 & 5 & 2 \end{bmatrix}$

Now, we can apply the reflection matrix for a reflection across the $x$-axis.

$\begin{bmatrix} 1 & 0 \\ 1 & -1 \end{bmatrix}\begin{bmatrix} -1 & -3 & 3 \\ 1 & 5 & 2 \end{bmatrix} = \begin{bmatrix} -1 & -3 & 3 \\ -1 & -5 & -2 \end{bmatrix}$

6. You only need to construct two perpendicular bisectors of a triangle to locate the circumcenter. The third can be drawn as a check that the other two properly located the point.

7. A reflection through the $y = x$ maps the point $(x, y)$ to the point $(y, x)$.

8. Since the cone and the square pyramid have the same dimensions of height and side length (or diameter in the case of the cone), the cone frustum will have the larger volume. The relationship will be

$V_{\text{square frustum}} \times \pi = V_{\text{cone frustum}}$

9. Answers will vary as any value for $t$ will generate a point. Sample:

For $t = 1$: $(x, y, z) = (4, 0, 0) + (1, 0, 1) = (5, 0, 1)$

For $t = 3$: $(x, y, z) = (4, 0, 0) + (3, 0, 3) = (7, 0, 3)$

10. 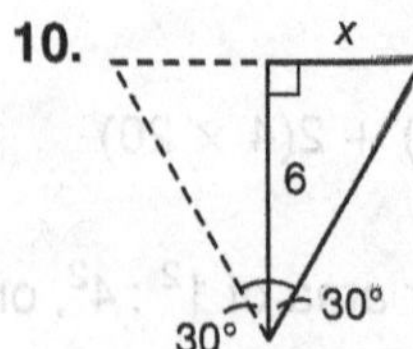


For the central angle: $\frac{360°}{6} = 60°$

$$\tan 30° = \frac{x}{6}$$

$$x = 6 \tan 30°; x = 2\sqrt{3}$$

Each side is two times this value or $4\sqrt{3}$ cm.

For the perimeter:

$$P = 6s = 6 \times 4\sqrt{3} = 24\sqrt{3} \text{ cm}$$

For the area:

$$A = \frac{1}{2}aP$$

$$A = \frac{1}{2}(6)(24\sqrt{3}) = 72\sqrt{3} \text{ cm}^2$$

11. $AE : AB = 15 : 21$ or $5 : 7$

$AF : AC = 20 : 28$ or $5 : 7$

Since $EF$ divides the sides $AB$ and $AC$ proportionally, $EF$ is parallel to $BC$.

12. The ratio of area is 1 : 16, so $\frac{x}{64} = \frac{1}{16}$, which means that $x = 4$ square feet.

13. great circle

14. Since each dimension will increase by a factor of 3, the area will increase by a factor of $3^2$ or 9.

15. $4x + 9 = 5x - 11; 20 = x$

This means that $5x - 11 = 5(20) - 11 = 89°$.

16. The largest area that she can enclose will be within a rectangle that is a square. So $P = 4s$, or $s = \frac{100}{4} = 25$ cm. The area can now be found:

$A = s^2$, so $A = (25)^2 = 625 \text{ cm}^2$.

17. magnitude $= \sqrt{25 + 49} = \sqrt{74} = 8.6$.

Choice **D** is correct.

18. $\overrightarrow{EB}$ bisects $\angle AEC$, so it divides the circle into two congruent arcs.

Let point $D$ be the point of intersection of $\widehat{AC}$ and $\overrightarrow{EB}$. Then,

$$m\widehat{BAD} = 180°$$

$$m\widehat{AD} = 180° - m\widehat{AB}$$

$$m\angle AEB = \frac{1}{2}(m\widehat{AB} - m\widehat{AD})$$

$$45° = \frac{1}{2}(m\widehat{AB} - (180° - m\widehat{AB}))$$

$$90° = 2m\widehat{AB} - 180°$$

$$270° = 2m\widehat{AB}$$

$$135° = m\widehat{AB}$$

19. $A = \frac{(3.14)(3960)^2}{180°}(77° + 56° + 90° - 180°)$

$A = \frac{(3.14)(3960)^2}{180°}(43°) = 11{,}762{,}942 \text{ mi}^2$

**20.** $\sin^2\theta + \cos^2\theta = 1$

$\cos^2\theta = 1 - \sin^2\theta$

$\cos\theta = \sqrt{1 - 0.12}$

$\cos\theta = 0.94$

**21.** Directionvector: $(3-4, -6-(-5), -2-(-1)) = (-1, -1, -1)$ or $(1, 1, 1)$

$(x, y, z) = (4, -5, -1) + t(1, 1, 1)$

For the point to be on the line:

$1 = 4 + t$ or $t = -3$

$-8 = -5 + t$ or $t = -3$

$-4 = -1 + t$ or $t = -3$

Since all three values of $t$ are the same, the point is on the line.

**22.** 39.6 in.; Eddie confused the terms "inscribed" and "circumscribed."

**23.** $\tan 30° = \frac{h}{9}$

$h = 9 \tan 30°$

$h = 5.2$ ft

**24.** 5 cm from the vertex:

$\frac{5}{20} = \frac{r}{4}$

$r = 1$ cm

$A = \pi r^2$

$A = (3.14)(1)^2$

$A = 3.14\ \text{cm}^2$

**25.** Direction vector:

$= (2 - 1, 5 - (-4), 8 - 6) = (1, 9, 2)$

Therefore, $(x, y, z) = (2, 5, 8) + t(1, 9, 2)$

For the point (4, 23, 12)

$4 = 2 + t$ or $t = 2$

$23 = 5 + 9t$

$9t = 18$ or $t = 2$

$12 = 8 + 2t$

$4 = 2t$ or $t = 2$

Choice **A** is correct.

**26.** The first statement is false, and the second statement is true. So, the disjunction is true, but the conjunctuon is false. Only their disjunction is correct.

**27.**

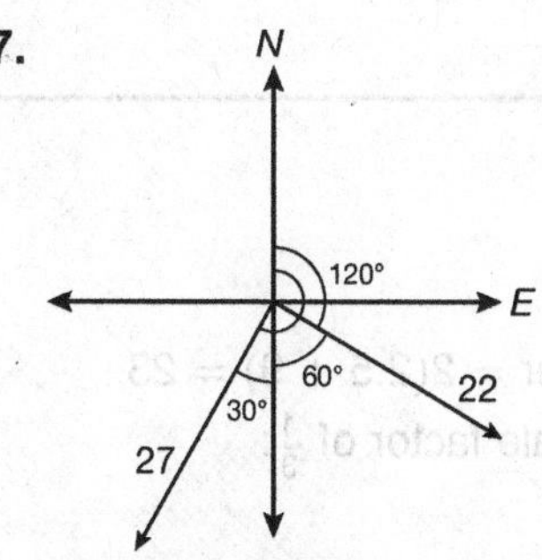


$c^2 = 27^2 + 22^2$

$c^2 = 1213$

$c = 34.8$ mi.

**28.**

For a regular octagon, the central angle of each triangle is $\frac{360°}{8} = 45°$

From the diagram:

$\tan 22.5° = \frac{1.5}{a}$

$a = \frac{1.5}{\tan 22.5}$

$a = 3.62$ cm

$A = \frac{1}{2}aP$

$= \frac{1}{2}(3.62)(24)$

$= 43.4\ \text{cm}^2$

**29.** Since the reflection line for the two shapes is vertical, the slope is undefined.

**30.**

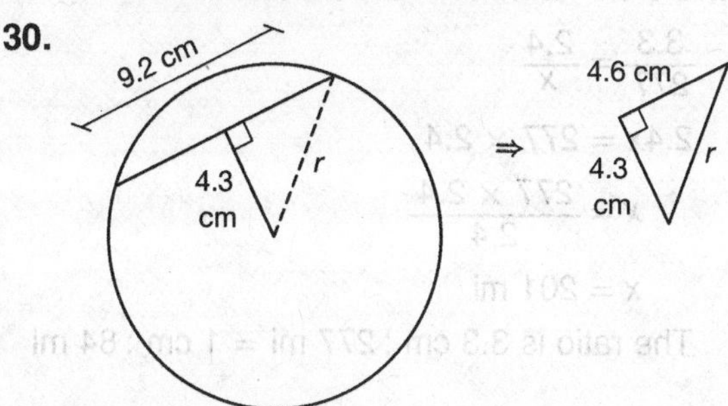


$r^2 = 4.3^2 + 4.6^2$

$r^2 = 39.65$

$r = 6.297$ cm

$d = 2r$

$d = 2(6.297) = 12.6$ cm

## LESSON 110

### Warm Up 110

1. dilation
2. current perimeter = 2(2.5 + 9) = 23
   Applying the scale factor of $\frac{1}{3}$:
   $23 \times \frac{1}{3} = \frac{23}{3}$
   The ratio of the original perimeter to the dilated perimeter is $23 : \frac{23}{3}$.
3. Only Choice **A** has rotational and line symmetry.

### Lesson Practice 110

a. Using a scale of 1 m to 0.5 cm:
$$\frac{l}{30 \text{ m}} = \frac{0.5 \text{ cm}}{1 \text{ m}}$$
$$l = 15 \text{ cm}$$
$$\frac{w}{15 \text{ m}} = \frac{0.5 \text{ cm}}{1 \text{ m}}$$
$$w = 7.5 \text{ cm}$$
See student work for scale drawing.

b. 10 in. : 555.5 ft means 1 in. : 55.55 ft

c. 200 mi : 1 ft = 3031 mi : *x* ft
$$\frac{200}{1} = \frac{3031}{x}$$
$$200x = 3031$$
$$x = \frac{3031}{200}$$
$$x = 15.2 \text{ ft}$$

d. 3.3 cm : 277 mi = 2.4 cm : *x* mi
$$\frac{3.3}{277} = \frac{2.4}{x}$$
$$2.4x = 277 \times 2.4$$
$$x = \frac{277 \times 2.4}{2.4}$$
$$x = 201 \text{ mi}$$
The ratio is 3.3 cm : 277 mi = 1 cm : 84 mi

### Practice 110

1. Answers will vary. Sample: Yvonne is correct. For the shape to be a rhombus all four sides would need to be the same length. There is no evidence that this is true, so the shape can simply be classified as a parallelogram.
2. Choice **D** is correct. All sides have the same length.
3. $12x = 360$
   $x = 30$
   Sum of measures of blue arcs:
   $6x = 6(30) = 180$
   $L = 2\pi r\left(\frac{m°}{360°}\right) = 2\pi(2)\left(\frac{180°}{360°}\right)$
   $= 2\pi$ in.
4. Either fixed point can be used as a position vector. The direction vector for both lines must be the same, or a scalar multiple of each other.
5. In a 45-45-90 triangle, the legs are of the same length. Therefore, the rod is 67 cm long.
6. $\begin{bmatrix} -10+8 & -30+0 \\ -5-4 & -15+0 \end{bmatrix} = \begin{bmatrix} -2 & -30 \\ -9 & -15 \end{bmatrix}$
7. $A = \frac{\pi(8)^2}{180°}(215° - 180°)$
   $A = \frac{\pi(64)}{180°}(35°)$
   $A = 39.1 \text{ cm}^2$
8. direction vector = (6 − 3, 9 − 1, 3 − (−2))
   = (3, 8, 5)
   Therefore, (*x*, *y*, *z*) = (3, 1, −2) + *t*(3, 8, 5) or (*x*, *y*, *z*) = (6, 9, 3) + *t*(3, 8, 5)
9. $(3x - 4)° = \frac{1}{2}(148°)$
   $3x - 4 = 74$
   $3x = 78$
   $x = 26$
10. Answers will vary. Any set of dilations that give a value of one when multiplied will cause the preimage to coincide with the image.
11. $x^2 = 8^2 + 12^2 - 2(8)(12) \cos 111°$
    $x^2 = 276.8$
    $x = 16.6$
    $P = 8 + 12 + 16.6$
    $P = 36.6$
12. There is no line symmetry, but there is rotational symmetry of order 2.

13. 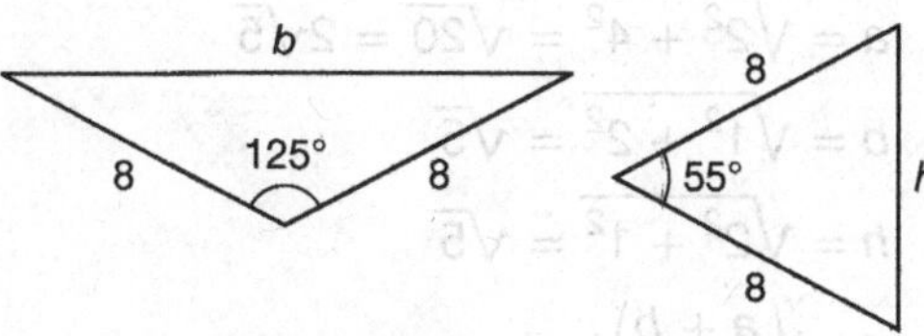


$b^2 = 8^2 + 8^2 - 2(8)(8)\cos 125°$
$b^2 = 201.4$
$b = 14.2$ in.
$h^2 = 8^2 + 8^2 - 2(8)(8)\cos 55°$
$h^2 = 54.6$
$h = 7.4$ in
$P = 2(b + h)$
$P = 2(14.2 + 7.4) = 43.2$ in.

14. The shape with the greatest number of sides will have the largest area, as it is closest to a circle. Choice **D** is correct.

15. The point of tangency is (−2, 4). The equation of the tangent line is $y = 4$. Circle $A$ has a radius of 2 units and circle $B$ has a radius of 4 units.

16. 12.1 cm : 139 mi
So 1 cm : 11.49 mi or 0.09 cm : 1 mi

17. Since $d = 2r$, $h = 3d$ becomes $h = 6r$.
$V = \pi r^2 h$
$V = \pi r^2(6r)$
$509 = 6\pi r^3$
$r = \sqrt[3]{\frac{509}{6\pi}}$
$r = 3$ m
Therefore, the height is 6(3) = 18 m.
$SA = 2\pi r^2 + 2\pi rh$
$SA = 2(3.14)(3)^2 + 2(3.14)(3)(18)$
$SA = 395.64$
$SA \approx 396 \text{ m}^2$

18. $11^2 = x(x + 8)$
$x^2 + 8x - 121 = 0$
Using the quadratic formula, we obtain
$x = \frac{-8 \pm \sqrt{64 + 484}}{2}$
$x = \frac{-8 \pm \sqrt{548}}{2}$
$x = 7.7$ or $-15.7$
Since $x$ must be positive, 7.7 is the only possible answer.

19. 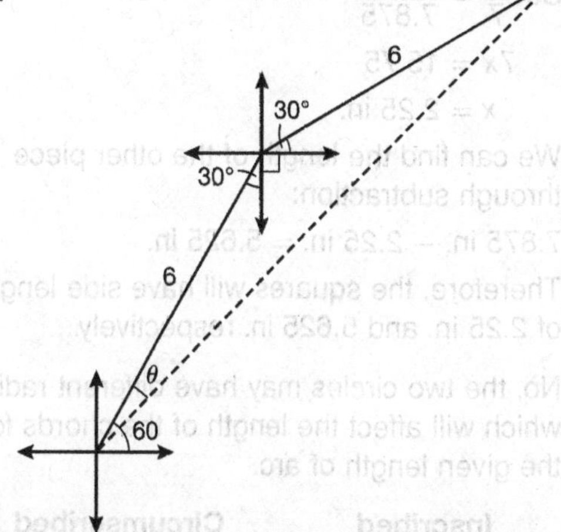


$x^2 = 6^2 + 6^2 - 2(6)(6)\cos 150°$
$x^2 = 134.35$
$x = 11.59$ mph
To find direction, we use the sine law:
$\frac{\sin 150°}{11.59} = \frac{\sin \theta}{6}$
$\sin \theta = \frac{6 \times \sin 150°}{11.59}$
$\sin \theta = 0.2588$
$\theta = 15°$
From the diagram, we can see that the direction is 45° north of east.

20. 4 ft : 36.0 million miles = $x$ ft : 483.4 million miles
$\frac{4}{36} = \frac{x}{483.4}$
$36x = 1933.6$
$x = 54$ ft

21. $A = \frac{(3.14)(4)^2}{180°}(98° + 110° + 100° - 180°)$
$A = \frac{(3.14)(16)}{180°}(128°)$
$A = 35.7 \text{ cm}^2$

22. Answers will vary. See student work.

23. She needs to cut the 31.5-inch material into 4 strips to complete squares. So $\frac{31.5 \text{ in.}}{4} = 7.875$ in. per strip. Since we now need to divide these sides into pieces in the ratio 2 : 5, we need to look at the fact that the strips need to be marked in 7 equal sections, and then cut at the 2 : 5 point.

So: $\frac{2}{7} = \frac{x}{7.875}$

$7x = 15.75$

$x = 2.25$ in.

We can find the length of the other piece through subtraction:

7.875 in. − 2.25 in. = 5.625 in.

Therefore, the squares will have side lengths of 2.25 in. and 5.625 in. respectively.

**24.** No, the two circles may have different radii, which will affect the length of the chords for the given length of arc.

**25.** **Inscribed** **Circumscribed**

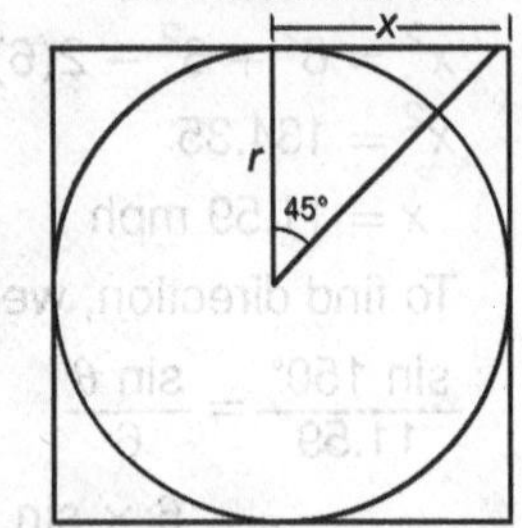


For the inscribed square:

$x^2 = r^2 + r^2$

$x^2 = 2r^2 \quad x = \sqrt{2}r$

For the circumscribed shape:

Since the tangent line $x$ and the radius are sides of an isosceles triangle, $x = r$. This means that the side length is $2r$.

**26.** Choice **C** is correct.

**27.**

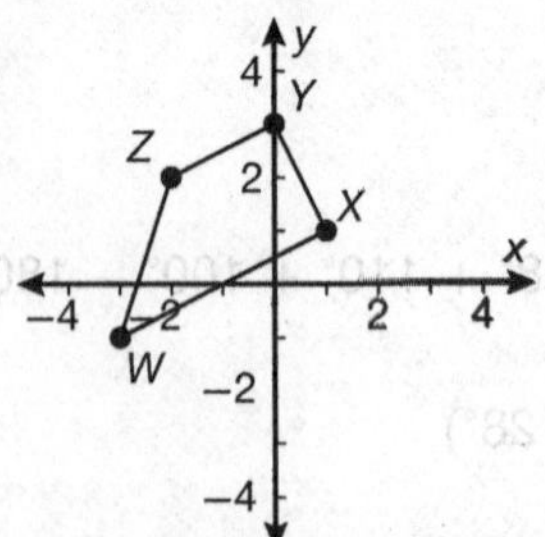


From the diagram, the shape can be seen to be a trapezoid. Side $YX$ and side $WX$ both have a slope of $\frac{1}{2}$, while the other two sides are not parallel. The slope of side $XY$ is −2, which means that this side is perpendicular to the two parallel sides, which means that its length will be equal to the height of the trapezoid.

Using the distance formula,

$a = \sqrt{2^2 + 4^2} = \sqrt{20} = 2\sqrt{5}$

$b = \sqrt{1^2 + 2^2} = \sqrt{5}$

$h = \sqrt{2^2 + 1^2} = \sqrt{5}$

$A = \left(\frac{a+b}{2}\right)h$ becomes

$A = \left(\frac{2\sqrt{5} + \sqrt{5}}{2}\right)\sqrt{5}$

$A = \frac{3\sqrt{5} \times \sqrt{5}}{2}$

$A = \frac{15}{2}$

**28.** The triangle has two equal sides, so it is isosceles.

**29.** $SA = 4\pi r^2$, and since $r = \frac{d}{2}$,

$SA = 4\pi\left(\frac{d}{2}\right)^2$

$= 4\pi\frac{d^2}{4} = \pi d^2$

**30.** $(-2x + 40)° = (3x - 15)°$

$-5x = -55$

$x = 11$

$(-2x + 40)° = (-2(11) + 40)°$

$= (-22 + 40)° = 18°$

Each angle measures 18°.

## INVESTIGATION 11

**1.** $\frac{a+b}{b} = \frac{a}{b}$

If $a = 1$

$\frac{1+b}{1} = \frac{1}{b}$

$b^2 + b - 1 = 0$

$b = \frac{-1 + \sqrt{1^2 - 4(1)(-1)}}{2(1)}$

$b = \frac{\sqrt{5} - 1}{2}$

**2.** $\frac{c+d}{c} = \frac{c}{d}$

If $c = \sqrt{5}$,

$\frac{\sqrt{5} + d}{\sqrt{5}} = \frac{\sqrt{5}}{d}$

$d^2 + \sqrt{5}d - 5 = 0$

$$d = \frac{-\sqrt{5} + \sqrt{\sqrt{5}^2 - 4(1)(-5)}}{2(1)}$$

$$d = \frac{5 - \sqrt{5}}{2}$$

3. $\frac{e+2}{e} = \frac{e}{2}$

$e^2 - 2e - 4 = 0$

$$e = \frac{2 + \sqrt{2^2 - 4(1)(-4)}}{2(1)}$$

$$e = \frac{2 + 2\sqrt{5}}{2}$$

$$e = 1 + \sqrt{5}$$

4. $a = bx$

5. $\frac{bx + b}{bx} = \frac{bx}{b}$

$b^2x + b^2 = b^2x^2$

$b^2x^2 - b^2x - b^2 = 0$

$b^2(x^2 - x - 1) = 0$

$x^2 - x - 1 = 0$

6. $x = \frac{1 + \sqrt{1^2 - 4(1)(-1)}}{2(1)}$

$x = \frac{1 + \sqrt{5}}{2}$

7. $\frac{b+h}{b} = \frac{b}{h}$

8. $\frac{2\sqrt{5} + h}{2\sqrt{5}} = \frac{2\sqrt{5}}{h}$

$h^2 + 2\sqrt{5}h - 20 = 0$

$$h = \frac{-2\sqrt{5} + \sqrt{20 - 4(1)(-20)}}{2(1)}$$

$$h = \frac{-2\sqrt{5} + 10}{2}$$

$$h = 5 - \sqrt{5}$$

9. 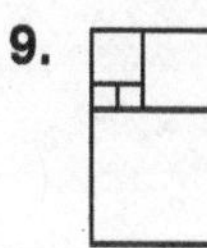

10.

11. 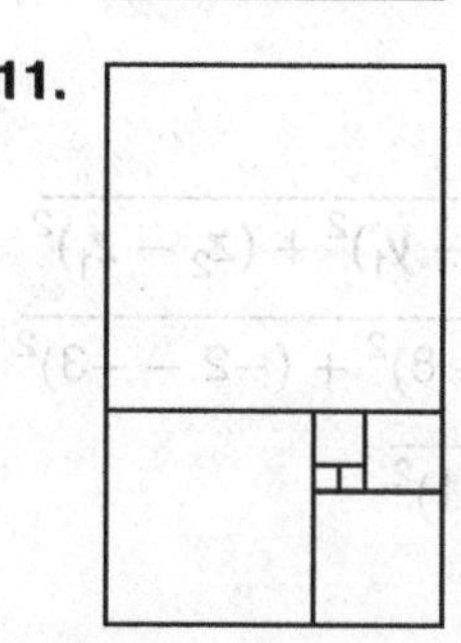

## Investigation 11 Practice

a. 1, 1, 2, 3, 5, 8, 13, 21, 34, 55

$\frac{1}{1} = 1$ $\frac{2}{1} = 2$ $\frac{3}{2} = 1.5$ $\frac{5}{3} = 1.6$ $\frac{13}{8} = 1.625$

$\frac{21}{13} = 1.6154$ $\frac{34}{21} = 1.6190$ $\frac{55}{34} = 1.6176$

b. As the Fibonacci sequence continues, the ratio of consecutive terms approaches the golden ratio.

c. 55, 89, 144, 233, 377, 610, 987, 1597

$\frac{89}{55} = 1.61818$ $\frac{144}{89} = 1.61798$

$\frac{233}{144} = 1.61806$

$\frac{377}{233} = 1.61804$ $\frac{610}{377} = 1.61804$

$\frac{987}{610} = 1.61803$ $\frac{1597}{987} = 1.61803$

d. As the squares of the golden rectangle increase, the ratio of the dimensions of the rectangle approach the golden ratio.

## LESSON 111

### Warm Up 111

1. equidistant

2. $d = \sqrt{(2 - -6)^2 + (-3 - -7)^2}$

$= \sqrt{(8)^2 + (4)^2}$

$= \sqrt{80} = 4\sqrt{5}$

3. Midpoint $= \left(\frac{8 + -2}{2}, \frac{-3 + 5}{2}\right) =$

$\left(\frac{6}{2}, \frac{2}{2}\right) = (3, 1)$

b. Midpoint $= \left(\frac{x_1 + x_2}{2}, \frac{y_1 + y_2}{2}, \frac{z_1 + z_2}{2}\right)$

$= \left(\frac{22 + 15}{2}, \frac{14 + -8}{2}, \frac{9 + -6}{2}\right)$

$= \left(\frac{37}{2}, \frac{6}{2}, \frac{3}{2}\right)$

$= (18.5, 3, 1.5)$

### Lesson Practice 111

a. $d_{RS} = \sqrt{(x_2 - x_1)^2 + (y_2 - y_1)^2 + (z_2 - z_1)^2}$

$= \sqrt{(0 - 6)^2 + (12 - 8)^2 + (-2 - -3)^2}$

$= \sqrt{(-6)^2 + (4)^2 + (1)^2}$

$= \sqrt{53}$

c. The first person is at (−40, 25, −300), and the second person is at (−25, 10, −250).

$d = \sqrt{(x_2 - x_1)^2 + (y_2 - y_1)^2 + (z_2 - z_1)^2}$

$= \sqrt{(-40 - -25)^2 + (25 - 10)^2 + (-300 - -250)^2}$

$= \sqrt{(-15)^2 + (15)^2 + (-50)^2}$

$= \sqrt{2950} \approx 54.3$

The skydivers are about 54.3 feet apart.

### Practice 111

1. The new center of the circle is at (−2, 5) and the radius remains the same.

$(x + 2)^2 + (y - 5)^2 = 36$

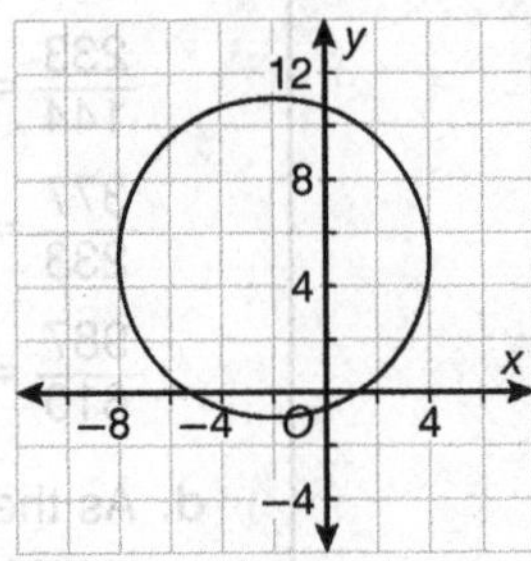


2. $(x, y) \longrightarrow (y, x)$

$(-2x, 3y) \longrightarrow (3y, -2x)$

3. Since T: $(x, y) \longrightarrow (-y, x)$, describes the transformation of each vertex of *JKLM*, then the angle of rotation is 90°.

The rotation matrix $\begin{bmatrix} 0 & -1 \\ 1 & 0 \end{bmatrix}$ indicates a 90° rotation.

4. Midpoint $= \left(\frac{x_1 + x_2}{2}, \frac{y_1 + y_2}{2}, \frac{z_1 + z_2}{2}\right)$

$= \left(\frac{-10 + -4}{2}, \frac{2 + -2}{2}, \frac{13 + 5}{2}\right)$

$= \left(\frac{-14}{2}, \frac{0}{2}, \frac{18}{2}\right) = (-7, 0, 9)$

5. The center of the circle is the orthocenter of the triangle. Therefore, $R = \frac{2}{3}h$ and $r = \frac{1}{3}h$.

6.

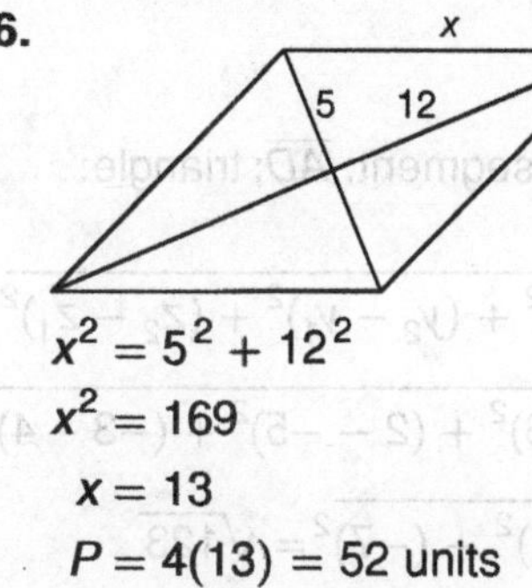


$x^2 = 5^2 + 12^2$

$x^2 = 169$

$x = 13$

$P = 4(13) = 52$ units

7. He is incorrect. The value $t = 3$ gives the point (13, 18, 17), not (13, 18, 16). This can be seen by solving for $t$ and $t \neq 3$ for all three sets of coordinates.

$3t + 4 = 13$

$3t = 9$

$t = 3$

$5t + 3 = 18$

$5t = 15$

$t = 3$

$4t + 5 = 16$

$4t = 11$

$t \neq 3$

8. Compare the surface areas of the triangular prism and the cylinder.

$h_T^2 = 10^2 - 5^2$

$h_T^2 = 75$

$h_T \approx 8.7$

$S_T = 2(10)(10) + 2\left(\frac{1}{2}(10)(8.7)\right)$

$= 200 + 87 = 287 \text{ ft}^2$

$S_C = \frac{1}{2}[2\pi(5)(10) + 2(\pi 5^2)]$

$\approx 236 \text{ ft}^2$

The triangular-prism-shaped frame will require more plastic.

9. The slope of all three equations must be 2 since the slope of the first equation is 2. The $y$-intercept can be any real number. Therefore, $p$ can be any real number. The second equation becomes $y = \frac{m}{2}x + 4$.

$\frac{m}{2} = 2$

$m = 4$

$3n = 2$

$n = \frac{2}{3}$

10. The first astronaut is at (−5, 3, −6), and the second astronaut is at (4, −3, 3).

$d = \sqrt{(x_2 - x_1)^2 + (y_2 - y_1)^2 + (z_2 - z_1)^2}$

$= \sqrt{(-5 - 4)^2 + (3 - -3)^2 + (-6 - 3)^2}$

$= \sqrt{(-9)^2 + (6)^2 + (-9)^2}$

$= \sqrt{198} \approx 14.1$ feet

11. $d_{VW} = \sqrt{(x_2 - x_1)^2 + (y_2 - y_1)^2 + (z_2 - z_1)^2}$

$= \sqrt{(3 - -4)^2 + (7 - -8)^2 + (-6 - 7)^2}$

$= \sqrt{(7)^2 + (15)^2 + (-13)^2}$

$= \sqrt{443}$

Midpoint $= \left(\frac{x_1 + x_2}{2}, \frac{y_1 + y_2}{2}, \frac{z_1 + z_2}{2}\right)$

$= \left(\frac{3 + -4}{2}, \frac{7 + -8}{2}, \frac{-6 + 7}{2}\right)$

$= \left(\frac{-1}{2}, \frac{-1}{2}, \frac{1}{2}\right) = (-0.5, -0.5, 0.5)$

12. $2(KL) = FG$

$2(5x - 12) = 4x + 18$

$10x - 24 = 4x + 18$

$6x = 42$

$x = 7$

$FG = 4(7) + 18 = 46$

13. $\begin{bmatrix} -4 & -4 & -4 & -4 \\ \frac{1}{2} & \frac{1}{2} & \frac{1}{2} & \frac{1}{2} \end{bmatrix}$

14. See Student work. The drawing should be any two triangles that are similar by Side-Angle-Side Similarity.

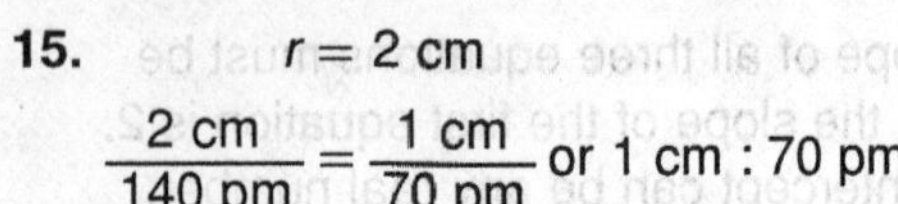



**15.** $r = 2$ cm

$\frac{2 \text{ cm}}{140 \text{ pm}} = \frac{1 \text{ cm}}{70 \text{ pm}}$ or 1 cm : 70 pm

**16.** $(x + 18) + 54 = 180$

$x = 108$

If $x = 108$, then the two angles are supplementary same-side interior angles.

**17.** When 15 is the smaller number:

$\frac{a + 15}{a} = \frac{a}{15}$

$a^2 = 15(a + 15)$

$a^2 = 15a + 225$

$a^2 - 15a - 225 = 0$

$a = \frac{15 \pm \sqrt{225 - 4(1)(-225)}}{2(1)}$

$a = 7.5 \pm 16.77$

$a \approx 24.27$ (since the side must be positive)

When 15 is the larger number:

$\frac{15 + b}{15} = \frac{15}{b}$

$b^2 + 15b = 225$

$b^2 + 15b - 225 = 0$

$b = \frac{-15 \pm \sqrt{225 - 4(1)(-225)}}{2(1)}$

$b = -7.5 \pm 16.77$

$b \approx 9.27$

**18.** $\frac{4^3}{32} = \frac{6^3}{x}$

$64x = 6912$

$x = 108$ ounces

**19.** Since it is an isosceles trapezoid and has a right angle, the adjacent base angle is also a right angle. Then, by the Same-Side Interior Angles Theorem, the other two angles are also right angles. Hence, the quadrilateral is a rectangle.

**20.** The triangle is small because the equation $A = \frac{\pi r^2}{180°}(m\angle A + m\angle B + m\angle C - 180°)$ reduces to $A = \frac{\pi r^2}{180°}$.

**21.** Label the vertical segment between the two triangles $y$ and solve:

$y^2 = 15^2 - 12^2$

$y = 9$

$x^2 = 12^2 - 9^2$

$x = \sqrt{63} = 3\sqrt{7}$

**22.** $B_1 = 25^2 = 625$

$B_2 = 15^2 = 225$

$V = \frac{1}{3}h(B_1 + \sqrt{B_1 B_2} + B_2)$

$V = \frac{1}{3}(21)(625\sqrt{(625)(225)} + 225)$

$= 8575 \text{ cm}^3$

**23.** Sample: line: $\overleftrightarrow{BD}$; segment: $\overline{AD}$; triangle: $\triangle ABD$

**24.** $d_{AB} = \sqrt{(x_2 - x_1)^2 + (y_2 - y_1)^2 + (z_2 - z_1)^2}$

$= \sqrt{(-1 - -6)^2 + (2 - -5)^2 + (-3 - 4)^2}$

$= \sqrt{(5)^2 + (7)^2 + (-7)^2} = \sqrt{123}$

**25.** Choice A: The dimensions of the base of the building would be 6 feet by 8 feet.

Choice B: The dimensions of the base of the building would be 12 meters by 16 meters.

Choice C: The dimensions of the base of the building would be 600,000 cm by 800,000 cm.

Choice D: The dimensions of the base of the building would be 36 inches by 48 inches.

Choice **B** is correct.

**26.** $A = \frac{1}{2}aP$

$A = \frac{1}{2}a(n)(s)$

$s = \frac{2A}{na}$

**27.** $L = \frac{1}{2}Pl$

$L = \frac{1}{2}(5)(6.2)(4)$

$L = 62 \text{ in.}^2$

**28.** $P = 4s$

$A = s^2 \rightarrow s = \sqrt{A}$

$P = 4\sqrt{A}$

**29.** $\triangle ABC \sim \triangle CBD$; $\triangle ACD \sim \triangle CBD$; $\triangle ABC \sim \triangle ACD$

30. a. 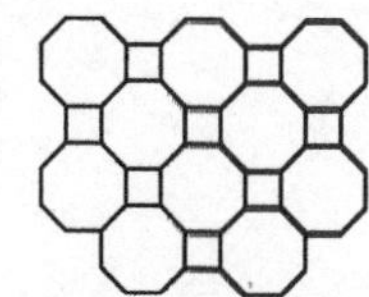

b. Translation symmetries based on vectors from the center of one octagon to the center of any adjacent octagon; Rotational symmetries based on rotations of 90° about center of any tile; Reflection symmetries with lines of symmetry through centers of any two adjacent tiles

## LESSON 112

### Warm Up 112

1. sector

2. Let $x = AD = DB$, then:
$x\sqrt{2} = 4$ so $x = 2\sqrt{2}$

$$A = \frac{1}{2}bh$$

$$= \frac{1}{2}(4)(2\sqrt{2}) = 4\sqrt{2} \approx 5.7 \text{ in.}^2$$

3. $\frac{30°}{360°}(\pi 3^2) = \frac{270\pi}{360} = \frac{3\pi}{4} \approx 2.36 \text{ cm}^2$

### Lesson Practice 112

a. $A_{sector} = \pi r^2\left(\frac{m°}{360°}\right)$

$$A_{sector} = \pi(48)^2\left(\frac{90°}{360°}\right)$$

$$A_{sector} = 576\pi \text{ mm}^2$$

$$A_{triangle} = \frac{1}{2}(48)(48) = 1152 \text{ mm}^2$$

$$A_{segment} = 576\pi - 1152 \approx 658 \text{ mm}^2$$

b. $A_{sector} = \pi r^2\left(\frac{m°}{360°}\right)$

$$A_{sector} = \pi(13)^2\left(\frac{157°}{360°}\right)$$

$$A_{sector} \approx 231.5 \text{ in.}^2$$

To find the height of the triangle:

$$\sin 23° = \frac{h}{13}$$

$$h \approx 5.1$$

$$A_{triangle} = \frac{1}{2}(13)(5.1) = 33.2 \text{ in.}^2$$

$$A_{segment} = 231.5 - 33.2 \approx 198 \text{ in.}^2$$

c. To find the radius of the circle:

$$\sin 30° = \frac{160}{r}$$

$$r = 320$$

$$A_{sector} = \pi r^2\left(\frac{m°}{360°}\right)$$

$$A_{sector} = \pi(320)^2\left(\frac{60°}{360°}\right)$$

$$A_{sector} \approx 53{,}617 \text{ m}^2$$

The triangle formed is a 30°-60°-90° triangle. So, the height of the triangle is $160\sqrt{3}$:

$$A_{triangle} = \frac{1}{2}(320)(160\sqrt{3}) \approx 44{,}341 \text{ m}^2$$

$$A_{segment} = 53{,}617 - 44{,}341 \approx 9276 \text{ m}^2$$

### Practice 112

1. $A_{sector} = \pi r^2\left(\frac{m°}{360°}\right)$

$$A_{sector} = \pi(11)^2\left(\frac{90°}{360°}\right)$$

$$A_{sector} = 30.25\pi \text{ cm}^2$$

$$A_{triangle} = \frac{1}{2}(11)(11) = 60.5 \text{ cm}^2$$

$$A_{segment} = 30.25\pi - 60.5 \approx 35 \text{ cm}^2$$

2. $10 = \frac{1}{2}(4 + x)$

$$20 = 4 + x$$

$$x = 16 \text{ cm}$$

3. $d_{PQ} = \sqrt{(x_2 - x_1)^2 + (y_2 - y_1)^2 + (z_2 - z_1)^2}$

$$= \sqrt{(-1 - 12)^2 + (7 - 11)^2 + (-5 - 10)^2}$$

$$= \sqrt{(-13)^2 + (-4)^2 + (-15)^2}$$

$$= \sqrt{410}$$

4. No. An equilateral triangle with side lengths of 10 cm has a larger area since it is regular.

5. Choice **A** is correct.

**6.** 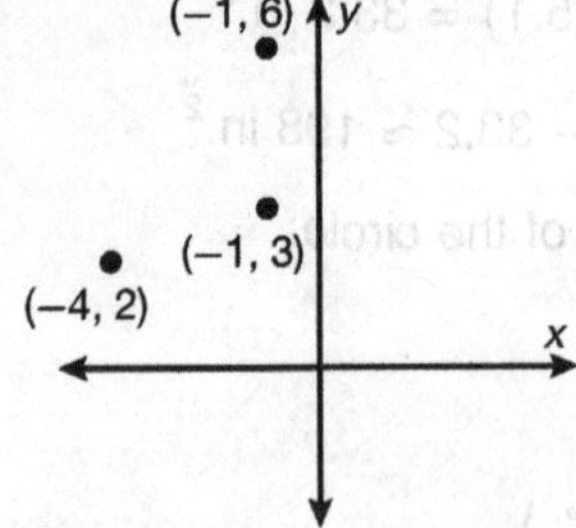


The other possible coordinates are (−4, 5), (−4, −1), or (2, 7).

**7. a.** $\begin{bmatrix} 2 & 4 & 2 & 0 \\ 2 & 0 & -2 & 0 \end{bmatrix}$

**b.** $\begin{bmatrix} 0 & -1 \\ 1 & 0 \end{bmatrix}\begin{bmatrix} 2 & 4 & 2 & 0 \\ 2 & 0 & -2 & 0 \end{bmatrix}$

$$= \begin{bmatrix} (0)(2) + (-1)(2) & (0)(4) + (-1)(0) & (0)(2) + (-1)(-2) & (0)(0) + (-1)(0) \\ (1)(2) + (0)(2) & (1)(4) + (0)(0) & (1)(2) + (0)(-2) & (1)(0) + (0)(0) \end{bmatrix}$$

$$= \begin{bmatrix} -2 & 0 & 2 & 0 \\ 2 & 4 & 2 & 0 \end{bmatrix}$$

**c.** 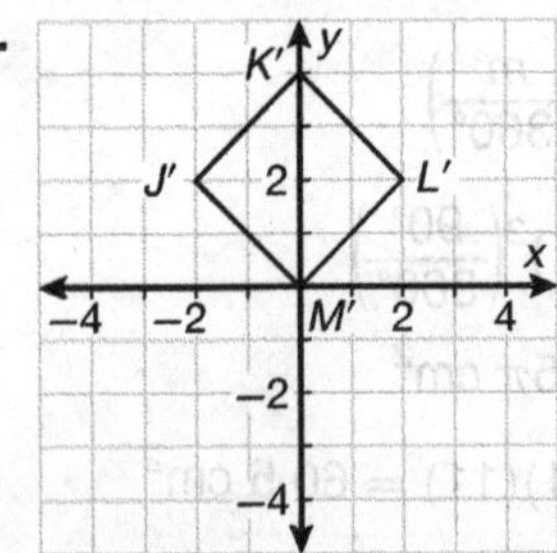


**8.** The sides of the first square are 6 cm.

$(6x)^2 = 900$

$36x^2 = 900$

$x^2 = 25$

$x = 5$

**9.** $\frac{8 \text{ ft}}{865{,}000 \text{ mi}} = \frac{1 \text{ ft}}{1.1 \times 10^5 \text{ mi}}$

or 1 foot : $1 \times 10^5$ miles

**10.** 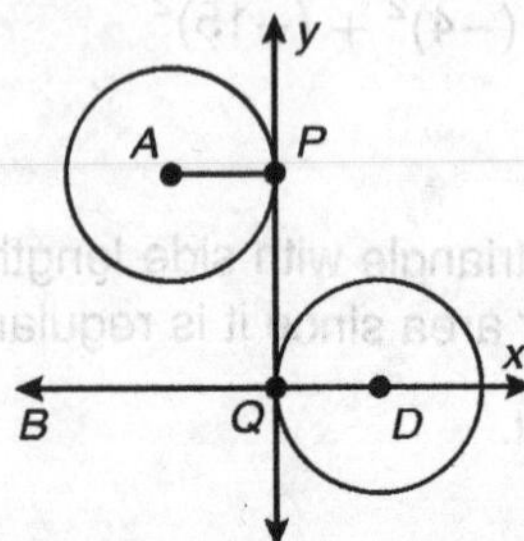


**a.** Yes, because if a line in the plane of a circle is perpendicular to a radius at its endpoint on the circle, then the line is tangent to the circle, and $\angle APQ$ is a right angle.

**b.** $\overleftrightarrow{BQ}$

**11.** $A_{sector} = \pi r^2\left(\frac{m°}{360°}\right)$

$A_{sector} = \pi(13)^2\left(\frac{60°}{360°}\right)$

$A_{sector} \approx 88.5 \text{ in.}^2$

Since the triangles formed on the left side are 30°-60°-90°, we can find the missing interior segments to each be $\frac{9}{\sqrt{3}} \approx 5.2$ in.

$A_{triangle} = \frac{1}{2}(10.4)(9) = 46.8 \text{ in.}^2$

$A_{segment} = 88.5 - 46.8 \approx 41.7 \text{ in.}^2$

**12.** Parallel Postulate

**13.** No. The radii of the circles may be different, which will affect the length of the arcs for a given length of a chord.

**14.** Choice **A**: This is true because $\frac{15}{10} = \frac{3}{2}$.

Choice B: $\tan^{-1}\left(\frac{14}{16}\right) \approx 41.2$

$90° - \tan^{-1}\left(\frac{16}{14}\right) \approx 41.2$

Choice C: $180° - \tan^{-1}\left(\frac{4}{2}\right) \approx 116.6$

$\tan^{-1}\left(\frac{1}{2}\right) \approx 26.7$

Choice D: $\tan^{-1}\left(\frac{20}{15}\right) \approx 53.1$

$90° - \tan^{-1}\left(\frac{3}{4}\right) \approx 53.1$

**15.** Sample: A pentagon inscribed in a circle. A circle circumscribed about a pentagon.

**16.** The slope of the line perpendicular to $y = -\frac{3}{2}x - 6$ is $\frac{2}{3}$.

$y = \frac{2}{3}x + b$

$-1 = \frac{2}{3}(1) + b; -\frac{5}{3} = b$

$y = \frac{2}{3}x - \frac{5}{3}$

To find the point of intersection, set the equations equal to each other.

$\frac{2}{3}x - \frac{5}{3} = -\frac{3}{2}x - 6$

$\frac{13}{6}x = -\frac{13}{3}; x = -2$

$y = -\frac{3}{2}(-2) - 6 = -3$

The point closest to $D$ is $(-2, -3)$.

**17.** $A_{sector} = \pi r^2\left(\frac{m°}{360°}\right)$

$A_{sector} = \pi(5)^2\left(\frac{36°}{360°}\right)$

$A_{sector} = 2.5\pi \text{ in.}^2$

To find the height of the triangle:

$\sin 36° = \frac{h}{5}; h \approx 2.9$

$A_{triangle} = \frac{1}{2}(5)(2.9) = 7.25 \text{ in.}^2$

$A_{segment} = 2.5\pi - 7.25 \approx 0.6 \text{ in.}^2$

**18.** $\frac{-7 + x}{2} = 2$

$-7 + x = 4; x = 11$

$\frac{3 + y}{2} = -4$

$3 + y = -8; y = -11$

$\frac{8 + z}{2} = 9$

$8 + z = 18; z = 10$

The other endpoint is $(11, -11, 10)$.

**19.** $V_{cone} = \frac{1}{3}\pi r^2 h$

$V_{frustum1} = \frac{7}{24}\pi r^2 h$; height $= \frac{1}{2}h$

$V_{frustum2} = \frac{7}{48}\pi r^2 h$; height $= \frac{1}{4}h$

$$\frac{V_{frustum1}}{V_{cone}} = \frac{\frac{7}{24}\pi r^2}{\frac{1}{3}\pi r^2} = \frac{7}{8}$$

$$\frac{V_{frustum2}}{V_{cone}} = \frac{\frac{7}{48}\pi r^2}{\frac{1}{3}\pi r^2} = \frac{7}{16}$$

Neither. He would fill it between one-fourth and one-half of the height of the cone because at this level the frustum's volume is more than half of the cone's volume.

**20.** $AC = LN = 4.6$ cm

$LM = AB = 9.3$ cm

$MN = BC = 3.2$ cm

**21.** If the value $t = 0$ is chosen, the point is $(0, 0, 0)$.

**22.**

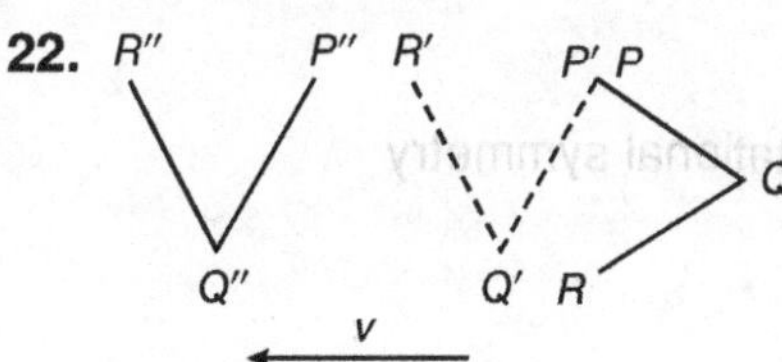


**23.** $L = Ph = (2\pi r)(h) = 2\pi(2)(3) \approx 37.70 \text{ in.}^2$

**24.** $(8 - 4 - 4 - 4, 3 + 2 + 2 + 2) = (-4, 9)$

Choice **C** is correct.

**25.** Central angle $= 180° - 2(26°) = 128°$

$A_{sector} = \pi r^2\left(\frac{m°}{360°}\right)$

$A_{sector} = \pi(3.2)^2\left(\frac{128°}{360°}\right)$

$A_{sector} \approx 11.4 \text{ ft}^2$

To find the height of the triangle:

$\sin 52° = \frac{h}{3.2}; h \approx 2.5$

$A_{triangle} = \frac{1}{2}(3.2)(2.5) = 4 \text{ ft}^2$

$A_{segment} = 11.4 - 4 \approx 7.4 \text{ ft}^2$

26. $D_{O,1}(x, y) \longrightarrow (x, y)$

27. $(x + 7) + (x - 11) = 2x - 4$
Since $2x - 4 < 2x + 1$, these three lengths cannot form a triangle.

28. All consecutive angles of rhombuses are not necessarily perpendicular. Choice **D** is correct.

29. $$\text{Midpoint} = \left(\frac{x_1 + x_2}{2}, \frac{y_1 + y_2}{2}, \frac{z_1 + z_2}{2}\right)$$
$$= \left(\frac{12 + -4}{2}, \frac{3 + 7}{2}, \frac{3 + -9}{2}\right)$$
$$= \left(\frac{8}{2}, \frac{10}{2}, \frac{-6}{2}\right)$$
$$= (4, 5, -3)$$

30. $\frac{1}{2}(n - 2)180° = 1260°$
$90°(n - 2) = 1260°$
$n - 2 = 14$
$n = 16$

## LESSON 113

### Warm Up 113

1. angle of rotational symmetry
2. a. 5
   b. 2
3. There are two digits that exhibit rotational symmetry. They are 1 and 8.

### Lesson Practice 113

a.

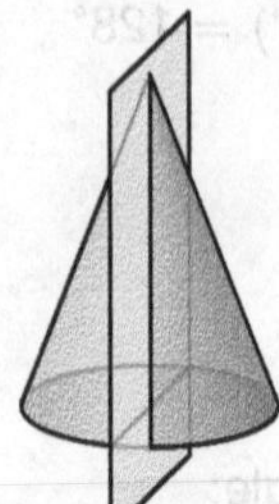

b. No, the solid does not have rotational symmetry through this axis.

c. Sample: Any plane through opposite vertices of the square and the pyramid's vertex, or an axis from the vertex to the squares center, with angle of symmetry 90° and order 4.

### Practice 113

1. Yes, the solid has plane symmetry.

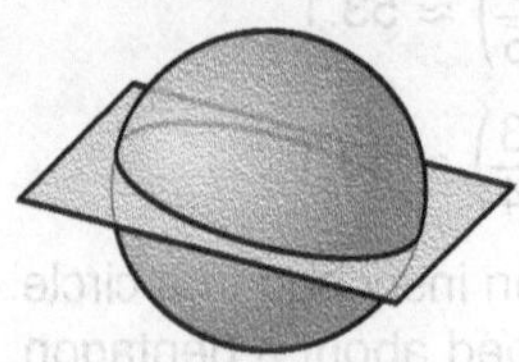

2. Length of the larger rectangle:
$\frac{4}{3} = \frac{l}{9}$
$3l = 36$
$l = 12$
Width of the larger rectangle:
$\frac{4}{3} = \frac{w}{3}$
$3w = 12$
$w = 4$
$P = 2(12) + 2(4) = 32$ ft

3. $$d_{CD} = \sqrt{(x_2 - x_1)^2 + (y_2 - y_1)^2 + (z_2 - z_1)^2}$$
$$= \sqrt{(3 - 6)^2 + (4 - -3)^2 + (-2 - 8)^2}$$
$$= \sqrt{(-3)^2 + (7)^2 + (-10)^2}$$
$$= \sqrt{158}$$
diameter $= 2\sqrt{158}$

4. $A = lw - \pi r^2$
$A = (48)(24) - \pi(2^2)$
$\approx 1139$ in.$^2$

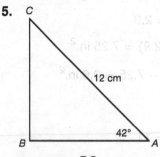

5. C, B, A; 12 cm; 42°

$\sin 42° = \frac{BC}{12}$

$BC = 12 \sin 42° \approx 8.02$

$\cos 42° = \frac{AB}{12}$

$BC = 12 \cos 42° \approx 8.92$

$P = 12 + 8.02 + 8.92 = 28.94$ cm

6. It would take at least 2 regions to represent a geometric probability of $\frac{1}{2}$. Choice **A** is correct.

7. To reflect the image across the *y*-axis:

$$\begin{bmatrix}-1 & 0\\0 & 1\end{bmatrix}\begin{bmatrix}2 & 6 & 4\\1 & 1 & 5\end{bmatrix}$$

$$=\begin{bmatrix}(-1)(2)+(0)(1) & (-1)(6)+(0)(1) & (-1)(4)+(0)(5)\\(0)(2)+(1)(1) & (0)(6)+(1)(1) & (0)(4)+(1)(5)\end{bmatrix}$$

$$=\begin{bmatrix}-2 & -6 & -4\\1 & 1 & 5\end{bmatrix}$$

To rotate 180°:

$$\begin{bmatrix}-1 & 0\\0 & -1\end{bmatrix}\begin{bmatrix}-2 & -6 & -4\\1 & 1 & 5\end{bmatrix}$$

$$=\begin{bmatrix}(-1)(-2)+(0)(1) & (-1)(-6)+(0)(1) & (-1)(-4)+(0)(5)\\(0)(-2)+(-1)(1) & (0)(-6)+(-1)(1) & (0)(-4)+(-1)(5)\end{bmatrix}=\begin{bmatrix}2 & 6 & 4\\-1 & -1 & -5\end{bmatrix}$$

8. $A_{sector} = \pi r^2\left(\frac{m^\circ}{360^\circ}\right)$

$A_{sector} = \pi(3.2)^2\left(\frac{90^\circ}{360^\circ}\right)$

$A_{sector} \approx 8.04 \text{ in.}^2$

$A_{triangle} = \frac{1}{2}(3.2)(3.2) = 5.12 \text{ in.}^2$

$A_{segment} = 8.04 - 5.12 \approx 2.92 \text{ in.}^2$

9. Fibonacci sequence: 1, 1, 2, 3, 5, 8, 13, 21, …
Sum of the first 6 = 20
Sum of the first 7 = 33
Sum of the first 8 = 54

10. Either $c - 7 = 3 - a \longrightarrow c = 10 - a$ and $d - 6 = -1 - b \longrightarrow d = 5 - b$ or $c - 3 = 7 - a \longrightarrow c = 10 - a$ and $d - (-1) = 6 - b \longrightarrow d = 5 - b$

11. $\cos 60^\circ = \frac{3.5}{x}$

$x = \frac{3.5}{\cos 60^\circ} = 7$ inches

12. $\frac{n(n+1)}{2} = \frac{90(90+1)}{2} = 4095$

13. Yes, the solid has rotational symmetry. The order of symmetry is 4 and the angle of rotational symmetry is $\frac{360^\circ}{4} = 90^\circ$.

14. $30 = \frac{4}{3}\pi r^3$

$r \approx 1.928$

$\frac{1.928 \text{ in.}}{140 \text{ pm}} = \frac{1 \text{ in.}}{72.61 \text{ pm}}$ or

$\frac{1.928 \text{ in.}}{140 \text{ pm}} = \frac{0.01 \text{ in.}}{1 \text{ pm}}$

15. She has graphed $y \leq 1.5x + 2$. The line should be dashed instead of solid.

16. If the tangent of the first angle is 0.75 or $\frac{3}{4}$, the tangent of the other angle is $\frac{4}{3}$.

17. $A_{sector} = \pi r^2\left(\frac{m^\circ}{360^\circ}\right)$

$A_{sector} = \pi(28)^2\left(\frac{90^\circ}{360^\circ}\right)$

$A_{sector} = 196\pi \text{ cm}^2$

$A_{triangle} = \frac{1}{2}(28)(28) = 392 \text{ cm}^2$

$A_{segment} = 196\pi - 392 \approx 224 \text{ cm}^2$

18. The *y*-intercept is at +1. The slope is $\frac{-2}{1}$ or −2. This makes the equation $y = -2x + 1$. Choice **B** is correct.

19. Midpoint $= \left(\frac{x_1 + x_2}{2}, \frac{y_1 + y_2}{2}, \frac{z_1 + z_2}{2}\right)$

$= \left(\frac{4.5 + -2.5}{2}, \frac{3.25 + 6.75}{2}, \frac{8.6 + -2.6}{2}\right)$

$= \left(\frac{2}{2}, \frac{10}{2}, \frac{6}{2}\right) = (1, 5, 3)$

**20.** The solid has both plane symmetry and symmetry about an axis.

**21.** $EF = FG = 12.2$

$EG = 35.7 - 2(12.2) = 11.3$ in.

**22.**

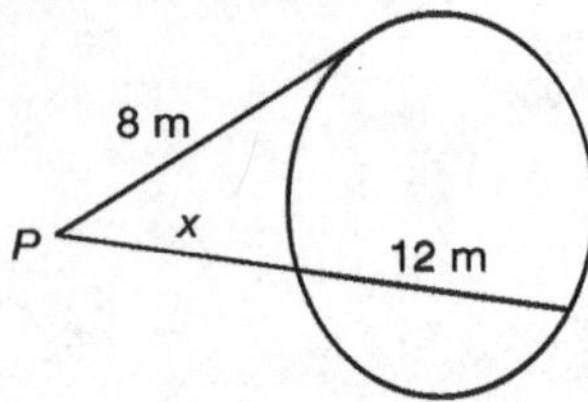


$$x(x + 12) = 8^2$$
$$x^2 + 12x - 64 = 0$$
$$(x + 16)(x - 4) = 0$$

$x = 4$ cm (because $x$ must be positive)

The secant is 16 m long.

**23.** $A_{\text{sector}} = \frac{1}{4}A_{\odot} = \frac{1}{4}\pi r^2$

$A_{\text{triangle}} = \frac{1}{2}r^2$

$A_{\text{sector}} - A_{\triangle} = \frac{1}{4}\pi r^2 - \frac{1}{2}r^2$

$= \left(\frac{1}{4}\pi - \frac{1}{2}\right)r^2$

**24.** $m = \frac{4 - 0}{2 - -4} = \frac{4}{6} = \frac{2}{3}$

**25.** $x^2 = 25^2 + 15^2$

$x^2 = 850$; $x \approx 29.15$ lb

**26.** Let $h$ = height of the larger cone

Let $x$ = height of the smaller cone

$V_{\text{larger cone}} = \frac{1}{3}\pi r^2 h$ $\frac{1}{2}V_{\text{larger cone}} = \frac{1}{6}\pi r^2 h$

$\frac{1}{6}\pi r^2 h = \frac{1}{3}\pi r^2 x$

$\frac{1}{2}h = x$ or $h = 2x$

The height of the larger cone is twice the height of the smaller cone.

**27.** $P = 32$ cm

The maximum area would be the square with side lengths of 8. The area is $8^2 = 64\text{ cm}^2$.

**28.** The solid has plane symmetry but does not have symmetry about the given axis.

**29.** $V - E + F = 2$

$V - 22 + 10 = 2$; $V = 14$ vertices

**30.** No, since the direction vectors are both the same (5, 1, 0) and point $A$ is not on the line connecting $C$ and $D$.

## LESSON 114

### Warm Up 114

**1.** inequality

**2.** $4x + 5 < -x - 5$

$5x < -10$; $x < -2$

**3.** The slope of the line is 2 and the $y$-intercept is $-3$. Since the line is dashed, the inequality is $y < 2x - 3$.

**4.** Choice A: $3\sqrt{10} - 13 < 2\sqrt{10} + 2$

$-3.51 < 8.32$

Choice B: $3(42) - 13 < 2(42) + 2$

$113 \nless 86$

Choice C: $3(15) - 13 < 2(15) + 2$

$32 \nless 32$

Choice D: $3(\sqrt{253}) - 13 < 2(\sqrt{253}) + 2$

$34.72 \nless 33.81$

Choice **A** is correct.

### Lesson Practice 114

**a.** First graph the lines $y = x$ and $y = -2x + 5$. Since both inequalities use > and <, use a dashed line for both. Shade the region above $y = x$ and below $y = -2x + 5$.

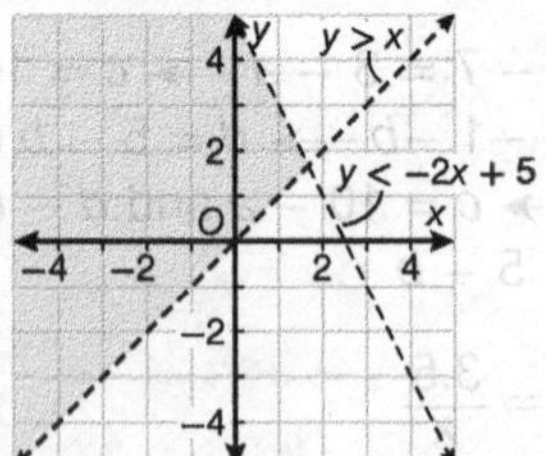


**b.** First graph the lines $y = x + 1$ and $y = -2x - 1$. Since both inequalities use $\le$ and $\ge$, use a solid line for both. Shade the region that represents the solution for the system of inequalities.

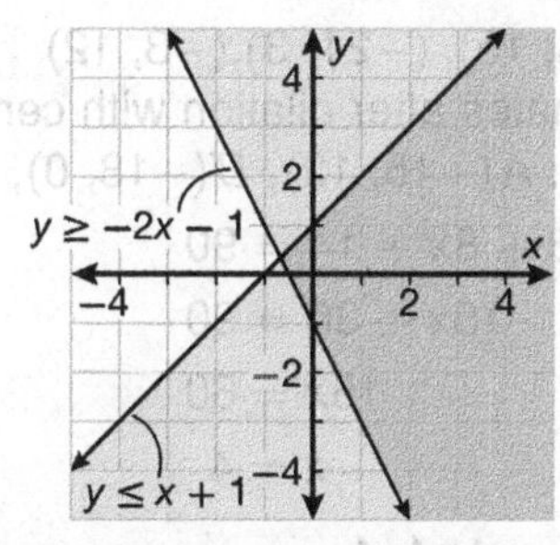


**c.** First graph the lines $x = -3$, $y = -2x$, and $y = x - 1$. Since all three inequalities use > and <, use a dashed line for all three. Shade the region above $x = -3$ and $y = x - 1$ and below $y = -2x$.

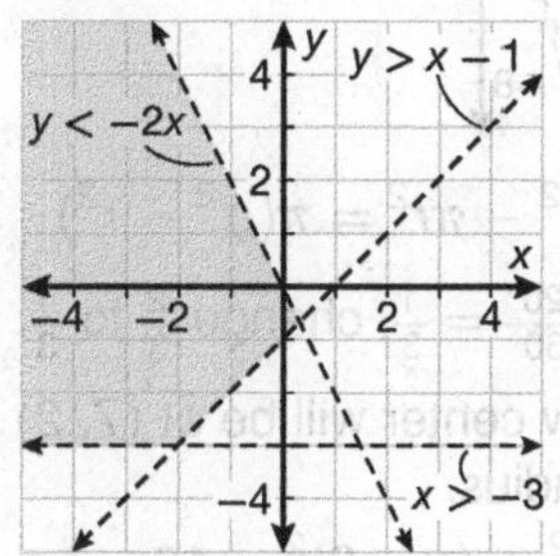


**d.** First graph the lines $y = x - 5$ and $y = -2x - 4$. Since both inequalities use > because it is only above the region, use a dashed line for both. Shade the region above $y = x - 5$ and above $y = -2x - 4$.

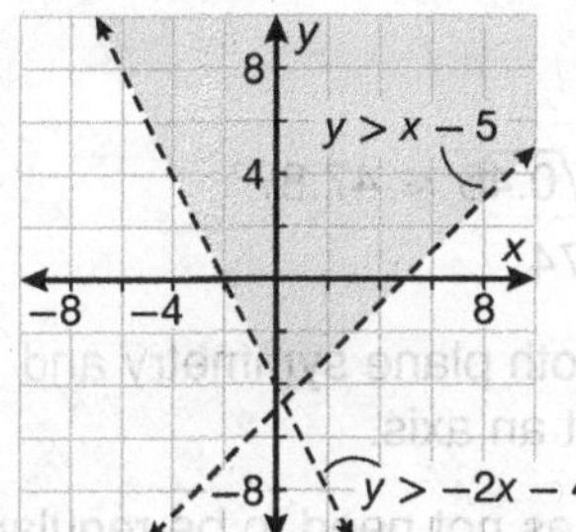


## Practice 114

**1.** No, the solid does not have plane symmetry.

**2.** The sum of the legs squared must be $17^2 = 289$. Sample: 15 and 8 because $15^2 + 8^2 = 289$.

**3.** $\cos \theta_1 = \dfrac{17}{33}$

$$\theta_1 = \cos^{-1}\frac{17}{33} \approx 59°$$

$$\sin \theta_2 = \frac{17}{33}$$

$$\theta_2 = \sin^{-1}\frac{17}{33} \approx 31°$$

**4.** The line connecting the points (3, 5, 11) and (5, −13, −1) is given by the equation $(x, y, z) = (3, 5, 11) + t(1, -9, -6)$ and when $t = 1$, the point is (4, −4, 5). Also, when $t = 2$, the first line $(x, y, z) = (-2, 0, 1) + t(3, -2, 2)$ produces the point (4, −4, 5). Since these two nonparallel lines contain the same point, this point must be where they intersect.

**5.** $180° - 2(63°) = 54°$

$$A_{\text{sector}} = \pi r^2\left(\frac{m°}{360°}\right)$$

$$A_{\text{sector}} = \pi(15.5)^2\left(\frac{54°}{360°}\right)$$

$$A_{\text{sector}} \approx 113 \text{ cm}^2$$

To find the height of the triangle:

$$\sin 54° = \frac{h}{15.5}$$

$$h \approx 12.5$$

$$A_{\text{triangle}} = \frac{1}{2}(15.5)(12.5) \approx 97 \text{ cm}^2$$

$$A_{\text{segment}} = 113 - 97 = 16 \text{ cm}^2$$

**6.**

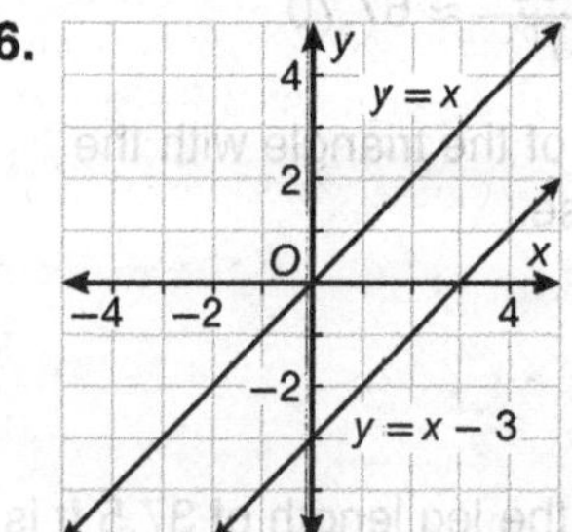


No solution

**7.** $V = \frac{4}{3}\pi r^3 = \frac{4}{3}\pi(10^3) \approx 4188.79 \text{ m}^3$

**8.**

**9.** Find the distance between (0, 0, 0) and (6, 6, 6).

$$d = \sqrt{(x_2 - x_1)^2 + (y_2 - y_1)^2 + (z_2 - z_1)^2}$$

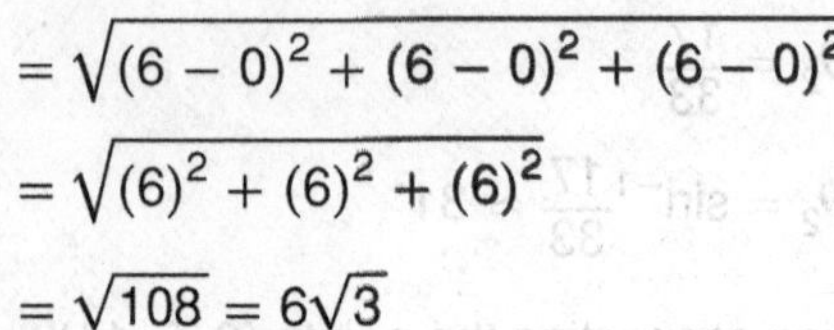

$= \sqrt{(6-0)^2 + (6-0)^2 + (6-0)^2}$

$= \sqrt{(6)^2 + (6)^2 + (6)^2}$

$= \sqrt{108} = 6\sqrt{3}$

**10.**

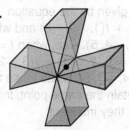

**11.** A zero-magnitude vector has no direction.

**12.**



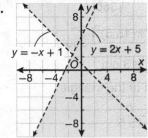

**13.** $m\angle L = 180° - 98° - 35° = 47°$

$$\frac{50}{\sin 47°} = \frac{LN}{\sin 98°}$$

$$LN = \frac{50 \sin 98°}{\sin 47°} \approx 67.70$$

**14.** First, find the leg of the triangle with the 53-foot hypotenuse.

$$\frac{1}{\sqrt{2}} = \frac{l}{53}$$

$l \approx 37.48$

The triangle with the leg length of 37.5 ft is slightly larger in area.

**15.** The golden ratio is approximately 1.6.

$$\frac{A}{B} = \frac{1.9}{1.17} \approx 1.6$$

$$\frac{E}{C} = \frac{0.68}{0.42} \approx 1.6$$

$$\frac{G}{B} = \frac{1.89}{1.17} \approx 1.6$$

$$\frac{H}{G} = \frac{3.06}{1.89} \approx 1.6$$

**16.** Coordinates of $A$, $B$, and $C$ after translation with center at the origin: $(-6, 5)$, $(-7, 1)$, $(-1, 4)$

Coordinates after dilation with scale factor of 3: $(-18, 15)$, $(-21, 3)$, $(-3, 12)$

Coordinates after dilation with center at $(3, -3)$: $A'(-15, 12)$, $B'(-18, 0)$, $C'(0, 9)$

**17.** $7x + 16 + 8x + 14 = 90$

$15x + 30 = 90$

$15x = 60$

$x = 4$

**18.**

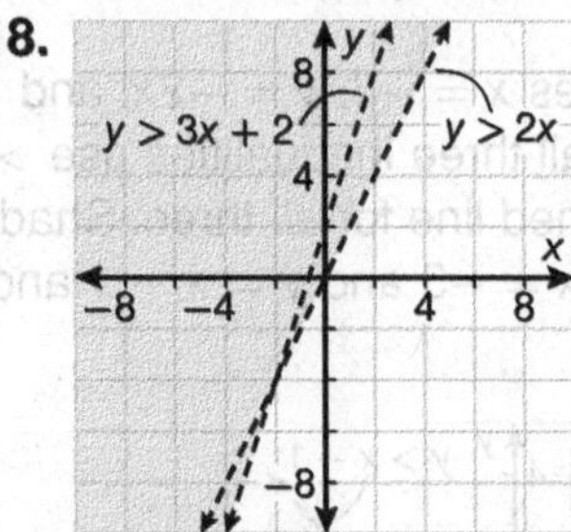



**19.** $A = \pi g^2 - \pi r^2 = \pi(g^2 - r^2)$

**20.** Since $\frac{120°}{360°} = \frac{1}{3}$, change $\frac{2}{3}$ to $\frac{1}{3}$.

**21.** The new center will be at (7, 2) with the same radius.

$(x - 7)^2 + (y - 2)^2 = 16$

Choice **C** is correct.

**22.** $\frac{8}{10} = \frac{9}{IF}$

$8IF = 90$

$IF = 11.25$

**23.** $\cos\theta = \sqrt{0.45}$

$\theta = \cos^{-1}\sqrt{0.45} \approx 47.87°$

$\sin 47.87° \approx 0.74$

**24.** The solid has both plane symmetry and symmetry about an axis.

**25.** The polygon does not need to be regular. Imagine a kite or a rhombus, which can have a circle inscribed in it and yet can be inscribed within a circle.

**26.**

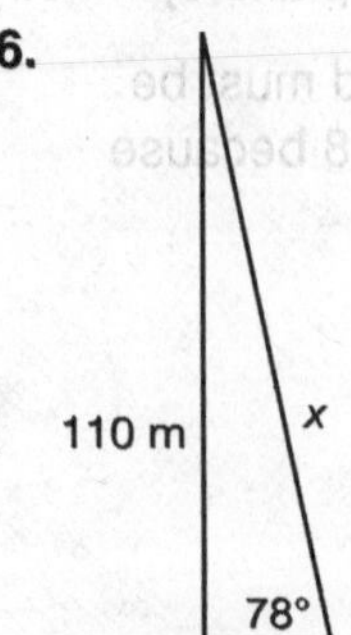

$\sin 78° = \frac{110}{x}$

$x = \frac{110}{\sin 78°} \approx 112$ meters

**27.** $A = lw - 2lw - 10(lw)$
$= (50)(35) - 2(3)(7) - 10(2.5)(2.5)$
$= 1645.5 \text{ ft}^2$
$1645.5 \text{ ft}^2 \div 0.5 = 3291$ bricks

**28.**

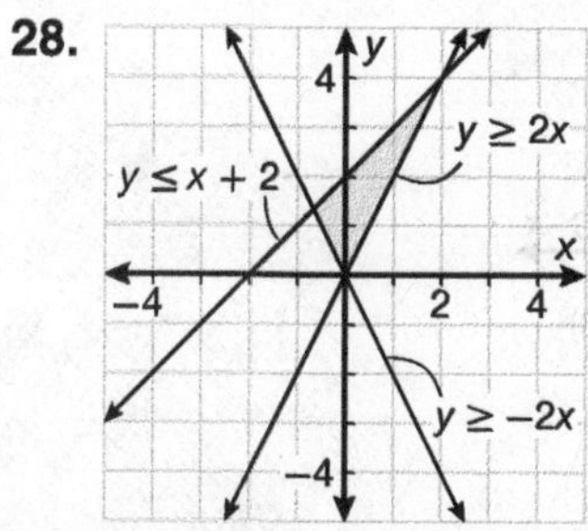


**29.** $13.6^2 = 8.7^2 + 10.1^2$
$184.96 = 75.69 + 102.01$
$184.96 \neq 177.7$
Stacy is not correct.

**30.** Select a point to perform the transformation on.
$P(-1, 3) \rightarrow P'\left[\frac{4}{5}(3) - \frac{3}{5}(-1), \frac{4}{5}(-1) + \frac{3}{5}(3)\right]$
$= P'(3, 1)$
$m_{PP'} = \frac{3-1}{-1-3} = \frac{2}{-4} = -\frac{1}{2}$
The line perpendicular to this line is $y = 2x$.
This is a reflection across the line $y = 2x$.

## LESSON 115

### Warm Up 115

1. composite figure
2. $S = L + 2B = Ph + 2(lw)$
$S = (2(8) + 2(5))(4) + 2(5)(8)$
$S = 184 \text{ cm}^2$
$V = lwh = (8)(5)(4) = 160 \text{ cm}^3$
3. $S = L + 2B = 2\pi rh + 2(\pi r^2)$
$S = 2\pi(3)(10) + 2\pi(3^2)$
$S \approx 245.04 \text{ in.}^2$
$V = Bh = \pi r^2 h = \pi(3^2)(10) \approx 282.74 \text{ in.}^3$

### Lesson Practice 115

**a.** $S = L_1 + L_2 = \frac{1}{2}P_1 l_1 + \frac{1}{2}P_2 l_2$
$l_1^2 = 3^2 + 4^2$
$l_1^2 = 25$
$l_1 = 5$
$L_1 = \frac{1}{2}(2\pi)(3)(5) \approx 47.1$
$l_2^2 = 3^2 + 6^2$
$l_2^2 = 45$
$l_2 \approx 6.7$
$L_2 = \frac{1}{2}(2\pi)(3)(6.7) \approx 63.1$
$S = L_1 + L_2 = 47.1 + 63.1 = 110.2 \text{ cm}^2$

**b.** $V = V_{cone} + V_{cylinder}$
$V = \frac{1}{3}(\pi r^2)(h) + (\pi r^2)(h)$
$V = \frac{1}{3}(\pi 7^2)(12) + (\pi 7^2)(22)$
$V \approx 4002.4 \text{ m}^3$

**c.** $V = lwh - lwh$
$V = (11)(9)(15) - (2)(2)(15)$
$V = 1425 \text{ in.}^3$

**d.** $V = lwh + lwh$
$V = (8)(5)(5) + (4)(5)(2)$
$V = 240 \text{ ft}^3$

### Practice 115

1. $S = (100)(25) + (25)(25) + 4\left(\frac{1}{2}(25)(15)\right)$
$S = 3875 \text{ in.}^2$
2. $\begin{bmatrix} -4 & -4 & -4 \\ -8 & -8 & -8 \end{bmatrix}$
3. Sample: triangle and quadrilateral
4. The solid has both plane symmetry and symmetry about an axis.
5. $29 = \frac{1}{2}(114 - x)$
$58 = 114 - x$
$-56 = -x$
$x = 56°$

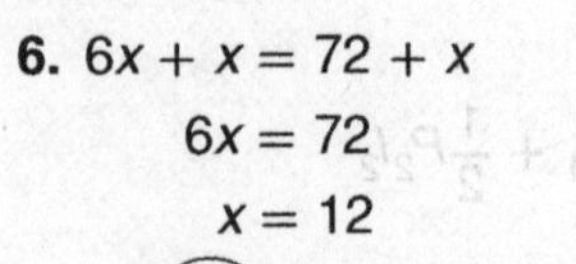



**6.** $6x + x = 72 + x$

$6x = 72$

$x = 12$

$m\widehat{NP} = 7(12) = 84°$

**7.**

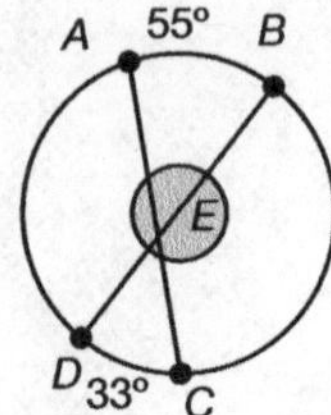


$m\angle AEB = \frac{1}{2}(55 + 33) = 44°$

**8.** No, they cannot be a triangle because they all lie on the same great circle, so they are considered collinear.

**9.**

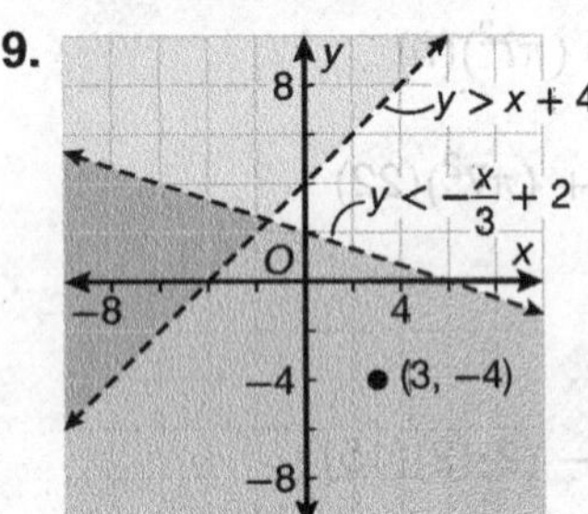


Yes, (3, −4) is in the solution set.

**10.** $A_{sector} = \pi r^2\left(\frac{m°}{360°}\right)$

$A_{sector} = \pi(5.2)^2\left(\frac{120°}{360°}\right)$

$A_{sector} \approx 28.32 \text{ m}^2$

To find the height of the triangle:

$\sin 120° = \frac{h}{5.2}$

$h \approx 4.50$

$A_{triangle} = \frac{1}{2}(5.2)(4.50) = 11.7 \text{ m}^2$

$A_{segment} = 28.32 - 11.7 \approx 16.62 \text{ m}^2$

**11.** $V = V_{sphere} + V_{cylinder}$

$V = \frac{4}{3}\pi r^3 + \pi r^2 h$

$V = \frac{4}{3}\pi(2)^3 + \pi(2)^2(4)$

$V \approx 83.8 \text{ cm}^3$

**12.** $2(x + 7) + 2(3x - 37) = 180$

$2x + 14 + 6x - 74 = 180$

$8x - 60 = 180$

$8x = 240$

$x = 30$

vertex angle $= 2(30 + 7) = 74°$

base angles $= 3(30) - 37 = 53°$

**13.**

(0, 6) cannot be the fourth vertex.

Choice **A** is correct.

**14.** Sample: A circle inscribed in a triangle; A triangle circumscribed about a circle

**15.** Sample: *If there is a power outage, then the dryer will not work. If the dryer does not work, then the clothes will not dry. If there is a power outage, then the clothes will not dry.*

**16.** disjunction: $y > 3x - 2$ or $2x - y > 1$

(3, 4):

$4 > 3(3) - 2$

$4 \not> 7$

$2(3) - 4 > 1$

$2 > 1$

(3, 4) is a solution.

(2, 3):

$3 > 3(2) - 2$

$3 \not> 4$

$2(2) - 3 > 1$

$1 \not> 1$

(2, 3) is not a solution.

**17.** $V = lwh - lwh$

$V = (76)(38)(44) - (10)(10)(76)$

$V = 119{,}472 \text{ m}^3$

18. $\frac{12 + x}{2} = 4$

$12 + x = 8$

$x = -4$

$\frac{7 + y}{2} = -3$

$7 + y = -6$

$y = -13$

$\frac{1 + z}{2} = 6$

$1 + z = 12$

$z = 11$

$Y(-4, -13, 11)$

19. $J(2, 4) \rightarrow J'\left[\frac{1}{2}(2), \frac{1}{2}(4)\right] = J'(1, 2)$

$K(2, -3) \rightarrow K'\left[\frac{1}{2}(2), \frac{1}{2}(-3)\right] = K'(1, -1.5)$

$L(-3, -3) \rightarrow L'\left[\frac{1}{2}(-3), \frac{1}{2}(-3)\right]$

$= L'(-1.5, -1.5)$

$M(-3, 4) \rightarrow M'\left[\frac{1}{2}(-3), \frac{1}{2}(4)\right] = M'(-1.5, 2)$

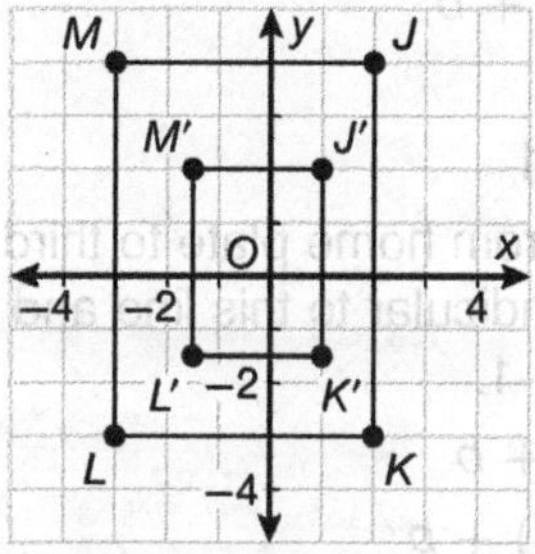


The larger quadrilateral is four times the area of the smaller quadrilateral.

20. She incorrectly matched up corresponding parts and found the similarity ratio to be 1 : 2, but it is actually 2 : 5. The value of $x$ is 12.5.

21. $d_{AB} = \sqrt{(-3 - 1)^2 + (1 - 4)^2}$

$= \sqrt{(-4)^2 + (-3)^2}$

$= 5$

$d_{EF} = \sqrt{(-5 - -1)^2 + (-1 - -4)^2}$

$= \sqrt{(-4)^2 + (-3)^2}$

$= 5$

$d_{BC} = \sqrt{(1 - 4)^2 + (4 - 0)^2}$

$= \sqrt{(-3)^2 + (4)^2}$

$= 5$

$d_{FG} = \sqrt{(-1 - 2)^2 + (-4 - 0)^2}$

$= \sqrt{(-3)^2 + (-4)^2}$

$= 5$

$d_{CD} = \sqrt{(4 - 0)^2 + (0 - -3)^2}$

$= \sqrt{(4)^2 + (3)^2}$

$= 5$

$d_{GH} = \sqrt{(2 - -2)^2 + (0 - 3)^2}$

$= \sqrt{(4)^2 + (-3)^2}$

$= 5$

$d_{AD} = \sqrt{(-3 - 0)^2 + (1 - -3)^2}$

$= \sqrt{(-3)^2 + (4)^2}$

$= 5$

$d_{EH} = \sqrt{(-5 - -2)^2 + (-1 - 3)^2}$

$= \sqrt{(-3)^2 + (-4)^2}$

$= 5$

$m_{AB} = \frac{4 - 1}{1 - -3} = \frac{3}{4}$

$m_{BC} = \frac{4 - 0}{1 - 4} = -\frac{4}{3}$

$m_{CD} = \frac{0 - -3}{4 - 0} = \frac{3}{4}$

$m_{AD} = \frac{1 - -3}{-3 - 0} = -\frac{4}{3}$

$m_{EF} = \frac{-1 - -4}{-5 - -1} = \frac{3}{-4} = -\frac{3}{4}$

$m_{FG} = \frac{-4 - 0}{-1 - 2} = \frac{4}{3}$

$m_{GH} = \frac{3 - 0}{-2 - 2} = -\frac{3}{4}$

$m_{EH} = \frac{3 - -1}{-2 - -5} = \frac{4}{3}$

$AB = 5 = EF$, $BC = 5 = FG$, $CD = 5 = GH$, and $AD = 5 = EH$; slopes of $\overline{AB}$, $\overline{BC}$, $\overline{CD}$, and $\overline{AD}$ are $\frac{3}{4}$, $-\frac{4}{3}$, $\frac{3}{4}$, and $-\frac{4}{3}$, while slopes of $\overline{EF}$, $\overline{FG}$, $\overline{GH}$, and $\overline{EH}$ are $-\frac{3}{4}$, $\frac{4}{3}$, $-\frac{3}{4}$, and $\frac{4}{3}$, so consecutive sides are perpendicular and thus all interior angles in both quadrilaterals are right angles; therefore, $ABCD \cong EFGH$. Both quadrilaterals are squares.

**22.** $L = \frac{1}{2}Pl$

$70 = \frac{1}{2}(7s)(2)$

$s = 10$ in.

**23.** $V = V_{cylinder} + \frac{1}{2}V_{sphere}$

$V = \pi(17^2)(40) + \frac{1}{2}\left(\frac{4}{3}\pi(17)^3\right)$

$V \approx 46{,}606.6 \text{ ft}^3$

**24.**

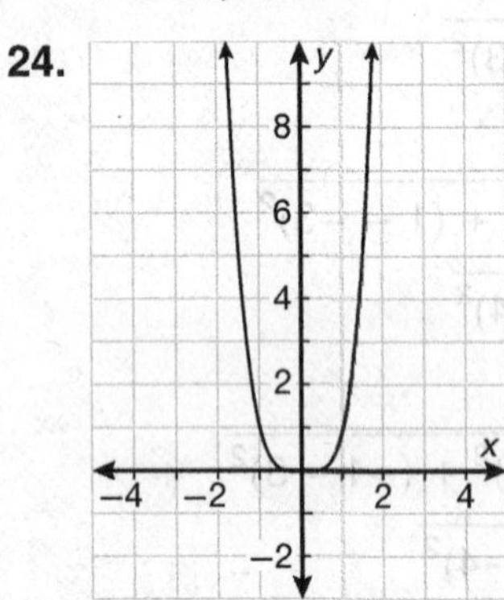


It has a line of symmetry at the $y$-axis. It does not have rotational symmetry.

**25.**

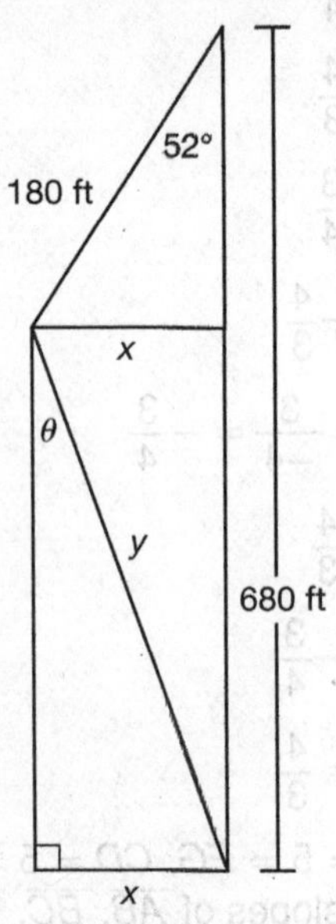


$y^2 = 680^2 + 180^2 - 2(680)(180) \cos 52°$

$y^2 \approx 494{,}800 - 150{,}714$

$y \approx 587$ ft

$\sin 52° = \frac{x}{180}$

$x = 180 \sin 52° \approx 142$

$\sin \theta = \frac{142}{587}$

$\theta = \sin^{-1}\frac{142}{587} \approx 14°$

**26.** LL Congruence Theorem

**27.** $\frac{360°}{120} = 3°$

**28.** $2x + 1 = \frac{1}{2}(14)$

$2x + 1 = 7$

$2x = 6$

$x = 3$

$DF = 2(3) + 1 = 7$

**29.** First find the equation of the line from home plate, (3, 2), to first base, (5, 4).

$m = \frac{4-2}{5-3} = \frac{2}{2} = 1$

$y = 1x + b$

$2 = 1(3) + b$

$b = -1$

$y = x - 1$

The line from home plate to third base will be perpendicular to this line and have a slope of $-1$.

$y = -1x + b$

$2 = -1(3) + b$

$b = 5$

$y = -x + 5$

The area of a foul ball would be anything below each of these lines. therefore, the disjunction is $y < x - 1$ or $y < -x + 5$.

**30.** $m\angle JKL = 2x$

## LESSON 116

### Warm Up 116

1. function

2. $m\angle C = 90°$

$\frac{65}{\sin 90°} = \frac{56}{\sin A}$

$$m\angle A = \sin^{-1}\frac{56 \sin 90°}{65} \approx 59°$$

$$m\angle B = 180° - 90° - 59° = 31°$$

3. $\dfrac{20}{\sin 51°} = \dfrac{x}{\sin 78°}$

$$x = \frac{20 \sin 78°}{\sin 51°} \approx 25.2$$

4. $y^2 = 45^2 + 40^2 - 2(45)(40) \cos 95°$

$y^2 = 3625 - -313.76;\ y \approx 62.8$

### Lesson Practice 116

a. $\sec\theta = \dfrac{1}{\cos\theta};\ \cos\theta = \dfrac{y}{z};\ \sec\theta = \dfrac{z}{y}$

$\csc\theta = \dfrac{1}{\sin\theta};\ \sin\theta = \dfrac{x}{z};\ \csc\theta = \dfrac{z}{x}$

$\cot\theta = \dfrac{1}{\tan\theta};\ \tan\theta = \dfrac{x}{y};\ \cot\theta = \dfrac{y}{x}$

b. $1 = \csc^2\theta - \cot^2\theta$

$1 = 2^2 - \cot^2\theta$

$\cot^2\theta = 3;\ \cot\theta = \sqrt{3}$

c. $\cot\theta = \dfrac{x}{2.02} = 1.19$

$x = (1.19)(2.02) \approx 2.40$ miles

$y^2 = 2.02^2 + 2.40^2;\ y \approx 3.14$ miles

### Practice 116

1. No, it will not break, because with the balloon's radius doubled, the new radius is 3.4 inches. So the elastic band, which acts as a circumference, will be stretched to only $(2\pi)(3.4) = 21.4$ inches.

2. $A_{sector} = \pi r^2\left(\dfrac{m°}{360°}\right)$

$A_{sector} = \pi(13)^2\left(\dfrac{90°}{360°}\right) = 42.25\pi \text{ in.}^2$

$A_{triangle} = \dfrac{1}{2}(13)(13) = 84.5 \text{ in.}^2$

$4(A_{segment}) = 4(42.25\pi - 84.5) \approx 193 \text{ in.}^2$

3. Since $\sec\theta = \dfrac{\text{hypotenuse}}{\text{opposite}}$ and the hypotenuse will always be longer than the side opposite, the quotient will be either less than –1 or greater than 1. Choice **C** is correct.

4. Excluding the bases from each cone:

$\pi rl + \pi rl = (3\sqrt{13} + 15)\pi$

$\pi r(\sqrt{13}) + \pi r(5) = 3(\sqrt{13} + 5)\pi$

$\pi r(\sqrt{13} + 5) = 3(\sqrt{13} + 5)\pi$

$$r = \frac{3(\sqrt{13} + 5)\pi}{\pi(\sqrt{13} + 5)}$$

$r = 3$ units

5. 3.6 miles per hour forward

6. The only reason a system will have no solutions is if the lines are parallel. There is no solution because the lines never intersect on a plane.

7. (3, 4) is in the region and (0, 0) is not.

8. Since ∠1 and ∠2 are complementary, m∠1 + m∠2 = 90°. By the Vertical Angles Theorem, ∠1 ≅ ∠3. Therefore, m∠1 = m∠3. By substitution, m∠2 + m∠3 = 90°, so ∠2 and ∠3 are complementary.

9. She has placed the *z*-coordinate first in her ordered triplet, when it should be last. The three-dimensional coordinates are (3, 2, 0) and (4, 5, 0).

10. $V = V_{prism} + V_{pyramid} = lwh + \dfrac{1}{3}Bh$

$V = (6)(6)(9) + \dfrac{1}{3}(6)(6)(8)$

$V = 420.0 \text{ in.}^3$

11. $d_{LM} = \sqrt{(-3-1)^2 + (-3 - -1)^2}$

$= \sqrt{(-4)^2 + (-2)^2} = \sqrt{20} = 2\sqrt{5}$

$d_{MN} = \sqrt{(-3 - -3)^2 + (-3-2)^2}$

$= \sqrt{(0)^2 + (-5)^2}$
$= 5$
$d_{LN} = \sqrt{(1 - -3)^2 + (-1 - 2)^2}$
$= \sqrt{(4)^2 + (-3)^2}$
$= 5$

Since $LM = LN$, the figure is an isosceles triangle.
$P = 5 + 5 + 2\sqrt{5}$
$= 10 + 2\sqrt{5}$

**12.** The solution of a conjunction is the intersection of solutions, while the solution to a disjunction is the union of all the solutions. While the inequalities may have no solution in common, they always each have a solution, so the union cannot be empty.

**13.** $2y - 5 = 52 - y$
$3y = 57$
$y = 19$
$P = 2(19) - 5 + 52 - 19 + (2(3(19) + 14))$
$= 208$ mm

**14.** $B_1 = \pi(3^2) \approx 28.27$
$B_2 = \pi(1^2) = 3.14$
$V = \frac{1}{3}h\left(B_1 + \sqrt{B_1B_2} + B_2\right)$
$V = \frac{1}{3}(5)\left(28.27 + \sqrt{(28.27)(3.14)} + 3.14\right)$
$\approx \left(\frac{1}{3}(5)\right)(40.83)$
$\approx 68.1 \text{ cm}^3$

**15.** $7(2x - 6) = 5(x + 3)$
$14x - 42 = 5x + 15$
$9x = 57$
$x \approx 6.33$

**16.** They are not the same. The secant ratio never has a value between 1 and 0, because it is the reciprocal of the cosine, and the reciprocal of a number less than 1 (which cosine always is) will always be greater than 1. A similar argument shows that the secant cannot take a value between 0 and −1, and the same holds for the cosecant. Neither can be equal to 0 because zero has no reciprocal.

**17.** Sample:

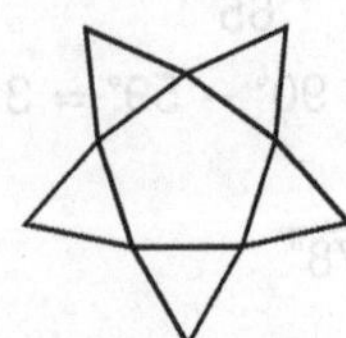

**18.** $d_{YZ} = \sqrt{(x_2 - x_1)^2 + (y_2 - y_1)^2 + (z_2 - z_1)^2}$
$= \sqrt{(5 - -5)^2 + (5 - -5)^2 + (5 - -5)^2}$
$= \sqrt{(10)^2 + (10)^2 + (10)^2}$
$= \sqrt{300} = 10\sqrt{3}$

**19.** $S = L_{cylinder} + S_{sphere}$
$S = 2\pi rh + 4\pi r^2$
$S = 2\pi(5)(10) + 4\pi(5)^2$
$S \approx 628.3 \text{ mm}^2$

**20.** $(x, y) \rightarrow (-x, -y)$
$X(-3, -2) \rightarrow X'(3, 2)$
$Y(-1, 1) \rightarrow Y'(1, -1)$

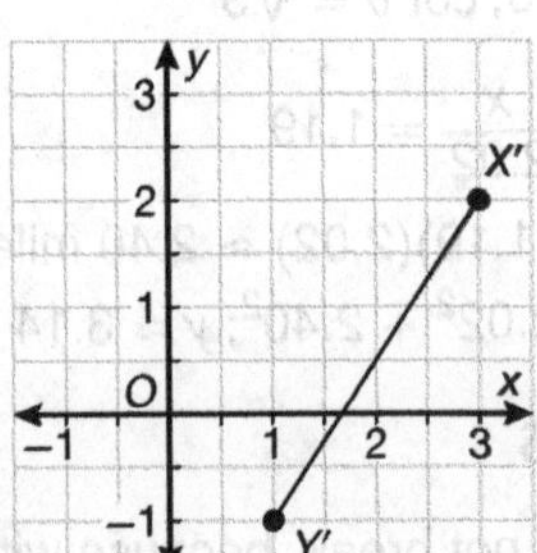


**21.** The point of tangency is located at (−2, 0). The equation of the tangent line is $y = 0$.

**22.**

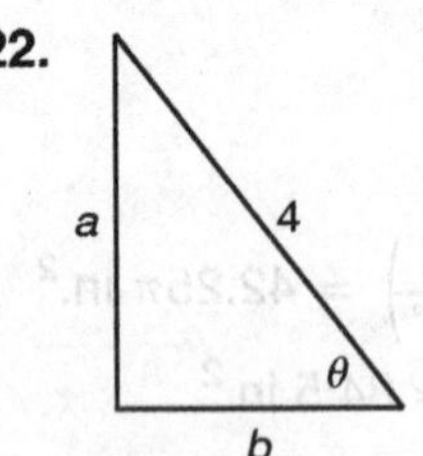


$\tan\theta = \frac{a}{b} \rightarrow \cot\theta = \frac{b}{a}$

$\sin\theta = \frac{a}{4} \rightarrow \csc\theta = \frac{4}{a}$

$\cos\theta = \frac{b}{4} \rightarrow \sec\theta = \frac{4}{b}$

**23.** $(x + 5)^2 = 8^2 + 7^2 - 2(8)(7)\cos 86°$
$(x + 5)^2 \approx 113 - 7.81$

$(x + 5)^2 \approx 105.19$
$x + 5 \approx 10.26$
$x \approx 5.26$

**24.** $\cos\theta \cdot \tan\theta = \cos\theta \frac{\sin\theta}{\cos\theta} = \sin\theta$

$\sin\theta = 0.8$
$\theta = \sin^{-1} 0.8 \approx 53°$
$\cos 53° \approx 0.6$

**25.** The pattern for the next three steps will be +2, +4, +6. The next three steps will be 19, 23, and 29.

**26.** For a given perimeter, a circle contains the greatest area of any possible shape.

**27.** Yes, the solid has rotational symmetry. The order of symmetry is 12. The angle of rotational symmetry is $\frac{360°}{12} = 30°$.

**28.** $\sin\theta = \sqrt{1 - \cos^2\theta} = \sqrt{1 - \frac{1}{\sec^2\theta}}$

$= \sqrt{\frac{\sec^2\theta - 1}{\sec^2\theta}} = \frac{\sqrt{\sec^2\theta - 1}}{\sec\theta}$

**29.** The new center is (−10, 11) with the same radius. $(x + 10)^2 + (y - 11)^2 = 81$

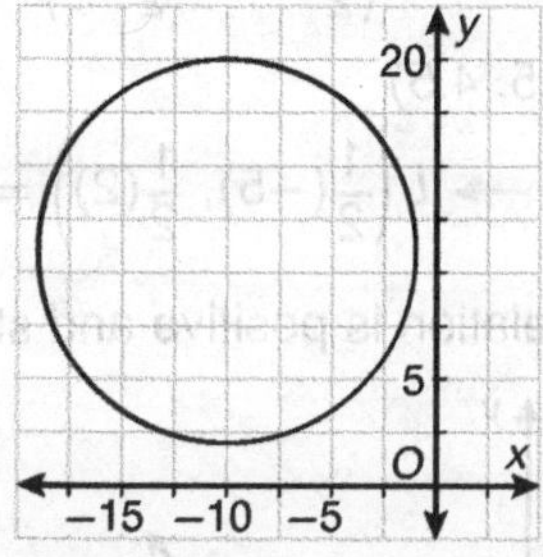


**30.**

| Statements | Reasons |
|---|---|
| 1. $m\angle ABM = m\angle ACM$, $m\angle AMB = 90°$, $m\angle ACM = 90°$ | 1. Given |
| 2. $m\angle AMB = m\angle ACM$ | 2. All right angles are congruent. |
| 3. $AM = AM$ | 3. Reflexive Property of Equality |
| 4. $\triangle BAM \cong \triangle CAM$ | 4. AAS Theorem |

## LESSON 117

### Warm Up 117

**1.** parallel

**2.** Midpoint $= \left(\frac{x_1 + x_2}{2}, \frac{y_1 + y_2}{2}, \frac{z_1 + z_2}{2}\right)$

$= \left(\frac{5 + 1}{2}, \frac{7 + 1}{2}, \frac{-2 + -6}{2}\right)$

$= \left(\frac{6}{2}, \frac{8}{2}, \frac{-8}{2}\right)$

$= (3, 4, -4)$

**3.** $m = \frac{10 - 8}{10 - 4} = \frac{2}{6} = \frac{1}{3}$

Choice **C** is correct.

### Lesson Practice 117

**a.** In A, the line has a slope that does not represent the data, so it is not a good choice. In B, the line goes through the points and the slope shows the trend of the data, so it is a good choice. In C, the line has the correct slope, but it lies too far from the data points, so it is not a good choice.

**b.** It is a weak, negative correlation.

**c.** There is a strong positive correlation.

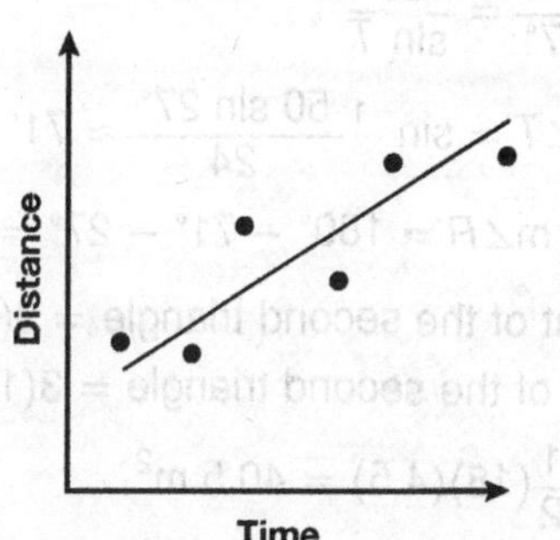


**d.** By examining the scatterplot, it is apparent that it will be complete in about 62 months.

### Practice 117

**1.** The error is in using 5 as the height. The Pythagorean Theorem must be used to find the height.

$h^2 = 5^2 - 4^2$
$h = 3$

The height is 3.

$V = \frac{1}{3}\pi(4^2)(3) + \frac{1}{3}\pi(4^2)(3)$

$V = 16\pi + 16\pi = 32\pi$

The correct solution is $32\pi$, or approximately 100.5 units$^3$.

2. always

3. First, find the width of the roof.

$w^2 = 8^2 + 5^2$

$w^2 = 89$

$w \approx 9.43$

$A \approx 2(55)(14) + 2(10)(14) + 2(9.43)(55) + 2\left(\frac{1}{2}(8)(10)\right)$

$\approx 1820 + 1037 + 80$

$\approx 2937 \text{ ft}^2$

4. $45 - y = 2y + 12 + 31 - y$

$45 - y = y + 43$

$-2y = -2$

$y = 1$

5. $(RT)^2 = 50^2 + 53^2 - 2(50)(53)\cos 27°$

$(RT)^2 \approx 5309 - 4722$

$RT \approx 24$

$\frac{24}{\sin 27°} = \frac{50}{\sin T}$

$m\angle T = \sin^{-1}\frac{50 \sin 27°}{24} \approx 71°$

$m\angle R = 180° - 71° - 27° = 82°$

6. height of the second triangle = 3(6) = 18 m

base of the second triangle = 3(1.5) = 4.5 m

$A = \frac{1}{2}(18)(4.5) = 40.5 \text{ m}^2$

7. 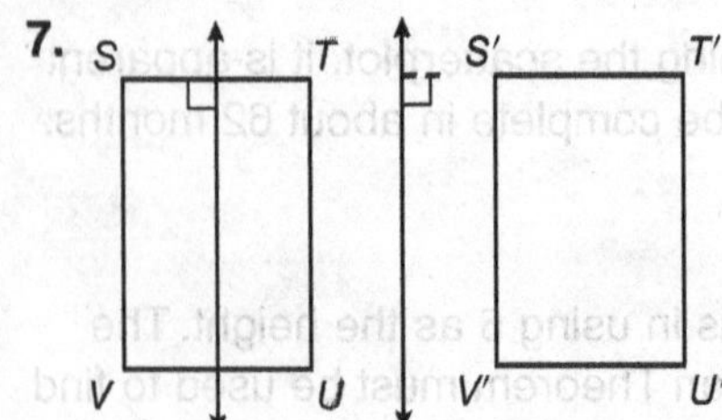


8. 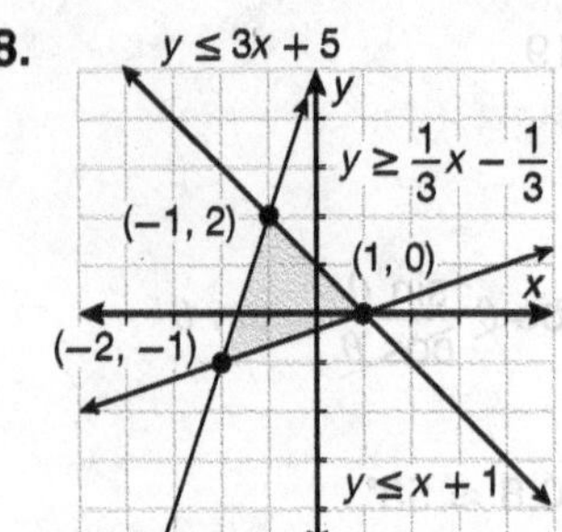


The vertices are (−2, −1), (−1, 2), and (1, 0)

Sample: (0, 0)

9. $\frac{9.5}{12} = \frac{LJ}{12}$

$12LJ = (12)(9.5)$

$LJ = 9.5$

10. First perform the translation.

$J(1 - 3, 3 + 4) = J(-2, 7)$

$K(0 - 3, 5 + 4) = K(-3, 9)$

$L(-2 - 3, -2 + 4) = L(-5, 2)$

Now, perform the dilation.

$J(-2, 7) \rightarrow J\text{'s}\left(\frac{1}{2}(-2), \frac{1}{2}(7)\right) = J'(-1, 3.5)$

$K(-3, 9) \rightarrow K'\left(\frac{1}{2}(-3), \frac{1}{2}(9)\right)$

$= K'(-1.5, 4.5)$

$L(-5, 2) \rightarrow L'\left(\frac{1}{2}(-5), \frac{1}{2}(2)\right) = L'(-2.5, 1)$

11. The correlation is positive and strong.

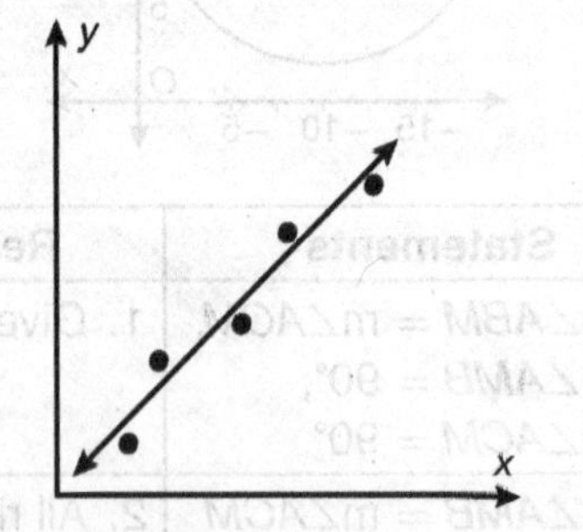


12. Since, $1 = \csc^2\theta - \cot^2\theta$

$\cot^2\theta = \csc^2\theta - 1$

$\cot\theta = \sqrt{\csc^2\theta - 1}$

$\tan\theta = \frac{1}{\sqrt{\csc^2\theta - 1}}$

**13.** $x(x + 20) = (75)(100)$
$x^2 + 20x - 7500 = 0$
$$x = -\frac{-20 \pm \sqrt{400 - 4(1)(-7500)}}{2(1)}$$
$x \approx -10 \pm 87$
$x \approx 77$
Route $\approx 77 + 20 \approx 97$ m

**14.** A negative correlation would be expected. As the absences increase and assignments are missed, the student's grades can be expected to decrease.

**15.** $\frac{130°}{360°}(\pi r^2) = 12$
$r \approx 3.25$ m

**16.** $l = 2w$
$(2w)w = 50$
$2w^2 = 50$
$w = 5$ m
$l = 10$ m
1m : 1 in.

**17.** Extending the scatterplot to June, the next point would be at the top of the graph or approximately 18.5 hours.

**18.** By substituting the equation of a line into the equation of the circle, the largest possible polynomial is a quadratic in one variable. A quadratic function in one variable has at most two solutions. Hence, there are at most two points of intersection between a line and a circle.

**19.** There are zero lines of symmetry. The rotational symmetry has an order of 2.

**20.** The cosecant ratio never has a value between 1 and 0, because it is the reciprocal of sine, and the reciprocal of a number less than 1 (which sine always is) will always be greater than 1. A similar argument shows that cosecant cannot take a value between 0 and −1. Choice **D** is correct.

**21.** $8y = 66°$
$y = 8.25$
$m\,\widehat{WX} = 8.25 + 4 = 12.25°$
$m\,\widehat{WY} = 66° + 12.25° = 78.25°$

**22.** $\begin{bmatrix} -1 & 0 \\ 0 & 1 \end{bmatrix}\begin{bmatrix} 2 & -3 & -2 \\ 2 & 6 & -6 \end{bmatrix}$

$= \begin{bmatrix} (-1)(2) + (0)(2) & (-1)(-3) + (0)(6) & (-1)(-2) + (0)(-6) \\ (0)(2) + (1)(2) & (0)(-3) + (1)(6) & (0)(-2) + (1)(-6) \end{bmatrix}$

$= \begin{bmatrix} -2 & 3 & 2 \\ 2 & 6 & -6 \end{bmatrix}$

The triangle was reflected in the $y$-axis because when the triangle matrix is multiplied by the reflection matrix $\begin{bmatrix} -1 & 0 \\ 0 & 1 \end{bmatrix}$, the result is the image matrix.

**23.** A regular square pyramid has 4 plane symmetries. They are the planes containing the lines of symmetry of the square base.

**24.** Assume a right triangle $VBN$ has an obtuse angle. Let $\angle V$ be right and $\angle N$ be obtuse. Then $m\angle B + m\angle N = 90°$, so $m\angle N = 90° - m\angle B$. By the definition of obtuse angles, $m\angle N > 90°$. Substituting, $90° < 90° - m\angle B$, which simplifies to $0° > m\angle B$. By the Protractor Postulate, a triangle cannot have an angle with a measure less than zero, so the assumption is contradicted and a right triangle cannot have an obtuse angle.

**25.** $L = \frac{1}{2}Pl = \frac{1}{2}(10)(10) = 50 \text{ in.}^2$

**26.** $\frac{4^3}{12^3} = \frac{17.2}{V}$
$(64)(V) = (1728)(17.2)$

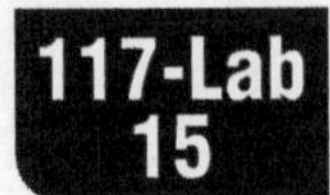


$64V = 29{,}721.6$

$V = 464.4 \text{ m}^3$

**27.** It is known that $\tan\theta = \frac{\sin\theta}{\cos\theta}$. Since $\cos^2\theta + \sin^2\theta = 1$, $\cos\theta = \sqrt{1 - \sin^2\theta}$. Substitute to find that $\tan\theta = \frac{\sin\theta}{\sqrt{1 - \sin^2\theta}}$.

**28.**

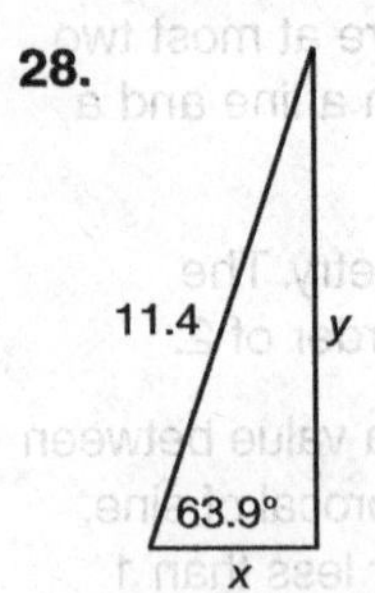


$x = 11.4 \cos 63.9° \approx 5.02$

$y = 11.4 \sin 63.9° \approx 10.24$

So, the vertical vector is $10.24 - 9.8 = 0.44$

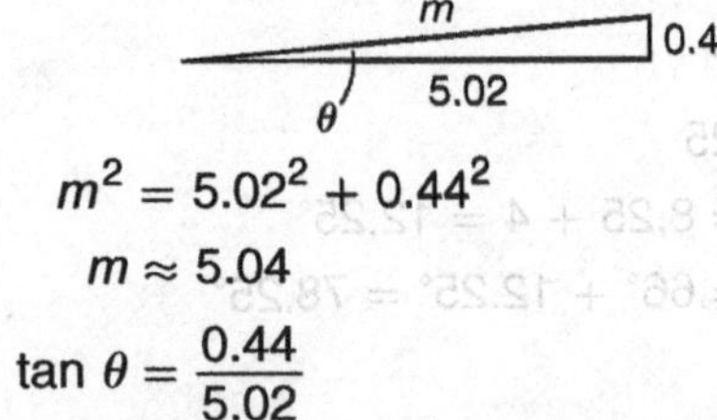


$m^2 = 5.02^2 + 0.44^2$

$m \approx 5.04$

$\tan\theta = \frac{0.44}{5.02}$

$\theta \approx 5°$

$5.04 \text{ m/s}^2$ at 5° to the horizontal

**29. a.** 3, 4, 7, 11, 18, 29, 47, 76, 123, 199; The tenth spiral would contain 199 seeds.

**b.** $3 + 4 + 7 + 11 + 18 + 29 + 47 + 76 + 123 + 199 = 517$ seeds

There are 517 seeds altogether in the first 10 spirals.

**30.** Choice **B** is correct.

## LAB 15

**7.** The graph shows that there is a negative relationship in the data. The test for 1000 pounds might have been conducted on a bookshelf with a structure default.

**8.**

Y1=-.676607X+1453.32

X=1800 Y=235.4274

Sample: It may not be accurate because the outlier point is causing the best fit to be inaccurate.

**9.**

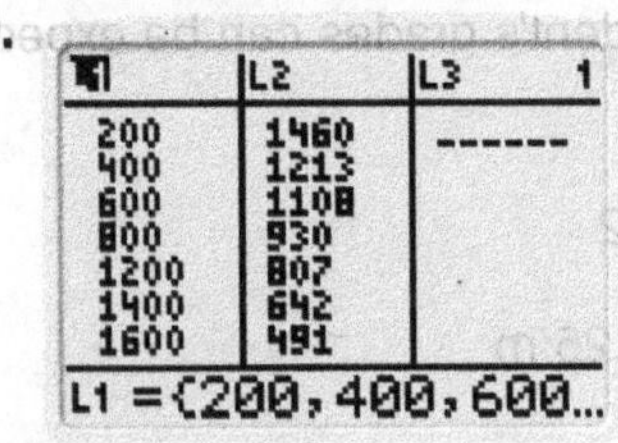

| L1 | L2 | L3 |
|---|---|---|
| 200 | 1460 | ------ |
| 400 | 1213 | |
| 600 | 1108 | |
| 800 | 930 | |
| 1200 | 807 | |
| 1400 | 642 | |
| 1600 | 491 | |

L1 ={200,400,600...

**10.**

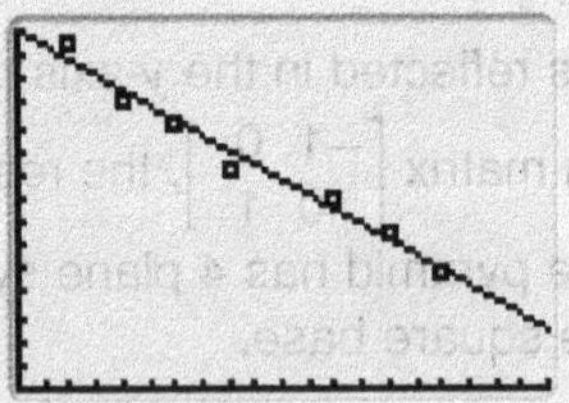

**11.**

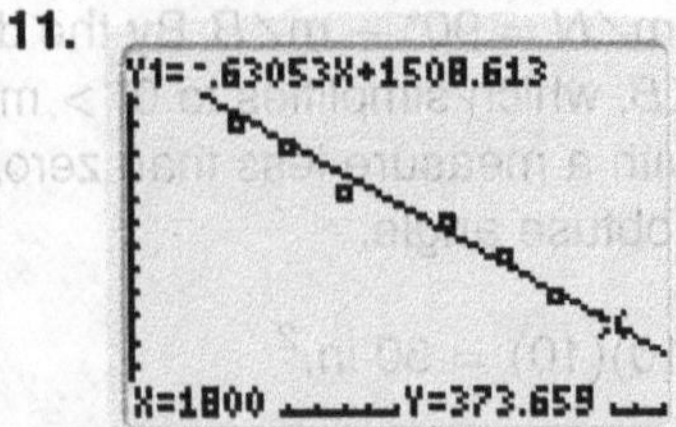


Sample: Yes, the graph and the estimate changed. Taking out the outlier made the line of best fit slightly more accurate.

## Lab 15 Practice

See student work. Sample: Removing a point that is not an outlier has little effect on the line of best fit. A good estimate can still be made. You can choose an outlier using personal judgment—if it is the only extreme value, it should probably be eliminated, whereas multiple extreme values may not need to be eliminated.

# LESSON 118

## Warm Up 118

**1.** origin

**2.** $\begin{bmatrix} 1 & 0 \\ 0 & 1 \end{bmatrix} + \begin{bmatrix} -1 & 4 \\ 3 & 0 \end{bmatrix} = \begin{bmatrix} 1-1 & 0+4 \\ 0+3 & 1+0 \end{bmatrix}$

$= \begin{bmatrix} 0 & 4 \\ 3 & 1 \end{bmatrix}$

**3.** Choice **A** is correct.

## Lesson Practice 118

**a.** $\det = x_1y_2 + x_2y_3 + x_3y_1 - y_1x_2 - y_2x_3 - y_3x_1$

$\det = (5)(2) + (4)(0) + (5)(6) - (6)(4) - (2)(5) - (0)(5)$

$\det = 10 + 0 + 30 - 24 - 10 - 0$

$\det = 6$

**b.** $\det = x_1y_2 + x_2y_3 + x_3y_1 - y_1x_2 - y_2x_3 - y_3x_1$

$\det = (-2)(2) + (1)(3) + (0)(-4) - (-4)(1) - (2)(0) - (3)(-2)$

$\det = -4 + 3 + 0 + 4 - 0 + 6$

$\det = 9$

**c.** $A = \left| \frac{1}{2} \det \begin{bmatrix} 1 & 4 \\ 2 & 3 \\ 1 & -4 \\ -1 & -4 \\ -2 & 0 \\ -1 & 4 \end{bmatrix} \right|$

$A = \left| \frac{1}{2}[1(3) + 2(-4) + 1(-4) + -1(0) + -2(4) + -1(4) - 4(2) - 3(1) - -4(-1) - -4(-2) - 0(-1) - 4(1)] \right|$

$A = \left| \frac{1}{2}(3 - 8 - 4 - 0 - 8 - 4 - 8 - 3 - 4 - 8 - 0 - 4) \right|$

$A = \left| \frac{1}{2}(-48) \right|$

$A = |-24| = 24$ square units

**d.** $A = \left| \frac{1}{2} \det \begin{bmatrix} 0 & -35 \\ -70 & 35 \\ -35 & 70 \\ 35 & 70 \\ 70 & 35 \end{bmatrix} \right|$

$A = \left| \frac{1}{2}(0(35) + -70(70) + -35(70) + 35(35) + 70(-35) - -35(-70) - 35(-35) - 70(35) - 70(70) - 35(0)) \right|$

$A = \left| \frac{1}{2}(0 - 4900 - 2450 + 1225 - 2450 - 2450 + 1225 - 2450 - 4900 - 0) \right|$

$A = \left| \frac{1}{2}(-17{,}150) \right|$

$A = |-8575| = 8575$ square feet

## Practice 118

**1.** $A = \left| \frac{1}{2} \det \begin{bmatrix} -5 & 7 \\ -1 & 15 \\ 5 & 2 \\ 0 & -8 \\ -10 & -3 \end{bmatrix} \right|$

$A = \left| \frac{1}{2}(-5(15) + -1(2) + 5(-8) + 0(-3) + -10(7) - 7(-1) - 15(5) - 2(0) - -8(-10) - -3(-5)) \right|$

$A = \left| \frac{1}{2}(-75 - 2 - 40 + 0 - 70 + 7 - 75 - 0 - 80 - 15) \right|$

$A = \left| \frac{1}{2}(-350) \right|$

$A = |-175| = 175$ square units

**2.** This is a weak, negative correlation.

**3.** $A = \left| \frac{1}{2} \det \begin{bmatrix} 5 & 7 \\ 7 & 0 \\ 1 & -5 \\ -6 & 2 \end{bmatrix} \right|$

$A = \left| \frac{1}{2}(5(0) + 7(-5) + 1(2) + -6(7) - 7(7) - 0(1) - -5(-6) - 2(5)) \right|$

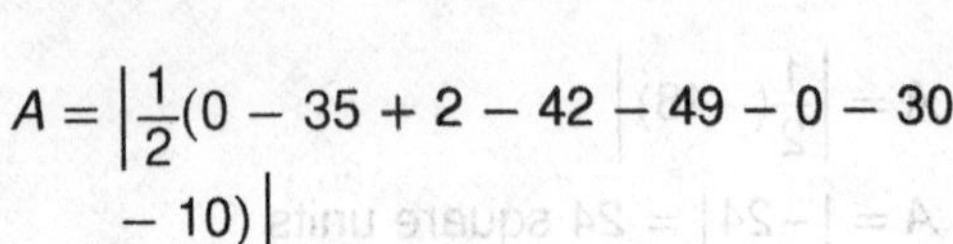

$$A = \left|\frac{1}{2}(0 - 35 + 2 - 42 - 49 - 0 - 30 - 10)\right|$$

$$A = \left|\frac{1}{2}(-164)\right|$$

$A = |-82| = 82$ square yards

4. The values for csc $\theta$ and sec $\theta$ are undefined. These values approach positive infinity or negative infinity but there is no actual value when $\sin\theta = 0$ or $\cos\theta = 0$, because there cannot be a zero in the denominator of a fraction.

5. $d = |4 - 3| = |1| = 1$

6. Since $\overline{TA}$ is a diameter of the circle, the arc that subtends it has a measure of 180°. According to Theorem 64-1, the angle that $\overline{TA}$ forms with the tangent is half of 180°, which is 90°. Therefore, $\overline{TA}$ is perpendicular to the tangent.

7. $V = \pi(16^2)(28) - \pi(6^2)(28)$
$V \approx 19{,}352.2 \text{ cm}^3$

8. $\det = x_1y_2 + x_2y_3 + x_3y_1 - y_1x_2 - y_2x_3 - y_3x_1$
$\det = (5)(5) + (4)(1) + (2)(4) - (4)(4) - (5)(2) - (1)(5)$
$\det = 25 + 4 + 8 - 16 - 10 - 5$
$\det = 6$

9. $A_{sector} = \pi r^2\left(\frac{m°}{360°}\right)$

$A_{sector} = \pi(5)^2\left(\frac{90°}{360°}\right)$

$A_{sector} = 12.5\pi \text{ in.}^2$

$A_{triangle} = \frac{1}{2}(5)(5) = 12.5 \text{ in.}^2$

$A_{segment} = 12.5\pi - 12.5 \text{ in.}^2$
Shaded area: $\pi(5)^2 - (12.5\pi - 12.5)$
$= 18.75\pi + 12.5$

10.

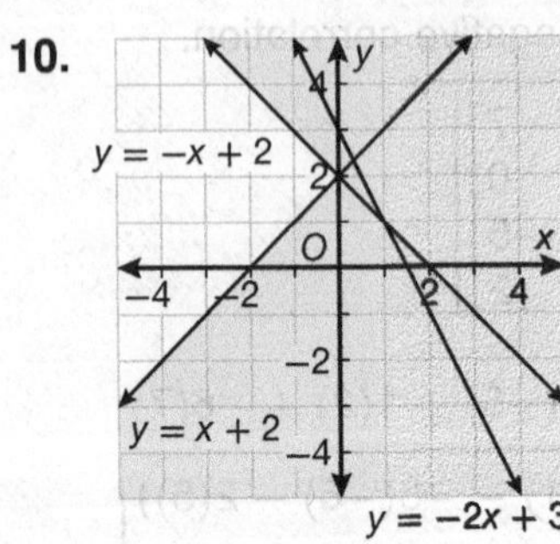


No, $y > -2x + 3$ is already included in the region.

11.

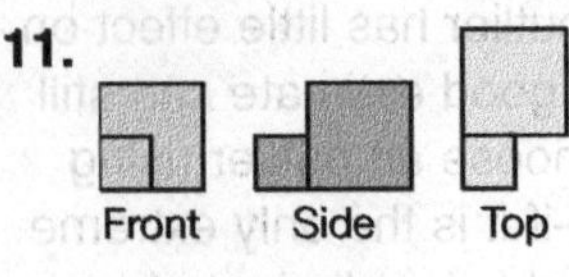


12.

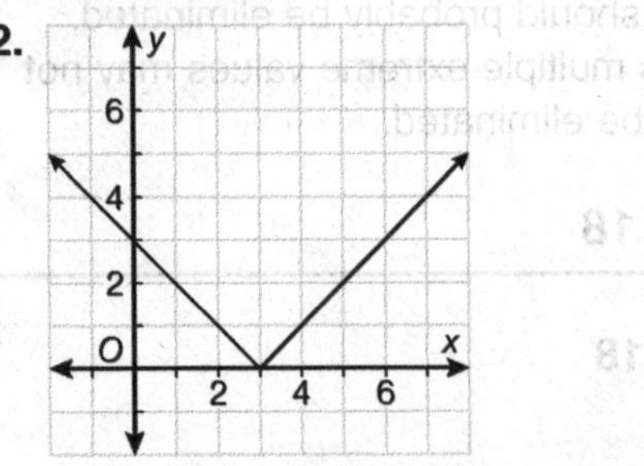


$x = 3$ is the equation of the line of symmetry.

13. The radius of the inscribed circle is $5\sqrt{3}$ in.
Circumference $= 2\pi(5\sqrt{3}) = 10\pi\sqrt{3}$ in.
Area $= \pi(5\sqrt{3})^2 = 75\pi \text{ in.}^2$
The radius of the circumscribed circle is 10 in.
Circumference $= 2\pi(10) = 20\pi$ in.
Area $= \pi(10)^2 = 100\pi \text{ in.}^2$

14. There is exactly one counterexample: an angle bisector divides a 180° angle into two right angles.
Choice **C** is correct.

15. The slope of the line perpendicular to $y = 12x - 4$ is $-\frac{1}{12}$.

$y = -\frac{1}{12}x + b$

$1 = -\frac{1}{12}(4) + b$

$\frac{4}{3} = b$

$y = -\frac{1}{12}x + \frac{4}{3}$

16. $\begin{bmatrix} 1 & 2 \\ 0 & 0 \end{bmatrix} = (1)(0) + (0)(2) - (2)(0) - (0)(1)$
$= 0 + 0 - 0 - 0 = 0$

17. Let $r$ be the radius of the circle of the cross section.

$\frac{h}{H} = \frac{r}{R}$

$rH = hR$

$r = \frac{hR}{H}$

$A = \pi r^2 = \pi\left(\frac{hR}{H}\right)^2$

**18.** No. Although the slope represents the trend in the data, the line does not go through the data points.

**19.** $x^2 + x^2 = 16^2$
$2x^2 = 256$
$x^2 = 128$
$x \approx 11.3$
$P = 2(11.3) + 16 = 38.6$ feet

**20.** $(x - 6)^2 + (y - -2)^2 = 5^2$
$(x - 6)^2 + (y + 2)^2 = 25$

**21.** $L = \pi rl$
$l^2 = 24^2 + 4^2$
$l^2 = 592$
$l \approx 24.33$
$L \approx \pi(4)(24.33) \approx 305.74 \text{ in.}^2$
$3(305.74) \approx 917.22 \text{ in.}^2$

**22.** $m\widehat{UV} = 180°$
$m\angle VTU = \frac{1}{2}(180°) = 90°$

**23.** The first airplane is at (35, −140, 1), and the second airplane is at (−300, 95, 2.25).

$d = \sqrt{(x_2 - x_1)^2 + (y_2 - y_1)^2 + (z_2 - z_1)^2}$
$= \sqrt{(35 - -300)^2 + (-140 - 95)^2 + (1 - 2.25)^2}$
$= \sqrt{(335)^2 + (-235)^2 + (-1.25)^2}$
$= \sqrt{167{,}451.5625} \approx 409.2$

The airplanes are about 409.2 miles apart.

**24.** $\frac{3^2}{4^2} = \frac{15.3}{A}$
$9A = (16)(15.3)$
$A = 27.2$ square units

**25.** Since the tan 0° = 0, cot 0° is undefined. Choice **B** is correct.

**26.** $V = lwh - (2lwh)$
$3000 = (18)(12)(x) - (2)(3)(3)(x)$
$3000 = 216x - 18x$
$3000 = 198x$
$x \approx 15$ inches

**27.**

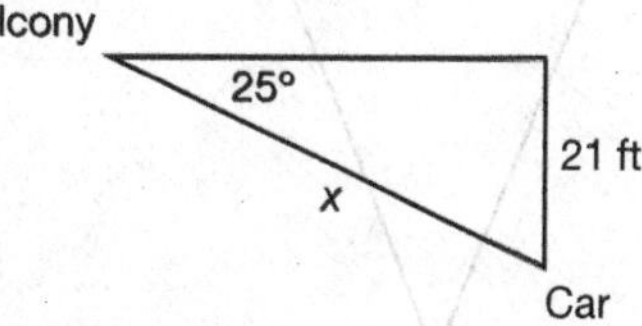


$\sin 25° = \frac{21}{x}$

$x = \frac{21}{\sin 25°} \approx 50$ feet

**28.** Reena's line is a better fit, since her line has a slope that represents the data, and includes the data. Oscar's line includes the data, but the slope of his line does not represent the data well.

**29.** $A = \left|\frac{1}{2}\det\begin{bmatrix} 0 & 2 \\ -3 & 1 \\ -2 & -1 \\ 1 & -1 \\ 3 & 1 \end{bmatrix}\right|$

$A = \left|\frac{1}{2}(0(1) + -3(-1) + -2(-1) + 1(1) + 3(2) - 2(-3) - 1(-2) - -1(1) - -1(3) - 1(0))\right|$

$A = \left|\frac{1}{2}(0 + 3 + 2 + 1 + 6 + 6 + 2 + 1 + 3 - 0)\right|$

$A = \left|\frac{1}{2}(24)\right|$

$A = |12| = 12$ square units

**30.** The lines are parallel and distinct. When you graph the inequalities, their graphs do not intersect. So there is no solution to this system of inequalities.

## LESSON 119

### Warm Up 119

**1.** frustum

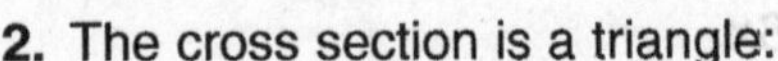



2. The cross section is a triangle:

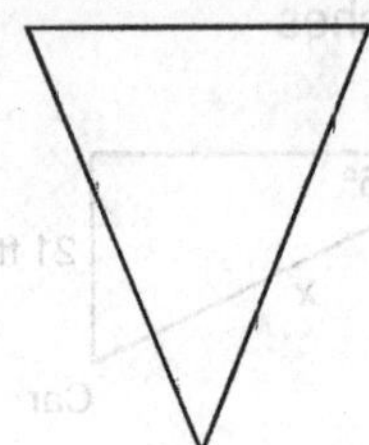

3. $r = \frac{6}{2} = 3$ and $h = 8$, so

$$V = \frac{1}{3}\pi r^2 h$$
$$= \frac{1}{3}\pi(3)^2(8)$$
$$= \frac{1}{3}\pi(9)(8) = 24\pi$$

The volume is $24\pi$ in.$^2$.

4. $$V = \frac{4}{3}\pi r^3$$
$$972\pi = \frac{4}{3}\pi r^3$$
$$\frac{3}{4\pi} \cdot 972\pi = \frac{3}{4\pi} \cdot \frac{4}{3}\pi r^3$$
$$729 = r^3$$
$$r = \sqrt[3]{729} = 9$$

The radius is 9 cm.

## Lesson Practice 119

a. Each interior angle in a regular octagon measures 135°. At least 3 octagons need to be placed at each vertex. So each vertex would have total measure 135° × 3 = 405°. But this is > 360°, the angle of a point on a plane. So octagons would not construct a Platonic solid.

b. 5 equilateral triangles meet at each vertex. Each angle measure in an equilateral triangle is 60°.

60° × 5 = 300°

The sum of angles is 300°.

c. Each interior angle in a square measures 90°. Four faces: 4 × 90° = 360°. But 360° is the angle of a point on a plane. So squares would form a tessellation, not a solid.

## Practice 119

1. Brittney confused csc $\theta$ with sec $\theta$.

Correct solution: $\sin\theta = \frac{1}{\csc\theta}$

2. $$F + V = E + 2$$
$$7 + 10 = E + 2$$
$$17 = E + 2$$
$$17 - 2 = E$$
$$15 = E$$

3. Tetrahedron; Only this Platonic solid is formed from a single vertex opposite a base.

4. Choice **A** is correct; Two end triangles overlap when folded.

5. The dimensions are still 7 units by 3 units by 5 units, since they do not change under a rotation.

6. Use the Law of Cosines to determine $QR$:

$$c^2 = a^2 + b^2 - 2ab\cos C$$
$$QR^2 = (70)^2 + (45)^2 - 2(70)(45)\cos 42°$$
$$QR^2 = 4900 + 2025 - 6300(0.7431) \approx 2243$$
$$QR \approx \sqrt{2243} \approx 47.4$$

Therefore, $P = a + b + c$

$$P \approx 70 + 45 + 47.4$$
$$P \approx 162.4$$

The perimeter is about 162.4 units.

7. The slope of the line is $m = 8$. If the line makes (counterclockwise) angle $\theta$ with the positive $x$-axis,

$$\tan\theta = m = 8$$
$$\theta = \text{Tan}^{-1}(8) \approx 82.9°$$

8. Since the convex polygon contains the origin, draw lines to each vertex from the origin. As long as the vertices of the polygon are ordered counterclockwise, the area of the polygon is the sum of the areas of the triangles:

$$A = \frac{1}{2}\begin{vmatrix} x_1 & y_1 \\ x_2 & y_2 \end{vmatrix} + \frac{1}{2}\begin{vmatrix} x_2 & y_2 \\ x_3 & y_3 \end{vmatrix} + \ldots + \frac{1}{2}\begin{vmatrix} x_n & y_n \\ x_1 & y_1 \end{vmatrix}$$
$$= \frac{1}{2}(x_1y_2 - x_2y_1) + \frac{1}{2}(x_2y_3 - x_3y_2) + \ldots$$
$$+ \frac{1}{2}(x_ny_1 - x_1y_n)$$

$$= \frac{1}{2}(x_1y_2 + x_2y_3 + \ldots + x_ny_1 - x_2y_1 - x_3y_2 \ldots - x_1y_n)$$

$$= \frac{1}{2}\begin{vmatrix} x_1 & y_1 \\ x_2 & y_2 \\ \vdots & \vdots \\ x_n & y_n \end{vmatrix}$$

This is the formula in Lesson 118 (changing the order of the vertices only changes the sign).

**9.** $A_{rect.} = lw = (40)(18) = 720$

The base of each triangle is $b$, where

$2b + 18 = 28$

$2b = 28 - 18 = 10$

$\frac{2b}{2} = \frac{10}{2}$

$b = 5$

The height of each triangle is $h$, where

$c^2 = b^2 + h^2$

$13^2 = 5^2 + h^2$

$169 = 25 + h^2$

$h^2 = 169 - 25 = 144$

$h = \sqrt{144} = 12$

$A_\triangle = \frac{1}{2}bh = \frac{1}{2}(5)(12) = 30$

The radius of the semicircle is $r = \frac{8}{2} = 4$

$A_{semicircle} = \frac{1}{2}\pi r^2 = \frac{1}{2}\pi(4)^2 = \frac{1}{2}(16\pi) = 8\pi$

Therefore,

$A = A_{rect.} + 2A_\triangle - A_{semicircle}$

$A = 720 + 2(30) - 8\pi$

$A = 780 - 8\pi \approx 754.9$

Area of pattern is about 754.9 in.$^2$

**10.** If all side lengths are multiplied by $a$, then each term in the summation of the determinant area formula is multiplied by $a^2$. Hence, the total area is multiplied by $a^2$.

**11.** $\tan\theta = \frac{\text{opp.}}{\text{adj.}}$

$\tan 29° = \frac{x}{14}$

$x = 14 \tan 29° \approx 7.76$

**12.** The first astronaut is following the line $(x, y, z) = (3, -1, 4) + t(6, 3, 7)$. The second astronaut is following the line $(x, y, z) = (-49, -15, -2) + u(11, 4, 6)$. The astronauts meet only if the lines intersect:

$(3, -1, 4) + t(6, 3, 7) = (-49, -15, -2) + u(11, 4, 6)$

$x$-coord: $3 + 6t = -49 + 11u$

$3 + 49 + 6t = 11u$

$52 + 6t = 11u$

$y$-coord: $-1 + 3t = -15 + 4u$

$15 - 1 + 3t = 4u$

$14 + 3t = 4u$

By elimination,

$52 + 6t = 11u$

$\underline{-2(14 + 3t) = -2(4u)}$

$24 = 3u$

$\frac{24}{3} = \frac{3u}{3}$

$8 = u$

$14 + 3t = 4u = 4(8) = 32$

$3t = 32 - 14 = 18$

$\frac{3t}{3} = \frac{18}{3}$

$t = 6$

Substitute in $z$-coord. equation:

$4 + 7t = -2 + 6u$

$4 + 7(6) \stackrel{?}{=} -2 + 6(8)$

$4 + 42 \stackrel{?}{=} -2 + 48$

$46 = 46$

So lines do intersect.

**13.** Choice **C** is correct. For strong positive correlation, points lie close to an upward-sloping line.

**14.** Each axis of rotation passes through a vertex and the center of the opposite face. Since there are 4 vertices, there are 4 axes.

**15.** By Theorem 86-1,

$AE \cdot BE = CE \cdot DE$

$x \cdot 9 = 3 \cdot 12$

$9x = 36$

$\frac{9x}{9} = \frac{36}{9}$

$x = 4$

16. $A = \left| \frac{1}{2} \begin{vmatrix} 2 & 3 \\ 4 & 5 \\ 1 & 6 \end{vmatrix} \right|$

$= \left| \frac{1}{2}(2 \cdot 5 + 4 \cdot 6 + 1 \cdot 3 - 4 \cdot 3 - 1 \cdot 5 - 2 \cdot 6) \right|$

$= \left| \frac{1}{2}(10 + 24 + 3 - 12 - 5 - 12) \right|$

$= \left| \frac{1}{2}(37 - 29) \right| = \left| \frac{1}{2}(8) \right| = 4$

The area is 4 square units.

17. $V = \frac{1}{3}Bh$

$V = \frac{1}{3}(lw)h$

$V = \frac{1}{3}(20)(10)(6) = 400$

Volume is 400 $ft^3$.

18. The scale factor of 0 reduces all lengths to 0. Therefore the diameter of the circle becomes 0, so the image is a point.

19. Solve inequalities for $y$:

$2x + 3y > 1$

$3y > 1 - 2x$

$\frac{3y}{3} > \frac{1 - 2x}{3}$

$y > -\frac{2}{3}x + \frac{1}{3}$

1st region is above line $y = -\frac{2}{3}x + \frac{1}{3}$.

$x - 3y \geq 1$

$-3y \geq -x + 1$

$\frac{-3y}{-3} \leq \frac{-x + 1}{-3}$

$y \leq \frac{1}{3}x - \frac{1}{3}$

2nd region is on and below line $y = \frac{1}{3}x - \frac{1}{3}$.

$5y - 4x \geq 10$

$5y \geq 4x + 10$

$\frac{5y}{5} \geq \frac{4x + 10}{5}$

$y \geq \frac{4}{5}x + 2$

3rd region is on and above line $y = \frac{4}{5}x + 2$.

The solution is the conjunction of 1st region with the disjunction of 2nd and 3rd regions:

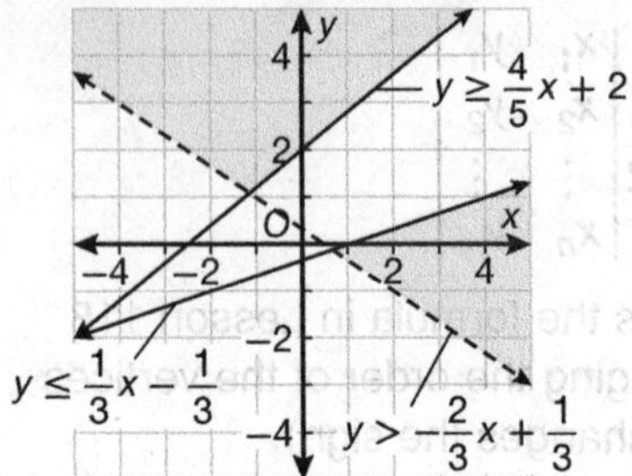


20. By the Pythagorean Theorem,

$a^2 + b^2 = c^2$

$x^2 + 10^2 = 20^2$

$x^2 + 100 = 400$

$x^2 = 400 - 100 = 300$

$x = \sqrt{300} = \sqrt{3}\sqrt{100} = 10\sqrt{3}$

The value of $x$ is $10\sqrt{3}$ yd.

21. The central angle of each sector is $\frac{360°}{5} = 72°$, so the area of each segment is

$A_{segment} = A_{sector} - A_{triangle}$

$= \frac{72}{360}\pi(3)^2 - 2\left[\frac{1}{2}(3\sin 36°)(3\cos 36°)\right]$

$= \frac{9}{5}\pi - (4.27975)$

$\approx 1.375$

Therefore, the combined area is 5(1.375) ≈ 6.9 square inches.

22. $(x, y) \rightarrow (x + 3, y)$

$(x, -3) \rightarrow (x + 3, -3) = (3, -3)$

$x + 3 = 3$

$x = 3 - 3 = 0$

23.

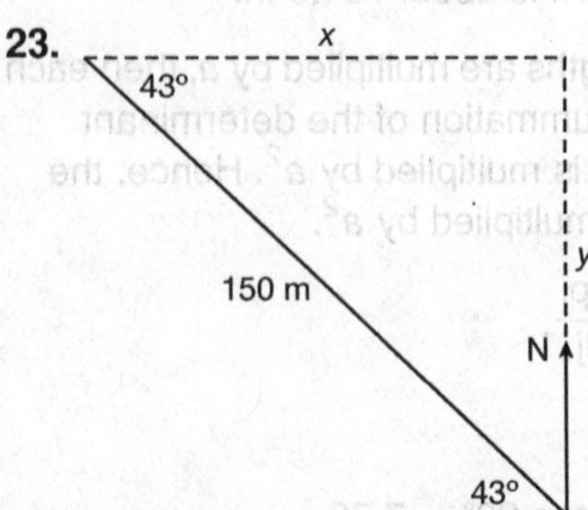


Westward: $\frac{x}{150} = \cos 43°$

$x = 150 \cos 43°$

$x \approx 109.70$

Northward: $\frac{y}{150} = \sin 43°$

$y = 150 \sin 43°$

$y \approx 102.30$

Westward, by $109.70 - 102.30 \approx 7.4$ m

**24.** Definition of a rhombus: A quadrilateral with 4 ≅ sides. Since a square has 4 ≅ sides, the statement is always true.

**25.** Jar: $r = \frac{3.5}{2} = 1.75$, $h = 5.75$

$$V_{jar} = \pi r^2 h = \pi(1.75)^2(5.75) = \pi(3.0625)(5.75) \approx 55.32$$

Scoop: $r = \frac{1}{2}$ or 0.5

$$V_{scoop} = \frac{1}{2}\left(\frac{4}{3}\right)\pi r^3 = \frac{2}{3}\pi(0.5)^3 = \frac{2}{3}\pi(0.125) \approx 0.26$$

The remaining volume is $55.32 - 0.26 \approx 55.1$ in.$^3$

**26.** Let $s$ represent side length of the triangle.

Inscribed in circle:

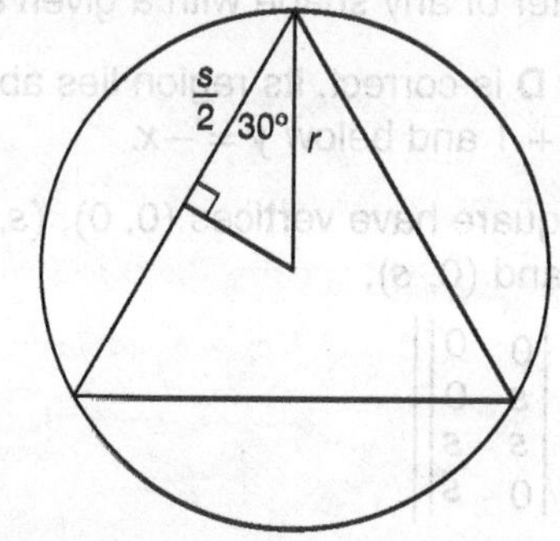


$$\frac{s/2}{r} = \cos 30°$$

$$\frac{s}{2r} = \frac{\sqrt{3}}{2}$$

$$s = (2r)\frac{\sqrt{3}}{2} = r\sqrt{3}$$

Circumscribes circle:

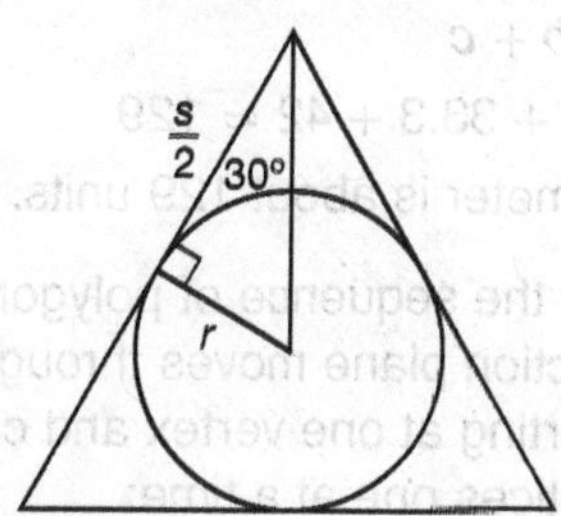


$$\frac{r}{s/2} = \tan 30°$$

$$\frac{2r}{s} = \frac{\sqrt{3}}{3}$$

$$2r(3) = s\sqrt{3}$$

$$6r\sqrt{3} = s\sqrt{3}\sqrt{3} = 3s$$

$$\frac{6r\sqrt{3}}{3} = \frac{3s}{3}$$

$$2r\sqrt{3} = s$$

**27.** $1 + \tan^2 \theta = \sec^2 \theta$

$$\tan^2 \theta = \sec^2 \theta - 1$$

$$\tan \theta = \pm\sqrt{\sec^2 \theta - 1}$$

$$\tan \theta = \pm\sqrt{\left(\frac{3}{2}\right)^2 - 1}$$

$$\tan \theta = \pm\sqrt{\frac{9}{4} - 1}$$

$$\tan \theta = \pm\sqrt{\frac{5}{4}} = \pm\frac{\sqrt{5}}{2}$$

**28.** Let $a$ and $b$ represent lengths of sides opposite 91° and 38° angles, respectively; let $C$ be angle opposite side of length 42 units. By the Triangle Angle Sum Theorem,

$$m\angle A + m\angle B + m\angle C = 180°$$

$$91° + 38° + m\angle C = 180°$$

$$129° + m\angle C = 180°$$

$$m\angle C = 180° - 129° = 51°$$

By Law of Sines,

$$\frac{a}{\sin A} = \frac{c}{\sin C} \qquad \frac{b}{\sin B} = \frac{c}{\sin C}$$

$$\frac{a}{\sin 91°} = \frac{42}{\sin 51°} \qquad \frac{b}{\sin 38°} = \frac{42}{\sin 51°}$$

$$a = \frac{42 \sin 91°}{\sin 51°} \qquad b = \frac{42 \sin 38°}{\sin 51°}$$

$$a \approx 54.0 \qquad b \approx 33.3$$

Therefore,

$P = a + b + c$

$\approx 54.0 + 33.3 + 42 \approx 129$

The perimeter is about 129 units.

**29.** Consider the sequence of polygons as the cross-section plane moves through each solid, starting at one vertex and crossing other vertices one at a time:

Tetrahedron: △, quadrilateral, △

Cube: △, quadrilateral, quadrilateral, quadrilateral, △

Octahedron: quadrilateral, hexagon, hexagon, hexagon, quadrilateral

Dodecahedron: △, quadrilateral, pentagon, hexagon, ...

Icosahedron: pentagon, octagon, ...

Answer: icosahedron and dodecahedron

**30.** By the Law of Sines,

$$\frac{a}{\sin A} = \frac{b}{\sin B}$$

$$\frac{a}{\sin 110°} = \frac{15}{\sin 40°}$$

$$a = \frac{15 \sin 110°}{\sin 40°} \approx 21.93$$

## LESSON 120

### Warm Up 120

1. rotation
2. All angles are right angles; opposite sides are ∥; opposite sides are ≅; diagonals are ≅
3. Choice **D** is correct.

### Exploration 120

3. The line appears on both sides of paper. A Möbius strip has only one side (and only one edge).
4. A Möbius strip becomes one long strip with a twist. The cut gave the strip a second edge. It is now twice as long, because the Möbius strip had one side that was twice as long as the object itself.

### Lesson Practice 120

**a.**

∞ ꝏ B

Yes; because both shapes divide a two-dim. space into 3 regions.

**b.** B; The given object divides the plane into 5 regions; only shape B also divides the plane into 5 regions.

**c.** No division (no holes): {1, 2, 3, 5, 7}

Division in two regions (one hole): {4, 6, 9, 0}

Division in three regions (two holes): {8}

### Practice 120

**1.** Point matrix: $\begin{bmatrix} -2 & 4 & 6 \\ 3 & 8 & -1 \end{bmatrix}$

$$\begin{bmatrix} -2 & 4 & 6 \\ 3 & 8 & -1 \end{bmatrix} \rightarrow \begin{bmatrix} -2+4 & 4+4 & 6+4 \\ 3-3 & 8-3 & -1-3 \end{bmatrix}$$

$$= \begin{bmatrix} -2 & 4 & 6 \\ 3 & 8 & -1 \end{bmatrix} + \begin{bmatrix} 4 & 4 & 4 \\ -3 & -3 & -3 \end{bmatrix}$$

Transformation matrix is $\begin{bmatrix} 4 & 4 & 4 \\ -3 & -3 & -3 \end{bmatrix}$.

**2.** For an $n$-sided regular polygon, the ratio of the area to the perimeter increases as $n$ increases. Since such polygons tend toward a circle, a circle has a lower ratio than all regular $n$-gons. Investigation shows that non-regular polygons have larger ratios than regular polygons with the same number of sides, which implies a circle has the least perimeter of any shape with a given area

**3.** Choice **D** is correct. Its region lies above $y = 3x + 1$ and below $y = -x$.

**4.** Let a square have vertices (0, 0), ($s$, 0), ($s$, $s$), and (0, $s$).

$$A = \left| \frac{1}{2} \begin{vmatrix} 0 & 0 \\ s & 0 \\ s & s \\ 0 & s \end{vmatrix} \right|$$

$$= \left| \frac{1}{2}[(0)(0) + (s)(s) + (s)(s) + (0)(0) - (s)(0) - (s)(0) - (0)(s) - (0)(s)] \right|$$

$$= \left| \frac{1}{2}(2s^2 - 0) \right| = s^2$$

5. Since all three chords are congruent, the minor arcs are also congruent:

$$\widehat{LKJ} \cong \widehat{KJN} \cong \widehat{JNM}$$
$$m\widehat{LKJ} = m\widehat{KJN} = m\widehat{JNM}$$
$$m\widehat{LK} + m\widehat{KJ} = m\widehat{KJ} + m\widehat{JN} = m\widehat{JN} + m\widehat{NM}$$

First equation:

$$m\widehat{LK} + m\widehat{KJ} = m\widehat{KJ} + m\widehat{JN}$$
$$m\widehat{LK} = m\widehat{JN}$$
$$2x - 35 = x - 3$$
$$2x - x = -3 + 35$$
$$x = 32$$

Second equation:

$$m\widehat{KJ} + m\widehat{JN} = m\widehat{JN} + m\widehat{NM}$$
$$m\widehat{KJ} = m\widehat{NM}$$
$$m\widehat{KJ} = (3x - 5)^\circ$$
$$m\widehat{KJ} = (3(32) - 5)^\circ = (96 - 5)^\circ = 91^\circ$$

6. Possible response: No; for example, consider point $X(1, 0)$. With given order,

$$X(1, 0) \rightarrow X'(1, 0)$$
$$\rightarrow X''\left(-\frac{1}{2}, -\frac{\sqrt{3}}{2}\right) \rightarrow X'''\left(\frac{1}{2}, -\frac{\sqrt{3}}{2}\right)$$

But with the order of the first two transformations switched,

$$X(1, 0) \rightarrow X'\left(-\frac{1}{2}, -\frac{\sqrt{3}}{2}\right)$$
$$\rightarrow X''\left(-\frac{1}{2}, \frac{\sqrt{3}}{2}\right) \rightarrow X'''\left(\frac{1}{2}, \frac{\sqrt{3}}{2}\right)$$

So the resulting image of $X$ is different.

7. Use Theorem 79-1:

$$m\angle A = 0.5(100 - 20) = 40^\circ$$

8. False; For example, $\theta = 50^\circ$ makes the equation untrue.

9. Label the top left vertex $A$, and the bottom right vertex $B$. Then $\triangle ADF \sim \triangle FDB$, so

$$\frac{AD}{FD} = \frac{FD}{BD}$$
$$\frac{4}{FD} = \frac{FD}{9}$$
$$4 \cdot 9 = FD \cdot FD$$
$$36 = FD^2$$
$$FD = \sqrt{36} = 6$$

10. $$\left|\frac{1}{2}\begin{vmatrix} 2 & 5 \\ -3 & 1 \\ 1 & -6 \end{vmatrix}\right|$$

$$= \left|\frac{1}{2}[(2)(1) + (-3)(-6) + (1)(5) - (-3)(5) - (1)(1) - (2)(-6)]\right|$$
$$= \left|\frac{1}{2}(2 + 18 + 5 + 15 - 1 + 12)\right|$$
$$= \left|\frac{1}{2}(51)\right| = 25.5$$

The area is 25.5 square units.

11. $$\tan\theta = \frac{\text{opp.}}{\text{adj.}} = \frac{50}{1500} = \frac{1}{30}$$

$$\theta = \text{Tan}^{-1}\left(\frac{1}{30}\right) \approx 1.91^\circ$$

The angle of depression should be about 1.91°.

12. Determine midpoint $M$ of base, which is also midpoint of $\overline{RT}$:

$$M(x, y, z) = \left(\frac{x_R + x_T}{2}, \frac{y_R + y_T}{2}, \frac{z_R + z_T}{2}\right)$$
$$= \left(\frac{1+3}{2}, \frac{1+(-1)}{2}, \frac{2+2}{2}\right)$$
$$= \left(\frac{4}{2}, \frac{0}{2}, \frac{4}{2}\right) = (2, 0, 2)$$

Determine the vector $\overrightarrow{MV}$ and check it is perpendicular to vectors $\overrightarrow{RS}$ and $\overrightarrow{ST}$, implying it is perpendicular to the plane of the base:

$$\overrightarrow{MV} = \begin{bmatrix} x_V - x_M \\ y_V - y_M \\ z_V - z_M \end{bmatrix} = \begin{bmatrix} 2-2 \\ 0-0 \\ 6-2 \end{bmatrix} = \begin{bmatrix} 0 \\ 0 \\ 4 \end{bmatrix}$$

$$\overrightarrow{RS} = \begin{bmatrix} x_S - x_R \\ y_S - y_R \\ z_S - z_R \end{bmatrix} = \begin{bmatrix} 3-1 \\ 1-1 \\ 2-2 \end{bmatrix} = \begin{bmatrix} 2 \\ 0 \\ 0 \end{bmatrix}$$

$$\overrightarrow{ST} = \begin{bmatrix} x_T - x_S \\ y_T - y_S \\ z_T - z_S \end{bmatrix} = \begin{bmatrix} 3-3 \\ -1-1 \\ 2-2 \end{bmatrix} = \begin{bmatrix} 0 \\ -2 \\ 0 \end{bmatrix}$$

All 3 vectors are perpendicular.

Therefore, $\overrightarrow{MV}$ is an altitude of the pyramid, so the height equals $MV$:

$$h = MV = |\overrightarrow{MV}| = \sqrt{0^2 + 0^2 + 4^2} = 4$$

The height is 4 units.

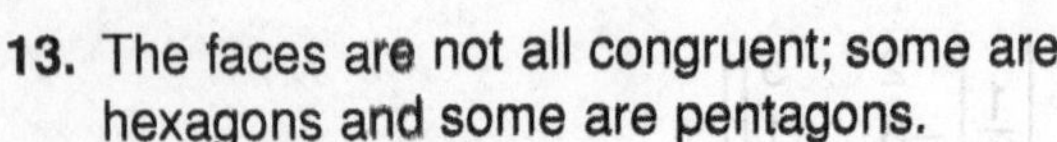



13. The faces are not all congruent; some are hexagons and some are pentagons.

14. Choice A; A, a, P, and p all have one hole.

15. The larger triangle is similar to the smaller triangle, after enlargement by a scale factor of 2. Therefore,

$$\frac{7x-12}{AB} = 2$$
$$7x - 12 = 2AB$$
$$7x - 12 = 2(x+6)$$
$$7x - 12 = 2x + 12$$
$$7x - 2x = 12 + 12$$
$$5x = 24$$
$$\frac{5x}{5} = \frac{24}{5}$$
$$x = 4\frac{4}{5} \text{ or } 4.8$$

16. Possible net:

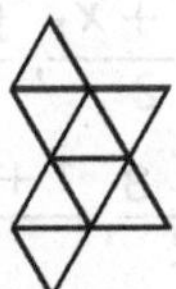

17. $S = 4\pi r^2$
$$= 4\pi(15)^2$$
$$= 4\pi(225)$$
$$= 900\pi \approx 2827$$
The surface area is 2827 $cm^2$, to nearest square centimeter.

18. Radius $r$ satisfies
$$\sin\left(\frac{70°}{2}\right) = \frac{75/2}{r}$$
$$r = \frac{37.5}{\sin 35°} \approx 65.38$$
Therefore,
$$A_{segment} = A_{sector} - A_{\Delta}$$
$$= \left(\frac{x}{360}\right)\pi r^2 - \frac{1}{2}r^2 \sin x°$$
$$\approx \left(\frac{70}{360}\right)\pi(65.38)^2 - \frac{1}{2}(65.38)^2 \sin 70°$$
$$\approx 2611.2 - 2008.4 \approx 603$$
The area is 603 $yd^2$, to nearest square yard.

19. Use the distance formula for side lengths:
$$XY = \sqrt{(x_2 - x_1)^2 + (y_2 - y_1)^2}$$
$$= \sqrt{(1-(-2))^2 + (1-3)^2}$$
$$= \sqrt{3^2 + (-2)^2} = \sqrt{13} \approx 3.6$$
$$YZ = \sqrt{(x_2 - x_1)^2 + (y_2 - y_1)^2}$$
$$= \sqrt{(-1-1)^2 + (-3-1)^2}$$
$$= \sqrt{(-2)^2 + (-4)^2}$$
$$= \sqrt{20} = 2\sqrt{5} \approx 4.5$$
$$XZ = \sqrt{(x_2 - x_1)^2 + (y_2 - y_1)^2}$$
$$= \sqrt{(-1-(-2))^2 + (-3-3)^2}$$
$$= \sqrt{1^2 + (-6)^2} = \sqrt{37} \approx 6.1$$
Use the Law of Cosines for the first two angle measures:
$$c^2 = a^2 + b^2 - 2ab\cos C$$
$$YZ^2 = XY^2 + XZ^2 - 2(XY)(XZ)\cos X$$
$$(\sqrt{20})^2 = (\sqrt{13})^2 + (\sqrt{37})^2 - 2\sqrt{13}\sqrt{37}\cos X$$
$$20 = 13 + 37 - 2\sqrt{481}\cos X$$
$$20 = 50 - 2\sqrt{481}\cos X$$
$$2\sqrt{481}\cos X = 50 - 20 = 30$$
$$\frac{2\sqrt{481}\cos X}{2\sqrt{481}} = \frac{30}{2\sqrt{481}}$$
$$\cos X = \frac{15}{\sqrt{481}}$$
$$m\angle X = \cos^{-1}\left(\frac{15}{\sqrt{481}}\right) \approx 47°$$
$$c^2 = a^2 + b^2 - 2ab\cos C$$
$$XZ^2 = XY^2 + YZ^2 - 2(XY)(YZ)\cos Y$$
$$(\sqrt{37})^2 = (\sqrt{13})^2 + (\sqrt{20})^2 - 2\sqrt{13}\sqrt{20}\cos Y$$
$$37 = 13 + 20 - 4\sqrt{65}\cos Y$$
$$37 = 33 - 4\sqrt{65}\cos Y$$
$$4\sqrt{65}\cos Y = 33 - 37 = -4$$
$$\frac{4\sqrt{65}\cos Y}{4\sqrt{65}} = \frac{-4}{4\sqrt{65}}$$

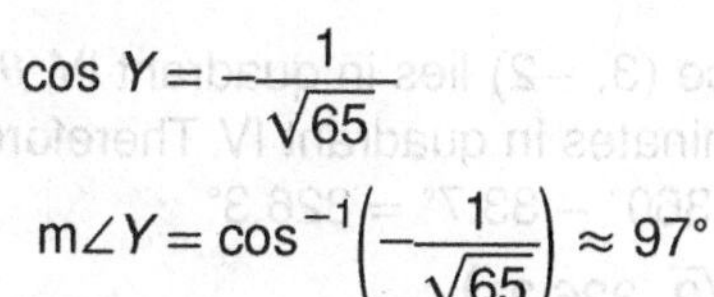

$$\cos Y = \frac{1}{\sqrt{65}}$$

$$m\angle Y = \cos^{-1}\left(-\frac{1}{\sqrt{65}}\right) \approx 97°$$

Use the Law of Sines for the third angle measure:

$$\frac{\sin Z}{XY} = \frac{\sin X}{YZ}$$

$$\frac{\sin Z}{3.61} \approx \frac{\sin(46.8°)}{4.47}$$

$$\sin Z \approx \frac{3.61\sin(46.8°)}{4.47} \approx 0.589$$

$$m\angle Z \approx \sin^{-1}(0.589) \approx 36°$$

Side lengths are $XY \approx 3.6$, $YZ \approx 4.5$, $XZ \approx 6.1$; Angle measures are $m\angle X \approx 47°$, $m\angle Y \approx 97°$, $m\angle Z \approx 36°$

**20.** $F_V = F_N \sin\theta = 12\sin 55° \approx 9.83$

$F_H = F_N \cos\theta = 12\cos 55° \approx 6.88$

**21.** Use the one-dimension Midpoint Formula:

$$x = \frac{a+b}{2},\ y = \frac{c+d}{2}$$

Midpoint of $x$ and $y$ is:

$$\frac{x+y}{2} = \frac{1}{2}\left(\frac{a+b}{2} + \frac{c+d}{2}\right)$$

$$= \frac{1}{2}\left(\frac{a+b+c+d}{2}\right)$$

$$= \frac{a+b+c+d}{4}$$

The midpoint of the two midpoints is the average (mean) of the four values $a$, $b$, $c$, and $d$.

**22.** No; No pushing or pulling of string will undo the knot.

**23.** Consider circle sector with central angle $x°$ and isosceles $\triangle$ with leg length $r$ and central angle $x°$.

$$A_{\text{sector}} = \left(\frac{x}{360}\right)\pi r^2;$$

$$A_\triangle = \frac{1}{2}bh$$

$$A_\triangle = \frac{1}{2}\left(r\cos\left(\frac{x°}{2}\right)\right)\left(2r\sin\left(\frac{x°}{2}\right)\right)$$

$$A_\triangle = r^2\cos\left(\frac{x°}{2}\right)\sin\left(\frac{x°}{2}\right)$$

Therefore,

$$A_{\text{segment}} = A_{\text{sector}} - A_\triangle$$

$$= \frac{x}{360}\pi r^2 - r^2\cos\left(\frac{x°}{2}\right)\sin\left(\frac{x°}{2}\right)$$

$$= r^2\left(\frac{x}{360}\pi - \cos\left(\frac{x°}{2}\right)\sin\left(\frac{x°}{2}\right)\right)$$

**24.** Let ||grams be $P_1$ and $P_2$.

| | Statements | Reasons |
|---|---|---|
| 1. | Area of $P_1 = bh_1$ | ‖gram Area Formula |
| 2. | Area of $P_1 = A$ | Given |
| 3. | $bh_1 = A$ | Trans. Prop. of =, Steps 1 and 2 |
| 4. | Area of $P_2 = bh_2$ | ‖gram Area Formula |
| 5. | Area of $P_2 = A$ | Given |
| 6. | $bh_2 = A$ | Trans. Prop. of =, Steps 4 and 5 |
| 7. | $bh_1 = bh_2$ | Trans. Prop. of =, Steps 3 and 6 |
| 8. | $\frac{1}{b}(bh_1) = \frac{1}{b}(bh_2)$ | Mult. Prop. of = |
| 9. | $h_1 = h_2$ | Simplify |

**25.** He has assumed that the open can has a hole in it, but since the opening does not extend all the way through the can, it can be thought of as a very deep indentation, which is not a topologically distinct alteration to make.

**26.** $d = \sqrt{(x_2 - x_1)^2 + (y_2 - y_1)^2 + (z_2 - z_1)^2}$

$$= \sqrt{(-2-2)^2 + (7-5)^2 + (1-6)^2}$$

$$= \sqrt{(-4)^2 + 2^2 + (-5)^2}$$

$$= \sqrt{16+4+25}$$

$$= \sqrt{45} = \sqrt{9}\sqrt{5} = 3\sqrt{5}$$

**27.** Weak positive correlation

28. Yes. If force is applied to a spoon, tines could be pulled out of the curved part of the spoon, and the remainder of the material redistributed to form the fork. The reverse would be true for a fork being forced into the shape of a spoon.

29. Let $\angle 1$ be Taryn's position and $\angle 2$ be Amanda's position. Does not make a difference; Since $\angle 1 \cong \angle 2$ and thus $m\angle 1 = m\angle 2$, $\triangle$ formed by players is isosceles, and so Shirley is equidistant from the other two.

30.

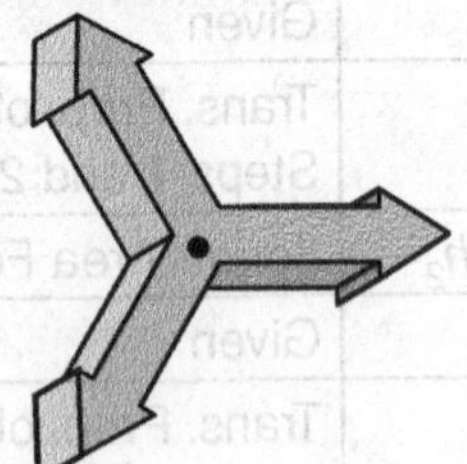

## INVESTIGATION 12

**a.1.** $(4 \cos 180°, 4 \sin 180°)$
$(-4, 0)$

**a.2.** $(1 \cos 270°, 1 \sin 180°)$
$(0, -1)$

**a.3.** $(3 \cos 360°, 3 \sin 360°)$
$(3, 0)$

**b.1.**
$$r = \sqrt{(-3)^2 + (-3)^2} = \sqrt{18} = 3\sqrt{2}$$
$$\theta = \tan^{-1}\left(\left|\frac{-3}{-3}\right|\right) = 45°$$
Since $(-3, -3)$ lies in quadrant III, $\theta$ terminates in quadrant III. Therefore, $\theta = 180° + 45° = 225°$
$(3\sqrt{2}, 225°)$

**b.2.**
$$r = \sqrt{(0)^2 + (2)^2} = \sqrt{4} = 2$$
$\theta = \tan^{-1}\left(\left|\frac{2}{0}\right|\right)$ which is undefined.

Since $\theta$ terminates on the positive $y$-axis, the value of $\theta$ is 90°.
$(2, 90°)$

**b.3.**
$$r = \sqrt{(3)^2 + (-2)^2} = \sqrt{13}$$
$$\theta = \tan^{-1}\left(\left|\frac{-2}{3}\right|\right) = 33.7°$$
Since $(3, -2)$ lies in quadrant IV, $\theta$ terminates in quadrant IV. Therefore, $\theta = 360° - 33.7° = 326.3°$
$(3\sqrt{2}, 326.3°)$

**c.**

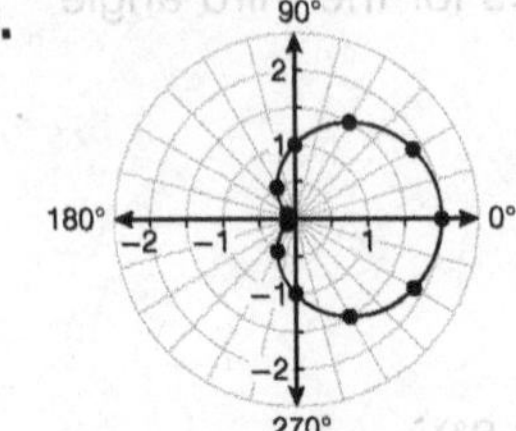


cardioid; The graph of $r = 1 + \cos\theta$ is a rotation of the graph of $r = 1 + \sin\theta$ clockwise about the pole by 90°.

**d.**

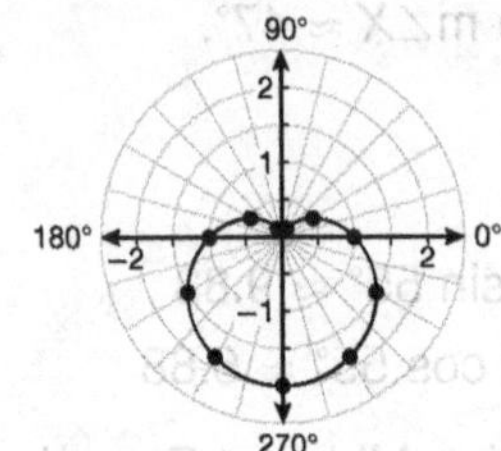


cardioid; The graphs are 180° rotations of each other.

## ORDER OF OPERATIONS AND ABSOLUTE VALUE

### Skills Bank 1

**a.** $|8| = 8$

**b.** $|-157| = 157$

**c.** $(2 + 3)^2 = (5)^2 = 25$

**d.** $2 + 3^2 = 2 + 9 = 11$

**e.** $2 - |-4| = 2 - 4 = -2$

**f.** $|2 - (-4)| = |2 + 4| = |6| = 6$

## PROPERTIES OF ARITHMETIC

### Skills Bank 2

**a.** Assoc. Prop. Add.

**b.** Assoc. Prop. Mult.

**c.** Distributive Property

**d.** Com. Prop. Mult.

**e.** Id. Prop. Mult.

**f.** Closure Property of Multiplication

## CLASSIFYING REAL NUMBERS

### Skills Bank 3

**a.** real, rational, integer **b.** real, rational

**c.** real, rational, integer, whole, natural

**d.** no

## RATIOS, PROPORTIONS, AND PERCENTAGES

### Skills Bank 4

**a.** $\frac{4.50}{3} = \frac{18}{x}$; $x = 12$

12 bus tickets can be bought with $18.

**b.** $\frac{3}{100} = \frac{x}{70}$; $2.1 = x$

It takes 2.1 pounds of lye to make 70 bars of soap.

**c.** ($12.50)(0.50) = $6.25
$12.50 + $6.25 = $18.75
A widget sells for $18.75.

**d.** ($120)(0.40) = $48
$120 − $48 = $72
The price of the reduced shoes is $72.
($72)(0.10) = $7.20
$72 − $7.20 = $64.80
After the 10% discount, the shoes cost $64.80.

## ESTIMATION

### Skills Bank 5

**a.** 1.5 **b.** 32,900 **c.** 516,202 **d.** 0.01

## EXPONENTS AND ROOTS

### Skills Bank 6

**a.** $2^5 = 2 \times 2 \times 2 \times 2 \times 2 = 32$

**b.** $3^{-2} = \frac{1}{3 \times 3} = \frac{1}{9}$

**c.** $\sqrt{16} = 16^{\frac{1}{2}} = 4$ **d.** $\sqrt[3]{27} = 27^{\frac{1}{3}} = 3$

**e.** $5^{-3} = \frac{1}{5 \times 5 \times 5} = \frac{1}{125}$

**f.** $\sqrt[3]{8} = 8^{\frac{1}{3}} = 2$

## SCIENTIFIC NOTATION AND SIGNIFICANT FIGURES

### Skills Bank 7

**a.** $7.8 \times 10^4$ **b.** $7.80001 \times 10^4$

**c.** $7.800010 \times 10^4$ **d.** $7.8001 \times 10^{-2}$

## UNITS OF MEASURE

### Skills Bank 8

**a.** $(10 \text{ yd})\left(\frac{36 \text{ in.}}{1 \text{ yd}}\right) = 360 \text{ in.}$

**b.** $(24 \text{ cm})\left(\frac{1 \text{ m}}{100 \text{ cm}}\right) = 0.24 \text{ m}$

**c.** $(1240 \text{ in.})\left(\frac{1 \text{ mi}}{63{,}360 \text{ in.}}\right) = 0.02 \text{ mi}$

**d.** $(120 \text{ mi})\left(\frac{1760 \text{ yd}}{1 \text{ mi}}\right) = 211{,}200 \text{ yd}$

**e.** $(400 \text{ m})\left(\frac{1 \text{ km}}{1000 \text{ m}}\right) = 0.4 \text{ km}$

**f.** $(2 \text{ km})\left(\frac{100{,}000 \text{ cm}}{1 \text{ km}}\right) = 200{,}000 \text{ cm}$

## CONVERTING UNITS AND RATES

### Skills Bank 9

**a.** $15 \text{ in.} \times \frac{2.54 \text{ cm}}{1 \text{ in.}} \approx 38.1 \text{ cm}$

**b.** $1.89 \text{ qt} \times \frac{946 \text{ mL}}{1 \text{ qt}} \approx 1787.9 \text{ mL}$

c. $2.02 \text{ mi} \times \frac{1.609 \text{ km}}{1 \text{ mi}} \approx 3.3 \text{ km}$

d. $2.714 \text{ g} \times \frac{0.0353 \text{ oz}}{1 \text{ g}} \approx 0.1 \text{ oz}$

e. $3.14159 \text{ kg} \times \frac{35.3 \text{ oz}}{1 \text{ kg}} \approx 110.9 \text{ oz}$

f. $508 \text{ mL} \times \frac{0.034 \text{ oz}}{1 \text{ mL}} \approx 17.3 \text{ oz}$

g. $\frac{9.8 \text{ m}}{1 \text{ sec}} \times \frac{60 \text{ sec}}{1 \text{ min}} \times \frac{3.281 \text{ ft}}{1 \text{ m}} \approx \frac{1929.2 \text{ ft}}{\text{min}}$

$\approx 1929.2 \text{ ft/min}$

h $\frac{42 \text{ L}}{1 \text{ min}} \times \frac{1000 \text{ mL}}{1 \text{ L}} \times \frac{1 \text{ min}}{60 \text{ sec}} = \frac{700 \text{ mL}}{1 \text{ sec}}$

$= 700 \text{ mL/sec}$

i. $\frac{50 \text{ km}}{1 \text{ hr}} \times \frac{0.621 \text{ mi}}{1 \text{ km}} \approx \frac{31.1 \text{ mi}}{1 \text{ hr}} \approx 31.1 \text{ mi/hr}$

j. $\frac{8.3 \text{ lb}}{1 \text{ gal}} \times \frac{28.350 \text{ g}}{1 \text{ oz}} \times \frac{16 \text{ oz}}{1 \text{ lb}} \times \frac{1 \text{ gal}}{4 \text{ qt}}$

$\times \frac{1.057 \text{ qt}}{1 \text{ L}} \approx \frac{994.9 \text{ g}}{1 \text{ L}} \approx 994.9 \text{ g/L}$

## CALCULATING PERCENT ERROR

### Skills Bank 10

a. Jarrell's measurement is 0.1 feet off. As a percentage: $\frac{0.1}{8} = 0.0125 = 1.25\%$

b. Susanne's measurement is 0.1 pounds off. As a percentage: $\frac{0.1}{1.3} = 0.0769 = 7.69\%$

c. Mae's measurement is 0.1 cups off. As a percentage: $\frac{0.1}{1.9} = 0.0526 = 5.26\%$

## MEASURES OF CENTRAL TENDENCY

### Skills Bank 11

a. List the numbers in order: 0, 0.4, $\frac{1}{2}$, 2, 3, $\pi$, 4, 8, 200

The median is 3.

b. $\frac{12 + 2 + 7 + 15 + 9 + 1 + 8 + 2}{8} = 7$

c. square

d. mean: $\frac{7 + 3 + 6 + 1 + 2 + 3 + 7 + 9}{8} = 4.75$

median: {1, 2, 3, 3, 6, 7, 7, 9}; 4.5

mode: 3 and 7

## PROBABILITY

### Skills Bank 12

a. There are 12 marbles to draw from. 6 of them are black. Therefore, the odds of drawing a non-black marble is $\frac{6}{12}$. After the first draw, there are only 11 marbles left, and 5 of them are non-black, so the probability of drawing a second non-black marble is $\frac{5}{11}$. To find the probability of both of these events happening together, multiply the two probabilities:

$\left(\frac{6}{12}\right)\left(\frac{5}{11}\right) = \frac{30}{132} = \frac{5}{22}$

b. There are six outcomes on any number cube. In the first roll, the probability of rolling a 3 is $\frac{1}{6}$. In the second roll, the probability of rolling a 3 is $\frac{1}{6}$. To find the probability of both of these events happening together, multiply the two probabilities: $\left(\frac{1}{6}\right)\left(\frac{1}{6}\right) = \frac{1}{36}$

c. There are eight equal outcomes for this spinner. In the first spin, the probability of not spinning a 4 is $\frac{7}{8}$. In the second spin, the probability of not spinning a 4 is also $\frac{7}{8}$. To find the probability of both of these events happening together, multiply the two probabilities: $\left(\frac{7}{8}\right)\left(\frac{7}{8}\right) = \frac{49}{64}$

## THE COORDINATE PLANE

### Skills Bank 13

a–d.

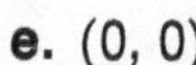



**e.** (0, 0)

## EVALUATING EXPRESSIONS

### Skills Bank 14

**a.** $4(2)^2 - 3 = 4(4) - 3$
$= 16 - 3 = 13$

**b.** $\frac{9}{2(-2) + 3} = \frac{9}{-4 + 3}$
$= \frac{9}{-1} = -9$

**c.** $3((-2) + 2(5)) = 3((-2) + 10)$
$= 3(8) = 24$

**d.** $4(1.5) - 3 = 6 - 3 = 3$

**e.** $\frac{3(-3) + (-3)^2}{-3} = \frac{-9 + 9}{-3}$
$= \frac{0}{-3} = 0$

**f.** $(2)(6) + 3(2) = 12 + 6 = 18$

## SOLVING LINEAR EQUATIONS AND INEQUALITIES

### Skills Bank 15

**a.** $\frac{2 - x}{2} = x$
$2 \cdot \frac{2 - x}{2} = 2 \cdot x$
$2 - x + x = 2x + x$
$2 = 3x$
$\frac{2}{3} = \frac{3x}{3}; \frac{2}{3} = x$

**b.** $46 - 3h = 7$
$46 - 3h - 46 = 7 - 46$
$-3h = -39$
$\frac{-3h}{-3} = \frac{-39}{-3}; h = 13$

**c.** $\frac{-y}{2} < 14$
$2 \cdot \frac{-y}{2} < 2 \cdot 14$
$\frac{-y}{-1} < \frac{28}{-1}; y > -28$

**d.** $2p - 5 > 3p$
$2p - 5 - 2p > 3p - 2p$
$-5 > p$

## TRANSFORMING FORMULAS

### Skills Bank 16

**a.** $A = bh$
$\frac{A}{b} = \frac{bh}{b}$
$\frac{A}{b} = h$

**b.** $\frac{20}{3x} = y$
$3x \cdot \frac{20}{3x} = 3x \cdot y$
$20 = 3xy$
$\frac{20}{3y} = \frac{3xy}{3y}$
$\frac{20}{3y} = x$

**c.** $A = \frac{1}{2}bh$
$2 \cdot A = 2 \cdot \frac{1}{2}bh$
$\frac{2A}{h} = \frac{bh}{h}$
$\frac{2A}{h} = b$

**d.** $\frac{2}{3}(3p + 8) = q$
$\frac{3}{2} \cdot \frac{2}{3}(3p + 8) = \frac{3}{2} \cdot q$
$3p + 8 - 8 = \frac{3}{2} \cdot q - 8$
$\frac{3p}{3} = \frac{\frac{3}{2} \cdot q - 8}{3}$
$p = \frac{1}{2}q - \frac{8}{3}$

## FUNCTIONS

### Skills Bank 17

**a.** Answers will vary. Sample answer: (4, 2) and (4, −2) both fit the relation and lie in the same vertical line.

**b.** Answers will vary. Sample answer: $x = 0$

**c.**

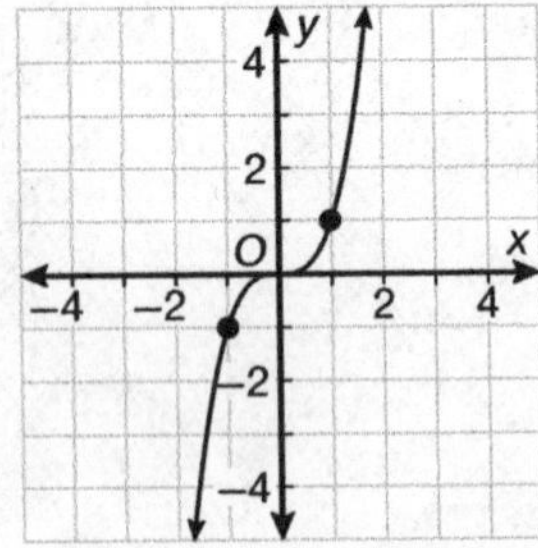

Check students' work; yes

**d.** $y = |x|$

## BINOMIAL PRODUCTS AND FACTORING

### Skills Bank 18

**a.** $(x)(x) + (x)(3) + (-5)(x) + (-5)(3)$
$= x^2 + 3x - 5x - 15$
$= x^2 - 2x - 15$

**b.** $(2x)(1) + (2x)(-x) + (-5)(1) + (-5)(-x)$
$= 2x - 2x^2 - 5 + 5x$
$= -2x^2 + 7x - 5$

**c.** $(x + 3)(x + 1)$ **d.** $(x - 6)(x + 3)$

## LINES IN POINT-SLOPE AND STANDARD FORMS

### Skills Bank 19

**a.** $4x + 5y - 4x = 13 - 4x$
$5y = -4x + 13$
$\frac{5y}{5} = \frac{-4x + 13}{5}$
$y = -\frac{4}{5}\left(x - \frac{13}{4}\right)$

**b.** $4 \cdot y = 4 \cdot \frac{3}{4}x + 4 \cdot 6$
$4y = 3x + 24$
$4y - 4y = 3x + 24 - 4y$
$0 - 24 = 3x - 4y$
$3x - 4y = -24$

**c.** $2x + 2y - 2x = 6 - 2x$
$\frac{2y}{2} = \frac{6 - 2x}{2}$
$y = 3 - x = -(x - 3)$

Check students' work.

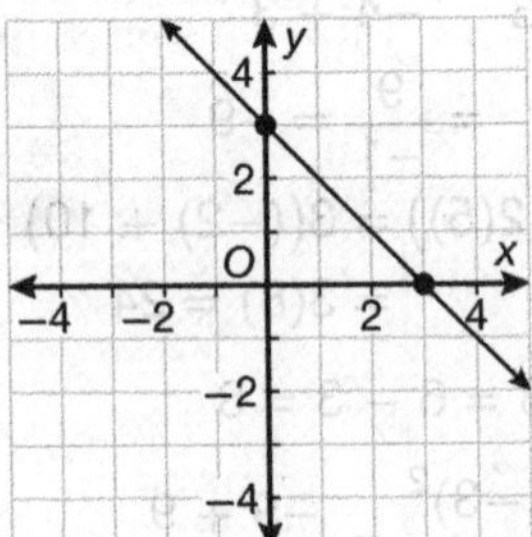

## QUADRATIC EQUATIONS AND FUNCTIONS

### Skills Bank 20

**a.** $(x + 3)(x - 5) = 0; x = \{-3, 5\}$

**b.** $x = \frac{-b \pm \sqrt{b^2 - 4ac}}{2a}$
$= \frac{-3 \pm \sqrt{3^2 - 4(3)(-6)}}{2(3)}$
$= \frac{-3 \pm \sqrt{9 + 72}}{6} = \frac{-3 \pm \sqrt{81}}{6} = \frac{-3 \pm 9}{6}$
$= \left\{\frac{-12}{6}, \frac{6}{6}\right\} = \{-2, 1\}$

**c.** Check students' work; axis of symmetry: $x = -1$, vertex: $(-1, -9)$

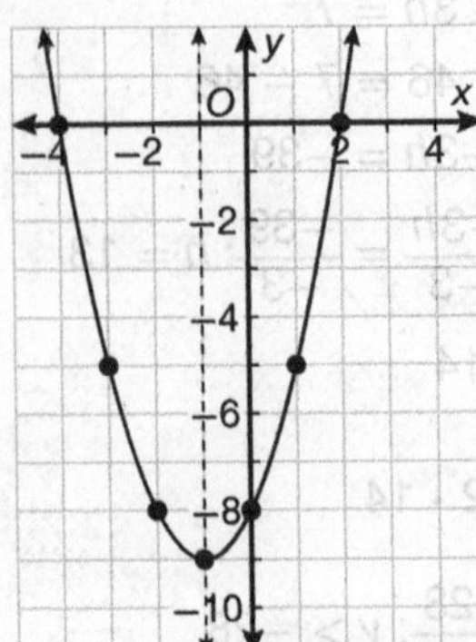

## DISPLAYING DATA

### Skills Bank 21

**a.** Circle graph; The data represents parts of a total.

**b.** Check students' work.

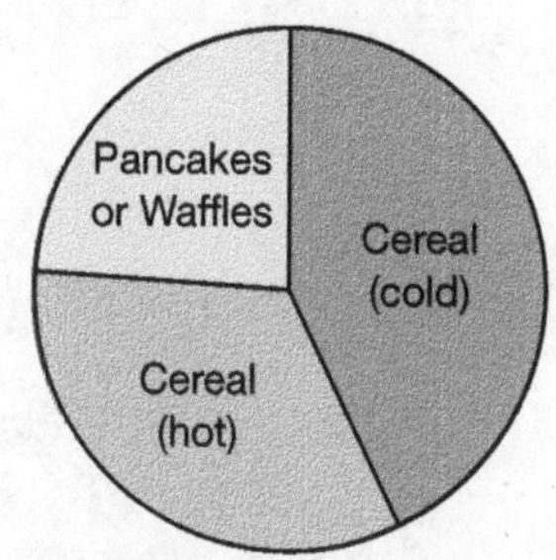


**c.** Check students' work.

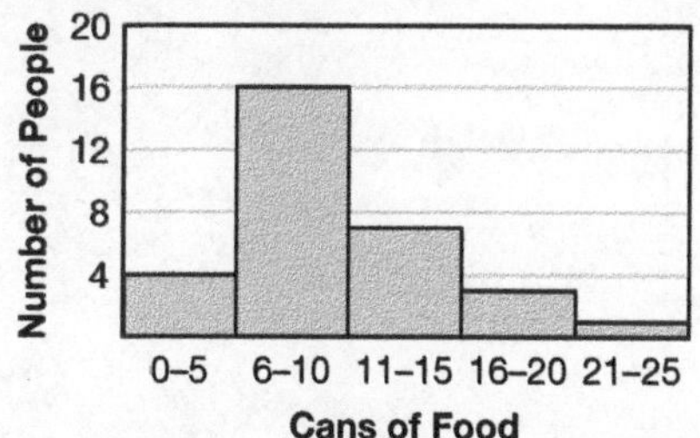


## PROBLEM-SOLVING PROCESS AND STRATEGIES

### Skills Bank 22

**a.** Understand: The problem asks how tall Alicia's brother is. We can use a ratio to determine the answer.

Plan: In the ratio, we will compare Alicia's height to the height of her brother, and then compare the Alicia's photo height to the photo height of her brother.

Solve: $\frac{5}{x} = \frac{2}{1.8}$; $4.5 = x$

Alicia's brother is 4.5 feet tall.

Check: Does the answer make sense? Alicia is taller than her brother in the photograph and also taller than him in real life. The answer is not too small (for example, 1 foot would be too small for a person), but not too large either. The answer, 4.5 feet, seems right.

**b.** Understand: The problem asks how much change Hoon gets from \$20. However, we do not know exactly how much he tipped. We will need to find this out.

Plan: The tip is given as a percentage. To find out what 15% of \$16 is, we have to convert the percentage to a decimal and multiply by the cost of the meal. Adding the tip to the meal cost will give us the total price. Then, we will subtract that amount from \$20.

Solve: The tip is given by: $0.15 \times \$16 = \$2.40$

Next, we add the tip to the price of the meal: $\$16 + \$2.40 = \$18.40$

Finally, we will subtract the total price from \$20: $\$20 - \$18.40 = \$1.60$

Hoon will get exactly \$1.60 change.

Check: Does the answer make sense? One good way to check is to subtract only the price of the meal from \$20: $\$20 - \$16 = \$4$. If Hoon had not left a tip at all, he would have received back \$4. Since he did leave a tip, he received less change (and not more change). The answer, \$1.60, seems right.

**c.** Understand: The problem asks for the probability of getting an odd number in two consecutive spins. The first thing we need to do is determine the probability of getting an odd number in one spin.

Plan: First, we will find the probability of getting an odd number in one spin. Then, we will square that number since the probability of getting a second odd number is not affected by the first spin.

Solve: The probability of getting an odd number in one spin is: $\frac{5}{9}$. The probability of getting two odd numbers consecutively is: $\frac{5}{9} \times \frac{5}{9} = \frac{25}{81}$. The probability of getting two odd numbers on two spins is $\frac{25}{81}$.

Check: Does the answer make sense? One way of estimating it would be to assume the spinner only has two equal sections, one even and one odd. Then, the probability of getting two odd numbers is $\frac{1}{2} \times \frac{1}{2} = \frac{1}{4}$ or 25%. $\frac{25}{81} \approx 31\%$, which makes sense since the probability of getting an odd number is slightly above $\frac{1}{2}$. The answer, $\frac{25}{81}$, seems right.

## DISPLAYING DATA

### Skills Bank 21

a. Circle graph: The data represents parts of a total.

b. Check students' work.

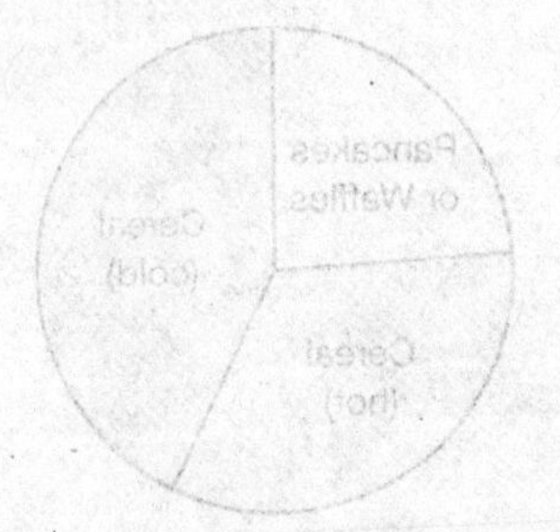


c. Check students' work.

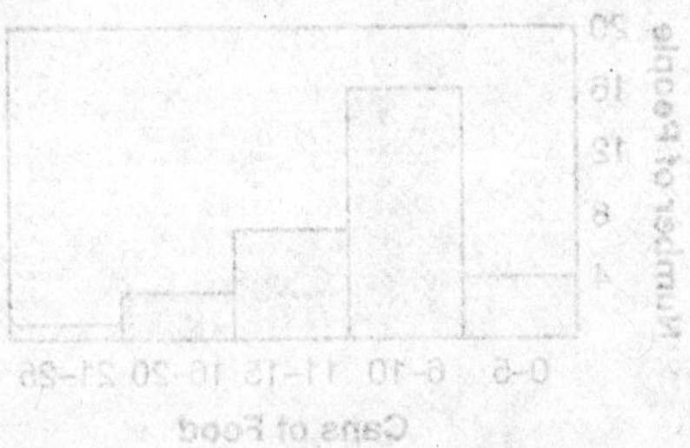


## PROBLEM-SOLVING PROCESS AND STRATEGIES

### Skills Bank 22

a. Understand: The problem asks how tall Alicia's brother is. We can use a ratio to determine the answer.

Plan: In the ratio, we will compare Alicia's height to the height of her brother, and then compare the Alicia's photo height to the photo height of her brother.

Solve: $\frac{5}{x} = \frac{2}{1.8}$; $4.5 = x$

Alicia's brother is 4.5 feet tall.

Check: Does the answer make sense? Alicia is taller than her brother in the photograph and also taller than him in real life. The answer is not too small (for example, 1 foot would be too small for a person), but not too large either. The answer, 4.5 feet, seems right.

b. Understand: The problem asks how much change Hoon gets from \$20. However, we do not know exactly how much he tipped. We will need to find this out.

Plan: The tip is given as a percentage. To find out what 15% of \$16 is, we have to convert the percentage to a decimal and multiply by the cost of the meal. Adding the tip to the meal cost will give us the total price. Then, we will subtract that amount from \$20.

Solve: The tip is given by: $0.15 \times \$16 = \$2.40$

Next, we add the tip to the price of the meal: $\$16 + \$2.40 = \$18.40$

Finally, we will subtract the total price from \$20: $\$20 - \$18.40 = \$1.60$

Hoon will get exactly \$1.60 change.

Check: Does the answer make sense? One good way to check is to subtract only the price of the meal from \$20: $\$20 - \$16 = \$4$. If Hoon had not left a tip at all, he would have received back \$4. Since he did leave a tip, he received less change (and not more change). The answer, \$1.60, seems right.

c. Understand: The problem asks for the probability of getting an odd number in two consecutive spins. The first thing we need to do is determine the probability of getting an odd number in one spin.

Plan: First, we will find the probability of getting an odd number in one spin. Then, we will square that number since the probability of getting a second odd number is not affected by the first spin.

Solve: The probability of getting an odd number in one spin is: $\frac{5}{9}$. The probability of getting two odd numbers consecutively is: $\frac{5}{9} \times \frac{5}{9} = \frac{25}{81}$. The probability of getting two odd numbers on two spins is $\frac{25}{81}$.

Check: Does the answer make sense? One way of estimating it would be to assume the spinner only has two equal sections, one even and one odd. Then, the probability of getting two odd numbers is $\frac{1}{2} \times \frac{1}{2} = \frac{1}{4}$ or 25%. $\frac{25}{81} \approx 31\%$, which makes sense since the probability of getting an odd number is slightly above $\frac{1}{2}$. The answer, $\frac{25}{81}$, seems right.